# MEETINGHOUSES OF EARLY NEW ENGLAND

# MEETINGHOUSES OF EARLY NEW ENGLAND

Peter Benes

University of Massachusetts Press
AMHERST AND BOSTON

*To Jane, Tuska, and Mina*

Copyright © 2012 by University of Massachusetts Press
All rights reserved
Printed in the United States of America

LC 2011050380
ISBN 978-1-55849-910-2

Designed by Dennis Anderson
Set in Adobe Caslon Pro by Westchester Book
Printed and bound by Thomson-Shore, Inc.

Library of Congress Cataloging-in-Publication Data

Benes, Peter.
Meetinghouses of early New England / Peter Benes.
pages cm
Includes bibliographical references and index.
ISBN 978-1-55849-910-2 (cloth : alk. paper)   1. Public buildings—New England—History.   2. Wooden churches—New England—History.   3. Vernacular architecture—New England—History.   4. New England—Church history.   I. Title.
NA4210.B46 2012
726.50974—dc23
2011050380

British Library Cataloguing in Publication data are available.

Frontispiece. *The Old Church Truro*. Meetinghouse built in 1720 on the Hill of Storms, Truro, Massachusetts. Demolished in 1840. Watercolor by Edwin Whitefield, circa 1860–1870. Courtesy of Historic New England.

# Contents

| | | |
|---|---|---|
| | Introduction: A New England Icon Reconsidered | 1 |

### PART I: THE BACKGROUND

| | | |
|---|---|---|
| 1 | The Meetinghouse and the Community | 13 |
| 2 | The Meetinghouse and the Church | 29 |
| 3 | The Builders | 49 |
| 4 | Seating the Congregation | 62 |

### PART II: THE ARCHITECTURE

| | | |
|---|---|---|
| 5 | Meetinghouses of the Seventeenth Century | 77 |
| 6 | Meetinghouses of the Eighteenth Century | 118 |
| 7 | Meetinghouses of the Early Nineteenth Century | 204 |

### PART III: CONCLUSIONS

| | | |
|---|---|---|
| 8 | Some Theoretical Models | 221 |
| 9 | Meetinghouse Architecture as Puritan Ecclesiology | 239 |
| 10 | A Fleeting Image | 264 |

| | |
|---|---|
| Epilogue | 273 |
| Appendix A: Tables | 281 |
| Appendix B: Chronological checklist of meetinghouses in New England and Long Island, 1622–1830 | 289 |

| | |
|---|---|
| Appendix C: Pinnacles, pyramids, and spires, 1651–1709 | 347 |
| Appendix D: Enlargements of meetinghouses in New England by cutting the frame, 1723–1824 | 348 |
| Appendix E: Citations of exterior painting, 1678–1828 | 350 |
| Appendix F: Citations of interior painting, 1656–1817 | 359 |
| Appendix G: Meetinghouse replications in New England, 1647–1828 | 364 |
| Notes | 375 |
| Works Cited | 403 |
| Acknowledgments | 429 |
| Index | 431 |

Fully annotated versions of Appendixes B-G and a complete bibliography, including sources cited only in the appendixes, are available online at

http://scholarworks.umass.edu/umpress.

# MEETINGHOUSES OF EARLY NEW ENGLAND

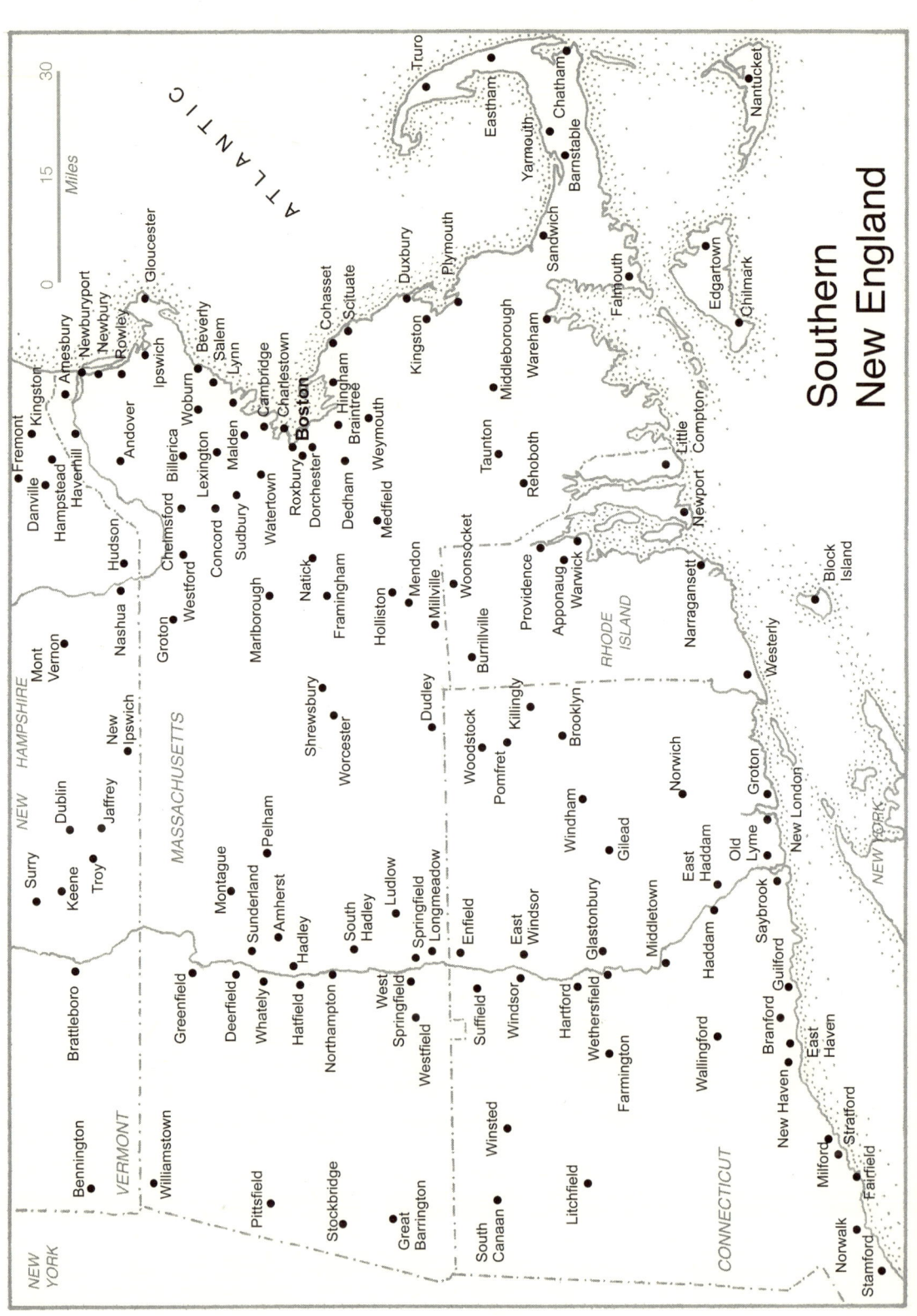

INTRODUCTION

# A New England Icon Reconsidered

THE NEW ENGLAND meetinghouse has long held a place in the American imagination as a cultural and historical icon. Meetinghouses have stood for the community. They have enshrined traditional New England religious values. They have been a symbol of permanence, stability, democracy, and religious reform. From their belfries could be seen the spires of meetinghouses in adjoining parishes, a metaphorical link to an orderly network of "primitive" Christian communities and a visual link to the Baroque and Italianate taste of English architects, such as Christopher Wren and James Gibbs. The meetinghouse bell, the emblematic center of each community, summoned parishioners to the Sabbath meeting, marked days of fasting and thanksgiving, accompanied funerals, and warned of emergencies. These iconic features were eulogized by nineteenth-century New England parish and town historians—that wonderful generation of storytellers who loved to inform their readers that, as children, they were filled alternately with terror and hope that the sounding board would fall on the minister's head and that the dropping of hinged pew seats sounded to them like the rattle of musket fire.[1]

A closer look at the evidence suggests that many of these ideas are unfounded or only partly true. The builders of most New England meetinghouses, for example, saw them as temporary structures; many had not even been completed when they were taken down and replaced by a larger one. And a widespread pattern of neighborly and sectarian rivalry challenges the notion that meetinghouses represented community stability. At least thirteen recorded instances are known when one faction of "aggrieved" neighbors stole, burned, or cut in half the principal timbers of a meetinghouse on the night before its scheduled raising, hoping to see it relocated to a more desirable location.[2] One such faction so diverted the workers that a large section of the frame fell, injuring several people.[3] Sectarian controversies were equally confrontational. In the 1790s Congregationalists and Baptists in Rehoboth, Massachusetts, vying for control of the town's meetinghouse, precipitated what historians later called the "longest meeting" ever held in New England—a day-and-night takeover by outnumbered Baptist elders and members of their congregation who lectured, read, sang, and exhorted in a continual chain of exercises designed to prevent the Congregational minister from preaching. After two weeks the exhausted Baptists left the building. They subsequently lost in court.[4] In the same decade the town of Fitchburg, Massachusetts, was called together ninety-nine times in a failed effort to site a proposed meetinghouse; the debates became so acrimonious that audiences from neighboring towns "flocked" to the meetings to watch the proceedings.[5]

Were meetinghouses democratic institutions? Inequality, gender bias, and social control were built into every step of the parish system. Committees, always made up of landed Caucasian men, monitored virtually every social interaction. One committee separated the community into ranks of importance by assessing age, estate, and parentage; a second committee divided the meetinghouse into descending levels of "dignities"; a third committee decided where each individual would sit, assigning pews like a grade-school seating chart; and a fourth spelled out the exiting precedence to be followed when the service was over.

And as for bells and English architects, relatively few New Englanders heard bells before 1800, and only one steeple in the region (the 1775 First Baptist meetinghouse in Providence) is known to have actually been copied from an English architect's design. Most parishioners were summoned to the religious service by a raised red flag, the beat of a drum, or the sound of a conch or trumpet.

The term *meetinghouse* first occurs in written usage in March 1632 in the journal of Massachusetts governor John Winthrop (1588–1649), who alludes to the "new meeting house" at Dorchester whose thatch had been blackened by a small explosion of powder.[6] By "meeting house" he meant little more than the structure that had recently been erected in that town for the purpose of holding public meetings and church services. The term was significant to him and many others in the new Puritan colony of Massachusetts Bay because implied in its use was a definition of *church*. To the members of the Church of England, who largely remained behind in England during the initial migration to Massachusetts and Connecticut, a church was an ecclesiological and architectural reality—a sacred building for worship with all the accompanying texts, vestments, surplices, calendars, rituals, prayer books, and organs that defined the Anglican service. To a Puritan like Winthrop, a church was a social concept—a covenanted body of people gathered to practice Christian teachings. Where the church held religious services was unimportant. This idea was reflected in the somewhat tortuous but explicit statement issued in 1680 by the second Boston synod that "there is now *no place* which renders the Worship of God more acceptable for its being there performed."[7] It is also reproduced in a frequently cited remark about meetinghouses by the English Puritan preacher Isaac Chauncy in 1697 (often incorrectly attributed to Richard Mather or Cotton Mather), "There is no just grounds from Scripture to apply such a *Trope* as church to an House for Publick Assembly." Chauncy added, "There is no House or artificial building in Scripture called a Church."[8]

That John Winthrop and other New Englanders readily called the Dorchester structure a "meeting house" without offering competing (and religiously loaded) terms such as *church, chapel, temple, tabernacle, kirk,* and *synagogue*[9] suggests a unity of expectations among his Puritan listeners and correspondents. In the Netherlands, Rev. Francis Johnson, pastor of a Brownist congregation in Amsterdam, worshiped in what he called a "preaching house." (In one unusual instance an English Anabaptist congregation in Amsterdam worshiped in a converted kitchen called a "bakehouse" [*backhuys*].)[10] In England, however, Reformed services that included the sacraments had long been held at clandestine "meetings" that took place in private homes, school houses, barns, ships, fields, and woods—but sometimes openly in Anglican churches. Legal depositions by English Barrowists (followers of the separatist Henry Barrow [ca. 1550–1593]) arrested in the woods in 1593 frequently cited their attendance at "meetings." But English Puritans adopted the term, too. Samuel Rogers, for example, a young clergyman who attended Puritan worship soon after his graduation from Emmanuel College, Cambridge, employed it in his 1634–38 diary: "Went to Dix:[on's] for a meeting; but I cannot find the presence of Christ as faine I would." Elsewhere he wrote, "We have had our weekly meeting this night, the L[ord] left me not."[11]

In Massachusetts Bay these new public spaces were sanctioned by law and attendance became mandatory. They were now called "meeting houses" because by this time the word *meeting* had already begun to mean a place for the religious conventicles usually forbidden under Elizabethan and Jacobean law.[12] American Puritans of all sects and denominations, whose earlier worship in England had meant attending "meetings," readily added "house" to describe their religious edifices. A New World expression accepted by most Reformed seventeenth-century English colonists, the term lasted both in England and in North America. A hundred fifty years after Winthrop had cited the explosion in the Dorchester meetinghouse, Rev. Ezra Stiles (1727–1795) still called Congregational houses of worship "meetings" (and Anglican houses of worship "churches")—at least in the abbreviated privacy of his diary—as did Mary Vial Holyoke of Salem, Massachusetts, writing in the 1770s and 1780s. It was more than just a verbal conformity. Like other Protestant clergymen, Ezra Stiles frequently preached in secular locations—the courthouse in East Greenwich, Rhode Island, or the "Old Town House" in Providence—before these congregations had built their own houses of worship.[13]

In current usage the term *meetinghouse* has developed both architectural and economic definitions. Architectural historians, such as Edmund W. Sinnott, distinguish a meetinghouse plan by the so-called short-side alignment of the main entry and pulpit. In a Reformed meetinghouse the pulpit and entryway face each other across the narrow dimension of the building. In an Anglican church the principal entry and the pulpit usually face each other along the main alley from one end of the building to the other.[14] To some social historians, however, a meetinghouse is defined by those who paid for it, not by its architectural layout. To them the structure is a meetinghouse if it was erected and maintained by public taxation. Though the town's Congregational society (or competing Baptist, Presbyterian, or Methodist societies) occupied the meetinghouse for religious services, the building was also available for civic purposes.

The New England "meetinghouses" discussed here encompass both definitions. They include all houses of worship—regardless of their architectural alignment—built by public taxation for Congregational and Presbyterian religious societies.[15] They also include all houses of worship raised privately by Quakers, Shakers, Anglicans, Lutherans, Methodists, Covenanters, Presbyterians, Universalists, Congregationalists, separating Congregationalists, Seventh-Day or Sabbatarian Baptists, Six-Principle Baptists, and members of Dutch Reformed churches. The numbers are staggering. Documents show that more than 2,189 houses of worship in New England and related communities in Long Island were raised between 1622 and 1830 (see Appendix A, Table 1). Eighteenth-century ecclesiastic surveys and early nineteenth-century population estimates suggest that an additional 300 were probably paid for and raised by Congregational parishes in the region and another 50 by Baptist and Anglican parishes. But these figures lack documentation. The building rate was prolific—an average of 10 to 15 new structures each year. More than a third of all meetinghouses were replacements for earlier ones, some for the second, third, fourth, or even fifth time—evidence that they were seen as temporary. Towns welcomed the opportunity to tear down these structures and replace them with newer ones because the old ones looked decrepit or had become too small or had fallen out of fashion. Towns were also constantly reshaping and enlarging their meetinghouses either by adding lean-tos or by cutting the frame to insert sections. Some meetinghouses were moved from place to place like luggage. After worshiping for years in a local schoolhouse, the separatists in Rowley, Massachusetts, purchased the old meetinghouse of the town's Second Society in 1769, took it down, and moved it to Bradford; in 1782 they took it down again and reassembled it back in Rowley near the schoolhouse where they had originally worshiped.[16] These changes were relatively easy because most meetinghouses were made of wood, in contrast to those in England, where forests were already depleted in the sixteenth century and the use of wood for building was long in decline. About 95 percent of the meetinghouses built in New England and Long Island were timber-frame structures similar to barns, millhouses, warehouses, and schoolhouses; their framing techniques had much in common with wooden bridges.

Because Reformed meetinghouses were seen as temporary, survival rates are low. Of an estimated 338 meetinghouses erected during the first-period architectural style (roughly between 1622 and 1770), about 15 structures still stand, or approximately 4 percent. Most of these survivals are meetinghouses of small Baptist or Quaker congregations, or those raised for Native Americans. Out of an estimated 1,155 structures built during the second-period architectural style (roughly between 1699 and 1820), about 190 remain—a survival rate of a little more than 16 percent—and most of those have undergone major renovations, relocations, and restorations that have obscured their original appearance. The survival rate of Reformed meetinghouses built during the third-period architectural style (roughly 1790 to 1830), however, is much higher, because in those years architects and building contractors had come into the picture and brick and stone had begun to replace wooden posts and beams. More than half of the 603 meetinghouses built during this period are still standing, and in many of these, Baptist, Unitarian, Methodist, Trinitarian, Presbyterian, Congregational, and Roman Catholic congregations continue to meet. (By contrast, of the 93 Anglican churches built during these periods, 46 still remain, or 49 percent.)

The architectural history of meetinghouses is best revealed by the transitions from earlier styles to newer ones. Perhaps the most important years are 1639 to 1640, when several large, newly formed parishes in eastern Massachusetts and Connecticut—chiefly made up of affluent London-based immigrant groups—established what we now consider a "New England" meetinghouse style. Also important are the opening two decades of the eighteenth century, when second-period styles gradually took over from the first, and the final decade of the eighteenth century and the first decade of the nineteenth when Federal or third-period meetinghouse styles took over from the second. In all three transitions, however, we are dealing with a limited body of evidence. Almost nothing is known of New England meetinghouses before 1642—the year when Sudbury, Massachusetts, signed a contract with John Rutter, the earliest record of the form. Out of approximately 562 structures raised during the next two transition periods, 1701–20 and 1791–1810, details about individual structures are available for about one-quarter. Of the remaining three-quarters, we know only these meetinghouses were built, but no descriptions are available.

New England meetinghouses have attracted the attention of numerous scholars, one of the earliest of whom was Henry M. Dexter, whose article "Meeting-Houses" was published in the *Congregational Quarterly* in 1859. Like Dexter's study, Noah Porter's 1883 article "The New England Meeting House" and Charles A. Place's 1922 article "From Meeting House to Church in New England," most studies of New England meetinghouses have been based on survivals.

Among the leading works are Eva A. Speare's *Colonial Meeting-Houses of New Hampshire,* Edmund W. Sinnott's *Meetinghouse and Church in Early New England,* Harold W. Rose's *The Colonial Houses of Worship in America,* and Peter Mallary's *New England Churches and Meetinghouses.* Others, however, are based on church and town records or, like Alice Morse Earle's *The Sabbath in Puritan New England* and Ola E. Winslow's *Meetinghouse Hill, 1630–1783,* compiled from documentary materials.[17] Of the record-based studies, four have proven the most systematic and insightful. J. Frederick Kelly measured and studied eighty-seven still-standing houses of worship for his magisterial *Early Connecticut Meetinghouses,* published in 1948; he also prepared a full documentary examination of earlier meetinghouses and churches at each site. Kelly's work led to Anthony N. B. Garvan's *Architecture and Town Planning in Colonial Connecticut,* which devotes its final chapter to public buildings. Garvan was the first to study European prototypes, and he coined the phrase "plain style" to describe first-period forms. John Coolidge added to Garvan's hypothesis, speculating on the original source of American meetinghouse designs in his 1961 article "Hingham Builds a Meetinghouse." Marian Card Donnelly carried this comparative approach one step further in her highly influential *New England Meeting Houses of the Seventeenth Century,* published in 1968, as well as in articles for the *Journal for Architectural History* and *Old-Time New England.*

In the past forty years, a new group of scholars skilled in material culture redefined our understanding of New England history and its ecclesiastic architecture. Donald R. Friary examines the full cultural and social range of Anglican architecture in New England in a study that still ranks as the best source on this subject. Frederic C. Detwiller combed the archives of the Society for the Preservation of New England Antiquities, now Historic New England, to uncover drawings by the self-taught architect Thomas Dawes and established his ties to Charles Bulfinch. Robert B. St. George and Robert Trent identified the migration of seventeenth-century English joiners and pew builders in eastern Massachusetts and perhaps more than anyone else reshaped our understanding of Garvan's "plain style." Philip D. Zimmerman along with this author, compiled a loan exhibition at the Currier Gallery of Art, Manchester, New Hampshire, titled *New England Meeting House and Church: 1630–1850* that addresses the larger world of architecture, Sabbath-day customs, and Communion ware in the Reformed tradition. This exhibition provided the setting for a conference on meetinghouses at Dublin, New Hampshire, the papers of which were variously published in the *Annual Proceedings of the Dublin Seminar for New England Folklife* and *Old-Time New England,* addressing meetinghouse architecture, framing, color, comfort, replication theories, and porch designs. Zimmerman also completed a doctoral thesis on southern New Hampshire ecclesiastical architecture in the early nineteenth century. William Lamson Warren studied meetinghouses in Oxford and Southbury, Connecticut. Richard Bushman studied the Brattle Square Meetinghouse and Christ Church in Boston, pinpointing the urban Anglican assault on Congregational houses of worship in the eighteenth century. And Kevin M. Sweeney's pioneering study "Meetinghouses, Town Houses, and Churches" moved up the date when communities in Connecticut and the Connecticut Valley typically built townhouses or town halls—a decision that left meetinghouse builders free to concentrate on the intended ecclesiastic purpose of their structures.

Two important recent studies of New England meetinghouses are Gretchen Buggeln's *Temple of Grace* and Carl Lounsbury's "God Is in the Details," both of which, like Kevin Sweeney's study, address the larger issue of change. Buggeln's work examines the transformation of Georgian-style meetinghouses in the late eighteenth century into Federal, Greek Revival, and Gothic churches whose form was dominated by a new Republican aesthetic and the privatization of the Congregational parish. While the subject of Lounsbury's study is the 1833 meetinghouse in Wapwallopen, Pennsylvania, his excellent analysis of ecclesiastical architectural change in the American Northeast extends well into New England.

These authors have all followed Noah Porter's original thesis that through a progressive adoption of newer architectural styles and decorative codes the seventeenth-century "meetinghouse" gradually evolved into the nineteenth-century "church," a process that matched the final legal disestablishment of church and state in New England between 1807 and 1832. This study follows the same paradigm, but it focuses on the relationship between Reformed and Anglican worshiping practices in the region before 1830 and the competing influence of "progressive" and "conservative" parishes. It is tempting, but probably ultimately misleading, to say that Congregationalists simply followed the lead of the Anglican Church in eighteenth- and early nineteenth-century New England. All the evidence suggests that New England Congregationalism occupied the middle ground in a larger spectrum of English Protestantism that ran from high-church Episcopalians and extended to low-church Episcopalians and Presbyterian and Congregational parishes and ended with Quakers and Baptists and independent sects or sectaries, such as the Sandemanians, Rogerenes, and Shakers. While Congregationalists were always in the majority in New England, they and other Protestant groups routinely imitated Anglican churches when building their meetinghouses. But it is also true that Anglican, Presbyterian, and even Dutch Reformed congregations imitated Congregational practices.

Scholars have not always agreed, however, on whether seventeenth-century New England meetinghouses were a uniquely American building form or whether they were based on English or European antecedents. Edmund Sinnott sees in seventeenth-century meetinghouses "no close resemblance to any communal or ecclesiastical structure of the Old World."[18] His view conforms to those of others who postulate that the source of these structures was local or "originate[s] more in residential than ecclesiastical architecture."[19] Even as recently as 1993 Kevin Sweeney called the form "basically an original architectural expression."[20] But Anthony Garvan, John Coolidge, and Marian Donnelly are less sure. While Garvan thinks that the first generation of builders practiced an "architecture of negation," he nevertheless postulates the existence of a Protestant plain style that may have derived from Huguenot and Dutch Reformed traditions.[21] Coolidge, in contrast, states outright that "nothing about the [Hingham, Massachusetts] edifice is demonstrably American," and he is the first to cite Per Gustaf Hamberg's classic work *Tempelbygge för Protestanter*.[22] Donnelly, whose research is in part dependent on Garvan's study, takes a closer look at specific Huguenot "temples," such as those in Lyon and Charenton, France, in 1586 and 1623, suggesting these displayed the same centrally mounted pulpit and surrounding galleries that dominated New England meetinghouse architecture in the mid-seventeenth and early eighteenth centuries. While pointing out that a systematic study of European Protestant ecclesiastic architecture had yet to be written, she indicates that these structures, and others like them, might have been well known to English and Dutch nonconformists immigrating to the New World.

Several studies of European Protestant architecture have shed additional light on the question of European influences. Central to these is the Swedish-language work Coolidge cites: Per Hamberg's study of the origins of Lutheran, Huguenot, and Dutch Reformed houses of worship. Although the work was not available to English readers until its posthumous translation in 2002, under the title *Temples for Protestants*, it draws together the basic concepts later articulated independently by Garvan and Donnelly. Hamberg describes in some detail the influence of the designer Jacques Perret on sixteenth- and seventeenth-century Huguenot temples and traces the evolution of the round, or octagonal, form in the Netherlands. European perspectives were also voiced at a conference held in Princeton, New Jersey, in 1995 titled "Calvinism and the Arts." (The papers were compiled and published in *Seeing beyond the Word: Visual Arts and the Calvinist Tradition*.) Two of the contributors, Christopher Stell and Hélène Guicharnaud, searched early records and a few surviving Protestant structures in England, France, and the Netherlands in their examinations of European Reformed church architecture. In 1997, Keith L. Sprunger, a student of exiled English churches in sixteenth- and seventeenth-century Holland, published a new interpretation of early Calvinist architecture in Europe. Based on published tracts, records, and correspondence, his article, "Puritan Church Architecture and Worship in a Dutch Context" describes the exchanges between Separatist and Puritan exiles in Middleberg, Leiden, and Amsterdam on the issue of reusing "tainted" properties. Separatists worshiped in the houses they lived in, whereas the more numerous Puritans either reused Catholic churches or built new meetinghouses following a "Classic Dutch" tradition of architecture.

Like Donnelly and Hamberg, these authors have provided much of the groundwork supporting the belief that seventeenth-century New England houses of worship derived from those built in Europe. Their efforts were followed by a new generation of architectural and church history students in England, among them Andrew Spicer, whose *Calvinist Churches in Early Modern Europe*, published in 2007, puts together the most informed and influential statement yet on Protestant church architecture in sixteenth- and seventeenth-century Europe.

Several architectural preservationists, archaeologists, and restorers have also applied their expertise to surviving examples of New England houses of worship. Brian Powell and Andrea Gilmore, a team working for Building Conservation Associates of Dedham, Massachusetts, undertook a long-term archaeological investigation of the 1681 Old Ship in Hingham, Massachusetts, the oldest meetinghouse still standing in New England. Their detailed four-volume report, issued in April 2007, is one of the most comprehensive examinations of any New England house of worship written to date. Jan Lewandoski, a professional timber-frame builder, has published several articles on the restoration of meetinghouse frames and steeples in *Timber Framing*.

The primary issue addressed here is the blossoming of a stunning but ultimately impermanent New England vernacular tradition of ecclesiastical architecture.[23] The causes of this impermanence are found to lie in the ties between the region's meetinghouse builders and the wide availability of original growth forests, the shifting role of the meetinghouse in an era of rapidly evolving Protestant liturgy and spiritual practices, and the larger interface between Anglican and Reformed worshiping traditions. These connections are viewed against New England patterns of parish autonomy, the likelihood that early meetinghouse styles in New England were clearly intertwined with past English and European practices, the overall "refinement" of the Congregational service, and the gradually weakening civic control over church affairs.

The parish-by-parish examination offered here helps bring the subject down to a manageable scale. According to the 1648 Cambridge Platform of Church Discipline, the size of a gathered congregation "ought not to be of greater number than may ordinarily meet together conveniently in one place; nor ordinarily fewer than may conveniently carry on church work."[24] Because an average meetinghouse could accommodate no more than eight hundred to a thousand people, the task of raising meetinghouses rested on about a hundred to two hundred families—figures that conform to those compiled by Ezra Stiles in the 1760s.[25] Thus, the houses of worship built in the region before 1830 were erected by neighbors who knew each other well and who nourished their independence from other towns and parishes around them. Although these decision makers were always landed men, their choices were made through committees that spoke for the wider community, and so the process was in its own way democratic. The same men who raised the meetinghouse also determined its dimensions and form, selected and paid their minister, and agreed on who could and who could not be a church member, who could be baptized, and who could take Communion. They also selected the translations the congregation sang in the religious service and whether their singing could be accompanied with pitch pipes or musical instruments. They even determined where the "small" girls sat, where the "large girls" sat, where the eligible maids and bachelors sat, and whether women could sit in chairs in the alleys and whether they could wear hats during the religious service.[26]

Fortunately, the same nineteenth-century local historians who recount tales about the childhood emotions that swept over them in church also provide considerable data on parish history and local meetinghouses no longer available elsewhere and reproduce verbatim a sizable number of contracts, receipts, account book entries, and building logs. While this study uses this secondhand evidence cautiously, it relies considerably on these historians' efforts.

In 1999 the Berkshire Family History Association uncovered a fascinating document passed by a town meeting in Pittsfield, Massachusetts, shortly after that community had raised its second meetinghouse in 1790. Concerned about the replacement cost of hundreds of windowpanes in a structure designed by the Boston architect Charles Bulfinch, the town in 1791 prohibited all games played with balls from the common, among them "any game called Wicket, Cricket, Baseball, Football, Cat, Fives, or any other game or games with balls . . . 80 yards of meetinghouse."[27] (The nearby town of Northampton passed a similar prohibition in the same year.)[28] In a notice published in the *Berkshire Genealogist* in 2000, the association observed that although Cooperstown, New York, was long thought to have been the site of the first game of baseball, played after 1839, the game was already causing problems in Pittsfield in 1791—reopening the debate about where and when the game got started.[29] Details like these bring the observance of the New England Sabbath close to the ebb and flow of everyday life. Meetinghouse architecture, a significant part of that life, circulated among towns like a vernacular language. This book is dedicated to identifying and understanding that language and interpreting its several dialects.

# PART I
# The Background

CHAPTER ONE

# The Meetinghouse and the Community

ALTHOUGH NEW ENGLAND meetinghouses were built primarily for public religious exercises, little about them was sacred for much of the seventeenth and eighteenth centuries. Best described as two- or three-tiered municipal halls (fig. 1.1), they were surrounded by hovels, horse stalls, horse blocks, well-sweeps, graveyards, "necessaries," carriage sheds, and Sabbath-day houses.[1] Inside they resembled an oversized, well-lighted, one-room schoolhouse with poor acoustics. Parishioners typically entered an unheated structure that showed the effects of years of water, snow, and mud tracked in by boots. The inside was dominated by an elevated pulpit or desk covered with a sounding board or canopy,

Figure 1.1. Stereoscopic view dated circa 1890 of the Rocky Hill meetinghouse built in West Salisbury, Massachusetts (which became part of Amesbury in 1886). Raised by Ambrose Palmer and Jacob Spofford of Georgetown, Massachusetts, in 1785. Courtesy of Historic New England.

Figure 1.2. *Interior of East Church, Salem* [Massachusetts]. The view shows box pews, two stoves, and a single stovepipe installed in a converted first-period (1717) meetinghouse in Salem's East Parish. Lithograph by Bufford and Company, circa 1847. Courtesy of the Peabody Essex Museum, Salem, Massachusetts.

colloquially described as a "coffee pot cover," with rows of benches, pews, and galleries facing it on three sides (fig. 1.2). Pews were confined, the occupants facing in several directions; some pews were furnished with small folding writing tables. The Communion table was often a hinged single leaf that hung down from the front rail of the deacons' pew to allow more seating space.

These buildings were crowded to capacity when in use and abandoned when not. They were cold and dark during the winter, compelling clergymen to wear fur skullcaps, gloves, and overcoats.[2] They were hot in the summer and sometimes showed evidence of pigeons, swallows, and bats. Special conveniences were provided for those who chewed tobacco. Sexual and other graffiti were visible in the stairwells and the backs of pews in the upper galleries (figs. 1.3 and 1.4). Household chairs were left in the pews along with foot warmers. Finish carpentry was likely to be incomplete: boards sometimes covered the windows, doors and door-casings were unpainted, and roofs were stained by leaks. Lead weights and pulleys were attached to the front door to allow it to be more conveniently kept closed. Signs were posted to restrain people from slamming seats or cutting them with knives.[3] In the corners of the building, benches were elevated a foot or more above the floor, and pews were sometimes suspended from tie beams like box seats—indications of the stagelike or arenalike quality of the meetinghouse interior noted by later architectural historians.[4] This theatrical effect was even more exaggerated in structures with two tiers of galleries, because

Figures 1.3 and 1.4. Sailboat and fish graffiti in the gallery of the Rocky Hill meetinghouse, 1785, West Salisbury, now Amesbury, Massachusetts. Located near the mouth of the Merrimack River, Salisbury was the home of numerous seamen and fishermen. Length of images approximately 3 inches. Courtesy of Historic New England.

the pulpit had to be raised another six feet so that those in the uppermost gallery could hear the minister.

These conditions, which varied with time and place, generally prevailed before 1790. Nevertheless, because meetinghouses were usually the only municipal building in the community, they were closely wedded to the social and cultural fabric of the neighborhood. Here were held the annual town meeting, town elections, parish and church meetings, and public events, such as important county trials, public executions, public punishments, and political and religious protests.[5] Meetinghouses provided safe places to store gunpowder because fires for heating were disallowed.[6] They were used as temporary barracks for soldiers on the march and as hospitals in times of war.[7] They were places to exhibit the works of panorama and historical painters and to hold singing exhibitions that capped off a winter's school taught by a psalmody teacher.[8] At the meetinghouse were celebrated the baptisms that marked the beginning of the religious life of virtually every individual in the community. The town's burying ground was usually located just outside the meetinghouse, with headstones frequently made by a local carver.

Nowhere is this communal intimacy better expressed than in the names individual meetinghouses acquired, many of which—then and now—begin with "Old" regardless of the age or condition of the structure. "Old White," "Old Sloop," and "Old Jerusalem" are typical names among Congregational, Baptist, and Presbyterian congregations in eastern New England. The Lutheran church in Alna, Maine, is called the "Old German Meeting House." Some were named after their founders, others for their appearance. In Porter, Maine, the "Old Bullockite" meetinghouse was named after Elder Jeremiah Bullock, a fundamentalist Baptist preacher; in New Haven, Connecticut, the White Haven Society, a separatist congregation founded in 1744, was known variously as the "Blue Meeting-house," the "Old Blue," or simply "The Blue." (It was also called "Mr. Bird's" or "Mr. Edwards's" meetinghouse, after its ministers.)[9] The meetinghouse of the Third Society in Boston, built in 1669, was initially called the "South Meeting House" to distinguish it from the town's "North Meeting House." But it became the "Old South" in 1716 after the formation of a neighboring society that called itself the "New South." Similarly, the 1712 meetinghouse of Boston's First Society, initially known as "The Brick" meetinghouse, became the "Old Brick" a few years later, in 1721, after a second brick meetinghouse, appropriately called the "New Brick meeting house," was built nearby.

Elsewhere in Massachusetts, Hingham's 1681 meetinghouse acquired the name the "Old Ship" from the appearance of the underside of its roof timbers (fig. 1.5).[10] Comparable architectural features inspired the "Old Tunnel" in Lynn, named after the funnel-like shape of its cupola.[11] At least two meetinghouses were named for the wood they were made from: the "Old Cedar" in Boston and

Figure 1.5. Trusses supporting the roof and belfry of the second meetinghouse built in Hingham, Massachusetts, in 1681. The appearance of these timbers led to its name, the "Old Ship." Photograph by Paul Wainwright, 2008.

"the Hemlock meeting house" in Colebrook, Connecticut. The "Old Tin Top," originally located on Richmond Street in Providence, Rhode Island, was named for the covering of its spire; when the building was floated down to Warwick, it kept its name. The unpainted meetinghouse the "Coffin" in Orford, New Hampshire, was named for its weather-blackened appearance; the "Old Round" in Richmond, Vermont, for its sixteen sides; the "Tory Hill Meeting House" in South Buxton, Maine, for the political inclinations of its minister; the "Potash meetinghouse" in Rochester, Vermont, for its closeness to a nearby potash factory; the "Still" in Amesbury, Massachusetts, reputedly for the intemperance of its founding minister; and the "Line meeting house" in Fall River and Tiverton for its location on the border between Massachusetts and Rhode Island. Perhaps the most unusual name is that given to the "Ohio Meeting House" in Hampton Falls, New Hampshire, for its remote location: trying to reach it was like traveling to the Ohio territory.

The use of colloquial or popular names for old structures is probably a reflection of their civic role. But these names also suggest an important distinction between Reformed and Anglican practice and in a sense symbolize the chief difference between these two Protestant denominations. American Episcopal churches were named for saints and biblical figures or reigning kings and queens. An Episcopal church established in Marblehead, Massachusetts, in 1714, for example, retains its original name, St. Michael's Church, and the Episcopal King's Chapel in Boston, which is older by far than most of the meetinghouses just cited, also retains its original name, though it was known as the "Stone Chapel" for about twenty years after the American Revolution. No Anglican house of worship in New England was ever colloquially referred to as "The Lord's Barn" or "God's Old Barn," as many Congregational and Presbyterian meetinghouses were in the eighteenth and nineteenth centuries. Nor was any Anglican house of worship ever given a name that included the word *Old*.[12]

Local histories offer abundant lore about meetinghouses, claiming, for example, that early houses of worship always had dirt floors stamped down by use, that they were made of notched logs, one piled on top of another, and that they were strong enough to protect against "marauding Indians." As communities grew and meetinghouse interiors became more ornate, children were reported to have played with the "squeaky" spindles in the opening of the pews and stared at the hourglass in front of the pulpit, willing it to run more quickly. One local history, Caleb Greenleaf's almanac, reports that when the Presbyterian meetinghouse was erected in Newburyport, Massachusetts, in 1756, "not one oath [was] heard and nobody hurt" and that when the frame was finally up, the raisers "stood up on the topmost point and sang . . . the Doxology."[13] Birds and animals were always a problem, especially the dogs that roamed the meetinghouse when it was in use. Occasionally strong men in the community—called "dog-whippers" in some towns, but "dog-pelters" in Antrim, New Hampshire—were charged with catching and caning them as they tried to enter the meetinghouse and levying a fine on their owners. The town of Reading, Massachusetts, permitted only the dogs of men who helped pay for caning services to remain in the meetinghouse "as recognized members of the congregation in regular standing." But in most communities dogs seem to have been tolerated, many of them allowed to sleep on the "broad stair" or turn-around halfway to the pulpit.[14]

Some stories were based on pure fancy and persist today in the common imagination of New England's antiquarians and history lovers. James Robinson Newhall (1809–1893), a judge in Lynn, Massachusetts, invented a fictitious diary in an effort to more effectively communicate local history in Essex County. Newhall's seventeenth-century "English traveler," whom he called Obadiah Turner, left a permanent mark on the popular image of meetinghouse life with the story about tithingman Allen Bridges's use of the sharp end of a rod to wake up a

Lynn farmer fast asleep in his pew. In Turner's account, the dreaming sleeper thought he had been attacked and exclaimed in a loud voice that resounded throughout the hall, "Cuss the woodchuck!" Newhall's imaginary story has insinuated itself into local legend and left the inaccurate impression that tithingmen carried a stick with a foxtail on one end and a thorn on the other.[15]

Other stories involve the supernatural. According to one account, the devil sometimes occupied the uppermost part of the belfry in the fifth meetinghouse in Ipswich, Massachusetts, and from there he liked to prey on unsuspecting parishioners and their children. The current minister of the Congregational church on the site of that meetinghouse will obligingly point out to skeptics the two stones on the ground at the base of the tower where the Evil One left his footprints after jumping down from his perch. This was presumably the same devil that came out of Hokomock Swamp to plague parishioners in South Bridgewater, Massachusetts, that gave the name "Devil's Roosting Place" to the meetinghouse in Livermore, Maine, and hid "amang the foremost and fattest" of the Scottish congregation in Peterborough, New Hampshire.[16] Another myth is that only a pail of milk can put out steeple fires kindled by lightning. Parish histories of the Unitarian Church in Groton, Massachusetts, and of the First Parish in Waltham, Massachusetts, both claim that steeple fires caused by electrical storms in 1770 and 1795 were successfully doused with milk.

Some local practices were grounded in long-standing artificers' or builders' traditions. According to an account book kept during the construction of the meetinghouse in Washington, New Hampshire, the building committee requested in August 1786 that "all the hewing timber should be cut in the old of the moon" in preparation for its erection in the fall of 1787—presumably to make sure it would be sufficiently dry twelve months later when the frame was raised.[17] The custom of "sitting on the sills"—perhaps a carryover from barn building—was a ritual of cooperative work and a public act of thanksgiving and prayer. A nineteenth-century historian of the First Church in Killingly, Connecticut, recalled a story that in 1714 "every male . . . over twenty-one in the whole town seated themselves around on the sills, and they just filled the sills." Rev. Ezra Stiles reported that during the erection of the 1717 structure in nearby North Haven, "all the Men in the Parish [were] at [the] Raising, & when they had finished Raising sat around on the Sill of the house which was about 30 by 40." In another instance Stiles used this custom as a measure of increasing population. After visiting East Hartford's meetinghouse in 1768, Stiles noted that Rev. Samuel Woodbridge told him that when the first meetinghouse was raised in 1735, the entire town "could sit on the Sills." Now, however, there were "400 Families."[18]

The commonly repeated story of the master framer being carried aloft with the first beam (usually holding a rum bottle in his free hand) is also based on customs associated with erecting large wood-frame buildings or bridges. An elevated position gave the builder a good vantage point from which to direct the work, and those laboring below him seemed to have preferred it. When Gen. John Fuller supervised the raising of the meetinghouse in Rockingham, Vermont, in 1787, he stood on the plate of the first bent as it was raised, lifting him twenty-three feet above the sill and twenty-five feet above the ground. Years later, Elias Carter, who at twenty-four built his first meetinghouse at Brimfield, Massachusetts, was described as going up with the first tie beam, "standing on the gallery girt."

A characteristic sequence of legal, communal, and social events preceded and followed the raising of any meetinghouse in New England. The first obligation was establishing the validity of its erection. Under the consensus of first-generation English immigrants, but also later under New England's colonial and early national laws, every town was required to provide a meetinghouse for public assembly and to hire a minister and a school teacher before it could be officially recognized as a town and elect representatives to the colony or state assembly. These buildings and services were usually funded by rates or taxes. But they also could be funded by "public" money. (Sandwich, Massachusetts, paid for its 1656 meetinghouse by selling in Boston a quantity of oil obtained from whales stranded on the beach.)[19] Once these requirements had been fulfilled, additional meetinghouses in the town's jurisdiction were allowed only by the creation of new "precincts" (also called "parishes" or "societies") within the town, requiring the approval of the colony legislature.

The formation of new parishes was often hotly contested because they decreased the tax revenues of existing parishes while increasing their tax burden. The division of Sudbury, Massachusetts, into eastern and western precincts, and the later subdivision of each into the constituent towns of Sudbury, Wayland, Stowe, and Maynard, followed an evolutionary pattern common to many early New England towns, particularly those whose boundaries in any way exceeded the traditional six-mile-square layout. In this pattern the initial seventeenth-century English settlers of Sudbury built their meetinghouse at an easterly location that was convenient to them. But as the town gradually filled up, the original location became increasingly burdensome to the newer western residents, who petitioned in 1708 to move the site to the center of town or to form a second precinct. The westerners claimed, "Many of our children and little ones [and] ancient and weak persons, can very Rarely attend the public worship." The petition was opposed by a majority of the town, including several west-side residents who preferred to put up with the inconvenience of travel rather than bear the expense of a second minister and meetinghouse. The court turned down the petition. Undaunted, the west-side group petitioned again the following year, and this time they won recognition as the Second Parish in Sudbury.[20]

A similar story with a different outcome took place in Newbury, Massachusetts, in 1712. Residents of the western "Plains" in Newbury had been frustrated time and again by their failure to win precinct status. They, too, had to walk miles and ford an icy river to attend worship. After several midnight confrontations with their opponents, they finally solved the problem by building their own meetinghouse without the town's approval and simply stopped paying taxes. The town appealed to the General Court of Massachusetts, which ordered the westerners to desist. In response, the Plains neighborhood "met with a gentleman Mr. Bridge, [a] churchman," who told them that if they petitioned to join the Church of England, he would protect them. Bridge, who was a "surveyor of the king's woods," helped them become a "pure Episcopal church" and got them in touch with the "diocesan," the bishop of London, to provide a minister and shelter from their "aggrieved brethren."[21]

Once a precinct was formed, it was necessary to site the meetinghouse. This effort, too, led to factional strife among neighborhoods vigorously competing to have it located near them. Few site controversies in New England stirred more extreme behavior than the ninety-eight-year "meetinghouse war" waged in the First Society in Lebanon, Connecticut, which pitted the older families in the southeastern district against the newer, increasingly numerous families of the northern and western districts. The controversy originated in 1706 when the proprietors of Lebanon agreed among themselves that the meetinghouse was to be "forever" fixed on the highway in the southeast sector of the town.[22] When the town proposed in 1724 to replace the first meetinghouse with a new one in the same place, however, the more recent residents in the northwestern sector offered so much opposition to the old location that the effort was stalled in court. The Connecticut General Assembly finally ruled in favor of the old site, while allowing the northwest residents the option of recovering their share of the new building's cost if they formed their own society. They did not do so and the dispute lingered. In 1772 the town voted to build a third meetinghouse on a more northerly site, but this time the descendants of the original southeastern residents went to court (fig. 1.6). Once again the assembly ruled to honor the original agreement. But in 1803 when it was time to rebuild for the fourth time, the northwest faction persuaded the assembly to allow a new northern site. This stratagem proved successful until it came time to tear down the old building. After the demolition began, large crowds assembled at the site to prevent (or to ensure) the "damnification" of the structure. The resulting court writs and counter arrests saw a number of the town's leading citizens confined in jail and precipitated the case's being tried in court. The affair was finally settled in 1804 with a financial judgment against the northern faction and the subsequent division of Lebanon into two societies.[23]

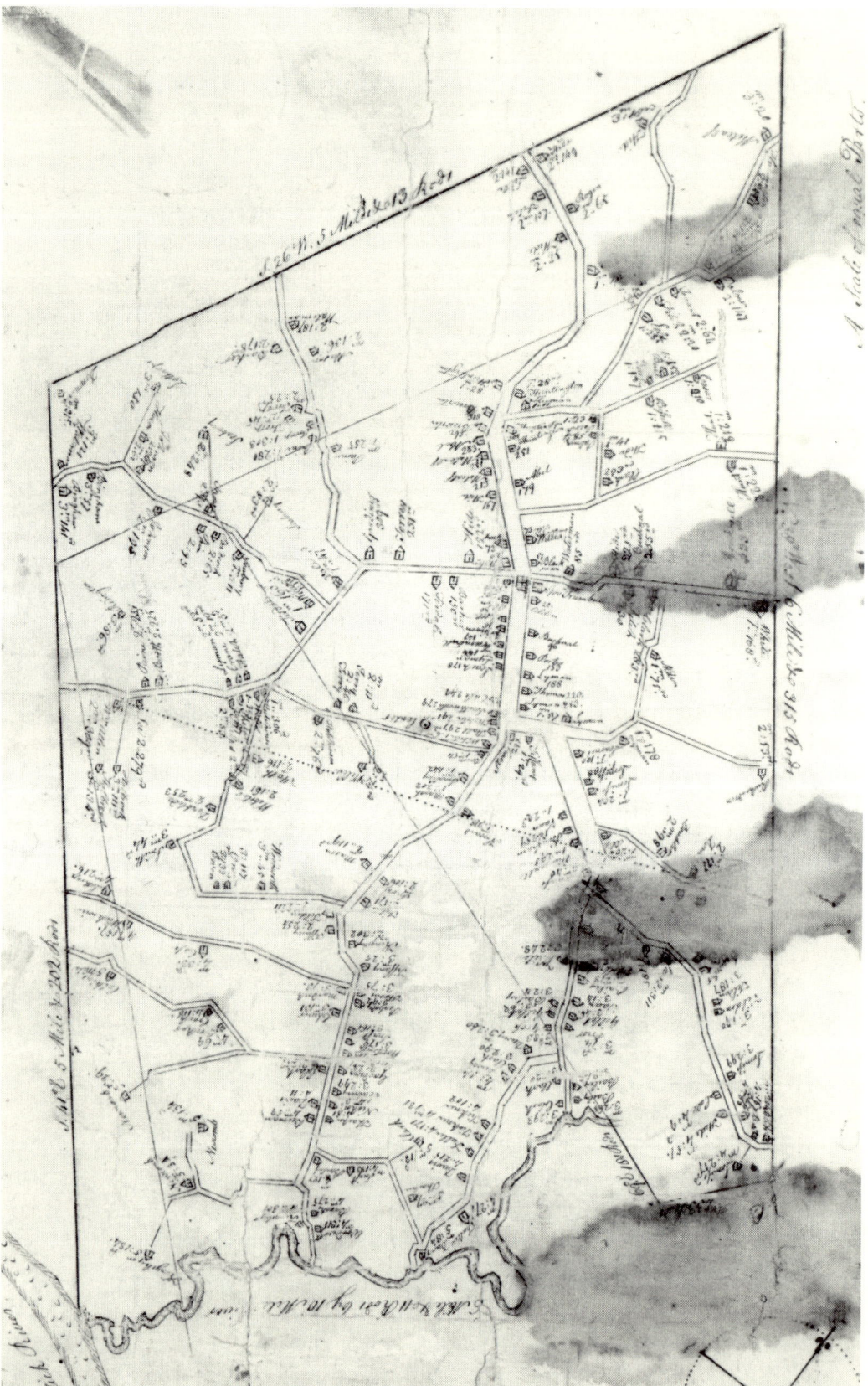

Figure 1.6. *A Plan of the first Society in Lebanon*, prepared by surveyor Nathaniel Webb, Lebanon, Connecticut, 1772. The plan gives the location of every house in Lebanon, names its owner, and provides its distance in miles from the meetinghouse located in the lower right quadrant.

Under some circumstances the principal landholders or proprietors assumed the responsibility of siting a meetinghouse rather than the town or parish body. When the sixty proprietors of Williamstown, Massachusetts, met in 1766 at Lieutenant Benjamin's tavern, they voted to build a forty-by-thirty-foot meetinghouse in the center of town, leaving it to a committee to finish the work. Two years later, with the frame still to be raised, an argument over the site arose because certain "men of influence" had moved into the center or southern part of the town and wished to have the meetinghouse near them. The proprietors again assembled and voted to disallow the town from having a say in the matter and then cast their own votes following a traditional system that reflected the acreage that each proprietor owned (rather than a show of hands). The resulting vote was 9,880 acres in favor of the old site (the "Square") and 5,035 acres against this location and in favor of one on Stone Hill Road.[24] A comparable arrangement between land and pew rights was followed in Abington, Connecticut, in 1753.[25]

As soon as a new meetinghouse was completed enough to be used for public worship, it acquired a variety of civic responsibilities that reflected the community's collective sense of order. Of primary importance was to "give a sign" indicating when to assemble for religious services and town or parish meetings—or to announce an emergency. A staff-mounted red flag or "colors" told people in 1676 in Chelmsford, Massachusetts, when it was time to gather on the Sabbath.[26] "Red bunting," raised "upon the public Worship of God," was still in use in Hartford, Connecticut, in 1727.[27] Drums were also common. Like sweeping the meetinghouse, drumming on the Sabbath was a function paid for by the town (fig. 1.7). In 1660 "goodman Edwards" of Wethersfield, Connecticut, received £2.5 a year for sweeping the meetinghouse floor, locking its doors, and summoning the inhabitants by drumming. The following year, apparently in acknowledgment of how well he performed his job, the town voted "that the Bell should be run no more to call the Assembly together, on the Sabbath and Lecture days, but that the Drum should be beaten at such times."[28] Edwards may have stood on the turret or platform of the meetinghouse roof, though he may also have beaten "the Drum round the town." Records show that calling the meeting together by drumming was still practiced in Longmeadow, Massachusetts, well into the 1740s, in Newtown, Connecticut, until 1763, and in North Guilford, Connecticut, in 1814.

A few communities used trumpets to call the meeting. Windsor, Connecticut, voted "to sound a trumpet" from the top of its meetinghouse in 1658, and Hatfield, Massachusetts, paid Jedediah Strong eighteen shillings a year for the same purpose.[29] A less expensive device, apparently favored in western Massachusetts and in the Connecticut River Valley north of Springfield, was the conch or "conk," which when blown correctly sounds like a horn. Conches were obtained from seamen working the West Indian trade. Records in Stockbridge,

Sunderland, Montague, South Hadley, Greenfield, Shelburne, Whately, Williamsburg, and Amherst all indicate that conches were used to warn meetings in these towns until the mid or late eighteenth century.³⁰ In a communication written in nearby Greenfield in 1894, one townsman remembered hearing his grandfather blow a conch and that "when the wind was right it is said that it was often to be heard several miles."³¹ After using a conch for more than twenty years, Whately voted not to "improve" anyone to blow its conch shell in 1795—probably the last time this practice was cited. Sunderland, in contrast, was less decisive. Having tried hoisting a red flag, the town voted to beat a drum but then reverted to a flag, went back to a drum, tried a "cunk shell" in 1745, returned to a drum from 1745 to 1754, and finally purchased a bell in 1754.³²

Figure 1.7. Oak and walnut drum, late seventeenth century, used to warn the meeting and announce public occasions in Farmington, Connecticut. The initials "L D" in brass tacks have not been identified. Diameter 23 inches. Connecticut Historical Society, Gift of William Porter.

Another civic function was to erect a "dial post" in a cleared area before the meetinghouse to measure time.[33] (These were later replaced by clocks mounted on the bell tower.) Sundials were often accompanied by signposts, usually nailed to a tree or post on the crossroads, indicating to strangers the direction and distance to the nearest towns. Wilton, Connecticut, set aside a "poplar tree" for this purpose in 1727.[34]

Meetinghouses also provided a place for public notices. Braintree, Massachusetts, voted in 1715 "that the publishments of Marriages for the future [are] to be set up upon the foreside [outside] of the most Public Doors of the meeting house in said Town." Plymouth, Massachusetts, voted in 1720 to place these notices on the little pillar under the gallery. In time, the "Public Doors" were replaced by a "box . . . with a glass door" such as the one that Jaffrey, New Hampshire, ordered attached to the outside of its meetinghouse in 1792. These boxes were moved whenever the meetinghouse changed location, and their use continued well beyond the separation of church and state. The town clerk of Windham, Maine, posted banns in a box attached to the town's meetinghouse in the nineteenth century that became a "source of unfeigned curiosity to all comers young and old."[35] Here, too, in keeping with a practice brought over from England, seventeenth-century bounty hunters nailed wolves' heads. Ipswich, for example, voted that "whosoever shall kill a Wolfe with hounds . . . he shall have paid him by the constable ten shillings . . . if with a trap or otherwise, he shall have five shillings: provided they bring the heads to the meeting house, and there nail them up." Hampton, New Hampshire, voted to provide ten shillings for anyone who killed a wolf and "nail[ed] the same to a little red oak tree at the northwest end of the meeting-house."[36]

The meetinghouse was also a site for the confinement and punishment of transgressors. The same carpenters who were paid to install the pulpit and pews were often hired to erect public cages, pillories, stocks, and whipping posts in a visible place—usually within sight of the front door. William Buell, the joiner who was commissioned to alter the "great Pew" in the Windsor, Connecticut, meetinghouse in 1661, was also paid "for a pair of stocks." Portsmouth, New Hampshire, ordered in 1662 that "a cage be made for the unruly and those who sleep in meeting or take tobacco on the Lord's Day . . . in time of public exercise." These customs continued into the first years of the nineteenth century. In 1802 Woodstock, Connecticut, ordered a new signpost and stocks, the post "to be square and painted white and [the] stocks to be painted red." Pillories were used in Salem until 1801 and in Boston until 1803.[37]

Perhaps the most visible public role for these buildings was as a setting for state occasions and for trials and executions. In October 1736 Boston's "Great Meeting-House" (meaning the Old Brick of the First Church) was the site for negotiating a treaty between the Province of Massachusetts and the chiefs of the Five Nations to "brighten" their chain of friendship. The main speaker among the Native Americans was prompted by another Native American who sat near him holding a handful of sticks representing the points to be raised.[38] Years later authorities in Maine District concluded a treaty with three Indian tribes at the Falmouth meetinghouse.[39]

Trials for murder and treason were routinely held in meetinghouses, especially if large crowds were expected. In 1717 Jeremiah Phenix, a victualler, was brought to trial in Boston for striking and killing Ralph Motershed with an iron hatchet. Judge Samuel Sewall (1652–1730) reported that the Suffolk County court assembled in the "Old Meetinghouse" (presumably either the Old Cedar of the South Church or the Old North of the Second Church) and that the trial continued for about five hours.[40] Almost sixty years later when the British were about to evacuate Boston, Col. Samuel Pierce of Dorchester, Massachusetts, wrote in his diary on 18 April 1776 that the "Court sat in our meeting-house to try the Tories."[41] In rural areas the tradition of holding circuit courts in meetinghouses was common. Virtually all of the trials held in Falmouth, Nantucket, Barnstable, and Worcester, Massachusetts, by Chief Justices Benjamin Lynde and his son Benjamin Lynde Jr. between the years from 1730 to 1780 met in local meetinghouses.[42]

So popular were these trials and executions that special provisions were made to accommodate the crowds. After a farmhand from Guinea, Africa, named Pomp was tried and condemned for the murder of his former owner, Charles Furbush, an Andover farmer and militiaman, he was brought in chains on Wednesday, 6 August 1795, to the First Parish meetinghouse in Ipswich, Massachusetts, to hear his funeral sermon. The town had previously hired Joseph Lord to shore up the two upper tiers of galleries to prevent their collapsing from the number of people who were expected. Rev. Levi Frisbie preached to an audience of about fifteen hundred people packed into ground-floor pews and two overflowing tiers of galleries. Built almost fifty years earlier as the fourth meetinghouse in Ipswich when the town was at the height of its ascendancy, the structure was still one of the largest and most elegant in Essex County. The pulpit and canopy were richly carved and mahoganized; gilded doors led to the outside; ornately crafted banisters ascended the gallery stairways; pews were spindled with delicately turned balusters. Rev. Levi Frisbie's sermon lasted approximately an hour. Immediately afterward Pomp was hanged in what may have been a portable scaffold set up on Ipswich's meetinghouse hill (fig. 1.8).[43] The following Sunday, August 10, a few hundred members the First Parish and their families convened for their usual Sabbath exercises.

Even large New England meetinghouses like the one at Ipswich did not have the capacity to hold all the spectators who wished to witness such dramatic proceedings. When Jason Fairbanks was put on trial in 1801 in Dedham,

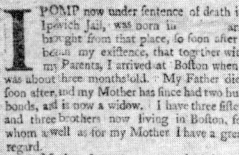

Figure 1.8. *Dying Confession of Pomp.* Broadside by Jonathan Plummer Jr. on the trial and execution of a condemned man at Ipswich, Massachusetts, 6 August 1795. Photograph courtesy of the Peabody Essex Museum, Salem, Massachusetts, BR910.42 DYING POMPEY.

Massachusetts, for killing his fiancée, Elizabeth Fales, the event was moved from the new Norfolk County courthouse across the street to Dedham's First Parish meetinghouse, a sixty-by-forty-six-foot structure that with its gallery space could accommodate up to fifteen hundred persons. When this space proved inadequate, the trial was relocated several hundred yards to Dedham Common, where it lasted three days. After Fairbanks was found guilty, a crowd of about ten thousand attended his hanging.

The votes taken by state legislatures disestablishing all Congregational and Presbyterian societies and ending tax support for religion in their jurisdiction gradually eliminated the civic use of the meetinghouse. In 1780 and 1790 Massachusetts and New Hampshire began the process to put an end to the privileged position of the Congregational Church by revoking its exclusive right to tax. Residents of these states now could pay taxes to support churches of their own choosing, a system that has been called by historians "general assessment." In practice it still discriminated against members of non-Congregational churches who lived in a town with only a Congregational church, or those individuals who came to be known as Nothingarians who shunned all organized religion. General assessment was legally dissolved in 1807 in Vermont, 1818 in Connecticut, and 1819 in New Hampshire, ending an arrangement long and bitterly opposed by separatist, Baptist, Quaker, Anglican, and Methodist denominations in these states whose numbers had significantly increased. In Massachusetts, however, the old system remained. But so broad was the popular dissatisfaction with these laws that printers prepared arguments against them to add to booksellers' or chapmen's portfolios. Boston's Nathaniel Coverly summarized this point of view in his 1812 broadside *On the Evils of State Religion Upheld by Law:* "The moment any religion becomes national or established by law its purity must certainly be lost, because it is then impossible to keep it unconnected with men's interests; and if connected, it must inevitably be perverted by them." Nathaniel Coverly's arguments were finally made into law in the Commonwealth more than two decades later in 1833.[44]

CHAPTER TWO

# The Meetinghouse and the Church

THE IPSWICH meetinghouse where Pomp was executed served the civic and legal needs of a major portion of eastern Massachusetts. Located in one of three shire towns of Essex County, this meetinghouse provided a seat of justice for a base population of about forty thousand that included Andover and Ipswich and most of the neighboring towns to the south and west. The church that actually worshiped at this meetinghouse, however, represented a small fraction of this number—about a thousand men, women, and children from the older and wealthier section of town. Ipswich had at least three other Congregational societies besides the First Church, each one with its own meetinghouse, elected parish officers, and a salaried clergyman. This small scale of parish life was typical of New England and Long Island, where churches were assembled from a geographic area of about three to six square miles and consisted of about two hundred families. This range was crucial to the evolution of the meetinghouse form and was the principal fulcrum around which all changes to it took place.

New England churches were made up of "covenanted" individuals, meaning they were formed by voluntary agreement entered upon by a select group of adult men and women. Under the Reformed system, they enjoyed full freedom to establish and follow their own rules while carefully watching how their neighbors followed theirs. Most put aside the traditional feast and saints' days of the Anglican Church, as well its bishop-centered hierarchy. But they did impose a social discipline of their own. As the state-sponsored or "established" institutions, Congregational and Presbyterian parishes hired educated and orthodox clergymen who were in effect town employees, their salaries and sometimes their housing paid by local taxes.[1] Equally important, this discipline gave the town or parish authority to enforce church attendance. While data are inexact, it is likely that during much of the seventeenth century about half the resident population participated in the weekly Sabbath exercises. (Nursing women and children under the age of thirteen generally stayed home.) In the prerevolutionary eighteenth century, attendance may have been about 40 percent of the general population.[2]

Reformed worship involved a devotional state of mind supported by faith, logic, and reason—and not simply a ritualized act. The service was a cerebral "exercise" in which the congregation and the clergyman participated through reading, praying, singing, exhorting, preaching, and prophesying. Sabbath exercises usually occupied about seven hours (8:00 AM to about 4:00 PM) with a short break for "nooning." Other special times were given to fasts, thanksgivings, and days of humiliation. Religious activities typically engaged a significant portion of a New Englander's time—roughly 15 to 20 percent of his or her waking life. Much of that time was spent in the meetinghouse.

The longest portion of the service was spent listening to the word of God through prayers and sermons, the two central acts in the New England agenda of worship. Prayers, usually spoken by the clergyman extemporaneously or "without a Prompter," often went on for more than an hour. Spontaneity could add to this time. Rev. Peter Thacher (1651–1727) noted in his diary, "I was near an hour and halfe in my first prayer and my heart much drawne out on it."[3] And Jasper Danckaerts, a Dutchman who kept a journal of his travels in the region in the 1680s, noted that on certain occasions, such as fasts, a minister in Boston could make "a prayer in the pulpit, of full two hours in length." Danckaerts added that as many as three clergymen relieved each other at the pulpit as they got tired.[4] Prayers had their own syntax and internal rhythm that reflected a strong dependence on Scripture. Increase Mather (1639–1723), who kept notes on his prayers, filled his listeners with what Charles Hambrick-Stowe calls a "whole Bible full of devotional resources."[5]

Sermons were equally long and usually explored or refined a biblical verse or a Scriptural commentary on a social or ethical problem. On a typical Sabbath the clergyman would organize and deliver a one-hour sermon in the morning and a one-hour sermon in the afternoon. Some clergymen also gave a lecture on Thursdays. Like prayers, sermons were not always written out. Rev. Thomas Smith (1702–1795) of the First Church of Falmouth, Maine (now Portland), recorded in his diary on 11 January 1759, "I preached a lecture entirely extempore, determining to do it but the moment before I begin." (Smith retained his position with that church until his death.)[6] Sermons and lectures were timed by an hourglass—a symbol of Protestant worship since the early sixteenth century—conspicuously housed in a wooden or wrought-iron stand attached on or near the pulpit and under the supervision of the deacon (figs. 2.1 and 2.2).[7] Published sermons suggest a delivery time consistent with one or two turns of the hourglass, but occasionally clergymen urged their listeners to "stay and take another glass." John Winthrop reported that Rev. Thomas Hooker (1586–1647) preached for two and a quarter hours in 1639 after he resettled in Hartford.

Like prayers, sermons had an internal rhythm and drew to a crescendo at the end, in keeping with the practice of saving the "best wine for the last." Together, prayers and sermons defined a public culture that saw each rite precipitating the stages of a Christian conversion that would eventually lead to personal salvation.[8]

Listeners were expected to take notes on the clergyman's discourse for use in their own private or family devotions and to help them develop a "hearing ear."[9] The number of published sermons has suggested to some that many of these were composed from notes taken by the congregation. Diaries in the late eighteenth and early nineteenth centuries, such as those by the cabinetmaker

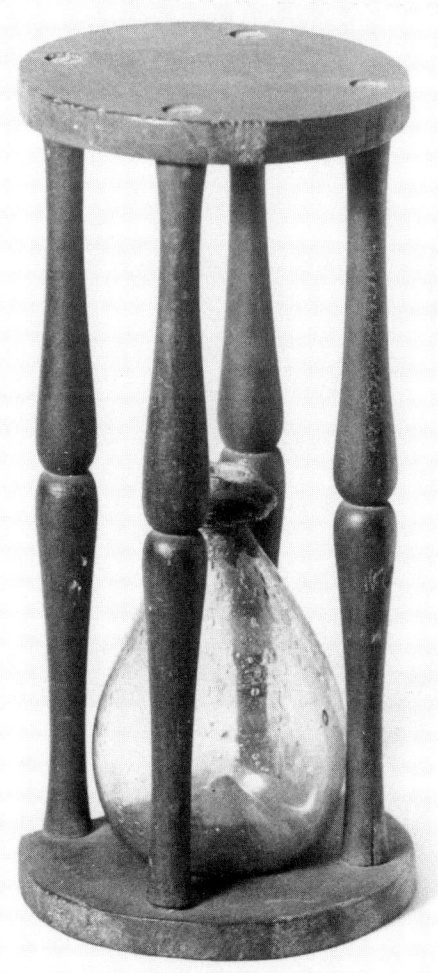

Figure 2.1. Hourglass used in Woodstock, Connecticut, in the eighteenth century. Height about 8 inches. Courtesy of the First Congregational Church, Woodstock, Connecticut.

Figure 2.2. Turned hourglass holder or "settle" used in the second meetinghouse in Rocky Hill, West Salisbury (now Amesbury), Massachusetts. The date 1729 may represent the year an hourglass was donated to the parish. Width of frame approximately 7 inches. Photograph by Arthur C. Haskell, circa 1933. Historic American Buildings Survey, Library of Congress, Washington, D.C. (The meetinghouse is now owned by Historic New England.)

Amzi Chapin and the housewife Elizabeth Porter Phelps, indicate that the weekly cycle of everyday life began with the Sabbath sermon.

The singing of psalms and hymns was an important part of the Reformed service throughout New England. Ezra Stiles reported in 1765 that in Andover,

Massachusetts, he heard "the venerable Mr. Saml. Phillips" preach, adding: "He began worship with asking for blessing and reading Scripture. He sings NE Version [i.e., the Bay Psalm Book] twice in forenoon & twice [in the] afternoon."[10] In the services in Andover, which were typical, the deacon sometimes read the psalms aloud before each singing. Some psalms were as long as 130 lines and could take a full half hour to read. In 1788, singing in Holden, Massachusetts, was usually "five times in a day."[11] Gilead, Connecticut, sang twice in the morning and three times in the afternoon. The congregation was expected to stand.

Other ministerial routines of the Sabbath included reading Scripture from the pulpit, prophesying, hearing public confessions, baptizing, celebrating Communion, collecting money for the poor, and disciplining church members. Rev. Ebenezer Parkman (1703–1782), of Westborough, Massachusetts, reported in his diary on 18 September 1748, "We this day began the public reading of Scriptures. In the morning after prayer, before singing, I read the first chapter of Genesis, and in the afternoon the first chapter of Mark."[12] Each one of these passages might take Parkman fifteen minutes to recite. Baptisms of newborn children, always a difficult ceremony in the cold winter months, took place every other week. Listening to public "relations"—conversions written by parishioners who were asking for church membership—was more infrequent, as was Communion, which typically took place six times a year.

In the two hundred years between 1630 and 1830 little changed in New Englanders' commitments of time and spiritual energy to their Reformed religion. Turmoil and reassessment followed King Philip's War in the 1670s; two periods of revivals in the 1740s and the early 1800s reawakened and gave new focus to religious life. But the same written covenants that held a religious society together in the seventeenth century were still being observed in the early nineteenth century. Sermons and prayers, which took one or two hours in the seventeenth century, continued to take one or two hours 200 years later. The same Communion and baptismal ceremonies that moved Samuel Sewall to tears on a Sabbath morning in 1688 were still practiced 150 years later.[13]

The revocation of the Massachusetts Bay charter in 1686, however, and the advent of a significant English influence in Boston brought on what Harry S. Stout terms a period of "Anglicization" of religious exercises that affected education, everyday life, and religious practices throughout New England. While Stout claims that the process "gilded the face of New England society but did not transform its soul," the spiritual effects of this process are nevertheless striking.[14] As the initial fervor of the first and second generations subsided, a significant egalitarianism manifested itself in matters involving church polity, church membership requirements, the role of the sacraments, and liturgical procedures that some historians see as a "declension" of religious zeal, and others as a change in focus that maintained religious fervor. However it is described, the effect was to make religion increasingly less intellectual and defiant and more ritualized or sacramental—that is less Calvinistic and more Congregational in its nineteenth-century sense.

This new emphasis is clearly revealed in religious architecture. Henry Ainsworth (1571–1622), one of the most outspoken of the early-seventeenth-century Separatists who left England for Holland, expressed the "Puritan" or "stainless" view of architecture in his defense of Brownist sects in 1604. "That all monuments of idolatry in garments or any other things, all Temples, Altars, Chappels, & other places dedicated heretofore by the Heathens or Antichristians, to their false worship, [should] . . . be raised and abolished, not suffered to remain, for nourishing superstition, much less employed to the true worship of God."[15] Elsewhere he criticizes seventeenth-century Anglicans or Anglican-leaning Puritans for continuing to use "Idol" Catholic churches for their services. "It remaineth then upon you to justify the use of these Massehouses, & to discover our error (if such it be) that reprove and condemn them."[16]

By contrast, mid-eighteenth-century New Englanders reintroduced the view that places of worship should be dedicated to that purpose. Terms such as "God's Tabernacle," "God's House," or "house for the worship of God" began to appear in town and parish records rather than the usual "meeting house."[17] Simultaneously, the physical setting of worship became more comfortable and visually rich through increased use of paint, textiles, and design. Some meetinghouses, such as the remodeled first-period meetinghouse of Rev. William Bentley (1759–1819), originally built in 1718 (see fig. 1.2), and the second Brattle Square house of worship, built in 1772, were even heated with large iron stoves.[18] Communities began to arrange for the consecration of new structures, a practice that became commonplace in the late eighteenth and early nineteenth centuries.

The process that Stout calls "Anglicization" brought about changes in four separate ecclesiastic areas: governance, membership, liturgy, and music. In the early period, gaining church admission was a structured—and usually difficult—process; men and women sat in different sections of the meetinghouse and used separate entries and stairwells, and the congregation faced the locus of collective religious authority seated before them in an expanded pulpit. In the later period, church admission procedures were less restrictive, families began to occupy their own pews, and men and women began to sit together "promiscuously" in the benches. Elders and teachers no longer crowded the pulpit and their offices were reduced or dropped. Bible reading and the Lord's Prayer—long avoided as a staple of Anglican liturgy—were reintroduced into the service. Psalmody was now taught in schools.

One of the most significant transformations was in church authority. Although each Church of Christ was autonomous in the Congregational system, by mutual agreement they all followed a set of rules formulated by bimonthly regional meetings and synods, of which the principal ones were the Cambridge platform of 1648 and the Saybrook platform of 1708. From the beginning, the selection of a minister and the choice of supporting church officers, such as teachers and deacons, were usually delegated to a small number of church elders. At the 1635 founding of the church in Newtowne (now Cambridge) a council of messengers gathered from surrounding communities chose seven Newtowne men to form the church membership; these seven in turn named Thomas Shepherd as the minister and one man as deacon. The choice was confirmed when the Reverend Mr. Shepherd received the "Right hand of fellowship" from his peers. At the 1638 founding of Dedham, Massachusetts, ten men (all former church members in England) polled themselves to see whether they were qualified to be "pillars" or "living stones" on which the church was to be based. The six that were selected then determined among themselves who would be the minister, who would be the "teacher," and who would be appointed as a ruling elder. These men in turn decided who was qualified to be a communicant, what constituted the grounds for excommunication, how often the sacrament was to be celebrated, and who would serve as deacons.[19]

During the first and second generations, this top-down practice was widely followed in New England, but increasingly these decisions were made by the church membership and eventually by the entire congregation.[20] The sixteenth provision of the Brattle Society's 1699 "Manifesto," for example, states, "We cannot confine the rights of choosing a Minister to the Communicants alone, but we think that every Baptized Adult Person who contributes to the Maintenance, should have a Voice in Electing."[21] Thus, what had begun as a decision of church communicants was extended to all qualified pewholders. This practice was stipulated in Massachusetts in 1692 under the new charter—a change that dovetailed into a requirement that towns pay the minister through taxes. A routine procedure soon ensued in which church and town shared responsibility. After the church members in Milton, Massachusetts, had narrowed down their selection to three candidates in 1728, they passed the matter over to the town for its "concurrence with the Church in their choice of a minister." The town's vote was recorded as "48 for Taylor Mr. Warren 2 Mr. Wadsworth had 1:3."[22] After 1730 each town and parish shared the role in selection throughout New England until the disestablishment laws were passed in the nineteenth century and churches became independent bodies.

Simultaneously, the roles of teacher and ruling elder were gradually allowed to weaken. Henry Ware, the nineteenth-century historian of the Second Church in Boston, notes that when the teacher and ruling elder of the church died unexpectedly in 1655, his position was not filled again. When the Reforming Synod convened in 1679, the "inconveniences" of the elder system as well as the loss of qualified men to fill the position were viewed as threatening to make

New England's churches "prelatical or popular." The last ruling elder of Boston's Third Church died in 1680. And in nearby Roxbury ruling elders were appointed during the tenure of the town's first two meetinghouses, but none after 1700. These numbers conform to Henry Dexter's view that ruling elders were chosen by some churches after 1700 but that most others had abandoned the practice. The Brattle Street Church never even mentions the term "elder" or "ruling elder" in its records.[23]

A related issue was church membership. Under the Puritan system, admission to the sacraments of baptism and Communion were restricted to church members. Applicants were interviewed by the elders and the minister, and their inclusion was approved by a meeting of the church. Proof of "saving grace" was codified in a written "relation" read aloud by the applicant to the entire congregation. These documents ran up to two pages in length and consisted of a formal profession of faith and the religious experiences that led up to conversion. When accepted, new communicants were permitted the rites of Communion for themselves and baptism for their children. Restricting admission to those who could qualify as "living saints" was a principal difference between Reformed and Anglican practices, because all members of an Anglican parish had access to church sacraments.

Faced with a declining number of communicants, late seventeenth- and early eighteenth-century New England churches initiated compromises to stabilize or increase membership and to keep the community involved with the church. The most radical—and contentious—approach was introduced at a synod held in Boston in 1662. In a very close vote, churches were encouraged to extend the privilege of baptism to parishioners who were not church members. Nonmembers could publicly "own the covenant," putting themselves under the jurisdiction of the church, and offer themselves and their children for baptism. The practice—called the "halfway covenant" by later generations—provoked what may have been the greatest and longest-lasting liturgical controversy among dissenting New England churches before 1820. At first only a few churches responded to this opportunity. Boston's Third Church, the towns of Chelmsford and Reading, Massachusetts, and Windsor, Connecticut, began the practice in the 1660s. After King Philip's War, a series of calamitous fires in Boston, and the political turmoil of the 1670s and 1680s, however, many older communities, including Roxbury, Charlestown, and Dorchester, adopted the practice. More followed in the 1690s and the first two decades of the eighteenth century. Eventually this ecumenical procedure was practiced on and off by virtually every congregation in the region before 1780, often at the discretion of the minister. But most New England churches eventually revoked the practice or simply let it die out, usually between 1775 and 1810.

The halfway covenant considerably changed the complexion of church membership. According to the church manual published by Cambridge, Massachusetts, Rev. Nathaniel Appleton baptized 1,747 children when he practiced the halfway covenant between 1717 and 1771. In that same period he allowed 714 persons to take full Communion and allowed almost a third of this number (214) to own the covenant in order to bring their children to baptism. Another 90 owned the covenant to be baptized themselves. In other words, about a quarter of all parents who received baptism for their children in Cambridge did so without full membership status.[24] The practice also precipitated a large number of divisions or separations. The Third Church in Boston, founded in 1669, was formed by a dissatisfied minority of the First Church who were denied the opportunity to baptize themselves and their children by "owning the covenant." Samuel Bird's church in New Haven separated from the First Church in 1744 on the same premise; they went on to build a house of worship known, from its exterior color, as the "Blue Meeting-house."

The practice of propounding public "relations" was also changing, though it accrued in small increments. Normally, a man or a woman seeking admission to the church wrote a short history of his or her conversion and read it before the assembled congregation. Sometimes women were excused from this obligation or asked to address their relations to the church communicants rather than the entire congregation. In Boston in 1633 the wife of Rev. John Cotton was not required to make an open relation because it was not "fit for women's modesty." In Dedham, Massachusetts, when a woman fainted several times in public as she spoke, she was examined in private.[25] Danvers, Massachusetts, permitted written (not spoken) confessions in 1689. Eventually many churches made reading of relations optional, reserving the actual decision to the minister in consultation with the elders. Cambridge, Massachusetts, made confessions optional in 1697; the Second Parish in Rochester, Massachusetts, made them optional in 1713.[26] Two periods in New England history seem to have triggered a greater number of compromises to the original written system for testing faith. After the New England earthquake of 1727, nine congregations are known to have abandoned or modified relations, and after the Revolution, seven are known to have done so.[27]

Some communities attempted to make church membership a right of every law-abiding parish resident. Open admission was associated with churches in eastern Massachusetts in the late 1680s and 1690s. The 1699 Brattle Society Manifesto allowed baptism to the children of "*any* professed Christian" and Communion to all those "of visible sanctity."[28] The policy was later associated with Solomon Stoddard (1643–1729) in the Connecticut River Valley. At the meeting during which Stoddard asked the Northampton church to abolish the narrative relation, he preached a sermon from Galatians 3:1 stating his support for a long-standing sacramental regulation "that the Lords Supper was a converting ordinance."[29] While Stoddard's example was not widely imitated, many churches in the Connecticut Valley practiced some form of open Communion in subsequent years. Questioning both the halfway policy and open admission became major issues in the 1740s during the Great Awakening religious revival. Stoddard's successor, Jonathan Edwards, tried to reinstitute strict standards for admission to full Communion, but he failed and eventually he was forced to resign his ministry. His perspective was repeated by "Calvinistic" Congregationalists in the early nineteenth century. In some instances, open admission revealed other faults in the New England system. In a case in New Milford, Connecticut, Rev. Daniel Boardman agreed to allow baptism to be administered to infants, even those born at seven months after their parents' marriage. He stipulated, however, that if the child were born in less than that time, parents had to "Walk the Broad Aisle" and make a public confession to the congregation.[30]

At least one American congregation outside of New England observed a form of Communion that nearly resembled Stoddard's. Ezra Stiles's diary records his dismay over learning in 1773 that the church in Charleston, South Carolina, practically opened the door to anyone in the street: "No Relation of experience, no confession of faith, no church covenant, no Charge, no Vote of the Brethren."[31]

Other changes involved Scripture reading. Reciting passages from the Bible in the pulpit—a ceremony called by its critics "dumb reading"—and forms of rote prayer were not practiced in early New England churches because of their association with formalism. But shortly after a leading Boston congregation announced it would read Scripture and recite the Lord's Prayer in 1699, some clergymen began to revive the practice. In his 1720 *Discourse Concerning the Publick Reading of the Holy Bible*, Rev. William Homes of Chilmark, Massachusetts, argues that the practice was "not part of the reformation from Popish Superstition." Rev. Cotton Mather in the *Ratio Disciplinae* of 1726 says, "This practice obtains in many churches among us, and that no offence is taken at it."[32] Nevertheless, the path back was slow in coming, the transition occupying the better part of the next fifty years. Proponents of change used gifts of Bibles as an inducement, sometimes offering to build a "drawer" for their donation under the pulpit. In 1772 Shirley, Massachusetts, was given a Bible by "Madam Hancock" (said to be the wife of John Hancock of Boston) on the condition that it be read as part of the public worship; the church and congregation accepted the gift and voted in favor of open reading.[33] But many outlying towns kept to the old ways. When Ezra Stiles passed through Massachusetts and Connecticut between 1769 and 1772, about half the congregations he visited did not read Scripture in the church service.[34]

The selection of Communion silver also went through modifications. Barbara Ward has distinguished between churches whose Communion pieces orig-

Figure 2.3. Silver two-handled cup made by John Hull and Robert Sanderson, Boston, Massachusetts, circa 1660–1678. Inscribed "ACE" on body. "The Gift of Mrs. Elizabeth Clement to the Church in Dorchester 1678." Diameter 3.5 inches. Photograph courtesy of the Museum of Fine Arts, Boston.

inated as bequeathed household items (standing cups, beakers, drinking glasses) (figs. 2.3 and 2.4) and those whose Communion pieces are more formally church-acquired (flagons, two-handled cups), generated by silversmiths at the request of deacons. She ties these preferences to positions taken by the recipient church on a variety of liturgical issues. Bequeathed household silver, sometimes inscribed with the donor's name, reflected a communicant's dependence on the clergyman and the hierarchical practice of serving Communion to the most important communicants first. Samuel Sewall, for example, suffered what he called a "humiliation" in 1724 when he was served the Communion wine after Madam Katharine Winthrop and in an inferior vessel. The use of flagons and two-handled cups, in contrast, tended to reinforce the egalitarian relationships between communicants, who passed the wine to each other rather than taking the vessel from the clergyman, and may have influenced the type of table used for this sacrament. Two trends soon appear: an increasing inclusiveness, as Communion was shared by a wider number of believers regardless of their status as church members, and an increasing adherence to Anglican ways.[35]

Another significant change in the public routine of eighteenth-century New England worshiping practices, which is frequently overlooked by historians, is the shift from sitting on gender-segregated benches to sitting with one's family in a "comfortable" pew. While based on social considerations (discussed in chapter 4), this change had an important liturgical element, because where one sat defined one's access to the word of God. Private pewing allowed the town's wealthy, its officers and magistrates, its military men, and even its handicapped residents and strangers to be treated differently from the rest of the congregation; they could expect to enjoy the places coveted by others. Some pew owners were allowed to bring their own furniture and build doors and windows to the outside. The issue of seating was not fully resolved for over a hundred years, but in the end it helped convert the Sabbath service from its ideal of a disciplined mental exercise to what amounted to a family affair.

More than any other factor, the use of music was a critical sign of increasing sacramentalism. Like the Lord's Supper, the practice of psalmody was regarded as a "converting" ordinance around which Reformed Christians built their everyday world of worship.[36] An early concern was the metrical translations of the Book of Psalms. Most seventeenth-century congregations arrived in the New World with Thomas Sternhold and John Hopkins's *Whole Book of Psalmes*—the

Figure 2.4. Wine glasses used for the Communion service by the First Congregational Church in Groton, Connecticut. England, mid-eighteenth century. Height 7½ inches. Connecticut Historical Society, Gift of Mrs. Howard B. Haylett.

"Old Version" first published in 1562 and used by the Church of England and English dissenters alike. But soon after the founding of Harvard College in 1636, several Hebrew scholars composed a newer version of the *Whole Book of Psalmes* known for its closeness to the original language. While disadvantaged by its tortured English phrasing, it allowed New England Puritans to replicate the early experience of Christian life. A modified version of this translation, printed in 1651, was used by almost every congregation in eastern Massachusetts, hence its name—the "Bay Psalm Book" or the "New England Version." It went through twenty-seven editions and reigned supreme in New England "for more than a century."[37]

A more lyrical translation became available in 1696 with the publication of *New Version of the Psalms,* a product of the English poets Nahum Tate and Nicholas Brady. With improved phrasing, this translation was easier to sing and eventually became the standard for the Church of England and American Anglicans. Tate and Brady was sung in Boston's King's Chapel in 1713 and was soon picked up by the New Brick in 1722, the West or Lynde Street Church in 1736, and Boston's Baptist Church in 1740. Tate and Brady remained in favor in rural eastern Massachusetts until 1760. A third translation, first published by the Englishman Isaac Watts (1674–1748) in 1717, was reprinted in Boston in 1741 under the title *Psalms of David Imitated.* This version became a favorite during the Great Awakening.

The provincial style of singing psalms was another source of contention. Few seventeenth-century New Englanders actually owned psalm books. Consequently, beginning with the second or third generation (1670 to 1710), most congregations followed a practice of "lining out," an earmark of the early-American nonconformist church experience.[38] The chorister, usually a church deacon, would choose one of about eight widely known tunes, announce his selection, and then read or sing the first line of the psalm. The congregation followed by singing the same line. The chorister then read the next line, and again the congregation sang it. The recitative reading and singing continued "line by line" until all verses were completed. The practice was common among dissenting sects in England, especially rural ones, as well as some Anglican churches in America. James MacSparran, the rector of St. Paul's Church in Narragansett, Rhode Island, for example, continued this practice until 1730.[39]

Many congregations, however, were forgetting the tunes. To counter this trend, reformers in Massachusetts, among them Rev. Thomas Walter and Rev. Thomas Symmes, encouraged congregants to attend a school to relearn old music, to learn new tunes, and to sing in parts. "Regular singing" or "singing by rule," as this movement was known, relied on "prickt" notes (notes that were pricked or embossed in the text) to outline the tune and trained talented parishioners to sing in harmony. The first such school was held at the Brattle

Square meetinghouse in Boston after 1720; others soon opened in Roxbury, Dorchester, Cambridge, Brookline, Reading, and Ipswich.[40] So closely was the singing-by-rule method associated with eastern Massachusetts that clergymen sometimes referred to it as the one "recommended by the Reverend Ministers of Boston." Singing by rule reached the Connecticut Valley after 1725 with the establishment of singing schools in Hartford, Windsor, and Springfield. By midcentury, singing by rule was practiced in about a third of New England's towns and parishes. At times, the issue involved the civil authorities. The town of Farmington, Connecticut, which practiced singing by rule, passed an ordinance in 1725 allowing town officials to prosecute anyone who sang "irregularly."[41]

A critical measure of the success of "regular singing" came when some congregations began to omit the "reading" of psalms, a practice they saw as a clear sign of New England's backwardness. While lining out ended in Boston after the 1730s, it continued in rural areas for many years, even after newly printed texts, such as Tate and Brady's *New Version* and Isaac Watts's *Psalms of David*, became widely available from New England printers and trained singers were ready to sing from them. Despite the best efforts of musical reformers, lining out dominated New England congregations through much of the eighteenth century. Many compromises were attempted. Some congregations sang all the way through during the opening and closing of the service but read the psalms line by line in the middle of the service (a practice called singing through "half the time"). Others read two lines at a time or an entire verse or even the entire psalm before they sang. Still others read the psalms only on Communion days but sang without reading in the Sabbath service.[42] As always there were instances of resistance—deacons who left the meetinghouse muttering "Popery! Popery!"[43] But change was inevitable. And when it finally happened, the suspension of recitative singing was a major turning point in the worship experience of a congregation and more than anything else consolidated the aesthetics of the service. Most rural congregations in New England omitted the reading of psalms between 1770 and 1790, though a few still observed this practice into the early nineteenth century, among them Ipswich, Westborough, and Stoughton, Massachusetts, and Chester, New Hampshire.

The end of recitative singing soon led to the practice of allowing trained singers to sit together in the pews or in special sections of the front gallery. Congregations voted to allow these practices in Boston in the 1750s, but apparently it was not tried until 1778 in Westborough, Massachusetts, when Ebenezer Parkman reported that the singers and their teacher sat together for the first time in a front pew on 8 February. Soon afterward the town voted that the singers could sit together in the gallery with the stipulation that the "Males [sit] in the Front Gallery on the Men's side, and the Females in the front Gallery on the Women's."[44] Some towns (such as North Bridgewater, Massachusetts, in 1801) even arranged singers' seats in circular form, a Renaissance-inspired idea unheard of among Puritans in the seventeenth century.[45]

Arguments over recitative singing also led to debates about the use of pitch pipes and "motions of the hand." Advocates hoping that these additions would improve the quality of singing were opposed by those who rejected "artificial" singing. But little by little these aids became part of the psalmody process. Pitch pipes, tuning forks, and homemade "whistles" (whose length could be regulated) were first introduced in the second half of the eighteenth century by choristers who wanted to keep the notes within the range of singers' voices (fig. 2.5). Special care was observed to minimize complaints. Kensington, Connecticut, allowed a pitch pipe as long as choristers used it "modestly," and some pitch pipes were even disguised as books to avoid inflaming the congregation. Swinging of the hand—a way of keeping time—was begun by congregations in the 1760s; but because it was seen as "ostentatious," Sterling, Massachusetts, outlawed the practice (as well as the pitch pipe) in 1770. Even as late as 1780, pitch pipes were disallowed in East Windsor, Connecticut.[46]

Next to come were musical instruments. According to Ezra Stiles, stringed or woodwind instruments made their debut in American churches in 1766 when Episcopal Trinity Church in New York City introduced the playing of

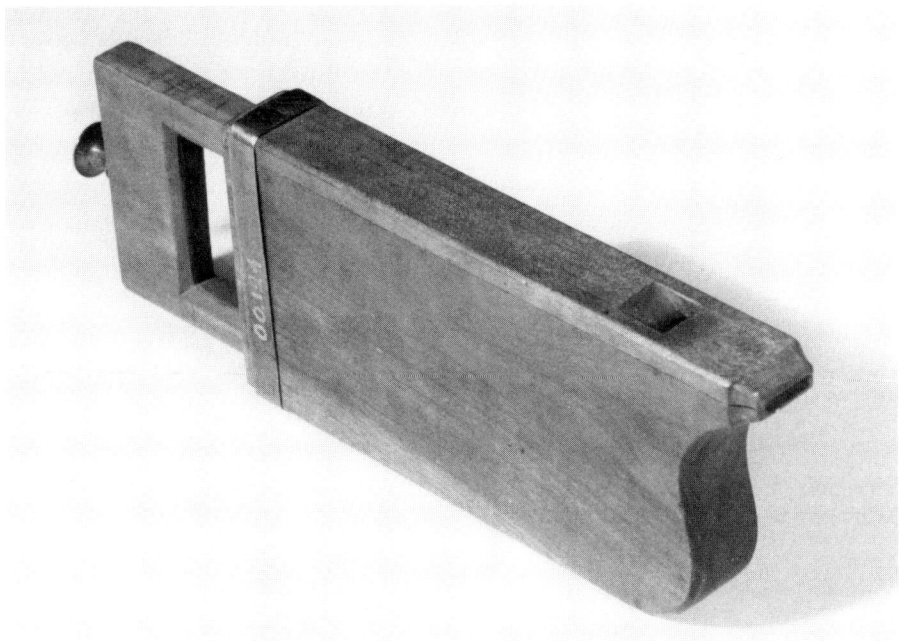

Figure 2.5. Pitch pipe used by Eliab Breck, a singing teacher in Sterling, Massachusetts, in 1806. Maple and brass. Length 7 inches. Courtesy of the Sterling Historical Society, Inc., Gift of Mrs. Alice Breck, granddaughter.

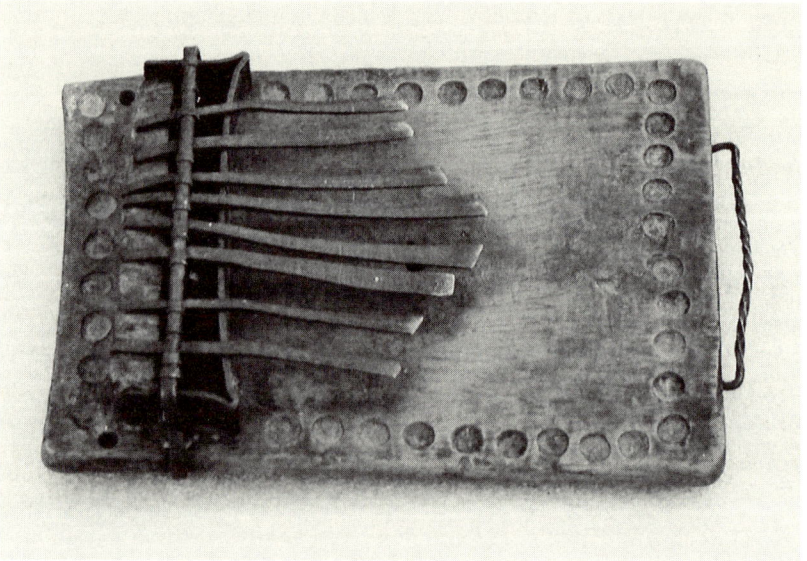

Figure 2.6. Mbira or sanza. Instrument probably used to set the pitch and accompany the dedication on New Year's Day, 1806, of the second meetinghouse in Bennington, Vermont. Possibly left by a runaway slave or purchased by a seaman visiting Africa. Wood and wrought iron. Height 7 inches, width 4.5 inches. Bennington Museum, Bennington, Vermont.

violins, bass viols, French horns, flutes, and hautboys to accompany singing in the service. He noted it was "the 146th year since the landing at Plymouth"—a wait of about six generations. The use of musical instruments soon spread to dissenting congregations, beginning with William Billings's introduction of the bass viol in Boston around 1770.[47] As always there were those who objected. The First Parish in Ipswich, Massachusetts, introduced a flute and violin in the 1790s—prompting one outraged parishioner (Dr. John Manning) to dance up and down the broad aisle while they played.[48] Chester, New Hampshire, added a "clarionet" and a tenor viol; and Georgetown, Massachusetts, a bassoon. Many rural parishes played whatever instruments were available. An African mbira or sanza, an eight-pronged vibrating device, is said to have been used at the dedication of the 1806 meetinghouse in Bennington, Vermont (fig. 2.6).

Bass viols, typically made by local woodworkers, had become popular in rural Massachusetts and New Hampshire by the beginning of the nineteenth century. James Harvey Bingham, for example, owned and played a bass viol in Claremont, New Hampshire (fig. 2.7). Their makers were often the ones who played them. Amzi Chapin of Springfield, Massachusetts, made scores of bass viols in his travels as a singing teacher in Appalachia in the early nineteenth century.[49] Many people, however, objected to their use or regarded them with derision. One woman in Littleton, New Hampshire, told the church meeting in 1815, "I will have you to know there will be no bass fiddler in heaven." A

Stratham, New Hampshire, deacon who agreed with her noted that musicians had introduced a fiddle into the church "as big as a hog's trough."[50]

It was only a matter of time before keyboard instruments were introduced into the meetinghouse. The first organ installed in a house of worship in New England was the one given to King's Chapel in 1713. (It had originally been a

Figure 2.7. Bass viol formerly owned and played in the church service by James Harvey Bingham of Claremont, New Hampshire. Height 46 inches. Early nineteenth century. New Hampshire Historical Society.

gift by Thomas Brattle to the Brattle Square congregation, but they declined it and gave it to their Anglican neighbor.)[51] Christ Church in Middletown, Connecticut, had an organ in use by 1756, as did Christ Church in Stratford.[52] The first Congregationalist organ in New England was an instrument of two hundred pipes installed in the meetinghouse in Providence in 1770.[53] Boston's First Church purchased one in 1785 though its pastor, Rev. Charles Chauncy, resisted the acquisition; the Brattle Society acquired one in 1790.[54] Norwich, Connecticut, voted for an organ in 1792 "soon after the Episcopal Church at the Landing installed one."[55] In all there were about twenty organs among New England Congregational parishes by 1800, and they sometimes aroused the same discomfort as the bass viols. When the town of New Braintree, Massachusetts, purchased an organ in 1806 a deacon remarked he would "rather hear the filing of his old saw than that noise." The rural equivalent of the organ was the melodeon. One was purchased by Littleton, New Hampshire, in the early nineteenth century; the town later added a seraphine (a reed harmonica) and a French horn.[56]

By focusing on those liturgical and musical innovations where data are available in sufficient quantity, we may now have a way of defining the New England church experience. As each congregation gave up its traditional Calvinist practices and assumed newer "Congregational," "Presbyterian," "Baptist," or even "Anglican" ones, it left behind a point of reference posted in time and place that indicates its position in a measurable continuum of ecclesiastic change. Progressive parishes were the first to end the practice of lining out; conservative parishes were the last. Progressive parishes were the first to read Scripture from the pulpit; conservative ones the last to do so. Progressive parishes were the first to sit "promiscuously"; conservative ones the last. The tipping point of each practice can be generally narrowed down to about one or two decades (and sometimes to one or two years), after which a majority of New England congregations followed the new way and a minority the old (see Appendix A, Tables 2 and 3). For example, most churches accepted the halfway covenant by 1690; about eighty years later, in the 1770s, many of these churches rejected it. Spoken or written relations were made optional in most parishes by around 1740. "Dumb reading" of the Bible was instituted between 1740 and 1750. Private pewing was introduced by 1710. Seating men and women together was widely practiced after 1750. Regular singing began around 1730; Watts or Tate and Brady replaced the old version or the Bay Psalm Book after 1760; singers sat together in the pews between the years 1770 and 1780; singers moved to the gallery after 1780; lining out was ended between 1780 and 1790; bass viols were permitted in the religious service around 1800.

There are some indications that these changes followed a geographic pattern. Most generally began in Boston and spread west into the Connecticut Valley, south into the Connecticut shoreline and Rhode Island, and north to New

Hampshire and Maine. While the Boston Synod of 1662 invited Connecticut churches to participate, most early adoptions of the halfway covenant occurred in eastern Massachusetts; Connecticut in a sense was obliged to catch up. The first religious societies to offer private relations for women were in Boston and eastern Massachusetts; the first to make relations optional were in eastern Massachusetts. Seven of the first nine religious societies that voted for "dumb reading" were Boston and Salem congregations; of these, the first three were the Brattle congregation, the New Brick, and Hollis Street. Comparable practices in rural eastern Massachusetts and Connecticut followed decades later in the 1750s and 1760s. The first professional schools teaching regular singing were held in Boston and its immediate suburbs in the early 1720s; these practices were picked up in the Connecticut River Valley after 1725 and introduced elsewhere in New England after 1730 and 1740. Four of the first six religious societies to adopt Tate and Brady's version of the psalms were located in Boston, with a heavy influx in eastern Massachusetts between 1740 and 1770. Seven of the first eight congregations that voted to sing "all the way through" were located in Boston. Beginning with the Brattle congregation in 1699, which voted "that the psalms in our public Worship be sung without Reading line by line," the new practice was adopted by King's Chapel, New Brick, Old South, the Baptist Church, and the First Church all before 1759.[57] Most others followed in the 1770s and 1780s. Boston was also the first to allow singers to sit together in a ground-floor pew, with eastern Massachusetts following in the 1760s and 1770s.

In three instances change went the other way, meaning the innovation originated in rural areas of New England and spread to populated coastal areas. The adoption of Isaac Watts's *Psalms of David Imitated* and his *Psalms and Hymns* began in western Connecticut and the Connecticut Valley. Of the first fourteen towns to sing Watts, eleven were located in the rural parts of Connecticut or the Connecticut Valley and only three were in rural eastern Massachusetts.[58] The practice of allowing singers to sit together in the gallery originated in central and eastern Connecticut in the 1750s and spread north into the Connecticut Valley in the 1760s. The inclusion of the bass viol, despite William Billings's purported role, was essentially a northern rural New England event and usually limited in Reformed congregations to central and northern New England. The viol was first adopted in Stratham, New Hampshire, in 1783, by Shirley, Massachusetts, in 1787, and then by Dublin, New Hampshire, and Shrewsbury, Wareham, and Westminster, Massachusetts.[59] Here the tipping point was between 1794 and 1806, when twenty-four congregations are known to have approved the use of this instrument. Bass viols almost never reached urban areas such as Boston—the nearest were Roxbury and Boston's Baptist Church in 1818—or secondary ports such as New Haven or Portsmouth; only two Connecticut examples are known (Guilford in 1796 and West Woodstock in 1801).[60]

Because many parish and church records are missing or incomplete, large gaps in information remain for many congregations. The statistical mean may not always characterize the experience of any one individual precinct or church body. And sometimes the record is unclear. Most nineteenth-century observers say that Stoddardism "thrived" in the Connecticut River Valley. David Flaherty found, however, that Connecticut churches were "less forward in dispensing with Relations, although traditionally less strict on admission to church membership." He cites the churches in Norwich, New Haven, and Windsor, which may have extended public relations longer than others.[61] But both the halfway practice and the variety and sophistication of retaining relations make these difficult to pin down.

Regardless of their imperfections, however, what the available data do provide is a theoretical template that can be generally applied to virtually every New England Protestant congregation regardless of its denomination. In this equation, religious societies that passed certain liturgical benchmarks signaled when and where they fit into a larger evolutionary continuum—possible clues to a more nuanced understanding of the architecture of their meetinghouses. Before we address that subject, however, we must first turn to two others: the building of the structures themselves and the manner of seating the congregation within them.

CHAPTER THREE

# The Builders

THE "ARTIFICIAL WORKMEN"[1] who erected New England's meetinghouses followed what amounted to a widespread agreement on what New England houses of worship should look like and how they should be constructed. This consensus was so broad that the raising and joining techniques workmen employed to build meetinghouses in parishes in the middle reaches of the Penobscot River in Maine were the same ones their colleagues used four hundred miles away in Stamford, Connecticut. And to most builders, the structure was a multi-storied wooden frame with several doors and multiple windows.

To raise this initial component—the frame—carpenters began by felling, curing, hauling, shaping, and numbering approximately 150 to 200 timbers, each one between six and sixty feet long. The timbers were drawn primarily from local stands of oak, beech, birch, white pine, pitch pine, and eastern cedar—all of them widely available in New England at the time. The principal timbers, commonly called "sticks," made up the basic rectangular shell of the structure. They consisted of sills, plates, posts, girts, and braces for the main body, and a variety of king posts, principal rafters, and ridgepoles for the roof. These were assembled at a communal raising and put together so skillfully that by one account the frame could be "turned upon one side, and rolled across the common . . . [and] not wreck the body of it."[2] Raisings, which always attracted hundreds of participants and spectators, were important social occasions in the early history of every community, providing a chronological milestone in the life of the town that set apart those "present at the raising" from those who came after. Samuel Sewall's diary tells us he attended the raising of the Charlestown, Massachusetts, meetinghouse in June 1716; he beat in the first treenail and stayed long enough to see the carpenters "raise the third post." He contributed an "angel," a coin worth about two pounds, toward the food and drink prepared for the workers, an important means of attracting help.[3]

The task Sewall witnessed in Charlestown was completed in two days—on the twentieth and twenty-first. This timing was about average in the seventeenth and early eighteenth centuries for raising frames, which usually required sixteen to twenty hours spread over two successive days. The frame of the second meetinghouse in Billerica, Massachusetts, was raised in two days in 1694. The town had summoned "all persons capable of labor" to arrive after seven in the morning by the second beat of the drum. "About forty and five hands of our town" came to help, the town records say, as well as "many others out of other Towns, some that came to inspect us and several that were helpful to us." They "concluded with a psalm of praise and returning thanks unto God by our Reverend pastor."[4]

Larger structures required more time. When the First Church in Salem, Massachusetts, planned its third meetinghouse in 1718, the building committee designed a seventy-two-by-fifty-foot structure with two tiers of galleries and a central turret or belfry. It took four days to raise the frame and a fifth day to raise the central turret.[5] Raisings that involved standing bell towers took longer. According to the diary of Deacon Ebenezer Hunt, an eyewitness to the event, the builders of the seventy-by-forty-six-foot meetinghouse in Northampton, Massachusetts, took twelve days, 6–17 September 1736. The work was supervised by Joseph Wright, who ordered it done in successive stages: laying down the sills, raising the posts and plates, installing the girts and beams, mounting the trusses and rafters, and raising the belfry tower. Each stage took about two days to complete. A rain delay required the town to send home its helpers and to hire sixty men at five shillings a day to finish the work. The town had to wait another two years before it raised a spire over the bell tower.[6]

Structures built in the later Georgian and Federal styles required double or triple this time. According to a journal kept by Dr. David Hunt in 1811, construction on the fourth meetinghouse in Northampton, supervised by the builder Isaac Damon (1781–1862), went on for eight weeks before the workmen reached the "octagon" on the spire. Following a design by Asher Benjamin, this building measured one hundred by seventy-six feet, with posts thirty feet high, and used a substantial four-story entry portico that supported the bell tower. Even then, the workmen still had to do the rough boarding, lay the floors, add shingling, and complete the spire above the octagon.[7]

It was never easy to recruit experienced hands to do this work, and most towns made attendance at these events mandatory for men over a specified age. Sometimes a town divided the task geographically. Hampton, New Hampshire, for example, issued an order in 1675 that required all men over the age of twenty to spend one day assisting in the raising of the new meetinghouse, beginning at "the Ringing of the Bell" at six o'clock in the morning. The work schedule was divided into two days. The first day all those "that live from Mr. Cottons House & so Round the town Eastward to the Lane by Herzon Levitts and so forward to . . . the path to Pascataqua [River]" were obliged to come; and the second day "all the Rest of the Towne from the west side of the Pascataqua way Round to Mr. Cottons House; & also all that live on the other side of the marsh towards Salisbury" were to come. Absentees would forfeit twelve pence "in money or else the constable to distrain."[8]

Hampton's meetinghouse was not big, its dimensions probably forty feet by forty feet with provision for a gallery. In the eighteenth century, when frames were much larger, builders needed many more hands. Winchendon, Massachusetts, required 111 men in 1792 to raise a sixty-by-fifty-foot twin-porch structure under the supervision of Ensign David Rice.[9] The demand for men was so great that towns regularly appealed to their neighbors for help. In 1781 Temple, New Hampshire, which planned to raise a fifty-five-by-forty-two-foot structure, voted to supplement their own labor by applying to the nearby towns of Peterborough, New Ipswich, and Wilton, for 15 men each, and 5 more from the "Slip" (an unincorporated parish).[10] Greenfield, New Hampshire, which required 100 men to raise the frame of its meetinghouse in 1795, asked for 9 men each from Peterborough, Temple, Wilton, Lyndeborough, Francestown, and Hancock and 6 from "the Society."[11]

Large numbers of men were needed because these structures enclosed a sizable internal void. Framers usually raised them in sections—either "bents" (the short-side frames) or "broadsides" (the long-side frames). These elements were preassembled on the ground and raised into a vertical position into mortises cut into the sill. They were lifted by the combined action of pulleys, derricks, gin poles, windlasses, winches, yoked oxen, chains, ladders, and human strength. Once the frames were in position, the final plate elements were raised and fastened and the roof trusses, ridgepoles, and rafters installed.[12]

The principal tools used in these operations were the gin pole and the spike pole. Gin poles and their associated tackle provided the basic lifting capacity to raise heavy pieces: bents, broadsides, individual timbers, and roof trusses. They consisted of a large post firmly embedded in the ground at the base of which was a metal fulcrum to operate a pivoting derrick. They were variously made from ironwood or oak with heavy iron tops with cyebolts for rigging, and even today abandoned examples of gin poles or their irons can be found imbedded in the framing of bell towers. Spike poles, or "pick poles," were handheld timbers between twelve and twenty feet long with an iron spike and ferrule fastened at one end. (The ferrule allowed quick disengagement when needed.) These poles were used to help lift each frame section as it was raised into position, to steady the frame as its base was installed into the mortise, and to stabilize it as the roof plate was secured. Ambrose Swalow of Chelmsford, Massachusetts, was paid thirteen shillings four pence for making "20 spikes and ferrules for Raising the meeting house" in 1711. Larger meetinghouses might require many more. Westford, Massachusetts, voted in 1770 to order "a hundred spick poles prepared" for the raising of its sixty-three-by-forty-four-foot meetinghouse with a post size of twenty-six or twenty-seven feet—making it high enough to include two tiers of galleries. A hundred spike poles could require as many as 150 workmen at the raising. Builders sometimes sent away for specialized equipment.[13] Boxford, Massachusetts, paid fifteen shillings for providing "the gear and Ropes . . . and blocks" to raise its thirty-four-by-thirty-foot meetinghouse in 1700; they were charged an additional five shillings to return the equipment home. Woburn, Massachusetts, sent a man to Boston to procure "tackle" on the eve of raising its third meetinghouse in 1748.[14]

Charles Clark has conjecturally reconstructed the 1773 raising of the meetinghouse frame in Wilton, New Hampshire, during which several men were killed. As Clark describes the process, the workers lifted up two principal broadsides with tackle and pick poles and inserted the remaining girts, plates, kingposts, and ridgepoles by means of a single gin pole mounted initially within the structure but relocated outside to insert the final frame members.[15] The master builder was Ephraim Barker, an experienced engineer. He had just completed the 1772 meetinghouse in nearby Amherst, where he had arranged "to hire the Gem [Gin]" post. Forty-five years earlier, Lt. Aaron Cleveland's 1728 contract to raise the fifty-five-by-forty-four-foot meetinghouse in Malden, Massachusetts, outlined a process similar to Barker's; he was asked to "provide a [single] Gin to Raise said frame."[16]

Each builder, however, selected the approach he would use to accomplish the task, which was determined by the size and location of the frame. When Billerica, Massachusetts, raised their meetinghouse in 1694, the builder appointed men "to find gin posts and others to dig holes for them," suggesting he expected to use more than one gin pole.[17] The lifting and steadying of timbers for large structures required at least four derricks and sometimes more. In 1792 the master builder Henry Wiggin was hired to raise the frame of a sixty-by-fifty-foot meetinghouse in the town of Newmarket (now Newfields), New Hampshire. He asked the town to provide, "4 Spruce spars for shores 44 feet long—6 inches at the top end. 8 raising shores 36 feet long, 4 inches at the top end, [either of] spruce or hemlock. 9 spruce spars 30 feet long, 4 inches at top end."[18] Presumably each forty-four-foot spruce spar was stationed at one corner of the frame. Wiggin may have employed gin poles in pairs, using the raising shores as temporary beams to support the framing section after they went up. This structure kept the bents or broadsides from toppling before the horizontal plate was attached. Wiggin's shores and spars were four to six inches wide at the top end, implying that each one was little more than a huge raw tree trunk needing about a dozen men or more to handle it.

Because the process involved the obligatory use of many local people, some towns inserted themselves into the decision of how a meetinghouse was to be raised. Despite the experience of known builders, Tewksbury, Massachusetts, voted in 1735 to raise the meetinghouse with "teacle" (tackle), presumably without a derrick. Shrewsbury, Massachusetts, on the other hand voted not to provide a gin to raise its new meetinghouse in 1766, as did Westford, Massachusetts, in 1770—though it is unclear whether the towns were voting not to use a gin or simply not to pay for it.[19] Townsend, Massachusetts, directed its committee to "provide jins and roaps" to raise its new 1770 meetinghouse, adding that they also provide "some person that can splice roaps if they breake, all at the towns cost." Greenfield, New Hampshire, voted in 1795 to raise its meetinghouse "with ladders"—a phrase that suggests that as each element was lifted up, it was steadied by workmen stationed on ladders.[20]

The final step in building a meetinghouse—finishing the structure—was never so dramatic as the raising, but it took much more time. Finishing consisted of boarding and shingling the roof, boarding and clapboarding the sides and ends, building galleries, window frames, and door frames, adding stairwells or stairwell porches, installing the pulpit and pews, and glazing the windows. The process sometimes took several years or even decades to complete. Falmouth, Maine, voted to build a meetinghouse in 1720 and chose the site in 1721. Workmen raised the frame that same year, enclosed it in 1722, completed the outside clapboarding in 1725, and put in seats and a pulpit in 1728. In 1740, the structure was converted into a town house when its replacement, subsequently called the "Old Jerusalem," was raised farther out on Falmouth Neck. Marlborough, Connecticut, took fifty-four years to finish a meetinghouse whose frame was raised in 1749. Workers completed the gallery in 1772, installed pews in the body in 1777, clapboarded the front and two ends in 1787, painted the inside of the meetinghouse and outer doors in 1789, plastered the inside in 1792, and completed the project by underpinning and laying the steps in 1803.[21] So great was the likelihood that these tasks fell well into the future, towns formulated specific instructions to allow for it. When Brookfield, Massachusetts, planned its second meetinghouse in 1715, they voted "to put in Gallery Pieces [horizontal girts] so that they may build galleries when they shall have occasion."[22]

THE TASK of supervising the building of a meetinghouse during the seventeenth and eighteenth centuries seems to have been an occasional trade and not one that provided steady employment. Out of approximately 1,460 documented meetinghouses built in New England between 1622 and 1790, the names of about 150 master builders are known. Fewer than twenty of these builders raised more than one structure; only six raised more than two. Judah Woodruff (1720–1799), for example, who was responsible for one of the finest eighteenth-century meetinghouse survivals in Connecticut, was a woodworker and house builder. In 1771 he was hired to build the new meetinghouse in Farmington. He went to

Boston with a colleague named Fisher Gay to procure finishing pine but found oak timber for the frame and bell tower locally. Woodruff, who served as an officer in the French and Indian campaigns and in the American Revolution, completed ten domestic houses before 1771 and four or five after the Revolution.[23] He was also a woodcarver, and according to an early town historian, his "carvings on the front of the pulpit, representing vines of the English ivy," and the "wondrous green vines" in the sounding board were greatly admired by subsequent generations.[24] Despite his considerable skills he is not known to have raised any other houses of worship.

For the years 1791 to 1830, in contrast, when approximately 729 meetinghouses were erected in the region, the identities of about eighty master builders are known. Of these, eighteen were responsible for multiple structures, some for as many as 14 or 16, indicating that these men were professional meetinghouse builders who were able to attract the bulk of the trade for themselves.[25]

Meetinghouse builders shared the essential characteristic of a background in structural carpentry—making or repairing large timber structures, such as watermills, windmills, barns, and bridges.[26] These projects required skill in handling and joining sizable timbers, as well as carpentry and woodworking expertise and experience in the design and assembly of foundations. When the town of Hingham, Massachusetts, voted in 1680 to build its second meetinghouse, it hired Charles Stockbridge (1634–1683) of nearby Scituate to erect the structure (figs. 3.1 and 3.2). Stockbridge, forty-seven at the time, was a mill owner, a wheelwright, and a millwright who had built a saw mill and corn mill in Scituate and more recently a water-powered mill in Plymouth. John Elderkin (1612–1687) of Norwich, Connecticut, who raised the first two meetinghouses in New London (1652 and 1679) and one in Norwich (1673), was a millwright with previous experience as a bridge builder. He had come to New England in 1637, having learned his trade in England. He was responsible for a bridge across the Shetucket River in Norwich that was later named after him. His son John Elderkin II in turn built the third meetinghouse in Norwich in 1711 as well as one at Norwich West Farms in 1717 (now Franklin, Connecticut).[27]

By the beginning of the nineteenth century, millwrights and bridge mechanics were still the dominating presence among New England meetinghouse builders. Isaac Damon—who besides erecting the meetinghouse in Springfield, Massachusetts, had recently completed ones in nearby Northampton and in Brattleboro, Vermont—was already well known for building several bridges across the Connecticut River; he later bridged the Penobscot, Mohawk, Hudson, and Ohio Rivers.[28] And as time went on, architects and designers not directly involved as contractors were introduced into the planning process, teaming with others to do more than one structure. The firm of Terry and Fillmore, which built the 1801 meetinghouse in Norwich, Connecticut, combined the carpentry expertise of Joseph Terry of Hartford and the architectural skill of Lavius Fillmore (1767–1850).[29]

At the same time, master builders were often men of political consequence or men with military or naval experience who came with a background of building forts, wharves, and ships; they were also used to commanding the hundred or more raisers needed for the assembly of the frame. About twenty of the known master builders after 1770 held ranks as colonels, captains, lieutenants, or cornets.

Figure 3.1. Woodcut view of the "Old Ship" (or "Old North"), the second meetinghouse in Hingham, Massachusetts, built in 1681 by Charles Stockbridge. One of four woodcut illustrations of local meetinghouses by Hosea Sprague, second half of the nineteenth century. Courtesy of the First Parish Old Ship Church in Hingham, Massachusetts.

Figure 3.2. Old Ship meetinghouse, Hingham, Massachusetts, photographed for the Historic American Buildings Survey 1941 by Frank O. Branzetti. Library of Congress, Washington, D.C.

Col. John Ames, a carpenter and cabinetmaker in Marlborough, Massachusetts, built at least four tower additions in Shrewsbury, Northborough, Townsend, and Ashfield and constructed the fourth meetinghouse in Marlborough that replaced a 120-year-old structure. Ames's influence carried over the Connecticut River to Buckland, where he raised a meetinghouse in 1793.[30] Some builders were closely involved in the political events of the period. Daniel Hemenway (1719–1794), who was responsible for meetinghouses in Shrewsbury, Worcester, and Northborough, was Shrewsbury's delegate to the convention that framed the Massachusetts constitution.[31]

As in most early American trades, the expertise needed for framing these structures was held in families—primarily between fathers and sons but also among brothers as well as brothers and nephews. A family that became preeminent builders and woodworkers in Essex County, Massachusetts, were descendants of Richard Jaques (ca. 1574–1653), a resident of Wiltshire, England, whose son Henry Jaques (ca. 1619–1687) settled in Newbury in 1648 and founded a line of joiners, turners, cabinetmakers, housewrights, and millwrights. Henry Jaques was hired in 1661 by the town to make "a gallery at both ends and all along on the west side of the new meeting-house, with three substantial seats all along and three pair of stairs" and to lay the meetinghouse floor. In 1675 he served on the committee to complete "the ministry house."[32] Henry Jaques's son, Serj. Stephen Jaques (1661–1744), a millwright and woodworker, contracted in 1700 to build Newbury's third meetinghouse for £530. It was to be sixty by fifty feet with a stud height of twenty-four feet and four prominent gables. (The structure was remembered in the nineteenth century for having "needles sticking from the timbers of the roof.") Stephen Jaques is also reputed to have made the Communion table for Newbury and was probably responsible for many of the interior fittings. In 1703 Stephen Jaques, now an ensign, worked with Benjamin Woodbridge and Henry Jaques (his nephew) to build a windmill. Numerous Jaques family members continued in the building and woodworking trades. Stephen's son Stephen Jaques (1686–after 1741) and his grandnephew John Jaques (1721–1803) were turners.[33]

Similar relationships continued in the mid-eighteenth century. Thomas Dick and John Dick of Pelham, Massachusetts, are credited by historians with having raised or worked on at least six meetinghouses in Worcester and Hampshire Counties. They were presumably brothers, since they both had children in Pelham between 1738 and 1759. They raised their first meetinghouse in Shutesbury, Massachusetts, where "Mr. Dix" was named as master builder in 1735 and again in 1739.[34] (Shutesbury lies immediately north of Pelham.) Another neighboring town, Petersham, credited Thomas Dick for painting its meetinghouse red in 1738 for the sum of £3.10.10. Two years later Bolton voted "that Thomas Dick should have the liberty to cut six sticks of lumber on any man's land in order to

Figure 3.3. Old Home Day, celebrated circa 1920 in Pelham, Massachusetts. The first meetinghouse in Pelham, completed by Thomas and John Dick in 1743, is seen in this photograph after the gallery was floored over and the building used as a town hall. Courtesy of the History Room of the Pelham Free Public Library, Pelham, Massachusetts.

build the Meeting-house." Thomas Dick and John Dick together signed the circa 1741 contract to build the meetinghouse at Pelham itself, a structure that still stands in that town (fig. 3.3).[35] Thomas Dick, then called an innholder, contracted to build the Charlemont meetinghouse in 1753; after the project was shelved, he was hired again in 1762.[36]

Perhaps the most unusual of New England's building conglomerates were the Spofford and Palmer families in eastern Essex County, Massachusetts, many of them residents of a well-known hill in Georgetown. Together they were responsible for about fourteen meetinghouses or meetinghouse enlargements in the late eighteenth and early nineteenth centuries, some of them standing to this day. They were active in Rowley, Andover, Newburyport, and Salisbury, and, like other meetinghouse carpenters, they also excelled in building sawmills and designing suspension and chain bridges.[37] The founder of this clan was Col. Daniel Spofford (1721–1803), a millwright and builder, who in his later years was known to have worn a green cap when he went about his work and a white wig when sitting in the deacons' seat at church. Daniel lived on "Spofford's Hill" (also known as Baldplate Hill), a site settled by John Spofford in the seventeenth century. At a family reunion held in Georgetown in 1869, his farm was called the "Old Col. Daniel Spofford homestead."

According to a short history by his grandson (a nineteenth-century Rowley physician), Col. Daniel Spofford served in the Seventh Regiment of the Essex County Militia and later as representative to the general court in 1776 and delegate to the state constitutional convention of 1780. He raised "several church edifices" and twice enlarged Salem's Middle Precinct (Peabody) meetinghouse, first by cutting it in half crosswise and later by cutting it lengthwise, adding two rows of pews with a broad aisle between them. Daniel trained his son Moody Spofford (1744–1828), who, according to the same history, was responsible for building meetinghouses in South Andover (1788), Groveland (1790), and "other churches" in eastern Essex County. Called an "eminent architect," Moody Spofford teamed with the bridge designer Timothy Palmer to create a model for the well-known suspension bridge spanning the Merrimack in 1794, the two working together in the shop on Spofford's Hill, giving "every timber and bolt in due proportion." The design was later patented, and Timothy Palmer went south with several Essex workmen and built the first bridges across the Schuylkill River at Philadelphia and the Potomac River at Washington.[38]

Colonel Spofford also trained two nephews and two of their colleagues. One nephew was Jeremiah Spofford (b. 1749), son of Daniel's brother Eliphalet (who also lived on Spofford's Hill). Jeremiah and his brother-in-law Samuel Adams of Rindge, New Hampshire, submitted the low bid to build the frame of the Jaffrey, New Hampshire, meetinghouse. A second was Jacob Spofford (b. 1755), son of Daniel's brother Deacon Abner Spofford. He too was called "an ingenious mechanic" and is credited with having invented a circular sawmill.[39] Jacob Spofford and Joseph Haskell joined Jeremiah in building the Jaffrey meetinghouse in 1775, returning to Essex County on the day the English burned Charlestown, Massachusetts. Later he teamed with his cousin Moody to help Timothy Palmer construct the Haverhill suspension bridge in 1794. Col. Daniel Spofford may have also trained Timothy Palmer's brother Ambrose Palmer, who worked with Jacob Spofford to build the Rocky Hill meetinghouse in West Salisbury and who is said to have been one of two men supplying lumber for the second meetinghouse of Newburyport's First Society in 1801. A third Palmer sibling, Andrew or Andrews Palmer of Newburyport, may also have been trained by Colonel Spofford; Andrew later built a meetinghouse at Arlington, Massachusetts (1804), and at Sudbury's First Parish, now Wayland, Massachusetts (1814).[40]

In central Massachusetts and eastern Connecticut, meetinghouse construction was dominated between 1804 and 1820 by the family of Timothy Carter, an English immigrant who is said to have arrived in the region in the 1760s carrying drawings and specifications, among them Batty Langley's *The City and Country Builder's and Workman's Treasury of Designs,* published in London in 1756.[41] Carter married Sarah Walker of Sutton, Massachusetts, in 1768 and had at least three sons. The two oldest were Timothy Carter Jr. and Benjamin Carter; the youngest was Elias Carter, born in Auburn, Massachusetts, in 1781. They were still boys when their father was killed in 1784 raising a meetinghouse

Figure 3.4. First Congregational Church, Leicester, Massachusetts, built in 1784 by Timothy Carter Sr., who lost his life there in an accident. The meetinghouse is shown in 1862 after the removal of its main door and its conversion to a church plan, leaving the two center windows spaced farther apart than the others. From John Nelson, *Pastor's Memorial*, frontispiece. Courtesy of the American Antiquarian Society.

in Leicester, Massachusetts (fig. 3.4), but all three continued in his profession.[42] Elias Carter (1781–1864) went on to become a major woodworker, builder, and architect. At the age of twenty-four he accepted a contract of $2,000 to assemble the third meetinghouse in Brimfield, Massachusetts, the town deducting $400 for providing manpower to raise the frame.[43] Carter or his trainees or subordinates went on to raise at least fourteen more meetinghouses between 1811 and 1820. The first was in Templeton and the last in Mendon.[44] Carter's price increased as his reputation grew. In Killingly, Connecticut, in 1818 Elias Carter's bill for "Said house per contract including glass" was $4,080.[45]

The success of family builders led to the forming of consortia among siblings and colleagues, who traveled long distances to obtain work. Abner Spofford, for example, joined Ambrose Palmer to form "Spofford and Palmer," a firm that used the Spofford family mill in Rowley. Elias's father, Timothy Carter, and his uncle, Benjamin Carter, formed a contracting firm under the name of Carter and Carter. Elias Carter made a partnership with Jonathan Cutting Jr. of Templeton, who helped him raise the meetinghouse in Templeton.[46] Later Elias Carter teamed with John Hulett, who dominated the meetinghouse field in western Massachusetts. These partnerships helped consolidate a regionwide profession that specialized in building houses of worship. Whereas seventeenth-century carpenters only occasionally took on large jobs, early nineteenth-century contractors became a professional commodity available to towns wishing to raise houses of worship. Contractors often passed around work with their colleagues. Peleg Kingsley, of Brattleboro, Vermont, was hired in 1811 to build the fourth meetinghouse of Northampton, Massachusetts; he in turn gave the work to Isaac Damon, who did most of the framing.

The task at hand, however, remained the same throughout the period: foundation layers, framers, carpenters, joiners, ironworkers, glaziers, and painters worked under a town-appointed committee and relied on local men to assist them. When Springfield, Massachusetts, assembled its second meetinghouse in 1677, the town had just finished a war with Algonkians that had held up its plan for three years. Designing the structure in the current style (a hipped roof, a turret, and a gallery),[47] the town called on John Allis, a housewright and woodworker from Hartford, to build the foundation, erect the frame, and to complete most of the windows and inside finish carpentry. The building committee hired three woodworking assistants, who helped with fastening the clapboarding, building the turret, and laying the roof boards and floors. To complete the project, they engaged a turner (Samuel Allis, John's brother), an ironworker, a glazier, and a glazier's assistant.[48]

More than 110 years later, when Westminster built its second meetinghouse in 1788, Massachusetts was one of thirteen former English colonies that had united as a new nation. Westminster, too, followed the current model (a twin-porch meetinghouse with stairwells on either end), and like Springfield, let the framing to an experienced master builder, Timothy Bacon. The town then broke down the work into portions and subcontracted them individually. The building committee gave the enclosing and shingling to one carpenter; the window frames, glazing, and sashes to another; the clapboarding to a third; and the inside finish carpentry to a local church deacon.[49] Even as historical circumstances changed dramatically, the process of building New England's houses of worship had actually changed very little.

CHAPTER FOUR

# Seating the Congregation

THE SUBJECT that most directly concerned committees in Springfield and Westminster was where the congregation would sit in their new houses of worship. Meetinghouse seating remained one of the most common topics of discussion at New England town and parish meetings for the first two hundred years of the region's history. Holding seating discussions was no doubt a continuation of past practices in Calvinist churches, especially those in seventeenth-century Scotland.[1] These discussions dealt with issues such as meetinghouse dimensions, the number and placement of galleries, the building of private pews, and access to pews from the outside. They also dealt with rules about measuring the "importance" of families, assigning "dignities" to the seats, providing for infirm, elderly, and deaf parishioners, and selling pews to raise funds for building and repairing the meetinghouse.

Between eight hundred and a thousand persons of all ages, ranks, and backgrounds were expected to fit into a forty-by-fifty-foot New England meetinghouse—the most common size before 1790. By Reformed tradition, women were seated on the minister's left and men on his right, separated by a narrow aisle running the width of the meetinghouse. This practice was followed by the church in New Haven, Connecticut, in 1647 and again in 1655; and according to Ezra Stiles's memory sketch of the floor plan of the second meetinghouse in New Haven, it was still being followed in the 1750s (fig. 4.1). This segregated tradition was widely observed among Congregationalists, Baptists, Presbyterians, and Quakers in New England before 1770 and among Quakers still at the beginning of the nineteenth century. Some towns reversed these positions. Longmeadow, Massachusetts, for example, arranged for women to sit on the "west side" of the meetinghouse in 1716, suggesting they sat on the minister's right.[2]

While special places were reserved for visiting strangers or for those who were hearing impaired, each remaining bench and pew was parceled out with great care by a committee assigned for the purpose. The "best" locations were those immediately to the left or the right of the pulpit or directly in front of it at

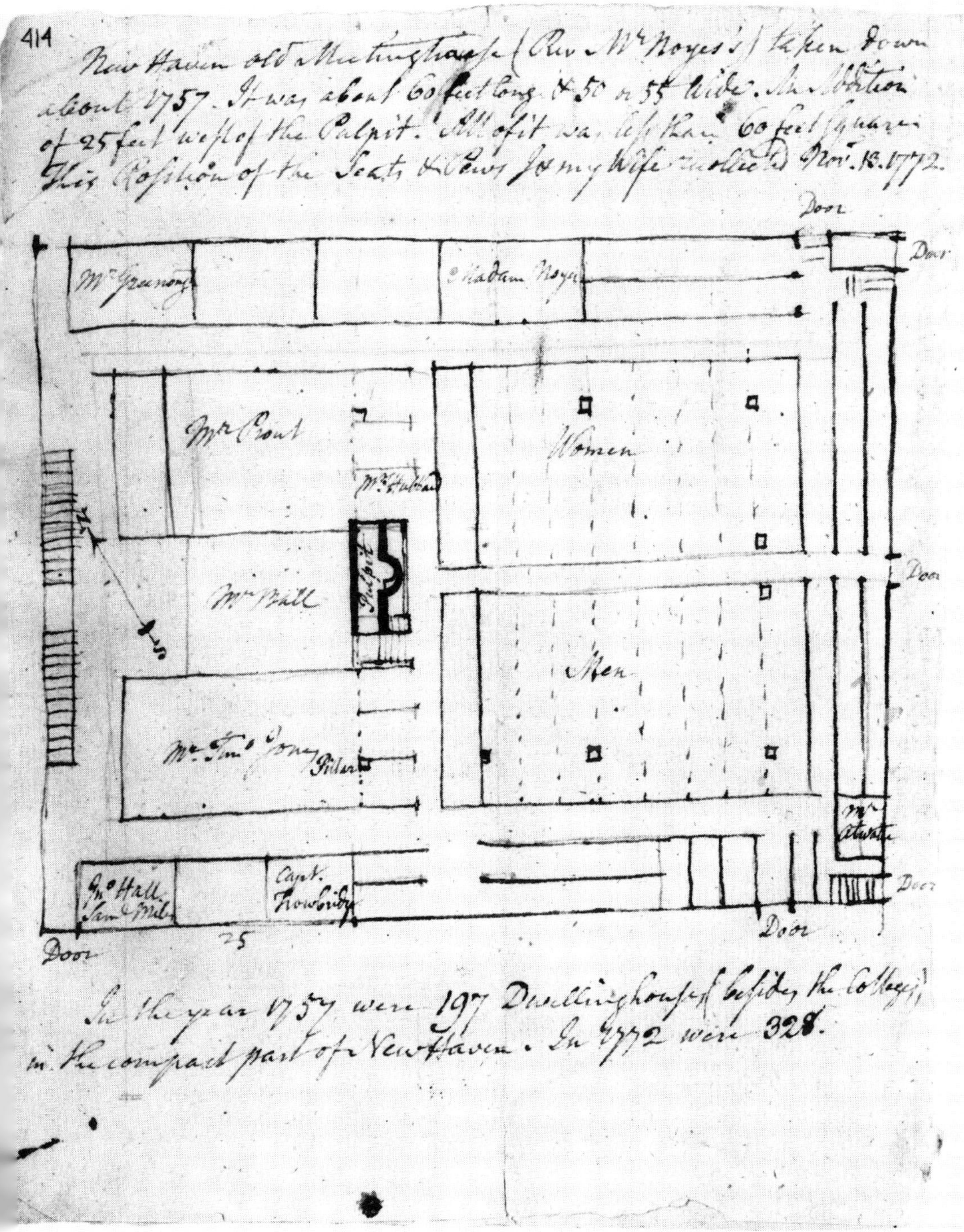

New Haven old Meetinghouse (Rev. Mr Noyes's) taken down about 1757. It was about 60 feet long & 50 or 55 wide. An Addition of 25 feet west of the Pulpit. All of it was less than 60 feet square. This Position of the Seats & Pews I & my Wife recollected Nov. 13. 1772.

In the year 1757 were 197 Dwellinghouses besides the Cottages, in the compact part of New Haven. In 1772 were 328.

Figure 4.1. Memory drawing by Ezra Stiles of the plan of the second meetinghouse in New Haven, Connecticut, showing the "Position of the Seats & Pews I & my Wife recollected Nov. 13. 1772," with women on the right and men on the left. This meetinghouse was built by Nathan Andrews in 1668 as a 55-by-35-foot structure. After the width of the meetinghouse was enlarged to 60 feet, the pulpit was centrally located. Beinecke Rare Book and Manuscript Library, Yale University.

the Communion table. Here sat the clergyman and his family; church teachers, deacons, and elders, principal landholders, and important militia officers. The distribution of pews and benches on the sides and far walls, many of them raised up to a foot above the level of the floor, followed an elaborate merit-based system to which every member of the community was expected to adhere.[3] Each head of household and his spouse were graded by their importance and assigned to a specific place appropriate to their "dignity." First-row pews in the gallery, pews near the doorways, and pews on the main aisle went to those with the most dignity; pews obscured by distance, stairwells, or supporting columns went to those with the least. Well established in sixteenth-century Tudor England, this practice placed wealthy parish residents in pews at the front, while the poor sat on benches at the rear.[4] In New England, these assignments were posted on a seating chart (fig. 4.2), a sheet usually nailed to the entrance of the meetinghouse, which subjected the community to a periodic review of individual worth unmatched for its frankness. To handle enforcement, each town appointed tithingmen—a type of meetinghouse police that one historian calls "grotesque" and "most

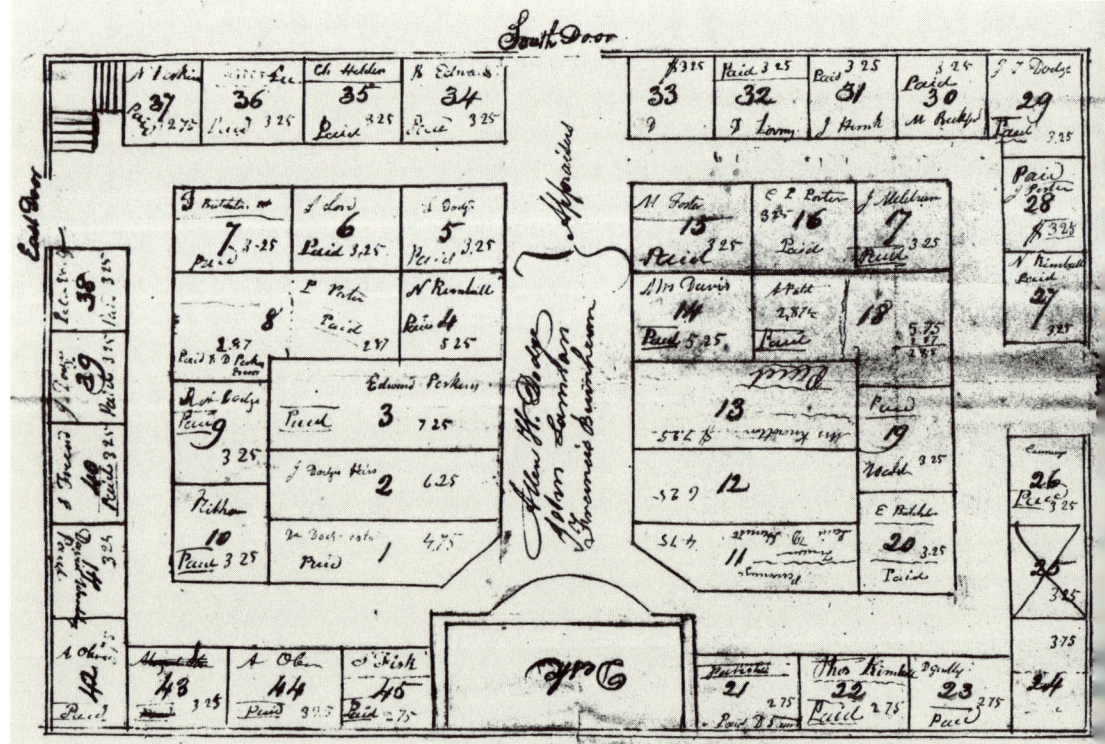

Figure 4.2. Ground-floor pew plan of the third meetinghouse in Wenham, Massachusetts, early nineteenth century. Built in 1748, the meetinghouse dimensions were 52 by 42 feet; stairs to the gallery are visible in the upper left near the east door. Wenham Museum Collection, Wenham, Massachusetts.

extraordinary"—to be in charge of security and decency.⁵ Largely ineffectual, the office of tithingman nevertheless was a required duty for most men before 1770. Initially most communities had only one or two tithingmen, who also catechized children and prevented Sabbath travel. But after the Reforming Synod of 1680 took up the matter, some towns appointed many more—each one responsible for a specific section of the town. According to a nineteenth-century clergyman at Ipswich, Massachusetts, "16 rods, used by tything men, being about 5 feet in length and one inch in diameter" were discovered in the closet under the pulpit when the meetinghouse was taken down in 1823.⁶

That seating plans were scrupulously enforced from the earliest period is suggested by a detailed set of instructions put into effect in 1662 in Cambridge, Massachusetts, not long after the deaths of two prominent members of the congregation. The committee that had made earlier placements in 1658 met again to distribute the seats that were now left vacant. They followed an order that resonates to this day. Stephen Day, the seventy-year-old printer, was relocated "2: Seats from the [Communion] table"; John Gibson was put "where Mr. Day was wont to sit"; Richard Eccles, where "Jno. Gibson was wont to sit"; and Benjamin Crackbone, where "Ri: [Eccles] was wont to sit." On the women's side the newly widowed Mrs. Upham was seated "with her mother"; Ester Sparkhawke was assigned "in the place where Mrs Upham is removed from"; and Joanna Winship in turn was put "in the place where Ester Sparhawke was wont to sit." On 11 January 1662/63, after several additional deaths, the committee met again to move Jonathan Taylor and Richard Eccles to the seats "where Br. Stedman & Mr Robins sat" and James Hubbard where "Jno. Taylor sat."⁷

In formulating seating assignments, towns generally drew on a committee of civil, clerical, and military authorities. The 1662 Cambridge seating committee consisted of selectmen, deacons, and elders. In the New Haven Colony, the deputies to the general court joined with the church deacons in 1647 to seat the fifty-by-fifty-foot meetinghouse raised eight years earlier by William Andrews. In this instance the committee put "Mr. Gov. Eaton and Dep. Gov. Goodyear" in the first seat directly to the left of the pulpit. Mrs. Eaton and the wives of other leading families occupied the same rank across the main alley on the women's side. Nine years later, Eaton and Goodyear were still occupying the same bench, but new seats between them and the pulpit had been installed for the deacons, four elderly men, and three elderly women.⁸ Hartford, Connecticut, appointed Capt. John Allyn to seat the First Church in 1685; six years later he was one of three military officers and two deacons to perform the same task. Westfield, Massachusetts, in 1679 and again in 1703, appointed a succession of deacons, "foundation men" of the church, and prominent military officers to allocate seats. In some instances the task was given entirely to church officers. Milton,

Massachusetts, selected Rev. Peter Thatcher and its three deacons to seat the meetinghouse in 1705.[9]

When the decisions about seating were particularly difficult, however, older men were often called on. In 1671 the Beverly selectmen delegated three men who were communicants but not officers of the church: Roger Conant, Richard Brackenbury, and Ens. William Dixey, a militia officer. All three had settled in Salem during the years 1630 to 1634, and all were seventy years old or older.[10] The task of seating the new forty-by-twenty-foot lean-to addition to the overcrowded Marblehead meetinghouse in 1672 proved so difficult the town's selectmen refused to have anything to do with the matter. A special committee of four men, all in their seventies, was given the task to "rectify any disorders with due care that such as have been formerly seated may keep their places as many as conveniently can." These four men were virtually all who were left from the first generation of Marblehead settlers.[11]

Town records reveal that the task of assigning seating was sometimes confusing and difficult. The seating committee in Windsor, Connecticut, took the equivalent of five days between 23 February and 18 March 1730 to make up their minds. They consumed nineteen meals and spent four shillings "for drink" in the process and in the end asked their minister, Rev. Samuel Mather, for another "part of a day" before the task was completed.[12] Seating committees were often challenged by their constituents or were themselves divided in their feelings. The town of Sunderland, Massachusetts, voted in 1738 "to throw up all that hath been done [so far] in seating the meeting house" and appoint a committee of nine men to seat the "Meeting House in this Method: the three oldest by themselves, and the Middle aged by themselves, and the three youngest by themselves: and then bring their Locatings & compare them together and when agreed to bring their seating to the town to see if the Town will approve of it."[13]

Seating committees were also kept from selecting locations for themselves. Woburn and Haverhill appointed a second committee to "seat the seating committee."[14] In at least one instance a seating committee was drawn from outside the community. After Stafford, a town in north central Connecticut, improved its meetinghouse in 1746, the town appointed a seating committee made up of the Stafford town clerk, Zebulon West, and Deacon Tyler Boath of Tolland and Deacon John Mirick of Willington.[15] And in Belchertown, Massachusetts, the responsibility was passed in 1783 to the "sisters" of the church, possibly the first such occasion in New England where female church members were given this right. (The sisters failed to agree and passed the task back to the men.)[16]

Most towns tried to spell out the rules under which seaters estimated an individual's or a family's rank in the parish. The instructions voted by Northampton, Massachusetts, in 1737 were typical: "1st to have respect principally to men's estate. 2nd to have regard to men's age. 3rd that some regard and respect be had to men's influence but in a lesser degree."[17] Out of seventy-four parishes in New England whose rules are known for the period 1650 to 1800, respect for age and "ancient persons" is cited in sixty-four instances; rate or estate in sixty-three; usefulness, influence, qualifications, and place in twenty-one; dignity or honor in nine; military rank in nine; parish rate in nine; parentage or descent in three; piety and poor hearing in one instance each. In general, old, wealthy men and women whose families had served the community were accorded the greatest public respect; young landless men, unmarried women, servants, and slaves the least.

A closer look at particular towns reveals that the issue could be more complex. One of the most complete sets of seating instructions on record was prepared after Beverly, Massachusetts, built its second meetinghouse in 1682. These rules specified a series of "degrees" by which every propertied male adult was numerically ranked for seating purposes. Under its guidelines, every year of age over twenty-one counted one degree; the ranks of captain, lieutenant, and ensign, respectively, counted twelve, eight, and four degrees; every shilling of rate paid on real estate counted three degrees; every shilling paid on personal estate counted one degree; every six degrees assigned to a parent counted as one degree to each of his sons; and a living father, grandfather, or great-grandfather each counted one degree.[18]

Like others, Beverly's formula weighted age more than any other single factor, with each year of age producing the same number of degrees as every ten pounds of estate. But the town's emphasis on parentage reveals a bias against newcomers. Under these rules, a forty-one-year-old ensign owning £120 in real estate and £60 in personal estate whose grandfather was still alive in the community and whose father was a major landowner could have up to 40 percent of his degrees from his birthright. A wealthy farmer or trader of the same age, however, newly arrived in the community could be ranked lower even if he owned twice the real and personal estate of the ensign. This bias is seen occasionally in town votes, such as one taken in Cambridge in 1662, that made it impossible for newcomers to advance except through the death of those ranked above them. Milford, Connecticut, voted that no person "shall be removed out of his present seat except to a higher."[19] Windsor, Connecticut, in 1718 said "age and estate to be considered, [but] none to be degraded."[20] Lexington, Massachusetts, warned its committee "not to degrade any person" and reminded everyone "to bring in their ages to the selectmen" before the seating plan was issued.[21]

Notably missing from the Beverly document is any attempt to give credit for occupations other than military ones. Farmers, teachers, storekeepers, merchants, physicians, sea captains, and mill owners are never cited. Equally absent in the Beverly document—as in all such New England documents—is any reference to church membership. While the community's oldest and most respected residents may or may not have been church members (and many probably were), their "piety" or membership in a body of regenerated saints was not a factor in where they were seated. This practice is evident in the 1647 seating list in New Haven, which shows communicants, identified by the terms "Bro.[ther]" and "Sister," placed side-by-side with nonmembers, identified by their surnames, but no male church members in the first three seats. These were occupied by Governor Theophilus Eaton and Deputy Governor Goodyear, among others.

Issues of gender discrimination and social leveling also surface in these assignments. In 1703 Brookhaven, Long Island, reserved the Communion table for all freeholders who had paid or proposed to pay more than forty shillings toward the salary of Rev. George Phillips. It further stated that "no women are permitted to sit there, except Col Smith's Lady, nor any woman-kind." (The difference between "women" and "woman-kind" is lost to history.)[22] Elsewhere a social agenda emerges that was alternately reactionary and progressive. Shortly after Westfield, Massachusetts, completed its second house of worship in late 1721, the town's seating committee revised its earlier rules that made one year of age equal to one pound in the list by making one year equivalent to three pounds. This system privileged age over assessment. But the committee also stipulated that only a third part of "what Estate he hath by heir or by marrying of a widow" would be counted. Thus, self-acquired estate was given three times the value of estate acquired by inheritance or marriage, a clear and somewhat radical statement quite different from the one established by Beverly. Finally, Westfield specified that any portion of estate that is "advanced by negroes shall be excluded & cast out." This restriction may have reflected a widespread practice in the Connecticut River Valley, where the ownership of agricultural and household slaves was relatively common. Similar rules were passed in the South Parish of Andover, Massachusetts.[23]

Seventeenth- and eighteenth-century towns also formed committees that specified which group of seats was esteemed better than others. New construction and especially the introduction of galleries, stairwell porches, and elevated pews required towns to "dignify" the meetinghouse, which meant quantifying the rank of each interior seating space in decreasing levels to allow the seaters to make their assignments. As a rule, spaces in most meetinghouses were divided into four or five dignities, each of which was defined by its prominence and nearness to the pulpit. But this division could easily increase. In 1703, when Westfield installed galleries and two new pews in its thirty-six-foot-square meetinghouse (built in 1672), the town had to add new dignities among the existing ones: "The fore pew to be in Dignity between the fore seat in the body & the Table. And the second pew to be in Dignity between the first & second seat in the body. And the fore Gallery is accounted to be in Dignity between the 3rd & 4th in the body."[24] In all, the 1703 vote divided the meetinghouse into twelve dignities, beginning with the "Table" at the pulpit and ending with the second tier of gallery seats. Other communities went further. The 1717 meetinghouse in Sunderland, Massachusetts, and the 1737 meetinghouse at the Turkey Hills Society in East Granby, Connecticut, were each ranked into fourteen dignities by their seating committees in 1728 and 1749. These were both relatively small, forty-five by thirty-five and forty by thirty-five feet, and literally every bench and pew was counted.[25] Redding, Connecticut, specified but did not approve fourteen dignities in 1763. Perhaps the highest number was the seventeen devised in 1802 in Southington, Connecticut, by a seating committee that symmetrically graded each pair of thirty-two pew spaces on the ground-floor level.[26]

The constant demand for pews led many individuals to build their own. One seventy-year-old resident in Sudbury, Massachusetts, tired of sitting in a row next to other worshipers, stole unseen into the meetinghouse, removed two benches, and installed a new pew in their place. The selectmen immediately ordered it nailed up and undertook an investigation to determine who was responsible. (The culprit later admitted to the deed, saying he did not "intend any evil by it.")[27] In other instances parishioners asked for permission to build pews with the expectation that they pay for them. Medford, Massachusetts, in 1696 allowed its leading citizen, Maj. Nathaniel Wade, to construct a pew in its new meetinghouse provided it "not go beyond the first bar of the window." Later, when similar permission was given to another individual, the town required the owner to take in one or two persons not belonging to his family "whom the town may name."[28]

Pew owners sometimes took advantage of lax supervision and made some surprising architectural changes. After Boston's second meetinghouse was consumed by fire in 1676, the town stipulated that no pews "with a door into the street" would be allowed.[29] We do not know how many New England meetinghouses had pew doors leading to the street, but the practice may have been common. In 1715 Medford gave Ebenezer Brooks "a pew in the part of their meetinghouse joining to the minister's pew" and allowed him "to make a door into said pew on the outside of said meeting-house." The committee that took this step may have done so to benefit the minister because the twenty-seven-by-twenty-four-foot meetinghouse had only one doorway. Twenty-one years later, after the town had built a larger meetinghouse, it "voted that John Bradhaw, jun., should have liberty to cut a door-place and make a door at the south end of the meetinghouse into his pew." But the practice of allowing outside doors from pews went too far in Framingham, Massachusetts, which found its meetinghouse so broken up with individual doors leading to the outside that in 1715 the town drew the line at three principal doors—"and the rest of the doors to be clapboarded up."[30]

Private ownership eventually led to shared ownership. One of the first examples of shared ownership was the "liberty" given in 1668 to five men in Newbury,

Massachusetts, to build a pew for their wives "at the east end of the south gallery to the pulpit," placing them among their friends and in a good position to hear the sermon. A similar vote taken in Newbury in 1677 allowed several young women to build a "pew or new seat" in the south corner of the women's gallery. Three men who objected to the "new seat," however, forcibly entered the building by breaking a window and demolished the pew and the chairs within it.[31] Despite this incident and others like it, the practice of group ownership of pews flourished and took on a social meaning. A vote by the Long Society in Preston, Connecticut, in 1759 allowing Peter Pride and "five young men" to "build a Pew over the men's Gallery Stairs" also stated that "Miss Anna Mix and five young Women more belonging to said Society" had permission to "Build a Pew over the Woman's Gallery Stairs." While little is known of the actual circumstances of these votes, they do suggest a form of gender equality or even group courtship. Similar pew building permissions were extended to young men and women in Brimfield, Massachusetts, in the same decade.[32]

The issue of private pewing became much more complex when men and women began to sit together. Approximately thirty-eight votes allowing "promiscuous seating" are known before 1780, many taking place after the completion of a new meetinghouse or after pews were installed for the first time in the meetinghouse.[33] In 1713, for example, about the same time the construction of a new meetinghouse was completed, Guilford, Connecticut, voted that "men & women [shall] sit together in the meeting house in the pews." Neighboring Stratfield voted to allow one man to sit with his family in 1718, a year after their meetinghouse was completed.[34] But the majority of the votes allowing private pews took place between 1750 and 1770. Invariably they were preceded by a series of compromises. At first only the clergyman sat with his family. In Wrentham, Massachusetts, that practice was established in 1721. Later provisions allowed the principal pewholders—usually ranking military officers, landed farmers, and share-owning seamen—to sit with their wives, children, and relatives, while the rest of the meetinghouse, including those in smaller pews, remained divided by men and women. Amherst, Massachusetts, voted in 1738 to place "the Males together and Females together, except the two pews next to the East End of the Pulpit."[35] Four years later all men and women occupying pews in Amherst were seated together. Another compromise was to allow all pew holders on the ground floor this privilege, but not the gallery pews or benches. The final accommodation was to permit this positioning throughout the meetinghouse, possibly excepting a few benches and pews reserved exclusively for unmarried men or unmarried women. Apprentices, indentured servants, black household slaves, Native Americans, and the "wretched boys" (usually between ten and fifteen years of age) continued to be relegated to the upstairs where they would be out of sight. Like the suspension of lining out in the singing of psalms, the acceptance of mixed seating throughout the meetinghouse probably did more than anything else to change the Sabbath experience of eighteenth-century Protestant churchgoers.

The granting of private pews led to the formation of legal associations whose purpose was to own and administer them. According to a "Pewman's Bond" written into the town records of Windsor, Connecticut, seven members of the First Society each contributed five pounds toward the building of a gallery pew in 1718. The terms of this bond were restrictive and required that no one could sell his right without the consent of all the others.[36] Pew associations like this lasted well into the eighteenth century and sometimes beyond. According to a record book still extant in the late nineteenth century, the fourteen proprietors of a pew in the first meetinghouse in Fitzwilliam, New Hampshire, convened on 1 August 1791, "choosing a moderator to Govern said meeting . . . [as well as] a Clerk." The society voted that "Rocksene Amadon shall set in said Pew on John Osgood's right." On two later occasions the group stipulated that if any "person or persons shall put into said Pew any of the Town's people on more than two Sabbaths in a row, they shall forfeit his right in said Pew." Later it decided that "if any person or persons shall behave himself out of order on the Sabbath shall quit his right."[37] Membership in pew societies helps explain some unusual valuations in eighteenth-century legal documents. When the household inventory of Abel Flint of Lincoln, Massachusetts, was taken in 1789, for example, a value of twenty shillings was placed on "one Seventh part of two thirds of a pew in Lincoln"—his share of a pew that had been subdivided at least twice, first into thirds, and then two of those thirds into seven parts.[38]

The increase in private pewing also led to a bidding process to determine which families sat where. An initial form of this method was to give the choice of the best pews to families who paid the highest parish rates. In 1760 the First Society in Pomfret, Connecticut, distributed the pews of its new meetinghouse among the forty-three persons who were the highest taxpayers in the parish. "He that is highest in the list," the document reads, is "to have the first choice, he that is next highest, the next choice, and so on, till they have done drawing."[39] Under these circumstances, the act of choosing seats and dignifying the meetinghouse became redundant because they were accomplished by bidding. After 1760, auctioning pews became a common means of paying for new meetinghouses, greatly reducing the powers of seating committees and virtually eliminating an individual's age in the selection process. A vote taken in 1800 in Newton, Massachusetts, to begin selling pews, stipulates that the "ancient mode of seating parishioners" would be replaced by a process of auctioning.[40]

Because competitive bidding ranked a meetinghouse as explicitly as the decisions of the early seating and dignifying committees, it is possible to combine all three sources of data to plot the movement of the most desirable locations.

Seating "morphology" in the seventeenth century was defined by proximity to the Communion table. In New Haven, Hartford, and Cambridge, benches or pews immediately beside the table were set aside for those with the highest dignity. This pattern continued into the eighteenth century. Brookline, Massachusetts, in 1713 assigned a £5 value to the pew "next [to] the Pulpit on the west," but only £3 to the pew "on the right hand of the coming in at the east Door."[41] Roxbury's seaters in 1740 gave the highest value (£49.3.4) to the four pews immediately surrounding the pulpit and the minister's pew and placed a second dignity (£36.17.6) on pews clustered near the entrances.[42]

As pewing became "promiscuous" and was extended into the main body and portions of the gallery, the "best" locations gradually became those where parishioners might best be seen or to those that had a good perspective on other members of the congregation. Framingham, Massachusetts, drew up a schedule of dignities in 1715 that gave seats in the front gallery the same importance as the second and third seats in the body even if they were farther away from the pulpit.[43] In 1741 Millbury, Massachusetts, designated the best value to four pews in the center of the house, which sold for 7.6.0, or almost twice the price of those next to the pulpit.[44] And by mid-century, the worth of pews on the south wall (meaning those farthest from the pulpit) also began to exceed those near the pulpit. In 1749 when the First Parish in Ipswich had just completed its new meetinghouse, the four highest prices paid for pew rights were located on either side of the main front door. The same valuation took place in 1754 in Duxbury, where the highest bid (£20.13.4) paid was for a pew at the left of the front door. (The pew next to the pulpit was auctioned at £19.9.4.) Curiously, the minister's pew itself sometimes accompanied this move to the south wall. After the erection of its new meetinghouse in 1756, Cambridge, Massachusetts, put the minister in the "back row" with the town's eminent families.[45]

This trend is succinctly revealed in two dignity schedules dated twelve years apart that survive from Murrayfield (now Chester), Massachusetts, a town that built its first meetinghouse in 1767. Murrayfield set aside the entirety of a town meeting in 1773 for designating seats, a process repeated again in 1785. Each document divides twenty-seven ground-floor pews into four dignities. In 1773 the two pews immediately before and on either side of the pulpit were ranked "D[ignity]1"; those on the south wall were assigned "D[ignity]4. In 1785, however, the two pews on the south wall directly to the left and right of the front door were upgraded to "Dignity 1st"; the four pews along the broad alley had been improved from dignities three and four to "Dignity 2d"; and the pew to the right of the west door had been raised from dignity four to "Dignity 2d." Clearly, in Murrayfield it was as prestigious in 1785 to sit by one of the entrance doors as it was to sit before or beside the pulpit in 1773.[46]

These trends did not always reflect the complete range of usage, especially among societies that still kept to the old ways and appointed seating committees to allocate pews. Southington, Connecticut, which continued to name seating committees well into the 1780s, put virtually all persons over the age of sixty in pews of the first or second dignity (located principally around the pulpit), regardless of their estate evaluation; the committees placed middle-aged wealthy men between thirty and forty on their periphery. New Milford, a relatively new community in rural western Connecticut that had built its first meetinghouse in 1719 and a second in 1752, maintained a seating committee even as late as the first decade of the nineteenth century. In April 1802, New Milford's committee put fifteen of the highest ranked families (those valued at over two thousand dollars) in pews immediately to the right, left, and directly in front of the pulpit, collectively identifying them as part of the "First Rank" of the six-rank list. This arrangement was virtually identical to the original 1754 seating plan in New Milford, which put the first rank in five pews closest to the pulpit, assigning the sixth dignity to pews by the doorways.[47]

At this point New Milford was still in the earliest phase of its seating evolution. But other parishes were well on their way to a third and final stage that paralleled the shift by builders and architects to a long aisle and a church plan. This last phase emphasized the central aisle, and it became typical in the Federal period. Eight of the nine highest prices paid in 1799 to raise funds for the Bulfinch-designed meetinghouse in Lee, Massachusetts, were for pews located on either side of the passageway between the pulpit and the main door.[48] In the pew sale of Roxbury's 1803 fifth meetinghouse, the auction prices of the fourth, fifth, and sixth rows of pews on the main aisle were twice those of identical pews in the sixteenth row on the same aisle (the ones near the entrance).[49] So desirable were main aisle locations, they were advertised in the newspapers. On 9 January 1805, Robert T. Paine Jr., a recent Harvard graduate and an actor in Boston's new theaters, placed a notice in the *Columbian Centinel* offering for sale "One of the best situated Pews in the middle or broad aisle of the Rev. Mr. Emerson's meeting house, No. 57."[50] We do not know whether anyone purchased Paine's pew. But within two years the Old Brick was torn down and replaced by an equally massive building with a four-tiered front portico and a main alley almost twice the length of its predecessor.

The story of seating had now come full circle. What had started out in the seventeenth century as a Calvinist-inspired effort to produce places of worship that were auditories, in which hearing the preached word was emphasized and architecturally facilitated, had now been supplanted by a system favoring individual parishioners and their families who wanted to see and to be seen by the rest of the congregation on the central aisle. The newer practices clearly gave the meetinghouse an Anglican emphasis. One last issue remained: who would be the first to exit. The earliest known discussion of exiting procedures in the meetinghouse took place in 1754 when Pepperell, Massachusetts, voted that the fore seat in the front and side galleries was to exit before the second seat in the galleries—apparently for the sake of safety.[51] Nine years later Shirley, Massachusetts, was much more explicit and voted that each seat in the meetinghouse "shall go out on the Sabbath days according to their dignity"—a small but unsubtle way of emphasizing a family's "place" in the town's society.[52] Neighboring Groton instituted the same policy two years later.[53] Thereafter, exiting protocols became part of the parish vocabulary governing seating. In 1790 Holden, Massachusetts, required that the congregation keep their seats until the minister and deacons had left the building.[54] Hubbardston, Massachusetts, stipulated in 1803 that the fore seats were to rise and leave only after the minister came down from the desk; then the body seats; then the lower pews, and finally the galleries.[55] Sudbury, Massachusetts, drew up the most explicit exiting document in the region when it voted in 1796 that as soon as "Divine Service" was over, "Pew Holders in the body of the Meeting House . . . [shall] fling their pew Door wide open so as not to obstruct the passage of the people in the alleys—that the Speaker pass out first then the pew holders to pass on after as fast as Conveniently may be out at the front Door, then those that sit in the next seat."[56] The text went on for each passageway until the entire structure was emptied.

The votes speak for themselves. New Englanders were now following meetinghouse exiting procedures as complex and hierarchical as those by which they were originally seated. That they gave the matter any attention at all was a sign that some of them were becoming impatient to leave.

PART II

# The Architecture

CHAPTER FIVE

# Meetinghouses of the Seventeenth Century

## Sources of the Design

THE LACK of prior Christian houses of worship presented both an opportunity and a dilemma for first-generation New Englanders. In England and the northern Netherlands, churches were available in virtually every parish. During periods of Puritan ascendancy and especially during the Commonwealth period they were typically stripped and refitted for Reformed Christian services. The Westminster Confession of 1646 allowed Reformed congregations to assemble in Anglican and Catholic churches because "no place is capable of any holiness under pretence of whatsoever dedication or consecration . . . [and their use] for worship among us should be continued."[1] In New England, colonists were not obliged to remake older Anglican or Catholic churches; but they did have to address the issue of building large structures almost immediately.

Once European settlement was consolidated in Massachusetts and Connecticut, meetinghouses were built on a wood frame or "girt" fabric whose technology was based on English domestic, barn-building, bridge-building, or mill-making traditions.[2] Over the next eighty-five years (1630–1715), two principal meetinghouse forms evolved in the region. One form resembled large barns or school houses and included numerous windows. These meetinghouses were laid out in a square (or nearly square) plan, with a plate high enough to accommodate one or two tiers of galleries; they were typically covered with a hipped roof and surmounted by a central turret. Those built in the second form followed a long or rectangular plan with a relatively low plate. The first, called a "four-square" meetinghouse after the "4:square roof" cited in a Cambridge document in 1649, was the more important of the two.[3] Though not always dominant, the form was widely prevalent. Out of 176 Reformed first-period structures whose dimensions are known between 1622 and 1715, 68 followed an exactly square shape—most commonly thirty or forty feet. But many others (approximately half that number) came fairly close to this ratio, combining a high plate, a hipped roof,

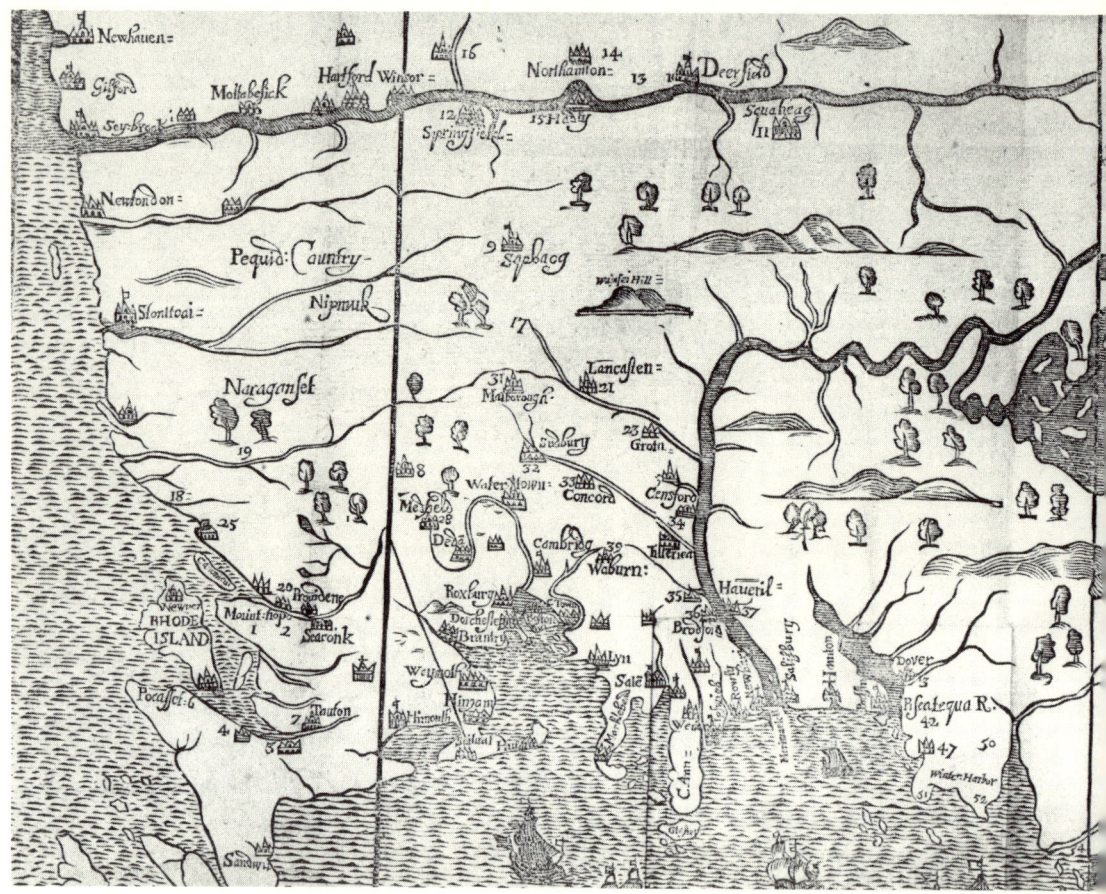

Figure 5.1. Detail from *A Map of New England*, published in William Hubbard's *The Present State of New-England. Being a Narrative of the Troubles with the Indians* (1677). John Foster (1648–1681). The map indicates the location of Hartford, New Haven, and Boston as they were perceived in the seventeenth century. The principal rivers are the Connecticut and the Merrimack; the vertical line in the center indicates the southern boundary of the Province of Massachusetts Bay. North is to the right. While the image is probably a second- or third-hand engraving of Foster's original, it reveals individual structures—likely meetinghouses—at the center of each community. Overall dimensions of the map are 12 by 15 inches. Library of the Boston Athenaeum.

and an almost square design whose length exceeded the width by only a few feet. Dimensions are unknown, however, for approximately 172 meetinghouses during this same period.

While four-square forms have been documented in Massachusetts Bay as early as 1632 (in Cambridge and possibly Lynn), three large houses of worship built in New England in the late 1630s and early 1640s may have provided models for others (fig. 5.1). One was the 1638 meetinghouse in Hartford built by the congregation of Rev. Thomas Hooker, who had spent almost two years in the Netherlands and was familiar with Reformed building practices. Hooker and his sizable following had resettled along the Connecticut River in 1636 after the group had declined to remain in Massachusetts. The erection date of their meetinghouse is known from a "weather cock" (possibly a dated flag vane) removed from the belfry or turret when the house was taken down in 1737—a fact noted years later in the diary of Rev. Daniel Wadsworth (1704–1747). Though details are sketchy, this was a framed structure (later repairs called for "new ground sills"). It was covered with clapboards and may have had fifty-by-fifty-foot dimensions and a "pyramidical" roof (meaning hipped), at the top of which were a turret and a bell taken by the congregation from Cambridge. Galleries were installed in 1644, 1660, and 1664, and a covered outside porch led to the "chambers" upstairs used for trials and meetings of the general court. The house served the Hartford Church and a variety of civic functions for ninety-nine years, during which it was repaired many times.[4]

A second model was a meetinghouse built in 1639 by the founders of New Haven, Connecticut. Rev. John Davenport (1597–1670), formerly of Oxford and London—who had also recently spent time as a preacher in Amsterdam—declined the opportunity to stay in the Boston area, and like Hooker, he determined to settle a new colony in Connecticut with his followers. Accordingly, he and Theophilus Eaton explored the country along the seacoast west of the Connecticut River and finally fixed on Quinipiack as the place for their settlement. To meet the long-range requirements of the new colony, New Haven set aside £500 to build the first large meetinghouse in New England whose dimensions are known from town records. At "fifty foot square," it may have been the largest such structure in New England and one provided with all the essential components of the four-square meetinghouse: a hipped roof, gallery seats for about sixty men, and a turret in the center of its roof surmounted by a banistered and railed platform.[5] The builder was William Andrews (d. 1676), a joiner of some wealth (he was assessed at £150), who became a proprietor of the new colony and was given a lot in one of the squares. Despite recurring problems with rotting timbers (extra pillars may have been installed to support both the turret and a portion of the gallery in 1651, 1656, and 1659), this house was used by the town for thirty years.[6]

A third candidate for a model was the 1640 meetinghouse of the First Church in Boston. Almost no details survive of the "Old Meeting House," as it was called by Rev. Benjamin Colman's biographer, Ebenezer Turell, in 1749; but the building must have been substantial. Gov. John Winthrop's journal notes that the total cost was £1,000, one-third of which was raised by selling the old building. This sum compares with £400 paid to John Sherman for the forty-by-forty-foot meetinghouse built in Watertown in 1656 and the £437 (plus the value of the old house) given to Charles Stockbridge for the fifty-five-by-forty-five-foot Old Ship in Hingham in 1681. John Winthrop also tells us that a young child broke her arm and shoulder in 1643 when she fell eighteen feet from the gallery to the floor. This is an unusually high gallery, and the structure may have been fitted with a second gallery in 1675.[7] In 1694 the First Church designated two deacons and a third church member to determine the "convenience of making a middle door at the North side, and shutting up the two corner doors, and about a porch to the east side." The house was large enough to accommodate Boston's First Church for more than seventy years, and the brick structure that replaced it may have been a masonry equivalent of the original 1640 design.[8]

A question that draws continuing debate among scholars is, Did the Hartford, New Haven, or Boston builders simply "make up" the four-square design as they went along or did they have a specific precedent or tradition in mind? If they did make up the design, it would have been an "American" design; if they followed a tradition, it would have been an English or European one. Arguing strongly in favor of an American origin is the lack of any real English precedent for domestic architecture.[9] While the late sixteenth-century Burntisland kirk in Fife, Scotland, erected by cloth merchants and seamen at the close of the sixteenth century, provides a Scottish precedent, there is no evidence that the hipped-roof and turreted four-square form was ever built in England at any point in the seventeenth century either as a wood-frame structure or as a brick or stone one. Christopher Stell's inventory of nonconformist chapels and meetinghouses in central England proves this point conclusively for Gloucestershire and surrounding central English counties. East Anglia, from where many of New England's emigrants originated, provides little more.[10]

A second argument for an American origin is linguistic. The Massachusetts Bay colony may have been the first group of English speakers to use the term *meeting house*—doing so within two years after the initial Puritan settlement in Boston. By contrast, English Puritans were still calling their houses of worship "meetings," and English separatists and nonseparating Puritans in Holland were calling them "houses for public assembly" or just "houses." John Winthrop used the term *meeting house* for the house of worship in Dorchester in his journal in March 1632, and the rapidity with which colleague communities such as Cambridge, Boston, and Charlestown echoed him in 1632 and 1633 suggests they were dealing with a new architectural concept—and hence a new architectural form.[11]

Arguing in favor of a European origin, however, is a growing body of evidence that Protestant meetinghouses built in Scotland, France, and the Netherlands between 1590 and 1690 shared many of the same characteristics of the classic early New England four-square types—the vertical orientation, the hipped roof, the extensive gallery space, the focus on the central pulpit, and the lack of a central alley. These concepts were part of a new Calvinist architectural radicalism that denied the special sanctity of houses of worship and designated these buildings for public meetings and a place for town offices and living quarters. This radicalism may explain why all early English colonists, like Winthrop, fell so readily into the linguistic usage of *meeting house* to describe their houses of worship, revealing their prior exposure to Protestant worship in England and Europe. Although some Reformed congregations in Europe merely adapted the fabric of abandoned Anglican and Catholic churches to their needs, the Puritan, Presbyterian, Huguenot, Dutch Reformed, and, in some instances, Lutheran congregations in Europe and America who were designing new religious buildings from the ground up may have drawn from this radical viewpoint. All faced analogous, though clearly not similar, social and political circumstances, and all may have come to the same architectural conclusions.

Anthony Garvan and Marian Donnelly are inclined to this view. Both have suggested, but are unable to prove, that the four-square form may have come from a French Huguenot tradition that flourished in France before the revocation of the Edict of Nantes in 1685 and the destruction of their meetinghouses by Catholic authorities. One early Huguenot "temple"—the Paradis, built at Lyon, France, in 1566—took the form of an oval; a gallery, reached by outside staircases, went all the way around the structure. In the center stood an elevated high pulpit and canopy; a raised section behind the pulpit provided a place for a Communion table (figs. 5.2 and 5.3). The 1623 Huguenot temple at Charenton, on the outskirts of Paris, had two tiers of galleries, and the pulpit was raised at least to the height of the first gallery (fig. 5.4). This structure, designed by the architect Salomon de Brosse, was said to have seated four thousand worshipers.[12]

At least six scholars or commentators working between the 1950s and the 1990s have reinforced Garvan's and Donnelly's hypothesis. The first was Per Gustaf Hamberg, who points out that designs for "square temples" were proposed for Huguenot congregations at the end of the sixteenth century by the architect and city planner Jacques Perret. He also points out that architects who owned copies of Perret's design books introduced octagonal churches into the Netherlands. Square and octagonal plans with turreted roofs and one or two tiers of galleries became the Protestant standard in both countries. A typical example is the Willemstad Reformed Church (built in 1596) pictured in Hamberg's work as a single-story octagon. The design followed Perret's model and provided benches for men and women on the ground floor and stairs on either side of the pulpit leading to "three tiers of pews against the walls *en manière de théâtre.*"[13]

A study of Huguenot architecture by Hélène Guicharnaud published in 1999 confirms many of Hamberg's ideas. She indicates that French law stipulated that Protestant temples must be located away from major Catholic population centers and must have no physical resemblance to Catholic churches. Guicharnaud distinguishes between basilican and centralized configurations, the latter of which are octagon and dodecahedron (sixteen-sided) plans with two tiers of galleries, a dormer window for each section, and a turret. She also says temples were popularly known as "barns" (*granges*), "pies" (*godiviaux*), or even "rats'

Figure 5.2 and 5.3. Two views of the interior of the Huguenot temple at Paradis, Lyon, France, circa 1566. Both are attributed to Jean Perrissin (ca. 1536–1611). *Above:* Drawing showing benches, raised pulpit, and galleries. Archives municipales de Lyon 1GG 86, Lyon, France. *Below: Temple De Lyon, Nommé Paradis.* Paint on wood. Bibliothèque de Genève, Centre d'iconographie genevoise.

nests" (*nids à rats*)—a parallel to the radical communal intimacy experienced later in New England. These varied forms are amply demonstrated in René Laurent's historical study of French Protestant church architecture and in Bernard Reymond's more comprehensive study of Protestant religious architecture, both issued in 1996.[14]

Keith Sprunger makes a similar argument his 1997 study of approximately forty exiled English churches founded in the Netherlands in the sixteenth and seventeenth centuries. He discusses the disputes among separating and nonseparating English dissenters, who differed on the issue of reusing the Catholic chapels, finding that Brownists or Barrowists wanted to tear them down because they were desecrated, while others were willing to strip them and reuse the shell. Typically the most fundamental congregations, such as those led by Henry Ainsworth and Francis Johnson, acquired residences where they both lived and preached; in contrast, the nonseparating congregations, such as those led by John Paget, who put his congregation under the jurisdiction of the Amsterdam Classis, used former Catholic churches assigned to them. In the end, when these

Figure 5.4. *Templum Charantony*. Interior of the 1623 three-tier Huguenot temple at Charenton, France, as seen during divine service. Two tiers of galleries are shown lined with standing worshipers. Watercolor by Achilles Werteman de Basle, collected in "album amicorum" by Franz. C. Deublinger, circa 1648. The Royal Library, Copenhagen, Denmark.

congregations were able to afford to build their own structures, they followed a Calvinist tradition of vertical orientation on a square or octagonal format.[15]

More recently, Andrew Spicer pointed out that the Huguenot tradition observed in the Paradis was repeated in the Netherlands after 1566 when the regent Margaret of Parma temporarily allowed Protestant worship in Flanders and Holland. A wave of temple and church building followed that basically outlined the Protestant form. The temple at Ghent, built between 1566 and 1568, had a pulpit on the north side. According to a contemporary observer, Marcus Van Vaernewicjck:

> This temple was then octagonal and surrounded by a gallery.... It was largely built of wood, like the churches of Muscovy, except that the spaces between the posts had been filled with brickwork set in tanner's mortar. Both the lower and upper storeys of the building were lit by numerous windows ... looked at from both the outside and inside, the temple resembled a lantern or riding school, only much larger ... the building measured 150 feet in length and 130 feet in width.[16]

Together, these studies suggest strongly that the same Calvinist radicalism that influenced the architecture of Protestant houses of worship in Reformation Europe may have also extended to North America. A closer look at the post-Reformation house of worship at Burntisland Parish—a sixty-foot-square masonry structure raised in 1592—provides additional evidence (figs. 5.5 and 5.6).[17] Contemporary with Willemstad and the Paradis Temple, the Burntisland kirk supported its roof and central tower on four massive stone pillars, one of which held the pulpit. The structure was remodeled at least three times in the eighteenth, nineteenth, and early twentieth centuries. A wooden steeple was replaced by a turret around 1750; corner buttresses and a larger masonry central tower were added in 1822; and a portico in 1907. But enough remains to indicate it had a centrally located pulpit, a second-floor "loft" (or gallery) on four sides, a "squat" central turret topped by a wooden spire, and a hipped roof. The builder was probably John Roche, a mason, who is also credited as being the architect. Locally, it has always been called "typically Dutch," suggesting it was copied from Amsterdam's Noorderkerk, the Scottish church in Rotterdam, or even the Grand Temple in La Rochelle, but these Dutch and Huguenot examples postdate Burntisland by many decades.[18] The most recent thinking, by Andrew Spicer, is that the building was a "sturdy home product" or a "home-spun solution to the demands of Reformed worship." Either way, the Burntisland kirk may be one of the best precedents found yet for the four-square form of the first-period New England style.[19]

Carrying this one step further, the idea of a Huguenot or Dutch origin, or a combination of the two, of the early American meetinghouse form is also supported by Dutch Reformed houses of worship found in Long Island and in the Hudson River area of New York colony, as well as some Quaker meetinghouses in New Jersey. The 1715 stone meetinghouse erected by the Dutch Reformed congregation in Albany, New York (fig. 5.7), virtually duplicates both the 1592 Burntisland kirk and the 1697 Rotterdam Scottish Church. But it also has much in common with Boston's three-tier Old Brick: the square, hipped roof extends upward at an angle of about forty degrees; a roofed belfry and bell surmount its apex; a front portico or porch provides stairs to the gallery. Only the use of large two-story compass windows differentiates the exterior of the two buildings.

Equally important are a number of six-sided and eight-sided meetinghouses raised in Long Island and New Jersey communities among Dutch Reformed congregations. One of the first was the 1681 octagonal meetinghouse in Bergen, New Jersey, constructed in stone by a congregation that had ties to Dutch communities in Long Island. The anonymously written "Brief History of Old Bergen Church" provides a memory picture and tells us the "archways over the door and windows were ornamented with small bricks imported from Holland."[20] Similar structures were built elsewhere. According to the nineteenth-century historian Nathaniel S. Prime, the stone meetinghouse in New Utrecht, New York, was erected "in the usual octagonal form" in 1700; Bushwick, New York

Figure 5.5. Burntisland Parish kirk, Fife, Scotland, erected by mason John Roche in 1592. This meetinghouse was heavily altered in the eighteenth and early nineteenth centuries, with stone buttresses added to each corner and a wooden turret replaced with a stone tower. Photograph by Ian Macdonald, 2007.

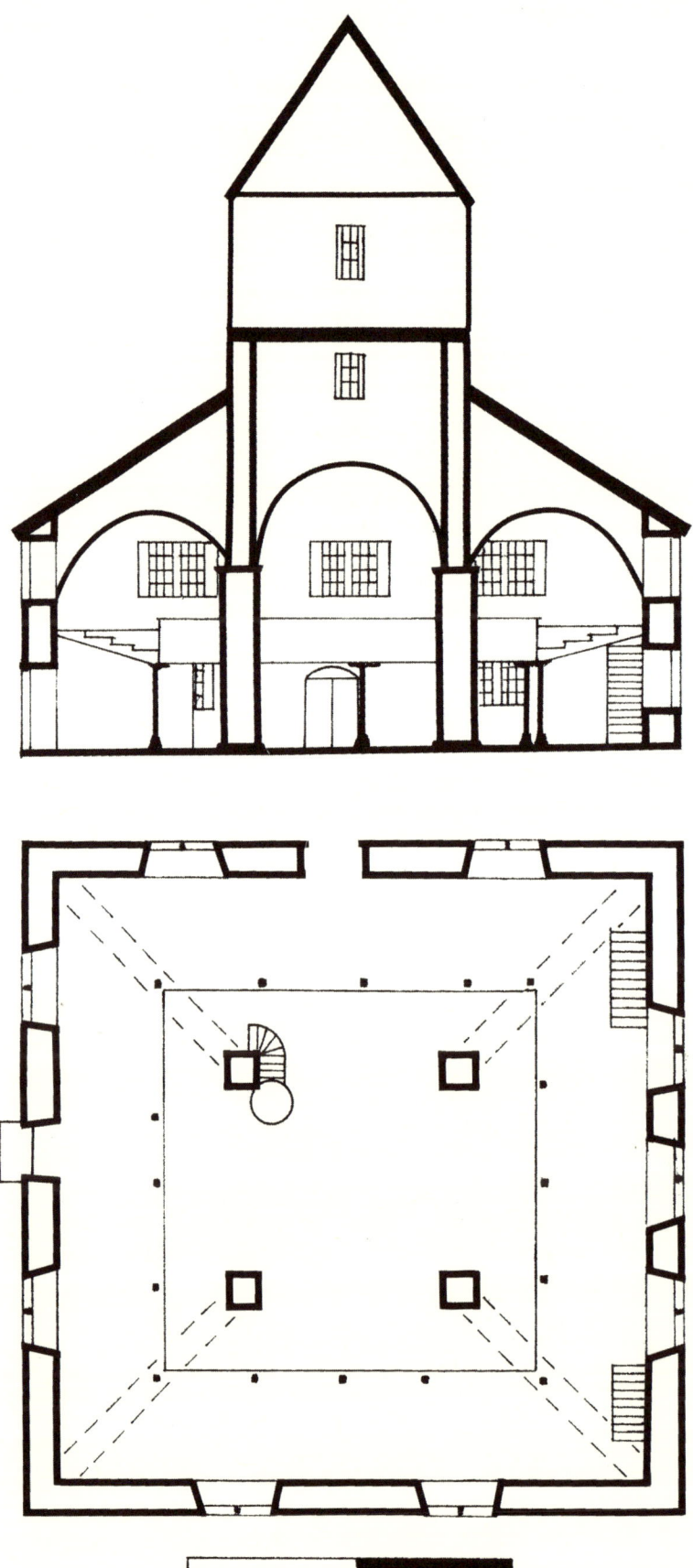

Figure 5.6. Conjectural original elevation and plan of the 60-by-60-foot kirk, Burntisland Parish, Fife, Scotland, based on George Hay, *Architecture of Scottish Post-Reformation Churches*, and a seventeenth-century drawing by John Slezer. Illustration by the author.

(now part of Brooklyn), built an eight-sided meetinghouse in 1710 that was used until 1840 (fig. 5.8); Jamaica, Long Island, raised an eight-sided stone meetinghouse in 1715. The only such structure in New England's first period was the 1698 meetinghouse in Fairfield, Connecticut—located just across Long Island Sound—which was seen and recorded by the Maryland physician Alexander Hamilton on his way north to Boston in 1744. Hamilton also noted the example in Jamaica, as did the diarist Joshua Hempstead, who called it "a Dutch 8 square meetinghouse" in 1749.[21]

A real possibility exists that, like the term *meetinghouse* itself, some elements of the New England architectural concept were taken from the American colonies back to England and possibly to other parts of Europe. The likelihood is greatest during the Commonwealth period, when many New Englanders returned to England either as clergymen or simply as visitors. Horton Davies, for

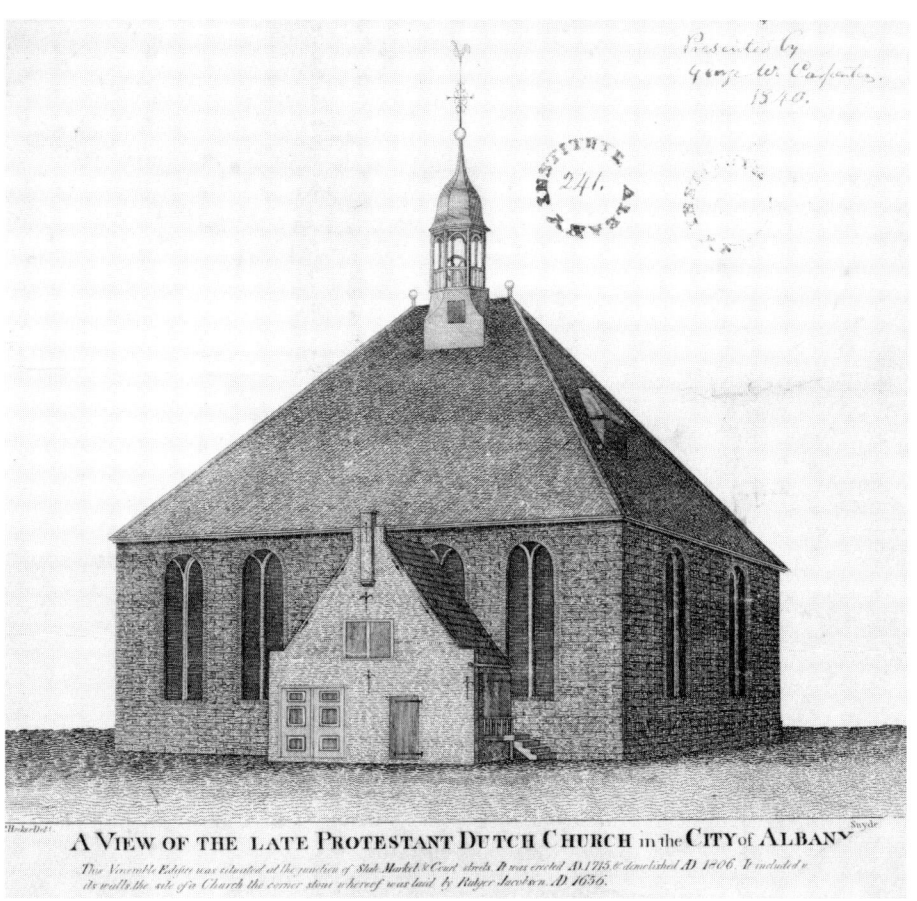

Figure 5.7. *A View of the Late Protestant Dutch Church in the City of Albany.* The second meetinghouse in Albany, New York, was built of stone in 1715. Drawing circa 1806 by Philip Hooker (1766–1836). Ink on laid paper. Courtesy of the Albany Institute of History and Art, Albany, New York, Gift of George W. Carpenter.

THE OLD BUSHWICK CHURCH L.I. BUILT IN 1711.
Drawn by Cornelia T. Meeker.

Figure 5.8. *The Old Bushwick Church L.I. Built in 1711.* Image of the first meetinghouse in Bushwick (now Brooklyn), New York. Nineteenth-century Long Island historian Nathaniel S. Prime called this shape "the usual octagonal form" among Dutch Reformed congregations. Image drawn by George Hayward after Cornelia T. Meeker; 1864 lithograph. Picture Collection, The New York Public Library, Astor, Lenox and Tilden Foundations.

example, claims that the New England meetinghouse, "in all its austerity . . . was an authentic, native product later to be copied by English dissenters."[22] Christopher Stell points out that the nonconformist stone chapel at Toxteth Park, Liverpool, where Richard Mather taught school and preached before coming to New England in 1635, was conceived as an orthodox Anglican chapel. But later, under the nonconformists' leaders, the building was converted and many elements of the New England style were incorporated: an elevated pulpit situated on the long side opposite the entrance doors. a Communion table set below the pulpit, and a gallery on three sides. There may be scores like it. Other English houses of worship—including the 1693 Old Meeting at Norwich, Norfolk County, and the 1707 Rook Lane Chapel built by dissenting wool merchants in the market town of Frome, Somerset County—appear to conform to some New England prototypes. With dimensions of fifty-five by forty feet, Rook Lane is a masonry structure with a hipped roof, a principal entry on the long side, flanking exterior stairwell porches, and a second-story gallery. Excepting its classic eighteenth-century parapet wall and pediment, as well as the two large interior columns supporting the roof, Rook Lane Chapel is essentially similar to the typical twin-porch New England meetinghouse such as the one in Rockingham, Vermont.[23] This "reversed" transatlantic process may have also characterized the importation of New England's religious culture into England, including early psalmody translations. The 1640 Bay Psalm Book, for example, was reprinted in England in 1647 and ran through at least twenty editions, the latest in 1754.[24]

In the end, however, the evidence of a European origin is overwhelming. The architectural concepts followed by the first-period New England meetinghouse builders appear to have been part of a vibrant Protestant tradition just coming to its peak in the first decades of the seventeenth century. The tradition was initially brought to England by exiles fleeing the depredations of the Catholic Duke of Alva, but it soon blossomed into a recognized style of Protestant architecture.[25] Some important French Protestant temples and Dutch Reformed and Scottish meetinghouses were already several decades old (or more) when Hartford, New Haven, and Boston built their meetinghouses in 1638, 1639, and 1640. These included the Burntisland kirk, the Paradis temple, the Reformed Church at Willemstad, and two Huguenot temples at La Rochelle illustrated in a 1620 bird's-eye-view map by Martin Zeiller (fig. 5.9). The first Zeiller image is a six-sided masonry structure with a central turret; the second, a four-square (masonry?) structure with dormer windows on each side that in some respects resembles the Burntisland kirk and the 1699 Ipswich, Massachusetts, meetinghouse. (Zeiller's illustration even suggests that pinnacles were used on two of the corners.) Other examples include a timber-framed, twelve-sided temple at Le Petit-Quevilly near Rouen, with two tiers of galleries and multiple double doors, begun in 1600 and completed in 1601 (figs. 5.10 and 5.11), and the square-form Remonstrants' temple in Amsterdam (fig. 5.12), consecrated in 1630, which reveals two tiers of galleries with benches.[26]

Except for their occasional octagonal or twelve-sided shapes, these European designs have much in common with the New England four-square form, and first-generation builders probably knew of these structures and were guided by them. Of the three makers of the "American" models we have discussed, William Andrews, who built the 1639 New Haven meetinghouse, may be a likely candidate for having brought these ideas to New England. The Quinipiack planters came from a tightly knit group of professionals that emigrated as a unit from England. Their leader, John Davenport, had recently spent time in the Netherlands, and they are known to have adopted other aspects of classical or European town planning in their fledgling colony. John Brockett, the land surveyor who laid out the original bounds for New Haven, followed a concept introduced by the Roman engineer and architect named Marcus Vitruvius Pollio, whose writings encouraged planners to divide new towns into nine equal squares

Figure 5.9. A view of La Rochelle, France, taken in 1620, showing two Huguenot temples *(13 and 14)* and a medieval church *(26)*. Detail from a perspective map in Martin Zeiller's *Topographia Galliae*, Section 7, between pages 60–61. University of Delaware Library, Newark, Delaware.

diagonally oriented away from prevailing winds.[27] De Brosse himself may have followed a Vitruvian model for his design of Charenton.[28] While we have no evidence that William Andrews or other New England builders were familiar with Huguenot meetinghouses, all three "American" builders found similar "Protestant" solutions to provide meeting spaces for their communities. That they chose four-square meetinghouses rather than octagonal ones and designed wood frames rather than stone or brick walls may have been less important than that they were following a well-established European formula for Reformed ecclesiastic architecture whose bell towers were mounted centrally and whose interior

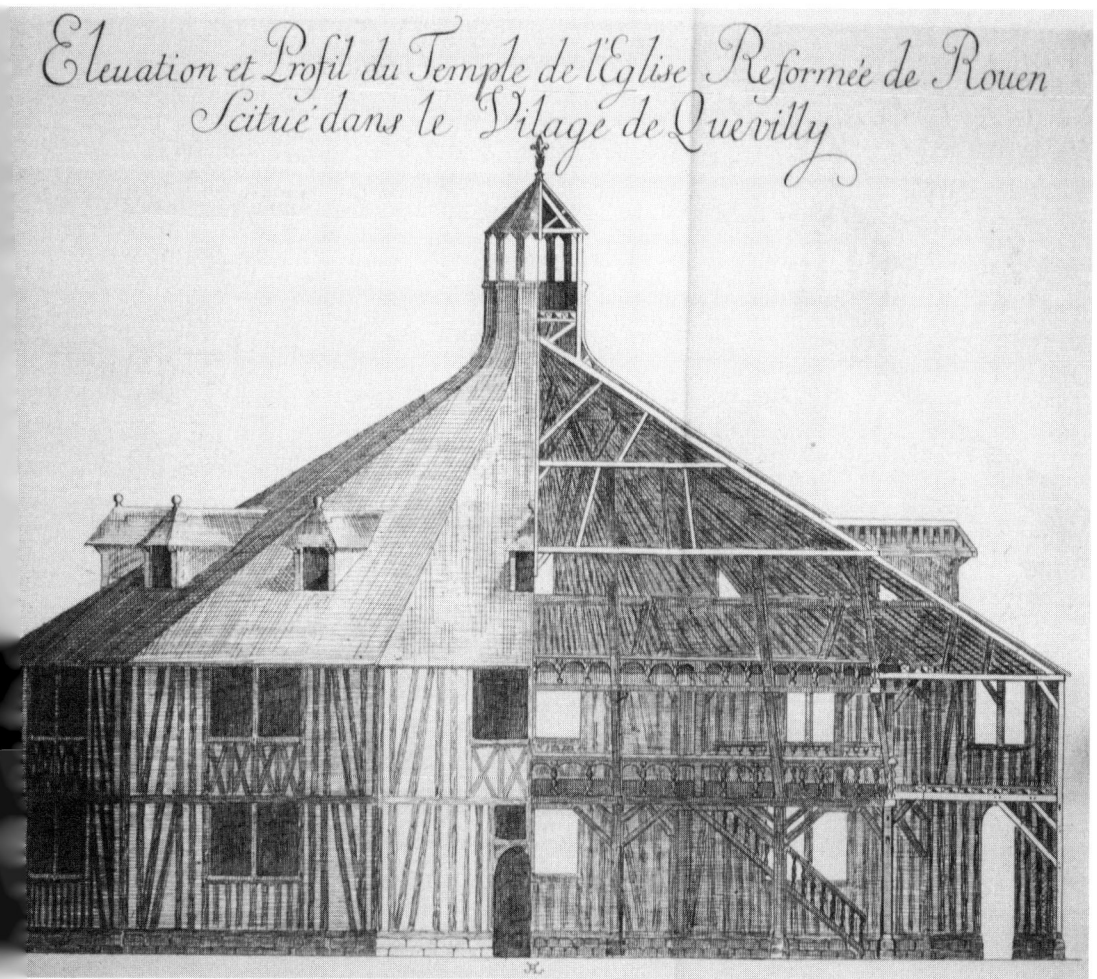

Figure 5.10. *Eleuation et Profil du Temple de l'Eglise Reformée de Rouen Scitué dans le Vilage de Quevilly.* Engraving of the twelve-sided Huguenot temple at Le Petit-Quevilly, near Rouen, France, built 1600–1601. Combined exterior view and interior section showing timber construction, galleries, and turret. From Philippe LeGendre, *Histoire de la persécution faite à l'Eglise de Rouën sur la fin du dernier siècle* (Rotterdam, 1704). Facsimile engraving by Jules Adeline (1874). Widener Library, Harvard College Library, Fr 7082.70.4.11.

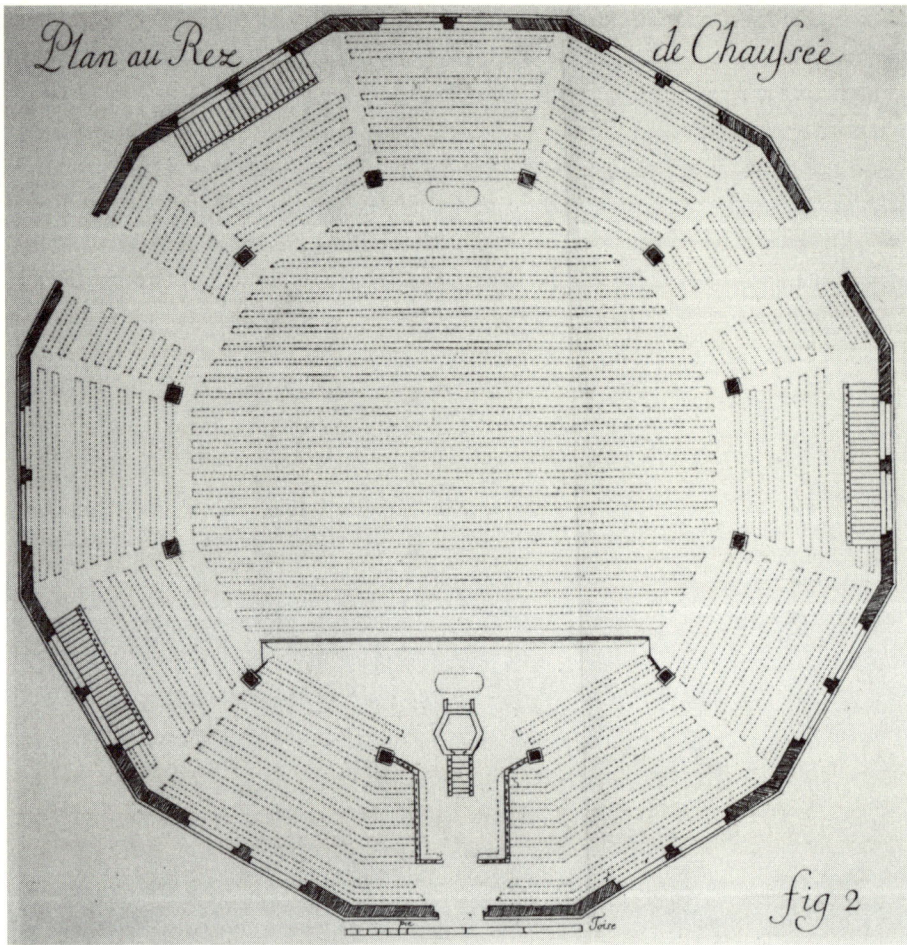

Figure 5.11. *Plan au Rez de Chaussée*. Ground-floor plan of the twelve-sided Huguenot temple at Le Petit-Quevilly, near Rouen, France, built 1600–1601. The circle of twelve inner posts supports two tiers of galleries as well as the roof. From Philippe LeGendre, *Histoire de la persécution faite à l'Eglise de Rouën sur la fin du dernier siècle* (Rotterdam, 1704). Facsimile engraving by Jules Adeline (1874). Widener Library, Harvard College Library, Fr 7082.70.4.11.

pews and benches were arranged *"en manière de théâtre"*—in short, a Protestant house of worship grounded on Calvinist principles and articulated through vernacular English barn-building and bridge-building traditions.

## The Four-Square New England Meetinghouse

While there are no contemporary descriptions of the 1638–40 meetinghouses erected in Hartford, Boston, and New Haven, good descriptions exist for those built after 1660 and occasional visual material for structures built after 1690. A contract prepared in 1658 between the selectmen of Malden, Massachusetts, and the carpenter Job Lane supplies excellent details. Lane was to build a "good strong, Artificial meetinghouse . . . of thirty three foot square, sixteen foot stud between joints, with doors, windows, pulpit, [and] seats." The contract stipulates "that all the sills, girts, main posts, plates, beams and all other principal timbers shall be of good and sound white or black oak" and that the "walls be made up on the outside with good clapboards, well dressed lapped and nailed. And the Inside to be lathed all over and well struck with clay, and upon it with lime and hard up to the wall plate." The contract further requires that the roof be covered with boards and short shingling. Three doors would offer access, and six glazed windows would provide light on three sides in addition to the usual two behind the "desk" (meaning pulpit). The roof of Malden's meetinghouse had a turret—in this instance six feet squarc in size "with rails about it," accessed from within by a ladder.[29]

Figure 5.12. *Templum Christianum Amsterdami*. Section of Remonstrants' temple in Amsterdam, as seen through the pulpit wall. Consecrated in 1630, it reveals the timber structure with two tiers of galleries and a raised pulpit. Engraving by Frans Brun (ca. 1600–ca. 1648), Amsterdam, 1630. University of Amsterdam Library (UvA), Special Collections Pr. G 35b.

The appearance of the Malden roof is unknown. Later accounts suggest that it was hipped with a relatively high pitch. But a description of the circa 1656 meetinghouse in Taunton after it was hit by lightning suggests that some early four-square roof types were not always peaked. The bolt, according to an account in the *Boston News-Letter* of 5 August 1706, "split the wooden button on the top of the vane spindle . . . destroyed the biggest part of the covering of the Turret boards, shingles and timber, and so descended on the proper roof of the Meeting-House, which is almost flat, and ript up the boards and shingles for about 10 foot." This description indicates that the roof of Taunton's turreted meetinghouse had an unusually low angle of pitch.

The outside appearance of four-square meetinghouses built at the end of the seventeenth century can be gained from a sketch taken by twenty-three-year-old Dudley Woodbridge as he traveled from Cambridge, Massachusetts, to the Connecticut River Valley in October 1728. He drew (and labeled) an elevation of the thirty-by-thirty-foot meetinghouse in Deerfield, Massachusetts, built in 1694, showing a hipped roof surmounted by a turret and a belfry, one on top of the other (figs. 5.13 and 5.14). Elsewhere on this page Woodbridge sketched two other meetinghouses that appear to be much larger and furnished with two tiers of galleries, but these are unidentified and may have been products of his imagination. Nevertheless, like the Deerfield example, each has a high-pitched roof and a centrally located belfry. The sense of verticality is the most striking feature of the four-square design, and in some instances, the upper third floor was reserved as a chamber, such as in Wethersfield and Farmington, Connecticut.[30]

Noticeable, too, is the amount of light Woodbridge's Deerfield structures let in, particularly in the upper floors through second-floor and dormer windows. This feature is consistent with the findings of the architectural investigator Brian Powell, who recently commissioned a reconstruction drawing of the Old Ship meetinghouse in Hingham. Powell led a team that examined the building in 2006 and 2007 and found evidence of large second-floor windows, three on the narrow sides and four on the long sides (in addition to the pulpit window). Above these were large gable windows (fig. 5.15). Powell suggests that the size and number of windows may have been chosen deliberately by the three-man building committee, whose instructions to examine other meetinghouses in the neighborhood included a mandate "to give the town the best light they can therein."[31] This mandate matches a central concept in Puritan religious thinking, which equated hearing the Gospel with entering a "Land of Light."[32] An alternate reading of the Hingham text suggests that "light" in the building committee's instruction may have meant "guidance."

What is not in doubt is the "sharp" incline of four-square roofs in the latter half of the first period, as well as their prominent gable windows. Nathan Andrews (1639–1712), son of the joiner William Andrews, received the contract to

Figures 5.13 and 5.14. *Delineated at Deerfield, Deerfield Meeting house* and *Dwelling houses*. Pen and ink and watercolor drawings in a diary kept by Dudley Woodbridge (1705–1790) during his trip to the Connecticut Valley, 1–10 October 1728. Shown are the Deerfield meetinghouse and examples of domestic housing as well as two hypothetical or unidentified meetinghouses that he may have encountered; the detail illustrates the second meetinghouse in Deerfield, Massachusetts. Courtesy of the Massachusetts Historical Society.

Figure 5.15. Reconstruction of the Old Ship meetinghouse in Hingham, Massachusetts, built in 1681 by Charles Stockbridge. Based on architectural investigations undertaken by Brian Powell and Andrea Gilmore in 2006 and 2007. Drawn by Marty Saunders, a church member. Courtesy of the First Parish Old Ship Church in Hingham, Massachusetts.

build New Haven's second meetinghouse in 1668. The original dimensions of this second building were fifty-five by thirty-five feet, but Williams was asked to widen it into a square format in 1698 after the town failed to receive bids for a brick alternative. This meetinghouse is illustrated in the James Wadsworth 1748 map of New Haven, which shows an angle of incline of about forty-five degrees (fig. 5.16). This structure served the First Church until it was replaced by one of brick in 1757—a useful life of almost ninety years.

Two other views of four-square meetinghouses reveal the same roofline. An early surveyor's plat of the 1699 meetinghouse in Ipswich shows a structure whose gables were almost as high as the turret (fig. 5.17). This sixty-six-by-sixty-foot first-period meetinghouse with twenty-six-foot posts was raised by Abraham

Tilton and Abraham Perkins and was one of the largest four-square types in its time. It had two dormer windows on one side and three on the other; a large flag weather vane stood at the peak of the roof.[33] Stephen Jaques's 1700 contract for Newbury, Massachusetts, specified a sixty-by-fifty-foot meetinghouse with a twenty-four-foot plate supporting a hipped roof whose angle of incline was over forty degrees. Jaques built an octagonal central turret with a spire. The original design included four large dormer windows, suggesting room for a second tier of galleries. The dormer window layout in Ipswich and Newbury may have been typical. When Middleborough, Massachusetts, raised its second meetinghouse in 1700, its builders extended the gable windows all the way up to the ridgeline creating "four gable ends."[34] The result was a nearly square structure, thirty-six

Figure 5.16. Image of the second meetinghouse in New Haven, built by Nathan Andrews in 1668, showing a large paneled double door with a cap, two corner doors, two small dormer windows, and a single turret. Detail from the unsigned *Plan of the City of New Haven Taken in 1748*, attributed to James Wadsworth (1730–1817). Beinecke Rare Book and Manuscript Library, Yale University.

Figure 5.17. Detail, "... *the foot way now in Contest.*" View of the third meetinghouse in Ipswich, Massachusetts, drawn by a surveyor to contest a right-of-way claim in 1717. This meetinghouse was raised by Abraham Tilton and Abraham Perkins in 1699; its dimensions were 66 by 60 feet with 26-foot posts, the roof "with 2 [or] 3 gables on every side, with one Teer of Gallery round said house." Courtesy of the Peabody Essex Museum, Salem, Massachusetts.

feet on one side, thirty feet on the other, with a stud height of sixteen feet—high enough to accommodate one and a half tiers of galleries.

Two of the largest meetinghouses of the first period were located a few hundred yards from one another on Marlborough Street in the center of Boston. One was the seventy-five-by-fifty-one-foot Old Cedar built in 1669 for the newly formed Third or South Church. Besides its size, the house was unusual because of the political circumstances that accompanied its erection. Before it was raised, the Third Church had waged a drawn-out legal battle with the Massachusetts Bay Colony, headed by Gov. Richard Bellingham with support from selectmen and the First Church, over the propriety of building a meetinghouse without permission from the deputies and Boston's two existing congregations. The South Church countered they had a right to build it because it was on private property, not a gift from the town, and they went ahead relying on outsiders. The committee hired a builder in Braintree, Massachusetts, Lt. Robert Tweld (ca. 1620–1697), who also served on a committee to rebuild Braintree's corn mill that had been destroyed by fire and whose inventory indicates he owned woodworking tools.[35] Tweld arranged to have the frame timbers, presumably made of cedar, prepared outside of Boston and carried to the site on the road between Roxbury and the North End in seventy cartloads from a place fourteen miles away (probably Braintree itself); an additional thirteen cartloads came from the Muddy River forests northeast of Boston. On 1 October 1669 "many Brethren in Neighboring Towns" arrived in Boston to help raise the structure, "and so the work was carried along gradually, to the completing thereof." The William Burgis–William Price view of 1722 (fig. 5.18) indicates it had a central bell turret perched at the apex of what may have been four or six substantial gables, some parallel to one another in the characteristic M pro-

Figure 5.18. "Old Cedar," seen on the right *(10)*, was the first meetinghouse of the Third Church, Boston, erected 1669. The image reveals three gables and a raised turret with a pyramid at each corner. The lean-to just below it may be one of its three stairwells. From William Burgis and William Price, *A South East View of the Great Town of Boston in New England in America*, 1725. I. N. Phelps Stokes Collection, Miriam and Ira D. Wallach Division of Art, Prints and Photographs, The New York Public Library, Astor, Lenox and Tilden Foundations.

file. It had two tiers of galleries and three porches; the porches and the roof were covered with sheet lead reputedly purchased at a cost of two thousand pounds.[36] When it was demolished in 1729, the *Boston Weekly News-Letter* reported on 28 April that the main timbers of the Old Cedar "were decay'd to Rotteness: and the ends of all the Summers . . . turn'd to Powder" and that as a precaution the belfry was removed separately before the workmen toppled the house.

The Old Brick, located just opposite the colony's town house on Cornhill Square, was three feet shorter and three feet wider than the Old Cedar and was built by the First Church to replace its predecessor, which had burned in the Boston fire of 1711 (fig. 5.19). It, too, supported two tiers of galleries on three sides

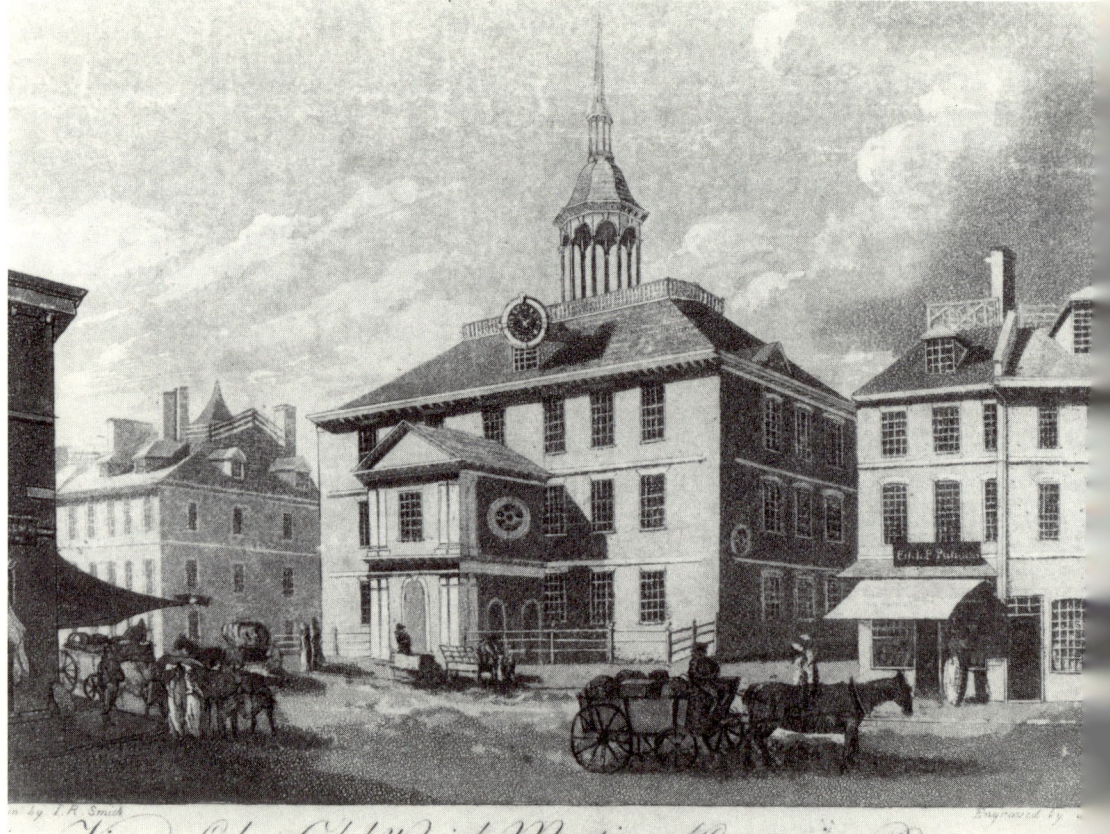

Figure 5.19. *View of the Old Brick Meeting House in Boston, 1808.* Aquatint by James Kidder from a drawing by T. R. Smith of the third meetinghouse of the First Church in Boston. The best-known example of the four-square meetinghouse, the 72-by-54-foot "Old Brick" in Boston was completed two years after the society's second meetinghouse was consumed by the fire of 1711. Furnished with a front stairwell porch and clock, and two tiers of galleries, the Old Brick was the largest meetinghouse in New England until the Old South was raised in 1729. This early-nineteenth century illustration shows it with a pilastered two-story stairwell porch, which replaced the original porch in 1784. Courtesy of the Massachusetts Historical Society.

and was furnished with a turret and belfry in the center of its four-square roof. The bell, "procure[d] . . . here, at the Church's risk," was presumably in place when the meetinghouse was opened to its parishioners in 1713. The turret quickly decayed and in 1726 an entirely new one was made, presumably a copy. This is the belfry seen on the William Burgis 1728 map of Boston just behind a huge lozenge-faced clock.[37] It was protected under a hexagonal or octagonal framework that supported an ogee-shaped cupola, which allowed the bell to peal without the sound's being impeded by windows or louvers. Curiously, only two of the many prints and paintings of the Old Brick suggest the existence of a bell mechanism underneath the cupola. One is Henry Pelham's *The Bloody Massacre perpetrated in King Street Boston on March 5th 1770*, which reveals a bell-wheel within the pillars. (Imitations of this drawing by Paul Revere and Jonathan Mulliken show the same feature.) The second is an 1808 painting by John Rubens Smith. The structure served the First Church for ninety-six years.[38]

## Other Early Meetinghouse Forms

Small congregations may have preferred the long house, so called after the "long brick [meeting] house with a leanto" cited in the Branford, Connecticut, records of 1699.[39] Approximately twenty-three are known from descriptions or dimensions given in town records between 1638 and 1710. The actual number, however, may have been higher. A classic one-story long house was built in Edgartown, Martha's Vineyard, in 1665. Its dimensions were thirty-three by nineteen feet with a plate height of eight feet, an elevation that made it difficult to install galleries. Other long houses were constructed in 1639 in Marblehead, Massachusetts (forty by twenty [?] feet), and in 1662 in Hadley, Massachusetts (forty-five by twenty-four feet).[40] Many long houses were topped with turrets for bells or lookouts. In 1645 a "tower" was placed at each end of the forty-five-by-twenty-five-foot Springfield, Massachusetts, long house, one of which was designed as a "watch-house."[41]

The known proportions of other long houses suggest that the short dimension was usually a little more than one-half its length—for example the forty-by-twenty-two-foot meetinghouse in Hampton, New Hampshire, built in 1640.[42] But their sizes varied considerably. The largest long houses in the region exceeded sixty feet in length. The cedar-covered meetinghouse built by Saybrook, Connecticut, in 1676 was sixty feet long and thirty feet wide; its sixteen-foot posts suggest it was provided with a tier of galleries. The meetinghouse built in 1640 in Windsor, Connecticut, has been calculated by one church historian to have been seventy feet long and thirty-six feet wide, possibly the result of later additions.[43] And they appear to have been well made. Dedham's thirty-six-by-twenty-foot girt meetinghouse, "fabricated" in 1638, was constructed of newly felled oak and pine assembled on a two-foot stone foundation or "carfe." Records indicate it was twelve feet "between the upp[er] and nether sill" and "daubed" (probably meaning the inside walls were plastered). Thatch was used for the roof. The town also ordered a pair of casement windows installed on the backside for the "officers seat"—the earliest documented instance of a pulpit window in a New England house of worship. Dedham added a decorative "pyramid" in 1651.[44]

The advantage of a long house was that its frame was simpler to build. Framers may have preferred a short span rather than the complex trusses and rafters needed for square structures. What is not known is the form of the roofs. Were they pitched like New England meetinghouses built in the following century? Or were they fitted with high multiple gables that formed the usual M profile? The only detailed evidence of a long house roof is a memory drawing of the 1683 meetinghouse in Plymouth, Massachusetts, a forty-five-foot long house shown with a pitched roof and a small central bell tower. This meetinghouse was expanded in 1712 with lean-tos to increase its width to forty feet (fig. 5.20), and it is possible that when this work was done, an earlier M-shaped gabled roof (as shown with a turret in the upper right-hand corner of the top drawing) was replaced by a pitched one.

That some long houses were little more than an adaptation of an English barn refitted to suit the purposes of a meeting hall is suggested by two instances in New England when builders were directed to follow agricultural or domestic specifications. In 1651, New London, Connecticut, voted that its meetinghouse was to be "the same dimension of Mr. Parke his barn." And in 1659 when Rehoboth, Massachusetts, was enlarging its 1646 meetinghouse, the town specified that it be "shingled as well as Goodman Payne's house."[45] These examples suggest that the two congregations may have previously gathered in actual barns or houses for their religious services, in keeping with a practice followed in France and the Netherlands, and in New England from the seventeenth well into the nineteenth century. The similarity in design between barns and meetinghouses explains why old meetinghouses in the region were often sold off for reuse as barns and why so many nineteenth-century parish historians colloquially refer to their meetinghouse as "the Lord's Barn."[46]

New Englanders may also have brought over to America what Nigel Yates has called the Anglican response to the Protestant Reformation.[47] Recent evidence has revealed that English dissenters and nonconformists had developed the long-form meetinghouse well before their arrival in New England. Christopher Stell reports that thatched and wood-frame cottages were turned into meetinghouses by dissenting sects in western and eastern England, possibly as early as the late sixteenth century, but certainly by the early seventeenth century.[48] Some of these were long houses in the sense defined here. Bramhope

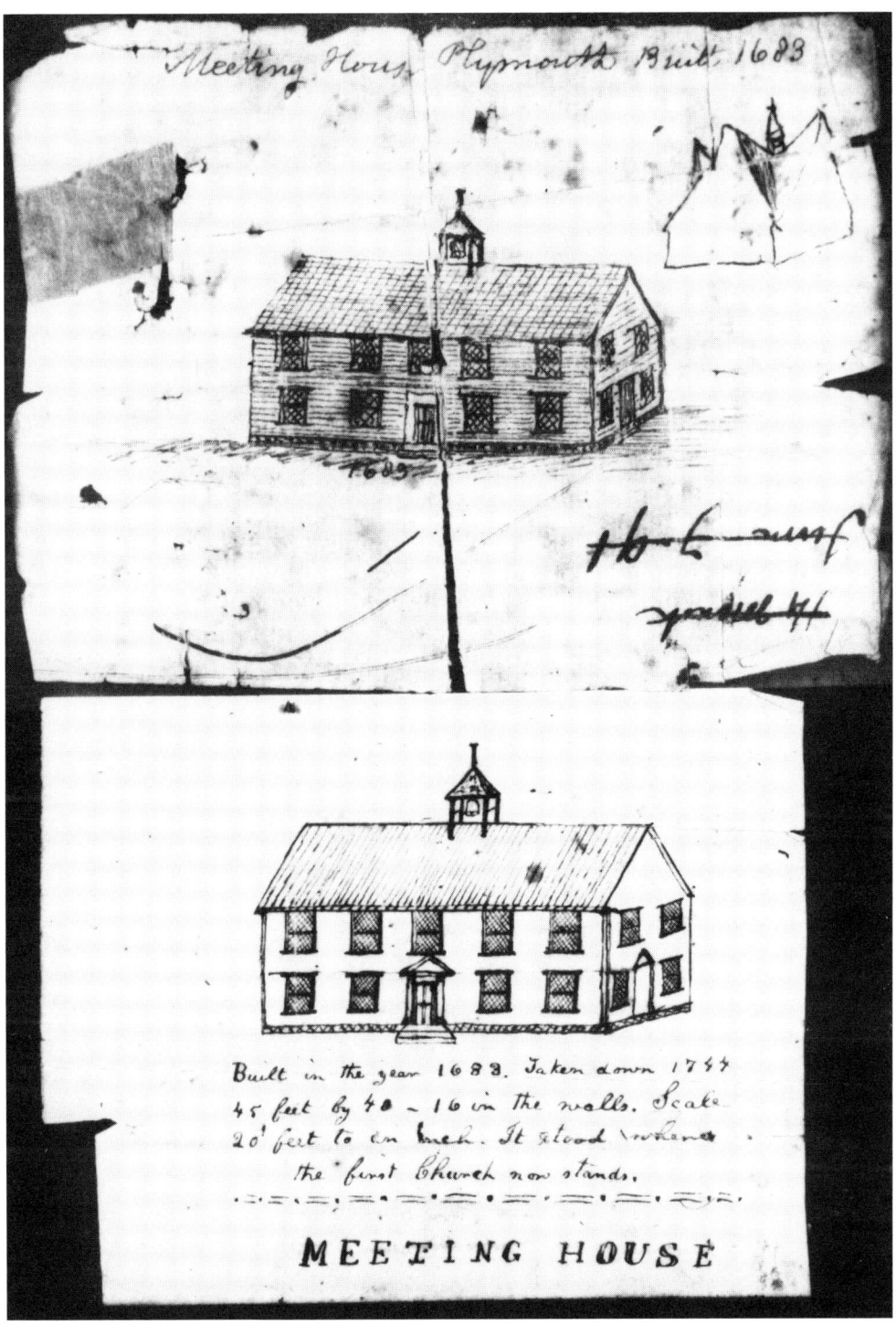

Figure 5.20. *Meeting House.* Late eighteenth-century memory drawings of the second meetinghouse in Plymouth, Massachusetts, built 1683 in the form of a "long house." Possibly by Samuel Davis (1765–1829). The two views show a pitched roof surmounted by a small central bell tower. The lower caption identifies its dimensions as 45 by 40 feet, but the structure shown here may represent the original appearance of the meetinghouse before it was expanded 18 feet by lean-tos in 1712. The building was struck by lightning in 1715. Courtesy of the Pilgrim Hall Museum, Plymouth, Massachusetts.

Chapel in Yorkshire, a one-story structure of stone built in 1649, was 60 feet long and 17.5 feet wide, a design similar to that of an animal shed. Bramhope had two entrances on the south or long side, but the Communion table (and possibly the pulpit) was located on one of the narrow ends. Other long forms include the meetinghouse in Guyhirn, Cambridgeshire, a brick and stone structure 44 by 24 feet. The form persisted in England into the early eighteenth century. The well-known "Old Meeting" in Norwich (built in 1693), one of the best survivals of Puritan architecture in England, is a rectangular hall with seating on three sides and the pulpit in the center of the long side.[49]

Other, more practical approaches to the task of building a meetinghouse included building on posts sunk into the ground, creating what historical archaeologists today call "earthfast" structures, as opposed to those underpinned with stones. At least two first-period meetinghouses in New England were built in this style. One is known from a 1659 document contracting for a thirty-by-eighteen-foot meetinghouse in Norwalk, Connecticut, stipulating that it "be set upon posts in the ground, 12 foot in length, that there be a 10 foot distance from the ground to the ———." Because only a fragment of the document remains, it is not known whether this meetinghouse was elevated off the ground like seventeenth-century English market halls or whether the floor lay on ground-based sleepers. The second example is revealed in the archaeological work done at the site of the 1706 meetinghouse in Duxbury, Massachusetts, where investigators in 2008 found evidence of postholes comparable to those described in Norwalk. Similar sunken post traditions exist for seventeenth-century meetinghouses in Woburn and Billerica, Massachusetts, and domestic parallels have been found in Plymouth Colony and possibly in Guilford, Connecticut.[50]

Finally, the traditional "log cabin" championed by so many nineteenth-century historians may well have characterized at least some meetinghouses that functioned as temporary defensive forts. According to William Bradford's history of the Plymouth Colony, a timbered, horizontal-roofed fortification built in 1622 "served them also for a meeting house, and was fitted accordingly for that use."[51] Beyond that, about thirty-seven examples of block houses or "logg houses"—a fairly unusual term in seventeenth-century and eighteenth-century meetinghouse contracts—are "remembered" by historians writing between 1780 and 1880. But only a few are documented. Most of these were of hewn logs laid horizontally. John Huchinson's 1657 contract in Portsmouth called for a structure "40 feet square & 16 feet wall plate high—A flat Roof & substantial turret with a gallery about it. Substantial Ground sills, wall plates & side posts of oak . . . the sides to be of Logs 9 Inches thick, let into the side posts with a rabbet[.] 12 windows well fitted 3 substantial doors, a complete pulpit to reach the two middle posts, the side of the house planed 6 foot high[,] the floors to be laid with oak sleepers."[52] This structure was clearly a defensive fort. And a few towns actually erected palisades or stone embankments around their meetinghouses to enhance their security. In 1667 Dover, New Hampshire, voted to build a wooden eight-foot palisade approximately one hundred feet long on each side. Each log was to be twelve inches thick, and a "sconce" or lookout was raised at two corners. In 1675 Topsfield erected a stone wall around its meetinghouse five to six feet high and three feet thick at the bottom, with a watchhouse at the southeast corner within the wall.[53]

New England's frontier communities continued to use the defensive "log" form well into the eighteenth century. When Concord, New Hampshire—then called Rumford—built its first meetinghouse at "Penny Cook" in 1727, the new town voted for "a block house twenty-five feet in breadth and forty feet in length" for the security of the settlers.[54] It was three years before a floor was laid and another thirteen before pews and a gallery were installed. Similar log houses were constructed in nearby New Hampshire towns such as Chichester in 1731 ("timber" six inches thick), Suncook or Pembroke in 1733 ("good hewn logs"), and Boscawen in 1736 (same width as Rumford . . . "built of logs").[55] All of these may have followed the Portsmouth model of using sawn or hewed horizontal timbers let into the side posts.[56]

Even after the threat of war had subsided, however, log meetinghouses—relatively quick to build—were raised for the sake of convenience as temporary measures by newly settled late eighteenth-century frontier towns. These structures were generally made of horizontally laid round timbers requiring little or no preparation. Shelburne, Massachusetts, voted in 1769 that "every man does his Equal part or pays his money to building a Round Log Meetinghouse this Spring." Thirteen years later the town of Barnard, Vermont, called for all able-bodied men to "meet at the center on the 15th of this month with axes in order to peel bark and cut timber for said house."[57]

The evidence learned from these various forms—four-square houses, long houses, earthfast houses, and log houses—argues that New England's dissenting congregations had developed architectural formulas that differentiated their houses of worship from the forts, barns, dwelling houses, bridges, and mills from whose fabric they had sprung. While these structures were intended as ecclesiastic buildings and fitted with ecclesiastic furniture, such as pulpits, pulpit windows, Communion tables, and baptismal stands, they also included purely civil architectural elements seldom seen elsewhere in the first-period colonial landscape. Thirty-one meetinghouses built before 1700 are cited as having a turret or "penthouse." William Andrews's 1639 meetinghouse in New Haven boasted an "upper" turret over the lower turret—an image in line with Dudley Woodbridge's diary illustrations—as did the West Springfield meetinghouse of 1702.[58] Even small meetinghouses had turrets. The twenty-by-twenty-foot meetinghouse in Lynn, Massachusetts, was given one in 1662; the twenty-two-by-twenty-two-foot meetinghouse in Mendon, Massachusetts, in 1669 had a turret gathered into a seven-foot square.[59]

First-period meetinghouses also had bells. Approximately 82 of the 330 structures built at the height of the first period had belfries or turrets that could serve as belfries; about half of these are known to have bells. Cambridge, Massachusetts, hired a parishioner for "ringing the bell" in 1632; a "bellrope" is cited in the records of Watertown in 1647.[60] Like drums and red flags, bells marked purely civil functions—funerals, emergencies, royal birthdays—or simply indicated the passage of time. In four-square meetinghouses, such as those at Hatfield and Northampton, Massachusetts, belfries were hung above or within the turret in the apex of the roof. In long houses, bells were housed in small cupolas, known as "lanthornes" or "coneys" from their simultaneous use as beacons, located either in the center or at one end of the roof.

Seventeenth-century meetinghouses also had wrought-iron elements not usually seen in domestic or agrarian architecture. John Gilbert, an ironworker and glassworker who in 1678 installed the windows of the second meetinghouse in Springfield, Massachusetts, was paid for "1 dozen Iron Casem$^{ts}$" at a cost of five and a half pounds.[61] Woburn, Massachusetts, paid for "iron work for . . . casements" for its meetinghouse in 1701. The western precinct of Watertown, Massachusetts, installed "Irons for casements" on the meetinghouse they were building in 1721.[62] John Gilbert may also have been responsible for the wrought-iron weather vane erected on the Springfield turret. Weather vanes usually took the form of an iron flag (reputedly made from discarded kitchenware), often indicating the date the structure was raised. (In 1698 Newton, Massachusetts, ordered that a "vane . . . [be] set upon the turret of the meeting house.")[63] The several extant flags in the region's historical collections show that these vanes (and the poles they were fixed to) were decorated with traditional iron-workers' designs: fleurs-de-lis, hearts, cloverleafs, and curled and twisted shapes (fig. 5.21).

Among the civil elements of the exterior were ornamental roof fixtures mounted at the apex or the base of the gables or on the turret itself. At least ten meetinghouse "pyramids" are cited in New England records through 1709, and one additional example has been identified from the 1725 Burgis–Price view of Boston (see Appendix C). Little is known of these fixtures, which were also called "pyks" or "pinnacles."[64] That they were decorative is suggested by a vote in Roxbury, Massachusetts, in 1658 "that some pinakles or other ornament be set upon each end of the house." This use conforms to their traditional role as "pyramidal or conical ornaments used to terminate a gable buttress"—apparently as a way of exhibiting wealth or status.[65] Most meetinghouse pyramids seem to have been installed in pairs or multiples. Haddam, Connecticut, ordered "tooe pramedyes [pyramids] at each end" of their new meetinghouse in 1673. But other towns set them off against other features. In 1651 the contract for improving Dedham's meetinghouse called for a "penthouse" on one side of the building and a "pyramedy" [pyramid] on the other. Their size is uncertain. Pinnacles erected on seventeenth-century domestic dwellings were approximately two feet high, but those associated with meetinghouses may have been much larger.[66] Joseph Parsons, a carpenter in Northampton, Massachusetts, hired in 1694 to repair the meetinghouse, was paid for "sawing two stocks for Preamady [pyramids]"—suggesting not only that he was making two of them, but that they were formed from large timbers.[67] The pinnacles on the four corners of the bell tower over Boston's 1669 South meetinghouse may have been up to ten or twelve feet high.[68] The style (and the use of the term *pyramid* or *pinnacle*)

Figure 5.21. Flag weather vane used on the second meetinghouse (1663–1748) in Wenham, Massachusetts. 1688. Copper and iron. Width of flag 15.5 inches. Wenham Museum Collection, Wenham, Massachusetts.

continued into the eighteenth century when Norwich, Connecticut, ordered that its pyramid be mended in 1705; Norwalk allowed for a "pinnicle" on its new belfry in 1709.[69]

Marian Donnelly, who first addressed the issue of pyramids in the *Journal of the Society of Architectural Historians* in 1960, has suggested that these ornaments had little if any ecclesiastic significance and simply may have been a medieval ornament that identified the structure as a community gathering place.[70] And she may be entirely right because they also appear on seventeenth-century and early eighteenth-century public buildings and churches in Maryland and New York, and they may have been equivalent to the "lanthorn" erected by the town of Windsor, Connecticut, in the center of its meetinghouse sometime before 1658. But there remains the possibility they had a secondary importance in New England—one that later became crucial in the transformation of the seventeenth-century meetinghouse into a nineteenth-century church: meetinghouse pyramids and pinnacles may have been an early form of the steeples and spires of the eighteenth and nineteenth centuries going by another name. That is, their purpose on the meetinghouse may have been fundamentally ecclesiastic. The use of pinnacles and pyramids in Congregational and Anglican turret and bell-tower architecture in eighteenth-century Massachusetts argues that they were.[71] And if so, they may have been the common link between first-period architecture and the two periods that followed. Pinnacles and pyramids touched on the two principal threads or strands that guided New England's meetinghouse design before 1830. One was to identify a municipal building in its status as a public hall or gathering place; a second was to identify it as a place of worship. Over the next hundred years both strands evolved, but the second won out decisively.

## First-Period Interiors

Within, the first-period meetinghouse revealed a dependence on English furniture traditions and ecclesiastic forms. The dominant interior features—the pulpit, the pulpit window surrounds, the pulpit canopy, the elders' or deacons' seats, the gallery front, and the Communion table—formed a focused unit that was designed and decorated in current woodworking styles and that followed accepted ground rules for Protestant houses of worship. While an absence of survivals greatly limits our knowledge of these features, a few interiors can be reconstructed from architectural fragments or from partial descriptions in seventeenth-century meetinghouse contracts.

In most instances the same carpenter who erected the frame also completed the interior finish work and accessories. John Allis, the carpenter hired by Springfield, Massachusetts, to build its second meetinghouse, followed this dual role in

Figures 5.22 and 5.23. Two panels from the pulpit made in 1655 by John Houghton (1624–1684) in Dedham, Massachusetts, for the first meetinghouse in Medfield, raised in 1654. Oak. Diamond, height 12 inches; rectangular panel height 7 inches, width 14 inches. Collection of the Medfield Historical Society. Photograph by Daniel Farber.

1677. According to a detailed account, Allis was paid to lay the foundation and raise the frame at a cost of a little more than £140. He remained on the job to complete interior elements, such as the pulpit, the canopy, the deacons' seat, and the stairs leading to the gallery. His brother in turn was paid for turning and installing "6 doz. Of bannist's at 4s," turning two great pillars and seven posts. The "five week diet" John Allis received from the town during his stay suggests that he, or he and his brother, completed the work in about thirty days.[72]

The same account indicates that Springfield's pulpit was "raised on a frame"—meaning it probably resembled the capsule pulpit made for the 1654 meetinghouse in Medfield, Massachusetts, which has been reconstructed from two surviving fragments (figs. 5.22 and 5.23). According to Robert Blair St. George, the Medfield pulpit was made in nearby Dedham by the carpenter John Houghton and was possibly based on a prototype in oak still standing in Holy Trinity Church in Blythburgh, Suffolk. The design was fairly common in England and consisted of a self-standing, six-sided desk with elaborately carved and wainscoted front and sides, devised to hold one person (fig. 5.24). The pulpit was elevated on "pillars," or posts, with steps leading to the desk. Its relatively small size may be inferred from the fact it was carted from Dedham to Medfield by "Brother Bullen" after its completion—making it comparable to the Huguenot pulpits of the late sixteenth century (fig. 5.25).[73]

The traveling pulpit used by Rev. Daniel Takawampbait (ca. 1652–1716), a Native American leader of the praying town of Natick, Massachusetts, provides a clear contrast to Houghton's work. Takawampbait was active in the late seventeenth and early eighteenth centuries in Native communities in central and eastern Massachusetts. His pulpit, which may date from the years 1690 to 1710, looks like a small chest of drawers about four feet high with a hinged desk (fig. 5.26). The upper portion, perhaps made by English-trained carpenters, fits

Figure 5.24. Conjectural reconstruction of the pulpit made in 1655 by John Houghton (1624–1684) in Dedham, for the 1654 Medfield meetinghouse. Drawing by Alice Gray Read. From Robert B. St. George, "Style and Structure," 9.

Figure 5.25. Elevated pulpit and canopy in the circa 1566 Huguenot temple at Paradis, Lyon, France. Detail from *Temple De Lyon, Nommé Paradis*. Paint on wood. Bibliothèque de Genève, Centre d'iconographie genevoise.

into and at one point could be detached from the bottom two-thirds. The lower portion, said to have been made by two members of the Indian congregation in Natick, was added later and features four "horsebone" feet and chatter marks in the woodwork. The top and bottom are decorated by horizontal stripes, a Native design, though possibly an imitation of seventeenth-century wainscoting. It is believed Takawampbait traveled to Native communities carrying the upper third of the pulpit in a cart.[74]

The Springfield and Medfield examples, like the surviving Takawampbait pulpit, suggest an initial congruence between dissenting and Anglican pulpit forms in the early seventeenth century: they were intended for a single occupant. At the same time, other evidence reveals that first-period pulpits were also designed to hold more than one person—especially during 1660–90, when lay elders and two ordained ministers—a pastor and a teacher—played prominent roles in New England church life. Job Lane's 1658 contract for Malden called for a "pulpit and cover [canopy] to be of wainscot to contain five or six persons"—a phrase that suggests a more substantial pulpit where church officers sat facing the congregation, perhaps all housed under the canopy. Some seats may have been at a lower level beneath the pulpit desk, but in meetinghouses without a second-floor gallery they may have been at the same level as the desk and on either side of it.[75] A vote taken in Lynn, Massachusetts, directed that the number of persons "sit[ing] in the pulpit" in 1691 at the Old Tunnel meetinghouse should be no more than eight men—and listed them by name. Four of these

Figure 5.26. "Travelling" pulpit used by Rev. Daniel Takawampbait of the First Congregational Church of Natick, Massachusetts. The upper portion once detached from the lower two-thirds. Wood unknown and untested, circa 1690–1710. Height approximately 36 inches. Courtesy of the First Congregational Church, Natick, Massachusetts. Photograph courtesy of the Natick Historical Society, Giovanna Vitelli, photographer.

eight were termed "senior." Additionally, Lynn assigned three men to the deacons' seat, presumably installed below the desk, and ten more "at the [Communion] table," possibly stationed on the ground floor at the same level with the pews. In all, these improvements were designed to hold about twenty-one men. Lynn's pulpit was now getting crowded.[76]

The data from Lynn may not have been typical of all seventeenth-century meetinghouses, but it does conform to the model that historians have traditionally reconstructed to describe the floor plan of the first meetinghouse in New Haven, the one raised by William Andrews in 1639. According to Edward Atwater, the pulpit was arranged in 1656 into four tiers. The highest was the bench immediately behind the pulpit where the "teaching elders" sat; then came the pulpit desk; just in front of the desk at a slightly lower level was the seat of the "ruling elder"; and just in front and lower still was the seat for the deacons. These church officials sat directly facing the congregation. But Atwater's data also suggest that as many as eight men and seven women—presumably the founding members of the church—were seated between the pulpit and the governor's and magistrates' pews. It is possible that these fifteen people also faced the congregation, creating what in effect was a central focus of worship.[77]

Pulpits like those in Malden, Lynn, and New Haven that seated between four and twenty-one people were in all likelihood attached to the wall, not free standing like the Medfield example. This construction is suggested by language in two other period contracts. The first, prepared for the 1657 forty-by-forty-foot log meetinghouse in Portsmouth, New Hampshire, specified a "complete pulpit . . . to reach the two middle posts." The second, prepared in 1681 for the 1663 meetinghouse in Topsfield, Massachusetts, instructed the carpenters to design a "wainscot" pulpit "ten foot Long and if the room will give way . . . [and] to be longer & for breadth as the room will give way." Both descriptions indicate that carpenters were designing the pulpit to fit between the two central posts, making it a flattened, wall-attached structure rather than a freestanding capsule or a centrally located one.[78]

When meetinghouses were enlarged to accommodate more benches and pews, however, wall-attached pulpits were sometimes left in their former place, in effect being converted into self-standing types. When enlarging the New Haven meetinghouse with a twenty-five-foot addition on the north side, Nathan Andrews made a "square" structure fifty-five by sixty feet. In Ezra Stiles's 1772 recollection of a seating plan of this meetinghouse, the old pulpit was still located near the middle of the structure; benches, pews, and a tier of galleries faced the pulpit from all four sides.[79] Much the same happened in the 1714 meetinghouse of Boston's New North Society, whose initial dimensions were sixty-five by forty-eight feet with thirty-five-foot posts. In 1719 the meetinghouse was enlarged on the pulpit or north side by an eighteen-foot lean-to, making a sixty-five-by-sixty-six-foot structure. The pulpit and the elders' and deacons' seats remained in the center of the meetinghouse. According to an early nineteenth-century historian of the parish, the preacher had to "turn to each part of the audience in succession, and make his particular addresses."[80] This preaching arrangement may have been remarkably similar to the one favored by the Reformist Huldrych Zwingli (1484–1531) at the Grossmünster church in sixteenth-century Zurich, where he positioned himself in the center aisle of his church in an elevated pulpit surrounded on all sides by his followers, some standing with him at the desk.[81]

Communion tables varied as much in type and size as did pulpits. Malden's 1658 table was attached to the deacons' pew and devised "to fall down, for the Lord's Supper"—an arrangement probably typical of small meetinghouses throughout the seventeenth and eighteenth centuries, since space about the pulpit was always greatly in demand.[82] The area had to contain other fixtures, such as the raised benches or pews for the deacons, banistered stairs rising to the pulpit, a frame for holding the hourglass, and an iron stand for supporting the baptismal basin. That some tables were freestanding is suggested by one that Stephen Jaques is credited by tradition as having made for the First Church in Newbury, Massachusetts, in 1700. Jaques's heavily reinforced oak table was about five feet wide and four feet deep.

Because Reformed congregations generally favored taking Communion in a sitting posture rather than kneeling, some tables may have been fairly long. Scottish congregations sometimes took Communion at a table permanently occupying the length of the center aisle of the church. And there are some American equivalents to this arrangement. In 1671 Brookhaven, Long Island, voted to seat all those who paid forty shillings toward the salary of Rev. George Phillips at the Communion table. This too may have been a long table, and (if only to help support the minister) it may have been crammed into the interior of Brookhaven's twenty-eight-foot square meetinghouse.[83] Dorchester, Massachusetts, in 1677 installed a large pew "at the table" just in front of the pulpit. The records indicate that the pew accommodated fourteen persons in 1693 and twelve persons in 1698; an additional three deacons and three men sat "at the end next to it."[84] Chelmsford, Massachusetts, repaired its meetinghouse in 1702, enlarging it to allow installation of "a long table from one alley to another."[85]

The size of these tables may have been dependent on the manner of practicing Communion. Perhaps Dorchester inclined toward a form of Presbyterianism and favored long tables and matching vessels to promote collegiality. Other churches, such as Boston's First Parish, may have favored hierarchy and precedence and therefore a smaller table. While the issue does not seem to have been resolved in the seventeenth century, we do know that about a hundred years after Brookhaven's vote, Protestants in North America were still seated at long tables—some apparently extending the length of the meetinghouse as they did in Scotland. Ezra Stiles reports in 1773 that in South Carolina "the New England Meeting or Congregational Church at Charleston has a Communion Table 1½ or 2 feet wide along the broad Alley at which 60 Communicants sit, and the rest (Total 150 Communicants) draw near in 12 nearest adjoining Pews, and the Deacons carry the Elements."[86]

Seventeenth-century pews are rarely cited in the records, in part because few congregations actually built them. Some pews were located next to or before the pulpit. According to the 1652 town records of Windsor, Connecticut, William Buell was paid for making "the Eldr's pew, Deacon's Pew, Magistrate's Pew, and their Wives' Pew." He was later asked to divide the great pew into two, one part for the magistrates and one for others, and that it "be raised equal with short seats."[87] Robert Trent, who examined fragments of pews like these from the first meetinghouse in Marblehead, Massachusetts, reports that they reveal "high-quality joiner's work" and that they resemble chest fronts. He concludes that they were indistinguishable from English joinery of the same period and went through rapid stylistic changes (fig. 5.27).[88]

Not all first-period pews were stationed close to the pulpit. Some were attached to tie beams or gallery posts. A 1672 vote taken in Portsmouth, New Hampshire, stated, "Nehemiah Partridge and five or six more people have the free liberty to build a pair of stairs up to the westward beam within the meeting house and [build] a pew upon the beam." A 1679 vote in Braintree, Massachusetts, allowed William Rawson "the privilege of making a seat for his family, between or upon the two beams over the pulpit, not darkening the pulpit."[89] While we do not know whether this meant in back of or to one side of or directly in front of the pulpit, the proposed placement of this pew on two overhead beams suggests considerable variety may have existed in their locations.

Several "round" seats or pews are cited in connection with the second meetinghouse in Norwalk, Connecticut—a forty-foot square structure built in 1678 and replaced by the town in 1723. An agreement in 1686 called for three men of "substance," one of them Thomas Fitch, to be "seated in the round seat." The next paragraph in the records required that five more men "be seated in the round seat" and four men be placed in the seat immediately behind it. About a year later, however, after Fitch had been selected king's commissioner, the town voted to put him in the "upper great round seat." It is possible that these seats surrounded a round or half-round Communion table or possibly even overlooked the pulpit. But we have little idea of what "great" and "upper" actually meant in this context.[90]

Unlike meetinghouse exteriors, which were seemingly designed to distance themselves from Anglican and Catholic houses of worship, meetinghouse interiors—especially those associated with the pulpit and pulpit surrounds—

Figure 5.27. Pew door used in the first (1639) and second (1695) meetinghouses in Marblehead, Massachusetts, attributed to John Norman (1612–1672) or John Norman Jr. (1637–1713), working in 1659. Oak. 38¼ by 20 5/16 inches. Collection of the Marblehead Museum and Historical Association. Photograph by Daniel Farber.

followed ecclesiastic forms patterned after those of the Church of England. A possible exception was the placement of the pulpit, which in Anglican churches was a little offset from the main alley, though most small Anglican churches put the pulpit against the long wall just as Congregational meetinghouses did. Anglicans also gave greater prominence to the altar than did the Puritans, who favored folding tables. That a visual aesthetic governed these forms is implied by repeated references to terms such as "manner," "fashion," and "proportion" in the specifications given to carpenters. When Wethersfield, Connecticut, built its first meetinghouse in 1647, the building committee contracted with Joshua Jennings to follow the "wainscot, according to the seats [in the] Hartford Meeting House." John Huchinson's 1657 contract for the meetinghouse in Portsmouth, New Hampshire, called for a "main pillar with braces of oak to be suitably carved . . . [as well as] the arch work." Job Lane's 1658 Malden agreement specified a "wainscot" pulpit and canopy. Did these terms reflect artisanal traditions that accompanied trained woodworkers immigrating into eastern and southern New England in the seventeenth century—or were they specifically ecclesiastical? We do not know. Clearly the artisanal traditions that went into the interior design of the first-period meetinghouses go far beyond the "Protestant plain style" Garvan describes, reflecting, in addition, an established English or European taste. These traditions may have been more pervasive than we now surmise.[91]

CHAPTER SIX

# Meetinghouses of the Eighteenth Century

## Anglicans Come to New England

PINNACLES AND wainscoted pulpits were still widely in use in the 1680s and 1690s when new political and denominational elements entered the architectural equation. Despite the colonists' best efforts to forestall it, the English under James II revoked the Massachusetts Bay charter and sent an English governor, Edmund Andros (1637–1714), to preside over the newly formed Dominion of New England in 1686. Though the governor's term was brief, his installation led to the founding the next year of the first permanent Anglican parish in New England and the building of King's Chapel in Boston in 1688. A relatively modest spire-topped, wood-frame structure located on Tremont Street, this church was designed to serve the religious needs of Anglicans and the English governor in Boston. Andros had earlier deeply offended Boston residents when he held Anglican services in the meetinghouse of Boston's Third Church over the objections of its officers. The dimensions of the Anglican church on Tremont Street were fifty-four by thirty-six feet with a stud height of twenty feet; its standing belfry was ten feet square and rose twenty feet above the roof. The structure was contracted to three housewrights from Weymouth, Massachusetts, and followed a "platt" drawn up by a Boston surveyor named Philip Wells. Because the document specifies "five windows in the front five windows in the rear and two windows at each end," the design may not have followed the traditional axial or "church" plan used by Anglicans in Virginia and later in Boston in the construction of Christ Church in 1723. Instead, the main entrance may have been on the "front" side, meaning one of the long sides, with the pulpit directly opposite (fig. 6.1). A "table" was mentioned as an accessory, but the contract did not specify an altar, a nave, or a chancel.[1]

Within two years Andros was evicted, and a replacement government took over selected by William III and Mary II, who occupied the English throne in 1689. By then cultural shifts were already under way. Dancing schools, finishing academies, and musical training—which incorporated Restoration cultural practices that had always been anathema to the founding Puritans—were soon flourishing in eighteenth-century Boston. King's Chapel itself was an architectural confirmation of the new royal hegemony in New England, which led the way to a succession of English-appointed governors until the outbreak of the American Revolution in 1775.

Under these new influences, the seventeenth-century meetinghouse underwent radical changes. While some were limited to urban areas and ports of entry, others were distributed throughout the New England region. These changes included the adoption of round-top windows, a pitched roof, self-standing bell

Figure 6.1. Detail from William Burgis and William Price's view of Boston, showing the first King's Chapel, erected in 1688. *A South East View of the Great Town of Boston in New England in America*, 1743. Courtesy of the American Antiquarian Society.

towers, stairwell porches and additional pew space, Georgian-finish carpentry, and colorful exterior and interior paint. Because Georgian designs were also novel among Englishmen in the Chesapeake at this time, their appearance in early eighteenth-century New England may have been simply a reflection of prevailing English styles rather than drawn from denominational imitation. But the existence of an Anglican community in Boston whose ties to radical Puritanism were at best compromised, or at worst wholly antithetical, made everyone predisposed to new ideas.

The founding of King's Chapel came at a point when turreted, four-square meetinghouses were still dominant. In 1688 some of the largest examples of the first-period style were yet to be raised: Ipswich, Massachusetts, in 1699, Newbury, Massachusetts, in 1700, Stamford, Connecticut in 1702, Farmington, Connecticut, in 1709, North Andover, Massachusetts, in 1711, and York, Maine, in 1713. Boston was to build the Old Brick following a first-period plan in 1712, and Salem was about to complete four such meetinghouses between 1701 and 1718. Nevertheless, the revocation of the charter and the demise of the four-square meetinghouse were closely related. Had James II not allowed his commissioners to revoke the charter, and had his successors to the English throne postponed the founding of conforming Anglican parishes, the Georgian architectural innovations introduced by the Brattle Square congregation, the New North, and the Old South might have been delayed by several decades; in rural areas this postponement might have lasted half a century.

While no Reformed New England parish or religious society is on record as having imitated King's Chapel, the structure carried the English and European "codes" of Anglican or high-church architecture. These codes in effect provided a temptation that mainstream Congregationalists, Baptists, and Presbyterians were unable to resist. Urban New Englanders found themselves, as Richard Bushman explains, in a state of "provincial inferiority." Rather than "leading the Protestant Reformation as in 1630 and so the whole religious world," Bushman continues, "educated New Englanders knew they lived on the periphery of European culture." Stephen Nissenbaum tells us that provincial society also missed out on traditional Anglican or European celebrations, such as Christmas and Easter.[2] Knowingly or unknowingly, builders of the eighteenth-century New England meetinghouse thus gradually adopted the churchlike or churchly forms of Anglican houses of worship. Especially after 1699 when major urban meetinghouses were being erected by private associations of pew proprietors, Anglican houses of worship became something to covet rather than something to avoid. Throughout the eighteenth century, towns and parishes began to "Georgianize" their meetinghouses by amending the form of their windows and roofs, making their dimensions oblong, following classical architectural orders, adding bell towers with spires, painting with "stone" colors, and, for many, eventually shifting to brick or stone.

The process, however, went both ways. Anglican church forms in America evolved briskly in the hundred years between 1660 and 1760, often going well outside the conventional English idiom if indeed such a thing existed. In Tidewater Virginia, Anglican builders drew on traditional axial plans that centered the altar at the far end of the main alley. Buildings in Maryland in turn were more "box like" or square, with the altar to the right of the main entryway.[3] In New England, Anglicans copied many aspects of Puritan and Congregational houses of worship, such as their proportions and their shallow cancels and long-wall entrances. It is even possible that they attempted to adopt Puritan codes so that they might better fit in, mute possible objections, recruit converts, or raise money. These efforts led to an architectural competition in which each denomination tried to outdo the other. The Second Anglican Society in Rhode Island actually built a meetinghouse, not a church. When originally erected in Narragansett in 1707, St. Paul's Church followed an eighteenth-century Congregational plan, the pulpit facing the main entry across the narrow dimension.[4] (The Communion table, surrounded by rails, stood at the east end.) This arrangement was retained when the church was moved to Wickford in 1800 (figs. 6.2 and 6.3). In Marblehead, Massachusetts, St. Michael's Church was erected in 1714 as a Puritan "square" (48 by 48 feet) with three hipped roofs on one side and a roof-mounted tower 17 feet square with a tapered spire on the other. (The top of the spire was said to be 103 feet off the ground.)[5] St. Peter's Church in Salem, built in 1733, was also built on a "meetinghouse plan" with the pulpit facing the principal door on the long end.[6] And a nineteenth-century woodcut of the 1734 Trinity Church in Boston, among the largest houses of worship in New England, illustrates that this gambrel-roofed structure was outside any known idiom of Anglican or Puritan architecture (fig. 6.4). Over time, eighteenth-century Anglicans and Reformed Congregational and Presbyterian societies created houses of worship that began to resemble each other. Except for its pew orientation and a chancel at the east end, the original form of the 1773 Anglican church in West Claremont, New Hampshire, for example, is scarcely different from other small Congregational meetinghouses of the same period.[7]

One reason for the similarity between Anglican and nonconformist houses of worship in New England was the continued preference by most meetinghouse and church builders for wood-frame construction, despite the availability of stone and the relative ease of making bricks. Out of 1,668 houses of worship of all denominations built in New England and Long Island before 1800, only 8—Boston (1632), Guilford (1643), Stamford (1671), Jamaica (1690), Braintree (1696), New Utrecht (1700), Boston (King's Chapel, 1749), and East

Figures 6.2 and 6.3. Exterior and interior views of St. Paul's Church in Wickford, Rhode Island. This Anglican church took a "meetinghouse form" with the pulpit (on left) opposite the doorway (on right), but the builders nevertheless made sure to use compass-headed windows. Exterior photograph by Stanley P. Mixon, 1940. Interior photograph by Arthur W. LeBoef, 1937. Historic American Buildings Survey, Library of Congress, Washington, D.C.

Figure 6.4. *View of Old Trinity Church,* Boston, built by John Indicott in 1734. Wood engraving by Abel Bowen of Boston, circa 1828. Published in *The American Magazine of Useful and Entertaining Knowledge,* 1834. Courtesy of the American Antiquarian Society.

Haven (1772)—were built of stone; only 8, most of them in Boston, were built with brick. All the others were wood-frame structures with a few temporary "log" ones. This reliance on timber frames and wood finish work allowed meetinghouse builders to take advantage of a new infusion from England of fashionable eighteenth-century Georgian architectural and decorative styles without incurring the enormous costs of brick and stonework. The use of classical architectural orders in bell towers, bell-tower spires, exterior doorways, pulpits, and pulpit window surrounds was readily transferred to wood and followed codified and written formulas found in published plans and design books. Style-conscious terms such as *modillions, cornices, capitals,* and *pediments* entered into meetinghouse contracts and sometimes even into town and parish records. They occur regularly enough to suggest that community interest in Georgian styles ran high.

A second reason for the similarity of building forms was the common Protestant heritage of the parishes and churches that built them. Despite the important differences between a church led by archbishops and bishops and one led by consociations, elders, and church communicants, New England denominations had more in common with each other as Christians than they had differences as competing sects. As English Protestants, Congregationalists, Baptists, Presbyterians, and Anglicans all spoke the same language, celebrated many of the same sacraments, sang the same hymns, and recited the same Lord's Prayer. In short, some were simply more "Reformed" than others. The Protestantism that allowed two eighteenth-century Yale-educated divinity students to give up their parishes, travel to England to take Episcopal orders, and return as Anglican priests, also served radical sects such as Quakers and Six-Principle Baptists. For their part, having separated themselves from papacy, bishops, and clerical vestments in England, leaders of dissenting but established sects were constantly looking to see what they had left behind. Some of their ministers may have been convinced that written prayer books and open Communion were beneficial in the region; others simply liked the Anglican style. At the same time, Anglican leaders sometimes looked on Congregational church polity as a model. Boston's Trinity Church, for example, thrown on its own financial resources after its founding, soon became familiar with the New England spirit of church government—in effect becoming an association of private pew proprietors no different from those governing the Brattle Square or New North Societies.[8]

## The Compass-Headed Window

The most obvious "Anglican" feature that began to appear on eighteenth-century New England meetinghouses was the "arch'd" or compass-headed window—an architectural code identifying European and English houses of worship that goes back at least as far as the early sixteenth century and perhaps earlier. In England both Anglican and nonconformist ecclesiastic architecture observed this code. Eleven of the fourteen Protestant houses of worship of the seventeenth and eighteenth centuries Christopher Stell cites in a 1999 study had such windows, as did virtually all of those cited in his earlier inventory of Protestant chapels in interior counties of England. Typically, these windows are distributed throughout the structure, marking it as a building used for religious services. The Liverpool chapel where Richard Mather taught school as a young man had compass-headed windows on the ground floor and in the gallery.[9]

In New England, however, first-period meetinghouse builders are not known to have employed compass-headed windows. There are no graphic sources pointing to them, and they fail to show up in contracts and town votes. But once they were introduced into the region by the Anglican King's Chapel in 1688,

Figure 6.5. Painted wooden window cap used on St. Michael's Church, Marblehead, Massachusetts, in 1714, one of two discovered during work reclapboarding the building in 1978. Width 45 inches. Courtesy of St. Michael's Church, Marblehead, Massachusetts.

they became an architectural trademark in New England, identifying Anglican houses of worship. Compass-headed windows appear on Boston's 1723 Christ Church, Newport's 1725 Trinity Church, and Boston's 1734 Trinity Church—as well as on rural churches, such as Narragansett's 1707 St. Paul's Church and the 1770 Trinity Church in Brooklyn, Connecticut. Even when money was unavailable to pay for the windows, Anglican builders simulated this code using painted panels. The trompe l'oeil window caps restoration architects recovered from St. Michael's Church in Marblehead, are two of an estimated eight placed over the windows, giving the appearance of an Anglican-style building (fig. 6.5). A close inspection of these panels reveals that square or sash lights were overpainted on an earlier set of diamond quarrels sometime after the latter went out of fashion early in the eighteenth century.[10]

By contrast, most dissenting parishes in New England (an estimated 95 percent of those that built meetinghouses between 1740 and 1820) reserved half-circular windows for illuminating the pulpit. How soon this compromise was initiated is not clear; it may have been in the late seventeenth century but possibly not until 1740 or 1750. Reliable data are not available. The earliest survival with this feature is Boston's 1729 Old South. But this meetinghouse may not be a good indicator because all windows were half-circular in that structure (fig. 6.6). The two compass-headed pulpit windows found on the 1747 Cohasset meetinghouse seem to be original, and in nearby Hingham a similar pair can be dated to its renovation in 1755. At some point after that the practice became widespread, appearing on most eighteenth-century survivals throughout New England including those at Alna, Maine; Salisbury, Massachusetts; Sandown, New Hampshire; and Rockingham Vermont. The style even reached the isolated community

Figure 6.6. Interior view of the 1729 Old South meetinghouse, Boston, Massachusetts, showing the use of compass-headed windows extending throughout the building, including the pulpit window. Historic American Buildings Survey, undated photograph taken circa 1950 to 1960. Library of Congress, Washington, D.C.

Figure 6.7. North view of the "Old Bullockite" meetinghouse built in Porter, Maine, in 1818, showing the compass-headed window providing light to the pulpit. Named after Elder Jeremiah Bullock, a fundamentalist Baptist preacher, this house was one of the last eighteenth-century meetinghouse types raised in New England. Photograph taken in 1936 by Josiah T. Tubby. Historic American Buildings Survey, Library of Congress, Washington, D.C.

of Millville, Massachusetts, in 1769, and was still observed almost fifty years later in Porter, Maine, in 1818 (fig. 6.7).

Rather than looking at compass-headed windows solely as a means of distinguishing between New England's Anglican and Reformed denominations, we must also see them as highlighting a sense of class, style, and education within the dissenting fraternity. Second-period Congregational builders readily introduced the compass form whenever professional designers or architects were involved in the initial planning of a meetinghouse, and that usually would have been when building in an urban or wealthy setting. If we can believe the accuracy of the 1725 and 1743 Burgis–Price views of Boston, six of the seven new meetinghouses (the 1712 Old Brick always excepted) raised in that town during the three decades between 1699 and 1731 employed compass-headed windows in their bell towers; three (the New North, the New Brick, and the Old South) used compass windows throughout the structure. These windows also appeared in the fourth meetinghouse of Ipswich's First Parish in 1749 and the brick meetinghouse in New Haven in 1757. Their use continued in urban settings throughout much of the eighteenth century, such as in the second Brattle meetinghouse (1772), though sometimes they were placed selectively. For example, windows on the second floor of the North Church meetinghouse in Salem (1772) were arch topped, while others were square. And they were used by Baptist meetinghouse builders under similar circumstances. In 1729 Richard Munday (ca. 1685–1739), an early professional architect in Rhode Island, installed compass-headed windows on the lower floors of the Seventh-Day Baptist meetinghouse in Newport; Joseph Brown, architect of the First Baptist meetinghouse in Providence, built in 1774 and 1775, employed them throughout the building.

Even when used minimally in the pulpit window, the net effect of arched or compass-headed windows was the same in New England as it had been in England and Europe. The windows identified the structure as ecclesiastic through a "taught" form—raising it above the status of a barn, a meeting hall, or a commercial storage building. It is hard to overstate the full impact of this innovation. To enter the 1729 Old South was to be literally surrounded by its forty-one large windows, including the pulpit window, each one with an arch top and each one brilliantly illuminating the interior. It was now impossible to see a compass-headed window in England or in New England without knowing that that structure was intended for worship.

## A New Roof Alignment

A second step in this architectural metamorphosis involved the hipped or four-square roof. Sometimes offset by large dormer windows, hipped roofs had characterized Puritan New England meetinghouses and Dutch Reformed houses of worship in New York. They have been traced to prototypes among Calvinistic sects in Scotland, in the Netherlands, and in France—though they were seldom used in English nonconformist architecture. In New England the shift away from this architectural feature began just before the close of the seventeenth century when the Brattle Society proprietors or "undertakers" built in Boston a seventy-two-by-fifty-two-foot meetinghouse—disparagingly known by its early critics as the Manifesto Church—with a pitched or "flat" roof that extended between the end gables (fig. 6.8).[11] The roof's twenty- or twenty-five-degree angle of pitch was about half that of four-square meetinghouses—hence the colloquial period term *flat*. In addition, the builders added a prominent balustrade along the edges of the roof, a detail not seen in any other meetinghouse on the Burgis–Price view. When completed in 1699, the meetinghouse of the Brattle proprietors was the largest in New England and exceeded by one foot that of its neighbor, Old Cedar of the Third Church.[12]

To a generation accustomed to worshiping in meetinghouses that looked like poorly maintained haystacks, this shift was unprecedented—though not because it was an innovation.[13] Log houses, long houses, and even four-square houses may have had pitched roofs, though most of these were considered provisional or temporary buildings.¹⁴ Rather, the shift was unprecedented because the Brattle proprietors were from among the wealthiest merchant families in North America, and there was nothing provisional or temporary about their meetinghouse. This contravention of a Reformed architectural practice that went back a hundred years or more to the earliest Scottish, French Huguenot, and Dutch Reformed

Figure 6.8. Detail of William Price and William Burgis's view of the 1699 Brattle Square meetinghouse, Boston, showing its "flat" roof—the first to appear on an important urban congregation in New England. The bell tower and prominent balustrade seen in this detail were added in 1717. From *A South East View of the Great Town of Boston in New England in America*, 1743. Courtesy of the American Antiquarian Society.

meetinghouses must have been disheartening to some Boston residents. In 1699 the majority of the town's meetinghouses were already halfway through or close to the end of their lifetime. The "Old Meeting House" of Boston's First Church was now fifty-nine years old and had recently added a "platform" to its roof. The Old Cedar of the Third Church was thirty years old, and the Old North of Boston's Second Church was twenty-two years old. Each was laid out on the usual four-square plan with a dormer roof, a turret, a bell coney, and multi-tiered galleries; each represented the height of New England's Puritan style.

News of the Brattle Society's break with the past quickly reached outlying towns in Massachusetts that were considering the replacement of their structures. Twenty-five miles southeast of Boston the Second or South Parish in Scituate, Massachusetts, voted in October 1706 for a first-period type. The structure was to have a "square form," with "dimensions . . . 46 feet in length and 44 feet in breadth, and 20 feet between joints, and a sloping roof [meaning a hipped roof] with a turret upon it suitable to hang a bell on." This was a standard first-period design, and everything seemed ready to proceed. A month later after more debate, however, the parish voted to eliminate the galleries and make the building longer and narrower: "50 feet in length and forty feet in breadth, and 20 feet between joints." They then voted for a "flat roof [meaning pitched] of about ten feet rise"—virtually the same pitch as the meetinghouse of the Manifesto Church.[15]

It is unknown whether the Second Parish in Scituate actually followed through with this plan. New England town meetings returned to controversial issues again and again to allow the community time to come to an agreement. Arguments between factions in favor of pitched roofs and those in favor of hipped roofs soon appeared elsewhere. When Andover, twenty-five miles north of Boston, hired a new minister, Thomas Barnard, in 1707, the town enlarged his parsonage by adding a lean-to and increased the dimensions of his wife's pew. The town also decided to replace its thirty-eight-year-old meetinghouse, specifying a design that virtually imitated the meetinghouse of the Manifesto Church. It was to be "sixty-foot long, and forty-foot wide and twenty-foot stud and with a flat roof." Since the project would require a major financial outlay, dissenters in South Andover—who were some distance from the meetinghouse—began to talk of a parish division. As a compromise, the town meeting voted for a structure "fifty-six foot long, fifty foot wide and twenty-two foot stud and with a square roof without dormers [but] with two lucernes on each side." But their decision came too late. The south faction received approval from the Massachusetts legislature to build its own meetinghouse and rapidly did so in 1709. Now reduced in population, the north faction took a third vote in 1711 to build a structure "Fifty foot long, Forty-five foot wide, and Twenty-four foot between Joints, and with a [gathered] Roof like Salem-village meeting house"—a first-period design.[16]

Scituate and Andover both considered the new roof style, and Andover later rejected it because of a political standoff with a breakaway parish. The first towns in rural Massachusetts that can be documented to have built in this style were Concord and Chelmsford, two Middlesex County towns that almost simultaneously accepted this design when they were replacing meetinghouses in the years 1709 to 1711. Concord may have started the process a few months in advance. After agreeing in 1709 that their existing forty-two-year-old structure was in "decayed condition," Concord appointed a committee of six men to research the issue and present several models to choose from. When the committee reported on 20 January 1710, they offered two designs. One was a mostly square structure fifty-five by sixty feet, with two galleries and the usual "bevel Roof," that is, a larger version of Concord's existing period-one structure. The alternative offered was what the planners called an "English Built" roof with end-to-end gables on a slightly more rectangular dimension of sixty by fifty-two feet. As in Andover, the decision was marked by considerable controversy. To resolve it, the inhabitants voted "by papers" writing "E" for English or "B" for bevel. The count was sixty-six in favor of the "English moad" and twenty-seven for the old style. The resulting meetinghouse, completed by Charles Underhill in the fall of 1711, was sixty feet long and fifty feet wide, with a plate height of twenty-eight feet and two tiers of galleries. Its pitched roof was unbroken by the usual dormers or lucarnes (fig. 6.9). It is not known why the townsmen called it an "English Built" roof, though the term seems to indicate that the older gathered design was regarded as a European "Protestant" style of roof associated with the Netherlands and France.[17]

Even before Concord had raised the frame of its new meetinghouse, Chelmsford—twelve miles north—was halfway through the process of making the same decision. In a vote taken in September 1710—eight months after Concord had chosen theirs—the town agreed on the "bigness" of its new meetinghouse and decided on a structure "52 feet in length, 42 foot in breadth, and twenty four foot between joints." The contract also called for a "25 foot spar, and a turret to hang the bell in." If we assume that "spar" referred to the principal rafter, it indicates a building covered by a pitched roof resembling a somewhat smaller version of Concord's meetinghouse but with the addition of a belfry turret. Chelmsford's town meeting completed the contract by adding a "coving" (curved overhang) to the underside of the roof, reimbursing several private individuals, including the minister, who had originally underwritten this feature.[18]

That same year Rumney Marsh, a coastal village in what is now Revere, Massachusetts, built a pitched-roof meetinghouse with financial help from Boston merchants who owned farms there. (As he did in Charlestown, Samuel Sewall came to Rumney Marsh at the raising to drive a pin into the frame.)[19] And three years later Concord's "English" roof was imitated by its new neighbor,

Figure 6.9. Detail. *Plate II. A View of the Town of Concord,* showing the 1711 meetinghouse in Concord, Massachusetts, with an "English" roof. British troops in the foreground. From Amos Doolittle's engraving of Concord center taken in 1775. Photograph from the collection of the Lexington, Massachusetts, Historical Society.

Lexington, recently formed from the east portion of Concord. The new parish had won recognition as a town and voted in 1713 to build a meetinghouse "on the plan of the one at Concord."[20]

With one Boston meetinghouse and at least three rural neighbors providing the impetus for change, building committees in eastern New England who planned meetinghouses between 1712 and 1720 now had to choose between two competing roof styles. In Boston the First Church, which was replacing the fire-gutted "Old Meeting House" in 1712, voted to ignore the new style and build a brick version of a four-square structure—its size of seventy-two by fifty-four feet exceeded the width of the Brattle church by two feet. But two years later town authorities allowed the proprietors of the New North, a new society formed by "seventeen substantial mechanics" who separated from the North Church, to build a "timber" meetinghouse on Major Richard's pasture, with the specification of a "flat roof."[21] Two years after that the breakaway New South congregation did the same. In 1715 Lynnfield and Falmouth, Massachusetts, and Hampton, New Hampshire, all selected pitched roofs. After that year more parishes in eastern New England built structures with pitched roofs than did not.

Towns in central and southern New England followed the same trend. In 1712, only one year after Concord had raised its "English" roof, Guilford, Connecticut, more than 120 miles southwest of Concord or Boston, built a three-tier sixty-eight-by-forty-six-foot structure with a pitched roof. Others quickly followed. Hadley, Massachusetts, voted for a "flattish roof" in 1713; both parishes in Middletown, Connecticut, voted for identical pitched-roof structures in 1714; Stratfield (now Bridgeport), Connecticut, voted for a "long roof" in 1716; East Haven, Connecticut, voted for a "straight roof or barn fashion" in 1714 and again in 1717; Wallingford voted to imitate Guilford in 1717; Westfield, Massachusetts, stipulated a roof built in "barn fashion with a bell Coney upon the middle" in 1719.[22] The speed with which the concept reached Connecticut and the Connecticut Valley suggests that some form of regionwide exchange was taking place—spreading by word of mouth through traveling merchants, justices, and militia officers or even through clergymen exchanging pulpits with their colleagues. It was not just neighbors imitating other neighbors; it was a rare instance of towns adopting a communicable idea.

Within a decade, gathered or four-square roofs had become a stylistic liability. Towns with first-period roofs that did not want to bear the cost of a replacement chose to modify them—in other words to make them more acceptable to current taste. Votes were taken to remove dormers and lucarnes or to change the roof design from gathered to pitched. In 1726, twenty-six years after Stephen Jaques had completed a classic first-period structure in Newbury, Massachusetts, the town stipulated "that the four gable ends in the Roof of the meeting house be Taken Down and that each Part opened thereby be well timbered and boarded and shingled." That same year Mansfield, Connecticut, decided to add twenty feet to its twenty-four-by-twenty-four-foot structure and rebuild the roof "the contrary way." And in 1745 Middleborough, Massachusetts, replaced its forty-five-year-old hipped roof with a pitched one.[23]

The shift to pitched roofs raised new issues of pew alignments and passageways. Most urban Anglican churches gave prominence to the long aisle leading from the main door to the Communion table; this arrangement also gave a visual perspective on the service. By contrast, first-period floor plans of Puritan meetinghouses usually omitted alleys or filled them with chairs or benches. But now meetinghouse committees were reconsidering these alignments. When Medway, Massachusetts, voted to finish its new pitched-roof meetinghouse in 1749, the question was asked in town meeting "whether the Precinct will have an Alley three feet and a half wide straight from the great double doors to the

Pulpit." Medway voters, who first opposed this new style, subsequently met on many occasions to reconsider. Finally, as the nineteenth-century historian Ephraim Jameson records, "at a crowded meeting, they polled the house. All in favor went to one side; all opposed, to the other." In the end, a "majority of four [voted] in favor of the alley."[24]

Pitched or English-style roofs nevertheless were met with hesitation by conservative societies or those outside the influence of the larger port towns. East Windsor, Connecticut, voted to raise a forty-foot-square meetinghouse in 1713, specifying that the "roof of the new meeting house shall be as this is"—meaning their first meetinghouse erected about 1695.[25] When Framingham, Massachusetts, enlarged its 1698 meetinghouse, the town voted in 1715 to have a roof "the same form and workmanship as [nearby] Marlborough"—a four-square structure built 1688.[26] In 1716 Milton, Massachusetts, chose a "Roof to be built with chamfer beams and with four Posts for a turret if need be"—a first-period style.[27] Salem, Massachusetts, raised two meetinghouses with "tunnel" roofs and central turrets, one in 1717 and one in 1718. Isolated towns, such as those on Cape Cod, continued to build tunnel roofs and central turrets until 1730.[28] The last gathered roofs with central belfries were erected in eastern Massachusetts: Andover in 1734 and Plymouth in 1744.

The new pitched roofs had an immediate impact on New England's architectural landscape. They generated structures whose rooflines made the meetinghouse appear longer even if the actual dimensions were unchanged. Gone was the centrally mounted defensive platform or turret at the apex of the roof. Gone was the central bell coney and bell that was tolled from a rope hanging in the main aisle. Replacing it was an "English" structure without these early Scottish, Huguenot, and Dutch Reformed features. Meetinghouses with pitched roofs became the most common type built in New England and Long Island in the eighteenth century—an estimated 1,150 built at the height of the second period, many appearing as plain, spireless buildings. The style was still being followed in country parishes well into the first and even the second decade of the nineteenth century. But more than altering the landscape, the pitched roof helped create what in effect was a new spatial geography. There were now two architectural axes in the meetinghouse, neither of which existed there before. One axis, visible from within, extended on the short side between the double doorway to the pulpit—this was the "main alley" that so perturbed Medway's citizens. The second axis, visible from the outside, ran along the roofline from one gable end to the other. This feature generated a distinctive "face," or façade, on the side with the double door—an architectural element lacking in multidoor seventeenth-century houses of worship that were accessed from virtually any side and even from doors leading from the outside to individual pews. As long as these two axes remained at right angles, the structure would be viewed as a period-two "meetinghouse plan." When late eighteenth-century builders redesigned the axes to run parallel to each other, they opened the way to New England's Federal, or third-period, "church plan."

## The Standing Bell Tower

The second exterior feature that gave this new architectural "face" an Anglican character was the standing bell tower. To this day the "tower [rising] from the ground," as Medford, Massachusetts, called it in 1768, remains the most permanent visual symbol of eighteenth-century religious life in New England.[29] With its associated spires, clocks, cupolas, steeples, octagons, lanterns, weather vanes, compass windows, and Palladian windows, bell towers have inspired the public imagination for three centuries—though only one out of every seven meetinghouses built at the height of the second period had such standing towers and even fewer had bells in them (see Appendix A, Tables 1 and 4). Moreover, throughout the first and second periods, towns were raising freestanding belfries near but not attached to the meetinghouse. Rowley, Massachusetts, built a frame in 1658 near its 1639 meetinghouse to receive a bell. Chelmsford voted in 1716 to raise a separated twelve-by-twelve-foot "bell-house" fourteen feet high for its new meetinghouse. Bedford voted for a twelve-foot-square bellhouse in 1753; and nearby Lexington raised a similar bell tower when the town was given a 463-pound bell in 1761. The Lexington tower, illustrated in Amos Doolittle's well-known 1775 engraving of Lexington Common (see fig. 6.34), was located on "Belfry Hill," a rise about fifty feet from the meetinghouse. It was a small building capped by a hipped roof and turret reinforced by lattice work; a door at ground level allowed entry. Lexington's belfry survived into the age of photography (fig. 6.10).[30]

The dominance of the bell tower was architectural and ideological. In the public eye, meetinghouses without attached bell towers remained places of assembly; those with a cupola and spire rising 100 to 190 feet off the ground, however, were ecclesiological statements and presumably were seen as "house[s] of God." Standing bell towers continued a medieval Christian tradition of cathedrals and campaniles that went back a millennium or longer but had been avoided by Puritans, Huguenots, and Dutch Reformed congregations because they wished to, or were obliged to, distance themselves from Catholic and Anglican practice. In the same breath that they denounced saints' days, legislated against the celebration of Christmas, and hesitated to use the architectural term *church*, seventeenth-century New Englanders by deed (if not explicitly by word) renounced the use of bells in any part of the religious service or even as a musical instrument. The most radical of the dissenting sects—the English Quakers—took this one step further. They caustically labeled Anglican churches and chapels "steeplehouses," a term as highly charged in Quaker jargon as "hireling ministry."[31] Pinnacles and pyramids notwithstanding, no standing bell tower, spire, or steeple is known to have ornamented any of the approximately 338 dissenting meetinghouses built in New England and Long Island in the first-period style; no standing tower appeared on any Baptist meetinghouses before 1775.

Figure 6.10. Separated bell tower built in Lexington, Massachusetts, in 1761 after the town was given a bell. Photograph circa 1880 from the collection of the Lexington, Massachusetts, Historical Society.

Because few early New England bell towers survive, understanding them requires considerable reliance on documentary sources, some of which contain critical terms whose meanings are not always clear. We know, for example, that William Bentley's 1797 diary notation that the recently constructed meetinghouse in Westford, Massachusetts, had copied a "steeple" from nearby Chelmsford refers to an open octagonal belfry with a shallow entry portico, because the Westford meetinghouse and tower still stand. (Bentley also wrote an extensive diary description of Chelmsford's bell tower in 1793 when he took a similar trip.)[32] We do not know, however, what is meant in the record of a vote taken much earlier, in 1713, Hadley, Massachusetts, to put a "balcony" at one end of the roof of its new forty-by-fifty-foot meetinghouse.[33] Sylvester Judd, who wrote a detailed history of Hadley in 1863, claimed that this "balcony" was a standing tower housing a bell—the first in Hampshire County. He may be right, but if he is, we would have to draw the unlikely conclusion that Hadley built the first such "dissenting" tower in New England, predating Boston examples by at least a year. And before Chelmsford voted to install their twelve-foot-square separated tower, they had voted earlier, in 1710, for a "turret to hang the Bell in" but without adding a "steeple" over it. Regrettably we do not know whether *steeple* was another name for a seventeenth-century pinnacle or pyramid or whether something more substantial was involved, such as the spires and cupolas erected later in Boston.[34] If the latter is correct, it is a stunning discovery because it puts Chelmsford three years ahead of Boston. But that, too, is unlikely. Eighteenth-century records seldom distinguish clearly between a centrally mounted belfry, an end-mounted belfry, or an attached standing tower with a belfry—each of which might be called a "tower," a "belfry," a "steeple," a "cupola," or a "spire," or a "battlement."[35]

Engravers and printmakers added to the ambiguity through their free use of artistic license. The best graphic sources for understanding Boston's early bell towers are the views by William Burgis, John Harris, and William Price, the artist, the engraver, and the publisher, respectively, who together created graphic vistas of the town between 1723 and 1743. Price published several states of *A South East View of the Great Town of Boston in New England in America*, whose detail provides unmatched views of meetinghouses and their bell towers. It is now known, however, that William Price (1684–1771), a distinguished churchman and organist, may have conspired with his colleagues to add steeples and imaginative finials and weather vanes on Anglican churches where they never existed; he even included meetinghouses that may not have existed.[36]

Yet the same reasons that made bell towers controversial now make them a superb indicator of the pace of architectural change. Spires, steeples, and bell towers became rallying points for innovative and conservative forces within the community. They were seen—figuratively—on the cultural and ecclesiastical horizon at a distance of hundreds of miles, perceptions that easily crossed colony and state borders. And they were widely admired, especially by the towns that built them. When reporting to the New Haven, Connecticut, assembly in 1747 that Woodbury's new steepled meetinghouse was located exactly where the site committee had set the stake, the town clerk, Joseph Minor, added that "for its Bigness, Strength, and Architecture, it Does appear / Transcendantly Magnificent!"[37]

Standing bell towers followed a different timetable from virtually all other architectural aspects of the meetinghouse. They were replicated in fast-moving tracks that spanned long distances easily; they were also denominationally fluid, appearing simultaneously on Anglican, Congregational, Presbyterian, and Baptist structures. Since religious practices of the Reformed congregations that dominated in New England differed from the Anglican tradition chiefly in scale, wealthy urban societies unimpeded by an inherited Puritan aesthetic or doctrinal hesitation were able to mimic and compete with the "codes" or external appearances of Anglican churches without seeming to do so. This was especially true of those societies founded by private pewholders whose meetinghouse builders designed standing bell towers as a transitional feature. In the resulting competition, the nonconformists had one distinct advantage. They were perfectly willing to design "temporary" structures—which they had to do anyway because of constant demographic expansion. By contrast, Anglicans usually thought more of long-term use because they were not a state church and were not required to take in the ranks of a growing town.

The history of these towers begins in Boston. The earliest "steeplehouse" in the town was King's Chapel, whose parishioners may have walked through the bell tower to enter the sanctuary. The warden's account book reveals that on 30 July 1689 £4.4.9 was paid "for work done in the steeple and hanging the Bell."[38] The 1743 Burgis–Price view of Boston depicts its belfry "ten feet square" rising "twenty feet above the roof" surmounted by a modest peaked or hipped roof.[39] Projected from its center was a tall mast bearing a large crown halfway up—signifying the King's Church—and at the very top was a weathercock. The distinguishing feature of the tower was that the bell deck and bell mechanism were enclosed within its upper stage.

On the evidence of late seventeenth- and early eighteenth-century Massachusetts and Virginia survivals or illustrations, the hipped roof of King's Chapel's bell tower may have followed a provincial architectural style common to Church of England bell towers throughout North America. The Old Brick Church (later named St. Luke's Church) built on the Isle of Wight plantation in Virginia between 1677 and 1685 (making it roughly contemporary with the first King's Chapel) has a comparable tower, as does St. Michael's in Marblehead, and St. Peter's in Salem. A period image of St. Peter's shows a standing bell tower in 1733 almost twice the height of the two-story church; the towers of both churches have a hipped roof and support the bell in their uppermost stage.[40]

By contrast, dissenting Protestants in Boston made do with belfries installed centrally in turrets, an architectural tradition that had been well established among Reformed meetinghouses in Europe since the late sixteenth century. These turret-mounted belfries may have been considerably higher than the one on King's Chapel, but they were still mounted on the roofs—the critical indicator of their congregation's dissenting persuasion. While these belfries and bell towers played no part in the Congregational liturgy, they did provide a civic and architectural rivalry—particularly after St. Michael's Church in Marblehead raised a spire 103 feet high in 1714.

Perhaps in response to this, during a period of rapidly expanding population and economic growth, three newly formed Congregational religious societies in Boston almost simultaneously erected meetinghouses with standing bell towers or added them to existing structures. The first may have been the New North (fig. 6.11). According to the permission given them by the town in 1713, they were allowed to erect "a timber Meeting House 65x48x35 [with a] flat roof and battlements [possibly meaning a castellated tower]" on Hanover Street. The structure was raised the following year. The congregation must have attracted many new worshipers, because the meetinghouse was enlarged five years later, in 1719, with an eighteen-foot lean-to containing additional ground-floor pews and two tiers of galleries.[41] A bell was given to the congregation that same year by John Frizell, a Boston merchant. A second bell tower in Boston was raised by the New South in 1716 that was "finished after the Ionic order.[42] A third one was raised by the Brattle proprietors, the same affluent but controversial congregation that built the first "English roof" in New England. The Brattle's spire can be dated from an entry in Samuel Sewall's diary on 24 June 1717: "Mr. [Benjamin] Colman's New Steeple is raised."[43]

According to the Burgis–Price views and two broadside illustrations showing the Boston skyline during earthquakes (figs. 6.12 and 6.13), all three towers were roughly similar in design.[44] The bell deck and bell were housed within the upper part of the tower and projected sound through four circular or compass-topped windows. The roof, however, comprised a battlement capped by a single high pointed spire. These features were presumably inspired by earlier seventeenth-century towers designed by London architects, or possibly they were merely a much larger version of the "pinnacles" erected on New England meetinghouses in the previous century.[45] In each instance the builders located their tower on one of the shorter ends of the meetinghouse, and the main double door remained on the long side.

In 1721 a fourth Boston congregation that had just separated from the Old North built a brick meetinghouse that soon became the largest and most architecturally sophisticated house of worship in Boston. Designed by Edward Pell (1687–1736), one of the leading painter-stainers in the metropolis, the New

Brick had two tiers of galleries, three entrance porches, and a standing bell tower and steeple surmounted by a 172-pound brass weathercock made by the coppersmith Shem Drowne (figs. 6.14 and 6.15). Like others in the town, the tower was on the narrow end of the building, creating a vertical extension of the west entrance stairwell porch. But this time the bell deck and bell were placed in an

Figure 6.11. Detail from William Burgis and William Price's view of the 1714 New North meetinghouse in Boston, showing an octagonal steeple rising from the top of the bell tower battlements. This may have been the first "dissenting steeple" in New England. *A South East View of the Great Town of Boston in New England in America,* 1743. Courtesy of the American Antiquarian Society.

6.12 and 6.13. Two broadside views of the Boston townscape during the 1744 and 1755 earthquakes, suggesting that ghouse steeples were attached to their towers without intervening bell housing. *Above: Earthquakes, Tokens of God's Power rath*, woodcut, 1744. Rare Books Division, The New York Public Library, Astor, Lenox and Tilden Foundations. *Below: uakes Improved*, woodcut, 1755. Courtesy of the American Antiquarian Society.

Figures 6.14 and 6.15. Two views of the 1721 New Brick meetinghouse in Boston, taken approximately one hundred years apart. *Left:* William Burgis and William Price's view taken in 1725, *A South East View of the Great Town of Boston in New England in America*, 1743. *Right: New Brick.* From Abel Bowen's *Picture of Boston*, taken before 1840. This steeple type became common throughout eastern Massachusetts and northern Connecticut in the eighteenth century, but the compass-headed windows seen here were usually found only in urban areas. Courtesy of the American Antiquarian Society.

open belfry above the tower and were protected from the elements by an ogee-roofed cupola supported on an octagonal frame. The New Brick was the first congregation in New England to place the bell in this exposed position, but it soon became a regional feature characteristic of about three out of four of the standing bell towers erected in the region between 1720 and 1790.

Now, however, the denominational competition began in earnest. When Christ Church, the second Anglican parish in Boston, was formed in 1723, its place of worship far exceeded the New Brick in its internal appointments, but it lacked the massive vertical dimensions. Like the first King's Chapel, Christ Church did not have a spire; instead, a low hipped roof protected the bell tower. But because the shell and much of the interior have survived, Christ Church is the first Anglican house of worship in New England known to have been designed on a basilican plan; entry into the audience chamber was through the attached bell tower with the main aisle, pulpit, Communion table, and chancel at the opposite end.[46]

In 1729 dissenting builders made their final architectural statement in Boston before the mid-century. That year the Third Church replaced its sixty-year-old cedar meetinghouse with a brick structure whose ninety-five-by-sixty-eight-foot dimensions surpassed even those of the Old Brick and the New Brick. Designed by Robert Twelves, and built by the masons Joshua Blanchard and Nathaniel Emmes (who left their initials in the cornerstones), the plan of the new building may have been based on an Anglican church, St. James's in Piccadilly, London, completed by Christopher Wren (1632–1723) between 1676 and 1684. The "Old South Meetinghouse," as it was soon called, had a standing tower with a bell located above the tower and protected by a "blind" ogee cupola surmounted by a two-stage spire whose top rose to 180 feet—a design seen by one nineteenth-century historian as a "Gothic spire with a clothing of Italian architecture."[47] The 1729 Old South spire, still standing in downtown Boston, is the earliest surviving decorative treatment of a New England meetinghouse in a provincial Georgian mode. Possibly derived from an earlier Wren design at St. Antholin's Church, London, the spire was ornamented with dentilled modillions, a balustrade, an octagonal belfry stage with turned corner posts, a "lantern" stage, and a surmounting spire and split banner weather vane (fig. 6.16).[48]

By 1730 then, the town's skyline was known for its two older turreted meetinghouses, five newer Congregational meetinghouses with spired bell towers, and two Anglican church houses with spireless bell towers. At this point the scene shifts to Rhode Island and to Connecticut's coastal towns. Appropriately, the first bell tower to appear outside of Boston was raised in the one community whose traditional mercantile and maritime ties to England and to the English Caribbean made it a cultural rival to Boston's supremacy. Newport, the third oldest town in the Colony of Rhode Island, was the home of a new and rapidly growing Anglican community nurtured under the leadership of Rev. James Honeyman. In 1725 Honeyman persuaded Trinity Church to replace an earlier house of worship with an architecturally ambitious steepled church designed by Richard Munday, who is said to have followed the original lines of Boston's Christ Church. The appearance of the steeple is not now known, but two pieces of evidence suggest that it was not surmounted by the hipped tower that characterized most other Anglican churches in America: it is called a "spire" in the records, and it fell down during a gale in 1731. The destruction was so complete it was not replaced until 1760.[49]

Before it fell, however, Newport's Trinity tower was ostentatious enough to come to the attention of an influential coastal town in Connecticut. Guilford, about fifteen miles east of New Haven, had been making plans to add a belfry and bell to its imposing three-tier meetinghouse erected in 1712. Confusion still lingers about the steps they took. An initial vote, made by the town meeting in 1724, or one year before Newport's Trinity was raised, passed to the Guilford

Figure 6.16. The Old South meetinghouse *(10)* of the Third Church in Boston, as seen in the William Price and William Burgis view. Erected 1729, this house was the third brick meetinghouse in New England and features the same compass-headed windows as the New Brick. The tower on the left *(55)* is the Irish meetinghouse raised the same year. From *A South East View of the Great Towns of Boston in New England in America*, 1743. Courtesy of the American Antiquarian Society.

building committee surplus money from its mill operations to purchase a bell "like that in Mr. Colman's meeting house in Boston." At that time Rev. Benjamin Colman (1673–1747) was minister of the Brattle Square Church, and it is fair to presume that the town expected a bell tower similar to the one attached to his meetinghouse. In December 1725 the committee set aside "Timber and Materials for building a Steeple to the Meeting House at the west end thereof with a suitable Belfry and Spire." But the following January, after plans for Trinity's tower (or the completed tower itself) had become known in Guilford, the town voted that, instead, "the belfry and spire of the meeting house in this Society shall be built in the Fashion and proportion of the Belfry and Spire at Rhode Island." Then, two months later, the January 1726 vote was "repealed," and the society proceeded with another design.[50]

According to contemporary observers, the Guilford bell tower "was the first steeple built in the Colony of Connecticut." Again, no description of this tower survives; the tip of the spire was 120 feet off the ground, an indication that the bell itself may have been as high as 90 feet from the ground. A memory drawing by Charles D. Hubbard made many years after its replacement in 1828 shows a standing five-story tower surmounted by a squared belfry with an opening on each side. The steeple, which apparently lacked a cornice, had four inwardly curving sides and was topped by a cockerel (fig. 6.17). The installation, however, encountered problems: the tower swayed so severely in the earthquake of 1727 that the bell tolled of its own accord and in 1732 the motion of the bell was said

Figure 6.17. Memory painting of the second meetinghouse in Guilford, Connecticut (1712), showing the bell tower erected in 1726, the first example in Connecticut. Watercolor, 18 by 12 inches, by Charles D. Hubbard, circa 1900. Connecticut Commission on Culture and Tourism, Henry Whitfield Museum Collection.

to have so rocked the entire meetinghouse that the axis of the bell had to be rotated ninety degrees to stabilize its movement against the length of the building rather than against its width.[51]

With models available in eastern Massachusetts, Rhode Island, and along the Connecticut shoreline, standing bell towers now appeared with increasing frequency, most of them financed by private subscription. In Charlestown, Massachusetts, the seventy-two-by-fifty-two-foot meetinghouse whose raising was witnessed by Judge Sewall in 1716 acquired a steepled bell tower before 1723.[52] Nearby Milton erected a fifty-by-forty-foot meetinghouse in 1728 that had a belfry and bell, presumably on the same plan. In New Hampshire the North Parish in Portsmouth erected a bell tower and spire on the east side of its twenty-year-old, three-decker meetinghouse in 1730, and Exeter added a bell tower to its new structure in 1731.[53] Towns in central and southern Connecticut and Rhode Island joined them. Milford and Wallingford followed Guilford in 1728.[54] Newport's two Congregational churches built spired meetinghouses within a few years of each other (1729 and 1733). Both hired Cotton Palmer from Taunton, Massachusetts, who, like Robert Twelves, was among the earliest known designers working for Congregational religious societies in the colonies.[55]

In the meantime, the Anglican establishment in eastern Massachusetts began to rethink its approach to bell towers, looking for guidance from the same Gothic or medieval decorative traditions that had inspired Christopher Wren's church architecture in London after the fire of 1666. In 1733 the newly formed St. Peter's Parish in Salem, Massachusetts, contracted to build a forty-six-by-thirty-five-foot church with a twelve-foot-square entry bell tower that rose approximately forty-six feet from the ground. The vestry committee paid Jonathan Mackmallun, a St. Peter's parishioner, £1 12s for turning four balls for "the Pinnacles of the Tower," presumably one for each of the corners of the battlement. John Holliman, a Salem gravestone maker and painter-stainer, received the contract for painting much of the outside woodwork. This initial version of St. Peter's steeple was destroyed by lightning in 1741 and replaced by the hipped roof visible on two paintings of this church by George Augustus Perkins before it was pulled down in 1833.[56] What the original St. Peter's tower might have looked like before it was struck by lightning is suggested by two details of William Burgis and William Price's view of Boston purporting to indicate the recently completed tower for Trinity Church. The first was a paster prepared in 1736, or two years after Trinity was raised, showing eight identical pinnacles on the battlement, the same design as St. Peter's but with twice as many pinnacles (fig. 6.18).[57] The second is a new state of the Burgis–Price plate prepared in 1743 where Price added a huge central spire within these eight pinnacles capped by a weather vane and a huge bishop's miter—a greater elaboration of the same theme (fig. 6.19).

res 6.18 and 6.19. Progressive
ution of Trinity's bell tower
in William Burgis and William
e's views of Boston between the
s 1736 and 1743. While Trinity
rch itself is hidden by Fort Hill,
ell tower emerges behind it, first
pinnacled tower (in the "paster"
e left), second as a spire capped
large bishop's miter. The evidence
ests that both views are fictitious.
Drawn by the author from Reps,
ton by Bostonians," 38–39.
t: Detail from *A South East View
Great Town of Boston in New
and in America.* Courtesy of the
rican Antiquarian Society.

As we now know, period diarists (and one early nineteenth-century woodcut view) argue convincingly that Trinity's two bell towers existed only in the imagination of William Price.[58] Although Trinity's records indicate that a bell taken as spoils from the reduction of Quebec was installed on its roof in 1759, there is no evidence that it was actually mounted in a standing bell tower. And the English captain Francis Goelet's diary plainly states that Trinity Church, which Goelet saw during a visit to Boston in 1750, is "modern" with a "very neat little organ," but that "having no steeple, [it] looks more like a Prespeterian [Presbyterian] meeting house."[59]

Price was also involved in a second and more substantial challenge to Boston's Reformed churches. Having successfully attracted financial support in 1740 both abroad and at home, he persuaded his fellow vestrymen at Christ Church to erect a high steeple over the existing tower. The Anglican builder John Indicott installed the new work, which was said to have been designed by Price. It was an academically inspired structure whose weather vane rose 190 feet off the ground (fig. 6.20) and cost more than twelve hundred pounds—approximately double

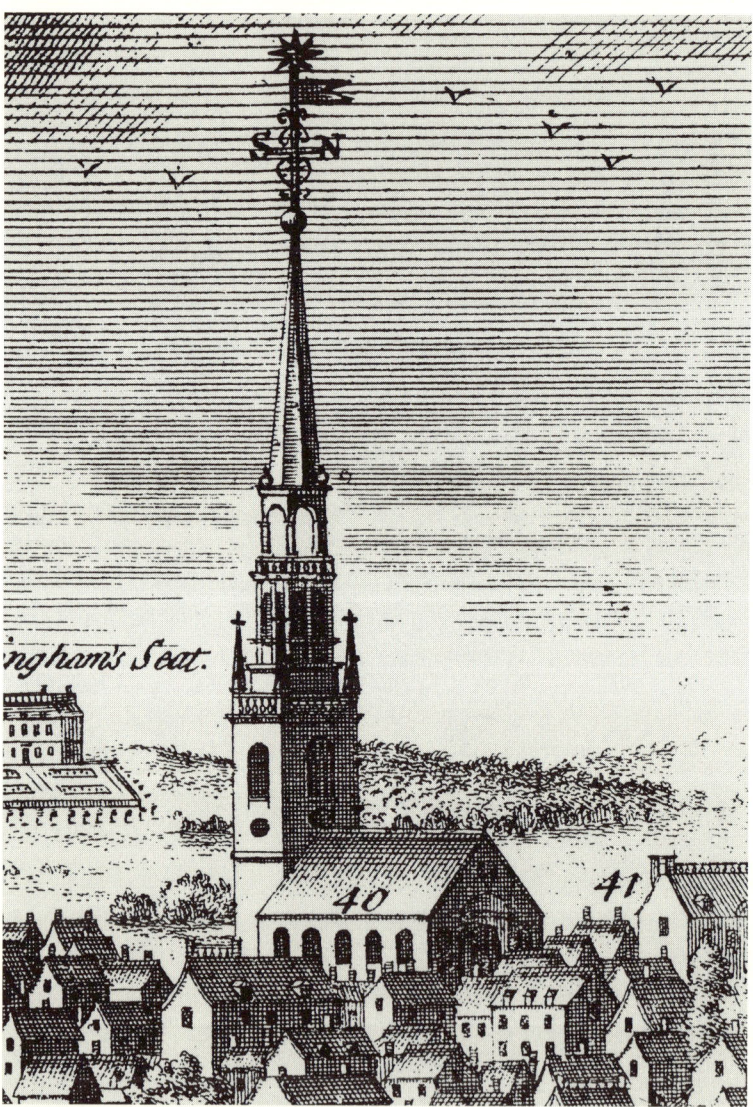

Figure 6.20. Detail from William Burgis and William Price's view, showing Christ Church, Boston, with a three-stage steeple erected in 1740, said to have been designed by William Price. "Dr. Cutler's Church" now possessed the first Anglican steeple in Massachusetts. *A South East View of the Great Town of Boston in New England in America*, 1743. Courtesy of the American Antiquarian Society.

Figure 6.21. Sketch of the 1723 meetinghouse *(a)* in Watertown, Massachusetts, taken by Dudley Woodbridge as he began his trip to the Connecticut River Valley on 1 October 1728. The structure on the right *(b)* is the 1721 meetinghouse in Natick, Massachusetts. Courtesy of the Massachusetts Historical Society.

that of an entire rural meetinghouse of similar proportions. It contained the first peal of bells brought into North America. While no accurate depiction of this spire survives, the Price view of 1743 and the Paul Revere views of 1770 and 1774 indicate that it was made up of three square stages, each smaller than the one below it, and each set off by obelisks or turned finials. The two uppermost stages were relieved by double- and single-arched openings. The tower of "Dr. Cutler's church" quickly became the most prominent landmark in Boston and was so well known it attracted a professional acrobat, who climbed it in 1756 and "flew" off it on ropes. Like so many others damaged in high winds, the spire fell down in an 1804 storm. The 1806 Charles Bullfinch-designed replacement of the original is said to have followed the basic arrangement of Price's design.[60]

The steeple on Christ Church, completed in 1740, marks a stylistic milestone in the evolution of New England's mid-eighteenth-century houses of worship—not surpassed until the surge of new building activity that took place just before and after the Revolution. Congregational building committees favored three general spire styles. The first was the simple tapering spire that surmounted a tower whose top story housed the bell—a design previously seen at the New North and Brattle meetinghouses. A rural version of this design was specified in 1728 in Aaron Cleveland's contract with Malden, Massachusetts, which limited him to a square steeple rather than the conventional octagon. He was instructed to "Board and shingle the steeple the pike of it and provide and put up the weather Cock and Ball upon the Top of said Steeple and board and clapboard the sides of said Steeple with four oval Windows in the Square of said Steeple."[61]

A comparable tapering spire is found in Dudley Woodbridge's sketch of the 1723 meetinghouse in Watertown, Massachusetts (fig. 6.21), one of the towns he passed through on his way to Deerfield in 1728. It is also seen in a bell tower erected at the Spruce Creek meetinghouse in Kittery, Maine, in 1734, illustrated in a 1739 division of land prepared by surveyor John Godsoe (fig. 6.22).[62]

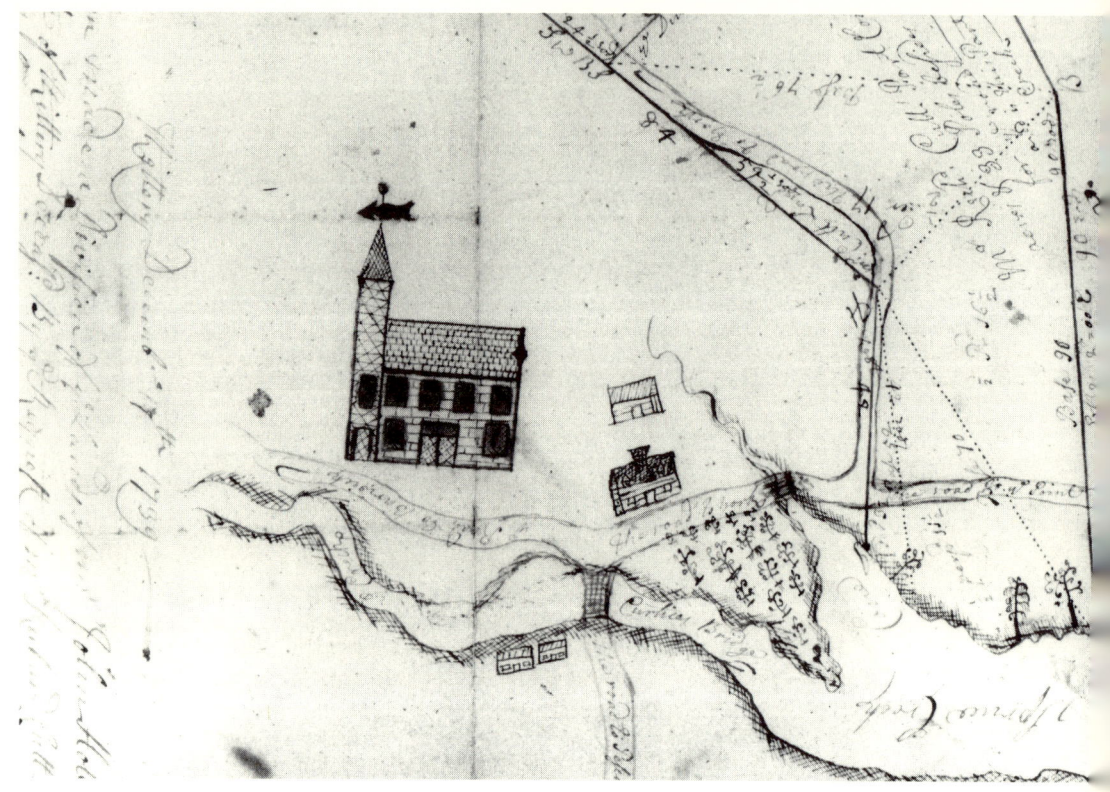

Figure 6.22. *Division of yᵉ Lands of mr. John Hole Late of Kittery Deceas:ᵈ*. Image of the 1734 Spruce Creek meetinghouse in Kittery, Maine, drawn for John Godsoe's survey in 1739, showing a simplified early steeple used in rural New England; copy by Tobias Leighton, town clerk, circa 1740. Town of Kittery, Maine. Photograph by Douglas Armsden, courtesy of Richard M. Candee.

The second style favored by Congregationalists predominated in eastern Massachusetts, northern Connecticut, and southern New Hampshire. In these spires, the bell was housed in an ogee cupola supported on eight pillars—the type first installed on the New Brick. Usually the openings were arched, the cornice of the tower was dentilled, and a rail or battlement typically surrounded the bell. This design was so widely used that one eighteenth-century document refers to it as the "common form."[63] In Boston a succession of prints tells us the older tapering spires were considered retrograde after 1750 and were taken down and replaced by the cupola. The older spire of the New North—seen in prints by William Burgis and in Burgis–Price views in 1723, 1725, and 1743—was transformed into the cupola style in Paul Revere's prints of 1770 and 1774. Much the same transformation took place with the New South.[64]

Besides these period visual sources, the cupola spire is also seen in memory pictures and occasional survivals. The 1763 meetinghouse of the First Church in Worcester, illustrated and photographed before being taken down in 1887, features this design (fig. 6.23) as does the 1769 meetinghouse in Medford illustrated in a lithograph print by Benjamin Champney in 1840.[65] Surviving steeples are found in Amherst, New Hampshire (steeple erected in 1771), Hampstead, New Hampshire (steeple erected in 1793), and Cohasset, Massachusetts (steeple erected in 1799). Typically these spires were surmounted by gilt vanes or weathercocks replacing the earlier iron flags. An Amesbury, Massachusetts, man was paid £8 5s in 1750 "for [making] the spindle of the meeting house," on which the

Figure 6.23. *Old South Church in Worcester as it was in 1817.* Memory drawing by William White Smith in 1882 of the 1763 meetinghouse in Worcester, Massachusetts. Courtesy of the American Antiquarian Society.

Figure 6.24. Weathercock attributed to Thomas Drowne (1715–1795), son of Shem Drowne (1683–1774) of Boston, installed on the "pyramid" of the third meetinghouse in Newbury, Massachusetts, in 1772 to replace a first-period flag vane. Gilt sheet copper, iron, lead, glass eyes. Height 32 inches, length 46 inches. Photograph © 2011, Museum of Fine Arts, Boston. Accession 2008.1401.

vane presumably turned. Newbury, Massachusetts, ordered a new "copper weather cock on the top of the pyramid" in 1772 when it installed a new steeple on its old meetinghouse (fig. 6.24).[66]

A third spire type was based in Connecticut, especially in towns along the Long Island shoreline. These appear to have followed the Guilford model or some derivation of it. The belfry was located above the tower and was protected by a squared cupola surmounted by a high four-sided spire apparently known as a "Squaw's cap" because of its conical appearance.[67] In virtually all cases, the roof lacked a cornice. No examples of these bell towers survive, but occasional evidence from memory pictures, paintings, drawings, and views suggests they may have been common. Examples include Wallingford (1728), Milford (1728), New Haven (1757), and Stratfield (1769–71) (fig. 6.25). About two-thirds of the sixteen bell towers built for Congregational meetinghouses in coastal Connecticut seem to have followed the "Squaw's cap" model. This model is also found on Anglican churches in coastal Connecticut, such as those on Christ Church in Stratford (1743) and on Trinity Church in New Haven (1753). Presumably builders chose the design because they were familiar with this form of construction.

In the 1760s, however, rival Anglican and Congregational bell-tower builders once again came into focus, and again two wealthy congregations in Rhode Island and Connecticut occupied center stage. Having waited for more than thirty years with a spireless tower, Newport's Trinity Church built a replacement tower in 1762 that virtually duplicated William Price's heavily corniced

Figure 6.25. Conjectural or memory view of the meetinghouse raised in Wallingford, Connecticut, in 1717, with a bell tower added in 1728, showing a "Squaw's cap" steeple gathered vertically on four sides. From Davis, *History of Wallingford* (1870), 120, Widener Library, Harvard College Library, US 14903.5.5.

square-stage design on Christ Church—even to the point of imitating the layout of the rounded windows and the uppermost "lantern" (figs. 6.26 and 6.27). Its completion was an important occasion for the town, and Ezra Stiles noted in his journal the height of the vane (140 feet) and of the "first Ball" (110 feet). (Stiles also reported that the "mast" of the spire was made of rotten wood and soon fell down in a storm.)[68]

Two years later, when Wethersfield, Connecticut, voted to replace its seventy-eight-year-old period-one meetinghouse, the building committee chose an ambitious eighty-by-fifty-foot design, the seventh brick meetinghouse in New England. (J. Frederick Kelly tells us that townspeople were eventually permitted to pay taxes for the building with onions at a rate of three pence a rope.) The design called for a stairwell porch at one end and a standing bell tower on the other, but rather than following the conventional Connecticut "Squaw's cap" design or the more "common" Massachusetts one, Wethersfield did in 1764 what the town of Guilford had considered and then apparently chose not to do in 1726: follow the fashion and proportion of the belfry and spire at Rhode Island. John Chester, who helped underwrite the construction, replicated the square-staged spire recently erected on Trinity Church with all its pinnacles, balls, and pyramids. While there is no evidence that John Chester himself went either to Boston or to Newport to examine these structures, he or someone else must have done so because Wethersfield's tower almost exactly matches Newport's 1762 design.[69]

Wethersfield's decision considerably widened the choices available to building committees, designers, and carpenters erecting bell towers in the Connecticut Valley and Massachusetts. Congregational use of Anglican ecclesiastic forms had been employed before, but now it was brought out into the open. Hatfield, Massachusetts, which built (or rebuilt) its bell tower shortly after 1764, adopted a Price-style steeple, perhaps copying the one at Wethersfield. (Hezekiah May and James Mitchell, both of Wethersfield, had earlier been involved in the building of Hatfield's meetinghouse when first raised in 1750.)[70] Four years later, in 1768, when building a new meetinghouse, the nearby town of Longmeadow instructed its committee, "To Make Enquiry and Get the Best Information they Can Concerning the Building the Top of the Steeple of said House Whether by Building another Square or Building in the Common Form."[71]

In effect, Longmeadow was deciding between following Wethersfield's example ("another square") and following the "common" form already well established in eastern Massachusetts. Decades later similar language was still being used by parish authorities in the region. When adding improvements to their meetinghouse in 1801, east Amesbury, Massachusetts, twice attempted to make up its mind whether to add an ornamented bell tower to the structure—considering either "a Cubaloe [cupola] or a spire." The parish meeting finally

Figures 6.26 and 6.27. Bell towers of (*above*) Trinity Church, Newport, Rhode Island (raised 1725; tower replaced 1762) and (*below*) the meetinghouse at Wethersfield, Connecticut, erected in 1764. Lithograph by Robertson, Seibery and Shearman, New York, 1860, after a drawing by J. P. Newell. Courtesy, American Antiquarian Society. Photograph by Stanley P. Mixon, 1940. Historic American Buildings Survey, Library of Congress, Washington, D.C.

gave up on the issue and left it up to the building committee, which eventually built a tower with a simple cupola.[72]

The dispersal of bell-tower and steeple designs in some instances followed the now familiar neighbor-to-neighbor routes. When Manchester, Massachusetts, wanted in 1753 to add a tower and steeple to a meetinghouse they had built in 1719, the town voted to raise it "from the beams and upwards near the form of Gloucester New Meeting house standing in the Revd Mr. Rogers his parish." Rev. John Rogers, who had recently been installed as minister over the newly formed Fourth Parish in Gloucester, had just built a meetinghouse whose belfry was mounted on the roof—presumably a less costly approach than building it from the ground up. Manchester's model was located less than seven miles away.[73] Elsewhere, when Brookline, Massachusetts, was considering the form and height of its new steeple in 1771, the town instructed its carpenters that "Said Steeple be not higher than Doctor Boyles [Byles] Steeple is," meaning the meetinghouse steeple of the Hollis Street Society in Boston.[74]

But in other instances eighteenth-century bell-tower imitations readily traveled much greater distances, a characteristic more common of bell-tower and meetinghouse design in the early nineteenth century. The prized and expensive innovations introduced into Boston and Rhode Island between 1715 and 1729 were literally "heard" throughout New England—distances did not matter. By citing Rev. Benjamin Colman's bell in 1724, Guilford's voters were ready to build a bell tower based on a model that few in the town had seen. That they changed their minds and voted instead for the "Fashion and proportion" of Newport's Trinity spire in 1726 did not bring the model any closer. Falmouth, Maine, when adding a bell tower in 1760, "copied the one at York," a community thirty-five miles to the south that few parishioners had ever visited. Guilford and Falmouth took these votes because the cultural and economic conditions for spanning these distances—meaning private money—had long been in place. When Wallingford, Connecticut, was considering a replacement for its old period-one meetinghouse, the town noted that "particular men" (that is, wealthy individuals and not the society or the town) were willing to pay for a tower and steeple, and they were authorized to do so. The town built its new meetinghouse in 1717 and added a privately funded tower in 1728. But their actual decision took place in 1716, three years after Boston selectmen had approved of New North's battlements and one year before Benjamin Colman's Manifesto congregation is known to have raised their tower in 1717. Guilford and Wallingford, in other words, were prepared to build a bell tower at just about the same time as the New North and the New South in Boston.[75]

This willingness by communities to approve the construction of bell towers supported by private money eventually transformed New England's meetinghouse architecture. Freed from public scrutiny, Congregational building committees increasingly transferred bell-tower work to professional architects and builders who had access to copybooks or who themselves had trained as designers. This practice paralleled a tradition among wealthy Baptists and Anglicans. We have seen that Richard Munday designed Newport's Trinity and Seventh-Day Baptist churches and that William Price, a professional cabinetmaker, designed the tower for Christ Church in Boston. But New England's Congregational societies were doing the same by the 1730s. The First Parish in Hartford, Connecticut, hired Cotton Palmer—who had previously erected the bell towers and spires in Newport in 1729 and 1733—to plan a new meetinghouse in 1737 (for which he was paid £1); he also designed and supervised the building of "the spire above the bell deck" (for which he was paid £250).[76] Norwich, Connecticut, voted to build a bell tower for its new meetinghouse in 1750 that included "a handsome Steeple raised on the beams at the North End of the House Modeled within according to the plan herewith Exhibited"—evidence that a designer or architect was involved in the process.[77]

To any Englishman seeing them for the first time, most of these meetinghouse bell towers must have seemed provincial. This response was probably inevitable, for despite the long-held belief that these bell towers followed an "English" design, the only known transatlantic bell-tower imitation in New England rises above the meetinghouse of the First Baptist Church in Providence, Rhode Island, built in 1774 and 1775. The self-taught architect Joseph Brown (1733–1785), one of four highly successful brothers who dominated merchant life in that colony, took on the task of designing the new meetinghouse. Brown had access to English stylebooks and used them to bring a definitive version of the Georgian architectural mode into the northern colonies (fig. 6.28). His colleagues even announced his source in the *Providence Gazette* of 10 June 1775, saying that the tower and spire were taken from "the middle Figure in the 30th Plate of Gibbs Designs." (According to tradition, the copy of James Gibbs's *Book of Architecture* now in the Providence Athenaeum is the one Brown used.) The result was the virtual duplication in wood of the center one of three designs Gibbs had prepared for St. Martin-in-the-Fields, a church built of stone in London in 1726 (fig. 6.29).[78]

Nevertheless, the completion of the First Baptist meetinghouse in Providence marks the zenith of the prerevolutionary or Georgian mode in the Anglican and Congregational bell-tower "competition." What had started out in Boston in 1688 as a single Anglican tower standing amid a field of Congregational turrets had escalated into a sustained ballet in which clocks, cupolas, lanterns, spire heights, square stages, weather vanes, compass windows, and octagonal stages signaled the growing taste and financial means of New England's regional life. It also marks the emergence of a significantly changed cultural landscape. When the New North raised its battlements in Boston in 1714, much distrust still existed between Anglicans and Reformed denominations. By 1775, even as this distrust was escalating into the political and military arena, any real sectarian differences in Congregational, Baptist, and Anglican bell-tower architecture were lost in the heady atmosphere of the classical and Italianate detail of English and European copybooks. In the end, it might be said that the competition in urban New England resulted in a tie. The 1729 Old South, Christ Church with its 1740 spire, and the 1774 First Baptist meetinghouse all drew on European or European-inspired bell-tower designs that had little or no denominational content except that they were generically "ecclesiastic" or "Christian." While Cutler's 190-foot tower briefly made Christ Church a Boston landmark unsurpassed by its peers, it soon became one among many others of equal or better quality.

Figure 6.28. *A S.W. View of the Baptist Meeting House, Providence, R.I.* Built 1774–1775 after a design by self-taught architect Joseph Brown. Engraved by Samuel Hill (1766?–1804) for the *Massachusetts Magazine*, August 1789. Library of Congress Rare Book and Special Collections Divisions, Washington, D.C.

Figure 6.29. Three steeple designs prepared for St. Martin-in-the-Fields. Plate 30, James Gibbs, *Book of Architecture*, 1728. Providence Athenaeum.

By 1774, Providence, like Newport and Boston, had evolved into a sophisticated and architecturally refined metropolis.

## Adding Space: Enlargements, Galleries, and Stairwell Porches

By incorporating opposing stairwell porches into their new meetinghouse in 1764, John Chester and his Wethersfield colleagues stopped well short of creating an outright imitation of the exterior of Newport's Trinity Church. Their purpose was practical. In the words of the Wethersfield committee that recommended them, stairwell porches ensured that the assembled congregation was not "interrupted by such as go into the galleries in time of worship, and that there may be more room in the house."[79] A reminder of the region's continuing demographic expansion, galleries and stairwell porches—vernacular in their design in almost every respect—were also an architectural inheritance of Europe's Calvinist building traditions, and they continued to dominate eighteenth-century meetinghouses at least until the 1790s. Outside stairwell porches were sizable and easily identified at a distance. But more important, they created a countervailing perception that in a sense nullified the "ecclesiastical" or "Anglican" presence of a standing bell tower and clearly identified a Reformed tradition practiced since the time French Huguenots built Paradis Temple in 1566. There is a special irony here. The very same exterior porches that gave New England meetinghouses their "first-period" look became the principal stylistic avenue for redesigning meetinghouses into third-period churches.

Except in those rare instances when a town or precinct became extinct, New England communities usually doubled in size every twenty years. The pressure of an expanding population prompted communities to raise and tear down their meetinghouses regularly—amid public quarrels over whether to enlarge them, move them, replace them, or leave them alone. Towns routinely found ways to increase their seating capacity. An early option was to create space by adding lean-tos running parallel to the ridgepole. Four towns in New England and one on Long Island are known to have added lean-tos to their seventeenth-century long houses. Marblehead built a lean-to in 1672 that was twenty feet wide; the resulting structure was forty feet square. Hadley added six-foot lean-tos on either side shortly after they raised the original structure in 1662. Glastonbury, Connecticut, voted in 1706 to enlarge "by galleries or lean-tos, as the committee should judge best."[80] This practice was followed even with large buildings. New Haven virtually doubled the size of its meetinghouse by having Nathan Andrews add a lean-to behind the pulpit in 1698.[81] The New North's lean-to in Boston in 1719 included an upper and lower gallery.[82] An interesting early nineteenth-century lean-to option, employed only in New Hampshire, was to add a "swell" or half-circle extension to the long side opposite the pulpit and to cover it with

Figure 6.30. Meetinghouse in Claremont, New Hampshire, showing the 1808 semicircular addition to the long side of this 1783 structure. Photograph circa 1857. Collection of the Fiske Free Library, Claremont, New Hampshire.

a gathered roof. This method was followed in 1802 in Concord and imitated in 1808 by Claremont (fig. 6.30).[83] Nor were these lean-to enlargements limited to Reformed houses of worship. Faced with the same need to expand seating, St. Peter's Church in Salem, Massachusetts, added a two-floor galleried addition to the long side of its sanctuary virtually the same height and width as the house itself (fig. 6.31). As in Claremont and Concord, the addition was essentially a lean-to.

Another approach was to lengthen the house by extending the ends with additional framed sections. In 1709 Mendon, Massachusetts, added ten feet to the gable ends of their meetinghouse, perhaps expanding the hipped roof to the new corners. New London, Connecticut, may have done the same thing about 1740.[84] A more radical method—used by communities really hard-pressed for space—was to split the meetinghouse into two sections, haul one a few yards away with ox teams and frame the gap. This approach was done lengthwise and crosswise. Dorchester, Massachusetts, enlarged its fifty-two-year-old meetinghouse in 1795 by dividing it along the ridgepole and separating the two halves by fourteen feet. The standing bell tower, located on the narrow end of the structure, was moved half this distance, or seven feet, to be again aligned centrally. What had been a sixty-eight-by-forty-six-foot meetinghouse was now sixty-eight by sixty, and the new ridgepole was about eight feet higher. Two decades later the house was damaged in a storm, and the town voted to tear the structure down and rebuild.[85]

When buildings were cut crosswise along the broad alley, the two halves were also separated, and one or two additional bays added. Holliston, Massachusetts, split its sixty-two-year-old meetinghouse in 1787 in this fashion, adding fourteen feet to the center to create a structure that was fifty-four by thirty-two feet. In all, thirty-two such examples of frame enlargements, averaging between fourteen and eighteen feet, are documented (see Appendix D). So frequently was this technique used that when the town of Westborough, Massachusetts, decided to expand its meetinghouse in 1772, it named a "Committee to View some meeting houses that have been Cut in two & a piece put in the middle."[86] A visual representation of how this type of division was accomplished with yoked draft animals is given us by the French artist Charles-Alexandre Lesueur (1778–1846), who drew a meetinghouse being cut in half when he traveled through Rhode Island and New Bedford, Massachusetts, during his visit to America in 1816 (fig. 6.32).[87] His sketch shows about nine teams of oxen pulling away half of a meetinghouse, which has been mounted on wheels. In this instance the division

Figure 6.31. Schematic view of St. Peter's Church, Salem, Massachusetts, built 1733, seen from the southwest, showing the galleried lean-to on the long side added sometime in the late eighteenth century. Drawing by the author based on an 1833 watercolor by George A. Perkins at the Peabody Essex Museum.

Figure 6.32. *Énlèvement d'une moitié d'une église pour avoir la paix entre deux sectes religieuses.* [Removal of half of a church in order to have peace between two religious sects.] A sketch taken in New Bedford, Massachusetts, 1816, by Charles-Alexandre Lesueur, showing workmen separating two sides of a meetinghouse, mounting one-half on wheels and hauling it away with oxen. It was the same process used by parishes to enlarge the meetinghouse by pulling one-half from the other and framing in the space. Muséum d'histoire naturelle, Le Harve, France.

and relocation was apparently an attempt to settle a dispute between two competing religious sects who shared the premises, and though neither the incident nor the identity of the sects appears in local history accounts, Lesueur's wide experience as a naturalist and illustrator and the sketch's accompanying documentation make his explanation credible even though the scene looks like a typical crosswise expansion.

Much more common than any of these methods was to add gallery space—in effect continuing the old Huguenot tradition of building elevated or tiered seats and pews. Most New England communities designed meetinghouses with posts high enough (most often twenty feet) to accommodate galleries on three sides of the building (fig. 6.33). But even a meetinghouse with a plate height of ten to fifteen feet could provide gallery space on the side opposite the pulpit. Medford, Massachusetts, in 1699 added a "fore-gallery" equally divided between men and women to a structure that was fifteen feet high.[88] In 1699 Rochester, Massachusetts, built end-galleries in its first house of worship, which had a ten-foot plate height. This arrangement left parishioners in the gallery cramped under the ceiling. In their second house of worship, the Rochester townsmen allowed Timothy Ruggles Jr., a young lawyer, in 1733 to construct a third-floor pew on a beam over the gallery. (The pew's floor was no doubt higher than the plate.) Nineteenth-century New England historians called these pews "swallows' nests" or "roof pews."[89]

Many New England meetinghouses were designed high enough to accommodate two complete tiers of galleries, creating what we now call "triple deckers." Any structure with a plate height of twenty-seven feet or more was probably intended for two tiers of galleries. Under these circumstances the galleried space could almost double a building's seating capacity without altering its external shell. After Concord, Massachusetts, built its meetinghouse with two tiers of galleries in 1711, neighboring Lexington wanted to do the same but could not afford to. Later, when private donors made funds available, the town voted to increase the plate height "four feet upward." This change made room for a second, smaller tier, illuminated by a set of smaller windows located just under the cornice (fig. 6.34). Most Boston meetinghouses had two tiers of galleries, possibly beginning as early as 1675 when the First Church added what may have been a second tier to its 1640 meetinghouse. Salem built two meetinghouses each with two tiers of galleries (in 1711 and 1718) as did Charlestown (in 1716) and

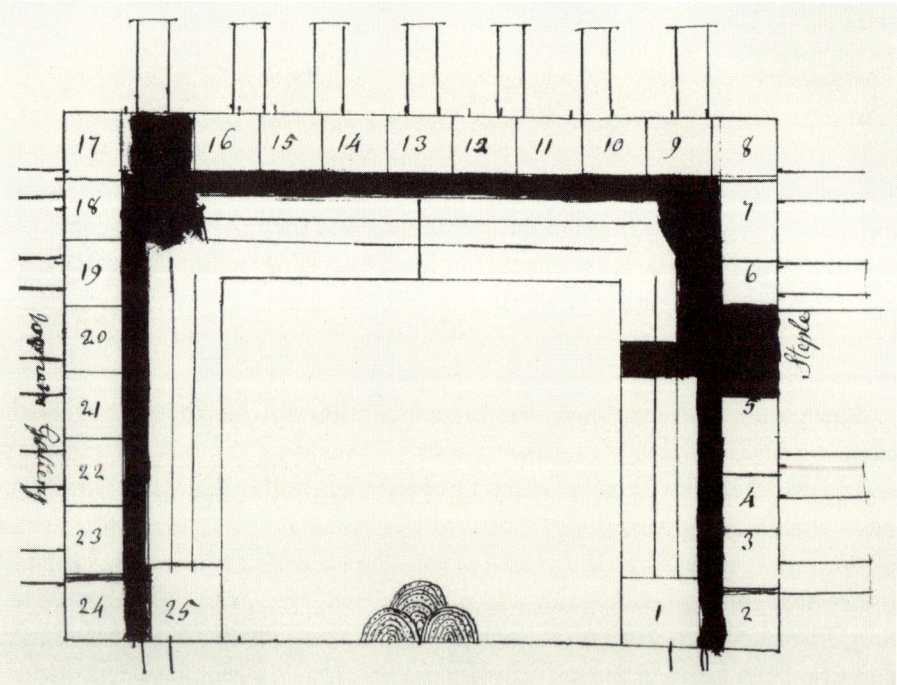

Figure 6.33. Gallery plan prepared by Samuel Lane of Stratham, New Hampshire, for the town's second meetinghouse in June 1767. Twenty-five pews surround three tiers of benches. The dark areas represent stairwells and aisles. The steeple is shown on the right, together with windows around the circumference. Stratham Town Records. Courtesy of the New Hampshire Division of Archives and Records Management.

Figure 6.34. Detail of the 1714 meetinghouse, Lexington, Massachusetts. From Amos Doolittle's engraving, *The Battle of Lexington. April 19th 1775. Plate I.* The design was to be "on the same plan as Concord," but with somewhat smaller dimensions. Its plate height was originally designed for one gallery, but a special vote added four feet to the plate height to allow one-and-a-half tiers of galleries, the uppermost illuminated by a row of small windows. A raised external belfry is located on the right. Courtesy of the Peabody Essex Museum, Salem, Massachusetts.

Framingham (in 1735). Even small meetinghouses were designed for two tiers. Wrentham, Massachusetts, provided the most extreme example of this plan in 1721 when the town built what amounted to a relatively modest meetinghouse (forty by thirty-eight feet) but specified a "height as may be most convenient and proper for two tiers of galleries one above the other." The resulting building was almost as high as it was wide.[90]

Galleries meant stairwells. Normally stairs were built in the southwest and southeast corners, where their presence would not intrude on the congregation's access to the pulpit. The early nineteenth-century pew plan of the third meetinghouse in Wenham, Massachusetts, reveals a single set of stairs in the southeast corner of the structure that took up about two pew spaces. But in the press to add pews, spaces became bargaining chips in the struggle between the townsmen who wanted to keep a neat meetinghouse and private individuals who wanted to build their own pews. Walpole, Massachusetts, allowed one of its church deacons in 1749 to "change" (presumably shorten) the stairs on the "westerly end of the meeting house and to build a Pew at his own Cost." Four years later the town "Voted to build one Pew over the Men's stairs and another over the Womens stairs, and another at the foot of the Womens stairs." When even this addition was found insufficient, the town elected to "shut up the [main] Alley" and to "Close the Body of seats," thereby creating even more space.[91]

As meetinghouses became filled with pews, towns began to create additional interior space by building entrance porches that served as stairwells to the gallery—in effect placing on the outside of the structure those architectural components that took up valuable space inside. Typically, outside stairwell porches were located in one of two places. In the single-porch model, a stairwell was attached to the center of the long side over the principal entry; in the twin-porch model, stairwells were attached on each end of the meetinghouse. These, too, frequently became bargaining chips between wealthy parishioners who wanted to build pews and the town meeting wanting to save money. Gilmanton, New Hampshire, voted in 1774 to grant Joseph Badger and Antipas Gilman "the privilege in the meeting-house for pews, which the stairs would occupy, provided they build two stairwell porches, one on the East and the other on the West end of the House."[92] To gain space for their pews, Badger and Gilman agreed to do the work.

Sometimes stairwells were added when other forms of enlargement were made. After Holliston increased the size of its meetinghouse by splitting it, the town also added a single stairwell porch in the center of the building. By eliminating the two flights of interior stairs, the town freed up two large spaces on the ground floor and two more smaller ones in the gallery, thereby gaining about 10 percent more pews.[93]

Stairwell types were place specific. Survivals, historic photographs, town and parish records, and nineteenth-century town histories reveal that at least sixty-eight meetinghouses were built with single porches (or single-porch additions) in New England between 1738 and 1810 (fig. 6.35). Among the earliest of these were the Second Parish in Wells, Maine (now Kennebunk) which voted to finish the galleries and build a "porch on the side fronting the road," and the East Parish in Barnstable, Massachusetts, which added a single porch when it enlarged its meetinghouse in 1756.[94] The majority of these (about 70 percent) were situated in remote towns bordering along the Maine, New Hampshire, and Massachusetts coastlines, with the highest concentration on Cape Cod and Plymouth County (fig. 6.36). Cape Cod alone had sixteen such porches before 1810. As one nineteenth-century Cape Cod historian notes, the single-porch meetinghouse in South Harwich built in 1792 "was in the uniform style in nearly all the towns of the Cape."[95]

In most instances a front stairwell porch was added to an existing, relatively old, meetinghouse when pews were added or when it was being enlarged. In 1760 when Harwich wanted to build more pews in its 1723 meetinghouse, the town built a front stairwell porch approximately ten feet square. Similarly, when nearby

Figure 6.35. *Old Universalist Meeting House.* View of the single-porch meetinghouse, built 1769, in southwest Scituate, Massachusetts, bordering Hanover. From John S. Barry, *Historical Sketch of the Town of Hanover,* 80. Widener Library, Harvard College Library, US 13288.5.5.

Chatham enlarged its 1730 meetinghouse in 1773 by adding a seventeen-foot section in the middle, it built a nine-by-ten-foot front stairwell porch.[96] But in later examples, especially meetinghouses raised after 1775, the single porch became part of the original design—suggesting that an architectural feature introduced for the purpose of increasing seating from 1750 through 1770, had, two decades later, evolved into a local or regional style. South Harwich's 1792 two-story front stairwell porch was part of the original contract.

Communities in eastern New England, however, that were wealthy enough to build standing bell towers typically aligned their outside stairwells opposite the tower: the tower base served as one stairwell and the opposing porch as a second. According to the *Annals* of James Blake (1688–1750), who as town clerk kept a log of all the notable occurrences in Dorchester, Massachusetts, the fourth meetinghouse in that town in 1743 had a 114-foot steeple at one end and a stairwell porch at the other, both 14 feet square.[97] Three years later, neighboring Roxbury rebuilt its 1740 steepled meetinghouse, which had burned in 1744, adding an opposed stairwell porch opposite the steeple privately paid for by Judge Paul Dudley.[98] During the next twenty years, towns such as Hamilton and Topsfield, Massachusetts, and Litchfield, Connecticut, raised new meetinghouses with similar stairwell arrangements. Communities adding standing bell towers to existing meetinghouses did the same. The Congregational society in Hanover,

168   Chapter Six

Massachusetts, voted to add a "women's porch" on the east end of its 1764 meetinghouse after the "men's" stairwell had been enclosed in the bell tower on the western end.[99] Implied here is the expectation that the men's and women's staircases should be similar.

Since it seemed to make good architectural sense to place a porch and bell tower on opposing ends of the meetinghouse, it was not long before it made

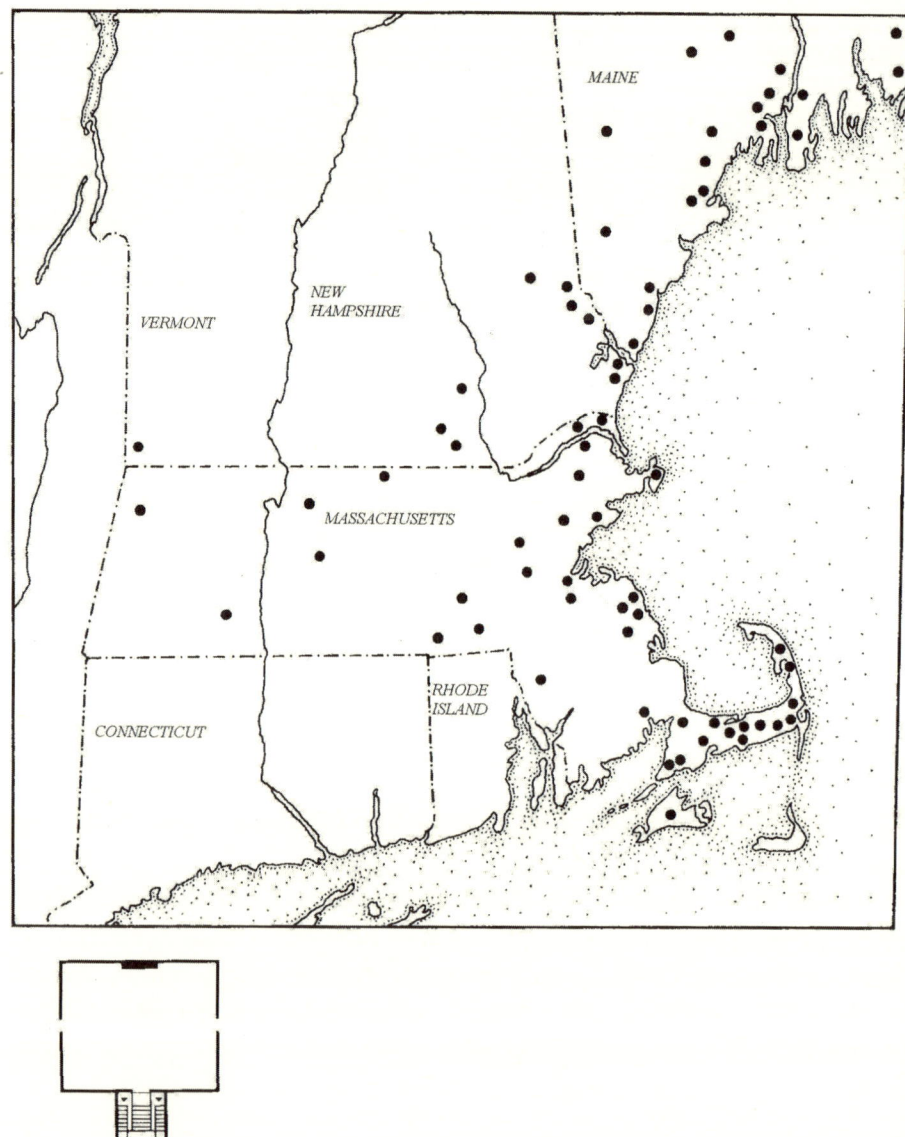

Figure 6.36. Distribution of sixty-nine known single-porch meetinghouses or single-porch additions, 1738 to 1810. Map by the author.

Figure 6.37. Twin-porch meetinghouse in Poplin, New Hampshire, now the town of Fremont. Built by public subscription in 1800, the meetinghouse served as a house of worship and as a town house through 1911. Each porch provides both an entrance to the meetinghouse and stairwell access to the gallery. Photograph by Paul Wainwright, 2008.

equal sense to build two such porches in the hope that when money became available the town or parish could add a bell tower. One of the first uses of the twin-porch plan was in New Braintree, Massachusetts, which in 1772 added a pair of stairwell porches on either end of a fifty-by-forty-foot meetinghouse that had been built in 1752.[100] The porches provided additional pew space because the old stairwells were now available for pews, but it also allowed the town eventually to build a belfry on one of the porches. A comparable strategy was behind the vote taken by the Second Parish in Boxford, Massachusetts, in 1774, which ordered a new meetinghouse "according to the same plan by which the meetinghouse in New Rowley [Georgetown] was built, excepting a steeple, instead of which we are to have a porch built at the other end of the meeting house."[101]

At least eighty-four twin-porch meetinghouses or twin-porch additions were erected in central and northern New England between 1772 and 1807, making it the predominant upland style. Typical is the meetinghouse in Poplin, New Hampshire, now Fremont, built in 1800, where two identical stairwell porches face each other at opposite ends of the building (fig. 6.37). In southern New

Hampshire the distribution of the style was focused in a sixty-mile-wide crescent formed by the Masonian grant. It was especially heavy in a "twin-porch" zone in the Contoocook River Valley of southern New Hampshire and the surrounding hill country of Hillsborough County, with significant numbers located in the adjacent highland areas of Cheshire County and Worcester County, Massachusetts (fig. 6.38). So densely concentrated was the style within New Hampshire's Contoocook zone that at the beginning of the nineteenth century

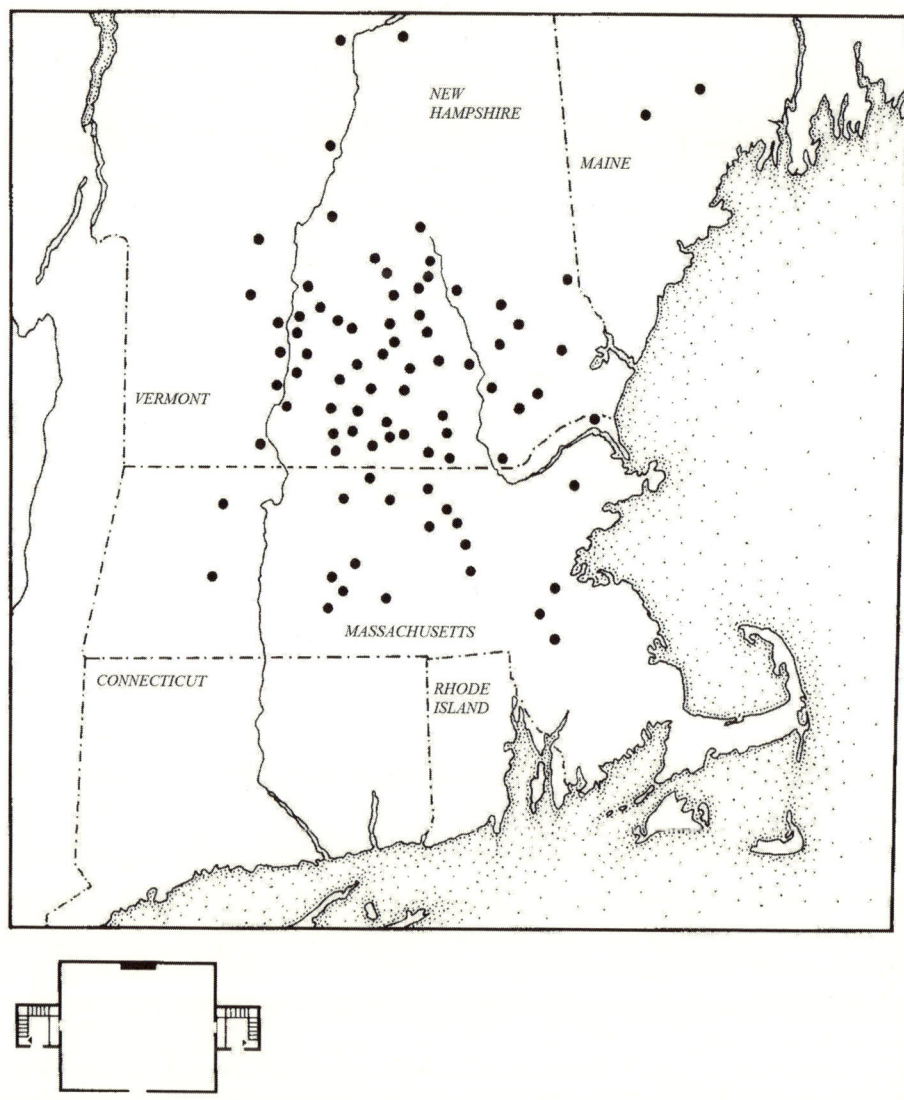

Figure 6.38. Distribution of eighty-four known twin-porch meetinghouses or twin-porch additions in New England, 1772 to 1807. Map by the author.

it was possible to ride north from Brookline to Bridgewater and pass through seventeen contiguous towns and see sixteen twin-porch meetinghouses.

Further examination reveals that the dispersal of stairwell forms in New England communities was linked to similarities in demographic, occupational, and economic circumstances. The single-porch plan spread freely along the northern and eastern New England coastlines into communities tied together by trade and packet routes and by a common dependence on fishing and shipbuilding trades. Its northernmost limit was the extent of settlement along the Maine coastline; its southernmost limit was Cape Cod. These communities had little expectation of underwriting a bell tower at any point in their future, and it made more sense to them to use single-porch additions rather than more expensive twin-porch plans.

The twin-porch plan was widely adopted among towns in central Massachusetts and southern New Hampshire whose second-generation meetinghouses (usually with dimensions of fifty by forty or fifty-five by forty-five feet) were becoming overcrowded. Unwilling or unable to assume the cost of the large, third-generation sizes such as were being built at Concord, New Hampshire, in 1751 (sixty-four by forty-six feet), or in Rindge in 1796 (sixty-six by fifty-two feet), towns whose populations exceeded one thousand or fifteen hundred after 1770 found that twin-porch designs forestalled the pressure of an expanding population without their having to build a new meetinghouse. These towns were no longer waiting for a natural increase in their population before adding twin exterior stairwells. Instead, they were including the porches in the original contract because that was the architectural practice they commonly witnessed around them.[102] The 1792 agreement for raising the meetinghouse in Canaan, New Hampshire, reads: "The dimension of said house are to be as follows: 42 feet in width and 52 feet in length, and the posts to be 26 feet long between joints, & the roof in proportion thereunto. Also, two porches, one at each end, each porch to be 12 feet square the posts to be 23 feet long."[103] Also, towns constantly borrowed from one another. When Milford, New Hampshire, added stairwell porches to its just-completed meetinghouse in 1786, the town's voters looked to their nearest neighbor, Temple, "to accept the plan of the porches" for their own.[104]

As the eighteenth century drew to a close, some New England towns were left unsatisfied by simply imitating single-porch or twin-porch models. Instead they combined the two and raised three-porch structures, the main porch providing a principal entry into the building and the two side ones providing stairwells to the second floor. Ashburnham, a central Massachusetts town located just below the New Hampshire border, built in 1791 as its second meetinghouse a sixty-by-forty-five-foot twin-porch structure, specifying an ambitious "cover

THE SECOND MEETING-HOUSE IN ASHBURNHAM, ERECTED 1791.

Figure 6.39. The triple-porch meetinghouse raised in Ashburnham, Massachusetts, in 1791 was equipped with two outside stairwells and a "cover" over the front door that may have contained stairwell access to the gallery. The structure contained forty-six pews below and twenty-five in the gallery. Horse sheds and carriage stalls are depicted at each side, with stone paving on the walkway and a horseblock in front. From Ezra Stearns, *History of Ashburnham*, 295. Andover-Harvard Theological Library, Harvard Divinity School, Harvard University, Brittle Book E844.

over the front door" with pilasters, compass window, and rustication.[105] Though seemingly "over-porched," the meetinghouse was a model of utility (fig. 6.39). The design offered seven points of access into the building: two on each end-porch, and three in the front entryway. Altogether five triple-porch structures were raised. Besides the one in Ashburnham, they were built in Shrewsbury, Massachusetts (ca. 1780), Westhampton (1783) and Andover, Massachusetts (1788), and Milton, New Hampshire (1803). While unusual, they do provide an emblematic connection to the sixteenth-century vernacular outside stairwells—such as those at the 1566 Paradis temple at Lyon, France—from which they had seemingly evolved.

We are now left with a vexing question. Why was the concentration of single-porch, twin-porch, and triple-porch stairwells in relatively well-defined geographical ranges of coastal and upland New England matched by what appears to be their total exclusion from meetinghouses in Rhode Island, Connecticut, and the lower Connecticut Valley? Many towns in these areas had little expectation of building bell towers, and most were expanding their populations as briskly as Massachusetts and New Hampshire. But none is known to have built a single-porch or a double-porch stairwell. Out of an estimated four hundred meetinghouses raised in Connecticut and Rhode Island during the eighteenth century, none was constructed with a single-porch stairwell, and only one was made with twin-stairwell porches (New London, Connecticut, or North Parish [Montville] in 1771). Only four Connecticut meetinghouses—Lebanon (raised in 1731 but enlarged in 1758), Wethersfield (1764), Brooklyn (1771), and Farmington (1771)—were built on an opposed bell tower-and-porch plan.[106] The remainder—99 percent—consistently used inside stairwells located on the southeast and southwest corners.

This difference does not appear to be an architectural issue. The key dimension guiding the use of outside stairwell porches on a meetinghouse was plate height: the higher the stud, the more likely builders would opt for a second tier of galleries rather than outside stairwells. Of 73 meetinghouses built in Connecticut between 1712 and 1766 whose plate size is known, the most common height was twenty feet (24 examples) followed by twenty-four feet (11 examples) and twenty-two feet (7 examples). A roughly similar ratio, however, existed in areas where porches were much more common. Out of 113 meetinghouses built in the same period in Massachusetts whose plate size is known, the most common height was again twenty feet (31 examples), followed by twenty-two feet (15 examples). Much the same ratio existed in Maine and New Hampshire where twenty-foot plate heights again outnumbered all others. So structurally, builders were dealing with an identical set of circumstances. Assuming that a minimum of nine feet was necessary for each tier of galleries, the "typical" meetinghouse throughout New England had at least one tier and may have been capable of receiving a second tier of galleries if it were needed.

A better understanding of regional stairwell variations may be found in nonarchitectural factors, such as the rate of meetinghouse rebuilding, population stability, and church attendance. Simply put, towns that did not build exterior porches either did not need to expand the seating capacities of their meetinghouses or found other ways of doing so—such as readily acceding to the local demands for new parishes. In Rhode Island these practices may have been a matter of colony and state law. Although populations were continually growing in that colony, the absence of an "established" religion and a wide range of denominations of Congregationalists, Separate Congregationalists, Baptists, Seventh-Day Baptists, and Quakers competing for church members kept attendance low for individual parishes. In Rhode Island, space was not a problem because there were already too many Protestant meetinghouses. Connecticut, however, stands out for different reasons. As New England's wealthiest colony,

Connecticut rebuilt its meetinghouses at a somewhat higher rate than other areas, thus providing its communities with larger spaces for worship. Connecticut's population also witnessed a constant migration out of the area, with large numbers of families moving to New York State and the Midwest. Moreover, like Rhode Island, the colony stood out for its numerous thriving Episcopal parishes. Ezra Stiles counted thirty Episcopal parishes in Connecticut in 1761 as opposed to five in Rhode Island, fifteen in Massachusetts, and two in New Hampshire. Each parish might account for a depletion in the ranks of nearby Congregational parishes by forty to eighty families.[107]

In the end, we are left with an architectural topography that was affected by distinct demographic, economic, and geographic patterns. On one hand was an unusually high concentration of single-porch meetinghouses in the relatively impoverished towns along the Massachusetts and Maine coastlines. On the other was a concentration of twin-porch meetinghouses among rapidly growing towns in the uplands of southern and central New Hampshire and Vermont. In between these two forms were opposed bell towers and porches raised through private money, and "porchless" meetinghouses, such as in Rhode Island, Connecticut, and western Massachusetts, where inside stairwells and the absence of exterior porches predominated. So clearly were the geographical lines drawn defining these concentrations that New Englanders living in the first decade of the nineteenth century might be known by the manner in which they reached the gallery of their meetinghouse.

## "Finishing" the Eighteenth-Century Meetinghouse

The pronounced geographical differences reflected in stairwell porches on eighteenth-century meetinghouses rarely show up in finish carpentry, and, when they do, they are more the product of shop or ornamental traditions than of demographic and occupational influences. Eighteenth-century exterior and interior forms belonged to three stylistic modes. First were the taught traditions passed down by succeeding generations of craftsmen. Second was the local interpretation of these taught traditions that sometimes assumed regional qualities. Third were the vernacular impulses that seemed to come from nowhere, producing designs such as the turned heart-perforated hourglass holder made in 1729 for the meetinghouse in Salisbury, Massachusetts, later installed in the 1785 meetinghouse in West Salisbury (now Amesbury). In general, whereas the exteriors of meetinghouses changed radically in the second period, the interior furniture—the pulpit, pulpit surrounds, principal pews, and gallery fronts—retained the forms they had acquired at the beginning of the eighteenth century. Access to light and space still dominated the meetinghouse, the pulpit was still a schoolhouse "desk," Communion tables still hung down from the deacons' bench, pew sides were still relieved by spindled openings, and "settles" were still being fashioned to house the pulpit hourglass (fig. 6.40).[108]

Nevertheless, though these basic forms were less subject to change, their handling by carpenters and joiners became considerably more influenced by Georgian decorative modes imported into New England through newly arrived plan books and by recent immigrants skilled in woodworking. Classical orders

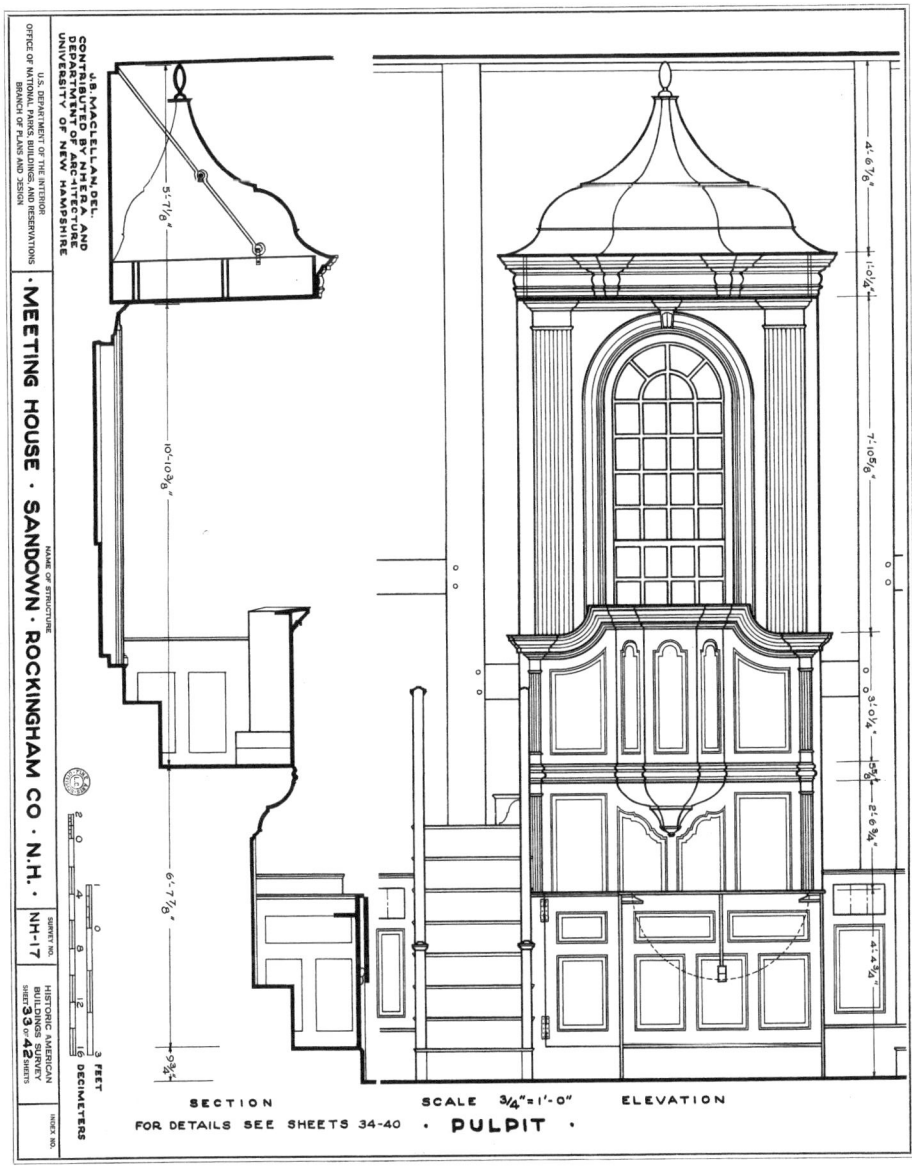

Figure 6.40. Architectural illustration of the pulpit installed at Sandown, New Hampshire, in 1773–1774. Drawn by J. D. McLellan for the Historic American Buildings Survey, 1936. Library of Congress, Washington, D.C.

began to appear in carpentry details. Outer surfaces became rusticated. Colors and textiles were introduced. Pulpits were now decorated with plush cushions and cloth hangings; pulpit surrounds were flanked by decorative columns; pulpit window surrounds and window casings were marbleized or mahogonized; canopies were ornamented by carved decorative emblems. While these "advances" were unrelated to the liturgical or architectural pretensions of compass-headed windows, gabled rooflines, and standing bell towers, they solidified the Georgian presence found in New England houses of worship by promoting a closer association to refined and patristic English taste. Carpenters and joiners were learning a new English artisanal aesthetic that in some ways was more superficial than seventeenth-century joinery but that nevertheless introduced a new decorative taste in public architecture (fig. 6.41).

The vocabulary of Georgian design was mentioned occasionally in town meetings. Bluehill, Maine, voted for covings for the roof of their new meetinghouse in 1792, specifying "what is called a double Cornish only." They also voted for "Crowns for the Windows" and in 1793 for porch doors to be "crowned with

Figure 6.41. Balcony and pewing in the 1785 Rocky Hill meetinghouse, Amesbury (formerly West Salisbury), Massachusetts, before restoration in the mid-twentieth century. Photograph by Arthur C. Haskell, Historic American Buildings Survey, Library of Congress, Washington, D.C.

pediments in manner with the front door."[109] More commonly these terms appeared in the written contracts issued by building committees or in plans submitted by carpenters and designers. These went far beyond the usual seventeenth-century instructions to provide a "plain" or "comely" appearance, and they help amplify our understanding of the full extent of English influence on meetinghouse architecture in the late colonial and post-Revolutionary periods. Whereas Aaron Cleveland's 1728 agreement for Malden's third meetinghouse ordered that the "handsome Galleries [openings] upon the Squares" of the steeple have modillions, later meetinghouse documents cite specific classical architectural orders.[110] The 1785 contract issued for the new meetinghouse in South Weymouth, Massachusetts, called for the outside doors to be "cased in the Doric order of architecture with their columns, consisting of bases and shafts, fluted . . . [as well as] their capitals and pitched pediments."[111] In 1787 the committee chosen by the town to complete the meetinghouse in Gardner, Massachusetts, ordered that "the inside . . . be finished according to the Ionic order of work."[112] Dunbarton, New Hampshire, a small town just south of Concord, specified in 1789 that the structure was to be finished on the inside and outside in "Tuscan order." And Warwick, Massachusetts, instructed its builder, Samuel Langley, to make for its 1786 meetinghouse an octagonal canopy whose "top [was] to be turned with an O.G." and "the entablature to be by the Corinthian order, except the modillion."[113]

Additional detail is occasionally provided by scale drawings that were prepared to accompany these instructions. Specifications for a pulpit, a pulpit window, and a canopy have been found in the papers of Maj. John Dunlap, a New Hampshire furniture maker, who prepared them about 1783 for the towns of Temple and Londonderry in southern New Hampshire (fig. 6.42). According to this document, the pulpit window was to be flanked by "capital[s]" and by "pillars eight inches wide" and topped by a "flowered OG and bead" molding. Below the canopy were "Eggs and Anchors Dentils." Under the desk was an "Inch and a half Cornice" set off with thirty-inch-high pillars using three flutes, and "near the End five flutes." A spiral finial was stipulated for the top of the canopy.[114]

Contracts naturally reflected a community's financial stake in the meetinghouse. Kensington, a Connecticut parish about twelve miles south of Hartford, voted in 1714 that its pulpit and pews should be built "battin [batten] fashion," presumably meaning with vertical siding whose joints are covered by narrow strips—a relatively inexpensive approach.[115] Woodstock, Connecticut, however, voted in 1720 that its pulpit and sounding board be "quarter-round wainscot, [with] fluted pilasters [on] each side its window" with the structure's lower windows "cased 'after the present fashion.'" The seats near the pulpit were also to be "quarter round wainscot" with the remainder of the seats done in "plain" work.[116] Similar terms entered into diary accounts. Alexander Hamilton, who passed through Boston in 1744, reported that the pulpit surrounds in the West or Lynde

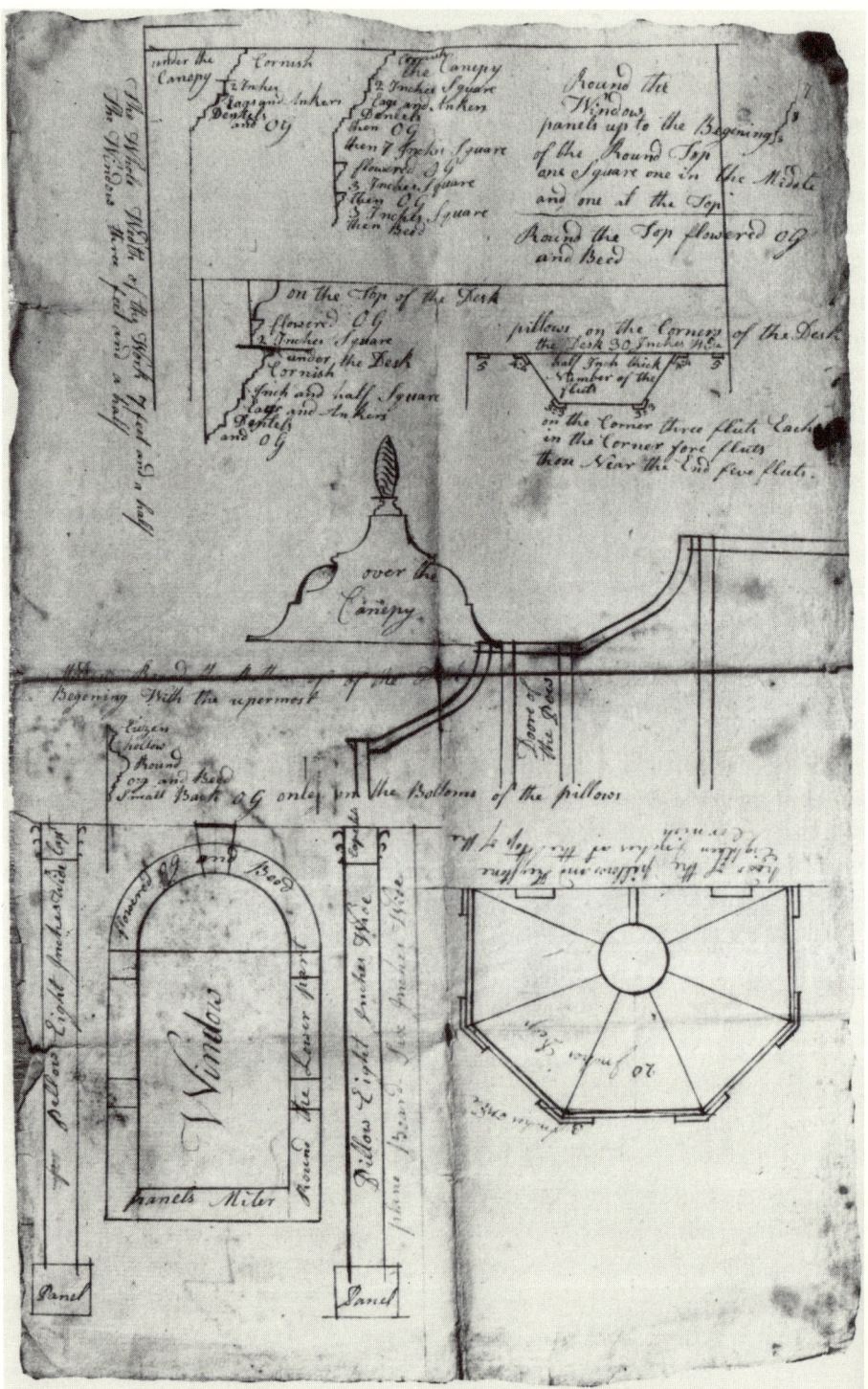

Figure 6.42. Working plan for a pulpit, pulpit window, and pulpit surrounds attributed to Maj. John Dunlap, Bedford, New Hampshire, last quarter of the eighteenth century. Said to have been used in Temple and Londonderry, New Hampshire, circa 1783. Private collection. From William N. Banks, "History in Towns," 716. Originally published in *The Magazine Antiques*, Brant Publications, Inc., October 1975.

Street meetinghouse in that town had a sounding board "supported at each side with pilasters of the Dorick order." He also noted that every window in the structure was "mounted with green curtains."[117]

Occasional examples of pulpits or pulpit fragments found in museum collections, church storage, and meetinghouse survivals help clarify these details. In 1714 East Haven voted for what may have been Connecticut Colony's second "flat"-roofed meetinghouse when it stipulated that its forty-by-thirty-foot frame be covered by a roof "jutted at each end"—a sign that the parish was looking ahead, not back.[118] But five years later when finish carpenters were completing the interior, they were told that the pulpit and seats were to "be in the form of the Branford meeting house," a first-period structure built in 1699 less than five miles away. The surviving three-panel oak front from the East Haven pulpit, built about 1719, now in the collection of the New Haven Museum and Historical Society (fig. 6.43), appears to be a transitional form between the self-standing

Figure 6.43. Joined oak pulpit front used in the first meetinghouse in East Haven, Connecticut, circa 1719. Height 33 inches, width 30 inches. New Haven Museum and Historical Society.

type built for Medfield (or even the "wainscot" pulpit built for Topsfield by Samuel Symons in 1681) and the wall-attached Georgian forms of the eighteenth century. There is no evidence suggesting it was part of a multiple occupant pulpit in which elders and deacons faced the congregation. The three panels supported the desk (now missing). Only in their construction are these panels linked to the first period, featuring a joined treatment of the pulpit rather than the batten construction then becoming popular among newly formed towns.

Nevertheless, East Haven and Branford were relatively recent Connecticut towns and were unlikely to have allocated their small resources for expensive pulpits. An example of a more decorative treatment is Richard Munday's 1729 pulpit for Newport's Seventh-Day Baptist congregation, now preserved with its canopy at the Newport Historical Society. Reached by a stairway with dramatically turned spiral balusters, the pulpit is supported by a wineglass stem and a circular base set off by ten Corinthian pilasters; the pilasters are continued behind the pulpit, leading to a heavily modillioned canopy that has the same profile as the pulpit itself.

Equally impressive are the pine pulpit and canopy built by Abraham Knowlton (1699–1751) and his son Abraham for the 1749 meetinghouse of the First Church in Ipswich. Like other eighteenth-century survivals, the Ipswich pulpit consists of an elevated platform and desk supported by a carved shell-form base; above hangs a decorated square canopy. In this instance, rather than the more common vertical projection in the front used in East Haven and Newport, Knowlton added a double-indented, curved podium whose massing resembles the bombé form characteristic of some fine Boston cabinet furniture of a slightly later date (fig. 6.44). The pulpit itself was flanked by "Corinthian Gilt Capital(s)." The canopy and pulpit were painted to imitate mahogany; for this purpose Knowlton charged the town for "white lead" and "amber." David Kimball's history of the Ipswich parish tells us the pulpit itself was designed and begun by Knowlton but was completed by his nineteen-year-old son after Knowlton succumbed to a chill he received while working in the belfry.[119]

Although Ipswich at this time was one of the most important seacoast towns in eastern Essex County, the ambitious decorative treatment of Knowlton's pulpit may also have been a function of a major 1747 rift in the Ipswich community when the southside residents of the town separated and built their own meetinghouse, hiring a Boston artificer to make the pulpit. Sensitive to potential competition from the new society, the First Parish instructed Knowlton to spare no effort in outdoing the "unpretentious" southside pulpit, which was said to have been simply "painted white." To ensure that Knowlton would not be held back, a group of Ipswich subscribers, who were still members of the First Parish, contributed considerable sums privately to help pay the costs. Sixty

Figure 6.44. Pulpit from the fourth meetinghouse in Ipswich, Massachusetts, designed by Abraham Knowlton of Ipswich, 1749, and probably completed by his son. Pine, painted in mahogany grain. Height 80 inches, length 96 inches. Courtesy of the First Church in Ipswich, Massachusetts.

years later the reputation of this pulpit continued to circulate. When William Bentley visited the First Parish meetinghouse in 1810, he noted in his diary that "a Mr. Knowlton entered into competition & let his pride assist this execution which was unexampled at that day."[120] Bentley was born ten years after the pulpit was built, and his informant may have been the Ipswich minister whom he was visiting.

Few designers or designer-carpenters equaled Richard Munday's or Abraham Knowlton's expertise in wood. But some kind of decorative treatment was common even in remote towns and parishes. A relatively untouched survival, housed in the basement of the 1773 First Parish meetinghouse in Shirley, Massachusetts, exhibits a full pulpit front with an edged modillion and six pilasters. A similar pulpit is still in use at the Congregational church in Shrewsbury. More modest ones are found in the 1785 Rocky Hill meetinghouse in West Salisbury (now Amesbury), Massachusetts, and in the Sandown and Danville, New Hampshire, meetinghouses (built in 1773 and 1755, respectively), all three of which are maintained as museums. Of these perhaps the best survival is Rocky

Hill, whose pulpit and pulpit canopy feature a dentilled cornice. Use of batten construction allowed even a parish as modest as the south precinct of Mendon, now Millville, Massachusetts, to offer its parishioners a decorated pulpit, pulpit surrounds, and canopy in 1769.

Comparable treatments embellished pulpit accessories such as the canopy, or sounding board, and the pulpit window surrounds. Always a mark of prestige in addition to amplifying sound, eighteenth-century canopies continued a tradition brought over from England in the seventeenth century practiced by both church and state authorities. (Pews reserved for Massachusetts governors in Boston meetinghouses, for example, had canopies suspended over them.) In eighteenth-century meetinghouses, their usual form was an octagon suspended by an iron rod or, equally commonly, five-eighths of an octagon—the three missing sides cut off by the wall where it was attached. The canopy of William Bentley's East Parish meetinghouse in Salem, Massachusetts, had this structure; two iron rods held it to the wall. A few canopies were hexagons—such as at the first meetinghouse of the Second Parish in Marblehead, built in 1716—or were large rectangles with a projection in the center matching the profile of the pulpit desk—such as at the fourth meetinghouse in Ipswich.

Canopy finials received special treatment. At least three Massachusetts finials assumed the shape of spirals or flames—Dorchester in 1743, Concord in 1744 (fig. 6.45), and Shrewsbury in about 1770—a design conforming to Georgian modes and probably carved by local furniture craftsmen. Two others—Berlin, Massachusetts, in 1787, and Jaffrey, New Hampshire, in 1775, were carved as pineapples; three are known in the form of acorns (Henniker, New Hampshire, and Newbury West Precinct and Ludlow, Massachusetts), and one in the shape of a pine cone (New Ipswich, New Hampshire).[121] Salem's Tabernacle and the meetinghouse in Westmoreland, New Hampshire, had a dove perched on the top of their sounding boards.[122] And a late nineteenth-century historian of Amesbury, Massachusetts, remembers an eagle "with his widespread wings" over the pulpit canopy at the 1761 Sandy Hill meetinghouse. One finial was unexpectedly flamboyant. The builders of Newburyport's Presbyterian meetinghouse in 1756 capped the pulpit canopy with a fifteen-inch rosette fashioned from a single piece of wood—probably by a ship carver—as a way to embellish the colossal one-hundred-by-sixty-foot proportions of the meetinghouse (fig. 6.46).[123]

In the Connecticut River Valley, local designs evolved. The shell-form pulpit base from Southington, Connecticut, installed in the town's second meetinghouse about 1757, is virtually identical to the base of the 1764 pulpit in Wethersfield.[124] Since the towns are about sixteen miles apart, it is likely that both bases were the product of the same craftsman or shop. Moreover, similar shells dated from the 1750s to the 1780s can still be found in more distant parts of the Connecticut River Valley and in areas that came under the influence of Connecticut Valley styles. These include the survivals at Ludlow (1783) and at East Hampton, Long Island (1750).

Contemporary authors recorded other instances of dramatic Connecticut River Valley themes. We have already witnessed the "English ivy" and "wondrous green vines" Judah Woodruff carved into the pulpit and sounding board at Farmington.[125] But perhaps the most vivid description is given by the American abolitionist author Harriet Beecher Stowe (1811–1896), whose father, Lyman Beecher (1775–1863), was the minister in Litchfield, Connecticut, in the early nineteenth century. (She, too, wondered what would happen if the pulpit canopy should fall on him.) In her reminiscences she reflects on her youthful impressions of the second meetinghouse in Litchfield, a substantial sixty-by-forty-five-foot building with a bell tower erected in 1762 and torn down in 1827: "How I did wonder at the panels on either side of the pulpit, in each of which was carved and painted a flaming red tulip, with its leaves projecting out at right

Figure 6.45. Flame finial from the canopy of the third meetinghouse in Concord, Massachusetts, erected 1711. Dating to about 1744, the pine finial is painted gold and red with a blue base. Height 17 inches. Concord Museum, Concord, Massachusetts.

Figure 6.46. Rosette finial from the canopy of the First Presbyterian Church, Newburyport, Massachusetts, built in 1756. Pine, diameter 15.5 inches. Historical Society of Old Newbury.

angles, and then at the grapevine, in bas-relief, on the front, with exactly triangular bunches of grapes alternating at exact intervals."[126] Stowe's descriptions are corroborated by the survival of three pulpit fragments from Litchfield's eighteenth-century meetinghouse. These consist of two pilaster capitals decorated with a six-petal rose, painted or dyed red (fig. 6.47), and an applied section of wood carved in the form of a vine stem. While no trace of other "flaming red tulip[s]" has come to light, the inspiration for it undoubtedly had much in common with the decorative and architectural motifs that have survived on furniture and doorways from Connecticut Valley towns such as Wethersfield, Hatfield, Deerfield, and Westfield. Similar six-petal roses are found on the pilaster capitals of the pulpit installed at the 1764 meetinghouse in Wethersfield. A photograph taken by Eva Speare in 1938 shows that this pulpit front consists of five panels—two on each side of the desk, each one flanked by pilasters with tulip capitals, and three beneath the desk flanked by pilasters ornamented with carved floral festoons.[127]

Two more complete fragments from this period have survived from the meetinghouse in East Hampton, Long Island, where Lyman Beecher was pastor before his installation at Litchfield. One is a pulpit front and shell-form base decorated with carved and painted vine-and-flower motifs within the vertical

Figure 6.47. Detail of a pilaster capital carved with a rose motif from the pulpit of the second meetinghouse in Litchfield, Connecticut, erected in 1762. Pine, width approximately 4 inches. Collection of the Litchfield Historical Society, Litchfield, Connecticut.

quarter moldings; pomegranates or flowers are picked out in red against a black background (fig. 6.48). The second is a pilaster capital from the pulpit surrounds that has the multiple-foliated "Corinthian" designs characteristic of the most ambitious Connecticut Valley doorways (fig. 6.49). Both show evidence of reapplications of their original red, black, yellow, and green colors.[128] This is the so-called Buell Pulpit named after Samuel Buell (1716–1798), the third minister in East Hampton, who served from 1746 to 1798. The design appears to match one pulpit in the Connecticut River Valley itself, remembered in 1883 by the former pastor of the First Church in Longmeadow. He recalled its being decorated by "carved work of grapes and pomegranates under the great sounding board."[129]

At least one Connecticut Valley pulpit motif can be linked to the designs of an eighteenth-century gravestone maker. This ornamentation is found on the pulpit surrounds of the 1783 meetinghouse in Ludlow, which was converted into a grange by extending the gallery into a second floor and cutting the pulpit window in half. While the lower half is now obscured, the upper is still visible, revealing carved vines, each growing from a mound, and each probably painted like the Litchfield examples to stand out against its background (figs. 6.50 and 6.51). Only a few hundred feet away is the Ludlow burying ground containing a gravestone produced by a family of carvers whose second generation signed their stones "C. Sikes" and "E. Sikes." Little is known of this family; they were active from the late eighteenth to the early nineteenth centuries, and their markers are distributed east of the Connecticut River in south-central Massachusetts and north-central Connecticut. They may have been the brothers

Figure 6.48. Carved and painted pulpit front and base installed in 1756 in the 1717 meetinghouse in East Hampton, Long Island. This is called the "Buell pulpit" after the Rev. Samuel Buell, the third minister, who assumed office in 1746. Pine; height 77 inches, width 33 inches, depth 17 inches. East Hampton Historical Society, Long Island, New York. Photograph provided by N. Sherrill Foster.

Figure 6.49. Carved and painted pilaster capital (or keystone) from the 1756 Buell pulpit installed in the 1717 meetinghouse in East Hampton, Long Island. Pine; height 17 inches, width 7 inches, depth 4 inches. East Hampton Historical Society, Long Island, New York. Photograph provided by N. Sherrill Foster.

Calvin and Elihu Sikes, born in Ludlow in 1779 and 1790, respectively. The likelihood that a Sikes family craftsman was responsible for the Ludlow pulpit vines is strengthened by the fact that three members of the Sikes family were in some way connected with the meetinghouse. Abner Sikes was part of a committee to locate the meetinghouse in 1774. John Sikes, born 1748 and the father of Calvin and Elihu, was one of a committee of five chosen in 1783 to erect the building. Pliny Sikes was ordered to "dispose of the lumber and other materials" after the completion of the interior in 1797.[130]

The Connecticut Valley decorative style extended well beyond its nominal borders. When Alice Morse Earle was compiling materials in the 1880s for *Sabbath in Puritan New England*, many eighteenth-century meetinghouses were still standing in eastern Massachusetts. She noted in her travels that communities well outside the Connecticut River subregion were using what appear to have been comparable motifs. The canopy in the 1784 Leicester, Massachusetts, meetinghouse was decorated with "a carved bunch of grapes or pomegranates"; the one in Shrewsbury, Massachusetts, with "carved and painted rosettes." In the latter instance we have a better sense of what Earle may have been talking about because two fragments from the Shrewsbury pulpit have been preserved (figs. 6.52 and 6.53). The first is a hollow, carved flame finial painted dark green with

Figures 6.50 and 6.51. Place-specific vine motifs in the Connecticut Valley. *Left:* Pulpit surrounds from the second meetinghouse in Ludlow, Massachusetts, built in 1783. Pine, height of image approximately 18 inches. *Right:* Detail of a gravestone made for Daniel, son of Lt. Isaac and Sybil Brewer, Ludlow, Massachusetts. Attributed to the Sikes family, circa 1790–1800. Photographs by the author.

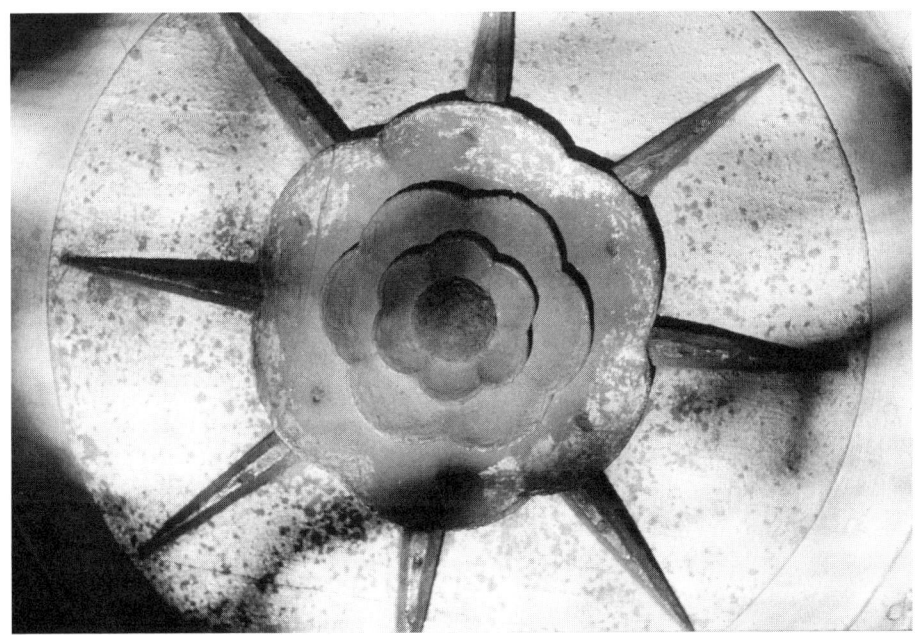

Figures 6.52 and 6.53. Flame finial (*right*) and escutcheon ornamental centerpiece (*below*) from the pulpit canopy of the meetinghouse in Shrewsbury, Massachusetts, raised in 1766. Carved and painted pine, circa 1770. Height of finial 14 inches; diameter of centerpiece 12 inches. From the collections of the Shrewsbury Historical Society, Shrewsbury, Massachusetts. Photographs by the author.

interior red; the second, a carved and painted multifoliated flower centerpiece designed for the underside of the canopy. They use the same green, gold, and red colors. And though neither has the vibrant red color and stylized designs of the Litchfield and East Hampton survivals, they do suggest that painted motifs related to those of the Connecticut Valley extended well into central Worcester County.[131]

The dissemination of these painted motifs and other academic and classical decorative orders on eighteenth-century meetinghouses followed the path of copybooks and shared plans and a neighbor-to-neighbor chain of imitations like those already witnessed in the seventeenth century. Of the almost 100 imitations that have been documented during the second period, about 1 out of every 5 concentrated on finish carpentry, including the construction of pulpits, pulpit windows surrounds, and pews. Most models were less than ten miles distant and virtually all were less than thirty. We can assume that craftsmen reinterpreted their models as they passed from one meetinghouse to another, though we do not always know what a particular pulpit or its pulpit surrounds looked like. When the brothers John and Thomas Dick were given a model by which to build Pelham's pulpit in 1743, for example, they were directed to make it in "Dignity like unto Hadley third Precinct [Amherst]"—a few miles west.[132] That Amherst's pulpit may have shared some elements of the Connecticut Valley style is suggested by a remnant shell-form decoration on a pilaster that is still seen on the second floor at Pelham. Very likely it represented the Dick brothers' interpretation of Hadley's "dignity."

Some records are highly specific and identify the names of the ministers whose pews, pulpit, or pulpit surrounds were being replicated. When South Weymouth, Massachusetts, was completing its new meetinghouse in 1785, the town drew on the decorative and architectural features that it had long admired in the meetinghouses of its neighbors. The same contract directing carpenters to case the outside doors in "the Doric order in architecture" also instructs them to make the pulpit, the sounding board, and the deacons' seat "in the same manner they are in the Revd. Mr. Taft's Meeting house." The contract further stipulates that the pulpit window be cased like the one in "Mr. Wibard meeting-house"—both to be painted in "lead color" with linseed oil as a base. Moses Taft and Anthony Wibard were clergymen in Braintree's first and third parishes, respectively (now Quincy and Randolph, Massachusetts), located at distances of approximately seven and eight miles. Taft preached in a relatively old meetinghouse raised fifty-three years earlier; Wibard, in a more recent one completed in 1763.[133] Regrettably we do not know whether these features were admired because they were traditional, dignified, comely, familiar, or simply inexpensive. Nor do we know whether their "manner" (meaning style) in any way matched the Doric treatment of the pillars and capitals. What we do know is that citing the ministers by name reveals how well known their respective "dignity[s]" resonated in the South Shore area of Massachusetts Bay, leading to a process that made the act of imitation sound almost personal.

## Architectural Colors

The painted treatment of wood specified in the 1785 South Weymouth contract provides still another demonstration of the growing public awareness of visual worship. Even if these surfaces were subdued, meetinghouses alive with architectural colors were a major change from first-period and early second-period practices. But the physical evidence of this most vernacular element in the eighteenth-century meetinghouse is almost always evanescent. To date few surviving meetinghouses have offered reliable color data; most information comes from town and parish votes as well as personal memories.[134] But colors, like bell towers, were a decisive component of changing fashion, and they make available critical information about the aspirations of the towns and parishes that selected them. They also provide a rare insight into the geography of architectural drift. More than any other element of the second-period New England meetinghouse, colors offer believable data by which the patterns of "cluster" dissemination can be clearly identified.

Seventeenth-century meetinghouses were infrequently colored or even stained. John Gilbert, who prepared the ironwork in 1678 on the 1677 meetinghouse in Springfield, was paid six shillings for painting the iron window casements and one shilling six pence for two quarts of oil, the first recorded application of color to a New England meetinghouse. Four years later Joshua Lincoln was paid five shillings for "coloring the casements" of the Old Ship meetinghouse in Hingham; he was also paid to color "other wood-work." Did this mean interior elements such as the pulpit, wainscoting, and gallery fronts? Did it include exterior doors and door frames? Most of these features, including the windows, were replaced when the Old Ship was remodeled in the 1750s. That the Hingham pulpit probably did have some color treatment is suggested by the discovery of fragments of verdigris paint on two surviving carved oak panels from the 1655 pulpit installed in Medfield, Massachusetts.[135]

The use of color in the early eighteenth century is a little more revealing but still inconclusive. The selectmen in Westfield directed in 1697 that their meetinghouse be repaired and painted "to make it comely and comfortable."[136] We do not know what this phrase means, however. A little more suggestive is a 1714 document that records Edward Pell, the painter-stainer and former apprentice to Thomas Child, as having been paid fifty-four pounds by the First Church of Boston "for painting the Brick meeting house." This was the same Edward Pell who seven years later designed the New Brick meetinghouse in

Boston with its innovative cupola tower. Fifty-four pounds was a substantial sum of money in 1714, and most likely his contract included the painting of casement windows and possibly the outside doors. If he did any interior work, it was probably limited to the pulpit and pulpit window. At some later point Pell, or another painter, applied a coat of the same light beige or stone color that is visible on James Brown Marston's 1801 view of this structure.[137] But painting was not limited to large urban meetinghouses. The west precinct in Watertown, Massachusetts, which in 1721 had just purchased Newton's meetinghouse to save themselves money, paid George Adams for two and a half days' work to apply "oil and Spanish Brown."[138] A second man was paid for "two oil cask[s] and 5 days Board."[139] The time given these tasks suggests they involved exterior surfaces and possibly the roof.

By the late 1720s more convincing evidence begins to appear that exteriors were being painted. Aaron Cleveland's 1728 contract for the triple-decker meetinghouse in Malden called for him to "color the outside [of] said house as followeth with a lead color" (presumably a medium to dark gray). The document included the "Steeple and [steeple] Galleries and all the Modillions and the fatheers [?] Weather Boards and Window frames with the cases Troughs & Trunks with the Shells over each Door."[140] A second example comes from Wallingford, Connecticut. According to the county historian Mary Mitchell, who was writing in the late 1920s, the New Cheshire Society in that town voted a "few years" after 1735 to "put on a good handsome paint on the meeting-house: in order to preserve the same from the weather."[141]

Much of the data before 1750, however, is inconclusive. In 1738 the builder Thomas Dick was paid £3.10.0 by the town of Petersham, Massachusetts, for "coloring the meeting-house." And in the next decade, in 1742 Madison, Connecticut, voted to "color our new meeting-house a lead color"; in 1743 Thomas Dick was paid for painting portions of the meetinghouse in Pelham, Massachusetts, "Askie color" (ashen gray or blue); and in 1744 Samuel Harriman was paid £20 for "Redding the meeting-house" of the Second Parish in Rowley (now Georgetown, Massachusetts), two years after Daniel Spofford enlarged the building. Most of these citations offer tantalizing information but leave unclear whether interior or exterior surfaces were involved. At least one Rowley historian writing in 1840 was convinced that "Redding the meeting-house" involved an outside coat, but that phrase too may just as well have referred to interior woodwork.[142]

Much more data are available from later in the eighteenth century. In 1748 the newly created Second Parish in Mendon, Massachusetts (later renamed Milford), voted "to color the Meeting House doors, window frames, weather boards, corner boards, eve troughs and the two bottom boards." Mendon was an old, relatively impoverished town in central Massachusetts, but the vote of its second parish is the first documented use of color painted on specific places on the exterior of a meetinghouse—in this instance on every outside surface except the roof.[143] The result may have been startling and provocative. The neighboring town of Westborough, the home of the diarist Rev. Ebenezer Parkman, refused in 1754 to "culler the outside of the meeting house," perhaps thinking that Mendon had taken the idea of exterior decoration to excess.[144] (Westborough did vote to color the pulpit.) And other towns applied exterior colors sparingly. The First Parish in Rowley set aside eight pounds in 1764 for "painting the Windows, Doors, Covens [coves?], Corner Boards, Wash boards & Spouts of the Meetinghouse."[145]

After the mid-eighteenth century, New England towns may have been applying exterior color routinely. The First Parish in Ipswich hired Thomas Lawlor in 1755 to prime, paint, and gild portions of both the inside and outside of their new meetinghouse; his account included 52½ pounds of white and stone color, 1½ gallons of boiled oil, 1 quart and a pint of turpentine, and 6½ pounds of chocolate pigment for a total bill of more than £292—a price so high it may have also involved considerable exterior painting. Lawlor's bill, incidentally, is the first known meetinghouse reference to chocolate doors in New England, a hue that presumably simulated mahogany. Leominster, Massachusetts, voted to color the "outside" of its meetinghouse in 1753; that same year Hadley, Massachusetts, to "cover the body . . . with quarter-boards and [to] color it." North Brookfield, Massachusetts, colored its clapboards in 1756. Lebanon, Connecticut, painted the west side the same color as the tower in 1758. East Haven, Connecticut, even invoked the religious purpose of the meetinghouse in choosing a color. When the town voted to color the new clapboards recently installed on its thirty-year-old meetinghouse in 1748, the voters selected a paint—unfortunately of unknown hue—"suitable for the house of God."[146]

Whether motivated by a sense of reverence or simply by the desire to preserve wood, the exterior painting of buildings frequently involved the efforts of the entire town. Northfield, Massachusetts, asked farmers to "take extra pains with their flax fields" in 1788, and the following winter 42½ bushels of flax seeds were taken to Boston and exchanged for "paints and oil." The town's meetinghouse was then painted in the summer of 1789. In 1796 Jaffrey, New Hampshire, hauled 70 bushels of flax seed to a crushing mill at New Ipswich to provide oil for painting its meetinghouse. Four years later Jaffrey squared its account with Nathan Barnard, a "public spirited citizen," who was given one dollar for furnishing kettles and firewood "to boil the oil to paint the meeting house." Towns also drew on a variety of oils. Berlin, Massachusetts, added 2 barrels of fish oil to the 65 gallons of linseed oil used to paint its meetinghouse in 1794; Shrewsbury, Massachusetts, combined 32 gallons of fish oil with 29½ gallons of linseed oil for painting repairs undertaken on its meetinghouse in 1808.[147]

Jaffrey's and Berlin's accounts also record that each town procured a considerable amount of white lead to mix into its paint. Jaffrey received approximately 200 pounds by ox cart from Concord and Keene; Berlin procured 400 pounds from Boston. When used alone, fish oil and linseed oil were absorbed into wood. White lead oxide provided an opaque patina or body in which coloring pigments stood out clearly. If the procedures outlined in Hezekiah Reynolds's 1812 *Directions for House and Ship Painting* were being followed, the kettles would have been brass or copper and the oil allowed to "simmer or boil very gently over a slow fire, until clarified." Reynolds's directions reveal that white lead was purchased in a dry state and that it was finely ground and mixed with a color before being combined with boiled linseed oil. He advised that the mixture not be so thick as to "clog the brush; nor so thin as to run upon the board." The 1788 painting of the third meetinghouse in Northampton, Massachusetts (a 1736 steepled building, seventy by forty-six feet), required 700 pounds of white lead, 140 gallons of oil, and 200 pounds of spruce yellow. The 1794 painting of the 1779 twin-porch meetinghouse in Berlin, Massachusetts, involved 500 pounds of white lead and approximately 100 gallons of oil, as well as verdigris and Spanish brown. Both followed a ratio of five pounds of white lead for each gallon of oil.[148]

In all, 229 sources of evidence have been uncovered for exterior paint used on meetinghouses in New England and Long Island from 1678 to 1828 (see Appendix E). These involve approximately 182 structures, and they are documented primarily from town and parish records, diaries, town histories, and reminiscences, but also from other sources such as landscape paintings, school art, surveyors' diagrams, survivals, paint analyses, and meetinghouse names. Of these citations, approximately 131 offer a discernible idea of exterior pigmentation. Though not all is understood about them, they contrast strongly with the "white" and "plain colors" sometimes cited for ecclesiastic structures in Virginia and the Carolinas during this period and suggest that fifth-, sixth-, and seventh-generation New England and Long Island Puritans were intensely aware of color and had a taste for bright ones.[149] Fifty-one of the meetinghouses documented in New England and Long Island were painted with varieties of yellow (light yellow, straw color, spruce yellow, yellow ochre, French yellow, dirty, dark or dingy yellow). Thirty-five were white. Sixteen were stone color (dark stone color, bright stone color). Ten were red (red ochre or peach-blossom). Eight were orange or bright orange. Seven were blue or sky blue. Five were green (pea green, dark green, verdigris, or olive). Four were tan, brown, or Spanish brown. And four were shades of gray (lead, askie, or slate). Clearly, colors were overwhelmingly more popular than plain white. Just as clearly, white was only one of many colors and significantly predated the introduction of Greek Revival architectural motifs into New England in the 1830s when most New England meetinghouses and churches were painted uniformly white or stone color. Unclassifiable but still vibrant was the scheme voted in 1792 by the Second or South Parish in Harwich, Massachusetts, which ordered that the ends and porch of its new meetinghouse be colored with yellow ochre; the backside, roof, and the area above the jets red; the jets, corner boards, weatherboards, window frames, door casings, and window sashes white; and the ground boards and doors be "of chocolate color."[150]

Some colors—for example, reds and peach-blossom colors—showed little or no geographic distribution. The earliest application may have been the "redded" meetinghouse in the Georgetown Parish in Rowley in 1744, but there were others. From William Bentley's diary we learn that the second meetinghouse in Hatfield, Massachusetts, had one or more coats of exterior red paint before 1793. (Bentley was glad to see the red covered up with something more "ornamental.")[151] The four red meetinghouses nearest to Hatfield were the Orford Parish in Manchester, Connecticut (fifty miles distant), East Plymouth, Connecticut (sixty-one miles distant), and Washington and Alstead, New Hampshire (both about sixty-five miles distant). Washington and Alstead apparently shared a red ochre or barn red color, and it is possible that local historians simply ignored these colors because "redding" was an inexpensive treatment based on readily available iron-oxide colors. An inventory of a Boston house painter in 1684 indicates that "red Lead," "Vermillion," and other red pigments far outnumbered all others, followed by varieties of "Oaker."[152] Moreover, like Harwich, at least two other parishes colored the unseen "back side" of their meetinghouse red or Spanish brown, and the "front side" more elegant stone color or stone yellow (Chatham, Massachusetts, and Hampton, Connecticut).

But there was nothing common about peach-blossom exteriors, presumably created by combining white lead with red ochre. Three of these are known, though again they were not close to one another. One was the 1739 meetinghouse in Killingworth, Connecticut, that is said by a historian writing in 1870 to have been a "peach-blossom color" before it was replaced in 1816. A second was the 1760 meetinghouse in Norfolk, Connecticut, a hill town in Litchfield County, which was remembered as a peach-blow color by a historian writing in 1847. (The *Oxford English Dictionary* tells us "peach-blow" was an early nineteenth-century American term meaning peach blossom color.) (Both historians were ministers of the parish about which they were writing.) The third was in East Hampton, Long Island, known from an 1801 subscription circulated to have the meetinghouse painted "Light red or Peach Bloe [Blow]"—a document suggesting that peach-blow may have been a color of choice around the turn of the nineteenth century.[153]

Greens also lack a defined geography. One striking example is the 1747 meetinghouse in Cohasset, Massachusetts, whose color is known from a mourning picture made in memory of Joseph Joy, a Cohasset sea captain who died in a dockside accident in 1812.[154] Joy is commemorated by a watercolor memorial possibly drawn by his widow, Ellinor Nichols Joy, but more likely by one of his two surviving daughters, Emily or Harriet Joy. While neither the date nor the provenance of this mourning picture is positively known (the daughters were born in 1810 and 1812), the meetinghouse illustrated in the background harbor scene is virtually identical to a nineteenth-century representation by Hosea Sprague (fig. 6.54). Excepting some details of the tower and the baluster railing on the bell tower, the image closely resembles the Cohasset meetinghouse as it stands today and suggests that in 1812 the clapboards and tower were colored green and the accompanying baseboards, doors, and corner boards picked out in white. This color scheme matches the one given by William Bentley, who reported in 1795 that the new third meetinghouse in Lexington was painted "green . . . [with] Sashes & Corners of the House . . . painted white"—the very scheme illustrated in the Cohasset watercolor. Specifying green colors sometimes reveals unexpected detail. In 1790 Woodbury, Connecticut, determined that its meetinghouse would be "near the color of Mr. Timy Tomlinson except it be a little more of a greenish as it." And in 1798 Ashburnham, Massachusetts, took a vote to paint its 1791 meetinghouse a "pea green." The Ashburnham vote was later rescinded and the town chose white.[155]

Exterior colors of yellow fall into rough but relatively distinct geographical and chronological clusters. Yellows and yellow ochres make almost 37 percent of all known colors cited in New England town and parish records before 1830. In general, these were confined to Massachusetts, southern New Hampshire, and Maine, where yellow seems to have been the color of choice. (Yellow ochre was mined for painting houses in New Hampshire.)[156] By contrast, nine are found in Connecticut and none in Rhode Island. The ubiquity of yellow is revealed in old meetinghouse names in these states. The 1794 meetinghouse in Dracut, Massachusetts, still painted yellow when Edmund W. Sinnott saw it in the 1960s, was called "Old Yellow," as were meetinghouses in Rehoboth, Massachusetts, Monroe, New Hampshire, Topsham and Brunswick, Maine, and Milton Green, Connecticut ("Old Yaller"). Yellow meetinghouses are also found in survey maps and schoolwork art. A surveyor's 1823 drawing of Kensington, New Hampshire, shows the 1771 "Congregational Meeting House" as a warm yellow structure with its main door painted a bright orange.[157] A nineteenth-century school-girl-made watercolor map of the center of Rindge, New Hampshire, depicts the 1796 meetinghouse as a yellow building with a red roof.[158]

Typically renewed in cycles of ten or twelve years, yellows tended to drift to stone color, especially after 1788 when towns increasingly specified these shades in an attempt to simulate the building materials of classical architecture. "Bright stone color," "dark stone color," or "yellow stone color"—whatever their actual appearance—helped simulate dressed stone and contributed to the architectural

Figure 6.54. Second meetinghouse in Cohasset, Massachusetts, raised in 1747. One of four woodcuts depicting Hingham and Cohasset meetinghouses by Hosea Sprague, second half of the nineteenth century. Courtesy of the First Parish Old Ship Church in Hingham, Massachusetts.

deception implicit in provincial Georgian and Federalist decorative motifs. By 1796 Jaffrey, New Hampshire, had changed to "light stone color," and in 1802 nearby Winchendon, Massachusetts, had switched to "bright stone color"; three decades later most parishes had turned to "white" and "light yellow." Stone-colored clapboards could be picked out vibrantly with doorway and corner boards. In 1805 Hampton, Connecticut, ordered that its meetinghouse be painted "a Stone yellow . . . the door and bottom boards of a chocolate color." The "Old Sloop" in Scituate was painted a "Dark Stone Color, [and] the . . . Doors a Chocolate Color" in 1774. Canaan, New Hampshire, determined in 1794 that its meetinghouse would be painted "stone color, the roof Spanish Brown, and the doors a sky blue."[159]

As popular as yellow was in Massachusetts and southern New Hampshire, orange dominated a small portion of northeastern Connecticut. A vote taken on 26 April 1762 by Pomfret specified that its large new meetinghouse "be colored on the outside of an orange color—the doors and bottom boards of a chocolate color—the windows, jets, corner boards and weather boards, colored white."[160]

Although this area of eastern Connecticut was later known for its portrait and decorative painters, the source of this unusual color scheme is not clear. Nor do we really know for sure what "orange" meant in the eighteenth century. Was it a true pumpkin color or simply a more concentrated yellow? One nineteenth-century historian called the Pomfret color a "deep" orange. Another recalled being told that this scheme was the "newest, biggest, and yallowest" in Windham County.[161] Nevertheless, it is the first known use of orange, chocolate, and white pigments on a meetinghouse and may be the first known application of orange paint on any kind of building.

Pomfret's vote apparently impressed the neighborhood. At least four (and possibly five) towns in Windham County, Connecticut, and neighboring Worcester County, Massachusetts, quickly imitated Pomfret's orange. The first was Windham itself, the county seat and the only one to have a steepled meetinghouse. A second was Brooklyn, a town immediately south of Pomfret that voted to paint its old (1734) meetinghouse orange. Both took these votes in 1762.[162] A few years later, in 1768 and 1769, Hampton, Pomfret's neighbor to the southeast, ordered the workmen making repairs to its meetinghouse "to color the same something like the color of Pomfret meeting house"; Dudley, just north of Windham County in Massachusetts, voted "to Color our meeting house with an orange Color"; and Killingly Second, North, or Thompson Parish, Pomfret's immediate neighbor to the northeast, which was just widening its meetinghouse by inserting a fourteen-foot section, voted "that the coloring of the body of our meeting house shall be like Pomfret." Thompson Parish's roof was to be "colored Red."[163]

That the practice of using orange as an exterior color may have gradually drifted into other towns in central Massachusetts and southern New Hampshire is suggested by two additional pieces of evidence. Twenty-five years after it was initially selected in Pomfret, the color appears in 1787 on the meetinghouse in Holliston, Massachusetts, about thirty-seven miles to the northeast of Pomfret. The color also reemerges in the "bright orange" clapboards (with stone-gray doors) chosen for the meetinghouse in Gilsum, New Hampshire, in 1791.[164] The Gilsum vote is doubly important because it provides the only documented use of orange paint well outside the Pomfret "pocket" and because Gilsum was a cultural transplant from eastern Connecticut. Originally a Wentworth grant set aside under the name of "Boyle" in 1752, Gilsum was purchased and developed by a group of Connecticut proprietors living in Hebron, Bolton, and Ashford—towns within a twenty-mile radius of Pomfret. The first meetings of the Gilsum proprietors were held in Hebron in 1762. Of the forty-nine heads of household known to be residing in the town before 1791, thirteen had previously lived in Hebron and six in other parts of eastern and central Connecticut. The town's selectmen, officers, and committeemen were largely from Hebron, including those responsible for building the meetinghouse.[165] The presumption is that a plurality of the committee that built the town's new meetinghouse remembered the orange meetinghouses from their childhoods in Connecticut, which suggests that New Hampshire's Connecticut-derived settlers brought with them this preference as part of their cultural heritage.

The story of blue or lead-color has less data but is equally curious. Initially blue and lead-colored meetinghouses seem focused along the Connecticut shoreline and parts of Long Island. For example, Milford erected a large three-tier meetinghouse with a bell tower in 1728; it was called the "blue church" by later historians, indicating it had an early coat of blue or lead-colored paint. The Second Parish in Guilford (now Madison) painted its meetinghouse "lead color" in 1742.[166] The so-called White Haven Society meetinghouse in New Haven was painted blue in 1761 and was known locally after 1764 as the "Blue Meetinghouse." (Abel Stiles, writing to Ezra Stiles on 18 February 1764, is the first person known to use the term, reporting, "there is a great whistness & silence among them, of the blue house since the ordination.") Later, the nineteenth-century New Haven historian Henry T. Blake drew attention to the coding of a colored lithograph print of the 1748 Wadsworth map of New Haven published by Thomas Kensett in 1808 where the printers marked each building on the map with "r" for red or "b" for blue to guide those who colored them. The White Haven meetinghouse was one of those marked "b."[167]

In the meantime the color had spread into rural Connecticut where at least five towns either voted for or applied blue or sky color. Gilead, the Second Parish in Hebron, chose "sky color" in 1749, as did Lebanon Crank (now Columbia) in 1753, and Westbrook, the West Parish in Saybrook, in 1763. Bethany, just northeast of New Haven, voted in 1774 "that the meetinghouse be colored blue, and the windows white." Griswold, a hamlet just northeast of Norwich that painted its meetinghouse in 1767, became known later as "Blue Pachaug," said to have been named after its meetinghouse color.[168]

Again we do not know what "blue," "lead-color," or "sky color" really looked like. Were any of these the vibrant "azure blue" that Henry Blake has suggested? Were they an "ultramarine" or "powder blue" as sold by Boston painter John Gore in 1761? These and Prussian blue in part depended on imported colors and were therefore the most expensive. Or were they all simply a grayish "lead" color that appeared "blue-like" on a clear day? Nor do we know whether blue had any iconic meaning. Anglicans in South Carolina and Virginia painted some of their ceilings with sky color and associated it with heaven.[169] And at least one nineteenth-century Connecticut historian has speculated that blue colors as an exterior paint articulated enthusiastic or separatist religious impulses.[170] His observation is echoed by the landscape historian John R. Stilgoe.[171] According to this point of view, the White Haven Society, a separatist church gathered in opposition to the Old Light minister Joseph Noyes of New Haven's First Church, selected blue as a symbol of resurrection—a way of letting their detractors in Noyes's Old Light Church know that they (and not Noyes's group) were on the right path to salvation. If so, it is entirely possible that "blues" and "sky colors" found in southern and eastern Connecticut and Long Island were a hallmark of eighteenth-century New Light enthusiasm—much as they were a generation later for Shaker societies that specified blue as an exterior color in the sect's Millennial Laws.[172] Like Isaac Watts's translation of the psalms and certain heart- and face-oriented spirit motifs found on Connecticut and Massachusetts gravestones, a blue meetinghouse may have been a way to communicate a new sense of hope in the aftermath of the Great Awakening.[173]

Because the data are inconclusive, these ideas cannot easily be proved or disproved. It is apparent that some of the most lively color groups—orange in Windham and nearby Worcester counties, and sky blue in New London, Tolland, and New Haven counties—were chosen in areas where religious sensibility was elevated and institutionally fragmented. Ezra Stiles drew a similar conclusion. After a visit to that area in 1769, he wrote in his *Itineraries:* "Whatever be the reason, the eastern part[s] of Connecticut . . . are of a very mixt & uncertain character as to religion." He added that "Exhorters, Itinerants, [and] Separate Meetings rose in that part," an emphasis shared by at least one other minister in that region who kept a diary similar to his. In Lebanon, religious excitement was so strong Rev. Jacob Eliot reported that in March and April 1742 "young men and Indians" regularly went about from parish to parish interrupting his service. He was obliged to wait an entire month before he could write in his diary that there were "No Exhorters at meeting."[174]

WITHIN, THE eighteenth-century house of worship complemented its exterior with patterns and treatments of its own. Overall, ninety-nine sources of evidence on interior color specifications have emerged between 1656 to 1817 (see Appendix F). Some treatments were muted. After approving new plastering work in 1713, the vestry committee at King's Chapel, Boston, voted to have the pillars, capitals, and cornice painted "wainscot Colur" before the scaffolds were taken down. But sometimes they were strikingly bold. In their architectural investigation of the 1681 Old Ship in Hingham in 2006 Brian Powell and Andrea Gilmore uncovered evidence of sponge or daub painting on the posts in an area that had been protected by the installation of a new pulpit. It consisted of red spots on a whitewash background, probably done in the 1720s or 1730s. While much of this evidence has degraded, they concluded after close study it was an intentional pattern rather than simply extraneous paint. If so, it reveals an early treatment of whitewash interior finish on a meetinghouse post that parallels domestic usage.[175]

The documentary record for interior paint is less tangible but probably more reliable. The most common pulpit or canopy color in the eighteenth and early nineteenth centuries was blue (nine examples). These display great variety. The third (1750) meetinghouse in Hatfield, Massachusetts, whose interior was photographed before its accidental destruction as it was being moved in 1982, revealed that the canopy, and probably the pulpit itself, was painted robin's egg blue.[176] Varieties of this interior color included "Prussian Blue" (Gilsum, New Hampshire, in 1791), "indigo blue wash" (Portsmouth, New Hampshire, in 1806), "sky blue" (Newport, New Hampshire, in 1810), and "Light-Blue" (Rowe, Massachusetts, in 1814).[177] Other common pulpit colors were "brilliant green," "rich sea green," "dark green," "dark olive-green," and "pea-green" (six examples); light stone or stone color (three examples); lead color (two examples), mustard (two examples), and one example each of clay color and red.[178] William Bentley remembered in 1813 that the pulpit in the first meetinghouse in Arlington, Massachusetts, was a chocolate color at the time of the British occupation of Boston.[179]

Mahoganized, marbleized, and grained finishes were also common. According to secondhand descriptions, the interior walls of the meetinghouse in Wilmington, Massachusetts, were painted in the "dull red of old mahogany" sometime between 1767 and 1813; the pulpit was "grained in imitation of mahogany" and the sounding board was painted a "very light red."[180] In 1770 New Ipswich decorated its 1767 gallery breastwork and supporting posts "poppy red and grained in imitation of marble or Mahogany."[181] Black and blue marbled treatment may also have been common. According to one historian of Leicester (writing in 1860), the interior painting of the 1784 meetinghouse was "a kind of pointed block-work of shaded marble, unlike anything seen in nature, and rarely if ever in art anywhere else."[182] Two relatively untouched instances of this treatment survive in the meetinghouse in Sandown and the Rocky Hill meetinghouse. In both structures the pulpit and canopy, pulpit stair balusters and pulpit window casings, the attached Communion table, and gallery breastwork are marbleized or mahoganized. The pews, wainscoting, interior door elements, window frames, floors, stairs, and gallery benches are unpainted to this day. Color schemes that left large areas of unpainted surfaces may have been common. In 1785 South Weymouth, which had ordered its gallery paneling, pulpit, and pulpit canopy to be painted a "lead color" (along with all exposed girts, posts, plates, and casings), had the interior sashes of all windows painted white and the plaster work of the ceiling and walls whitewashed. All interior wainscoting, pews, deacons' seats, pulpit benches, and stairwells were to be left unpainted.[183]

The pattern of emulating one's close neighbors was also common. In 1768 Yarmouth, Massachusetts, chose to imitate the "form and fashion" of the canopy with its ironwork, Communion table, and deacons' seat as they were in Barnstable's east precinct, specifying an unknown but "fashionable" color.[184] Interior color even followed transmission patterns marked by ethnic and denominational settlement lines. When the Presbyterian congregation in Bedford, New Hampshire, was making improvements to its pulpit, the town voted in 1767 to paint it "the same color the Rev. Mr. McGregor's pulpit is, in Londonderry"—the point of origin of most Scotch-Irish towns in New England.[185]

Supplementing the use of color finishes were gilt surfaces, painted dates, and occasional political devices. These treatments are known from receipts, building contracts, and surviving fragments but also from second- and third-hand oral traditions reported by town and parish historians. Gilt surfaces were uncommon, but they did exist. The same invoice Thomas Lawlor presented in 1755 to paint the Ipswich meetinghouse also showed that he requested reimbursement for gilding portions of the inside doors. Lawlor's colleague, Richard Manning, was paid in 1756 to gild the baptismal basin and the hourglass.[186] The canopy in the third New Ipswich meetinghouse was gilded. Prominently displayed dates marking the erection of the meetinghouse or the date of its first use were more frequent, however. Amherst, New Hampshire, displayed "1774" "curiously painted in gold, in old English letters, on a panel in front of the singers' gallery." Rowley, Massachusetts, painted "1749" in large figures in two places on the gallery fronts just opposite the pulpit. Northampton, Massachusetts, displayed the date "1735" on the sounding board.[187] Patriotic emblems were sometimes chosen, such as the thirteen gilt stars, specifying the thirteen original states, painted on a frieze below the canopy in Marblehead or the red, white, blue, and gold stripes that are said to have emblazoned the sounding board in the 1790 Newbury, Vermont, meetinghouse.[188]

THE EVOLUTION of painted surfaces in eighteenth-century New England meetinghouse architecture falls into two divisions. The first, roughly from 1697 to 1750, saw oil, paint, tar, pitch, and sand as protection against the weather. It was a utilitarian preservative applied to iron and wood casements, to doors, to window casings, to roofs, and to downspouts. But in the second division, between 1750 and 1830, a different attitude evolved. While protection was still important, paint had transcended its earlier protective function and was now a vehicle to enter the world of "fashionable" or "handsome" style. Communities pictured themselves as part of a built Georgian landscape where interior and exterior surfaces of artificial structures "made a statement" if not to their neighbors then at least to themselves. Perhaps the most telling example is the meetinghouse in Gilead, an underpopulated second parish in a sparsely settled area of eastern Connecticut that in 1748 built a relatively small house of worship, forty-six by thirty-six feet with a post height of twenty-two feet. The congregation in this meetinghouse sat on benches, not in pews; the galleries were seldom filled. Nevertheless, not long after the structure was raised, the parish voted for "sky color" as an exterior paint. Then, a dozen years later, shortly after the parish began seating men and women together, it elected to treat its pulpit, canopy, breastwork, and gallery pillars with a coat of light red, "slightly striped with white"—a marbleized finish unprecedented for an isolated rural church in the 1760s.[189] Gilead churchgoers, for the first time sitting with their families, now worshiped in a meetinghouse whose exterior was dressed with the color of the sky and whose interior was resplendent with red marble—a visual feast that may have paralleled a trend taking place in New England at large. It was one of several signs heralding the third and last period of the region's meetinghouse architecture.

CHAPTER SEVEN

# Meetinghouses of the Early Nineteenth Century

THE INCREASING presence of compass windows, steepled bell towers, Georgian decorative modes, and interior and exterior colors in the eighteenth-century meetinghouse argues that New England's Reformed congregations were no longer satisfied to attend religious services in a school-like or "intellectual" setting. In the first period the material assemblage (the pulpit, the canopy, the pulpit surrounds, and the Communion table) that allowed church leaders to teach the Gospel and administer the sacraments was centralized in an enclosure characterized by its architectural "negation" (to use Anthony Garvan's term). In the second period, parishioners increasingly wanted to extend this sacramental space outward and to convene on the Sabbath in a "comely" and "elegant" place marked by gentility, comfort, and taste. This continued aspiration ushered in the Federal-period and Greek Revival houses of worship of the third period during which scores of towns and parishes followed the lead of Salisbury, Connecticut, which decided in 1798, "We will build a Meeting House in the modern style."[1]

By virtually every measure the "modern style" found builders deeply influenced by the Anglican formula. The eighteenth-century axial plans of the most important urban Episcopal churches in Massachusetts, Connecticut, and Rhode Island offered the principal entry through the bell tower; a main alley aligned along the length of the building; and a prominent altar, pulpit, and Communion table that provided the focus of the interior space. In a dramatic reversal, architects of third-period Reformed meetinghouses essentially adopted all three elements of this axial plan except the prominence of the altar, which remained excluded. The short end of the building was turned ninety degrees to "face" the street; the formal bell tower or "portico" was now a main entry; and the long aisle leading from the door to the pulpit was realigned along the principal axis of the building. These "improvements" came with new amenities, such as slip pews, pew cushions, curtains for the windows, chandelier lighting, heating stoves, and lavish use of gilt surfaces and decorative textiles to "dress" the pulpit.[2] No one could now argue that this was a "municipal" building or even a "schoolhouse."

The seeds of change were already present in the early eighteenth century. Because of restricted land use, the narrow end of two important Congregational meetinghouses in Boston—the 1721 New Brick and the 1729 Old South—actually did face the street. Edward Pell, the painter-stainer who "drew the plan" of the New Brick, sited its bell tower in one of two main thoroughfares of the town's North End (Hanover Street) and allowed for an entry into the bell tower that in part competed with the main entry on the long side.[3] Eight years later when Robert Twelves, the builder of the Old South, used the site of its predecessor (the Old Cedar) at the corner of Milk and Marlborough Streets, he was obliged to squeeze the new ninety-five-by-sixty-eight-foot dimensions into a location that had previously accommodated a seventy-five-by-fifty-one-foot structure. Twelves's layout, detailed years later by Maj. Thomas Dawes (1731–1809) when he was making improvements to the meetinghouse in 1770, shows that the best location for the bell tower was on the west side facing Boston's Marlborough Street, now Washington Street, the principal thoroughfare in South Boston.[4] Twelves's design encouraged parishioners to enter through the tower doorway—which thus served as a portico even though the "main" entry was still on Milk Street opposite the pulpit. Twelves subtly reinforced this shift by placing the interior stairwells to the two tiers of galleries on the west or tower side, not on the side facing Milk Street.[5]

It is unclear how many other Reformed houses of worship in Boston made similar compromises. John Bonner's 1743 map, *A New Plan of the Great Town of Boston*, indicates that Mather Byles's meetinghouse faced Hollis Street in much the same way.[6] According to a late nineteenth-century drawing of the second meetinghouse of Boston's First Baptist Church, raised in 1771, the structure was jammed into a narrow space that required builders to eliminate the main entry on the long side and install three entrances at one of its smaller ends, one of them leading to a two-floor stairwell porch.[7] Space was always at a premium in Boston, and positioning was a good way of getting large-dimension buildings to fit a restricted site.

A more effective compromise was made in Salem, Massachusetts, in 1772. After an internal dispute, the North Society separated from Salem's First Parish and hired as their minister the son (Rev. Thomas Barnard Jr.) of their former clergyman. While the two parties remained amicable, the North Society separatists were able to attract a prominent and wealthy group of Salem citizens, who raised a large meetinghouse and bell tower on a narrow piece of land at the corner of North and Lynde Streets (fig. 7.1). Like the builders of the Old

Figure 7.1. Painted view of the meetinghouse of the North Parish, Salem, Massachusetts, raised 14–16 July 1772, as the first Congregational house of worship in New England that was designed as a church. The cupola depicted here replaced the original spire that was taken down in 1796, deemed unsafe and too costly to maintain. Attributed to Thomas Davidson (1842–1918), circa 1900. Courtesy of the First Church in Salem, Massachusetts.

South, they put the bell tower and main entrance on North Street, the principal road leading to Beverly. As described in the society's *First Centenary,* published in 1873, the planners created a meetinghouse that in effect reproduced the Anglican axial formula in a Congregational setting. A seating plan (fig. 7.2) prepared by Abijah Northey, a parishioner, circa 1773 reveals that the bell tower on North Street served as a "porch" or portico whose three main entry doors led to a staircase to the gallery, the two main alleyways, and the pulpit at the other end. There were no side entrances, but two doors behind the pulpit opened to the outside. Boxed pews on the ground floor and the gallery ran north to south. No details about the meetinghouse designer are known.[8]

Raised over a period of three days, between 14 and 16 July 1772, Salem's North Society meetinghouse was the first nonconformist house of worship in New

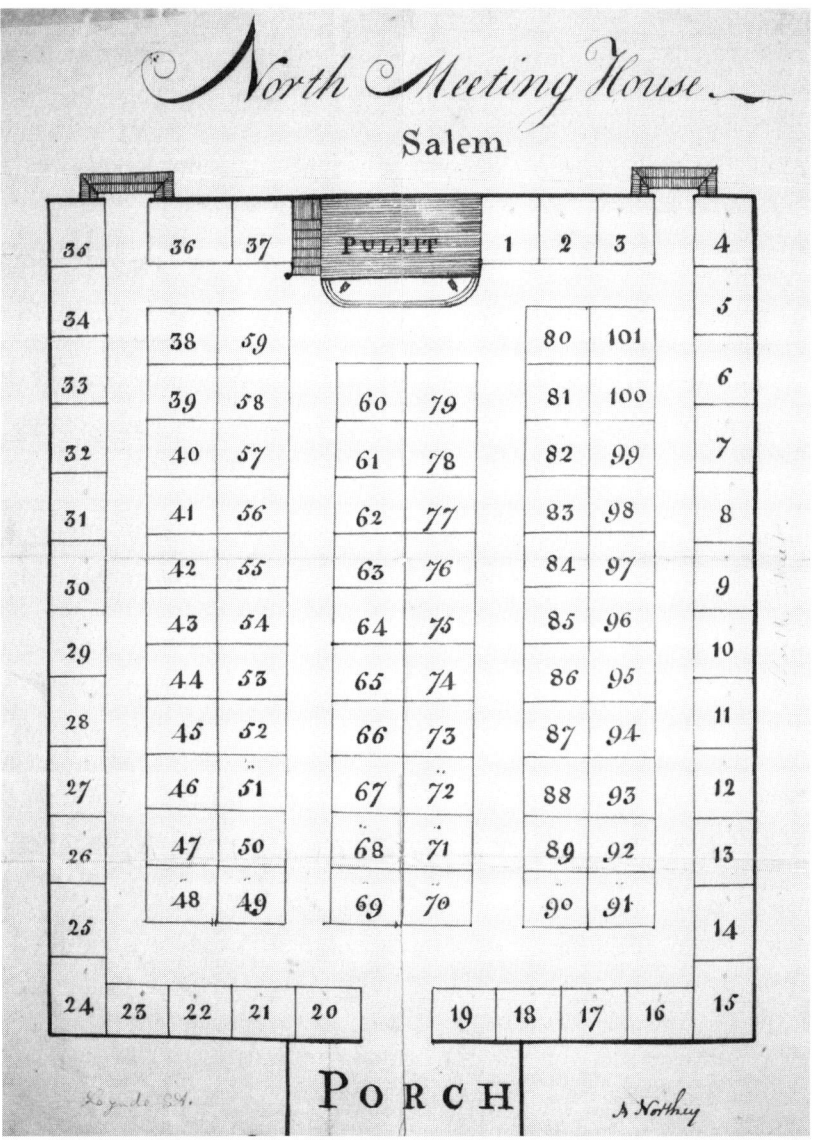

Figure 7.2. "North Meeting House – Salem." Pew plan, circa 1773, of the North Parish in Salem, Massachusetts. The diagram was made by Abijah Northey (1741–1816), a silversmith and merchant who was a member of a committee appointed by the proprietors to sell and convey pews. The "Porch" represents the bell tower with its three entry doors. Courtesy of the First Church in Salem, Massachusetts.

England to arrange its plan longitudinally and to eliminate the principal entryway on the long side. Almost immediately, two other dissenting parishes adopted the same plan. In Boston the proprietors of the Manifesto Church voted in February 1772 to replace their wooden 1699 meetinghouse with a new one of greater durability. The Brattle congregation was still home to many "aspiring aristocrats" in Boston, among them John and Samuel Adams, Joseph Warren, Samuel A. and Harrison Gray Otis, and Theodore Lyman. These men appointed a building committee that included two Massachusetts governors as well as proprietors with architectural experience and familiarity with design manuals. The committee considered two plans, one offered by the painter John Singleton Copley and a second by the architect-mason Thomas Dawes, a member of the Old South. Dawes's plan was chosen because Copley's idea was out of reach financially. Later that year the congregation built a ninety-by-seventy-five-foot brick meetinghouse with brownstone quoins and an elegant bell tower. The interior was designed in the latest English taste with ten Corinthian columns supporting the gallery and continuing upward to underpin the roof bay. Compass windows were distributed throughout the building, including a Palladian window in the entry portico. Dawes used the bell tower's base as the principal entry, though he kept the side entry; the main alley leading to the pulpit followed the alignment of the roof. The new house of worship was opened for services in July 1773.[9]

The next year, the First Baptist Society of Providence embarked on a similar scheme. To find the best plan for their meetinghouse, the building committee sent their architect, their chief carpenter, and a housewright to Boston "to view the different churches and meeting-houses there, and to make a memorandum of their several dimensions and forms of architecture."[10] Joseph Brown, Jonathan Hammond, and Comfort Wheaton most likely examined the Old South, the New Brick, and possibly Christ Church. But they took their principal lesson from the recently completed Brattle, because the large eighty-by-eighty-foot meetinghouse they designed (four times the area of the 1726 structure) mimicked the same "Anglican" codes as the Brattle, within and without, and used similar elements of Georgian design that had percolated through the Anglo-American world. As in the Brattle, the base of the Providence bell tower served as its principal entry; the pulpit was directly opposite with the main alley running along the roofline axis. Within, the ceiling bay was buttressed by ten columns that held up the gallery and that, like the new Brattle, continued upward to support individual window bays. The compass windows, quoins, dentiled cornice, "ox-eye" (oculus) pediment window, and "Dorrick Vernition" (Doric Venetian) pulpit window of the new meetinghouse were as ambitious and artistically refined as any found in Boston. The entire structure was set off with a tower steeple based on a design by James Gibbs. The frame was raised in August 1774, and the structure was opened for services in May 1775.[11]

On the eve of America's independence, three Reformed religious societies in New England's major port towns erected meetinghouses whose roofline paralleled the main aisle—the essence of the church plan. The outbreak of the American Revolution put an end to most attempts in the region to build new meetinghouses or to rebuild old ones. In 1776, 1777, and 1778, no more than 11 meetinghouses were raised—compared to the 83 built during the three preceding years of 1772, 1773, and 1774. But as the war subsided, construction resumed. Most towns and parishes continued to build houses of worship along the traditional second-period plan, either unwilling to commit their resources to structures like the Brattle Square or First Baptist meetinghouses or simply unwilling to change with them. Out of 172 Reformed meetinghouses built in the region in the fourteen years between 1776 and 1789, 170 are believed to have conformed to the second-period style; only 2 followed the new style.

The two exceptions were located at opposite ends of the new Commonwealth of Massachusetts, and neither one drew much notice. The "Old Tabernacle," built for the Third or Presbyterian Society in Salem after a 1774 fire destroyed its first structure, was purportedly patterned after Rev. George Whitefield's London Tabernacle Church. Raised in the fall of 1776 under the direction of the nineteen-year-old Salem carver and architect Samuel McIntire (1757–1811), it featured an unusual domed ceiling, possibly the first of its kind in New England. This structure had a front entry door at the base of the tower and no entry on the side, and the tower or narrow end faced the street.[12] The second exception was in Berkshire County in western Massachusetts, where in 1784 the First Parish in Stockbridge built a large meetinghouse, sixty by fifty feet, with a steeple reaching sixty-two feet high. Few details of its design survive, but the tower was placed "opposite the pulpit," meaning it was probably similar to Salem North's and the Old Tabernacle's plan.[13]

Neither Salem's nor Stockbridge's meetinghouse is known to have inspired any imitators. But because many communities were hoping to repair the damage left by the war (Ezra Stiles reports that in 1777 seven meetinghouses or Episcopal churches were burned by the British during their attack on New Haven alone),[14] towns were now seeking the help of a new corps of professional designers and architects. Thomas Dawes, the new Brattle meetinghouse architect, drew the plan for the renovation of the Old South after it was gutted and used as a riding rink by the British during the occupation. In 1784 and 1785 Dawes redesigned the interior of the Old Brick meetinghouse in Cornhill and added a two-story porch. Other religious societies in the area drew on Charles Bulfinch (1763–1844), a young Harvard graduate who was the maternal descendant of Charles Apthorpe (1698–1758), the wealthiest Bostonian of his day. Bulfinch, who brought with him the tastes of upper-class English society, completed the design for the three-stage bell tower of the new meetinghouse in Charlestown, Massachusetts, whose sixty-seven-year-old predecessor had burned during the British attack on the town. With a steeple height of 162 feet, the bell tower was still 28 feet lower than the one on "Dr. Cutler's" Christ Church, but it was at least as sophisticated, employing many elements of the Anglican code, including the extensive use of compass windows.[15]

Thomas Dawes became a colleague of Bulfinch's, both later collaborating on the 1789 Old State House colonnade and triumphal arch. But Bulfinch's reputation as a leading Federal-period designer soon began to grow. Fairfield, Connecticut, which in 1785 replaced a meetinghouse that had burned in 1779, voted for a pulpit according to Bulfinch's design—one raised on four, high, classical columns.[16] Two years later Bulfinch completed his first meetinghouse design—a replacement for the Hollis Street Church in Boston consumed by a fire in 1787. Bulfinch had just returned from an architectural tour of Europe, and he offered the Hollis proprietors a design inspired in part by Christopher Wren's St. Stephen's Church in London and in part by an Italianate twin-tower design of a church in Mistley, Essex, England, illustrated in Robert and James Adam's *Works in Architecture,* published in 1773–79. (Others have suggested it owes much to a twin-tower concept devised by Peter Harrison of Newport, Rhode Island, who was responsible for the second or stone version of King's Chapel in Boston and Christ Church in Cambridge.) Whatever the sources of the design may have been, the architectural result was unprecedented. Two towers, each placed on a front corner of the square building, were connected by an elaborate entry façade supported by four large Ionic columns that resembled a classical temple (fig. 7.3). The design was marked by a low-pitched roof and a heavy reliance on classical orders. The pulpit, located directly opposite the façade entry, lacked the usual sounding board because the domed ceiling presumably allowed even those farthest from the pulpit to hear every word of the sermon.[17] The builders and decorators spared no expense. Besides commissioning the "two Large Balls for the Cupolas," they ordered 96½ yards of crimson damask, 21 yards of fringe, and four tassels for the pulpit dressing; 9¼ yards of pink tammy for the curtains and pulpit window cushions; and three silk tassels for the pulpit itself. The society also arranged to paint and glitter two record books.[18]

Despite the publication of an engraving of the structure in the *Columbian Magazine of Philadelphia* in April 1788, Bulfinch's twin-tower Hollis Street design drew only three imitators, all in southeastern New England. The First Congregational Society in Providence, Rhode Island, hired the architect Caleb Ormsbee to design a double-tower meetinghouse in 1795, a building now known from an image on needlework samplers.[19] In 1809 William Bentley, during a

Figure 7.3. *An East View of the Meeting House in Hollis Street, Boston.* Engraving of the second Hollis Street meetinghouse in Boston, published in *Columbian Magazine of Philadelphia* in April 1788, opposite page 175. Engraver: J. [John] Vallance after a drawing by Charles Bulfinch. Courtesy of the John Carter Brown Library, Brown University.

visit to northern Plymouth County, Massachusetts, reported that the new meetinghouse in South Abington was "modeled upon the South Meeting in Boston [i.e., Hollis Street] with two turrets in front connected by a piazza & pediment." Bentley had earlier reported in 1806 that the 1798 meetinghouse in nearby Kingston, Massachusetts, had a "front pediment and two Cupolas," a structure virtually identical to the Hollis design that was illustrated in an 1876 town catalog.[20]

In the meantime, Charles Bulfinch's rising reputation soon reached the northernmost townships of the Housatonic Valley in western Massachusetts. Pittsfield, Stockbridge's neighbor to the north, decided in 1789 to replace its nineteen-year-old meetinghouse and chose Bulfinch to design the new one. This time Bulfinch greatly simplified the plan. He essentially began with a second-period meetinghouse with the narrow end and bell tower facing the street; he then converted the bell tower entry into a two-story portico that served as the principal entrance, aligning the main alley with the roof and eliminating the side entrance (fig. 7.4).[21]

The new Pittsfield meetinghouse proved so attractive that it was copied by the town of Taunton in southeastern Massachusetts in 1792, and after 1794 it set

Figure 7.4. "The Second Edifice (with Porch and Tower) Built in 1793." Sketch, circa 1830, showing the entryway of the meetinghouse in Pittsfield, Massachusetts, designed by Charles Bulfinch in 1789. This is one of three known contemporary images of this structure. From *Proceedings in Commemoration of the Organization in Pittsfield...*, opposite page 72. Widener Library, Harvard College Library, US 13411.10.8.

off a chain of imitations in western New England. The design reappeared with minor variations in ten towns over the next twenty-five years, all of them in the Berkshires and Housatonic range of western Massachusetts and in northwestern Connecticut. They were built by the same group of individuals, among them Joel Dickinson, Ebenezer Clark, John Hulett, Thomas Dutton, and Peter Powell. While they were not all identical, the designs always consisted of a pedimented eight-foot porch or portico whose sides were deep enough to accommodate doors on three sides; a bell tower with an open octagonal belfry; and a "Venetian," or Palladian, window located in the tower. The narrow end invariably faced the street.[22]

Bulfinch's success in Taunton and in the Berkshires gradually changed the equation for towns and parishes planning new meetinghouses in the early Federal Republic. In the years between 1785 and 1790 approximately 95 percent of meetinghouses built in New England followed traditional second-period styles, many of them "plain"—meaning without bell towers—and often furnished with single or double porches. Beginning in 1791, the number of third-period types gradually increased, and by 1794 as many third-period houses were being raised as second-period houses. The old style essentially ended by 1805 with only three built after that date. These were the twin-porch meetinghouse in Sullivan, New Hampshire, in 1807; the "plain" meetinghouse in Preston, Connecticut, in 1817; and the Bullockite meetinghouse in Porter, Maine, in 1818. Not surprisingly the holdouts tended to be far away from urban areas. Out of about 120 second-period meetinghouses built between 1789 and 1818, the bulk of these (70 percent) were for parishes in Maine, New Hampshire, and Vermont; by contrast only 4 percent were located in Connecticut. In the meantime, the total number of new meetinghouses continued to climb. Twenty-three were raised in New England in 1797; nineteen in 1798; and twenty-six in 1800. Most of these were in the new third-period style. This development was accompanied by a steady increase of bell tower additions to meetinghouses built between 1730 and 1770, many of them an extension of an existing stairwell porch. Of seventy-six bell towers raised in New England between 1785 and 1805, over half were additions to existing structures.

With this, the 175-year-old vernacular traditions of meetinghouse building came to an end. Towns unable or unwilling to hire architects found a temporary middle ground by retaining most aspects of a steepled eighteenth-century meetinghouse but realigning the pulpit and the short side that now faced the street—in other words doing much the same as Salem North Parish in 1772 or Stockbridge First Church in 1784.[23] At least eight towns followed this pattern between 1794 and 1802, among them Strafford, Vermont, in 1799 (fig. 7.5) and West Springfield, Massachusetts, in 1800.

Most towns, however, chose professional church designers. The principal author of this movement was Asher Benjamin (1773–1845), a carpenter born in rural

Figure 7.5. Meetinghouse in Strafford, Vermont. Built 1799 on a church plan, designated "transitional" by architectural historian Edmund Sinnott. Photograph by Jack E. Boucher. Historic American Building Survey, Library of Congress, Washington.

Hartland, Connecticut, who as a young man in about 1797 published *The Country Builder's Assistant* in Greenfield, Massachusetts, which was based on his experience with large buildings. His "Design for a Church" became one of several influential patterns for meetinghouses in Massachusetts, Vermont, and New Hampshire. This newer generation produced meetinghouses influenced by Federal taste but distinctly New England in their form, as architects and architect-builders worked to consolidate ecclesiastical design in a few hands. Asher Benjamin himself was responsible for at least thirteen meetinghouses; Isaac Damon is credited with having built thirteen; Elias Carter, a Worcester architect, raised at least fifteen. Others, such as Ithiel Town, Lavius Fillmore, David Hoadley, Charles Bulfinch, and Timothy Palmer, were responsible for scores more.

Generally, these men based themselves in an urban area such as Boston or New Haven. After working in Vermont and New Hampshire, Asher Benjamin moved to Boston, where he built the West Church in 1806 following plate 39 in his newly published *American Builder's Companion*.[24] (The portico or pavilion of this meetinghouse that supports the tower is notable for the massing of one square on top of another, the portico itself rising four stories high.) Benjamin prepared a similar design for Boston's Charles Street Church in 1807 and the First Church in Boston in 1808.

If necessary, towns went well outside their immediate area to find builders. After some discussion, Orange, Connecticut (Milford Third Parish), voted in 1810 that the ceiling of their new meetinghouse was to "be arch[ed]" and that the "pulpit be built on . . . one end of the house & the door or doors at the other"—a classic treatment of the church plan.[25] Unable to find a local builder, the town then called on David Hoadley (1774–1839), an architect-builder who had just completed an Anglican church at nearby Bethany and who was on his way to becoming a leading designer of meetinghouses in New Haven and Litchfield Counties.

Not all builders followed Asher Benjamin's lead. In planning the First Parish meetinghouse in Exeter, New Hampshire, in 1798, joiners Ebenezer Clifford and Bradbury Johnson placed the tower and a two-story portico in the center of the long side, with the pulpit directly opposite. Entry to the audience room was through a portico under the tower. At least three other towns in southern New Hampshire may have imitated Exeter's example.[26] Hopkinton, which built a twin-porch structure in 1789, added a two-story portico over the main door in 1800 and a tower over the portico between 1809 and 1811 (fig. 7.6); Milton did the same by erecting a central portico in 1803, in other words taking the first step like Hopkinton but without adding the tower. Private proprietors who built a Calvinistic Congregational meetinghouse in Henniker in 1801 also installed a belfry on the long side opposite the pulpit. Its narrow distribution indicates the long-side bell tower was a New Hampshire characteristic.

Adopting an architecturally designed church plan may have amended the appearance of the region's meetinghouses, but it did not change the traditional way of doing parish business. Realizing that neoclassical or Federal church plans were now "fashionable," and knowing how reluctant taxpayers were to spend town money, building committees drew selectively on their neighbors' meetinghouses to imitate those aspects that they liked best. That is, they reverted to

Figure 7.6. *Congregational Meeting-House / Hopkinton N.H. / 1826.* View of the 1789 twin-porch meetinghouse in Hopkinton after a pavilion and bell tower were built on the long side. The pavilion was added about 1800; the tower erected between 1809 and 1811. New Hampshire Historical Society.

design conduits commonly used earlier by builders in the seventeenth and eighteenth centuries. Westford, Massachusetts, raised a meetinghouse in 1794 that imitated the belfry and exterior color of the third-period meetinghouse recently put up in nearby Chelmsford; a year later the town copied Chelmsford's pulpit, canopy, and deacons' seats.[27]

Reversions like these became a common pattern. Hinsdale, Massachusetts, initially voted in 1797 for a "plain," meaning second-period, meetinghouse without a bell tower. Apparently not satisfied, the town decided later in the same year that "there be a convening porch annexed to said house"; then they decided to add a belfry and steeple above the convening porch. Two weeks later, on Christmas Day, they voted that the meetinghouse be built "according to the fashions of the present day," citing nearby Chester, Massachusetts, for exterior features and its immediate neighbor Pittsfield for interior arrangement.[28] Elsewhere, in 1805 Rocky Hill, Connecticut, built a meetinghouse "with a projection" on the plan of neighboring Middletown.[29] At least four rural or island congregations in Massachusetts imitated the "massing" Benjamin designed for Boston's West Church and for Boston's First Parish. These included Nantucket in 1809, Northampton in 1811, Bedford in 1816, and Springfield in 1818. Of these, only Northampton, which voted to build "in a manner equal to that of Mr. Emerson's meeting house in Boston [i.e., the First Church]," may actually have consulted Benjamin, who helped prepare a plan with Isaac Damon. Everyone else may have simply been taking Benjamin's idea.[30]

Not revealed in these documents is the fact that rural builders were now making meetinghouses that in their exterior alignment and most of their interior layout resembled Anglican churches. But how much had really changed? Pittsfield, Massachusetts, the town that is usually credited with ending the vernacular component of New England's meetinghouse story, kept the "Book of Credits" to help cover the enormous costs of building an urban structure in what had recently been a frontier community. The town asked landowning residents to sign up for individual timbers growing on their properties according to a list provided by the builder. A parish historian writing in 1889 summed up the process:

> Thus an eighty foot stick of timber came from Dr. Timothy Childs, the ridgepole from Stephen Fowler, two sills from Capt. Charles Goodrich, another sill, fifty feet in length, was brought by Zebulon Stiles, one of the first settlers of the town, Mrs. Stoddard and Mrs. Dickinson, the widows of two men prominent in the Revolution, together furnished a pillar twenty feet long and a pine beam of seventy feet, while Capt. Jared Ingersoll's timber lot in Lenox yielded one of the pillars for the belfry.[31]

Building Pittsfield's new meetinghouse was still a vibrant and neighborly effort in the third period as it had been in the first.

PART III

# Conclusions

CHAPTER EIGHT

# Some Theoretical Models

ONE OF the more salient characteristics of meetinghouses raised in New England and Long Island in the period 1622 to 1830 is the regional variety that thrived within a broader framework of uniformity. This variety goes to the very heart of the vernacular definition of their appearance, and understanding it will help us understand the meetinghouse form. Most parishes and towns followed what appeared to be a regionwide liturgical and social canon. They built "New England" meetinghouses and followed "New England" worshiping practices. Meetinghouses always faced south, with the pulpit on the north side. Behind every pulpit was a window that provided light for the minister to read his sermon. Separate men's and women's stairwells led up to the gallery; the Communion table folded down from the front rail of the deacons' pew for convenience. Nearby was a public burying ground. In a sense, to read one town history is to read them all. But clear variations existed within these larger norms, as well as differences in the time of their first implementation. The overall rate of new construction and church formation was so brisk that constant opportunity existed for the introduction of novel architectural ideas. Successful communities were eager to show their best face to their neighbors and incorporated innovative designs, the most recent decorative modes, and new interior arrangements in their houses of worship. Conservative neighbors, or impoverished ones, presumably watched with dismay and kept to their old ways.

Any study of the transfer of this canon must begin with the origin of the form during the Reformation. Architecturally, New England meetinghouses met four of the five basic criteria that differentiated Protestant Calvinistic houses of worship from Anglican and Catholic ones. In an argument first proposed by the separatist Henry Barrow in 1590, Reformed meetinghouses had to avoid the "old idolatrous shapes, with their ancient appurtenances, with their courts, cells, aisles, chancel, [and] bells." The most important step was to make a well-designed, permanent pulpit the chief liturgical center of the structure, emphasizing the role of the word of God as the principal feature in the religious service. By contrast, "lesser" church rituals, such as Communion and baptism, were performed on what was essentially impermanent furniture. The second criterion was to centralize the area of worship. The Protestant congregation faced the pulpit from all directions, creating what in effect was a school-like setting. The third and fourth criteria were to the ensure that the congregation remained attentive, using balconies to bring auditors closer to the pulpit and acoustics to amplify hearing by means of a canopy, dome, or ceiling that helped direct the voice of the minister to the congregation. Only in regard to the elimination of earlier Christian iconography was the New England Protestant experience different from that in Europe. As previously indicated, because there were no Catholic or Anglican churches in the wilderness of North America, as there were in France in the sixteenth century or in England in the seventeenth, there was no need to clear them of the "fretting leprosie" of their furniture and their images.[1]

Even so, a European traveler in the 1740s would have found noticeable deviations (if not outright confusion) in the region's houses of worship. Some meetinghouses were square with high hipped roofs, turrets, and prominent gables; others were rectangular with "English" roofs and high bell towers; still others were octagonal with conical roofs. A few were narrow and long, like horse stables; others were aligned vertically with one gallery superimposed on another. Parishioners along the eastern coastline gained entry to the gallery by a front stairwell porch; those in the uplands, by side stairwells. Some parishioners sat on plain benches facing the pulpit, the men separated from the women; others enjoyed private pews with special windows and doors opening into the street; still others found that the town had ordered such doors be clapboarded up. A few pulpits were small and in the form of a capsule, but many were massive and capable of seating ten or more people. Where one minister spoke under a carved and colonnaded canopy, others preached under a plain canopy suspended from the ceiling by an iron rod. Some meetinghouses reflected naïvely conceived architectural decorations; others displayed classical colonnades, dentiled cornices, compass windows, and intricately designed steeples.

If this visitor were a student of architecture, he or she might have recognized forty years later that the flow of ideas followed the course of certain landmark structures, particularly those belonging to the large urban Congregational, Baptist, or Anglican religious societies that defined the leading edge of innovation and style. As part of the wider Atlantic community, New England's ports of entry brought in carpenters trained in the centers of early Restoration, Georgian, and Federal fashion. Highly visible houses of worship, such as Boston's first Brattle Square meetinghouse, Boston's Christ Church, Newport's Trinity Church, Boston's Old South meetinghouse, Boston's second Brattle Square meetinghouse, Providence's First Baptist meetinghouse, and Boston's second Hollis Street meetinghouse, were all preeminent in the region for their refinement, innovation, and sophistication. Presumably they were models for rural communities who aspired to "good taste" in their houses of worship but without straying too far from the multifunctional Congregational meetinghouse.

Dominated by successful merchant families whose London and European business and political contacts acquainted them with the most recent English innovations, these urban congregations typically hired skilled craftsmen with some architectural training who had emigrated from England or who were colonial born but had trained in Europe. We suspect that Richard Munday, who drew the plans for Newport's Trinity Church and its Seventh-Day Baptist meetinghouse, may have been influenced by Christopher Wren.[2] We know, or at least presume to know, that William Price, the Boston cabinetmaker and print dealer who designed the 1740 bell tower at Christ Church, made numerous trips to London and employed at least one London journeyman; that Timothy Carter, the English immigrant who arrived in the region in the 1760s, carried with him drawings and specifications, among them *The City and Country Builder's and Workman's Treasury of Designs,* published in London in 1756; that Joseph Brown, the architect of the First Baptist Church in Providence, drew freely from a James Gibbs drawing to design its bell tower; that Charles Bulfinch had just completed a tour of Europe before he designed in 1787 the twin-tower Hollis Street edifice.[3]

Although some builders may have copied sophisticated English- or European-oriented urban models, in practice the diffusion of architectural ideas was never so simple or even cerebral. Over 190 instances of meetinghouse-related imitations made between 1647 and 1828 have been uncovered from town and church archives, from builders' contracts, and from the sale of buildings or building elements from one parish to another (see Appendix G). These documents cover a total of 263 architectural features typically citing an existing structure for the builder or carpenter to follow. They name specific items, such as the form of the meetinghouse, its dimensions, its roof type, or its exterior colors; these records also cite interior appointments: pews, pulpits, deacons' benches, galleries, wainscoting, Communion furniture, and interior colors. Designs for major additions that included porches, galleries, bell towers, steeples, and spires were sometimes borrowed. Even nonarchitectural items were copied—such as seating arrangements and the rules governing the "dignities" of pews and pulpits.[4]

To cite just one example, when the town of Surry, New Hampshire, met in 1789 to "finish" the meetinghouse they had raised in 1771, they voted to sell the work off to the lowest bidder and gave out the following instructions for the carpenters completing it:

> The whole of Said House [is to] be finished in the same form and as Near Like Keene Meetinghouse as the Bigness of Said house will admit of. . . . The outside of Said Meetinghouse is to be Glazed and painted like Keene meetinghouse also

the pulpit Window and the Canopy over the pulpit are to be finished Exactly like Keene, the inside of Said house to be plastered and whitewashed Like Keene meetinghouse, also the underpinning is to be well Repaired and pointed with Lime, also the pews in Said house are to be painted and numbered like Keene meetinghouse.[5]

The Surry instructions could not have been clearer. Except for its dimensions, which were about five feet smaller in both directions, the meetinghouse was modeled after Keene in every way possible.

While specifications as detailed as these address only a small fraction of the more than two thousand meetinghouses and churches built during this period, their insertion into the minutes of a town or parish meeting or a builder's contract appears to have been representative of a widespread process. The question we must ask is just where and in what manner towns and building committees perceived "fashion and proportion" or "the newest mode" when they gave directions to their carpenters.[6] Why, in other words, did Surry replicate the meetinghouse in Keene and not one in an urban community? Was it just because Keene, at seven miles distance, was closer than Portsmouth or Boston? Was it because they were unable to afford an urban model? Or did they simply put their trust in a rural ecclesiological aesthetic that excluded urban prototypes?

Models located at some remove were also a part of this transmission process. At least twenty committee votes chose models for architectural features that were more than fifty miles away (see Appendix A, Table 5). When Guilford, Connecticut, built a standing bell tower in 1726, the town voted to imitate the "Fashion and proportion of the Belfry & Spire at Rhode Island"—a tower and steeple that had just been erected on Trinity Church in Newport. The vote came shortly after the two Connecticut ministers sailed to London to take Episcopal orders, and the decision might be linked to the growing appeal of the Anglican Church in the Connecticut Colony.[7] In another instance, Northampton, Massachusetts, voted in 1810 to build a framed meetinghouse "in a manner equal to that of Mr. Emerson's meeting house in Boston"—the mammoth brick structure on Chauncy Place with a four-tiered porch and surmounting cupola, which had just replaced the Old Brick.[8] Guilford's consideration of the Newport tower spanned 127 miles on horseback, and about 80 miles by coastal vessel; Northampton's imitation of Boston's Chauncy Place meetinghouse carried 93 miles.

Some long-distance replications were a measure of population movements rather than hearsay or fame. In 1738 the town of Becket in Berkshire County, Massachusetts, used as its model the meetinghouse at Grafton (eighty-seven miles away in central Worcester County). Here the vote was actually recorded in Grafton by the Becket proprietors meeting many years before the Becket structure was built, clear evidence that the proprietors were voting for a new meetinghouse to resemble the one they all knew.[9] Much the same happened in

1768 when Salisbury, New Hampshire, specified a new meetinghouse with the same size as Kingston (fifty-five miles distant) and a pulpit like the one at Hawke (fifty miles distant). Here, too, proprietors were voting for features they were familiar with.[10]

Internal reasons sometimes led a community to select distant models. In 1743 Pelham, Massachusetts, located a little east of the Connecticut River, initially voted for a pulpit and canopy like those at Harvard, Massachusetts, about fifty-five miles away in eastern Worcester County. In this instance the two carpenters Pelham chose to do the work, Thomas and John Dick, had previously worked in towns near Harvard, and the community cited that pulpit because the Dick brothers had probably built it. (As we know, the Pelham building committee later changed its mind and voted for a pulpit whose "dignity" was like that of their nearest neighbor in Amherst.)

The preponderance of known replications, however, specifies a model close at hand. One hundred fifty-five committee votes (60 percent) cite models located at ten miles or under; another forty-eight (18 percent), at twenty miles or under. Many of these imitations were just three, four, or five miles apart. In 1714 Middletown Upper Houses (located in present-day Cromwell, Connecticut) elected to have the interior of its new meetinghouse finished like that of the South Society in Middletown. The two sites were about three miles apart by horseback; most if not the entire congregation of the new building knew the older one well because they had previously worshiped there. East Haven, Connecticut, chose in 1719 to have its pulpit and seats finished in the form of the nearby Branford meetinghouse. These two communities were less than five miles apart, and about one-third to one-half of the congregation had previously worshiped in Branford.[11] In some instances, towns and parishes even "replicated" themselves. East Windsor, Connecticut, voted in 1713 that its new meetinghouse roof "shall be as this is."[12]

Most imitations allude to the basic language of architecture—dimensions, form, post size, and joinery—signs that the process of diffusion was as much a vernacular transmission as it was stylistic. While many of these citations were little more than a way of specifying instructions to the carpenters, they do suggest some general trends. According to these records, 104 votes (40 percent) drew on models for the overall plan ("dimensions," "pattern" or "form," "posts," and "framing"): Chatham, Massachusetts, required the same "dimensions" as Eastham; Killingworth Farmers, Connecticut, stipulated posts "two feet shorter than . . . the First Society."[13] Another 91 (35 percent) addressed architectural details, including the design of pulpits (twenty-five examples), canopies (nine examples), interior or exterior colors (twenty examples), pews and seats (twenty-nine examples), Communion tables (two examples), and gallery breastwork (six examples). Together, basic architectural imitations accounted for about three out of every four that are documented.

In the absence of plan or copy books, most rural architectural fashions were perceived by towns through second-, third-, or fourth-hand imitations. As a result, the introduction of new styles may have usually followed a "nearest neighbor" manner of dispersal. The appearance of an innovation in one town alerted its neighbor to consider it, which in turn alerted the next neighbor, and so forth. In this scheme, much depended on who within the community traveled "abroad" and which direction they took. Blacksmiths and farmers in Surry, New Hampshire, were continually going to Keene to buy and sell goods and foodstuffs; it was natural that they thought of designing their meetinghouse like Keene's. Had Surry's population included several elite families—merchants, justices, and militia officers who typically traveled to major urban centers for trade, for court sessions, and for legislative meetings—they might have chosen an urban model.

The rate of dispersal was also controlled, however, by the rate of new construction or by decisions taken by the town to enlarge, repaint, or remodel its existing meetinghouse. Under these circumstances diffusion was quicker during periods of economic prosperity (as it was in the years just before the American Revolution) and slower in periods of war and depression (during and immediately after the Revolution). Finally, the actual character or design of the innovation may have weakened or become distorted the farther it traveled from its point of origin.

If we were to formulate a mental map of New England that reflects how a community compared itself to its neighbors, we might begin with a hypothetical square of nine towns arranged three by three in which the centermost town is our starting point. In this model, the "comfortable communion" with other parishes extends about six miles on every side. (One anonymous seventeenth-century commentator noted that the ideal form of towns was an area "square 6 miles every way. The houses orderly placed about the midst, especially the meetinghouse, the which we will suppose to be center of the whole circumference.")[14] The eight towns immediately surrounding this central point would likely figure prominently in the minds of building committees in charge of planning a new meetinghouse because they were familiar to most townspeople. The cordon of sixteen towns beyond the basic nine would be significantly less important but still within range of a man on horseback who could cover this distance in a day's or half-day's travel time. But major urban centers, such as Portsmouth, Newport, Boston, New Haven, and Providence, might show up only rarely in the town's cultural horizon. England might be off the map altogether except for travelers and those who read about new designs in pattern books and newspapers printed there.

From the very beginning, first-period styles were disseminated by imitation. Watertown, Massachusetts, agreed in 1654 with John Sherman, a tree warden and carpenter, "to Build a meeting house Like unto Cambridge in all points the

Cornish and fane [pennant] excepted and to have it finished by the Last of September in 1656."[15] In this instance, Watertown, which was spun off from Cambridge in 1634, drew not only from its nearest neighbor but also from its own point of origin. But the process easily went the other way. Westfield, Massachusetts, in 1672 voted to build its new meetinghouse after the "form" of Hatfield's, twenty miles to the north. Here Hatfield simply served Westfield as a model, having recently been settled by families immigrating from Springfield, Northampton, Windsor, and Hartford. In 1684 Windsor, Connecticut, voted to copy the fifty-by-forty-foot form of Springfield nineteen miles north on the Connecticut River built seven years earlier by John Allis of Hartford.[16]

In this process some meetinghouses stood out more prominently than others. The 1689 meetinghouse at Reading, Massachusetts, was the model for Billerica in 1693 and for Haverhill in 1696. Hatfield's thirty-by-thirty-foot form was not only the model for Westfield in 1672 but for Deerfield in 1694.[17] Some congregations even made a habit of copying the same neighbor. Hartford's Second Society probably imitated Hartford First's dimensions twice, once in 1670 and again in 1749. Wilton Parish, a subdivision of Norwalk, Connecticut, imitated Norwalk's "finishing" in 1741 and its construction in 1789.[18]

The same pattern of replication influenced roofs, seats, benches, and pulpits. Norwalk, Connecticut, directed in 1678 that the roof over its new forty-by-forty-foot meetinghouse be built following the style of Fairfield; Manchester, Massachusetts, voted in 1692 to have its roof "to be of the same form of Beverly or Wenham meeting house."[19] West Springfield chose seats like those in the First Society in 1702. Boxford, Massachusetts, told its builder in 1699 to design a pulpit "as good as" the one in nearby Topsfield and to make pews "to be set as in Andover." But when the North Parish in Andover voted for a new meetinghouse in 1711, it specified the "model of the seats to be like Bradford."[20]

Towns that found models beyond their immediate neighbors usually had a good reason for doing so. When Haverhill, Massachusetts, voted in May 1696 to replace its forty-nine-year-old meetinghouse with a new one, the town, like Hingham, sent its building committee to "look and view some meeting houses for dimensions," giving them ample time to do a good job. About two months later, on July 28, the committee reported that it had "been abroad at several places, taking dimensions of several meeting-houses, and having an account of the cost of them"—meaning they had gone twenty-two miles south and twenty-two miles west of Haverhill for their figures. After some discussion, the town ordered a structure fifty by forty-two feet whose interior was to be finished "after the pattern of the Beverly meeting-house," built in 1682, but whose exterior sides were to be installed "after the style of the Reading meeting house," raised more recently, in 1689—both of these were out of reach of most Haverhill residents.[21] The committee probably also examined but did not select as a model the fifty-by-forty-foot structure still under construction in Rowley (just across the Merrimack River), which had recently sent its own committee to visit Wenham and Beverly to report on size.[22] Why did Haverhill go to these lengths? Apparently its plans coincided with the aspirations of the newly chosen pastor, Benjamin Rolfe (served 1692–1708), who wanted a house of worship big enough for Haverhill's population. The nearest completed fifty-foot meetinghouse was located in Beverly with other large ones in Salem and Lynn.

When we examine specific instances of dispersal more closely, we learn that not all innovations traveled at the same rate or even in the same direction. The major portion of prototypes came from towns and parishes that were seen by others as regional leaders. In Massachusetts Bay, Beverly, Reading, and Wenham were frequently copied by newer communities around them; likewise, Hatfield was copied in the Connecticut Valley; and Guilford and Hartford were copied in Connecticut. These were not always important or highly populated port towns, though they were often older than the communities that imitated them. Some so-called leaders were distinctly rural and new—with imitations running against any perceived urban-to-rural or important-to-unimportant nearest neighbor models. Yarmouth, Massachusetts, copied Barnstable's interior colors in 1768 simply because they were right next door. Leaving aside the question whether one or the other was more typical of the New England experience as a whole, two distinctive patterns of diffusion seem to be at work during this period. Each pattern was associated with a specific group of architectural features, and each followed a distinctive manner of transmission.

Vernacular innovations, meaning those based on memory, convenience, and immediate need rather than on plan books or taught traditions, appear to have followed a "cluster" dissemination pattern that created well-defined, local pockets of usage within which communities attempted to imitate what their nearest neighbors were doing. These innovations usually had their origin in rural areas. Specifications for dimensions, locations of stairwells, pew designs, benches, gallery rails, and interior and exterior colors were often drawn from models located ten miles distant or under. Here, with this copying back and forth, is where the hypothetical eight towns immediately surrounding a community exerted their greatest influence.

These clusters defined the early meetinghouse landscape. Six Connecticut River Valley and Connecticut shoreline towns built fifty-foot-square structures similar to Hartford's second meetinghouse in 1638.[23] Smaller towns, such as Windsor, Connecticut, and Westfield and Springfield, Massachusetts, built lesser versions. Five eastern Massachusetts towns erected meetinghouses similar to the forty-foot-square dimensions Cambridge built in 1651.[24] Elsewhere, Wenham, Massachusetts, which built a four-square meetinghouse in 1663, may have begun a similar sequence when two neighboring communities (Manchester

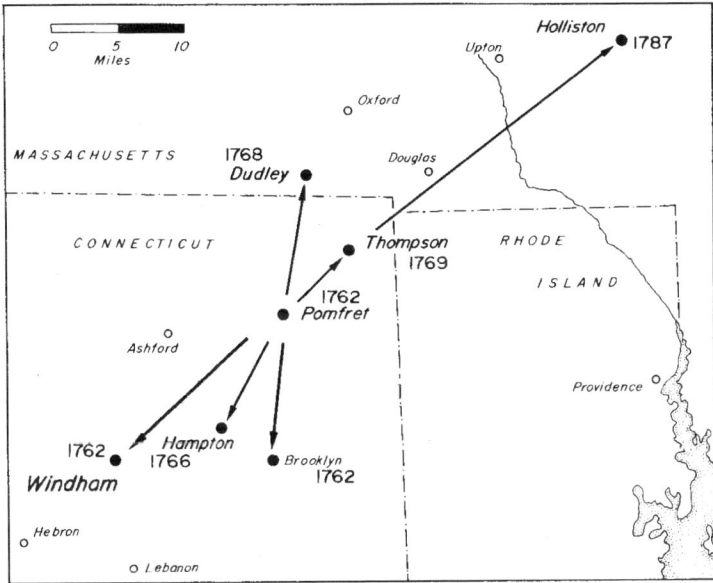

Figure 8.1. The "Pomfret cluster." Diffusion of orange as an exterior color for meetinghouses, 1762 to 1787, in Windham County, Connecticut, and neighboring towns in Massachusetts. Map by the author.

and Rowley) imitated aspects of its dimensions, roof, and interior components. The distribution of free-standing or separated belfries in three contiguous communities in Middlesex County, Massachusetts, reflects a narrower cluster. Little more than small sheds located at a short distance from the meetinghouse, these belfries became a local prototype: Chelmsford voted for theirs in 1716, Bedford in 1753, and Lexington in 1761.

The best examples of cluster distribution, however, are the eighteenth-century exterior painting practices discussed earlier. The orange first displayed in 1762 in Pomfret, Connecticut, was picked up by four or perhaps five surrounding towns between 1762 and 1769 (fig. 8.1). Their response to Pomfret's choice can only be described as immediate—the prime characteristic of cluster diffusion. The two later examples of orange coloration (Holliston in 1787 and Gilsum in 1791) were based on other factors, including hearsay and emigration into southern New Hampshire by Windham County residents. But what was Pomfret to these communities? Was it imitated because it was a regional leader? Probably not: Pomfret simply had an appealing idea. The area's civic leader was Windham, which later became the county seat and which had only recently erected the first steeple in that part of Connecticut. Yet Windham was one of two towns that immediately copied Pomfret's color. That many New England towns imitated the color of their neighbors' meetinghouses is suggested by evidence from southern New Hampshire, where yellow and yellow derivatives virtually excluded all other exterior colors in the 1770s and 1780s. Jaffrey copied Rindge, Temple copied

Wilton, Sandown copied Chester, and Surry copied Keene.[25] In this instance we do not know where the color originated, but some form of yellow or ochre was probably used on the meetinghouse in Wilton as early as 1773 or 1774.

By way of contrast, high-style innovations (such as rustication, pulpit and canopy design, the attached bell tower concept, spire arrangement, and the so-called church plan), which had their ultimate origin in schooled, Atlantic-wide and Anglican urban prototypes and architectural copybooks, appear to have followed "runs"—long-range linear dispersal routes that basically matched the availability of money to pay for them. Runs usually (but not always) followed established population dispersal routes by New England families emigrating into western Massachusetts, Vermont, and New Hampshire. Others traveled along the coastline, such as from Boston to Maine and Nova Scotia, or from Newport, Rhode Island, to Connecticut's port towns.

Two chains of imitation have been documented in western Massachusetts and southern New Hampshire that also reveal the rate at which the "modern style" actually moved across the New England landscape. The "Pittsfield run," called after that town's initial use of Charles Bulfinch's meetinghouse plan in 1790, involved ten communities in the Berkshires and its vicinity between 1794 and 1813. Six survivals, three recorded votes, three contracts, two shared builders, and a nineteenth-century woodcut help us follow its progress. Richmond, Massachusetts, instructed its builder, Thomas Dutton, in 1794 to make their meetinghouse "similar to the large meeting house in Pittsfield." Hinsdale, Massachusetts, contracted in 1797 to imitate the interior of the meetinghouse in Pittsfield; Salisbury, Connecticut, contracted in 1798 to imitate Richmond; Lee, Massachusetts (whose meetinghouse was built by John Hulett), voted in 1799 to adopt the plan of Richmond; Winsted, Connecticut, picked up the design in 1800 (seen on an 1836 John W. Barber woodcut); Washington, Connecticut, approved the design in 1801; South Canaan, Connecticut, in 1802; Westfield, Massachusetts, voted for Bulfinch's design in 1803. Lenox, Massachusetts, built the design in 1805; and Otis, Massachusetts (fig. 8.2), voted for the same construction as Winsted, Connecticut, in 1813.[26] The builder John Hulett may also have been involved with Richmond in 1794 and with the related survivals at Washington and South Canaan, Connecticut, raised between 1801 and 1804.[27] Two circumstances should be noted here. First, except for Richmond and Hinsdale, most towns seem to have acquired their design from a neighbor rather than Pittsfield—or for that matter from Bulfinch himself, who may have come to Berkshire County only once. Second, the design moved relatively slowly—a factor that reveals towns were still imitating each other, not following an architectural copybook or even an archetypical concept. The innovation covered the sixty-four miles between Pittsfield and Washington, Connecticut, in thirteen years, a rate of approximately five miles a year (fig. 8.3).

A more specific group of imitations offers much the same data but with greater precision. The "Templeton run" was a sequential group of porch and bell-tower designs that appeared on meetinghouses in central Massachusetts and southwestern New Hampshire between 1811 and 1823. Originating in Templeton, Massachusetts, where Elias Carter and Jonathan Cutting built a meetinghouse in 1811,

Figure 8.2. Congregational Church, 1813, Otis, Massachusetts, which followed the Pittsfield design. The town directed the builders to copy the 1800 meetinghouse at Winsted, Connecticut. Photograph by Jerauld A. Manter, circa 1960. New Haven Museum and Historical Society.

we know from survivals and documentary sources that at least eight imitations followed.²⁸ These began in Troy, New Hampshire, in 1815, and were repeated in Fitzwilliam, Dublin, Hancock, Acworth (fig. 8.4), Newport, and Jaffrey. It ended at Keene, New Hampshire, in 1829. In effect, the design moved into the north uplands covering a linear distance of 75 miles without making major lateral or rearward tacks before it returned to its base in Keene in 1829. If we include the

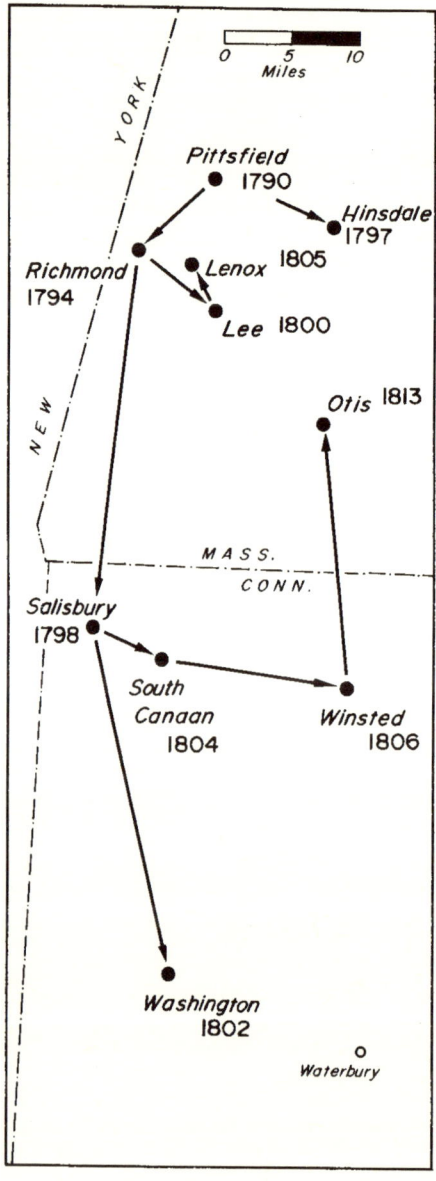

Figure 8.3. The "Pittsfield run." Diffusion of Charles Bulfinch's church design among towns in the Berkshire region of Massachusetts and Connecticut, 1790 to 1813. Map by the author.

8.4. Second meetinghouse in Acworth, raised in 1821, one of eight New Hampshire communities that chose a "Temple-[ty]pe" design, many of them replicating their immediate neighbors. Photograph by Ned Goode, 1959. Historic American [Buildin]gs Survey, Library of Congress, Washington, D.C.

Brimfield meetinghouse (burned in 1847) built under contract with Elias Carter in 1805 when the architect was only twenty-four years old, it covers a total northward distance of 111 miles over eleven years, a rate of transmission of approximately 10 miles a year—twice that of the Pittsfield example (fig. 8.5).[29]

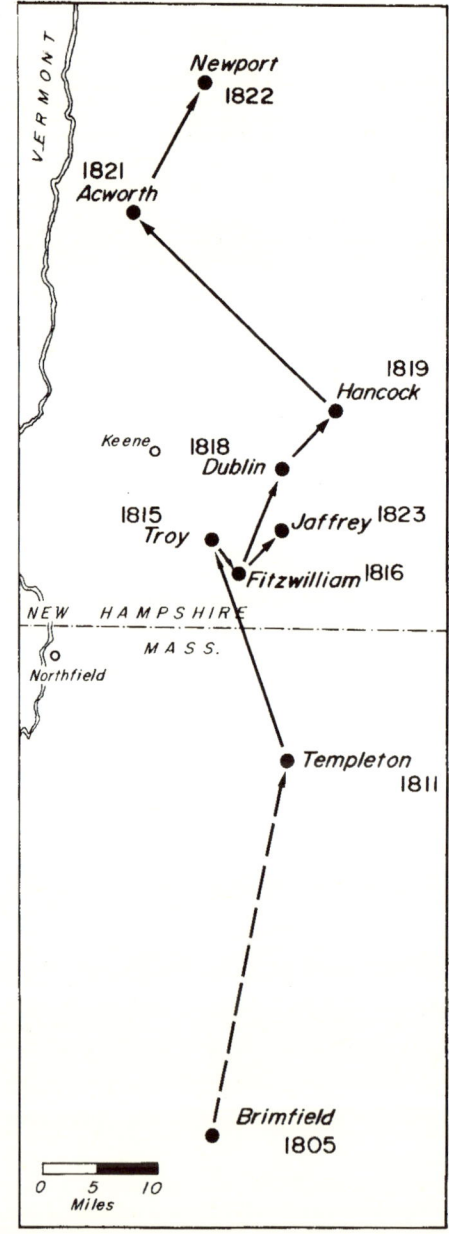

Figure 8.5. The "Templeton run." Diffusion of Elias Carter's church design among towns in central Massachusetts and southern New Hampshire, 1805 to 1823. The design then returned to Keene, New Hampshire, in 1829. Map by the author.

Like Pittsfield, the Templeton sequence advanced by the movement of individual builders and along the nearest neighbor model. Records of Troy, New Hampshire, indicate that in the summer of 1812 the town directed Captain Fuller and D. W. Farrar to examine the Templeton meetinghouse; Samuel Morse of Templeton did the finish carpentry. Dublin, in contrast, voted in 1817 to allow its committee to build "after the plan of Ashby or Fitzwilliam, or any other they may think proper."[30] Even if we did not have contemporary illustrations of the 1818 Dublin meetinghouse, we might accurately conclude that the committee chose the Templeton-style design in Fitzwilliam rather than the design attributed to Asher Benjamin in Ashby. The town hired as builders the same Jonathan Cutting and Samuel Kilburn who had been involved in raising the Fitzwilliam church.[31] Hancock voted in 1819 to "build a house nearly the size, construction, and form of the Congregational meeting house in Dublin" and hired Jacob Ames and Samuel Kilburn to do the work.[32] These decisions tell us the design was transmitted along a chain: Dublin imitated Fitzwilliam, not Templeton; Hancock imitated Dublin, not Fitzwilliam. More important, it tells us that these building committees perceived new designs in strictly local terms. For each of the three Templeton imitations whose documents have survived, the records cite an earlier model by location—usually the nearest town where such a model was standing—and not the name or reputation of the architect-builder responsible for constructing it.[33]

Among the many exceptions to these patterns was the vote taken by the newly formed town of Antrim, New Hampshire, in 1784 to copy the meetinghouse in Londonderry some forty miles away. In this instance, Antrim, a Presbyterian congregation that had just removed from Londonderry where most of the town grew up, plainly wanted a meetinghouse with which they were already familiar. Their builder, William Gregg, was himself a Londonderry native and most likely had been involved in the building of the Londonderry meetinghouse in 1769.[34] In a like manner, wealthy urban congregations might duplicate a feature close by either because it was convenient or because they sought to keep up with their neighbors. The New Brick congregation, a Boston church of considerable wealth that introduced New England's first ogee cupola on its bell tower, voted in 1766 to remake its deacons' seat "as lately been done at Mr. Cooper's [the Brattle Street meetinghouse] and the Old North [Boston's Second Church]"—two nearby congregations located within five hundred yards of them.[35]

In assessing these tentative hypotheses, we must keep in mind that these patterns of transmittal may have been determined as much by the level of financial investment they represented to a community as by their stylistic or innovative appeal. Towns and parishes erecting a standing bell tower usually relied on considerable amounts of donated money that supplemented tax revenue. With so much ventured in an idea by private individuals, a more distant source might be sought. Seats, galleries, and pews, however, were renovated or replaced almost every decade; window frames were rebuilt at approximate ten- or twenty-year intervals; a new coat of paint was applied every five or ten years. These alterations were perceived as such common occurrences that a nearby model would be satisfactory. Nor do we know whether imitations—distant ones and those from the immediate area—reflected a prevailing architectural taste or whether they were simply a convenient gauge of what the town expected from its builders and carpenters. In 1679 the Second Parish in Ipswich, Massachusetts, specified that its new turret be made "after the fashion, and in the proportions of" the one in Andover. Does this phrase reveal a hidden aesthetic? That is, did Ipswich like and admire Andover's turret because it was comely (and presumably Protestant), or were they simply using it dispassionately as a measure?[36]

New Englanders' sense of thrift and convenience also entered the equation. Parishes typically reused elements of their old meetinghouse when they raised a new one. John Elderkin II built the first meetinghouse at Norwich West Farms (now Franklin, Connecticut) in 1717 using the pulpit and seats from the structure his father had assembled in Norwich in 1673.[37] In 1711 North Andover, Massachusetts, ordered that the existing forty-two-year-old "pulpit in the North Precinct shall be set in our new meeting-house."[38] Sometimes parishes gave or sold their meetinghouse frames, pews, pulpits, and gallery seats to others. Rehoboth, Massachusetts, in 1720 donated its pulpit and the gallery facing to the recently formed Palmer's River congregation in that town.[39] New Milford, Connecticut, divided its old meetinghouse among four ecclesiastic neighbors, donating three-quarters of its body seats to the local Anglicans, the remaining seats to the town's Quakers, the pulpit to the Newbury Quakers, and the gallery seats to New Preston.[40] In a transfer like this a new parish might end up with old appointments just because it could not afford to pay for new ones.

In some instances new religious societies purchased an entire meetinghouse. As we have seen, two years after its founding in 1719, the west precinct in Watertown, Massachusetts, paid eighty pounds for the second meetinghouse in nearby Newton (built in 1697) so they would not have to bear the expense of building their own. They dismantled it, carried the frame components and other woodwork to its new location four miles away in fifty-seven horse-drawn cartloads, straightened the nails, and reassembled it with the help of a single gin pole and heavy rope supplied by Jonathan Coolidge of Newton. The only materials they needed to obtain were sleepers, shingles, pine boards, casements, glazing, and plaster.[41] Three comparable instances are known.[42]

The impulse for innovation, we should bear in mind, was always counterbalanced by a conservative aesthetic. The larger emphasis on what Anthony Garvan called a "Protestant plain style" is revealed by the age of the structures that were imitated (see Appendix A, Table 6). While some communities were copying new structures, many building committees selected models that were approaching or well past the halfway point of their useful life and were themselves about to be replaced. The majority of interior appointments (pulpits, deacons' seats, pews) were many decades old. Even turrets, a feature that revealed a community's status, were sometimes selected from old models—such as the Second Parish in Ipswich, imitating the ten-year-old turret in Andover in 1679. In short, building committees were just as likely to duplicate old models as they were new ones. Only colors and bell towers in the eighteenth century seem to be weighted toward new structures, perhaps because in some instances they represented radically innovative concepts.

Finally, there was a geographic element that may also have involved "class" and social standing. Coastal New England and interior New England may have functioned as two distinct cultural worlds in which architectural ideas circulated relatively freely within each area but that crossed the line into each other's domain only with difficulty. Out of 263 architectural features, only thirteen actually cite a Boston model or allude to a Boston-based carpenter or architect. Of these, two involved Anglican parishes copying Anglican forms and six involved Boston architects and designers working in a spate of building activity in the early national period. The remaining three—Guilford voting for a bell in 1726 like that in "Mr. Colman's meeting house," Ipswich Second Parish hiring in 1747 a Boston "artificer" to build its pulpit, and the First Baptist Society in Providence sending three men in 1774 to Boston to examine their "churches and meetinghouses"—represent less than 2 percent of known replications, each one involving an important coastal community; all the others usually cite rural prototypes, most of them close at hand.

Thus, the key models noticed by our hypothetical eighteenth-century English traveler may not have been the large urban Congregational, Baptist, or Anglican religious societies that defined the leading edge of innovation but those that represented the first breakthrough in a community's particular "world." For Boston congregations raising meetinghouses between 1714 and 1721 the model was the Manifesto Church with its "flat" roof in 1699 and the nearby New North Church with its battlements and spired bell tower. In Salem in 1772 it was the newly formed North Church with its "church plan." In rural Massachusetts, Concord's use of a "flat" roof in 1711 inspired Chelmsford, Lexington, and Lynnfield to do likewise. Guilford, Connecticut, also inspired local imitators when it introduced a standing bell tower in 1726; and Pittsfield, Massachusetts, led the way into the Berkshires with a new Federal church plan in 1790 when it used a Bulfinch design for its meetinghouse. These examples suggest that rather than being part of an Atlantic community, most New England towns existed in relatively confined cultural areas whose ecclesiastic architectural standards were based on those displayed by their neighbors—either those defined by their coastal commerce with other port towns or those defined by the ring of eight towns immediately around them. It also suggests why a narrow liturgical and architectural canon resulted in the simultaneous persistence of uniformity and regional variety. Because cultural perceptions were transmitted through second-, third-, and fourth-hand imitations, omissions and additions inevitably generated diversity. Many of these may even have been quite unintentional. The likelihood is that most meetinghouses, just like the Protestantism of their congregations, were as uniform as New Englanders knew how to make them.

CHAPTER NINE

# Meetinghouse Architecture as Puritan Ecclesiology

WHEN ELIAS CARTER's meetinghouse designs reached towns in southern and central New Hampshire in the 1820s, rural New England's ecclesiastic architecture had finally achieved the "Transcendantly Magnificent" stature proudly proclaimed by the Woodbury town clerk Joseph Minor in 1747.[1] Carter's meetinghouses, like those of Isaac Damon and other contemporary early nineteenth-century architects, reflected a new "Federal" aesthetic that increasingly isolated these public buildings for the specific exercise of religious worship. Frontier and upland communities, whose first meetinghouses often bore the signs of a struggling rural population, could now worship in an edifice whose principal purpose was to serve their Christian faith. Though many were still underwritten by the town, meetinghouses were upgraded to an environment free of baseball play, winter mud, stray dogs, biting winds, and signs warning occupants not to slam the seats. Treaties with Native Americans were no longer negotiated in them; capital trials no longer took place within; executions no longer took place outside. The aisles were now carpeted. The air was soon to be heated by stoves. Chandeliers hung from the ceiling. The walls echoed with the sounds of trained singers. Pulpits were decorated with crimson damask, fringes, and tassels, and even some record-keeping books were "painted and glittered."

Few of these advances toward comfortable "churchly" architecture were new to the third period. They were evident in Boston meetinghouse architecture as early as 1699. And though the term *church* does not normally appear in the legal idiom of town and parish records, it appears often enough to help us recognize the increasingly ecclesiastic role of the meetinghouse in the early eighteenth century. In 1700 Rev. Benjamin Colman called the Brattle Street meetinghouse a "new built church." Almost three decades later, in 1728, Westfield, Massachusetts, voted to raise fifty pounds for "a bell for the Church."[2] There were other signs, too. Norwalk, Connecticut, voted in 1723 that nothing was to be done in the meetinghouse "but what is consistent with, and agreeable to the most pure and special service of God, for which end it was built and now devoted." Leominster, Massachusetts, considered in 1740 whether "God's Tabernacle should be erected here." But it is also true that the issue was never entirely settled until the final disestablishment of Congregational and Presbyterian churches in the early nineteenth century. As late as 1817, a year after Bedford, Massachusetts, had completed its massive, Asher Benjamin–style meetinghouse, the town felt obliged to vote that "no town meetings, no training, nor choosing militia officers shall ever be held or done in the meetinghouse, and no other town business shall be done in said language house except by permission of the selectmen for the time being."[3]

The story of New England's early meetinghouse architecture centers on this transition. How did the vernacular "House[s] for Publick Assembly" (to use Isaac Chauncy's term), which readily shared municipal, legal, and ecclesiastic uses become transformed into architecturally designed churches devoted to the "special service of God"?

So far this study has revealed that meetinghouse styles were transmitted from one community to another like an idiomatic dialect. Indeed, towns and religious societies were just like individuals: they worked diligently to keep up with the styles of their neighbors. This awareness of what other towns were doing—a self-consciousness that characterized many aspects of Congregational polity and liturgical traditions—was the principal aesthetic impulse that created a "New England" style of meetinghouse architecture that encompassed subregional variations. Hingham's 1680 vote to send three men to view neighboring Massachusetts meetinghouses to compare "their number of Inhabitants with ours,"[4] or Haverhill's 1696 decision to imitate meetinghouses in Beverly and Reading, was probably repeated hundreds of times in New England. That this impulse to imitate was always part of a common civic aesthetic is documented in its most extreme form by Surry's imitation of Keene and the decision by ten Berkshire communities to adopt Bulfinch's Pittsfield design. It was an urge that pervaded every step taken by virtually every parish or religious society during the two hundred years under consideration.

We have also seen that the transmittal of this language followed predictable patterns as it moved from community to community. The first two or three rings of neighboring towns—those within a half-day's ride—exerted the greatest influence on local building committees. These structures helped determine dimensions, plate heights, exterior "forms," and rooflines. We have seen the transmission of simple design elements create local "clusters" of usage. Stairwells were defined by coastal in contrast to upland demographic patterns; exterior colors and bench joinery by neighborhood-based preference; pulpits by the "dignity" of individual ministers. By contrast, complex or costly improvements, such as colonnaded porches and bell towers, created long-range "runs" on a particular style that moved scores of miles following the availability of money, the movement of designers and carpenter-architects, and the dispersal of their publications.

Other studies have recognized that the acquisition of new architectural styles was also tied to the tastes, wealth, and piety of individual parishioners and of the community at large. These links have been closely examined by Richard Bushman and Gretchen Buggeln. Bushman, who sees in Boston's 1723 Christ Church an Anglicizing pattern for later eighteenth-century Congregationalists, finds similar imitations throughout the major cities of the English-speaking New World.[5] Buggeln studied the decisions of early nineteenth-century Connecticut towns facing the dilapidation of their eighteenth-century structures. As they built new meetinghouses, Buggeln notes, they followed a trail blazed by the sophisticated taste, vision, and financial means of leading pew owners who treated their meetinghouses like private assets—"advertisements" for the combined glory of neoclassical architecture and their own closeness to a state of grace. They introduced a "cult of sensibility," affirming that the meetinghouse where God reveals himself has a special sanctity.[6]

These points of view cannot be dismissed: neighbors imitate neighbors; money talks. John Winthrop's diary tells us the First Church of Boston paid a thousand pounds for its 1640 meetinghouse by soliciting private donations, thus avoiding the use of tax revenues. In 1669 the Third Church in Boston installed the first sheet-leaded roof in New England at a cost of two thousand pounds, again by private expense. The Brattle Square Society raised its "flat roof" meetinghouse in 1699 by a voluntary association of wealthy merchants. Private means paid for nearly all prerevolutionary eighteenth-century Congregational and Anglican meetinghouses in Boston, including the second meetinghouse of the Brattle Square Society toward which the merchant John Hancock alone gave a thousand pounds.[7] Private revenue built the spectacular second meetinghouse of the Hollis Street Society in Boston and the fourth meetinghouse of the First Church in 1808. Time and again, in Guilford and Wallingford and Portsmouth and Hartford, as well as in Boston, private wealth erected early bell towers.

Rhode Island congregations also relied on private money. Newport, long known for its competing and sometimes radical Baptist sects, saw its Seventh-Day Baptists raising a two-story meetinghouse in 1729 that displayed some of the earliest examples of Georgian taste in the region. The design, by Richard Munday, featured innovative architectural elements, such as a large central doorway, compass windows, intricately carved pulpit stairs, and lush interior paneling. It also produced the first vaulted ceiling of any meetinghouse in New England. Who paid for these luxuries? The Seventh-Day Baptist congregation in Newport included two goldsmiths, three former Rhode Island governors, a former colony treasurer, a former colony secretary, and an English-educated merchant (Henry Collins) with a reputation for sponsoring reading societies, libraries, and portrait painters in the community.[8]

Equally remarkable was the response of the First Baptist Church in Providence to their newly acquired wealth in the 1770s. Roger Williams and his seventeenth- and eighteenth-century Baptist successors in Providence met in private homes and unremarkable first-period meetinghouses for the first 140 years of their institutional existence. The society's first meetinghouse, raised in 1700, was a small twenty-by-twenty foot building ostensibly in the shape of a "hay cap" with a hole in the center of the roof that provided an outlet for a chimney. The society's second meetinghouse, raised in 1726, was a forty-by-forty-foot structure furnished with benches. As Providence became a mercantile powerhouse in the 1760s and 1770s, John Brown privately financed the society's third meetinghouse in 1774, the eighty-by-eighty-foot steepled structure whose elegance outranked the Boston meetinghouses its builders intended to copy. Even today the third meetinghouse is called the First Baptist "Cathedral."[9]

But these perspectives may be only part of the story. When the First Church in Boston, supported by one of the wealthiest congregations in New England, rebuilt their burned-out structure in 1712, they used a period-one style—while other congregations in the town were rapidly "modernizing" theirs. Twenty-two years later when the Second Parish in Andover, Massachusetts, voted to rebuild their meetinghouse, they also chose to follow "the same form and fashion as the old," a period-one structure. Both congregations enjoyed the same wealth and taste in decorative arts as found elsewhere in New England but preferred the old architecture, not the new. In contrast, Pittsfield, Massachusetts, a relatively isolated rural town 130 miles from Massachusetts Bay in an area that only recently had been a frontier, drew on a relatively unknown but brilliant Boston architect who played a pivotal part in transforming the design of ecclesiastical buildings in New England.

To understand why, our final inquiry goes beyond the general issues of taste and wealth to identify the characteristics of the leaders in this process—the individuals, building committees, congregations, and parishes who perceived and initiated the second and third architectural periods—and the characteristics of those who resisted them. Here we must reexamine the ideas raised in essays by Kevin Sweeney and Carl Lounsbury. In discussing the rise of sacramental piety, Sweeney equates the increasing aestheticism of the religious service with second-period architectural change. He notes that "changes in hymn singing and the reading aloud of Scripture increased the range of aural sensations found in worship service," adding that the third-period or "churchly" style was "another stage in the religious rehabilitation of the visible" by means of setting aside consecrated houses of worship.[10] Lounsbury, who sees this historical process applying to most Protestant denominations in North America, essentially adopts this view and states that "the softening of the hard edges of doctrine meant that the old Calvinist wariness of using physical objects to support worship for fear of idolatrous entrapment eventually gave way to an acceptance of objects as a means of enhancing the aesthetic atmosphere for worship." He takes this one step further, suggesting that the shift to the third-period meetinghouse styles reflected the shedding of a Calvinist heritage for a "rhetoric of republicanism" that transformed churchgoing in the nineteenth century.[11]

Using these positions as our initial points of guidance, we can begin with the larger premise that New England's Protestant history consisted of a prolonged struggle between those who wished to maintain a "pure primitive Church" and those who wished to see it broadened and modernized. According to this framework, "conservative" points of view were championed by the "visible saints"—the communicants and officers of the church.[12] They wished to keep the service as an intellectual or Calvinist event, to retain control over the selection of the minister, to preserve the role of elders, to appoint deacons for their lifetimes, and to maintain "authentic" (meaning untrained) musical practices. The congregation at large, however, supported "progressive" practices. They expected greater and more readily obtained access to the sacraments (the so-called halfway covenant or the Anglican model) and a more visual or sacramental experience of the service; they expected to share in the appointment of the minister, to disband the role of elders, and to improve musical education through singing schools. Though this dichotomy greatly oversimplifies the long-term equation and fails to include many nuanced alternatives representing opposite sides of the same coin, it does offer a starting point.[13]

To quantify and geographically chart these forces throughout New England, we have to go back to the evolution of liturgical practices discussed in chapters 2 and 4. By concentrating on areas where data are widely available from primary and secondary sources—the halfway covenant, reading Scripture, spoken relations, promiscuous seating, choice of psalmody texts, and singing practices—it is possible to compare the evolutionary corridor taken by individual congregations with the known chronology of their architectural change. In most instances the younger (but not always the wealthier) parishes that were the first to observe the modern liturgical practices were also the first to initiate architectural change. Older societies tended to reject change. Thus, the advance of new architectural taste—the "flat" roof, the standing bell tower, the compass window, the church plan, the bell-tower portico, and the final reorientation of the building to face the street—may have been governed by the same timetable that managed modifications in ecclesiological and liturgical practices (see Appendix A, Tables 2 and 3). Parishes that introduced them were also the ones that sold pews privately for meetinghouse maintenance and upkeep, who maintained good relations with their Anglican peers, whose meetinghouses were physically situated near Anglican churches, and who followed some Anglican prayer practices. Parishes that were slow to adopt these concepts or declined to consider them at all tended, in contrast, to retain the bevel roof and central turret, maintain the clustering of seating around the pulpit, delay the introduction of a main alley and compass windows, and postpone reorienting the meetinghouse so its portico faced the street. These parishes kept their distance from Anglican practices.

The best examples of so-called progressive parishes are the six religious societies founded in Boston between 1698 and 1731 that distanced themselves from the practices and architecture of the town's three oldest congregations. Recall that, as in Rhode Island, church congregations in Boston were independent and self-governing; after 1700 there was little governmental interference in Boston church life. Led by the affluent but controversial Brattle Square undertakers, these parishes flourished. The Brattle Society organized itself in 1698 with a church that opposed the Cambridge platform and chose as their first minister Rev. Benjamin Colman, a relative of one of the undertakers. As described by Richard Bushman, Colman "was the perfect choice for the Brattle Street pulpit, which was considered by some as halfway between Episcopacy and Congregationalism."[14] Not the first Reformed congregation in Boston that failed to meet a geographic identity (Baptists had organized a church in 1665 and Boston's Third Church was founded by seceders from the First Church in 1669), the Brattle nevertheless included a cadre of leading New England merchants who rose to power after the dissolution of the charter and England's Glorious Revolution in 1688. Among them were Thomas Brattle (1658–1713); Capt. Benjamin Davis (1649–1704); John Mico (d. 1718), who married Mary, daughter of Thomas Brattle; Thomas Cooper (d. 1705); and John Colman (m. 1694)—important owners of large mansions in the center of town. Colman and his congregation were on good footing with the Church of England and English writers and hymnodists. Benjamin Colman corresponded with Isaac Watts; he was friends with "Philomela," the English poetess Elizabeth Singer Rowe (1674–1737).[15]

Before hiring Colman, the undertakers gave him instructions that reintroduced some forms of Anglican worship in a Reformed church setting and challenged some of the central principles of Congregational polity. The congregation read the Bible during the church service and recited the Lord's Prayer ("all the Words of it together as it stands in the New-Testament").[16] More important was their disavowal of a "Publick Relation" to qualify admission for church membership as outlined in chapter 12 of the Cambridge platform. They also greatly broadened participation by allowing "every Baptized Adult Person who contributes to the Maintenance" (apparently meaning both male and female congregants) the right to elect the minister—thus extending the process to most pewholders.[17] The Brattle was also the first congregation in New England to omit the deaconizing of psalms (1699), the first to accept an organ given by one of its parishioners (1713), and the first to organize a singing school (1721).[18] These positions put them in conflict with most other congregations in the region, but in time basically all the innovations begun by Colman and the Manifesto Church were adopted by other Congregational churches in New England. His influence and reputation were still in evidence twenty-two years after his death. Ezra Stiles wrote in 1769, "Rev. Ch[auncey]. Whittelsey has begun read[in]g. Script[ure]. In pub[lic]. Worship in N[ew]. H[aven]. first Chh—in Dr. Colman's manner."[19]

Closely following Benjamin Colman's lead were the religious societies created in response to the town's surge in population and wealth between 1710 and 1740. Like the Manifesto Church, the New North, the New South, the New Brick, the Hollis Street, and the Lynde Street (or West) societies were owned by their pewholders. And like the Brattle, none was defined geographically; instead each represented church schisms or occupational groups. They embraced many of the practices begun by Colman long before others in New England. One society made relations optional and put an end to appointing "ruling elders" (New Brick in 1722).[20] Three societies were among the first in New England to read Scripture during the service (New Brick in 1729, Hollis Street in 1742, New North in 1750).[21] One gave the congregation the right to name the minister (New North, 1721).[22] One was the first society to observe a solemnity, "religiously set apart," on the day of its opening (North Church).[23] All five subscribed to Boston's earliest singing schools, with the Hollis Street congregation founding the first formal singing society in Boston. They were among the first to put aside the Bay Psalm Book and to follow Anglican King's Chapel by singing Tate and Brady's *New Version* (West Church in 1736, Brattle in 1753, New North in 1755) or Watts's *Psalms* (New Brick in 1751). Following the Brattle, they led all others by compromising or eliminating the practice of lining out (New Brick in 1729, New North in 1755).[24]

A central second figure in this group was Rev. Mather Byles (1707–1788), minister of the Hollis Street Society for forty-four years between its inception in 1732 and 1776 just after the British evacuation from Boston. A nephew of Cotton Mather's (he inherited his library), Byles was known for his wit, his ability with language, and his talent as a preacher. He was an avid proponent of organized music, author of *Poems for Several Occasions,* and a correspondent with English poets, including George Granville, Alexander Pope, and Isaac Watts. Byles was a friend to Boston Anglicans. While his connection to the society was dissolved for political reasons in 1776 (as a Loyalist he was arrested and disenfranchised), Byles continued his work as a writer of religious music and a leading proponent of music education.[25]

These six younger Boston religious societies set in motion the transition in meetinghouse construction from period-one styles to period-two styles by introducing key architectural elements. Among meetinghouses in Boston and other parts of eastern Massachusetts, and Connecticut and the Connecticut Valley, the Brattle raised the first urban meetinghouse with a pitched, "flat," or "English" roof—in the manner of Anglican churches then appearing in London. The choice of this style may have deliberately paralleled their choice of Communion plate, which favored large flagons over beakers and cups, again similar to Anglican practice.[26] Over the next two decades similar "flat" roofs accompanied by compass windows appeared at the New North, New South, New Brick, Hollis Street, and Lynde Street. In 1714 or 1715 the New North raised New England's earliest standing bell tower with battlements and a spired steeple—possibly the first church society in North America to do so. The New South, the Brattle, and the New Brick immediately followed. At least one meetinghouse (the New Brick) in addition "faced" its bell tower toward a principal street.

In the transition from second-period to third-period meetinghouse design, two Boston congregations from this early progressive group again led the way. Still representing the town's mercantile elite and newer professional classes, the Manifesto Church hired Thomas Dawes to build its "Anglicanized" second structure, designed on an axial plan in 1772. The second Brattle Street meetinghouse was the first in New England to be heated with "stoves" and the first to display a prominent Palladian window in the entrance foyer.[27] Elsewhere in Boston, when the 1787 fire destroyed the Hollis meetinghouse (and partially damaged Mather Byles's nearby home), the society responded by hiring Charles Bulfinch to design what became one of the first meetinghouses in New England with a dome and the first in New England with twin bell towers—a spectacular display of English Federal architecture that upturned 150 years of Huguenot, Puritan, and early Reformed traditions.

Providing a contrast is the conservatism of the two oldest societies in Boston—the First Church (Old Brick) and the Second Church (North Church). By nearly every measure, these churches were decades behind their younger neighbors in observing the liturgical practices identified with Colman. The First Church, founded under the guidance of Rev. John Cotton (1585–1652), played a leading role in the Antinomian controversy—an incident that defined New England's religious conformity and women's diminished role in church affairs. It resisted the formation of the Third Church in 1669 and strongly reaffirmed written relations. Later, under the guidance of the fifty-nine-year pastorate of Rev. Charles Chauncy (1705–1787), the society extended the election of the minister to the congregation at large in 1730, approved the halfway covenant in 1736, and retained spoken relations for church admission until 1756, when these confessions were allowed to be exhibited only to those who wanted to hear them. The First Church was probably the last society in Boston that deaconized the psalms (delaying the decision to sing all the way through until 1761). It retained the Bay Psalm Book, keeping the "old version" until 1761, when it finally turned to Tate and Brady. These changes were made thirty-one, thirty-seven, fifty-seven, and sixty-two years, respectively, after the Brattle Street Society adopted them in 1699.[28] Additionally the First Church had a history of postponing the musical training of its singers, waiting until 1758 before "encouraging" a singing school by a vote of the committee. Rev. Charles Chauncy resisted the introduction of musical instruments until shortly before his death in 1787.

Boston's Second or North Society, under the sixty-four-year leadership of Increase Mather and his son Cotton Mather (1663–1728), nearly duplicated this record except that it approved the halfway covenant somewhat earlier in 1693. In 1697 this church criticized the policy of a neighboring society in Charlestown that allowed the congregation at large to select the minister.[29] In 1699 Increase Mather composed a tract (*The Order of the Gospel*) that challenged the legitimacy of the Brattle Street congregation. The Brattle replied with *The Gospel Order Revived*, printing it in New York because they sensed that Massachusetts printers would not publish something hostile to the Mathers. Cotton Mather kept his comments to his diary: "I see Satan beginning a terrible shake in the churches of New England, and the innovators that have set up a new church in Boston (a new one, indeed!) have made a day of temptation among us. The men are ignorant, arrogant, obstinate, and full of malice and slander, and they fill the land with lies. . . . Wherefore I set apart this day again for prayer in my study, to cry mightily unto God." The Second Society kept to the old ways as long as possible: waiting until 1760 to share the privilege of electing the minister with the congregation at large, retaining a separate elders' seat at least through 1766, ending deaconizing in 1771, and making relations optional only in 1786 after they became affiliated with the New Brick.[30]

Two of these older societies worshiped in period-one structures for decades after this form was supplanted by Georgian and Federal styles. The First Society occupied the 1640 "Old Meeting House" for seventy years; after it burned in 1711, the society built the first-period Old Brick, which served the congregation for ninety-six additional years. The Second Society occupied its 1650 meetinghouse for twenty-six years; it built a first-period replacement in 1677, which it occupied for ninety-nine years until the British burned it for firewood. While little is known of either one of these structures, the second was illustrated on a 1768 map of Boston and on a woodcut of the North End home of Ebenezer Richardson (fig. 9.1). In both views the 1677 meetinghouse features a four-square roof and an attached "old-fashioned" bell tower possibly dating to the 1720s or 1730s.

Between these two extremes was Boston's Third or South Church, which, according to Mark Peterson, was a principal supporter of the halfway covenant, breaking away from the First Church in 1669 on that specific issue. But most accounts describe a congregation relatively slow in adopting the practices identified with a progressive society. While its pewholders were allowed the privilege of participating in the selection of a minister as early as 1712, church members did not include pewholders in their formal meetings until 1722 when the society needed money to repair the meetinghouse. Church admission required spoken relations until 1769. The church still retained the Bay Psalm Book in 1755, only replacing this version when their clergyman, Rev. Thomas Prince (1687–1758), issued his own translation of the psalms in 1758—the same year the church voted to discontinue deaconization. Its architectural history was mixed, however. Like its predecessors in Boston, the Old South worshiped in a period-one meetinghouse for the first sixty years of its existence. When accelerating wood rot required the society to condemn the structure in 1729, it voted for a

Figure 9.1. View of the second meetinghouse of the Second Society in Boston, built in 1677 and dismantled for firewood by the British occupiers during the Revolution, revealing a hipped roof and a turret-topped standing bell tower surmounted by a cockerel weather vane. The scene depicts a cartoon image of British customs official Ebenezer Richardson firing at a crowd in front of his house in the North End of Boston, near Theophilus Lillie's store. Woodcut from a broadside, *The Life, and Humble Confession, of Richardson, the Informer*. Boston, circa 1772. The Historical Society of Pennsylvania (HSP).

brick Georgian replacement that imitated aspects of Anglican Christ Church, well in line with the New Brick and the New South.[31]

The face-off between progressive and conservative religious societies in Boston was repeated elsewhere in the region with comparable consequences. For example, in New Haven County, Connecticut, the innovators were the towns of Guilford, Wallingford, Milford, and Stratford. A succession of votes taken by these towns between 1705 and 1743 placed four of the first five bell towers erected in Connecticut before 1750 in a tight arc around New Haven. Guilford in particular stands out as a liturgically progressive parish. The same year that this town completed its three-decker sixty-eight-by-forty-six-foot meetinghouse (1712), the community voted for men and women to sit together in the pews—probably the first in New England to do so. In 1748 the Guilford parish voted to discontinue lining out the psalms in the service—the fourth church body in New England to do so (after Boston's Brattle, King's Chapel, and New Brick), and the first in Connecticut. It was the first parish in Connecticut to introduce a pitch pipe and the first in Connecticut to accompany its psalms with a bass viol (in 1796) following up with flutes, a violin-cello, and a double bass viol. This was the same parish that decided to use private funds to build a belfry and spire in 1727 in imitation of Rev. Benjamin Colman's in Boston, then shifted over to imitate Newport's Trinity Church, but finally followed an unknown design.[32]

Guilford's neighbors were similarly progressive. Wallingford, located on the Quinnipiac River, voted to erect a meetinghouse patterned after Guilford's in 1716 and accepted private money to build a steeple. The structure was completed in 1717 and a bell tower added in 1728. Wallingford was a musically proficient town, voting to sing the new way and old way on alternate Sabbaths in 1731; it sent a "company of singing masters" to the South Church in Hartford in October 1769 with "several new pieces of music with instruments."[33] Milford, located on Long Island Sound about nine miles west of New Haven, completed in 1728 a three-decker meetinghouse 17 feet longer and 8 feet wider than Guilford's with an attached 95-foot bell tower. This construction followed a progressive seating vote by the town giving special preferences to "wives of Church officers" in 1705. After the 1728 meetinghouse was completed, the Milford church adopted the halfway covenant and the town voted to suspend its seating rules and to assign space to parishioners "by the money paid towards the building of the house"—one of the first to make this financial element explicit.[34] In 1743 Milford's neighbor Stratford built a three-decker meetinghouse with a 130-foot-high bell tower under comparable circumstances.[35]

The conservative element in this divergence was the First Church in New Haven, which retained the old "Puritan" ways amid this sea of change. Architecturally, the First Church of New Haven relied on two consecutive period-one structures for 118 years, from 1639 to 1757—despite recurring problems with overcrowding, wood rot, and water leakage. Faced with an increasing shortage of seating space in the 1680s and 1690s, the town authorized the builder Nathan Andrews to install seats over the women's stairs, a seat below the galleries, and a "hanging seat over the Galleries." Apparently not satisfied with these additions, the town in 1697 voted to build a new sixty-by-forty-foot meetinghouse of brick and stone, the cost of which was not to exceed five hundred pounds. But after receiving no bids, the town finally decided in 1698 to expand Andrews's original design.

New Haven did not have a bell tower until 1753 when the Anglicans raised Trinity Church; they did not have a Congregational bell tower until 1757 when the First Church built the brick meetinghouse their predecessors had originally planned in 1697—which included compass windows—using a design in many ways similar to Boston's Old South and possibly responding to similar internal circumstances. New Haven saw its second bell tower only in 1764 when the separatist White Haven Society erected theirs.[36]

Liturgically, the First Church of New Haven staunchly opposed the halfway covenant, its ministers in the 1670s seeing it as "an uncouth way and very unpleasant divinity." The church finally agreed to observe the practice in 1678, but separatist spin-offs in the eighteenth century rejected it. The church continued to require that relations be read before the entire congregation until 1751; it was still relying on written relations until Rev. Chauncey Whittlesey's ordination in 1758; and it began reading Scripture from the pulpit after 1769, decades behind congregations in Boston and other parts of Connecticut.[37] The First Church and the breakaway White Haven Society discontinued reading psalms only in 1771 when the itinerant singing master John Stickney taught his school in that town.[38]

Another set of circumstances, again involving first-period roof shapes and central belfries, surfaces between 1701 and 1718 in Salem, Massachusetts, the home of Massachusetts Bay's oldest congregation. Shortly after the deaths of several church leaders and the formation of two new religious societies, the town built four large meetinghouses, each one patterned after the "Great Meeting House" raised in Salem in 1670. These were constructed in the critical years when meetinghouse architecture was in transition from a first- to a second-period style—the last one raised about nineteen years after the Manifesto Church erected its "flat" roof, seven years after Concord had raised its "flat" roof, and about four years after the New North in Boston had erected its battlements and bell tower. Although these churches are pictured in early nineteenth-century drawings and paintings as well-advanced second-period structures, all four appear to have belonged to the first period.

Figure 9.2. *South Danvers in 1828*. View showing the tents and soldiery of Capt. William Sutton's Light Infantry encampment. The meetinghouse in the center was built in 1711 for the middle precinct in Salem, Massachusetts, as a period-one structure with two tiers of galleries and a four-square roof. The central turret was removed and the tower was added in 1774. The structure was cut and expanded twice by Daniel Spofford, first crosswise, and then lengthwise. Oil on wood. Attributed to Nathan Lakeman, 1804–1835. Copyright and Courtesy, The Peabody Institute Library, Peabody, Massachusetts.

The first of these examples was the forty-eight-by-forty-two-foot meetinghouse of Salem Village (now Danvers), built as a four-square structure in 1701. Few details are known of its design, except that its four-square roof was imitated by the north precinct of Andover in 1711. The second was the meetinghouse of the newly formed middle precinct in Salem (now Peabody), which gained its separation from Salem's First Parish in 1709 and built a meetinghouse. This structure had two tiers of galleries and a central turret. Approved by the parish vote in 1710, and raised in 1711, it dominated for years the center of what later became Peabody Square at the junction of Central Street and Gardner's Bridge at the millpond. As seen in an 1828 painting attributed to Nathan Lakeman, the structure had two doors almost side by side on the south side—the result of a later addition by Daniel Spofford of two bays—as well as a standing bell tower probably dating to 1774 when the roof was changed from a four-square turreted design to a gable-ended one (fig. 9.2).[39]

Salem's newly formed East Church soon joined this building boom. This society raised a sixty-by-forty-foot meetinghouse in 1717 with a "tunnel-shaped" roof cupola (presumably like the Old Tunnel in Lynn) "culminating in a belfry," with the bell rope hanging "down through the ceiling to the floor of the house"—again evidence of a first-period feature. This meetinghouse was enlarged and remodeled in 1770, with a fourteen-foot square tower and steeple attached to its western end. This is the meetinghouse that William Bentley occupied after his ordination in Salem in 1783, illustrated in a drawing by D. M. Shepard, the source of a lithograph published by the Essex Institute in Bentley's four-volume diary. In 1718 Salem's First Parish, acknowledging the "great decay" of its 1670 meetinghouse, replaced it with a seventy-two-by-fifty-foot four-square structure that had two tiers of galleries and a belfry in the center of the roof whose bell rope hung in "the broad aisle, half-way between the pulpit and the main entrance"—almost a duplicate of the 1670 structure. At some point, probably after 1770, the parish replaced the four-square roof with a gabled one and added a standing bell tower and an opposed porch. This remodeled version was illustrated by Abel Bowen of Boston for Charles Upham's history just after being taken down in 1826 (fig. 9.3).[40]

THE EXPERIENCES of Salem's four parishes were matched by other, older Massachusetts communities in coastal Essex and Middlesex counties, such as Medford, Lynn, Essex, and Beverly, whose inhabitants attended services in period-one structures or who built in that style after 1715.[41] Lynn continued to worship in a period-one meetinghouse with a centrally hung bell rope throughout much of the eighteenth century (fig. 9.4), as did Beverly, until 1770. Medford built a period-one meetinghouse in 1726. These two structures were imitated by Haverhill and Rowley. But younger or second-generation neighbors who were located in a periphery around them—such as the Second or North Parish in Beverly and societies in Chelsea, Reading, Topsfield, Wenham, Manchester, and Gloucester—all built second-period houses with standing towers or added towers to existing structures at a fairly early date. Thus, like the congregations in Boston and New Haven, older congregations in Essex and Middlesex counties were keeping to the old ways of meetinghouse design while congregations in their suburbs were introducing newer styles.

As in the First Church in New Haven, there is some evidence that conservative liturgical practices in the four Salem religious societies accompanied the decisions to keep first-period meetinghouse designs. While Salem's First Parish began reading Scripture in the service in 1736, the church retained the practice of lining out through the 1770s and required written relations until 1781.[42] A sign of the First Church's focus on its antiquity is revealed in 1826 when timber twice used in the "Great Meeting House[s]" of 1672 and 1718 was preserved and made into a Communion table in 1826—while other pieces were made into "curious relics."⁴³ In Salem's middle precinct, traditional seating practices were being followed. In 1724, for example, John Waters was given a pew for his wife and family, but Waters himself was seated in the "front fore seat in the gallery"—the usual sign that men were separated from women.⁴⁴ Lynn's First Church retained a pulpit that seated eight elders facing the congregation; three other men sat in the deacons' pew, and ten more were assigned to the Communion table. The church had accepted the halfway covenant by 1700 but rejected it in 1768. Later, in the 1770s, Salem's First Parish, its East Parish, and its Middle Precinct chose not to adopt a church plan when they were remodeling their meetinghouses, while the breakaway North Church and the newly formed Tabernacle Church were embracing third-period architectural concepts—the North Church in 1772 and the Tabernacle in 1776.⁴⁵

How these ecclesiastical and architectural perspectives were transferred from one community to another is illustrated by the two congregations in Andover,

Figure 9.3. *Meeting-House of the First Church—built in 1718.* View of the third meetinghouse of the First Church in Salem, Massachusetts, after its central turret was replaced by a bell tower circa 1770. The original 1718 structure had a four-square roof surmounted by a turret and belfry. Line engraving, signed "AB." Attributed to Abel Bowen, circa 1826. From Charles W. Upham, *Principles of the Reformation*, 50. Widener Library, Harvard College Library, US 13437.10.49.

Figure 9.4. *View of the First Congregational Meeting House, Lynn, Mass., in 1820.* Memory depiction of the 1682 "Old Tunnel" meetinghouse in Lynn, Massachusetts, as it was in 1820, seven years before the structure was taken down, moved, and reerected with a changed form. Artist unknown. Courtesy of Lynn Public Library.

Massachusetts. Here the liturgical evidence is much more complete than in Salem. Ezra Stiles, who visited Rev. William Symmes when he toured the area in 1768, reports that the First Parish in Andover "sing[s] Tate and Brady since 1765—don't read Scriptures—No admiss[ions] Without Relations—receive [Communion] Stand[in]g In Pews or Seats—not all Baptized—Deacons continue till death—Deacons not ordained—no ruling Eldrs nor ever had—most Fam[ilies] Pray &c." Four of these nine practices were hallmarks of a conservative church. When visiting the Second or South Parish in Andover, Stiles records "[I] kept the Sabbath at [south] Andover [and] heard the venerable Mr. Saml. Phillips aet. 79 preach. He began Worship with ask[ing] a bless[in]g & read[in]g Script[ure]s. He sings N.E. Version [1640 imprint of the Bay Psalm Book] twice in forenoon & twice Afternoon. Has Four Deacons, no ruling Elders. Two [tiers of] galleries. The Congrega[tion] about 500 Souls or 450 and yet a crouded Assembly."[46] Like the First Parish, the South Parish "use[d] Relations" for admission into church at least until 1773. It was one of the last parishes in New England to offer pews for choirs and trained singers, doing so in 1779; Deacon I. Abbott was still reading the Psalms in 1794.[47]

The leader here may have been Rev. Samuel Phillips (1690–1771), who comes through in Stiles's report almost as a caricature. Stiles refers to him as an "Old Light Calvinist" and an "Opposer of Mr. Whitefield & the Extraordinaries of 1741."[48] Phillips's 1880 biographer calls him a "Calvinist of the old school."[49] Phillips began preaching at Andover when he was twenty years old and served the Second Parish in Andover for sixty-one years. His tenure was two years longer than that of Rev. Charles Chauncy of Boston's First Church and was exceeded in length only by those of Ebenezer Gay of Hingham (1696–1787) and Joseph Adams of Newington, New Hampshire.[50] His published sermons on divinity are conservative and emphasize justification by faith over justification by works. In a 1766 publication he asserts that faith is "the alone Condition of our present Justification before God."[51] His nineteenth-century biographer says he preached past the turning of the hourglass and was known for his sternness, "which caused undue fear in many of his people, and especially among the young."[52]

Architecturally, Andover considered and rejected a "flatt roofe" at its town meeting in 1707, voting instead in 1708 for a "square roofe without dormans with two Lucoms on each side." When Andover's South Parish seceded on the issue of location a year later in 1709, the North Parish reconvened and reduced the size of its meetinghouse and again voted for a "Roofe like Salem village" (that is, a four-square roof). Later, when the North Parish reused its seventeenth-century pulpit, it already had seen more than forty years of service. This conservative point of view continued in Andover for the next three generations. In 1734, when Andover's South Parish raised its second meetinghouse, the parish specified the new one was to be built "after the same form and fashion as the old"—an ambiguous phrase, but one that nevertheless implies they were following aspects of the period-one style of their 1709 meetinghouse.[53] One year later, when neighboring Tewksbury was preparing to erect their first meetinghouse in 1735, they examined the old dismantled first-period Andover frame and found the timbers "all sound except for two or three sticks." (There is no evidence that they used it, however.)[54] Two generations later when planning a new meetinghouse in 1787, South Andover asked Moody Spofford to model the new one after the thirty-four-year-old meetinghouse in the North Parish, specifying there would be "nothing superfluous, but [be] plain and neat, not have any medallions [modillions], dentals, or carved work"—in effect ignoring a group of young professional architects in Boston just starting to receive commissions (fig. 9.5).[55] Eventually both Andover structures were remodeled and replaced, North Andover in 1835 and South Andover a few decades later. One observer to the dismantling in North Andover told Sarah L. Bailey, who was compiling the town's history in 1880: "If they had let it stand, it would have been better than the one they have now."[56]

Figure 9.5. Mid-nineteenth-century drawing of the 1788 meetinghouse in South Andover, Massachusetts, built by Moody Spofford. The original structure had three porches and was modeled after the one in Andover's north parish and without "medallions, dentals, or carved work." The former minister's son, Samuel Phillips Jr., was on the planning committee. The illustration shows the meetinghouse after the addition of a bell tower and its conversion to a church plan in the nineteenth century. Line engraving by Kilburn-Mallory, circa 1859. From George Mooar, *Historical Manual of the South Church in Andover, Mass.*, opposite page 32. Widener Library, Harvard College Library, US 13139.10.15.

In Newbury and Newburyport, the conservative group was the First Church of Newbury, the tenth oldest religious society gathered in Massachusetts Bay, which built its first meetinghouse in the "Old-Town" district in 1643. Opposed to them were three much younger Congregational or Presbyterian churches established in the "Waterside" district that built meetinghouses in 1725, 1756, and 1768; this part of town later incorporated as Newburyport. The First Church of Newbury was two decades behind the others in introducing reading Scripture into its service; it continued to sing the New England version of the psalms until 1761 when it adopted Tate and Brady; it failed to add musical instruments to the service in 1794 when the Presbyterians began using violins, bass viols, a clarinet, and a bassoon and the Congregationalists purchased an organ. Architecturally, the First Church of Newbury retained Stephen Jaques's 1700 first-period four-square meetinghouse for 106 years, removing two of the four dormers in 1726 and the remaining two about 10 years later (fig. 9.6). By contrast, each of the Newburyport societies built meetinghouses with "flat" roofs and large standing bell towers with spires in the "common" mode, the first raised in 1737 during a renovation. All three bell towers are seen in Benjamin Johnson's 1774 townscape of Newburyport and its harbor (fig. 9.7).[57]

An unusual example of a late first-period style is found in Plymouth, Massachusetts, the oldest Congregational society in New England. In 1744 Plymouth's First Church replaced its 1683 meetinghouse with what was probably one

Figure 9.6. *Old-Town Meeting-House, 1700–1806.* Woodcut illustration of the third meetinghouse in Newbury, Massachusetts, without the original dormer windows, which were taken down beginning in 1726. From Joshua Coffin, *A Sketch of the History of Newbury, Newburyport, and West Newbury* (1845), iii.

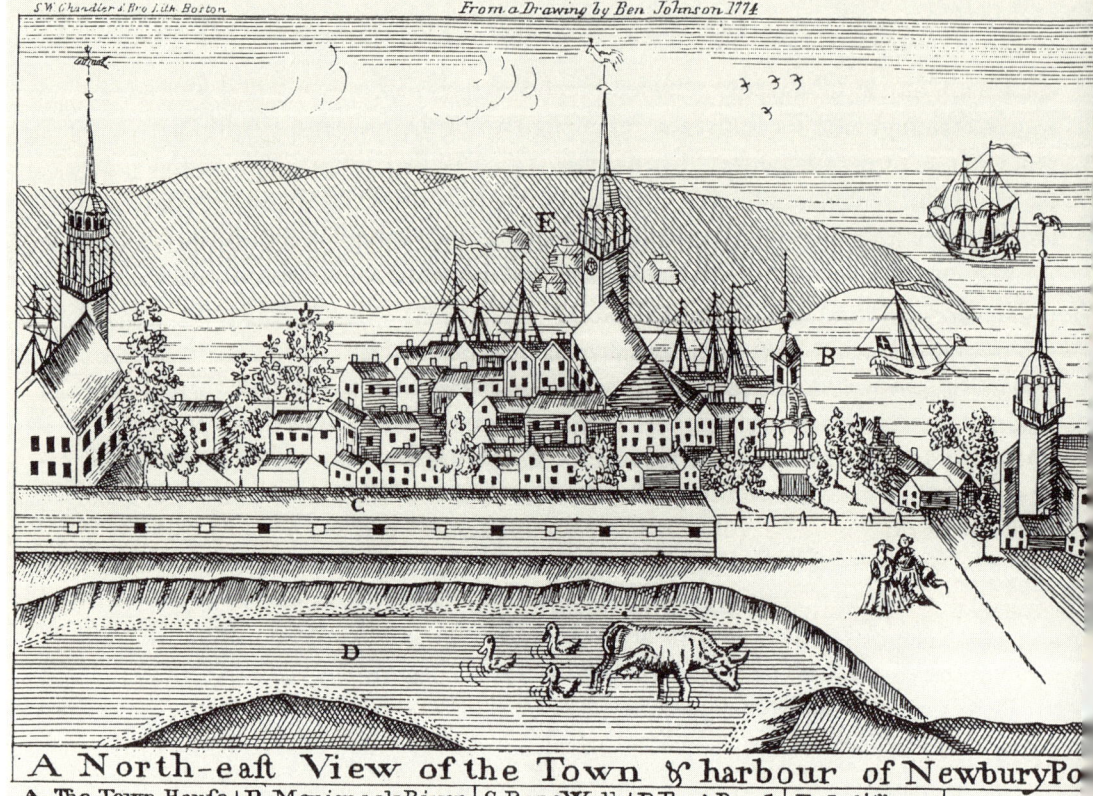

Figure 9.7. *A North-east View of the Town & harbour of NewburyPort*. Townscape by Benjamin Johnson, 1774, showing the three meetinghouses in Newburyport, Massachusetts, just before the Revolution. From a lithograph copy by S. W. Chandler, Boston, 1854. Historical Society of Old Newbury.

of the last four-square and turreted meetinghouse raised in New England (fig. 9.8). The diary of Rev. Nathaniel Leonard records that before the raising of this meetinghouse he led the congregation in singing one verse from Psalm 127, and four verses from Psalm 122, followed by a prayer. During the next three days he began each morning with part of the psalm and prayer. When the frame was erected, they sang nine verses from Psalm 115. The town felt so strongly about its new building they voted that any person who left a stove (meaning a foot warmer) in it would forfeit five shillings.

With its long tradition of separatism, characterizing the Plymouth church as "conservative" is not easy. But it was the same parish that sang from a 1612 psalm book (Henry Ainsworth's *Book of Psalmes: Englished both in prose and meter*) for sixty years, that changed to the Bay Psalm Book only in 1692 when the volume was over four decades old, and continued with the Bay Psalm Book until 1771 when it considered Tate and Brady. The congregation did not become liturgically "modern" until it finally chose Watts in 1786—much later than most other parishes. It was also a congregation that attempted to discard the halfway covenant at a relatively early date (1772) and kept written relations for church admission until 1823. Curiously, in the period after 1790 when New Englanders began to design their meetinghouses so that they faced the street, the parish removed the turret and replaced it with a centrally mounted standing bell tower over the front door on the long side (fig. 9.9), an architectural concept otherwise found in southern New Hampshire.[58] According to Peter Gomes, Rev. Chandler Robbins, who served during the 1780s and 1790s after Leonard's tenure, was "an upright and venerable pillar of orthodoxy, [who] did all within his power to preserve the faith of the fathers."[59]

Meetinghouses using traditional or first-period Puritan designs comparable to the one at Plymouth accompanied the movement of New Englanders north into Nova Scotia. A description provided by a descendant of a parishioner of James Murdoch's Protestant Dissenting Church in Halifax describes level after

Figure 9.8. Memory view of the third meetinghouse in Plymouth, Massachusetts (erected in 1744), showing a first-period hipped roof and central turret. Drawing possibly by Samuel Davis (1765–1829). Courtesy of the Pilgrim Hall Museum, Plymouth, Massachusetts.

Figure 9.9. Detail. *View of Town Square in Plymouth about 1828.* Third meetinghouse in Plymouth, Massachusetts, showing the portico and belfry added to the long side sometime after 1790. From a memory drawing by Doris Bartlett. Lithograph, circa 1840. Courtesy of the Pilgrim Hall Museum, Plymouth, Massachusetts.

level of gallery pews in what in effect was an imitation of the early seventeenth-century style of the temple at Charenton, France. Known alternately as Mather's Church or St. Matthew's Church, the 1754 Halifax structure was "a large square edifice, unpainted, and with no claim to architectural grace or beauty. It contained four tiers of pews, beside the wall pews, and would seat perhaps a thousand persons. It had a high square pulpit and canopy sounding board; the frame of the building was brought somewhere from New England, possibly from Machias, Maine, whence the frames of the old gambrel-roofed houses on Church Street are said to have been brought."[60] This massive "four decker" meetinghouse appears in an engraving of the governor's house in 1764.

While these transformations were taking place among the Congregationalists, Anglican parishes in New England were passing through some of the same liturgical changes, in some instances drawing disaffected Congregationalists into their fold. King's Chapel's choice of Tate and Brady's psalms in 1713 may have preceded their use in Boston's Congregationalist churches by several decades, but they too were replacing an older text (Sternhold and Hopkins) that no longer fitted their services. Much the same change was noted by Anglican minister Rev. James MacSparran in 1730 that the psalms should be sung without reading the first line—the same issue that faced Congregationalist denominations as they attempted to raise themselves up from their status as provincial colonists. Some Anglican parishes in fact were refuges for dissenters who were frustrated in their effort to follow a more refined manner of worship. After a major, unsuccessful struggle to improve singing in 1723 in the Second Parish in Braintree, Massachusetts, members of the congregation who wished to sing the "new" way seceded from the Second Parish and "publicly declar'd for the Church of England" in 1724—that is, they chose to become Anglicans because they wanted to sing more harmoniously.[61]

Anglican models may also have exerted a cultural influence. The decision by Salem's North Society in 1772 to design a meetinghouse on a church plan was as much a social and political one as it was architectural. The proprietors of the influential and successful North Society consisted of forty-two men and one woman, a widow, and included Edward Augustus Holyoke, a physician; Samuel Curwen, a judge and merchant; and Col. Benjamin Pickman, a merchant. "The original list," according to Salem historian James D. Phillips, had "a somewhat tory tinge." Frederic Detwiller agrees, reporting that the composition of the building committee for that work brought together the Royalist and aristocratic elements in Salem who wished to emulate what he called the higher "plane" of Anglican church architecture. And only a few streets away stood St. Peter's Church, the exterior of which was still basking in the red paint applied by John Holliman in 1741.[62] By no coincidence, perhaps, Salem's North Society changed its way of worship—beginning to read Scripture publicly in the service in 1772, ending relations in 1773, and discontinuing the practice of "propounding" prospective members in 1773.[63]

Berkshire County and the Housatonic towns of western Massachusetts may offer another example of these Anglican links. When Stockbridge set about planning a new meetinghouse in 1783, the town's selectmen and building committees must have been aware of the flourishing Episcopal parish in Great Barrington, their immediate neighbor about nine miles to the south. There in 1768 a vigorous parish, competing with perennially weakened Congregational and Dutch Reformed societies, had erected St. James's Church, a stately 71-by-40-foot structure with compass windows throughout and an attached tower and steeple 110 feet high. (Great Barrington's gilded weathervane was obtained in New York City for forty-one pounds.) The overwhelming presence of St. James's may have led Stockbridge in 1784 to build a bell tower "opposite the pulpit" in the third-period or axial or Anglican style. This structure in turn may have influenced Stockbridge's northern neighbor Pittsfield—then locked in a heated competition with Lenox and Lanesboro to become Berkshire County's sole shire town—to choose Charles Bulfinch to design a meetinghouse even more "churchly" than those of its neighbors. And this structure eventually led to a Housatonic Valley meetinghouse style that persisted in that area for years.[64]

On the outer edge of the spectrum were societies that declined to make any real changes in their places of worship or, for that matter, in their liturgical practices well into the nineteenth century. These groups were usually small and rural, however, but they clung tenaciously to the old ways. For example, a Baptist congregation in Warren, Rhode Island, led by Elder James Manning, raised its first meetinghouse in 1763, choosing square dimensions (forty-four by forty-four feet), a hipped roof with surmounting belfry, and a bell rope that "hung directly down in the center of the middle aisle."[65] Galleries were added in 1772. Other Baptist congregations built even smaller meetinghouses (twenty-eight by twenty-six feet) including the one at Apponaug in nearby Warwick, one of three of the same size built by Elder Peter Worden as he gathered converts in Rhode Island and Massachusetts. Even as late as the 1780s, rural congregations were still building meetinghouses with first-period features. In 1784 separatist supporters of the charismatic but reputedly alcoholic Amesbury, Massachusetts, clergyman Dr. Thomas Hibbert purchased land and built a meetinghouse with a "hopper-roof," a four-square design which—like Lynn's Old Tunnel meetinghouse—drew its name from the shape of the roof converging to a point at the top. In an attempt to avoid paying taxes to support his rival, Hibbert's group tried but failed to present themselves as Presbyterians. This was the same structure that was derisively nicknamed "The Still" by its opponents.[66]

Quaker examples of conservatism include the 1706 meetinghouse in North Pembroke, Massachusetts, photographed for the Historic American Buildings Survey in 1934 and 1987. This meetinghouse has separate entries for men and women as well as a floor-to-ceiling partition separating the sexes (both Quaker characteristics), but it also is a single-porch design like most meetinghouses in coastal Massachusetts. Two nearby Quaker survivals in South Uxbridge and East Sandwich, which are dated 64 and 104 years later, have been described by Edmund Sinnott as being in most respects similar to North Pembroke. These meetinghouses had benches facing the center table with galleries on three or four sides—a unique preservation of the special early Protestant link between the speaker and his audience.[67] At least some Quaker meetinghouses were square, such as the twenty-by-twenty-foot meetinghouse built in Woonsocket, Rhode Island, by John Arnold in 1719. But it is unclear whether they had hipped roofs. When traveling through Plymouth County in 1809, William Bentley noticed that the only "high square roofs" he observed in local meetinghouses belonged to Quakers—such as the one he found in Scituate. Bentley's phrase is imprecise, but it does suggest he was looking at four-square hipped roofs.[68]

While the data are incomplete, the link between architecture and church practices suggested here may provide a more nuanced understanding of the larger conversion of the first-period Puritan meetinghouse into a third-period Congregational church. Architectural historians traditionally have seen meetinghouse builders as navigating through a landscape of wealthy parishioners, newly imported English taste, the emerging presence of Anglican houses of worship, and a new Republican attitude—all of which came together to encourage major innovations in the period 1787 through 1810. What I am suggesting in this study is that the primary arena involved liturgical standoffs between older religious societies and their younger, mostly urban, counterparts—one side representing a "pure" Calvinist church and the other a more inclusive Congregational one.

It is possible to argue that the correlations described in this chapter were simply a matter of coincidence, that older religious societies retained first-period structures because people were used to worshiping in them; they knew them and wanted to keep them. Similarly, one could argue that Rev. Samuel Phillips of South Andover and Rev. Ebenezer Gay of Hingham were Calvinists or Old Light preachers just like many others in New England, that their views on relations, justification, and redemption were unrelated to the fact they both worshiped in period-one structures during their extraordinarily long tenures. But Ezra Stiles identified both Phillips and Gay as presiding over "the best State of any [church]—& nearly as perfect as this World will admit."[69] What he did not report was that the two men and their parishes were jealously conservative of their meetinghouses, consciously resisting the ostentation and new styles found in those of their neighbors.

Our judgment is that the story of Andover's and Hingham's meetinghouses goes well beyond mere happenstance. The choice made by Boston's First Church to rebuild in a first-period style in 1712 was as much an ecclesiological statement as it was an architectural one—a decision aimed at the perceived threat of a younger group who had abandoned some essential elements of the Cambridge platform in favor of a more comprehensive church. As the latter point of view gained greater adherents, builders drew on Georgian or Federal architectural practices in much the same way as their clergymen drew on the practices and liturgy of the Anglican Church. Five men set this conversion in motion. They were the Boston clergymen Rev. Benjamin Colman and Rev. Mather Byles; two self-taught architects Thomas Dawes and Asher Benjamin; and the Harvard-educated Charles Bulfinch. They introduced new tastes for innovative English and Federal architecture and new ideas about grace and holiness that were coupled with progressive church practices—both eventually becoming the regional norm. These five men take the full credit for extinguishing a longstanding "naïve" architectural tradition. Or should we say the full blame? Despite the best intentions of their builders, or perhaps because of them, meetinghouses had lost the Calvinist bloom of the wild vernacular rose.

CHAPTER TEN

# A Fleeting Image

WHETHER VIEWED as a weakening of sixteenth-century Calvinism, a gradual expansion of the sacraments, or the rhetorical republicanism of a new political era, the architectural transformation described here may have had a visual aspect to it that has hitherto remained obscure. The resurgence of English culture in eighteenth- and early nineteenth-century New England may explain the refined architectural motifs of entry porticos and bell towers designed in Federal and Greek Revival styles, but it also helps us better interpret the populist scope of New England's early nineteenth-century churchgoing experience. At the same time that Charles Bulfinch, Asher Benjamin, and Elias Carter were bringing the church plan into the region's rural communities, poorly trained and untrained artists were introducing painted religious images and religiously oriented decorative work into the pulpit area and its immediate surrounds. While almost no traces of these images have survived, the number of times they are cited in New England town histories, diary entries, and personal reminiscences, together with the compelling—if sometimes critical—detail of their descriptions, suggests that at least some rural meetinghouses were decorated with art whose ultimate purpose was similar to the "churchly" and "republican" changes taking place in meetinghouse architecture. In other words, the religious impulses that sought out Georgian and Federal aesthetics to refine urban and suburban meetinghouses were also drawing on naïve artisanship and image-making to "refine" isolated or rural ones.

One indication is the increasing use of painted or inscribed religious maxims, especially those that evoked attention to a newly built house of worship. William Bentley recorded three such maxims in a trip through northern Essex County in 1793. In the new meetinghouse in South Andover he found a pendant canopy with an inscription from Psalm 93:5: "Holiness becomes thy house O Lord, forever." The next day in Bradford, Massachusetts, he recorded a maxim from 1 Chronicles 16:29: "O worship the Lord in the beauty of holiness." It, too, was inscribed in gold paint on the canopy of the new meetinghouse and he noted that the clergyman used this text for the dedication of the house. Later that day Bentley also found the cipher "IHS" painted on the pulpit front of the meetinghouse in North Andover—the same congregation that had insisted that no "medallions, dentals or carved work" would be permitted on its new meetinghouse in 1788. Bentley notes that this was "not in the style of sentiment of the New England settlers" and concludes somewhat sourly that "the Catholic Church" (as he put it) had always existed in human nature.[1] Alternately, a cipher for In Hoc Signo or Jesus Hominum Salvator, the emblem was rarely used by Protestant churches in America. A parallel can be found in a blue-and-white earthenware plate used in the Communion service of the congregation in Concord, Massachusetts. Made in Lambeth, England, between about 1690 and 1711, the plate has religious symbols fired into its center including an upright cross, the letters "I.H.S.", and what appear to be three nails. It has come down with a history of use in Concord's First Parish, but there is no indication when it was introduced into the service.[2]

That these painted religious or semi-religious maxims were authorized by the community at large is suggested by a vote taken in Brimfield, Massachusetts, shortly after that community completed its 1805 meetinghouse. Pleased with the success of its native son Elias Carter, the town meeting voted to ask a sign painter to inscribe on the pulpit canopy, "My father's house shall be called a house of prayer for all people"—a paraphrase of Isaiah 56:7. The same informant who reported this vote remembered (and fortunately preserved) the "silk hangings" suspended behind it.[3]

A more visual symbol of the Christian deity was reported by Alice Morse Earle, who writes: "The pulpit of one old, unpainted church retained until the middle of this century [nineteenth] as its sole decoration, an enormous, carefully painted, staring eye, a terrible and suggestive illustration to youthful wrongdoers of the great, all-seeing eye of God."[4] The Divine eye as an emblem of God was a popular image among Protestants in the second half of the eighteenth century and an important symbol in Freemasonry, established in the colonies by the 1730s. A 1760 children's broadside uses verse from Isaac Watts's "The All Seeing God," published in 1715, to invoke a Calvinist vision of the human fate: "Almighty God, thy piercing eye / Strikes through the shades of night / And our most secret actions lie / All open to thy sight."[5] A frontier prophet in Vermont spoke in 1799 of visions of a "penetrating Eye" who "views with Impartiality, the most minute proceedings of his Creatures."[6] Anglicans shared a similar language. Jacob Bailey, a New Hampshire clergyman later known for his Loyalist sympathies, advised young women to avoid all that is impure, immodest, and indecent and to remember that the "all-seeing eye of God is upon you and he takes notice of your thoughts, words and behavior at all times."[7]

Other allusions to the Christian deity were created by the cast-iron or wrought-iron rods that suspended the canopy over the pulpit. In at least one meetinghouse in eastern New England, the rod was twisted into a rope by a late eighteenth-century metalworker and then "painted white, with streaks of gold," suggesting that the pathway to heaven comes from the preacher's text. In northern New England and in Maine, the canopies of three late eighteenth-century and two early nineteenth-century meetinghouses were suspended by a half-open hand—made from forged or cast iron or an iron core covered with a wooden or plaster sleeve (fig. 10.1). The symbolic intent is not known. The town house historian, Gwenda Smith, writes, "Here in Strafford [Vermont] it used to be said that any untrue words spoken in the pulpit would cause the hand to release its grip and send the sounding board crashing down on the offending speaker." In Thomaston, Maine, the hanger reached down (not up) and was described as a "well carved hand and arm let down from the ceiling, as if from a concealed giant reclining above it." The one in Strafford reaches up to hold a stirrup.[8]

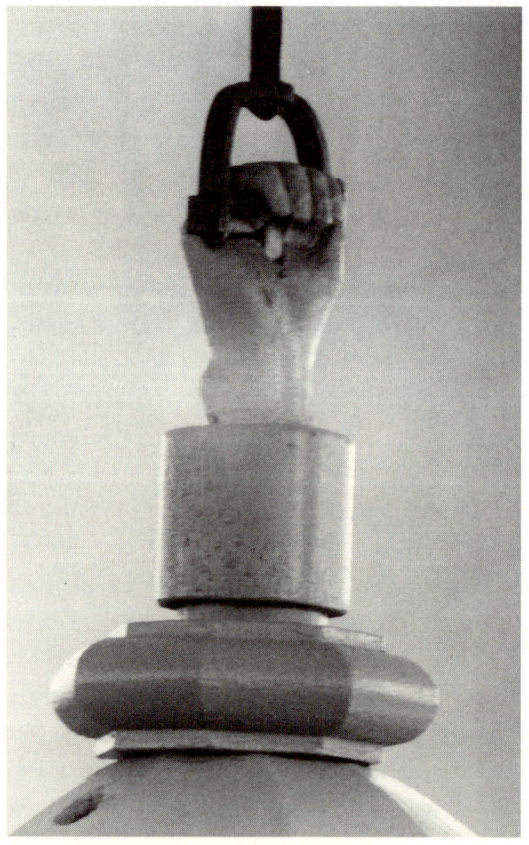

Figure 10.1. Ornamental hand holding up the canopy, Strafford, Vermont, built in 1799. Height from canopy to top of hand, approximately 18 inches. From Gwenda Smith, *The Town House*, 73. Photograph by Gwenda Smith.

Cherubim paintings in Congregational and Baptist meetinghouses are also known. According to Horace A. Keach, a nineteenth-century historian of Burrillville, Rhode Island, the Baptist meetinghouse erected there about 1770 was furnished before 1812 with "a lofty pulpit, above which is a painting representing cherubim, but a most rude and shabby daub." Presumably this was done when a steeple was added in 1812 and the interior remodeled. Elsewhere, an unidentified parish historian who wrote in 1886 of the 1734 meetinghouse in West Haverhill, Massachusetts, notes, "Some daring artist was allowed to paint the faces of two cherubs, one on each side of the pulpit window, where they looked upon the sober people, their rosy cheeks and laughing eyes making a grim contrast with their dim surroundings." He adds: "I have heard my mother (who was born in this parish) describe these crude paintings, and speak of the impression that the large blue eyes of one and the dark brown eyes of the other made upon her childish fancy." Benjamin Read, who compiled a history of Swanzey, New Hampshire, in 1892, notes that the pulpit of the 1796 twin-porch meetinghouse was "a large box with a door to enclose the minister—[and] was many feet above the floor; and above this on the wall were painted representations of seraphs or angelic beings." Francis E. Blake, a historian of Princeton, Massachusetts, remembered in 1915 that "back of the pulpit" of the 1796 meetinghouse "were some paintings 'supposed to represent angel faces,' and over the window caps on each side, was a figure of a cherub." "All these figures," he adds, "were obliterated during a subsequent repainting of the interior." In Sterling, Massachusetts, a story was still circulating in 1931 at the 150th anniversary of the town's founding that on a wall of the second meetinghouse built in 1799 "were painted two angels, one represented as ascending, singing 'Glory to God in the highest'; and the other as descending, singing, 'On earth peace and goodwill to men.'" Even as late as 1936, Abbie L. Phelps, as she alludes in a history she wrote of New Ipswich, New Hampshire, found evidence of "cherubs of the most distressing ugliness" in the 1812 meetinghouse.[9]

Painted images also appeared on the underside of belfries. According to a historian who had seen the building in the early nineteenth century, the plastered arch over the bell in the third meetinghouse in Durham, New Hampshire, was "painted a sky color interspersed with scattered clouds" in 1792.[10] Though this description invokes a tangible quality, we have little idea of the actual appearance of most of the others, especially those of angels. A hint is provided by a memory picture of the interior of the Baptist meetinghouse in Burrillville when it was used as a town house and a site for occasional preaching in Glocester, Rhode Island, in the first two decades of the nineteenth century. The image, which appears in the *Historical Pascoag Herald* of 1894, shows two winged cherubs' heads high above the pulpit—the pulpit window and the flue of the stove heating the hall dividing them (fig. 10.2). The heads are seen face on.[11]

Figure 10.2. *Interior of Old Town House—The Cherubim and Gallery*. Memory drawing of the gallery of the Old Town House, Burrillville, Rhode Island, as it appeared in 1812 with the cherubim behind the pulpit. The original meetinghouse was raised as a Baptist house of worship about 1770. From *Historical Pascoag Herald*, 1894. Photograph by Betty Mencucci. Courtesy of the Burrillville Historical and Preservation Society, Pascoag, Rhode Island.

Although the illustration lacks detail, it does suggest that Burrillville's cherubim may have been related to eighteenth-century Anglican decorating traditions. At least two trained artists working in Boston painted these types of images. John Gibbs (d. 1725) and his son John Gibbs Jr. (active 1729–1756) were churchmen and Boston artists of some ability who were well connected to King's Chapel, Christ Church, and Trinity Church. The three painted winged cherub heads attributed to John Gibbs Jr., now preserved in the collection of Trinity Church, Boston, are rare surviving examples of eighteenth-century New England ecclesiastical painting—probably prepared for the chancel or apse (fig. 10.3). They may have resembled the "6 Cherubims heads with festoons of Music" known to have been painted in Christ Church in Boston and subsequently painted over. At least some of these images were taken from Catholic sources, but it is also possible they came from within the Reformed or dissenting tradition.[12]

The likelihood that angels were popularly visualized in the lexicon of the early New England imagination is suggested by occasional images appearing as graffiti in the milieu of everyday life. One, dated to the early eighteenth century,

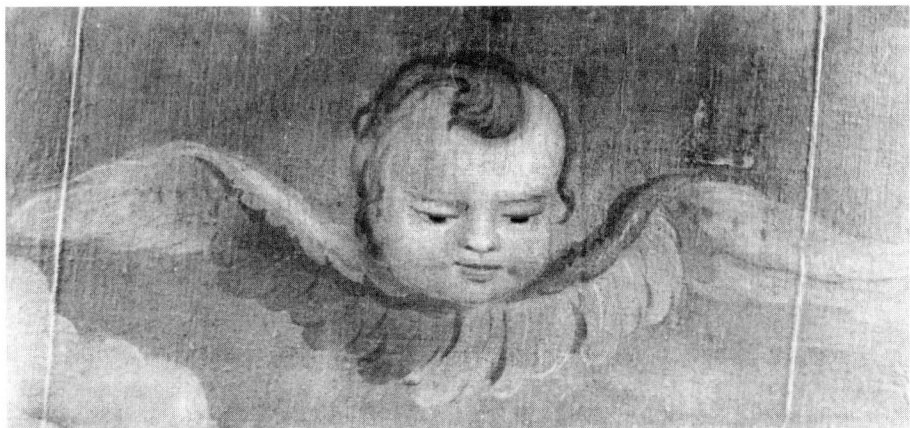

Figure 10.3. Winged cherub head with outstretched wings attributed to John Gibbs Jr. (active 1729–1756). Boston, circa 1755. Oil on canvas. Approximate width 40 inches. Photograph by Edward O. Miller Jr., courtesy of Bettina A. Norton. Trinity Church in the City of Boston.

is a winged angel head—and its reverse image—painted on an exposed upstairs beam of a privately owned house in Little Compton, Rhode Island, built between about 1750 and 1780 (fig. 10.4). Elsewhere, Boston probate records indicate that eighteenth-century New Englanders owned or collected religious images for display in their homes. Henry Guionneau, a Huguenot merchant, enjoyed "12 Pictures being 12 Apostles," and John Liddell, a gentleman, possessed a painting of Mary Magdalene. Anthony Stoddard owned an "Image of the Virgin Mary" valued at two pounds that he and Martha Stoddard kept in the second-floor principal chamber of their mansion house on King Street. Stoddard, a long-time member of Boston's Third Church, served as treasurer for the society and was personally responsible for financing the Old South in 1729.[13]

Some of these images, like the cherubs and death's heads carved on early New England gravestones, may have been primitively powerful—the visual equivalent of the language of the poet Edward Taylor, whose metaphysical verse variously describes how "Saints and Angells ravisht are in Glee" or unwittingly discovers his own "Gold-Fincht Angell Feathers dapled in / Hells Scarlet Dy fat."[14] Although mid-nineteenth-century commentators almost always derided these gravestone images, the art may have had considerable appeal in the late eighteenth and early nineteenth centuries. Some of the most interesting headstone designs in the region are transfigured skulls with emblems of "grace" attached to them (hearts, stylized mouths, eyes, wings, and flowers). Others are illuminated or radiant heads, some surrounded by sunlike beams. One carver in Haverhill, Massachusetts, depicted spirits as faces supported in the beaks of a pair of birds. And another carver in southeast Massachusetts, a member of the gravestone-making family of James New of Wrentham, pictured released spirits responding to the call of the trumpet as bubbling suns rising up or pushing up from the ground and floating into heaven (fig. 10.5).[15]

Other examples of angels commonly occur in samplers, mourning pictures, and quilts and in school art, diaries, and commonplace books. They are visual expressions of a larger naïve tradition that extends throughout almost two centuries of early New England history.[16] These remarkable "providences," as they were called, describe Puritan encounters with the invisible worlds of heavenly beings, devils, apparitions, and ghosts—witnesses who distinctly heard Jericho's trumpet, who saw visions of flaming swords in the sky, who described in detail their visits to upper and lower worlds. These went hand-in-hand with the region's constant search to find signs and evidence that brought heaven closer to earth or confirmed the righteousness of living saints. But they also go to the heart of the central paradox of the Reformed agenda. On one hand, church leaders were teaching that the will of God is unfathomable or incomprehensible. On the other hand, they were constantly uncovering the "sight of Heavenly things"—signs of the legitimacy and authenticity of their religious beliefs.

John Winthrop in wonderment learned in 1640 that a gnawing mouse had eaten out the Anglican book of "common prayer" in a bound volume—"every leaf of it"—providentially sparing only the Greek testament and the Psalms.[17] The diarist John Hull reported in 1668 that a man with a Bible under his arm was struck by a bolt of lightning that carried away "the whole book of Revelation," leaving the other parts "untouched."[18] Joseph Green, a teacher at the Roxbury Latin School in 1696, wrote in his commonplace book that "there shall be ten thousand times ten thousand holy angels waiting on Him to do His will. . . . Then the sun shall be darkened and the moon shall vanish, and the heaven and

Figure 10.4. Schematic drawing of two facing winged angel heads painted on an uncased upstairs beam in a privately owned house in Little Compton, Rhode Island. Eighteenth century. The design may have been part of a repeated pattern of angels and other images. Approximate width 24 inches. Drawing by the author from a 1979 photograph.

Figure 10.5. Gravestone of Sarah Allen, Bristol, Rhode Island, 1785, showing a trumpeting sun and responding souls rising from the earth under the phrase "Saints arising." Carving attributed to the shop of James New (1751–1835) of Wrentham, Massachusetts. Width 20 inches. Drawing by the author.

earth shall flee away before him, and his brightness shall exceed the brightness of the sun, moon, and stars."[19] In the eighteenth century, Elisabeth Mixer spoke in 1736 of seeing "heaven's gates opening," revealing angels wearing "sparkling crowns and diamonds."[20] In 1791 a "young man in Medford, near Boston" described "a true and wonderful relation of the appearance of three angels (clothed in white raiment) . . . together with the substance of the Discourse, delivered by one of the angels from the 3d chapter of Colossians, the 4th verse."[21] In 1799 Timothy P. Walker gave a detailed account of a sword thirty feet long that was carried by "an Angel or some Supernatural Being" with eyes like "lamps of fire." Behind it, in a reflection of light, was a "spacious scope covered with an innumerable host of Beings like unto Stars of Heaven."[22] Finally, there was Frederic W. Swan's *Remarkable Visionary Dreams of a Mulatto Boy, in Northfield, Mass.*, the 1822 testimony of a thirteen-year-old child whose dreams were written down by his mother as he approached the end of his life. Angels of all descriptions in bands or companies, and all sizes ("smaller," "great," "greater"), some singing, occur in every episode. One angel even appeared at the meetinghouse and told the boy, "This is my house, I set my servants to build it for a house of prayer."[23]

This populist imagery—as naïve as it was transitory—exists in sharp contrast to the visual role that Satan may have played among Anglicans in Virginia in the late eighteenth and early nineteenth centuries. Dell Upton cites a nineteenth-century account of two pictures from Bruton Parish Church in Williamsburg, Virginia. One of these hung in the students' gallery and depicted a satanic being in the fires of hell. The informant, "a member of an old Williamsburg family," wrote in 1840 that it made "a vivid impression on me[;] there were talons & beaks &c in the midst of horrible flames." Upton suggests that even if personified evil was gradually abandoned by Anglicans, Satan remained a "powerful force" among southern Evangelicals well into the nineteenth century.[24]

If we are correct in concluding that changing religious expectations reshaped the design of New England's houses of worship at the end of the eighteenth century, then we can safely assume that these same feelings had also generated an ephemeral decorating tradition that extended well into the third period of meetinghouse architecture. In the years just before the extinction of the folk impulse by an academic and industrial ethic, the angels and blue skies that had lain dormant in the hearts and imagination of New Englanders—and that permeate Edward Taylor's verse as they do the region's commonplace books—fleetingly became visible in the architectural painting found in meetinghouses in the waning years of their existence.

# Epilogue

THE NEW ENGLAND meetinghouse leaves a striking legacy of impermanence. Despite protestations to the contrary, most parishioners agreed with Isaac Chauncy's seventeenth-century view that meetinghouses were simply "places of assembly," presumably to be raised and demolished as the public saw fit. But New World demographics and Yankee parsimony also entered the picture. On one hand, rapid population expansion caused the "standing order" of Congregationalists to continually build larger and larger structures; on the other hand, towns just did not want to spend the money to make them permanent.

These two factors led to a succession of inexpensive vernacular wood-frame structures erected on a piecemeal basis. Between 1622 and 1830 an estimated 36 percent of all Reformed meetinghouses raised in the region were replacements for earlier ones. At least 519 parishes raised two meetinghouses; 169 raised three; 56 raised four; and 9 raised five. And these are only the documented examples; the actual number was likely higher. By contrast, Episcopal churches were usually marked by their relative permanence. While a few urban Anglican parishes rebuilt their churches or let them become derelict, the unbroken history of St. Michael's, Marblehead, Massachusetts; St. Paul's, Narragansett, Rhode Island; and Union Episcopal Church in Claremont, New Hampshire, was much more typical of the Episcopal tradition.

Many of the "lost" Reformed houses of worship were destroyed by fire; most, however, were replaced because they were indeed dilapidated. Time and again the record indicates that these buildings were dismantled and any salvageable materials were used as scantling and infill in their replacements. Parts of the first meetinghouse in Hingham, Massachusetts, built about 1635, are said to have been incorporated into the Old Ship in 1681 and are presumably still to be found in this structure.[1] Sometimes these materials were given as compensation. In Watertown, Massachusetts, "the seats of the old meeting house" were granted in 1654 to John Sherman, who added them to the four hundred pounds paid him for building the second meetinghouse in that town.[2] He or other joiners may have reused them in the second meetinghouse or have held onto them for different purposes. Old frames, floorboards, sleepers, and interior appurtenances thus became partial payments from one generation of workmen to another. In isolated instances the entire meetinghouse was sold or given away. Watertown's 1721 purchase of Newton's 1697 meetinghouse probably saved that Massachusetts town about half of what it would have cost to raise a new one.[3]

Meetinghouses that were not dismantled outright were sold at auction and moved by oxen or barges to a new location, where they were remodeled to serve other purposes. Southold, Long Island, voted in 1683 to convert its first meetinghouse into a jail, using it for that purpose until 1725.[4] The first meetinghouse in Woodbury, Connecticut, raised in 1681, was converted into a town house in 1747, then into an Episcopal church, later into a butcher's shop, and finally into a barn used by three successive farmers.[5] Litchfield's 1762 meetinghouse, abandoned in 1829 when the present Congregational church in that town was raised, became a public hall and—according to J. Frederick Kelly—eventually "a Moving Picture Theater."[6] And when the 1795 "Old Tin Top" in Providence, Rhode Island, was replaced in 1828 by a newer structure, the building was transformed into a riding circus; it then became a brewery. The 1795 meetinghouse in Chester, Connecticut, purchased by the town in 1847, was abandoned then resurrected and now serves as a musical theater.[7]

Meetinghouses were also turned into dwelling houses. The separatist meetinghouse in Windsor, Connecticut, which was built in 1761 as the Seventh Religious Society in that town, became the parsonage of Mr. Parsons after the two societies were reunited thirty years later.[8] But others were neglected and later converted into tenements. The story told about the 1714 meetinghouse in Oxford, Massachusetts, may not be typical, but it illustrates a point. The structure, put up for public auction a few years after it was replaced in 1748, was sold in 1752 to Jabez Holden, who made it into a dwelling house. Its ownership subsequently went through fifteen local families, who used it alternatively as a place of business (blacksmith's shop) or a dwelling house. The last owner in 1876 moved it from its former position fronting the common and let it out to tenants.[9] This same fate also befell several "round" (that is, sixteen-sided) meetinghouses in New Hampshire and Vermont in the early nineteenth century.[10]

More commonly, discarded meetinghouses served agricultural or industrial purposes. When the Congregational Society in Hatfield built its fourth church in 1849, the town's 1750 meetinghouse was moved to the rear of a nearby farmhouse and converted into a storage barn; fifty years later it was turned into a barn for drying tobacco.[11] Oak timbers from the 1732 meetinghouse in Kensington, Connecticut, "were used in a cow-house" on a local dairy farm in the town.[12] The "Bird meetinghouse" in Nashua (formerly Dunstable), New Hampshire, built for separatists in 1747, was first sold for use as a dwelling house and later as a factory. Edmund Sinnott, who saw this building in the 1950s, said it still retained some meetinghouse features.[13]

Finally, some discarded buildings, or portions of them, remained in place and served whatever purpose was offered to them—as sail lofts, manufacturing shops, park ornaments—or they were simply deserted and left to rot. The cupola of Lynn's 1682 Old Tunnel meetinghouse was taken to a nearby promontory in 1827 and used for years as a shoe shop until it was burned to celebrate the end of the American Civil War. In Andover, Massachusetts, old pews from the 1753 meetinghouse were converted into a fence in a neighboring yard in 1853 when the building was dismantled. The 1754 meetinghouse in Natick, Massachusetts, "was abandoned to the storms, until in an election-day frolic it was demolished and distributed among the woodpiles of the vicinity."[14]

Even the most exalted of these structures suffered from abandonment and neglect. Meetinghouses erected with considerable fanfare by one generation were dismantled or auctioned off by the next. The 1772 North or Lynde Street meetinghouse in Salem—the first Reformed church plan in New England—was "appropriated to manufacturing" when the church moved in 1836.[15] The building was then demolished. The twin-tower meetinghouse made in 1788 for the Hollis Street Church and the newer 1790 meetinghouse in Pittsfield—the two Bulfinch-designed structures that swept away 150 years of Reformed architectural tradition in New England—were each disposed of within decades after they were raised. In 1810 the dismantled Hollis Street meetinghouse was transported by raft to East Braintree (now part of Weymouth), where it was rebuilt without its towers and continued to serve as a church. It subsequently was converted into a schoolhouse and finally burned in 1897. The Pittsfield meetinghouse, damaged by fire in 1855, became part of the Maplewood Young Ladies' Institute, where it was turned into a gymnasium. It was photographed by the Historic American Buildings Survey in 1934 shortly before its demolition.[16]

The dissolution of the "standing order" in New England at the beginning of the nineteenth century did little to put an end to this process. Out of an estimated nine hundred jointly owned structures left stranded by the disestablishment laws passed between 1807 and 1832, approximately 95 percent continued to serve as meetinghouses for Congregational or Presbyterian religious societies, while the remaining 5 percent were retained by the town. But the actual transfer of ownership was never easy. Determining the rightful possessor of the meetinghouse, the parsonage, the land these were situated on, and any of the horse sheds and conveniences that came with them had to satisfy three or four sets of contenders. First was the town (or the proprietors or private owners) that had initially set aside land and still technically owned the structures on it. Second was the individual parish or precinct—many of them now Unitarian—that had assessed its members to pay for the building or make improvements by purchasing pews, porches, and bell towers. Third was the church, meaning those parishioners who had been admitted to full Communion. Few arrangements were able to satisfy all the parties. The settlement in the Dedham case of 1820, in which a court judgment gave the parish all rights to church property (over a separating faction of Trinitarian church members), explains why so many "First Churches" in Massachusetts are now Unitarian.[17]

In some instances, an attempt was made by the parish and town to share these assets. Under the terms set out by the town of Amherst, New Hampshire, the 1771 meetinghouse was sold at a nominal cost in 1833 to the First Congregational Church and Society in Amherst with the provision that the town could use the building for meetings as long as it liked. According to Eva A. Speare, "The bell, clock, belfry, and tower [were] to remain the property of the town, with the right to the Society to pass through the tower doors, ring the bell for funerals and public worship . . . 'without expense to the town.' Owners of pews were to have the right to them." In 1836 the society moved the meetinghouse across the street. Decades later it took over complete ownership of all parts except the town clock.[18]

In contrast, the meetinghouse in Washington, New Hampshire, built as a twin-porch structure in 1787, has remained in town ownership to the present. Initially, the Congregational Church of Christ in Washington continued to worship in the building after New Hampshire's Toleration Act was passed in 1819. The town, however, improved the structure by adding a belfry and bell on the east side in 1820. But when the church built its own house of worship in 1840 next door to the meetinghouse, the town assumed occupancy of the entire building. Town volunteers then installed a second-story floor and let it out to the Universalist Society and other groups; later the town partitioned the upstairs for an academy—all the while using the ground floor for municipal offices.[19] A similar sequence occurred elsewhere in New Hampshire. Milford variously used theirs as a post office, a library, and a fire station; Mont Vernon, for businesses and a historical society. In Milford, this process was reversed. The first floor of the town's "Eagle Hall" is once again serving as a church.[20]

Town ownership of meetinghouses was not limited to New Hampshire. In 1832, or the year before disestablishment was completed in Massachusetts, the congregation in Lynnfield split into Trinitarian and Unitarian factions, with the Unitarians retaining the use of the meetinghouse and the Trinitarians building next door. In 1836 when the meetinghouse was facing considerable repair, the Unitarians agreed with the town to fill in the second floor for their church, keeping the lower story as a meeting hall and town offices. Within a few years the Unitarians disbanded, and the meetinghouse reverted to the town. As reported by a late-nineteenth-century historian, the uses of the old meetinghouse were "simply astonishing." Besides occasional public worship, it was a site for "ordinations, prayer meetings, lectures, most all kinds of organizations, balls, parties, levees, town meetings, schools, caucuses, trials, conventions, anniversaries, war meetings, suppers and dinners, picnics, reunions, dancing-schools, writing schools, singing schools, lyceums, funerals, and parades." Later, when a new town hall was raised, the structure became a fire station.[21]

In all, out of 205 surviving New England and Long Island meetinghouses built before 1801, 136 (65 percent) still serve as houses of worship; 26 (12 percent) as town houses; 28 (14 percent) as museums or historical societies; and 15 (7 percent) as schools, granges, halls, theaters, or residences (see Appendix A, Table 7). Their subsequent use set the stage for what followed architecturally. With a few exceptions, meetinghouses that became the property of a church congregation were caught up in the vortex of early nineteenth-century fashionable architecture and the spread of Greek Revival taste. Edmund Sinnott's 1963 list of surviving second-period structures includes 23 that were "turned" so that the gable end faced the street—a process that usually involved converting the stairwell porch or standing bell tower into an entry portico.[22] (Another 52 were changed over to Federal or Victorian styles but may not have involved turning.) If we add to this list those that were turned but taken down before 1963, the actual number of turned meetinghouses may have been two or three times as large. The task was costly and difficult and involved jacking up the building, placing it on rollers, and swinging it and the attached bell tower (if it had one) ninety degrees, and lowering it onto a new foundation. One of the most visible examples is the meetinghouse in Groton, Massachusetts, built on the common in 1755, which variously served the First Parish as a house of worship, as a district court house, and as a place for town meetings until 1859. In 1795 a bell tower and stairwell porch were added on the far ends. In 1839, however, the rear stairwell porch was removed and the building was turned ninety degrees so that the bell tower faced the street; the second floor was filled in to create a smaller space for worship, and the first floor continued to be used by the town.[23]

Meetinghouses that remained exclusively the property of the town fared somewhat better, though not always. While some examples, like the one in Salem, New Hampshire, were moved to a more convenient location, they were never turned or made more "ecclesiastic" by a building committee wishing to keep up with the modern taste. Instead, towns and parishes measured their meetinghouses by a sense of thrift—and their convenience to the public—rather than by a sense of style. But these meetinghouses suffered too. As with church-owned structures, the first thing the town usually did was to fill in the second floor. The town of Henniker, New Hampshire, which took full ownership of the 1787 twin-porch meetinghouse in the nineteenth century, closed in the upper gallery with a floor and made it into a basketball gym, suspending the canopy in the stairwell, where it remains to this day; the lower floor still functions as a town house. A different story accompanied the 1783 meetinghouse in Ludlow, Massachusetts, when it was replaced by a new church in 1841. Here the structure was sold at auction to Increase Sikes for use as a sheep barn; Sikes later sold it to the town, which used it for years as a town hall but then allowed the local grange organization to occupy the first floor. The grange eventually came to own the building, which is now maintained by the Ludlow Historical Society.[24] The old meetinghouse in Merrimack, New Hampshire, used for years as a town house, suffered a different kind of fate. Today the only thing left of this structure is a picture postcard showing it with gaping holes in the roof and about to fall in on itself just before it burned in 1896.

Fewer than twenty second-period meetinghouses have escaped these devastating architectural changes. The best known are those in Cohasset, Amesbury, and Millville, Massachusetts; Brooklyn, Farmington, and Wethersfield, Connecticut; Jaffrey, Danville, Fremont, and Sandown, New Hampshire; and Alna, Bristol, and Waldoboro, Maine. All are active as churches or maintained by local historical societies. A few started out as churches, but as their congregations succumbed to demographic and population changes and were forced to disband, the sites became derelict. These structures eventually drew the interest of architectural preservationists who saw them as potential museums in the early and mid-twentieth century. The meetinghouse at Rocky Hill, West Salisbury (now Amesbury), Massachusetts, whose interior remained relatively intact after the decline of the church at the end of the nineteenth century, was acquired in 1941 by the Society for the Preservation of New England Antiquities, now Historic New England. It was benignly preserved and is open to visitors by appointment and for some events.[25] Similarly derelict meetinghouses at Hawke (now Danville) and Sandown, New Hampshire, became town property and are currently maintained by local associations.[26] These, together with examples in Alna and Waldoboro, Maine, are among the best representative structures of New England's eighteenth-century houses of worship.[27]

Extended neglect sometimes left restorers few options. The meetinghouse at Chestnut Hill in Millville, Massachusetts, which still has most of its interior wood fittings intact, was aggressively repainted throughout by the church after becoming rundown; the same was true of Rockingham, Vermont, whose interior was rebuilt and restored after suffering neglect. Both buildings are operated now as museums. An attractive but nevertheless compromised mid-twentieth-century restoration took place in the West Precinct in Barnstable, Massachusetts, which had Victorianized its 1719 meetinghouse in the mid-nineteenth century. After later generations allowed it to fall into disrepair, an effort was made in 1953 to restore the meetinghouse to its original form, done at considerable private expense. The building is now termed the oldest Congregational meetinghouse still in use in the world today.[28]

To this list must be added the Old South meetinghouse in Boston, whose brick shell and bell tower have withstood the effects of the British siege and a terrible fire in 1872, as well as the depredations of becoming a commercial site and a U.S. post office after the meetinghouse was abandoned by the Third Church in the nineteenth century. Slated to be torn down by a new owner in 1876, the structure survived through the grassroots efforts (fig. 11.1) of local store owners and benefactors such as Wendell Phillips, Oliver Wendell Holmes, and Mary Hemenway, widow of one of New England's wealthiest men, whose anonymous donation met the selling price demanded by the Old South Congregation, which had built a replacement church in Boston's Copley Square.

Figure 11.1. Old South meetinghouse, Boston, during fundraising efforts in the 1870s. Photographed by J. W. Black and Company, 1876. Courtesy of Historic New England.

Now administered by the Old South Association in Boston (formed in 1877), the site is heavily visited by tourists and is rented for meetings.[29]

The most successful preservation effort was the one undertaken by the Old Ship Church in Hingham, Massachusetts, whose Unitarian Universalist congregation still worships in this 1681 structure. Ten generations of custodians have ensured that this meetinghouse retains its outline as a period-one structure—collectively resisting repeated efforts to tear it down and build a larger or more architecturally ambitious structure. The attempts began in the first half of the eighteenth century with the question of adding private pews, a primary source of raising money for renovations or rebuilding. Like the Second Parish in Andover, the town refused to sell off pew spaces and instead kept to the old ways of seating the congregation. These votes took place in 1731, 1739, 1740, and 1752 during an exceptional population growth in eastern Massachusetts that saw Cohasset district become the Second Parish in Hingham in 1717 and South Hingham become its Third Parish in 1721. The house was finally enlarged in 1755 by expanding two walls and redesigning the pulpit area, but the entire issue came to a head in 1792 when votes were taken to add a standing bell tower and change the roofline to provide a "proper pitch roof . . . [to] correspond with the tower" (meaning to replace the gathered roof with a "straight" or "English" one). But a later meeting ordered the vote to "be dissolved."[30] Undismayed, proponents of change made an even more radical proposal in August 1792 to "take down the meeting-house and build a new one similar to a plan exhibited in the meeting which is on file." This proposal passed with sixty in favor and twenty-eight opposed. (The plan has not survived, but it was most likely a Bulfinch- or Benjamin-style meetinghouse.) But this idea was again reviewed at a meeting of the parish. Quoting from town votes, the nineteenth-century historian Calvin Lincoln tells us that in the end they decided not to take down the meetinghouse but instead to repair it "in its present form." It was a monumental decision and one that saved New England's only remaining first-period house of worship from demolition. Architectural preservationists are still applauding.

# APPENDIX A
# Tables

*Sources for all tables:* Town and county histories, parish and church records, town records, diaries, newspaper articles, and studies by architectural historians.

Table 1. Houses of worship raised in New England and Long Island, 1622–1830

| | Congregational, Presbyterian, and Baptist meetinghouses | | | | |
| Decade | First-period architectural style | Second-period architectural style | Third-period architectural style | Anglican churches | TOTAL |
|---|---|---|---|---|---|
| 1622–1630 | 2 | | | | 2 |
| 1631–1640 | 38 | | | 1 | 39 |
| 1641–1650 | 23 | | | | 23 |
| 1651–1660 | 31 | | | | 31 |
| 1661–1670 | 37 | | | | 37 |
| 1671–1680 | 46 | | | | 46 |
| 1681–1690 | 34 | | | 1 | 35 |
| 1691–1700 | 53 | 1 | | 1 | 55 |
| 1701–1710 | 47* | 2* | | 1 | 50 |
| 1711–1720 | 19* | 98* | | 1 | 118 |
| 1721–1730 | 3 | 114 | | 8 | 125 |
| 1731–1740 | 1 | 133 | | 9 | 143 |
| 1741–1750 | 1 | 145 | | 11 | 157 |
| 1751–1760 | 1 | 108 | | 3 | 112 |
| 1761–1770 | 1 | 165 | | 7 | 173 |
| 1771–1780 | | 140 | 4 | 1 | 145 |

(*continued*)

Table 1. (*continued*)

| Decade | Congregational, Presbyterian, and Baptist meetinghouses | | | Anglican churches | TOTAL |
|---|---|---|---|---|---|
| | First-period architectural style | Second-period architectural style | Third-period architectural style | | |
| 1781–1790 | 1 | 157* | 4* | 7 | 169 |
| 1791–1800 | | 77* | 150* | 8 | 235 |
| 1801–1810 | | 13 | 138 | 8 | 159 |
| 1811–1820 | | 2 | 117 | 13 | 132 |
| 1821–1830 | | | 190 | 13 | 203 |
| TOTAL | 338 | 1,155 | 603 | 93 | 2,189 |

*Estimated.

*Note:* First-period meetinghouses, found between 1631 and 1720, are distinguished by their "four-square" roofs and central turrets; second-period meetinghouses, found between 1699 and 1820, are known for their "flat" or "English" roofs and rectangular plan (a few have standing bell towers); third-period meetinghouses, found between 1770 and 1830, are known for their front orientation to the street, their entry porticos supporting a spire, and their "church" plan. A chronological list of meetinghouses and Anglican churches is provided in Appendix B.

Table 2. Congregational, Presbyterian, and Baptist religious societies in New England adopting new liturgical practices and patterns of seating, 1651–1830

| Decade | Halfway covenant | | Optional relations | Scripture reading | Private pewing | Men and women seated together |
|---|---|---|---|---|---|---|
| | Adopted | Rejected | | | | |
| 1651–1660 | 4 | | | | | |
| 1661–1670 | 12 | | | | 1 | |
| 1671–1680 | 10 | | | | 1 | |
| 1681–1690 | 7 | | | | | |
| 1691–1700 | 2 | | 1 | 1 | 5 | |
| 1701–1710 | 4 | | 2 | | 9 | |
| 1711–1720 | 2 | | 2 | 1 | 11 | 2 |
| 1721–1730 | 6 | | 10 | 3 | 4 | 6 |
| 1731–1740 | 5 | | 8 | 4 | 1 | 6 |
| 1741–1750 | 1 | | 7 | 7 | | 3 |
| 1751–1760 | | 2 | 11 | 8 | | 8 |
| 1761–1770 | 4 | 3 | 6 | 22 | | 7 |

Table 2. (*continued*)

| Decade | Halfway covenant Adopted | Halfway covenant Rejected | Optional relations | Scripture reading | Private pewing | Men and women seated together |
|---|---|---|---|---|---|---|
| 1771–1780 | 3 | 10 | 6 | 6 | | 3 |
| 1781–1790 | 1 | 7 | 4 | 5 | | 2 |
| 1791–1800 | | 6 | 4 | 3 | | 1 |
| 1801–1810 | | 3 | | 4 | | |
| 1811–1820 | | 4 | | 3 | | |
| 1821–1830 | | 3 | | 1 | | |

Table 3. Congregational, Presbyterian, Baptist, and Anglican religious societies in New England adopting new singing practices, 1691–1840

| Decade | Regular singing | Tate and Brady translation of the Psalms | Watts translation of the Psalms | Abandonment of lining out | Singers seated together | Singers seated in gallery | Bass viol accompaniment | Installation of an organ |
|---|---|---|---|---|---|---|---|---|
| 1700 | | | | 1 | | | | |
| 1710 | | | | | | | | |
| 1720 | 3 | 1 | | 1 | | | | |
| 1730 | 27 | 1 | | 1 | | | | |
| 1740 | 24 | 4 | | | | | | |
| 1750 | 6 | 1 | 11 | 1 | | | | |
| 1760 | | 16 | 25 | 3 | 1 | 1 | | |
| 1770 | 1 | 32 | 31 | 7 | 12 | 10 | | 1 |
| 1780 | 2 | 5 | 17 | 37 | 11 | 29 | | |
| 1790 | | | 10 | 41 | 5 | 23 | 5 | 2 |
| 1800 | | | 8 | 11 | | 10 | 26 | 7 |
| 1810 | | | 1 | 4 | | 1 | 17 | 5 |
| 1820 | | | | | | | 6 | 4 |
| 1830 | | | | | | | 5 | 2 |
| 1840 | | | | | | | | 1 |

Table 4. Attached standing bell towers raised by New England religious societies, 1680–1800

| Decade | Congregational, Presbyterian, and Baptist | Anglican | TOTAL |
|---|---|---|---|
| 1680–1690 |  | 1 | 1 |
| 1691–1700 |  |  |  |
| 1701–1710 |  |  |  |
| 1711–1720 | 3 | 1 | 4 |
| 1721–1730 | 9 | 3 | 12 |
| 1731–1740 | 9 | 2 | 11 |
| 1741–1750 | 18 | 2 | 20 |
| 1751–1760 | 14 | 1 | 15 |
| 1761–1770 | 31 | 2 | 33 |
| 1771–1780 | 18 |  | 18 |
| 1781–1790 | 12 | 1 | 13 |
| 1791–1800 | 49 | 2 | 51 |
| TOTAL | 163 | 15 | 178 |

Table 5. Meetinghouses used for prototypes by New England meetinghouse builders, 1647–1828, by distance from the new structure

| Architectural feature as prototype | 10 miles or under | 11–20 miles | 21–30 miles | 31–40 miles | 41–50 miles | Over 50 miles | TOTAL |
|---|---|---|---|---|---|---|---|
| Dimensions | 27 | 10 | 1 | 1 | 1 | 2 | 42 |
| Pattern, plan, or form | 26 | 12 | 3 | 4 | 1 | 9 | 55 |
| Posts | 2 |  |  |  |  |  | 2 |
| Framing | 2 | 3 |  |  |  |  | 5 |
| Interior | 3 | 1 | 1 |  |  |  | 5 |
| Exterior | 1 | 1 | 1 |  |  |  | 3 |
| Exterior ornamentation |  | 1 |  | 1 |  |  | 2 |
| Roofs | 5 | 1 |  |  |  |  | 6 |
| Pulpits | 15 | 2 | 4 | 1 | 1 | 2 | 25 |
| Canopies | 6 | 1 |  |  | 1 | 1 | 9 |
| Pews and seats | 24 | 3 | 2 |  |  |  | 29 |

Table 5. (*continued*)

| Architectural feature as prototype | 10 miles or under | 11–20 miles | 21–30 miles | 31–40 miles | 41–50 miles | Over 50 miles | TOTAL |
|---|---|---|---|---|---|---|---|
| Colors | 13 | 5 | 1 | | 1 | | 20 |
| Turrets | | 1 | | | | | 1 |
| Belfries, towers, steeples | 6 | 3 | 1 | | | 3 | 13 |
| Bells | | | | | | 1 | 1 |
| "Finishing" | 5 | 1 | 4 | | 1 | 1 | 12 |
| Porches, additions | 3 | 2 | | | 1 | | 6 |
| Gallery breastwork | 4 | 1 | 1 | | | | 6 |
| Ground pinnings | 1 | | | | | | 1 |
| Windows | 2 | 1 | 1 | | | | 4 |
| Communion tables | 2 | | | | | | 2 |
| Doors | | | 1 | | | | 1 |
| Floors | 1 | | 1 | | | | 2 |
| Stairs | | | 1 | | | | 1 |
| Ironwork | 1 | | | | | | 1 |
| Alleys | | | 1 | | | | 1 |
| Glazing | 1 | | | | | 1 | 2 |
| Entire meetinghouse | 4 | | | | | | 4 |
| TOTAL | 155 | 48 | 24 | 7 | 7 | 20 | 261 |

*Note:* Figures are for Congregational, Presbyterian, Baptist, and Anglican religious societies.

Table 6. Meetinghouses used for prototypes by New England meetinghouse builders, 1647–1828, by age in years

| Architectural feature as prototype | Under 1 year | 2–5 years | 6–10 years | 11–20 years | 21–30 years | More than 30 years | TOTAL |
|---|---|---|---|---|---|---|---|
| Dimensions | 4 | 8 | 6 | 8 | 4 | 7 | 37 |
| Pattern, plan, form | 11 | 14 | 10 | 11 | 6 | 1 | 53 |
| Posts | | | 1 | 1 | | | 2 |
| Framing | 1 | 1 | | 2 | 1 | | 5 |
| Interior | 1 | | 1 | 1 | | 1 | 4 |
| Exterior | | 1 | 1 | 1 | | | 3 |
| Exterior ornamentation | 1 | 1 | | | | | 2 |

(*continued*)

## Table 6. (continued)

| Architectural feature as prototype | Under 1 year | 2–5 years | 6–10 years | 11–20 years | 21–30 years | More than 30 years | TOTAL |
|---|---|---|---|---|---|---|---|
| Roofs | | | 2 | 1 | 2 | | 5 |
| Pulpits | 1 | 4 | 2 | 6 | 3 | 6 | 22 |
| Pews and seats | 2 | 6 | 2 | 7 | 9 | 3 | 29 |
| Colors | 6 | 2 | 4 | 3 | | 2 | 17 |
| Turrets | | | 1 | | | | 1 |
| Belfries, towers, steeples | 4 | 3 | 1 | 2 | 1 | 2 | 13 |
| Bells | | | 1 | | | | 1 |
| "Finishing" | 2 | 4 | 2 | 3 | | 1 | 12 |
| Porches, additions | 1 | 2 | 2 | | | | 5 |
| Galleries | | | 1 | 2 | | 3 | 6 |
| Ground pinnings | | | | | | 1 | 1 |
| Windows | | 1 | 1 | 1 | 1 | | 4 |
| Canopies | 1 | 2 | 1 | 3 | | 2 | 9 |
| Communion tables | | | | 1 | 1 | | 2 |
| Doors | | | | 1 | | | 1 |
| Floors | | | | 1 | 1 | | 2 |
| Stairs | | | | 1 | | | 1 |
| Iron work | | | | 1 | | | 1 |
| Alleys | 1 | | | | | | 1 |
| Glazing | | 1 | | 1 | | | 2 |
| Entire Meetinghouse | | | | | 1 | 3 | 4 |
| TOTAL | 36 | 50 | 39 | 58 | 30 | 32 | 245 |

*Note:* Figures are for Congregational, Presbyterian, Baptist, and Anglican religious societies.

Table 7. New England and Long Island meetinghouse survivals (built 1681–1800), by current disposition

| Decade | Church | Town house | Museum or historical society | School, grange, hall, theater, or residence | TOTAL |
|---|---|---|---|---|---|
| 1681–1690 | 1 | | | 1 | 2 |
| 1691–1700 | 1 | | 2 | | 3 |
| 1701–1710 | 4 | | 1 | | 5 |
| 1711–1720 | 6 | 1 | | | 7 |
| 1721–1730 | 4 | | 2 | 2 | 8 |
| 1731–1740 | 2 | 1 | 2 | | 5 |
| 1741–1750 | 4 | 2 | | 1 | 7 |
| 1751–1760 | 7 | | 3 | | 10 |
| 1761–1770 | 16 | 2 | 2 | | 20 |
| 1771–1780 | 18 | 3 | 3 | 1 | 25 |
| 1781–1790 | 26 | 5 | 5 | 2 | 38 |
| 1791–1800 | 47 | 12 | 8 | 8 | 75 |
| TOTAL | 136 | 26 | 28 | 15 | 205 |

*Note:* Figures are for Congregational, Presbyterian, Baptist, and Anglican religious societies.

APPENDIX B

# Chronological checklist of meetinghouses in New England and Long Island, 1622–1830

Entry date indicates year of the raising of the frame or completion of the exterior covering.

Town name in capital letters indicates the meetinghouse is still standing.

Roman numerals indicate sequence within a town or parish.

A "Separate church" identifies a religious society, usually Congregational or Baptist, formed without legislative, municipal, or parish permission.

Dimensions are given in feet.

Sinnott types 2, 3, and 4 refer, respectively, to second-period (2), Federal-period (3), and Greek-revival-period (4) structures as outlined in Edmund W. Sinnott's *Meetinghouse and Church in Early New England*.

1622  Plymouth, Mass. Fort "fitted . . . for . . . use as a meeting house."

1630  Charlestown, Mass. John Winthrop's house used as meetinghouse. "Great House."

1631  Dorchester, Mass., I. Palisade. Log tradition. Thatched. Loft. Fireplace? "Beating the drum."

1632  Boston, Mass. I (First Church). Stone, plastered with clay, thatched roof. Cost: £120.
Cambridge, Mass., I. Bell. Repaired with "four-square roof" 1649.
Lynn, Mass., I. About 20 × 20. Turret 1662. Moved to common 1682. Dismantled 1827.
Roxbury, Mass., I. Repaired 1646, 1656. Gallery, plaster, turret "pinakles" 1658. Bell 1660.

1634  Dover, N.H., I.
Ipswich, Mass., I. Gallery 1643. Sold for 50s 1647.
Salem, Mass., I. 20 × 17, 12 posts. 25-ft. addition to 20 × 45? Gallery, chimney 1639.
Watertown, Mass., I. "Bellrope" 1647. Gallery 1649.

1635 Concord, Mass., I.
Hartford, Conn., I. 40×40? Remembered as square. Replaced 1638.
Hingham, Mass., I. Private gallery 6 ft. wide. Posts and pillars turned.
Weymouth, Mass., I. 3 galleries, bell 1667.

1636 Charlestown, Mass., I. Temporary "between the town and the neck."
Scituate, Mass., I.
York, Maine, I.

1637 Hampton, N.H., I. Log tradition. Bell.
Plymouth, Mass., I. Bell.
Sandwich, Mass., I. Thatched roof tradition.

1638 Dedham, Mass., I. 36×20, 12 posts. Daubed, thatched; pyramid, bell 1651.
Duxbury, Mass., I.
Exeter, N.H., I.
Hartford, Conn., II. 50×50? Porch with stairs to "Chambers." Galleries 1644, 1660, 1664.
Providence, R.I. (Baptist), I. Roger Williams. Met in homes for 60 years.

1639 Braintree, Mass., I.
Charlestown, Mass., II. "Very comely built and large." Galleries rebuilt 1675.
Marblehead, Mass., I. 40×20? Gallery 1662, 2nd gallery and bell 1669. Enlarged to 40×40, lean-to added 1672.
Marshfield, Mass., I.
New Haven, Conn., I. 50×50. Gallery. Banisters. Rails. Platform. Turrets. Builder: William Andrews. Cost: £500.
Rowley, Mass., I. Framed (not log). Repaired 1671. Bell mounted on unattached tower 1673.
Southold, L.I., I. Log tradition. Used as jail after 1683, to 1725.

1640 Boston, Mass., II. (First Church, "Old Meeting House"). Clapboards, shingles. Cost: £1,000. Gallery. 2nd gallery 1675? Platform 1699.
Fairfield, Conn., I.
Hampton, N.H., II. 40×22, 13 posts. Builder: Richard Knight. Bell. West gallery 1649.
Portsmouth, N.H. (Anglican), I. Parsonage house and chapel.
Salisbury, Mass., I. Bell 1644. Enlarged 12 ft. 1652.
Saybrook, Conn., I (before 1640). 40×30.
Stamford, Conn., I.
Windsor, Conn., I. Thatched? Drum. Finish carpenter: William Buell. 2-gable roof, "Lanthorn" 1658. Enlarged to 70×30?

1641 Milford, Conn., I. 30×30. Gallery by 1696. Turret covered with lead 1718.

1642 Gloucester, Mass., I. Bell. 2 galleries 1686.
Sudbury, Mass. (First Parish or Wayland), I. 30×20, 8 posts. Framed. Builder: John Rutter.
Wenham, Mass., I. Rectangular. Plastered 1662. Galleries 1674.
Woburn, Mass., I.

1643 Guilford, Conn., I. 24×24. Stone, clay mortar. 4-sq. roof, thatched. Gallery. Porch.
Newbury, Mass., I.

1644 Branford, Conn., I. Log tradition. Enlarged 1679.
Eastham, Mass., I. 20×20. Thatched. Ports in the side.
Newport, R.I. (Baptist), I.
Reading, Mass., I. Log tradition? Rectangular. Galleries 1657.

1645 Dorchester, Mass., II. Daubed 1661. Shutters 1662. Gallery 1645, 1667. Detached bell frame. Moved 1671. Sold 1678.
Hempstead, L.I., I. 24×24.
Scituate, Mass. (Second or South Parish), I.
Southampton, L.I., I.
Springfield, Mass., I. 40×25, 9 posts. Shingled roof. Double studs. 2-turret "watch house." Builder: Thomas Cooper, J. Burr.

1646 Rehoboth, Mass., I. Enlarged 1659.

1647 Haverhill, Mass., I. 26×20. Builder: Thomas Davis. Enlarged 1659. Gallery 1667.
Ipswich, Mass., II. Bell. "Sheet" for the turret window. Used as fort. Builder: George Norton.
Wethersfield, Conn., I. 50×50? Galleries 1683.

1649 Malden, Mass. (Bailey's Hill), I.

1650 Boston, Mass. (Second Church or North), I. Burned 1676.
Flatbush, L.I. (Midwont) (Dutch Reformed). 60×28, 14 posts. Painted 1659.

1651 Amesbury, Mass., I.
Cambridge, Mass., II. "about 40×40 square." "4-square roof." Galleries 1670.
Natick, Mass., I.
Southampton, L.I., II. 30×24, 8½ posts. Builder: Ellis Post, Richard Post. Galleries 1652.

1652 East Hampton, L.I., I. 26×20 (or 26×26), 8 posts. Thatched. Gallery 1682.
Exeter, N.H., II. 20×20. Lean-to with chimney 1664. Gallery 1678.
New London, Conn., I. 30×30, 12 posts. 6 windows. 4 gables. Shingled. Turret. Builder: John Elderkin. Gallery 1671.

1653 Dover, N.H., II. 40×26, 16 posts. Plank construction? Builder: Richard Waldern. Turret 1665. Fortified 1667.
Edgartown, Mass.
Middletown, Conn., I. 30×20, 10 posts. Gallery 1665.
Sudbury, Mass., II. 40×24, 12 posts. Thatched. Clapboard. "Pinakles." 2 front gables. Builder: Peter King, Thomas Plympton.

1654 Medfield, Mass., I. Pulpit purchased 1655 from "John Hatton [Houghton]."

1655 Chelmsford, Mass., I. Seated 1678. Repaired 1708.
Chilmark, Mass. One-room meetinghouse. Builder: Thomas Mayhew. Turned into a dwelling house.
Northampton, Mass., I. Sawn timber, 26 × 18, 9 posts.

1656 Durham, N.H. (Oyster River), I. Builder: Valentine Hill.
Newport, R.I. (Second Baptist Church). 21 seceders.
Sandwich, Mass., II.
Taunton, Mass., I. Turret and vane. Builder: Harry Andrews.
Watertown, Mass., II. 40 × 40. Builder: John Sherman. Cost: £400. "Cambridge . . . pattern." Platform, galleries 1679.

1657 Berwick, Maine.
Marshfield, Mass., II. Builder: Ensign Eames, William Macomber.
Portsmouth, N.H., II. 40 × 40, 16 posts. 9-in. logs. "flat Roof." Builder: John Huchinson.

1658 Lancaster, Mass., I.
Malden, Mass., II. 33 × 33, 16 posts. Turret and rails 6 ft. sq. Builder: Job Lane. Galleries by 1684.

1659 Billerica, Mass., I. 30 × 24, 12 posts. "3' asunder." Thatched. Galleries 1679.
Norwalk, Conn., I. 30 × 18. "Set upon posts in the ground, 12 foot in length."

1660 Newton, Mass., I.
Rumney Marsh, Mass. (formerly Chelsea, now Revere). "Chapel of Ease" reported by Samuel Maverick about 1660.
Saco, Maine (Winter Harbor Congregation).
Swansea, Mass. (Baptist), I.

1661 Andover, Mass., I. Temporary.
Newbury, Mass., II. Builder: Henry Jaques. Porch for stairs and gallery by 1669.
Northampton, Mass., II. 42 × 42. Hipped roof. Turret and bell 1682. Galleries 1670. Dismantled 1738.
Stonington, Conn., I. Builder: Thomas Minor, Thomas Park.
Stratford, Conn., I. (Meetinghouse before 1661). Bell. Gallery added.

1662 Hadley, Mass., I. 45 × 24. 6-ft. lean-tos "on both sides . . . 36 breadth." Galleries 1698.
Marlborough, Mass., I. 36 × 18, 12½ posts. Burned 1675.

1663 Barnstable, Mass., I.
Jamaica, L.I., I. 26 × 26. Replaced before 1700.
Topsfield, Mass., I. Rectangular. Stone wall 1675. Galleries 1681–94. Dismantled, sold for £5.
Wenham, Mass., II. 24 × 24, 12 posts. Enlarged.

1664 Milton, Mass., I.
Salisbury, Mass., II. 46 × 30.
Wells, Maine, I.

1665　Amesbury, Mass., II. 30 × 25, 16 posts. Family pew 1696. Galleries 1699.
　　　Edgartown, Mass., II. 33 × 19, 8 posts.
　　　Groton, Mass., I. Thatched. Daubed. Gallery and 2 stairs. Burned 1676.
　　　Huntington, L.I., I. Rectangular. Enlarged 1686. Galleries 1707.
　　　North Kingstown, R.I. (Baptist).

1666　Brooklyn, L.I. (Dutch Reformed). Dismantled 1810.

1667　Concord, Mass., II. 34 × 26, 14 posts. "Square roof." Turret and bell. Vane 1673.
　　　Killingworth, Conn. (First Parish or Clinton), I.
　　　York, Maine, II. 28 (x 28), 16 posts. Turret with balusters. Builder: Henry Sayward. Galleries 1680.

1668　Fairfield, Conn., II. Bell 1685.
　　　Hatfield, Mass., I. 30 × 30. Galleries. Turret 1675. Bell 1682. Dormers 1688.
　　　Lyme, Conn. (Johnny Cake Hill), I. Log tradition.
　　　New Haven, Conn., II. 55 × 35. Turret. Dormers. Builder: Nathan Andrews. Enlarged 25 ft. 1698.
　　　Norwich, Conn., I. Lean-tos added.

1669　Andover, Mass., II. Bell 1675. "upper and lower galleries" 1696.
　　　Boston, Mass., I (Third Church, "Old Cedar"). 75 × 51. 3 porches. Cupola. Pinnacles. "sheete lead." Builder: Robert Tweld.
　　　Mendon, Mass., I. 22 × 22, 12 posts. "the Ruffes gathered to A 7 foote square wth a Turrett."

1670　Beverly, Mass., I. Gallery, turret 1671.
　　　Bradford, Mass., I. Galleries 1690.
　　　Hartford, Conn. (Second Parish), I. 50 × 50.
　　　Middletown, Conn., II. 32 × 32, 15 posts. Builder: John Hull. Gallery 1676.
　　　Salem, Mass., II ("The Great Meeting House"). 60 × 50, 20 posts. Turret. Chimney. Galleries.

1671　Bridgehampton, L.I., I.
　　　Brookhaven, L.I., I. 28 × 28 (or 26 × 30), 10 posts. Builder: Nathaniel Morton (or Nortens).
　　　Kittery, Maine (The Point), I.
　　　Newport, R.I. (Seventh-Day Baptist).
　　　Stamford, Conn., II. 30 × 30 (stone) to 38 × 38, 12 posts. Framed. Gallery platform. Turret.

1672　Farmington, Conn., I (before 1672). Gallery.
　　　Manchester, Mass., I. "Shall be builded 18 foot——cepting stud with too Gabell ends."
　　　Milton, Mass., II. "Nearly square" gallery.
　　　Newport, R.I. (Quaker), I. Dismantled.
　　　Oyster Bay, L.I. (Quaker), I. Builder: Samuel Andrews, John Feake. Cost: £20.
　　　Salem Village, Mass. (Danvers), I. 34 × 28, 16 posts. 2 galleries 1684.
　　　Westfield, Mass., I. 36 × 36, 14 posts. Galleries 1703.

Woburn, Mass., II. 40×40. Turret. Galleries 1678. Upper gallery 1694. Enlarged 20 ft. 1709. Dismantled 1752.

1673 Brookfield, Mass. (Quabaug), I. Burned 4 August 1675.
Dedham, Mass., II. 38×24, 26 posts. Turret and bell. Builder: John Baker, Daniel Pond. Enlarged to 38×38 1702.
Deerfield, Mass., I. Log tradition. Thatched. "To ye little house for a Meeting House."
Haddam, Conn., I. 28×24, 13 posts. 8 windows. "tooe pramedyes." Builder: John Clarke.
Norwich, Conn., II. Builder: John Elderkin. Enlarged 1689. Pyramids mended 1705.
Stonington, Conn., II. 40×22, 14 posts. Gallery. Builder: Thomas Minor, Thomas Park. Dismantled 1729.

1674 Bridgewater, Mass. (West Bridgewater), II. 40×26, 14 posts. Galleries.
Dunstable, N.H., I.
Rehoboth, Mass., II. Rectangular. Galleries lengthened 1701.
Roxbury, Mass., II. Galleries, porches 1708.

1675 Hampton, N.H., III.

1676 Eastham, Mass., II. "Steeple" (turret?) 1695.
Saybrook, Conn., II. 60×30, 16 posts. Cedar clapboards. Builder: William Bushnell.

1677 Boston, Mass., II (Second Church or "Old North"). Tower 1720? Dismantled for firewood by English 1776.
Dorchester, Mass., III. 50×45. Gallery. Pyramidal roof. Bell. Builder: Isaac Royal.
Marlborough, Mass., II. Thatched.
Springfield, Mass., II. 50×40, posts for galleries. Turret. Canopy. Slitwork. Builder: John Allis.

1678 Boston, Mass., I (First Baptist). Salem and Stillman Streets.
Hempstead, L.I., II. 30×24, 12 posts. Lean-to on each side. Builder: Joseph Carpenter.
Norwalk, Conn., II. 40×40, 16 posts. Roof like that in Fairfield.

1679 Ipswich, Mass. (Second Parish, Chebacco, or Essex), I. 42×36. Voted for turret like that in Andover.
New London, Conn., II. 40×40, 20 posts. 4 gables with pyramids. Turret. 2 galleries. Builder: John Elderkin, Samuel Lothrop. Burned 1694.
Sherburne, Mass. (Sherborn), I.
Swansea, Mass. (Baptist), II. 40×22, 16 posts. Moved to north Swansea in 1700.

1680 Edgartown, Mass., III. 20×20, 10 posts. "four cross galleries."
Groton, Mass., II.
Mendon, Mass., II. 26×24, 14 (or 16) posts. "a girt house." Builder: Samuel Hayward. Enlarged 10 ft. 1709.
Middleborough, Mass., I.

Scituate, Mass. (Second or South Parish), II.
South Kingstown, R.I. (Baptist).
Stratford, Conn., II. 48 × 42, 16 posts. Galleries and porch added.
Suffield, Conn., I.
Westerly, R.I. (Seventh-Day Baptist).

1681 Barnstable, Mass., II.
Derby, Conn., I. 28 × 20, 10 posts. Transom windows. Bannisters on seats. Drummer. Builder: John Hull. Enlarged 14 ft.
East Hampton, L.I., II. 2 tiers of galleries. Builder: Joshua Garlick.
HINGHAM, MASS., II ("Old Ship"). 55 × 45, 21 posts. Gallery. Undated single porch. Builder: Charles Stockbridge. Cost: £437. Enlarged 1730, 1755.
Wallingford, Conn., I. 28 × 24, 10 posts. Enlarged 16 ft. 1690, 20 ft. 1698. Galleries.
Woodbury, Conn., I.

1682 Beverly, Mass., II. 50 × 40. Galleries. Belfry in center of roof. Cost: £375.
Lynn, Mass., II ("Old Tunnel"). 50 × 44. Galleries. 4 pediments. Center bell tower. Porches 1716. Dismantled and moved 1827.
Scituate, Mass., II.
Weymouth, Mass., II. 45 × 40, 20 posts. 4 gables. 2 tiers of galleries. Builder: Jacob Nash. Burned 1751.

1683 Bristol, R.I., I. Square. Double galleries. Cap roof. Cupola and bell.
Plymouth, Mass., II. 45 × 22?, 16 posts. Enlarged 18 ft. to 45 × 40 1712. Cupola and bell. Lightning 1715.
Simsbury, Conn., I. 28 × 24, 14 posts. "piramides." Builder: Thomas Barber.
Southold, L.I., II. Gallery on east end.
Wrentham, Mass., I. 36 × 26, 16 posts. Gallery.
Yarmouth, Mass., II. 40 × 30, 13½ posts.

1684 Enfield, Conn.
Greenwich, Conn. I.
MASHPEE, MASS. (Indian Meeting House). Moved 1717. Now a tribal hall.

1685 Dartmouth, Mass. (Baptist). Removed to Tiverton, R.I.
Dunstable, N.H., II. Log tradition.
Isle of Shoals, N.H. 48 × 28. Belfry and bell.
Stow, Mass., I. 4 windows, 3 lights each. 2 double doors. Clay filled.

1686 Wethersfield, Conn., II. 50 × 50. "Dorman wind." Turret and bell. Galleries 1702. Pews 1715.
Windsor, Conn., II. 50 × 40. 2 tiers of galleries. Dormer windows.

1687 Lyme, Conn., II. 40 × 26, 14½ posts.

1688 Boston, Mass. (Anglican), I (King's Chapel). 54 × 36, 20 posts. Belfry 10 ft. sq. Architect: P. Wells.

Marlborough, Mass., III. Lasted 121 years until replaced 1809. Builder: John Newton, Moses Newton.
Sudbury, Mass. (Wayland), III. Builder: Daniel Pond.

1689 Jericho, L.I. (Quaker).
Newbury, Mass. (Second or West Parish), I. 30×30.
Reading, Mass. (Wakefield), II. Dormers 3 sides. Turret. Enlarged 1701.

1690 Chilmark, Mass. (Abel's Hill), I. Date approximate. Sold ca. 1724.
Jamaica, L.I., II. 40×40. Stone. Pyramidal roof (date in iron vane).
Mendon, Mass., III. 30×30, 16 posts. Enlarged 10 ft. on each end 1709. Builder: John Andruse.

1691 Greenwich, Conn., II. 32×26, 15 (or 16) posts. Clapboards and shingles.

1692 Lexington, Mass., I.
Manchester, Mass., II. 30×25, 16 posts. Belfry on top. Galleries.
Waterbury, Conn., I.
Woodstock, Conn., I. 30×26, 14 posts. Gable on each side. Builder: John Holmes.

1693 Glastonbury, Conn., I. Enlarged with galleries or lean-tos 1706. Burned 1734.
Oyster Bay, L.I. (Quaker), II.
Preston, Conn., I. 35×25, 16 posts. Gallery.

1694 Billerica, Mass., II. 2 days and 45 residents to assemble frame.
Deerfield, Mass., II. 30×30, "About 30 feet square." Turret. Gallery. Dismantled 1729.
Flushing, L.I. (Quaker), I.
New London, Conn., III. Enlarged 10 ft. on each end ca. 1740.
West Tisbury, Mass. I. Sold 1702.

1695 Danbury, Conn., I. 40×30.
East Windsor, Conn., I. Dismantled 1714.
Marblehead, Mass., II. Demolished 1824.
Medford, Mass., I. 27×24, 15 posts. Walls limed. Galleries.
Plympton, Mass., I. "Each side with a gable end." Sold as a barn 1716.
Stratfield, Conn. (Bridgeport), I.
Watertown, Mass., III.
Weston, Mass. (most westerly Watertown), I. 30×30. Farmers' meetinghouse.

1696 Braintree, Mass., II. Stone.

1697 Exeter, N.H., III. Gallery.
Gloucester, Mass., II. 40×40, 16 posts. Plastered.
Haverhill, Mass., II. 50×42, 18 posts. Galleries. Builder: John Haseltine. Bell taken down and put on hill.
Newton, Mass., II. Builder: John Brewer. Sold to West Watertown 1721.
Rowley, Mass., II. 50×40, 18 posts. Gallery. 4 gables and turret.

## Chronological Checklist of Meetinghouses

1698 Fairfield, Conn., III. 50×55? Hamilton 1744 says "octagonal" in *Itinerarium*.
Framingham, Mass., I. 40×30. Enlarged to 40×40 1715.
Gay Head, Mass. (Aquinnah).
Little Compton, R.I.
Windham, Conn., I. 35×24, 12 posts. Gable on each side. Galleries.

1699 Boston, Mass., I (Brattle Square or "Manifesto" Church). 72×52. Upper gallery. "Flat" roof. Steeple 1717.
Branford, Conn., II. Voted "long brick house" but 40×40 framed. Builder: Daniel Clark. Turret. Pyramidal roof. Galleries 1706.
Dartmouth, Mass. (Apponegansett) (Quaker). 35×30, 14 posts.
East Greenwich, R.I. (Quaker).
East Hartford, Conn., I.
Kittery, Maine (Second or North Parish or Long Reach). 35×20, 16 posts. Made into a school.
Kittery, Maine (The Point).
Ipswich, Mass., III. 66×60, 26 posts. "with 2 [or] 3 gables on every side." Galleries. Turret. Builder: Abraham Tilton, Abraham Perkins. Bell 1700. Clock 1702. Belfry 1712.
Newport, R.I. (Anglican), I (Trinity). 54×28 (probably).
Newport, R.I. (Baptist), II. Repaired 1783.
NEWPORT, R.I. (Quaker), II. 46×45. 2 tiers of galleries. 4-sq. roof. Auditorium called "Old Ship Room." Builder: John Jones. Additions 1808, 1857.
Rochester, Mass., I. 26×24, 10 posts. Galleries on 3 sides. Builder: Peter Blackmer.
Suffield, Conn., II. 40×40. 2 tiers of galleries.
Wells, Maine, II. Tower on roof. Enlarged 25 ft. 1735.

1700 Boxford, Mass., I. 34×34, 18 posts, to 34×30. Turret. Hipped roof.
Chatham, Mass., I. 22×22 (or 22×32), 13 posts.
East Greenwich, R.I. (Six-Principle Baptist). Upset by wind 1725.
LITTLE COMPTON, R.I. (Quaker).
Middleborough, Mass., II. 36×30, 16 posts. 2 ridge poles, 4 gables. 1½ tiers. Pitched roof 1745.
Newbury, Mass., III. 60×50. 24 posts. 4 gables. Builder: Stephen Jaques. Center turret and bell 1772.
New Utrecht, L.I. (Independent). Stone. "usual octagon form."
PORTSMOUTH, R.I. (Quaker). Double door. Similar to East Sandwich (1810).
Providence, R.I. (Baptist). 20×20. "Hay cap" shape, hole in roof for chimney. Builder: Pardon Tillinghast.

1701 Haddam, Conn. (Second or East Parish), I. 32×32. Turret shingled on all sides.
Hatfield, Mass., II. 45×45. Gables on 4 sides.
Salem Village, Mass. (Danvers), II. 48×42. Builder: Thomas Flint. Bell 1725.

1702 Berwick, Maine, II. 40×30.
Byfield, Mass., I.
Groton, Conn., I. 35×35. Stiles: 34×33. Galleries 1715.

Plainfield, Conn., I.
Stamford, Conn., III. 50×50. "ferrate" (turret?). Drum. Dismantled 1857.
West Springfield, Mass., I. 42×42. Turret 92 ft. 3 roofs, each one smaller. Builder: John Allys.
West Tisbury, Mass., II.

1703 Sandwich, Mass., III. Turret. Enlarged 15 ft. 1756, 1804.
SAYLESVILLE, R.I. (Lincoln) (Quaker). Enlarged 1745. Horse block.
Topsfield, Mass., II. 44×42.

1704 Falmouth, Mass., I.
Providence, R.I. (Quaker), I.

1705 Cambridge, Mass., III. Galleries.
Guilford, Conn. (Second or Madison), I. 35×35. Drum. Galleries 1712.

1706 Bradford, Mass., II. 48×40, 20 posts (seats copied by Andover).
Colchester, Conn., I. 40×40. Galleries. Drum.
Duxbury, Mass., II. 40×33, 17 posts. Postholes? Gallery. Builder: Samuel Sprague. Cost: £180. Enlarged 1754.
East Haven, Conn., I. 26×16, 17 posts; or 20×16, 7 posts.
Enfield, Conn., II. 40×40 or 38×38. Turret and belfry.
Greenland, N.H., I.
Lancaster, Mass., II.
Lebanon, Conn., I. 36×26 to 36×36, 16 posts.
Mansfield, Conn., I. 24×24, 14 posts. Enlarged 20 ft., roof set "contrary way" 1726.
Marshfield, Mass., III.
Medfield, Mass., II.
NORTH PEMBROKE, MASS. (Quaker). 28×28. Built in Scituate. Large single porch with 2 doors.

1707 Freetown, Mass., I. 36×36, 18 posts.
Kingston, N.H., I.
NARRAGANSETT, R.I. (Anglican) (St. Paul's). Moved from Narragansett to Wickford 1800.
Scituate, Mass. (Second or South Parish), III. 50×40, 20 posts. "flat roof of about ten feet rise." Enlarged 13 ft. 1745.
Southampton, L.I., III. Remodeled 1820.

1708 Dighton, Mass., I.
Dorchester, Mass. (Second Parish or Canton), I. 30×30.
Pembroke, Mass., I.

1709 Acushnet, Mass., I.
Andover, Mass. (South Parish), I. 56×50, 22 posts, "square roofe without dormans."
Barrington, R.I., I. 60×40? Gallery. Moved 1837.
Durham, Conn., I. 40×40, 20 posts. "Flat" roof, turret.

Farmington, Conn., II. 50×50. Turret and clock. "Court chamber" above gallery.
NORTH KINGSTOWN, R.I. (Six-Principle Baptist). 33×25. 1 story.

1710 Attleborough, Mass., I. 30×30, 16 posts. Galleries.
Brookhaven, L.I., II.
CHELSEA, MASS. (Rumney Marsh, now Revere), II. 34×30. "Flat" roof? Frame extant.
New London, Conn. (Waterford). Baptists formed church. 1710.
Norton, Mass., I.
Southold, L.I., III. 60×32.
Truro, Mass., I.

1711 Andover, Mass. (North Parish), III. 50×45, 24 posts. "Roofe like Salem-village." Builder: Samuel Snow.
Bushwick, L.I. (Brooklyn). Octagonal. Turret with bell. Demolished 1840.
Chelmsford, Mass., II. 52×42, 24 posts. "spar" 25 ft. "Terit to hang bell in." Unattached belltower.
Concord, Mass., III. 60×50, 28 posts. "English" or "flat" roof. 2 galleries. Builder: Charles Underhill. Tower 1791.
Coventry, Conn., I.
Hampton Falls, N.H., I.
Kensington, Conn., I. Galleries 1720.
NANTUCKET, MASS. ("Old North Vestry").
Newbury, Mass. (became Queen Anne's Chapel). 50×30.
Norwich, Conn., III. 50×50 or 50×45. Builder: John Elderkin II.
Salem, Mass. (Middle Parish or Peabody), I. 51×38, 24 posts. Turret. 2 tiers of galleries. Enlarged twice by cutting by Daniel Spofford. Bell tower 1774. Demolished 1836.

1712 Boston, Mass. III (First Church, "Old Brick"). 72×54, 34 ft. high. 3 decker. Turret. Belfry. Single porch.
Guilford, Conn., II. 68×46, 24 posts. 2 tiers of galleries. 3 tiers of windows. Steeple 1726.
Hamilton, Mass., I. 50×38, 20 posts.
Needham, Mass., I. Burned 1773.
NEWINGTON, N.H. 38×30. Sinnott: type 2. Bell added before 1744.
Portsmouth, N.H., III. 3 decker. Single porch. Belfry 1720. Spire 150 ft. 1730. Dismantled 1854.
West Hartford, Conn. (Fourth Parish in Hartford).

1713 BEVERLY, MASS. (North Parish). 50×40. Steeple 1751. Remodeled "Grecian style" 1838.
Dover, N.H. (Pine Hill), III. Builder: John Thompson Sr.
Hadley, Mass., II. 50×40. "Flattish" roof. "Balcony at one end" (standing belfry?).
Harwich, Mass., I.
Stow, Mass., II. 40×32, 20 posts.
Windham, Conn., II.
York, Maine, III. 50×50. "every way proportionable."

1714 Abington, Mass., I.
Boston, Mass., I ("New North"). 65×48, 35 posts. "flat roof & battlements." Enlarged 18 ft. north side. Steeple 1714? Replaced 1763. Demolished 1802.
Dracut, Mass., I. 30×25.
East Windsor, Conn., II. 40×40. Roof "as this is."
Groton, Mass., III. 50×40, to 40×35. Enlarged 1731. Belfry.
Killingly, Conn., I.
Lexington, Mass., II. 50×40, 28? posts. Like Concord. 2 tiers of galleries. Unattached belltower. Cost: £500.
Longmeadow, Mass., I. 38×38. Plastered. Gallery. Bell chamber.
MARBLEHEAD, MASS. (Anglican) (St. Michael's). 48×48, 23 posts. 17 sq. ft. Tower 50 ft. Spire 53 ft.
Oxford, Mass., I. 30×30, 18 posts.
Plympton, Mass., II.
Pomfret, Conn. (White's Plain), I.
Salisbury, Mass. (West Parish), I. 52×38, 24 posts.

1715 Amesbury, Mass., III. 45×35, 20 posts. Builder: S. Lunt. Removed to Sandy Hill 1761.
Brookfield, Mass. (Quabaug), II. 45×35. Gallery.
Brookline, Mass., I. 44×35. "diamond glass." Steeple, porch 1771–72.
Falmouth, Mass., II. 34×30, 18 posts. "with a flat roof as convenient." Galleries.
Hampton, N.H., IV. 60×40, 28 posts. 3 decker. Steeple or turret "from the beame upward."
Huntington, L.I., II.
Jamaica, L.I. (Dutch Reformed), I. Diameter 34 ft. Wooden. "octagonal." "8 [ft.] square."
LYNNFIELD, MASS. (Second Parish or Lynn). 30×25, 25 posts. Enlarged 14 ft. 1782. Town house 1836.
Medway, Mass., I. 34×28, 16 posts. "Roof to rise 4 feet from center of beam." Builder: John Richardson.
Middletown, Conn. ("Upper Houses," North, or Cromwell Parish), I.
Middletown, Conn., III. 60×40. Galleries. Enlarged 18 ft. 1740.
Southold, L.I. (Mattitick), I. Gallery. Builder: Nathaniel Warner. Used as sail loft after 1830.

1716 Boston, Mass. ("French" meetinghouse). Brick.
Boston, Mass. ("New South"). 60×55. Wood. Spire and steeple. "Ionic order."
Charlestown, Mass., III. 72×52. 2 tiers of galleries. Steeple? Burned 1775.
Dover, N.H. (Oyster River Parish).
Gloucester, Mass. (Second Parish or Annisquam West). Dismantled 1846.
Greenwich, Conn. (Second Parish), I. Pulpit "bluish color."
Kittery, Maine (Leighton's Point). 50×40, 25 posts. Single porch added. Demolished 1837.
Marblehead, Mass. (Second Parish), I (Holyoke's church). Dismantled 1832.
Middletown, Conn. (East Parish or Portland), I. 40×26. "on hill."
Newington, Conn.
Stratham, N.H., I. 48×36, 20 posts. Bell 1730.

Yarmouth, Mass., III. Enlarged 15 ft. 1768. Turret removed. Single porch added. Steeple.

1717 Dartmouth, Mass. (Acoaxet) (Quaker).
East Hampton, L.I., III (Buell's church). Gallery. Pulpit rebuilt 1756.
Kingston, Mass., I. 43×36, 20 posts. Steeple, bell, and porch 1764.
Littleton, Mass., I. Entrances on 3 sides. No gallery.
North Haven, Conn., I. 40×30.
Norwich, Conn. (Franklin or West Farms), I. Builder: J. Elderkin II.
Plainfield, Conn., II. 50×40, 20 posts. Planked ends and sides.
Rochester, Mass. (Quaker).
Rochester, Mass., II. 40×35, 20 posts. Pews on beams above the galleries 1733.
Salem, Mass. (Second or East Parish), I. 60×40. Central belfry. Enlarged 14 ft., steeple, porch added 1770.
Stratfield, Conn. (Bridgeport), II. 48×38, 24 posts. "Long roof." Gallery. Steeple 1769.
Sunderland, Mass. (Swampfield), I. 45×35 or 45×30, 18 posts. Galleries. Conch.
North Swansea, Mass. (Baptist). Single porch added probably after 1770.
Wallingford, Conn., II. 68×52. 2 tiers of galleries. Steeple voted 1716, built 1728.

1718 Ashford, Conn., I. 40×35, 18 posts. Enlarged 1795.
Bridgewater, Mass. (Second Parish or Bridgewater), I. 43×38, 18 posts.
Durham, N.H. (Durham Falls), II. 40×36, 20 posts. Belfry like that in Hampton.
Eastham, Mass., III.
East Haven, Conn., II. 40×30, 20 posts. Straight roof "barn fasyon." Jetted.
Easton, Mass., I. Glazed 1726.
Groton, Conn. (Baptist), I.
Northfield, Mass., I. 45×30, 18 posts.
Orleans, Mass. (Eastham), II. Single stairwell porch replaced stairs 1800.
Rehoboth, Mass., III. 2 sets of galleries (one above the other). Dismantled 1814.
Salem, Mass., III. 72×50. 2 tiers of galleries. Center belfry. Porch, steeple ca. 1770.
Westborough, Mass., I. 40×30, 18 posts.

1719 BARNSTABLE, MASS. (West Parish), I. Enlarged by 2 bays, tower, single porch added 1723?
Barnstable, Mass. (Second or East Parish; Cobb's Hill), I. Enlarged 15 ft., belfry, single porch added 1756.
Brunswick, Maine (Presbyterian), I. Single porch. Abandoned 1806.
Canterbury, Conn., I.
Danbury, Conn., II. 50×35. Enlarged 1745.
Derby, Conn., II. 40×32, 20 posts.
Durham, N.H. (Durham Point).
FLUSHING, L.I. (Queens, N.Y.C.) (Quaker), II.
Ipswich, Mass. (Second Parish, Chebacco, or Essex), II. 52×42, 21 posts. Center turret, bell rope.
Leicester, Mass., I. Galleries.
Manchester, Mass., III. 49×35, 20 posts. "Planket and not studed." Steeple 1753.
New Milford, Conn., I. 40×30, 20 posts.

Rehoboth, Mass. (West Parish or Palmer's River or Seekonk). Vertical plank construction.
Saco, Maine (Biddeford). 35 × 30.
Sutton, Mass., I. 40 × 36. Gallery.
Woonsocket, R.I. (Quaker). 20 × 20. Builder: John Arnold. "Small meeting-house" built adjoining in 1727.
Worcester, Mass., I. Builder: Mr. Constable. Spire 1743.

1720 Bellingham, Mass., I. 40 × 30, 18 posts.
Edgartown, Mass., IV. 40 × 30.
Fairfield, Conn. (Machamux) (Green's Farms or West Parish), I. 36 × 36, 16 posts.
Griswold, Conn., I. 45 × 35. Gallery.
Hebron, Conn., I. 30 × 24, 18 posts. Burned 1747.
Huntington, Conn. (Ripton), I. 50 × 40.
Newport, R.I. (Congregational), I.
Newtown, Conn. 30 × 36, 20 posts. Enlarged to 50 × 36 1720.
Rutland, Mass., I. 41½ × 30. Gallery.
Truro, Mass. (Hill of Storms), II. 40 × 36, 22 posts. Enlarged and single porch added 1765. Demolished 1840.
Warwick, R.I. (Quaker).
Westfield, Mass., II. 52 × 41. "Barn fashion with bell coney [on] middle." Burned 1803.
Woodstock, Conn., II. 46 × 37, 22 posts. Stiles: 50 × 40. Turret but no steeple.

1721 Amesbury, Mass. (East or Jamaco Parish), I. 45 × 35, 20 posts.
Boston, Mass. ("New Brick"). 3 porches, triple decker. Tower. Designer: Edward Pell. Demolished 1844.
Cohasset, Mass., I.
Falmouth, Maine. 36 × 28, 20 posts. Became town house. Burned 1775.
Haddam, Conn., II. 44 × 36, 20 posts.
Londonderry, N.H. (Presbyterian). 50 × 45. Gallery.
Natick, Mass., II. Gable over the door.
Newton, Mass., III. 57 × 45, 25 posts.
Shrewsbury, Mass., I. 40 × 32, 18 posts.
Stafford, Conn., I. 40 × 35, 20 posts.
Tolland, Conn., I. 30 × 30 to 45 × 35, 20 posts.
Watertown, Mass. (West Parish or Waltham), I. Purchased 1697 Newton meeting-house for £80.
Weston, Mass., II. Single porch 1755. Steeple, 2 porches 1800. Dismantled 1840.
Windham, Conn. (Second or Canada Society), I.
Wrentham, Mass., II. 40 × 38, posts for 2 tiers.
Yarmouth, Mass. (Second or East Parish or Dennis), I. Enlarged to 65 × 50 1761. 2-story single porch on south side.

1722 Bolton, Conn.
Brimfield, Mass., I. 45 × 40. Framed. Women seated on west side.
New London, Conn. (North Parish or Montville), I. 45 × 35, 20 posts.
Providence, R.I. (Anglican) (King's Church). 62 × 41. Tower added.

1723 BOSTON, MASS. (Anglican) (Christ Church). 70×51. Capped spire. Steeple by John Indicott 1740, rebuilt 1806.
Cheshire, Conn., I. 40×30, 18 posts. Builder: Henry Caner.
Eastham, Mass. (Wellfleet), I. 20×20.
Guilford, Conn. (Third Parish or North Guilford), I.
Harwich, Mass., II. Single porch 1760. Steeple 1760. Enlarged by opening frame to 72×45.
Lisbon, Conn. (Third Parish in Norwich or Newent), I.
Litchfield, Conn., I. 45×35, 20 posts.
Lynn, Mass. (Quaker).
North Branford, Conn. 40×30. Galleries.
Norwalk, Conn., III. Colored 1771. Burned by British 1779.
Providence, R.I. (Congregational). Tower added.
Ridgefield, Conn., I. 40×34, 28 posts.
Sherburne, Mass., II. 40×32, 20 posts. Enlarged 20 ft. 1769.
Swansea, Mass. (Baptist). 41×33, 22 posts.
Wallingford, Conn. (New Cheshire Parish). 40×30. Galleries 1726.
Watertown, Mass., IV. Steeple before 1728. Enlarged before 1775.
Weymouth, Mass. (Second Parish).

1724 Bridgewater, Mass. (Third Parish or East Bridgewater), I.
Centerbrook, Conn., I. 40×30, 20 posts.
Chilmark, Mass., II. 40×35, 20 posts. Cost: £448.
Fairfield, Conn (Anglican) (Trinity Church). Woodframe. Burned by British 1779.
Little Compton, R.I., II. 42×38, 20 posts.
Oyster Bay, L.I. (Baptist), I. 20×20. "Quadrangular pointed roof."
Southington, Conn., I. 26×16.
Stratford, Conn. (Anglican), I (Christ Church).
Sudbury, Mass. (West Precinct or Sudbury), I.
Westford, Mass., I.

1725 Freetown, Mass. (Quaker).
Hempstead, L.I. (Anglican), I.
Holliston, Mass. 40×32, 20 posts. Enlarged 14 ft., single porch added, colored orange 1787.
Hopkinton, Mass. 48×38, 20 posts.
Newburyport, Mass., I. 45×60. Enlarged to 80×60 1737. Steeple.
NEWPORT, R.I. (Anglican), II (Trinity). 70×46. Entry through tower. Architect: Richard Munday. Tower replaced 1762.
Portsmouth, N.H. (Plains). Blown down 1748.
PROVIDENCE, R.I. (Quaker), II. 30×70? Made a residence in 1844.
Rye, N.H., I.
Scituate, R.I. (Baptist).
Southport, Conn. (Anglican), I.
Sudbury, Mass. (Wayland), IV.

1726 Braintree, Mass. (Third Parish or Randolph), I. 44×32.
Fairfield, Conn. (Greenfield Hill or Northwest Parish), I. 52×46, 24 posts. Builder: Benjamin Darling, Samuel Thorp.
Medford, Mass., II. 52×38, 33 posts. Gathered roof, central turret?
Methuen, Mass., I. 40×35, 20 posts.
Preston, Conn. (Second Parish or Long Society), I. 43×35?
Providence, R.I. (Baptist), II. 40×40. Stiles: 30×40. Benches. Sold 1775.
Saybrook, Conn., III. 48×38. Steeple 1793. Dismantled 1838.
Stoneham, Mass., I. 40×36, 20 posts. Builder: Timothy Wright.
Walpole, Mass., I. 38×32. 3 decker: 2nd tier of galleries 1743.
Westbrook, Conn., I. 40×32, 10 posts. Sky color 1763. Steeple 1795. Demolished 1828.
Wilton, Conn. (Norwalk Second Parish), I.

1727 Columbia, Conn. (Second Parish in Lebanon or Lebanon Crank), I. Galleries.
Concord, N.H. (Rumford or Penny Cook), I. 40×25. "block house" (log tradition).
Groveland, Mass. (Bradford East Parish), I.
Kittery, Maine (The Point), II. Burned 1730.
Ledyard, Conn. (North or Groton Second Parish).
North Yarmouth, Maine, I. 50×40, 22 posts. Single porch, steeple, and vane added when enlarged 40 ft. in 1762.
Plymouth, Mass. (Second Parish or Manomet).
Uxbridge, Mass., I. 45×35, 19 posts.
Warwick, R.I. (Anglican) (Cowessett). 2 stories. Steeple and spire. Demolished 1764.
Windsor, Conn. (Poquonnock, north of Windsor), I.

1728 Attleborough, Mass., II. 50×40. 1-tier gallery.
Gloucester, Mass. (Third or North Parish).
Haddam, Conn. (Second or East Parish), II. 55×44.
Hanover, Mass., I (Central Meeting House). 48×38, 19 posts. Cost: £300.
Haverhill, Mass. (North Parish or Plaistow, N.H.), I. 36×48. No tower.
Killingly, Conn. (Second, North, or Thompson Parish), I. 50×40, 24 posts. Builder: John Comings. Enlarged 1769.
Meriden, Conn., I, 30×30. "Dog's Misery" considered but rejected as a location.
Middleton, Mass., I. 40×40, 22 posts.
Milford, Conn., II. 85×54. 2 tiers of galleries; 3 tiers of windows. Steeple 95 ft.
Milton, Mass., III. 50×40, 28 posts. Belfry and bell, "3½ cwt. grose."
Pembroke, Mass., II. 50×40, 22 posts. Enlarged 1764.
Southborough, Mass., I. 50×40, 20 posts. Dismantled 1807.

1729 Acushnet, Mass. (Quaker).
Bedford, Mass., I. Bell 1752.
BOSTON (Third Church), II ("Old South"). 95×68. Tower. Brick. Pulpit faced long side. Designer: Robert Twelves. Mason: Joshua Blanchard.
Boston, Mass. (Irish or Presbyterian), I. Converted barn.
Cranston, R.I. (Quaker). Enlarged 20 ft. 1819. Torn down 1955.
Deerfield, Mass., III. 50×40. Steeple in center of roof. Gallery. New steeple at north end, porch 1768. Stone color, chocolate doors 1769. Later yellow. Demolished 1824.

Malden, Mass., III. 55 × 44, 33 posts. Steeple. Builder: Aaron Cleveland. Cost: £1,040.
Newbury, Mass. (Second or West Parish; Pipe Stave Hill), II. 50 × 38, 20 posts.
New London, Conn. (Fort Hill) (Baptist). Square. Small, "high beyond a due proportion."
NEWPORT, R.I. (Congregational), II. 60 × 45. Steeple. Designer: Cotton Palmer.
NEWPORT, R.I. (Seventh-Day Baptist). 2 stories. Architect: Richard Munday. Moved; now part of Newport Historical Society.
Rocky Hill, Conn. (Stepney), I.
Rowley, Mass. (Second Parish or Georgetown), I. Enlarged 13 ft. 1742. "Redded" 1744.
Stonington, Conn. (Agreement Hill), III. Dismantled 1829.
Taunton, Mass., II. 56 × 46, 27 posts.
Voluntown, Conn. 30 × 26, 16 posts.
Waterbury, Conn., II. 50 × 40. "rude carved work on the interior."

1730 Chatham, Mass., II. 20 × 20. Single porch. Turret repaired 1741. Galleries. Enlarged 17 ft. and 9 × 10 porch added 1773.
Colchester, Conn. (Second Parish or Westchester), I. 40 × 32, 20 posts.
Exeter, N.H., IV. 60 × 45. 60 × 45. 2 tiers of galleries. Builder: John Folsom. Bell tower 1731.
Grafton, Mass. 50 × 40, 22 posts. Porches 3 sides.
Greenwich, Conn., III.
Killingworth, Conn. (Clinton), II.
KITTERY, MAINE (The Point), III. Sinnott: type 2 made 3, 1840.
Mendon, Mass., IV. 50 × 45, 24 posts. Opponents tried to cut down the frame.
Newmarket, N.H. (North Parish in Exeter), I.
Redding, Conn., I. 30 × 28, 2 stories.
Rochester, N.H., I. 40 × 35, 18 posts.
Rollinsford, N.H., I. Enlarged 16 ft. 1735.
Townsend, Mass., I. Builder: Henry Parker, Henry Jackson.
Trumbull, Conn., I.
WESTWOOD, MASS. (Baptist) (Clapboardtrees Meeting House). Remodeled 1834.
Wilmington, Mass., I. 46 × 30, 20 posts.

1731 Boston, Mass., I (Hollis Street). 60 × 40. Bell tower (base 11 × 11); spire. Burned 1787.
Canterbury, Conn., II. 50 × 45, 22 posts.
Chester, N.H., I. 50 × 38, 20 posts. Builder: Peter and Thomas Cochran of Londonderry.
Chichester, N.H. 35 × 25 to 35 × 16, 9 posts. Log: 6 in. thick.
JAMESPORT, L.I.
Lebanon, Conn., II. 60 × 46, 26 posts. Steeple. Enlarged 1758.
Lunenburg, Mass., I. 45 × 35.
New London, Conn. (Anglican) (St. James's). 50 × 50, 32 posts.
Newtown, L.I. (Jamaica) (Dutch Reformed). 50 × 40.
Portsmouth, N.H. (South Parish). Enlarged 24 ft. 1792. Single porch; bell tower before 1794. Church until 1826. Demolished 1863.
Raynham, Mass., I.
Scarborough, Maine (Black Point Society). 40 × 35, 20 posts.

Scituate, Mass. (Anglican) (St. Andrew's). Bell tower and bell. Enlarged 1753.
Stonington, Conn., III (Center meetinghouse). 2 tiers of galleries. Moved to Stonington Point 1786.
Sturbridge, Mass., I. 50 × 40, 21 posts.

1732 Braintree, Mass. (now Quincy), III. 61 × 41. Attached bell tower. Enlarged 1805.
BURLINGTON, MASS. 50 × 40, 23 posts. Redesigned 1847, 1888.
Glastonbury, Conn. (Second or East Parish), I. 45 × 35, 18 posts.
Harvard, Mass., I. 47 × 35, 20 posts. Square glass set in lead. Builder: John and Thomas Dick.
Kensington, Conn., II. 60 × 45.
Kingston, N.H., II. 55 × 45. 2 tiers of galleries. 100-ft. tower added.
Kingstown, R.I. (South Parish) (Presbyterian) (Tower Hill meetinghouse). Sold at auction after 1791; materials converted to house.
Mansfield, Mass., I.
NANTUCKET, MASS. (Presbyterian). Now a vestry.
Plympton, Mass. (Second or South Parish or Carver), I. Cut in half, 15 ft. added 1768.
Rehoboth, Mass. (Baptist) (Comer's or Oak Swamp Meeting House). Dismantled after 1834. Timbers for barn.
South Hadley, Mass. (Second Parish in Hadley), I. 40 × 30. No steeple.
Stamford, Conn. (Stanwich Society). 40 × 30.

1733 Falmouth, Maine (Second or Cape Elizabeth Parish).
Hampstead, N.H., I. Log tradition.
Hull, Mass., II. 30 × 36½. Bell.
Londonderry, N.H. (Second or West Parish).
NEWPORT, R.I. (Second Congregational Church). 60 × 40. Tower and steeple. Designer: Cotton Palmer.
Pembroke, N.H., I (Suncook). 30 × 24, 10 or 11 posts. "Hewn logs." Builder: Timothy Richardson.
Pomfret, Conn. (Second Parish or Mortlake).
Redding, Conn. (Anglican), I.
Roxbury, Conn., I.
Salem, Mass. (Anglican) (St. Peter's). 46 × 35, 25 posts. 12-ft.-sq. tower.
Southbridge, Mass., I.
West Tisbury, Mass., III. 35 × 30, 18 posts. 14 pews. Builder: Samuel Cobb. Enlarged 15 ft. 1768.
Woodbury, Conn. (Second Parish or Southbury), I. 46 × 35, 23 posts.

1734 Andover, Mass. (South Parish), II. 56 × 44, 30 posts. Cost: £108. "After the same form and fashion of the present one."
Arlington, Mass., I. 50 × 40, 24 posts. "Suitable" belfry. Sold at auction 1804 and made into a dwelling.
Boston, Mass. (Anglican) (Trinity). 90 × 60. Bell, but no tower? Builder: John Indicott.
Boxford, Mass. (Second Parish), I. Gallery and stairs.
Brooklyn, Conn., I. Galleries. Builder: Daniel Tyler.
Dudley, Mass.

Eastham, Mass. (North Parish or Wellfleet), II. Galleries. Single porch added in front 1792.
Haverhill, Mass. (Third or West Parish).
Hopkington, Mass. (Presbyterian).
Hudson, N.H., I. 40×35, 20 posts.
Jamestown, R.I. (Quaker), II.
Kittery, Maine (Middle Parish or Spruce Creek).
Litchfield, N.H. 45×35, 25 posts.
Lyme, Conn., III. 60×40, 24 posts. Tower. Bell. Steeple. Burned 1815.
Malden, Mass. (South Parish or Everett).
Newton, N.H. 40×30. Framed for galleries.

1735 Acton, Mass., I. 46×36, 21 posts. No steeple.
Berkley, Mass., I. 40×34, 18 posts.
Dedham, Mass. (West Parish).
East Hartford, Conn., II. 66×46, 27 posts.
Framingham, Mass., II. 55×42, 30 posts. 2 tiers of galleries.
Glastonbury, Conn., II. 56×44, 24 posts.
Hebron, Conn. (Anglican) (St. Peter's). 58×30.
Hempstead, L.I. (Anglican), II (St. George's).
Palmer, Mass. (Presbyterian), I. 30×36. Emblematic design in gable.
Petersham, Mass., I. 50×40, 21 posts. Colored in 1738 by Thomas Dick.
Sheffield, Mass., I. 54×35.
Tewksbury, Mass., I. 48×36, 14 posts (23 posts?). South Andover frame? Galleries. No steeple.
Upton, Mass., I. 40×30. Pulpit installed 1747.
Wallingford, Conn. (New Cheshire Parish). 64×45. Painted "few years later."
Winchester, N.H., I. 40×32, 18 posts.

1736 Boston, Mass., I (Lynde Street or West Church). Steeple. Barracks 1775. Dismantled 1806.
Boxford, Mass., II. 48×38, 24 posts. Finished 1745.
Cheshire, Conn., II. 64×45, 24 posts. Turret. Replaced by steeple 1790.
Dedham, Mass. (South Parish or Norwood), I.
Holden, Mass., I. 50×40, 22 posts.
Middletown, Conn. (North Parish or Cromwell), II. 55×30, 23 posts.
Northampton, Mass., III. 70×46. "Steeple or balcony at the end." Builder: Joseph Wright.
Salem, Mass. (Third or South Parish). Burned 1774. Predecessor of "Tabernacle."

1737 Billerica, Mass., III. 60×40, 26 posts.
Bridgehampton, L.I., II. 54×38.
Durham, Conn., II. 64×44, 25 posts.
East Granby, Conn. 40×35, 20 posts. Steeple 1796.
Guilford, Conn. (Second Parish or Madison), II. 60×40. Lead color. Steeple 1799.
Hartford, Conn., III. 66×46. Steeple. Designer-builder: Cotton Palmer.
Keene, N.H., I. 40×35, 20 posts.
Kensington, N.H., I. Galleries.

Londonderry, N.H. (Second or West Parish). Low in post.
Lynn, Mass. (Third Parish or Saugus). 44×36, 20 posts. Single porch, 3 doors.
Scituate, Mass., IV.
Stoughton, Mass. (Second Parish or Sharon).
Westminster, Mass., I. 45×35, 21 posts.
Wintonbury, Conn. (Bloomfield), I. 45×35.

1738 Amherst, Mass. (Hadley East or Third Precinct), I. 45×35.
Boscawen, N.H., I. 40×26. Built of logs.
Dunstable, N.H., III.
East Kingston, N.H. (Kingston Second Parish).
Ellington, Conn., I. 35×45, 20 posts.
Fairfield, Conn. (Green's Farms or West Parish), II. Burned by British 1779.
Gloucester, Mass., III. 75×60, 30 posts. Bell tower 75 ft. high. Steeple.
Granby, Conn. (East Parish or Turkey Hills or Simsbury).
Hampton, N.H. (Fourth Parish or North Hampton), I. 40×30.
Hardwick, Mass., I. 50×40, 22 posts.
Marshfield, Mass. (Second or North Parish).
New Boston, N.H., I. 30×45, 20 posts.
SALEM, N.H. 48×38, 22 posts. Became town house, moved.
Southport, Conn. (Anglican), II. 55×35, 20 posts. Steeple.
Swanzey, N.H., I. 50×40, 22 posts. Steeple 1738.
Tyngstown, Mass. (later Derryfield), I. 42×30, 20 posts. Abandoned. Burned 1751.
Wallingford, Conn. (Baptist). Began church 1735.
Wilton, Conn. (Norwalk Second Parish), II. 48×35, 22 posts.

1739 Amherst, N.H., I. 45×22, 22 posts.
Bridgewater, Mass. (West Bridgewater), III. 50×38, 22 posts. Spire and bell 1767.
Bridgewater, Mass. (Fourth or North Parish or Brockton), I.
Chester, N.H. (Presbyterian). 40×35 or 38×33, 20 posts. Dismantled 1793. Materials used in 1793 Long Meadow meetinghouse.
Franklin, Mass., I.
Harwinton, Conn., I. 50×35, 24 posts.
Kent, Conn., I. 50×40, 23 posts.
Killingworth, Conn. (Second Society or Killingworth Farms), I. 58×38, posts 2 ft. shorter than those of the First Society.
Mattapoisett, Mass., I.
New Canaan, Conn., I. 30×30. Gallery.
New Hartford, Conn., I. 50×40, 55×40.
New Salem, Mass., I. 45×35, 20 posts.
North Haven, Conn., II. 65×44. Steeple (square cap) 1798.
Stockbridge, Mass., I. 40×30. Conch (gift from Boston). Frame used for barn 1854.
Union, Conn., I. 45×35.
Wareham, Mass., I.

1740 Bernardston, Mass., I. 50×40, 23 posts. Re-pewed 1773. Colored yellow 1794.
Blandford, Mass. Pulpit 1759. Plastered 1786. Completed 1805.
Bolton, Mass., I. Builder: Thomas Dick.

Chester, Conn., I.
Cumberland, R.I. (Six-Principle Baptist). 30×25. 2 stories. Burned 1962.
New Fairfield, Conn.
Falmouth, Maine, II ("Old Jerusalem"). Enlarged 1759. Unattached belltower 1758. 120-ft. tower 1760.
Goshen, Conn., I. 46×34, 20 posts. 2 galleries, one above the other.
Littleton, Mass., II. 50×40, 23 posts.
Plymouth, Conn. (Anglican).
Preston, Conn., II. 48×38, 22 posts.
Roxbury, Mass., III. 62×42, 26 posts. Steeple. Burned 1744.
Shutesbury, Mass., I. 40×30, 20 posts. Builder: "D. Dix."
Simsbury, Conn., II. 50×40. Painted white 1782. Demolished 1830.
Windham, Maine, I. 40×30, 10 posts.

1741 Athol, Mass., I. Log tradition.
Branford, Conn., III. 64×44, 26 posts. Steeple 1803.
Canaan, Conn. (South Parish). 40×35, 20 posts, to 35×30, 18 posts.
Cornwall, Conn., I. 48×38, 24 posts.
Epping, N.H.
Gorham, Maine. 36×26, 20 posts. "shed." Log tradition?
Hollis, N.H., I. 22×20, 9 posts.
Lyndeborough, N.H., I. 35×30, 20 posts. Builder: Cornelius Tarbell.
Mendon, Mass. (Second or East Parish or Milford), I. 40×35. Colored 1748. Enlarged 14 ft., single porch added 1792.
Milford, Conn. (Second Parish, "Opposers").
Newburyport, Mass. (Anglican), I (St. Paul's).
Oxford, Conn., I. 38×32, 19 posts.
Watertown, Conn. (Westbury), I.

1742 Barrington, N.H., I. 44×36. Town hall 1840.
Boston, Mass. (Bennett Street).
Brentwood, N.H., I.
Buxton, Maine, I. Log tradition. 30×25, "9 feet stud of hune timber."
Colrain, Mass. Painted blue 1764.
Hadlyme, Conn. 46×35, 20 posts.
HINGHAM, MASS. (Second or South Parish).
Ledyard, Conn. (Separate church).
Leicester, Mass. (Quaker). 20×22. Made into a dwelling house 1791.
Leominster, Mass., I. 50×40, 23 posts, to 54×35, 22 posts. Painted 1753.
New Milford, Conn. (Quaker), I.
Sharon, Conn., I. 45×35, 20 posts (turned down a log house). Belfry 1743.
South Hampton, N.H.
Stratford, Conn., III. 60×40, 26 posts. Steeple 130 ft. high. Burned 1785.
Washington, Conn., I. Log. 30×26.
West Hartford, Conn. (Fourth Parish in Hartford), II.

1743 Attleborough, Mass. (Second or East Parish), I. 45×35. 1-tier gallery.
Bethlem, Conn. (Bethlehem Society or Woodbury East), I.

Bloomfield, Conn. (Anglican) (St. Andrew's).
Boylston, Mass. (North Shrewsbury). 45×35, 20 posts.
Dorchester, Mass., IV. 68×46. Steeple and porch, 14 ft. sq. 114 ft. high. Cost: £3,56 Enlarged 1795.
Exeter, N.H. (Second Parish, "seceders"). Steeple, gallery. Builder: Nathaniel Con ner. Dismantled and parts divided 1824.
Great Barrington, Mass. 45×35. Belfry 1745.
Ipswich, Mass. (West or Linebrook Parish). 60×40, 22 posts. 1-tier gallery. No stee ple. Moved and rebuilt 1828.
Lancaster, Mass., III.
Newburyport, Mass. (Separatist became Presbyterian), I.
Norwalk, Conn. (Anglican). 55×42.
PELHAM, MASS. 46×36. Painted "Askie Coler." Builder: Thomas and John Dick Undated single porch.
Rehoboth, Mass. (Six-Principle Baptist) (Round's church).
Spencer, Mass., I. 45×35. Stairs within.
Stonington, Conn. (Baptist). 40×30.
Stratford, Conn. (Anglican), II. Decorated door. 3 decker. 9 days to raise frame 130 ft. bell tower. Architect: Henry Dudley.
Suffield, Conn. (Second Parish or Ireland Plaine), I.
Tyringham, Mass., I. 40×35.
Warren, Mass. (Western), I. 40×40 to 45×35, 20½ posts.
Waterbury, Conn. (Anglican), I (St. James's).
Woodstock, Conn. (West Parish). 48×38. Foreseats like those in First Parish.

1744 Acushnet, Mass., II. Palladian window put in above door.
Bellingham, Mass. (Baptist), I. 35×30, 19 posts. (4th in Mass.).
Boston, Mass. (Irish or Presbyterian), II. Tower and spire.
Cambridge, Mass. (South Parish or Brighton). Tower and porch 1794.
Chatham, Conn. (Middle Haddam). 44×36.
Coventry, Conn. (North Parish).
Dorchester, Mass. (Third Parish or Stoughton), I. 45×35.
Greenwich, Mass. 40×30, 20 posts.
Killingly, Conn. (South Parish or Breakneck Hill), II. Moved 1757. Became town house
Mansfield, Conn. (North Parish).
Millbury, Mass., I. ("The Lord's Barn"). 40×35.
New Haven, Conn. (White Haven Society or Separate church) (the "Blue"). 60×44 Painted blue 1751. Bell tower 1764.
Plymouth, Mass., III. 72×68. Hipped roof with tower later moved to front. Demol ished 1831.
Plymouth, Mass. (Third Parish or Old Light Separate church).
Providence, R.I. (Beneficent Congregational). 40×36. Spire 100 ft.
Scarborough, Maine (Dunstan Society).
Westerly, R.I. (Quaker).

1745 Dracut, Mass. (Second Parish or Lowell), I. 45×35, 23 posts.
HAMPSTEAD, N.H., II. 50×40, 28 posts. Steeple, porch 1793. Town house 1852 Builder: Josiah Clark, Ethan Barker.

Killingly, Conn. (First or Middle Parish or Putnam Heights), III.
Marshfield, Mass. (Anglican) (Trinity).
Middlefield, Conn. 40×40.
Northborough, Mass., I. 46×36, 20 posts. Framer: Daniel Hemminway.
Norwich, Conn. (Franklin or West Farms), II.
Pepperell, Mass., I. 42×30, 20 posts.
Roxbury, Conn., II.
Sterling, Mass. (West Lancaster), I.
Waterbury, Conn. (Plymouth Church). 45×35, 20 posts.

1746 Belchertown, Mass., I.
Boston, Mass., I (Second Baptist Church). 45×33. Gallery.
Byfield, Mass., II. 56×45. Steeple 12-ft. sq. Enlarged to 70×45 ca. 1764. Burned 1833.
Hollis, N.H., II. 50×44, 23 posts.
New Milford, Conn. (Anglican), I.
Pelham, N.H. 28×24.
Pembroke, Mass. (Second Parish, now Hanson).
Plymouth, Conn.
Roxbury, Mass., IV. 62×42, 26 posts. Spire added to steeple. Cost: £2,905. Enlarged 1774.
Torrington, Conn., I ("Hemlock" meetinghouse). 30×30, 18 posts.

1747 COHASSET, MASS., II. 45×60. 2-story single porch 1767. Bell tower 1799.
Columbia, Conn. (Second Parish in Lebanon or Lebanon Crank), II. 64×46, 26 posts. Steeple 1792.
Concord, Mass. (Second Parish or Lincoln). Belfry and porches on 3 sides.
DUNSTABLE, N.H. (South Parish or Nashua) ("Bird's meetinghouse"). 40×38. Gallery.
Harwich, Mass. (Second or South Parish), I.
Hudson, N.H., II. 40×26.
Ipswich, Mass. (Third or South Parish). 60×40, 25 posts. No porch or tower.
North Guilford, Conn. (Anglican), I.
Sturbridge, Mass. (Separatist became Baptist), I.
Windham, Conn. (Third Parish or Scotland), I. 43×33, 20 posts. "with a handsome jeyht."
Woodbury, Conn., II. "Transcendantly Magnificent."
YORK, MAINE, IV. 70×50, 25 posts. Remodeled 1839. Made Victorian later.

1748 Canterbury, Conn. (Separate church).
Dorchester, Mass. (Second Parish or Canton), II.
Douglas, Mass. Glazed 1751. Plastered 1771. Colored 1793. Single porch.
Dracut, Mass., II. 45×35, 23 posts. Pine shingles. Gallery.
Gilead, Conn. (Second Parish or Hebron), I. 46×36, 22 posts.
Hebron, Conn., II. 60×48, 25 posts.
New Ipswich, N.H., I. Framed? Demolished 1748.
Oxford, Mass., II. Builder: David Baldwin. Cost: £640.
Rochester, Mass. (North Parish), I.
Sutton, Mass., II. 50×40, 22 posts. Tower and bell 1792.
Wenham, Mass., III. 52×42, 24 posts. Steeple pulled down 1759, replaced 1765.

Wilbraham, Mass., I. 45×35. Gallery. Moved 1794.

Woburn, Mass., III. 58×42, 24 posts. Builder: Joshua Thornton. Steeple? Enlarged, bell replaced 1772.

1749 Athol, Mass., II.

Berwick, Maine (North Parish), I.

BOSTON, MASS. (Anglican), II (King's Chapel). 71×60. Stone. Architect: Peter Harrison.

Bristol, Conn., I. 40×30.

Brookfield, Mass. (Second or North Parish), I. Twin porches added. Sold 1832.

Chester, N.H. (Long Meadow, later Auburn), I ("Little Meeting-house"). Dismantled 1793. Materials used in 1793 meetinghouse.

Easton, Mass., II. Porch and belfry 1794. Town hall 1816.

Hartford, Conn. (Second Parish), II. 66×46. Bell tower 16×16. Builder: Isaac Seymour.

Ipswich, Mass., IV. 63×47, 26 posts. Steeple. Builder: Daniel Heard. Finish carpenter: Abraham Knowlton.

Lunenburg, Mass., II.

Marlborough, Conn. 48×36. Gallery. Demolished 1841.

Medway, Mass., II. 42×33, 20 posts. Main alley. Doors to pulpit.

Middleborough, Mass. (Titicut), I.

Rowley, Mass., III. 60×42. Steeple and spire 12×12. Porch on other end.

Salisbury, Conn., I. 45×35, 20 posts.

Springfield, Mass., III. 60×46 (or 56×45), 25 posts. Bell tower.

Springfield, Mass. (Fifth Parish or Chicopee), I. 42×33. Entrances for men and women.

Suffield, Conn., III. 57×47. Gallery. Roof steeple. Builder: Joseph Howard. Replaced 130-ft. spire 1786.

Westborough, Mass., II. 50×40, 23 posts. 3 porches. Enlarged 14ft. 1773. Steeple 1800.

1750 Berwick, Maine, III. 70×47. Belfry and tall spire.

Brentwood, N.H., II.

Canterbury, N.H. 45×35. Twin porch added 1789.

Chelsea, Mass., II. Steeple mentioned 1749.

Dover, Mass., I. 42×34, 20 posts. No steeple. Gallery.

East Hampton, Conn. 46×36, 22 posts. Burned 1854.

Fairfield, Conn., IV. Replaced octagonal one, 60×44, 26 posts. 120-ft. steeple. Burned by British 1779.

Falmouth, Mass., III. 42×42. Enlarged, single porch added 1791.

Granville, Mass., I.

Hatfield, Mass., III. 56×45. "Belfry and tower with Gothic Points."

Medway, Mass. (Second or West Parish), I. 40×34, 20 posts.

Middletown, Conn. (Anglican). 50×36. Steeple. Bell 1759.

Middletown, Conn. (East Parish or Portland), II. 56×42.

Northford, Conn. 50×40.

Redding, Conn., II. 46×37.

Redding, Conn. (Anglican), II. 50×46.

Riverhead, L.I. (Wading River). 28×26.

Shelter Island, L.I. Builder: Brindley Sylvester.

Smithtown, L.I.
Sutton, Mass. (Baptist).
Ware, Mass., I. 40×35 to 30×25, 15 posts.
Warwick, R.I. (Baptist) (ca. 1750). 40×40, 2 stories.
Wells, Maine (Second Parish or Kennebunk). 30 ft. long. Enlarged 12 ft. 1752. Single porch 1755. Architect: James Hubbard.
Westerly, R.I. Indian church.
West Greenwich, R.I. (Baptist).

1751 ABINGTON, CONN. 48×39. Remodeled 1802, 1834.
Abington, Mass., II. 70×50, 26 posts. Side tower by 1796.
Bradford, Mass., III. Undated single porch.
Concord, N.H., II ("Old North"). 60×46, 28 posts. Spire 1783. Semicircle 1802. Burned 1870.
Ipswich, Mass. (Second Parish, Chebacco, or Essex), III.
Mansfield, Conn., II. 64×44, 25 posts. Steeple 1792. Turned 1839.
Norwich, Conn., IV. 70×48, 26 posts. Steeple on the beams. Burned 1801.
Washington, Conn., II. Steeple erected 1786.
Weymouth, Mass., III. Bell tower and steeple.

1752 Ashburnham, Mass., I.
Bridgehampton, L.I. (Separate church).
Falmouth, Maine (Quaker), I.
Gloucester, Mass. (Fourth or breakaway North Parish). Gallery 3 sides. Belfry.
New Braintree, Mass., I. 50×40. Twin porch addition 1772. Colored "dingy yellow."
New Canaan, Conn., II. 50×40. Bell tower 1797.
New Milford, Conn., II. 60×44, 27 posts. Steeple 1754.
Norton, Mass., II. 50×40, 20 posts, to 60×40, 25 posts. Steeple. Builder: William Coddington.
Peterborough, N.H., I. Repaired, enlarged 1761.
Reading, Mass. (Second or North Parish or Reading), I. 48×36.
Saco, Maine.
Southampton, Mass., I.
Tiverton, R.I. (Baptist), I.

1753 Andover, Mass. (North Parish), IV. Undated single porch. Dismantled 1835. Porch added to a dwelling house.
Barre, Mass., I.
Charlemont, Mass. 35×30, 18 posts. Only frame raised. Builder: Thomas Dick.
Dunbarton, N.H., I. 30×30, 10 posts. Log tradition.
East Windsor, Conn. (Second Parish or Scantic). 47×35, 21 posts.
Exeter, R.I. (Chestnut Hill) (Baptist, New Light). Fireplace near the center.
Falmouth, Maine (Third or New Casco Parish). Gallery.
Keene, N.H., II. 45×35, 22 posts.
Mason, N.H., I. 40×30.
New Haven, Conn. (Anglican) (Trinity). 58×38. 6-sided bell tower.
Shirley, Mass., I.

Southington, Conn., II. 70×35. Steeple 1797.
Stow, Mass., III. 50×40, 23 posts.
Templeton, Mass., I. 60×50.
Windham, Conn. (First Parish in Windham County), III. Steeple.
Windham, Conn. (Second or Canada Society), II. Builder: Thomas Stedman (20 years old).
Windham, N.H. (Presbyterian), I.

1754 Avon, Conn. (North Farmington), I.
Bellingham, Mass., II.
Bridgewater, Mass. (Third Parish or East Bridgewater), II. 56×45, 22 posts.
BROOKFIELD, MASS. (Third or South Parish). 55×45, 23 posts. Moved, became Roman Catholic church 1867.
Dunstable, N.H., IV. Used old materials.
Gloucester, Mass. (Fifth Parish or Sandy Bay or Rockport). 36×36. 2 stories. No belfry. Single porch.
HAMPTON, CONN. 55×45. Tower by 1794. Sinnott: type 2 made 4, turned 1838.
Natick, Mass., III.
New Ipswich, N.H., II. 50×40, 24 posts, to 32×22, 9 posts.
Tolland, Conn., II. 56×40. Steeple 1792. Dismantled 1838.

1755 Bedford, N.H., I. 40×50. 2 stories. Unattached belltower. Builder: Warren. Finish carpenter: Thomas and Josiah Warren. Painted 1762.
Brookfield, Mass., III. 55×45, 23 posts. Moved as town house. Sold 1809.
Brunswick, Maine (East Side).
GROTON, MASS., IV. 65×50, 26 posts. Belfry 1795. Porch opposite. Turned 1839.
HAWKE, N.H. (Danville). 49×37. Gallery.
Meriden, Conn., II. 60×50. Stiles: "about 64×44." Steeple 1803.
Montague, Mass., I. 2 windows behind pulpit. Conch. 2-story belfry 1801. Dismantled 1833.
New Britain, Conn., I. 45×35, 22 posts; revised to 80×64.
Nottingham, N.H., I.
Richmond, R.I. (Quaker).
Tyngsborough, Mass. (First Parish of Dunstable). Undated steeple blown down 1815.

1756 Cambridge, Mass., IV. 66×52. Steeple.
GREENLAND, N.H., II. Bell tower 1801. Remodeled 1834, 1881.
Hudson, Mass. Casement windows added. Coloring.
Merrimack, N.H., I. 50×34, galleries.
NEWBURYPORT, MASS. (Presbyterian), II. 100×60. Enlarged 1801.
New Preston, Conn., I. 36×26, 10 posts.
New Shoreham, R.I. (Block Island) (First Baptist Church), I.
Provincetown, Mass., I.
Rye, N.H., II. 60×40 to 58×40. Dismantled and used as stable in Portsmouth 1840.
Warren, R.I. (Baptist), I. 44×44. Hipped roof with small belfry "whose rope hung directly down in the center of the middle aisle." Gallery 1772.
Warwick, Mass., I. 35×30, 19 posts. Torn down 1787. Builder: Mason and Perry.

1757 Coventry, R.I. (Baptist). 28 × 26, 2 stories. Builder: Elder Peter Worden. 1st of 3 similar ones.
East Windsor, Conn., III. 60 × 45, 27 posts. Bell 1765.
HARPSWELL, MAINE (North Yarmouth). 40 × 35, 17 posts. Builder: Elisha Eaton Jr. Single porch 1774. Now town house.
Killingly, Conn. (South Parish).
New Haven, Conn., III ("New Brick meeting house"). 70 × 50. Stiles: 76 × 54.
North Bristol, Conn.
Windsor, Conn., III. 60 × 45, 24 posts. Steeple (square cap).
WOOLWICH, MAINE. Sinnott: type 2. Altered 1840s. No galleries.

1758 Bath, Maine. Single porch.
Carlisle, Mass., I. 40 × 30.
Dover, N.H., IV. 70 × 47. "belfry and tall spire."
Hinsdale, N.H.
Newcastle, Maine.
Riverhead, L.I. (Aquebogue), I. 33 × 24.
Weston, Conn. (Norfield Parish). 40 × 30, 19 posts.
Woodbridge, Conn. (Amity Society), I. 40 × 50.

1759 Bethel, Conn. 48 × 36, 21 posts. Sides: shingles 3 ft. long. Steeple 1818. Burned 1842.
Bridgewater, Mass. (Second Parish or Bridgewater), II. 64 × 50. Belfry.
Brookfield, Conn. 46 × 36, 20 posts. Steeple 1824.
Charleton, Mass. 40 × 50. Builder: Jonathan Upham. Cost: £26.
Derryfield, N.H. (Manchester), I. 40 × 35.
Lyndeborough, N.H., II. Single porch. Burned.
Newbury, Mass. (Second or West Parish), III. 54 × 49, 24 posts.
Pembroke, N.H., II. Builder: Ephraim Barker. Dismantled 1806? Private survival?
Rutland, Mass., II. 60 × 50, 24 posts. Burned 1830.
Topsfield, Mass., III. 54 × 42, 26 posts. Bell 1817.

1760 Agawam, Mass. (Springfield Sixth Parish, 1762; West Springfield Second Parish, 1774). "Never finished."
Charlestown, N.H., I. 34 × 20, 8 posts. "log house."
Gloucester, R.I. (before 1760). 30 × 20.
Greenfield, Mass. 45 × 35 to 50 × 40. Conch.
Norfolk, Conn., I. 50 × 40, 20 posts. Painted "peach-blow color."
Norwich Landing, Conn. (Anglican). 42 × 45.
Pomfret, Conn., II. 60 × 48, 24 or 25 posts. Builder: Thomas Stedman.
Providence, R.I. (Presbyterian) (before 1760). 53 × 35.
Providence, R.I. (Quaker) (before 1760). 28 × 39.
Providence, R.I. (Quaker, Warren Meeting) (before 1760). 28 × 38.
SHEFFIELD, MASS., II. 60 × 41. Turned 1819.
Wales, Mass. (Baptist). Sold to the town 1802.
Wallingford, Conn. (Anglican) (before 1760). 49 × 38.
Warwick, R.I. (Apponaug) (Baptist). 28 × 26. 1-tier gallery. Builder: Elder Peter Worden. 2nd of 3 similar ones.
Winchester, N.H., II. 44 × 34, 20 posts.

1761 Amesbury, Mass. (Sandy Hill), IV. Single porch. Rebuilt 1715 meetinghouse. Dismantled 1848.
Becket, Mass., I. 50×40, 22 posts. Steeple 1772.
Buxton, Maine, II. 45×35. "Proper stud."
CAMBRIDGE, MASS. (Anglican). 58×39. Bell. Architect: Peter Harrison.
Dartmouth, Mass. (Quaker) (Allen's Neck Meeting House).
DEDHAM, MASS., III. 60×46. Sinnott: type 2 made 3. Steeple, 2 porches. Enlarged 1819, 1857.
Hamden, Conn. (Carmel). 55×40. Turret by subscription.
Hampton, N.H. (Fourth Parish or North Hampton), II.
Newton, N.H., II. 58×40. Galleries. Tower 1816.
Oakham, Mass., I. 46×36. Dismantled and moved West Rutland meetinghouse. Gallery.
South Hadley, Mass., II. 60×45. Conch. Steeple and belfry 1791.
Vernon, Conn. 50×40, 24 posts, to 46×36, 22 posts.
Winchendon, Mass., I. 30×45, 20 posts.
Windsor, Conn. (North Parish), I. "Site" separatists.

1762 Bridgewater, Mass. (Fourth Parish), II. 64×50. Belfry (12×12, 85 ft. high). Porch 1789. Builder: Simeon Cary.
Brimfield, Mass., II. 20 posts.
Charlemont, Mass., I. 35×30, 18 posts. Never completed. Sold 1769. Builder: Thomas Dick.
Fairfield, Conn. (Greenfield Hill or Northwest Parish), II. 60×42. Steeple.
Granby, Mass., I.
HAMILTON, MASS., II. 60×54, 26 posts. Turned. Greek Revival.
Litchfield, Conn., II. 60×45. Steeple. Carved tulips and vines on pulpit.
Manchester, Conn. (Orford), I.
Monson, Mass., I.
New Boston, N.H., II. 50×40, 20 posts.
Newbury, Mass. (Fifth Parish) (Oliver Nobles's meetinghouse).
Northfield, Mass., II. 55×44. Builder: Hophni King. Steeple.
Princeton, Mass., I. 50×40. No steeple.
Woodstock, Conn. (North Parish or East Woodstock).

1763 Arrowsic, Maine. Single porch.
Bennington, Vt., I. 50×40. Single porch.
Bethel, Conn. (Anglican). 48×36.
Braintree, Mass. (Third Parish or Randolph), II. 60×45. Twin porch 1796.
Canton, Conn., I. Dismantled 1814.
Foxborough, Mass. Twin porch addition ca. 1780.
Hampton Falls, N.H. (Presbyterian).
NEWPORT, R.I. (Touro Synagogue).
Suffield, Conn. (Separatist).
Waldoboro, Maine, I. Log tradition.
Worcester, Mass., II (Old South). 70×50. Builder: D. Hemenway. Cost: £1,542. Bell tower, 2 porches. Dismantled 1887.

1764 Epsom, N.H. 50×40.
Falmouth, Maine (Portland) (Anglican). 50×29.
Gorham, Maine, II. Enlarged 30 ft. 1792.
Hanover, Mass., II (Central Meeting House). 62×43, 22 posts. Builder: Joseph Tolman. Steeple, opposing porch added.
Hartland, Conn., I. 45×35, 20 posts.
Holland, Mass. Pillars and pulpit painted "pee green" 1794.
Mansfield, Mass., II. 60×45. Moved 1872. Demolished 1888.
New Danbury, Conn. Burned by British 1777.
Richmond, Mass., I. 45×25.
Rindge, N.H., I. 50×40.
Royalston, Mass., I.
Topsham, Maine, I. Single porch voted 1770.
Wales, Mass., I. 45×35, 21 posts. Never finished. Removed to Willington, Conn.
Walpole, N.H., I. 56×42.
WESTMORELAND, N.H. 50×40, 20 posts. Moved 1779. Twin porches added.
WETHERSFIELD, CONN., III. 80×50. Opposed porch and steeple. Brick. Builder: John Chester (superintendent).

1765 Bethel, Conn., II. 60×45. Steeple 1793.
Coventry, Conn., II.
Haverhill, Mass., III. 66×48. Steeple. Dismantled 1837.
Haverhill, Mass. (Baptist). 60×42. Undated twin porch addition. Tower, turret, and bell added in 1801.
Hopkinton, N.H., I. 50×38, 22 posts. Burned 1789 following committee decision not to move it.
New Gloucester, Maine.
PAXTON, MASS. 50×40, 22 posts. Sinnott: type 2 made 3.
Portsmouth, N.H. (Sandemanian). Meetinghouse raised near Canoe Bridge.
SEABROOK, N.H. (Presbyterian). Town house 1893.
Stafford, Conn. (Second or West Parish).
Wapping, Conn., I ("Wapping Barn"). 60×40.
Warner, N.H., I. Log tradition.
Wilmington, Mass., II. 58×36. Pulpit grained mahogany.
Woodbury, Conn. (Third Parish or South Britain).

1766 Brookhaven, L.I., III.
Candia, N.H., I. 55×45. Gallery. Steeple and porch 1796. Burned 1828.
Fitchburg, Mass., I. Builder: Timothy Parker.
Methuen, Mass. (Second Parish). Pulpit "dressed" at same cost as in First Parish 1810.
New Milford, Conn. (Anglican), II.
Sharon, Conn., II. 60×40, 25 posts.
SHREWSBURY, MASS., II. 60×45, 27 posts. Builder: Daniel Hemenway. 3 porches. 1807 belfry. Turned 1834.
Wrentham, Mass., III. Cost: £1,500. Tower by subscription £190.

## Appendix B

1767 Ashfield, Mass., I. 48 × 36.
Bethlem, Conn., II. 60 × 43, posts as in "Old Society."
Canaan, Conn. (Second or East Parish). 50 × 40, 24 posts. Galleries 1787. "turret" 1797.
Charlemont, Mass. (Heath). 45 × 35, 20 posts.
Charlestown, N.H., II. 52 × 42, 25 posts.
Dighton, Mass. (Second Parish), I.
DIGHTON, MASS., II. 55 × 45, 24 posts. Became town hall.
Egremont, Mass.
Griswold, Conn. ("Blue Pachaug"), II. 66 × 42. No steeple.
LONGMEADOW, MASS., II. 56 × 42, 25 posts. Steeple 14 ft. sq., 54 ft. high.
Middletown, L.I. (formerly Middle Island).
Murrayfield, Mass. (later Chester), I. 45 × 40, 20 posts.
Newburyport, Mass., III.
Reading, Mass. (Wakefield), III. 70 × 50, 28 posts. Steeple and porch. Builder: David Nelson, Asa Todd.
Stratham, N.H., II. 63 × 45. Steeple 12 ft. sq. Builder: Josiah Clarke.
Watertown, Mass. (West Precinct or Waltham). Bell tower.
Wells, Maine, III. 65 × 46. Builder: Eleazer Kimball. Steeple 1770 by subscription.
Westford, Conn., I. Bought Brimfield, Mass., frame.
Westhampton, L.I.
Westminster, Vt. Twin porches added 1789. Spire 1793. Burned 1888.
Woodbury, Conn. (Second Parish or Southbury), II. 60 × 45 (like Litchfield).

1768 Ashford, Conn. (Second or Westford Hill Parish).
Berwick, Maine (Baptist).
Chesterfield, Mass., I.
DOVER, N.H. (Quaker). Front porch with 2 doors. (Single porch?).
Falmouth, Maine (Quaker), II. 40 × 32.
Great Barrington, Mass. (Anglican) (St. James's). 71 × 40. Tower 110 ft. Compass windows.
Hampton Falls, N.H. (Second Parish), II ("The Ohio"). 55 × 40.
Lanesborough, Mass., I. 60 × 43, 27 posts, to 58 × 40, 25 posts. Single porch.
Madbury, N.H.
Middletown, Conn. (Separate church). Meetinghouse held in "the Chambers . . . all in one."
Newburyport, Mass. (Titcomb Street), I.
New Ipswich, N.H., III. 60 × 54, 26 posts. Demolished 1816.
New Preston, Conn., II. 50 × 40, 22 posts.
Plymouth, N.H. (Ward's Hill), I. 50 × 40. Logs of uniform size. Gallery. Burned 1787.
Sag Harbor, L.I., I ("God's Old Barn"). "Beat of drum."
Salisbury, N.H. (Searle's Hill), I. Sold privately and moved to South Road, 1790.
Temple, N.H., I. 30 × 30, 12 posts.
Torringford, Conn. No steeple.
Warren, Conn., I. Gallery.
Winchester, Conn., I. 30 × 24, 9 posts.

1769 Ashby, Mass., I.
　Atkinson, N.H. 50×40.
　Bethany, Conn. 50×40. Steeple 1803.
　Boscawen, N.H., II. 40×25.
　Conway, Mass. 60×50? Porches, steeple added after 1796.
　Dedham, Mass. (South or Norwood Parish), II.
　Edgartown, Mass., V. 60×45. Pew owners permitted windows "upon their own cost."
　Goffstown, N.H., I. 40×38, 22 posts, to 30×30, 10 posts.
　Goshen, Conn., II. 64×44.
　Groton, Conn., II.
　Hardwick, Mass., II. Built by private subscription. Steeple added by the town.
　Hempstead, L.I., III.
　LONDONDERRY, N.H. (East Parish) (Presbyterian), II. 65×45. Steeple. Cut in half, 24 ft. added 1824.
　Londonderry, N.H. (Second or West Parish).
　Medford, Mass., III. 66×46. 2 porches, "with a tower from the ground."
　MENDON, MASS. (Third or South Precinct, now Millville) (Chestnut Hill Meeting House). 40×35.
　Pepperell, Mass., II. 60×45, 20 posts. Builder: Simon Gilson. Plain yellow building.
　Reading, Mass. (Third Parish or Wood-end). Later used as schoolhouse and town house.
　RICHMOND, R.I. (Six-Principle Baptist) ("Wood River Church").
　Rowley, Mass. (Second Parish or Georgetown), II. 55×40. Steeple and porch.
　Scituate, Mass. (Southwest Parish or Assinippi), I ("Old Universalist Meeting House"). Single porch. Demolished after 1832.
　Scituate, Mass. (Second or South Parish), IV. 72×48. Belfry and spire. Designer: Joseph Tolman. Demolished 1830.
　Shelburne, Mass., I ("Round Log Meetinghouse").
　Standish, Maine. Called "Old Church" in 1800.

1770 BEVERLY, MASS., III. 70×53, 28 posts. Bell tower. Enlarged 20 ft. 1795. Remodeled 1835.
　Brattleboro, Vt., I. Log tradition.
　Bristol, Conn., II. 65×45.
　BROOKLYN, CONN. (Anglican) (Trinity). 46×30. No tower. Compass windows. Architect: Godfrey Malbone.
　Burrillville, R.I. (Baptist) ("Old Town House") (1770?). Steeple. Painted cherubim.
　Cheshire, Mass. (Baptist). 28×26. Builder: Elder Peter Worden. 3rd of 3 similar ones.
　Colchester, Conn. (Second Parish or Westchester), II. 52×40. Steeple, bell.
　DIGHTON, MASS. (Baptist). 55×45, 24 posts. Steeple 1827. Sinnott: type 2.
　Fitzwilliam, N.H., I.
　Great Island, Maine (Sebascodigan Island). Single porch?
　Henniker, N.H., I. 30×20. Log tradition. Burned 1780.
　Lisbon, Conn. (Norwich Third or Newent Parish), II. Builder: Ebenezer Tracy.
　Marlborough, N.H. 45×35 to 50×40. Front porch, 1 side porch.
　New Durham, N.H. (Baptist). 42×35, 20 posts. Single porch, 1792.
　New Haven, Conn., I (Third Congregational or Fair Haven Church). 60×60. Taken from White Haven.

Pittsfield, Mass., I. 40×35, 20 posts. No belfry.
Pownalborough, Maine (Dresden) (Anglican). 60×32.
Reading, Mass. (Third or North Parish or North Reading).
Rowe, Mass., I.
Somersworth, N.H. Bell bought for meetinghouse.
South Britain, Conn. (Southbury). 45×35, 22 posts.
Troy, N.H., I. Builder: Stephen Church.
Upton, Mass., II. Belfry 1821. Dismantled 1848. Builder: Ezra Wood.
UXBRIDGE, MASS. (Quaker, Smithfield Monthly Meeting). 35×30. Brick. Cost: £206.
Wallingford, Conn. (Separate church). About 40×30. 2 floors. Disbanded 1787.
Wareham, Mass., II. Nearly square. Round top single porch in front.
Westerly, R.I. (Seventh-Day Baptist), II ("Spunk Meeting House").
Westford, Mass., II. 60×45, to 63×44, 26 or 27 posts. Tower. Burned 1793. Builder: Samuel Hall.
WESTMINSTER, CONN. (Canterbury). Builder: Sherebiah Butts. Turned. Sinnott: type 2 made 4 1835.
Williamstown, Mass., I. 40×30. Gallery.
Worthington, Mass. Moved 1792. Abandoned 1825.

1771 AMHERST, N.H., II. 75×45, to 70×40. Builder: E. Barker. Steeple and porch.
Boston, Mass., II (First Baptist Church). 57×53. No tower. Enlarged to 57×77, 1791.
BROOKLYN, CONN., II. 60×46, 26 posts. Builder: Daniel Tyler. Steeple, opposing porch. Colored white.
Chelmsford, Mass. (Baptist). 1729 meetinghouse from Westford.
Colchester, Conn. II. Builder: Isaac Fitch, Thomas Hall.
Deerfield, N.H. 65×45, 26 posts. (2 earlier frames dismantled).
Dublin, N.H., I. 50×38. Gallery. Twin porch addition ca. 1795.
FARMINGTON, CONN., III. 75×50. Builder: Judah Woodruff. Tower and steeple, spire 160 ft.
Haddam, Conn., III. 65×45. Builder: John Coach, Joseph Shailer.
Hudson, N.H. (Presbyterian). 50×30. Undated twin porch.
KENNEBUNK, MAINE., II. 57×46. Enlarged 28 ft. 1803. Spire 1803.
Kensington, N.H., II. Dismantled 1846.
Kent, Conn., II. 60×45, 26 posts. Steeple 1802.
Medfield, Mass. (Baptist), II. 31×31. Undated twin porch.
New London, Conn. (North Parish or Montville), II. 50×40? Undated twin porch. Dismantled 1847.
Ridgefield, Conn., II. 58×40, 24 posts. Steeple.
SURRY, N.H. 45×36 to 46½×36. Finished like Keene 1789. Twin porch 1791.
TOWNSEND, MASS., II. 60×45. Belfry and two porches added by John Ames when moved in 1804.
Westerly, R.I. (Seventh-Day Baptist), III.
Wolcott, Conn., I. 58×42.

1772 Andover, N.H., I. 30×20, 9 posts. 1 story. Torn down 1795 by opposers.
Bluehill, Maine, I.

Boston, Mass., II (Brattle Square). 90×75. Architect: Thomas Dawes. Brick with quoins.
BRISTOL, MAINE (Harrington meetinghouse). Moved twice. Sinnott: type 2, modified.
BRISTOL, MAINE (Walpole meetinghouse).
Bristol, Maine (Broadcove Parish or Bremen).
EAST HAVEN, CONN., III. 73×50. Stone with bell tower. Steeple 1794, 1797.
Francestown, N.H., I. Builder: John Quigley.
HUBBARDSTON, MASS. 50×40 to 45×45.
Lebanon, N.H., I. 48×34, 12 posts.
Lyndeborough, N.H., III. 50×40, 22 posts. Single stairwell porch over south door.
Manchester, Conn. (Orford), II. 54×40. Dismantled 1826.
Narragansett, R.I. Indian church. 25×25.
Newmarket, N.H. (West Society) (Presbyterian).
Newport, R.I. 30 or 35 ft. sq. Builder: Elder Dawson.
New Shoreham, R.I. (Block Island) (Free Baptist).
Northwood, N.H. (Baptist).
Plympton, Mass., III. 57×45.
Salem, Mass. (North Parish; Lynde and North Streets). Church plan. "large." Demolished after 1836.
Spencer, Mass., II. 56×47. Builder: David Baldwin. Twin porch. Tower, cupola 1802.
Stamford, Conn. (Baptist). Still standing 1868.
WALDOBORO, MAINE (Lutheran), II. 45×36, 20 posts. Single porch on end.
Watertown, Conn. (Westbury), II. Steeple 100 ft. high.
Windham, N.H. (Presbyterian).

1773 Athol, Mass., III. 56×46. Burned 1827.
Auburn, Mass. (Ward). 50×40, 24 posts. Belfry 1837.
Bristol, N.H. (Bridgewater), I. 35×35. 1 story.
Chesterfield, N.H. 60×45. Twin porch. Tower 1815.
CLAREMONT, N.H. (Anglican or Union Episcopal). Round window. Builder: Ebenezer Rice. Tower 1801. Extended 20 ft. 1820.
Conway, N.H.
Cornish, N.H. Twin porch. Dismantled 1804.
Gilford, N.H. (Baptist).
Hanover, N.H. Burned 1797.
Harvard, Mass., II. 66×45. Steeple 1794.
Hillsborough, N.H., I. 35×30, 9 posts. 1 gallery.
New London, Conn. (North or Chesterfield Parish). Abandoned.
Moultonborough, N.H.
Newport, N.H., I. 30×10 with fireplace. Square roof. Schoolhouse.
Putney, Vt. 45×35, 20 posts. Dismantled 1810.
Raynham, Mass., II. Builder: Israel Washburn. Steeple added.
Rehoboth, Mass. (West Parish, Palmer's River or Seekonk), II. 50×40. Dismantled 1813.
Rutland, Vt. (Congregational, 30 families).
SANDOWN, N.H. 50×44 or 54×48.
Shelburne, Mass., II. Conch. Demolished 1832.

SHIRLEY, MASS., II. 50×40. Tower, steeple 1804. Modified.
Southwick, Mass., I.
Uxbridge, Mass., II.
Washington, Mass., I.
Westfield, Conn. (north of Middlefield). 48×38. Used until 1848.
Whately, Mass. Builder: David Scott. Conch.
Wilton, N.H., I. 60×45, 27 posts. Twin porch. Builder: Ephraim Barker. Torn down 1845.

1774 Ashford, Conn. (Baptist).
Bow, N.H., I. Logs.
Boxford, Mass. (Second Parish), II. Twin porch. Builder: Stephen Barker.
Charlestown, R.I. (Baptist) ("Boss meeting house").
CHESTER, N.H., II. 60×45. Ogee spire 100 ft. Turned 1837.
East Greenwich, R.I. (Congregational). Lottery.
Freeport, Maine (Harraseeket).
Gilmanton, N.H., I. 60×45. Twin porch.
GILMANTON, N.H. (Baptist or Smith meetinghouse).
Gloucester, R.I. (Baptist). Lottery.
Gray, Maine, I.
HILL, N.H. 35×35. (New Chester). Builder: Enoch Osgood.
Hill, N.H. (Second Parish).
Hinsdale, Mass., I. 50×40. Height for galleries.
KENSINGTON, CONN., III. 60×42. Sinnott: type 2 made 3 1837.
LEE, N.H. (Quaker). Used as school.
Leominster, Mass., II. 50×60. Twin porch.
Meredith, N.H., I. 40×32, 8 posts.
Middletown, Conn. (Strict Congregationalist). 56×46.
Needham, Mass., II. 60×43. Builder: Adam Blackman. Tower 1811. Dismantled 1846.
New Gloucester, Maine. "block house."
Northbridge, Mass.
Plympton, Mass. (Second Parish or Carver), II. 42×37.
Pomfret, Vt. "Log Meeting house on the Chandler farm."
PROVIDENCE, R.I. (Baptist), III. 80×80. Church plan. Architect: Joseph Brown.
Raymond, N.H., I. 45×35, 21 posts. Frame built, dismantled, made into bridge 1775.
Scituate, Mass., V ("Old Sloop"). 66×48. Steeple opposing porch. Burned 1879.
Stafford, Conn., II.
WELLS, MAINE (Second Parish), II. 56×44. 2 stories. Single porch. Enlarged 1803. Steeple 1804. Dark yellow.
Wells, Vt., I.
Windham, Conn. (Third or Scotland Parish), II. Builder: Elisha Lillie.
Winthrop, Maine, I. 40×36. Glazed but never finished inside. Dismantled and sold 1785.
Worthington, Conn., I.

1775 Boxborough, Mass., I. Purchased old Harvard I meetinghouse 47×35, 20 posts.
Charlton, Mass., I.
ENFIELD, CONN., III. Portico 1848. Became town hall.

JAFFREY, N.H. 60×45, 27 posts. Twin porch. Builder: Samuel Adams, Jacob Spofford. Tower 1823.
Harvard, Mass. (Baptist). Purchased Leominster I meetinghouse. 45×35, 22 posts.
Lenox, Mass., I. 46×36.
Leverett, Mass. Single porch over front door 1785.
Sanbornton, N.H. 60×43½. No steeple.

1776 Packersfield, N.H. (Nelson), I. 30×25, 8½ posts. 3 windows. Builder: Church Tabor.
Salem, Mass. (Presbyterian after 1779) ("Old Tabernacle"). 78×62. Architect: Samuel McIntire. Bell tower 1805.
Tinmouth, Vt. "log house to meet in on the Sabbath."

1777 Peterborough, N.H., II. Galleries 1785. Sold 1829 for $75.
Rehoboth, Mass. (Freewill Baptist) (Iron's church).
Rollinsford, N.H., II. Burned 1778.
Windsor, Vt.

1778 Eastford, Conn., I. 45×35.
Fryeburg, Maine. 54×42. Gallery.
Lee, Mass., I. 48×36, to 50×36, 30 posts. 8-ft. projection in front ⅓ width.
Marlborough, Vt.

1779 Berlin, Mass., I. Twin porch.
Campton, N.H., I. Made from former residence.
Hartland, Conn. (Second Parish). No steeple.
Hudson, N.H. (North Parish), III.
Loudon, N.H. 56×42. Twin porch.
MONT VERNON, N.H. Twin porch. Converted and moved. Became town house.
Norwich, Vt.
Rollinsford, N.H., III.
Tinmouth, Vt., II. £400 for new meetinghouse.
Westport, Conn., III.
Wilbraham, Mass. (Baptist).
Williamsburg, Mass., I. 60×45. Conch. Spire 119 ft. Builder: Jonathan Warner.
Windham, Maine (Quaker).
Windsor, Mass. 50×40, 20 posts. Burned same year.
Windsor, Vt. (East Parish). "Nearly square, with a pointed roof."

1780 Alstead, N.H., I. 40×30. Upper for church, lower public meetings.
Hampton Falls, N.H., II. 65×40.
Northwood, N.H. 45×36. Twin porch.
Poultney, Vt. 45×35.
Reading, Vt. Log tradition.
ROCHESTER, N.H., II. Remodeled 19th century.
Weare, N.H. (Baptist). Logs hewn square.

1781 Burlington, Conn., I. 40×36.
Cummington, Mass. 45×35. Painted white 1806.

Darien, Conn. (East Stamford), I. 50×30, 20 posts.
Huntington, Mass., I. Log tradition.
Lyme, N.H., I. Frame used in store next door.
RICHMOND, N.H. (Baptist). 40×30. Gallery 3 sides.
Temple, N.H., II. 55×42, 24 posts. Twin-porch. Cost: £937.
Woodstock, Vt. Log tradition.

1782 Barnard, Vt. Peeled logs.
GOSHEN, MASS., II. 50×40. Posts 2 ft. shorter than Chesterfield. Twin porch. Moved.
GRANVILLE, MASS. (West Parish). Made Victorian.
North Adams, Mass., I. 38×30. Gallery.
ORANGE, MASS. 46×36. Turned 1832. Tower, belfry, spire 1832.
Turner, Maine. 35×35, 20 posts.

1783 Charlestown, Mass., IV. 72×52, 27 posts. Made 74×84. Steeple 162 ft. Architect: Charles Bulfinch. Builder: D. Goodwin.
Claremont, N.H. Twin porch. Builder: Ichabod Hitchcock. Moved 1790. Tower, semicircular addition 1808.
Hampden, Mass. Builder: Paul Langdon.
LUDLOW, MASS. Completed 1797, used until 1840. Became town house.
Northfield, N.H., I. 36×30.
Norwalk, Conn., IV (date estimated: 1723 meetinghouse burned by British 1779).
Salem Village, Mass. (Danvers) (Baptist). 60×45.
Southwick, Mass., II. Burned 1824.
WALPOLE, MASS., II. 60×40. Builder: Adam Blackman. Twin porch. Belfry 1791.
Westhampton, Mass., I. 50×40. 3 entrances covered by porches.

1784 Acworth, N.H., I. 50×40. Gallery. Moved 1821 and made into a townhouse.
Amesbury, Mass. (Separate church, became Presbyterian) ("The Still"). "Hopper" roof. Barn 1805.
Amesbury, Mass. (Second or West Parish), II.
Amherst, Mass. (Second Parish), I. Belfry and cupola 1822.
Barkhamsted, Conn. 50×40, 24 posts.
Boxborough, Mass., I.
Branford, Conn. (Anglican) (Trinity). "barnlike."
Bristol, R.I., II.
Leicester, Mass., II. Twin porch. Builder: Timothy Carter Sr. Belfry, steeple, 1790.
Middletown, Vt. Log tradition.
MILFORD, N.H. Galleries. Twin porch (copied Temple). Belfry 1803. Became town house.
New Milford, Conn. (Quaker), II.
Plainfield, Conn., III.
RICHMOND, R.I. (Baptist), II. 36×28, "usual height." Now town hall.
Royalton, Vt., I. 38×28 to 40×18.
Stockbridge, Mass., II. 60×50, 26 posts. Steeple 62 ft., opposite pulpit.
Sturbridge, Mass. (Baptist), II (Fiske Hill).
Tiverton, R.I. (Baptist), II.
Warren, R.I. (Baptist), II. 61×44. Tower 14 ft. sq. Spire 1800.

1785 Antrim, N.H., I. 50×40. Twin porch, sloping roofs. Builder: William Gregg.
Brandon, Vt. Town supported.
Brattleboro, Vt., II. 60×48. Twin porch.
Danby, Vt. (Quaker), I.
Easthampton, Mass., I. 52×42. No bell, no steeple.
Fairfield, Conn., V. Replaced the one burned by the British in 1779. Bulfinch pulpit.
Hartland, Vt.
Kingstown, R.I. (North Parish) (Baptist).
Lanesborough, Mass., II. 55×30. Gallery. Belfry and spire.
MILTON, MASS., IV. 66×52. Turned and enlarged 1835.
New London, Conn., IV. 70×50, 28 posts. Pictured with porch 1852.
New London, Conn. (Anglican) (St. James's). Dome and bell 1794.
Pawlet, Vt. Replaced because too small.
PHILLIPSTON, MASS., I. 50×40. Modified.
SALISBURY, MASS. (West Parish, now Amesbury), II ("Rocky Hill"). Single porch. 60×42. Builder: Ambrose Palmer, Jacob Spofford.
Stratford, Conn., IV.
WAKEFIELD, N.H. Upstairs became school.
Weare, N.H. 56×42. Gallery.
Weston, Conn., II. Moved and reerected Weston I frame.
Weymouth, Mass. (Second or South Parish), II. Bell tower with opposing. porch. 44 windows. Doric order.
Winchester, Conn., II. 46×56 to 50×40 to 54×40.
WOODBURY, CONN. (Anglican) (St. Paul's). 55×35. Bell tower.

1786 ADAMS, MASS. (East Hoosac) (Quaker). 2 side-by-side doors on long side.
Charlemont, Mass., II. 45×35, 20 posts.
Chilmark, Mass., III. "A porch entrance carrying stairs" = single porch? Gallery. 3 sides. No spire. Torn down 1842.
Danbury, Conn., III. 60×45. Spire 130 ft. high.
Deering, N.H. 55×45. 2 stories. Twin porch.
Gardiner, Maine (Anglican). 50×50. 1 story. Steeple with gilt sturgeon.
JAMESTOWN, R.I. (Quaker), III. 26×20. 1 story.
KEENE, N.H., III. 70×50. Belfry and steeple and opposing porch. Builder: Benjamin Archer.
New London, N.H. 50 ft. wide.
Prescott, Mass.
Raymond, N.H., I. Twin porch. Moved 1797. Used as town house.
Salem Village, Mass. (Danvers), III. 60×46, 27 posts. Belfry and steeple. Burned 1805.
Stonington Point, Conn., I. Purchased New London's pulpit and pews.
Torrington, Conn., II. Steeple 1797.
Walpole, N.H., II (Prospect Hill). Dome 1792. Town house 1825.
Warwick, Mass., II. 58×42, single porch. Builder: Samuel Langley.
Westerly, R.I. (Third Precinct, New Light) (Wilcox Church). Builder: Benjamin Palmer.
Winthrop, Maine, II (South Parish). 50×40. Builder: Adam Stanley from Attleborough, Mass. Single porch 1791. Became town house.

1787 Amherst, Mass., II. 65 ft. long. Belfry on west side 1791.
Enfield, Mass. Painted "sulphur color." Pews 1793. Belfry 1814.
Franklin, Mass., II. 62 × 40. Twin porch, each 14 ft. sq. Porch into belfry 1806.
Gardner, Mass. 45 × 60, 27 posts. Twin porch, each 12 × 14 ft.
HENNIKER, N.H., II. 60 × 45 to 50 × 40 to 55 × 40. Twin porch. Became town hall.
MIDDLE HADDAM, CONN. (Anglican).
Middleton, N.H. 52 × 42. Single porch.
Pittsfield, N.H.
Plymouth, N.H. (Ward's Hill), II. 56 × 44. Twin porch. Tower. Sold as barn, moved, became sawmill. Burned 1884.
ROCKINGHAM, VT. 54 × 44, 23 posts. Twin porch. Builder: Gen. John Fuller.
Sturbridge, Mass., II. Porch, steeple 1794. Turned. Burned 1908.
THETFORD, VT. Sinnott: type 2 made 3.
WASHINGTON, N.H., I. 60 × 50. Twin porch. Builder: Church Tabor.

1788 Alstead, N.H., II. Burned 1788.
Andover, Mass. (South Parish), III. 70 × 54. 3 porches. Builder: Moody Spofford. Cupola 1792.
Barnstable, Mass. (Baptist). Single porch. "Great porch all painted red."
Barnstead, N.H. 60 × 40, 24 posts. Twin porch.
Barre, Mass., II. 68 × 54.
Boston, Mass., II (Hollis Street). 72 × 60. Twin tower design. Architect: Charles Bulfinch. Builder: Josiah Wheeler.
Chester, Vt. (South Parish).
Embden, Maine.
Falmouth, Maine (Portland; Second Parish).
Gardiner, Maine.
Granville, Mass., II.
Hancock, N.H., I. 54 × 42, 25½ posts. Twin porch?
Haverhill, N.H. (Horse Meadow) (First Parish). 50 × 40 to 30 × 36. Dismantled 1882. Became barn.
Haverhill, N.H. (Second Parish) (Ladd Street).
JERICHO, L.I. (Old Jericho Turnpike) (Quaker). Gallery. Builder: Elias Hicks.
Petersham, Mass., II.
SOUTHAMPTON, MASS. Belfry 1822. Turned 1840.
Stoddard, N.H. Twin porch? Unused after 1838, converted to dwelling house.
Weare, N.H. (South Baptist). 56 × 45.
Westminster, Mass., II. 60 × 45. Twin porch: 14-ft. at each end. Builder: Timothy Bacon. Belfry 1807.
Whately, Mass. (became Baptist).

1789 ALNA, MAINE. Single porch. 51 × 41. 1 door. Builder: Joseph Carleton. Restored.
Ashfield, Mass. (Baptist). 1 story. "4 sided pointed roof."
BELCHERTOWN, MASS., II. Sinnott: "2 made 3 . . . 30 feet inserted."
Bernardston, Mass. (Baptist). Small. 1 story.
Brooksville, Maine.
CASTINE, MAINE. 65 × 50. Sinnott: type 2 made 3 1831. Used for town meetings.
Chester, Vt. (North Parish). 50 × 40.

Cornwall, Conn., II. 58 × 43, 26 posts. Dismantled 1840.
Deer Isle, Maine, I.
Dunbarton, N.H., II. 50 × 40, 25 posts. Single porch 13 ft. sq., 22 ft. high. Architect: Archibald Stinson. Builder: William Tenney.
Fairfield, Conn. (Green's Farms or West Parish), III. Replaced one burned by British.
Fitchburg, Mass., II.
Gray, Maine, II.
Hillsborough, N.H., II. 62 × 50, 28 posts. Twin porch. Builder: Ephraim Barker.
HOLDEN, MASS., II. Turned 1827.
HOPKINTON, N.H., II. 62 × 46. Twin porch 12 ft. sq. Middle belfry added 1809–1811. Turned 1829.
HOPKINTON, R.I. (Baptist).
MEDFIELD, MASS., III. Tower. Turned 1839. Belfry and porch removed.
Northfield, Conn. 50 × 38.
Royalton, Vt., II. 56 × 40. Twin porch.
Springfield, N.H.
Stoughton, Mass. (Second Parish or Sharon), II. Dismantled 1842.
Warner, N.H., II. 60 × 50. Gallery. Dismantled 1855.
Wells, Vt. "build a church thirty-six feet in length by one story and a half high." Never finished inside. Blown down 1847.
West Rutland, Vt.
West Stockbridge, Mass. 54 × 42, 23 posts. Steeple. Turned 1828.
Worcester, Mass. (Second Parish), I.

1790 ARLINGTON, MASS. (Baptist), I. Later used as dwelling house.
Benson, Vt., I. 24 × 40. "school-house meeting-house."
Bolton, Mass., II. 56 "and the width Handsom proportion thereto."
Brandon, Vt. (Baptist). Log house.
Castleton, Vt. 50 × 40. "side to the street . . . square pews . . . doors either end."
CENTERBROOK, CONN., II. Sinnott: type 2 made 4, turned 1839.
DARTMOUTH, MASS. (Quaker), II (Apponegansett meetinghouse).
Derryfield, N.H., II.
Fairfield, Conn. (Anglican) (Trinity Church) II.
Gilsum, N.H., I.
Groton, Conn. (Baptist), II.
GROVELAND, MASS. (Bradford East Parish). Builder: Moody Spofford. Sinnott: type 2, turned 1849.
Hampden, Maine (date estimated). Single porch. Became town house.
Hanover, N.H. (chapel, Dartmouth College). 50 × 36. Hipped roof. Moved 1833. Became barn.
Huntington, Mass., II. Gallery. Single porch opposite pulpit.
Mason, N.H., II. 55 × 45. Twin porch.
Middlefield, Mass., I. 52 × 44. Bell tower.
Newbury, Vt. 60 × 45. Twin porch? Painted white.
Pittsfield, Mass., II. 90 × 51. Church plan. Architect: Charles Bulfinch. Builder: Ebenezer Clark.
Plymouth, Conn., II.
Plymouth, Conn. (Anglican), II. 42 × 32.

SEABROOK VILLAGE, N.H. (date uncertain). Turned 1820.
TOWNSHEND, VT. Sinnott: type 2 made 3.
Weathersfield, Vt.
WILTON, CONN. (Second Parish in Norwalk), III. 54 × 40, 24 posts. Plan imitated Norwalk IV.

1791 Ashburnham, Mass., II. 60 × 45, 26 posts. "Pea green" color vote rescinded, painted white. 3 porches.
Bath, N.H., I. 30 × 30, 9 posts. One story.
Boscawen, N.H., III.
Bridgton, Maine. 45 × 35. Galleries. Single porch 1792.
Brookline, N.H. 40 × 30 to 38 × 28. Twin porch.
Chesterfield, Mass., II.
Chichester, N.H., II. 50 × 40.
Fairhaven, Vt. ("Lord's Barn"). Later used as a barn.
HADDAM, CONN. (Second or East Parish), III. 56 × 47. Architect: Lavius Fillmore.
Haddam, Conn. (South Parish) (Anglican) (St. Stephen's).
Jay, Maine, I.
Leicester, Mass. (Quaker).
Lynn, Mass. (Methodist), I. First Methodist house in Mass.
Milford, Conn. (North or Orange Parish). 36 × 30.
MILTON, CONN. (Litchfield Third Society) (Congregational). Moved 1828.
Pomfret, Vt., II. Twin porch. Canopy suspended by "hand."
Rochester, Mass. (North Parish), II. Replaced 1841.
Salisbury, N.H., II. 60 × 44 (52 × 40), 26 posts. Porch and steeple. Town purchased South Road meetinghouse.
SALISBURY, N.H. (Baptist). 52 × 40. Porches and small steeple. Remodeled 1839.
Springfield, Vt. 50 × 40, 21 posts. Porch and tower (after twin porch voted 1785).
Sullivan, N.H. Square. Builder: Thomas Spaulding. Painted like Keene. Disused 1801?
WEBSTER, N.H. (Corser Hill, south side). Builder: Samuel Jackman. Town house 1823.
Wolfeborough, N.H. 54 × 44. Single porch. Gallery. Became town house.

1792 Belfast, Maine (South Parish). 50 × 40. Sold 1830.
Belfast, Maine (West Parish). 40 × 40. 1 story.
Belmont, N.H. (Province Road). 1 story.
Bluehill, Maine, II. 50 × 40. Burned 1842.
CANTERBURY, N.H. (Shaker). Gambrel roof.
Chatham, Conn. (Methodist). 24 × 23.
Chelmsford, Mass., III. 64 × 48. Cost: £1,400. "Semicircular" windows in gallery. Posts (tower) 60 ft. Burned 1841.
Cumberland Center, Maine. Completed 6 years later.
Durham, N.H., III. 60 × 50. Builder: Edmund Thompson. Steeple arch: sky color and scattered clouds.
EAST PLYMOUTH, CONN. (Anglican).
Gilford, N.H. (Gunstock).
Gilford, N.H. (Upper Gilmanton).

Grafton, Vt.
Hartford, Conn. (Anglican), I (Christ Church). 90×44. Steeple fell when raised. Sold and moved 1829. Became Trinity Church. Burned 1853.
Harwich, Mass. (Second or South Parish), II. Single porch. Painted red, yellow, white, chocolate.
Holyoke, Mass. (Congregational and Baptist), I. Moved 1796.
IPSWICH, MASS. (Essex), IV. 44×62, 26 posts. Tower 12 ft. sq. Porch. Builder: Isaac Long, Jonathan Story.
Littleton, Mass., III. 55×40.
Mattapoisett, Mass. (Baptist).
Middlebury, Vt., I. "Large barn." Builder: Daniel Foot.
Newmarket, N.H., II (Junction of Newmarket and "Ash Swamp" Roads; East and West Societies). 60×50. Builder: Henry Wiggin. Galleries 3 sides. Steeple.
OXFORD, MASS. (Universalist). 46×43. "with porch or tower." Tuscan order.
Russell, Mass. (Baptist), I. Burned 1826.
SANDWICH, N.H. (Baptist). Turned 1847.
Scituate, Mass. (Universalist). Single porch.
Taunton, Mass., III. Church plan. Architect: Charles Bulfinch.
Washington, Mass.
Wendell, Mass. 55×40. Timbers cased.
Westminster, Vt. (Baptist). 2 floors. No steeple. Burned 1828.
Winchendon, Mass., II. 60×50, 27 posts. Twin porch. Builder: David Rice.
North Yarmouth, Maine (Second Parish).

1793 Boylston, Mass., II. 63×53. Cupola and bell.
BRIDGEWATER, MASS. (Third Parish or East Bridgewater), III. 68×54. Steeple and porch.
BUCKLAND, MASS., I. Stairwell porches at each end. Architect: John Ames. Sinnott: type 2 made 4 1846.
CANAAN, N.H. 52×42, 26 posts. Twin porch 12 ft. sq. Builder: William Parkhurst; fell during raising. Cost: £561. Pulpit: Maj. Levi George of Salisbury 1794.
CANAAN STREET, N.H. Sinnott: type 2, made 2 stories 1841. Church above, town hall below.
Chester, N.H. (Long Meadow), II. Replaced "Little meeting-house." Twin porch. Enlarged 1807.
Conway, N.H. (North Conway).
CORNISH, N.H. (Anglican) (Trinity). Builder: Philip Tabor.
GROTON, N.H. Reduced and lowered. Town meetings.
Hamden, Conn. (Separate church).
HANCOCK, MASS. (Shaker). Gambrel roof. 2 doors long side. Builder: Moses Johnson.
Hawley, Mass. 50×40. Painted yellow 1798.
Lebanon, N.H., II. Twin porch?
Lexington, Mass., III. About 70×50. Porches 3 sides. Belfry. Probably type 2.
Limington, Maine.
Middlebury, Vt., I. Religious meetings moved to "Deacon Sumner's barn."
Newport, N.H. Dismantled 1830 and made into a barn.

Northfield, N.H. Builder: William Durgin.
OXFORD, CONN., II. 56×40. Builder: Timothy Cande. Sinnott: type 2 with tower.
READFIELD, MAINE (Baptist). Moved to North Manchester, Maine. 1833.
Rowe, Mass., II. 50×40. Painted cream with green doors. Porch 1801.
Sunderland, Mass., II. 58×38, 25 posts. Tower and steeple.
Tamworth, N.H. 44×37, 10 posts.
Winsted, Conn., I. 50×40. 2 stories. Tower. Steeple. Dismantled and sold 1800.

1794 Brookfield, Mass., IV. 63×50.
Chester, Mass. (formerly Murrayfield), II. Hinsdale copied the exterior.
Colebrook, Conn. ("The Old Hemlock" meetinghouse). Dismantled 1842.
Croydon, N.H. Dismantled 1824 and converted into town hall.
DRACUT, MASS. (Second Parish or Lowell), III ("Old Yellow"). "same bigness as Pelham."
GILL, MASS. 50×40. Belfry 1795.
Lancaster, N.H. 26 posts. Twin porch.
LEMPSTER, N.H. 50×40. Twin porch. Dismantled and reerected 1822. Tower.
Middlebury, Conn.
MONKTON, VT. (Baptist). Now Grange hall.
NEW GLOUCESTER, MAINE (Shaker). Plain. Gambrel roof.
NEW SALEM, MASS., II. Sinnott: "late example" of type 2.
Norridgewock, Maine. 60×45.
North Yarmouth, Maine (N.W. Congregational Society). Dismantled 1839.
Otisfield, Maine.
Packersfield, N.H. (Nelson), II. 60×45. Gallery. Twin porch.
Richmond, Mass., II. 65×50, 25 posts. Porch west end. Copied Pittsfield. Builder: Thomas Dutton.
Rochester, Vt. ("Potash meeting house").
SABBATHDAY LAKE, MAINE (Shaker). Gambrel roof. Builder: Moses Johnson.
SOUTHFIELD, MASS. (New Marlborough).
Sutton (South), N.H. Builder: Daniel Page. Burned.
Tolland, Conn. (Methodist). Compass windows throughout including cupola.
West Boylston, Mass. (Boylston, Sterling, Holden), I.
WESTFORD, MASS., III. 65×48, 28 posts. Tower. Builder: John Abott and Moses Thomas.
Wilbraham, Mass. (Methodist). 40×34.
Winchester, N.H., III.
WINDSOR, CONN., IV. 75×55. Transitional. Builder: Ebenezer Clark, who also did Pittsfield.
WINSLOW, MAINE. Steeple 1830, removed 1884. Altered 1900.
Woburn, Mass. (Baptist). 40×40. Gallery. Single porch.
Wolcott, Conn., II.

1795 BRADFORD, N.H. 50×42. Twin porch. Town house 1838. Moved 1863.
Brookfield, Mass. (Baptist).
Brunswick, Maine (Baptist). Rebuilt as boarding house.
CHESTER, CONN. (Fourth Parish in Saybrook), II. Town house 1847, then theater.
Deer Isle, Maine, II. 54×48.

East Providence, R.I. (Baptist). "formed by Obadiah Holmes." Torn down 1879.
GREENFIELD, N.H. Builder: Hugh Gregg. Tower and steeple 1825. Floors filled 1848. Turned 1867.
Hanover, N.H. (meetinghouse, Dartmouth College). 66 × 60, 30 posts. Cost: £1,500. Tower and steeple. Burned 1931.
New Bedford, Mass., I. 40 × 45. Gallery.
Orford, N.H. ("The Coffin"). 60 × 40, 18 posts. Twin porch.
Providence, R.I. (Congregational), II. Twin tower like Hollis. Architect: Caleb Ormsbee. Burned 1814.
Providence, R.I. (Richmond Street), I ("Old Tin Top").
READFIELD, Maine (Methodist). Dragged by 50 yoke of oxen to present location.
Rumney, N.H. Converted to tannery.
Suffield, Conn. (Second Parish or Ireland Plaine), II.
SUTTON (NORTH), N.H. 50 × 40. Twin porch. Builder: John Harvey.
Sutton (South), N.H. 50 × 40 Twin porch. Builder: Daniel Page.
THOMASTON, MAINE (Baptist).
Topsham, Maine (Baptist) ("Old Yellow Meeting House"). 40 × 30.
WARDSBORO, VT. (Baptist). Moved 1834. Town hall and church.
Waterbury, Conn. (Anglican), II (St. John's, formerly St. James's). Torn down 1888.
Windham, Maine, III. 50 × 40. Single porch. Dismantled 1861. Sold for a barn.
Wintonbury, Conn. (Bloomfield) (Baptist). Small.

1796 Barnstable, Mass. (Centerville). 46 × 38, 21 posts. 3 doors.
BARNSTEAD PARADE, N.H. Twin porch. Builder: Richard Sinclair. Yellow. Remodeled 1866.
BOLTON, MASS. (Quaker). Moved to Old Sturbridge Village. Two doors.
DIGHTON, MASS. (Baptist or Elder Goff meetinghouse). Plain.
FALMOUTH, MASS. (West Parish) (Congregational). Moved 1857.
FOSTER CENTER, R.I. (Baptist).
Hallowell, Maine ("Old South Church").
Killingly, Conn. (Westfield).
Meriden, N.H. 60 × 50. Steeple and porch.
Methuen, Mass., II. "plan of the . . . lower Parish of Bradford."
Middletown, Vt. (Baptists and Congregationalists united). On the green.
Newburyport, Mass. (Harris Street) (Presbyterian), I.
Plainfield, Mass., I. 55½ × 42½.
Princeton, Mass., II. 70 × 55. Bell tower? Bell recast 1815.
RINDGE, N.H., II. 66 × 52. Steeple. Builder: John and David Barker. Remodeled 19th century.
Stratfield, Conn. (Baptist), I.
Swanzey, N.H., II. 62 × 45. Twin porch. Remodeled into town house 1850.
Thomaston, Maine. 50 × 50. 2 porches in front? Hand-suspended sounding board.
Tolland, Mass.
Tyringham, Mass., II.
Waterbury, Conn., III. 60 × 42. Steeple. Builder: William Leavenworth. Cost: £850.
Wells, Maine (Alewife) (Baptist ca. 1803).
Windsor, Conn. (Poquonnock), II.

1797 ANDOVER, N.H., II (Congregational). Twin porch.
Benson, Vt., II. 65×45. Bell.
BILLERICA, MASS. (Unitarian), IV. Bell tower. Sinnott: type 2 made 3, turned 1844.
Bowdoinham, Maine.
COVENTRY, R.I. (Six-Principle Baptist) (Maple Root Church).
Dublin, N.H. (now Harrisville) (Baptist). 40×30. Twin porch. Porches removed 1830. Moved 1840 and 1867.
Essex, Vt. Wood structure. Replaced 1840.
FALMOUTH, MASS. (East Parish or Hatchville). Single porch 16 ft. sq. Sinnott: type 2, turned 1842.
GORHAM, MAINE, III. Single porch. Sinnott: type 2.
Hampton, N.H., V.
Hampton, N.H. (Separate church).
Hanover, N.H., II.
Holderness, N.H. 36×30, 10 posts.
HOLDERNESS, N.H. (Anglican) (Trinity).
Jerico, Vt., I. "large, square-roofed, wooden structure."
Leyden, Mass. 50×40, to 46×36. 2 stories.
Montgomery, Mass., I.
Newington, Conn., II. About 50×40. Steeple on east end. Dismantled 1950s.
Orford, N.H. (West Parish).
Riverhead, L.I., II. 42×30.
Royalston, Mass., II.
Ryegate, Vt. 40×30, 20 posts. Twin porch.
STERLING, CONN. (Baptist).
SUDBURY, MASS. (West Precinct or Sudbury), II. 60×52. Porch and steeple.

1798 Charlotte, Vt. Wood.
Charlton, Mass., II. Builder: Jonas Ward.
EAST ALSTEAD, N.H.
EFFINGHAM, N.H. 46×36. 1 story.
EXETER, N.H., V. 80×60. 2-story bay and tower on side. Builder: Ebenezer Clifford, Bradbury Johnson, and James Folsom.
GRAFTON CENTER, N.H. (Baptist). Lower story made town hall.
HINSDALE, MASS., II. 52×45. "Convening porch." Belfry. Builder: Nathan Warner. Exterior copied Chester. Interior copied Pittsfield.
Hudson, N.H., (South Parish), IV. 50×40. Twin porch.
Kingston, Mass., II. 60×55, 25 posts. Bentley: pediment and 2 cupolas. Demolished 1851.
Marlow, N.H. Twin porch. Dismantled and removed 1845.
NEW HAMPTON, N.H. Lowered to 1 story. Town meetings.
Newport, N.H. (Baptist). 44×44. Twin porch. Sky blue pulpit.
NORTH YARMOUTH, MAINE (Yarmouth) (Baptist).
Palmer, Mass., II. Voted 50×40 (Twin porch); built 46×45. Porch at west end.
SALISBURY, CONN., II. 64×45. "in the modern stile." Copied Richmond, Mass. Builder: Moses Wells.
Tiverton, Mass. ("Line meeting house" between Massachusetts and Rhode Island.)
WEST CLARENDON, VT. (Baptist).

Williamstown, Mass., II. 76×56.
Windham, N.H. (Presbyterian), II. Town house late 19th century.
WINDSOR, VT., II ("Old South"). Pediment and bell tower.

1799 Camden, Maine. Gallery. Single porch.
Greenwich, Conn. (Second Parish), II. 52×40, 21 posts. Bell tower. Builder: Abraham Husted.
HENNIKER, N.H. (Quaker). 1 story. 2 doors close together.
Hollis, N.H., III. 68×54. Painted white.
Natick, Mass., IV. No belfry. Type 2. Gallery. Single porch. Builder: David Bacon. Painted yellow.
Portland, Conn. (Anglican). Later given as a town house.
Readfield, Maine (Methodist) (Kent's Hill). Made from existing frame.
Sterling, Mass., II. 75×70 or 60×55. 2 angels. Burned 1842.
STRAFFORD, VT. Bell tower. Canopy hand. Sinnott: transitional. Now town hall.
WARE, MASS., II. 57×44, 28 posts. Twin porch: "Porch at each end." Cupola on roof. Builder: Ezekiel Baxter.

1800 Agawam, Mass. (Sixth Parish in Springfield). Frame from old separatist meetinghouse in Suffield. Demolished 1966.
Alton, N.H. 50×40. One floor. Dismantled and put in storage.
BARRINGTON, R.I. Built by lottery.
BOSCAWEN, N.H. Sinnott: type 2, turned 1839 and 1940.
Brandon, Vt. (Baptist), II.
CORINTH, VT. Sinnott: transitional. Used as town hall until 1845.
Farmington Falls, Maine (Methodist).
FREMONT, N.H. (formerly Poplin). Twin porch.
Georgia, Vt. Builder: William Sprats. Finished 1802. Became town property before 1850. Restored 1936. Burned 1952.
GOSPORT, N.H. (Isles of Shoals). Stone.
Granville, Mass. (Baptist).
HEBRON, N.H. 2 stories. Builder: Benjamin Wood.
Hinesburgh, Vt.
Hubbardston, Vt. (Baptist). Log meetinghouse.
Lee, Mass., II. 65×50, 26 posts. Bell tower. Patterned after Richmond. Builder: John Hulett.
Merrimack, N.H., II.
MIDDLETON CORNERS, N.H. Sinnott: type 2. Frescoes. Church above, town hall below.
Monroe, N.H. (approximate date). 42×36. Gallery in back. Painted yellow.
New Braintree, Mass., II. 50×50.
NEWBURYPORT, MASS. (Anglican), II (St. Paul's). Builder: Stephen Toppan. Reading desk and pulpit to copy Trinity Church, Boston. Burned 1920.
NEW HAMPTON, N.H. (Baptist). Square. Spindle top. Unpainted pews.
Pownalborough, Maine (Dresden). Twin porch.
Reading, Mass. (Baptist). 38×34. Outside porch. Gallery.
Underhill, Vt.

Wallingford, Vt.
WEST SPRINGFIELD, MASS., II. Bell tower. Builder: Timothy Billings.
Winsted, Conn., II. Bulfinch type plan. Copied by Otis, Mass., 1813.

1801 Bow, N.H., II.
BRIDGEWATER, MASS. (West Bridgewater), IV. Shallow entrance bay.
Cavendish, Vt. 55×45.
FRANCESTOWN, N.H., II. 66×48. Builder: Joseph Bickford. Cost: $5,274.24. Bell 1808. Turned and enlarged 1834. Steeple changed 1855. Sinnott: type 3, perhaps 2 initially.
HARTLAND, CONN., II. 50×45, 25 posts. Steeple and spire. Builder: Daniel Bushnell.
Henniker, N.H. (Calvinistic Congregational). 60×45. Gallery. Belfry on long side opposite pulpit.
LANGDON, N.H. Twin porch. Builder: John Chandler. Belfry added, porches remodeled 1844. Church and town hall.
NEWBURYPORT, MASS. (First Society), III. Lumber from Ambrose Palmer, Daniel Spofford.
NORWICH, CONN., V. 70×50. Architect-builder: Joseph Terry, Lavius Fillmore. "Sky blue" interior dome.
OSSIPEE, N.H. (Leighton's Corner). 50×40. 2 stories. Low ceiling. Tower. Turned 1880.
Plymouth, Mass. (Third Church). 60×52. Cupola and bell.
Reading, Vt., II. Burned 1816.
Wintonbury, Conn. (Bloomfield), II. 50×40.

1802 Bath, Maine (North Parish). Gallery.
Bath, Maine (South Parish). Burned down by Know-Nothings.
Bath, N.H., II. 54×42, to 58×47. Builder: "Mr. Sargent."
BELLINGHAM, MASS., III. Town hall. Sinnott: type 2 with tower.
BOSTON, MASS., II ("New North"). Brick. Now Roman Catholic. Architect: Charles Bulfinch.
Campton, N.H., II.
Charlestown, N.H. (North Parish). Dismantled 1850.
CORNISH FLAT, N.H.
EAST WINDSOR, CONN. (North or Scantic Parish). 57×47. Sinnott: transitional, made 4, 1842.
GRANVILLE CENTER, MASS. (Federated).
Hollis (Little Falls), Maine. 2 meetinghouses voted.
Malden, Mass., III. Brick.
MILTON, CONN. (Anglican). Builder: Oliver Dickinson.
Monson, Mass., II. Cost: $3,000. Private contributions except $300.
PHIPPSBURG, MAINE (Congregational). Sinnott: type 2 made 4 1846.
SOUTH CANAAN, CONN., II.
WALES, MASS., II ("Union House"). Shared by Baptists, Universalists, and Congregationalists.
WAPPING, CONN., II. 60×44.

WASHINGTON, CONN., III. Builder: Peter Powell, Thomas Dutton.
WINDHAM, VT.
Woburn, Mass., IV. 55×60. 6×30 porch in front.

1803 Bristol, N.H. (Bridgewater), II. 49×38. Twin porch.
BURLINGTON, CONN., II. 60×45.
CORNWALL, VT. 50×20?
DANA HILL, N.H. (New Hampton). Small. 3 doors.
Epping, N.H., II.
Farmington, Maine. "at the Center." Twin porch. Tower 1827.
Landaff, N.H.
MILTON, N.H. 52×42. Builder: Caleb Wingate. Twin porch and portico. Became 1-story town house.
Nottingham, N.H., II.
ROXBURY, MASS., V. 68×81. Painted and ornamented.
Saco, Maine (Pepperellborough). Builder: Bradbury Johnson.
SOMERSET, MASS. (Baptist).
Southold, L.I., III. 60×40.
Stoneham, Mass., II. 50×46 or 56×46. Front porch and steeple.

1804 Arlington, Mass., II. 70×56, 30 posts. Builder: Andrew Palmer. Torn down 1840.
Brookline, Mass., II. 74×54. Double-porticoed porch under tower.
Canterbury, Conn., III. 60×45, 25 posts. Builder: Thomas Gibbs. Burned 1963.
Colchester, Vt. Schoolhouse, then barn, then stone schoolhouse.
East Greenwich, R.I. (Quaker), II.
Lebanon, Conn., III. Brick. Architect: Col. John Trumbull.
LEEDS, MAINE ("Old Meeting House").
Middletown, Conn., IV. (Presumed from Rocky Hill replication.)
MILLBURY, MASS. (Bramanville).
Poultney, Vt., II.
Rockport, Mass. (Universalist).
Salem, Mass. (Cambridge Street; Third Church). (South Meeting House). 80×66. Architect: Samuel McIntire.
Savoy, Mass.
SHREWSBURY, VT. ("Old Meeting House"). Shared with town.
SOUTH CANAAN, CONN., II. Bulfinch style.
ST. JOHNSBURY, VT. 62×44. Twin porch. Builder: John Stiles, Nahum Stiles. Reerected in center village 1845.
Warren, Mass. (Western), II. Burned 1814.
WEST DURHAM, MAINE (Methodist).
Westfield, Mass., III. 66×54. "procured from Mr. Bulfinch." Square belfry.

1805 BENNINGTON, VT., II. Architect: Lavius Fillmore.
Brimfield, Mass., III. 80×50. Gallery 3 sides. Builder: Elias Carter of Brimfield. Burned 1847.
Cornish, Maine. 50×40. Single porch.
Danby, Vt. (Quaker), II.

DORCHESTER, MASS. (Second Church). Builder: Oliver Warren. Sinnott: type 2.
EAST POULTNEY, VT. (Baptist). Builder: Elisha Scott.
LENOX, MASS., II. Builder: John Hulett.
Middletown, Conn. (Methodist), I. 42×32.
Newton, Mass., IV.
Pembroke, N.H., III. 60×45.
ROCKY HILL, CONN., II. 60×50. Porch projection 4 ft.
Salem, Mass. (Branch) (Howard Street). 74×62.
Salem, Mass. (Baptist).
Salem Village, Mass. (Danvers). 66×56, 28 posts. Brick.
Shrewsbury, Vt. (Universalist).

1806 BARRINGTON, R.I. (United Congregational).
Bethel, Maine.
BLOOMFIELD, CONN. (Anglican) (St. Andrew's). "Pews made of panels from earlier ones." Dismantled, moved, reerected 1830.
BOSTON, MASS. (Baptist Third Church). African American. Brick.
BOSTON, MASS. (Old West Church). Brick. 4-storied porch. Architect: Asher Benjamin.
BRIDGEWATER HILL, N.H. ("Old Town House").
Brunswick, Maine, II. Builder: Samuel Melcher. North gallery reserved for Bowdoin College students.
Cabot, Vt.
Ellington, Conn.
HARTFORD, CONN., IV. 102×64. Brick. Architect: David Wadsworth.
Ludlow, Vt. "Plain wood . . . devoid of steeple or ornaments."
MIDDLEBURY, VT., II. 78×58. Steeple 135 ft. Architect: Lavius Fillmore.
Middleton, Vt. (Baptist).
Milton, Vt.
Mount Washington, Mass., I. 24×30.
Newbury, Mass., IV. 61×51. Burned 1868.
NEWPORT, R.I. (Methodist) (St. Paul's).
PEACHAM, VT. Sinnott: type 3.
Salem, Mass. (Universalist).
STANDISH, MAINE. ("Old Meeting House"). Sinnott: type 3.
WOODSTOCK, VT. ("Old White").
Woodstock, Vt. (Methodist Episcopal).

1807 Acton, Mass., II.
BOSTON, MASS. (Charles Street Church). Massing portico. Brick. Architect: Asher Benjamin.
BRIDGEWATER, CONN. 52×40, 24 posts.
DUANESBURG, L.I. (Quaker). Center part operated pulleys and rope.
Framingham, Mass., III. 76×68 tower to 65×65. Tower in front.
Hallowell, Maine (Baptist). Burned 1868.
HINGHAM, MASS. (New North).
Jay, Maine, II (Baptist). Still used as town house in 1912.

Marlborough, Mass., IV. Architect: John Ames.
Marlborough, Mass. (West End), I.
NEW SALEM, MASS. Moved.
PORTSMOUTH, N.H. (Anglican), II (St. John's). Brick. Architect: Alexander Parris.
Salem, Mass. (Freewill Baptist).
Smithfield, R.I. Lottery.
SUDBURY, VT.
Sullivan, N.H., II. 49×37. Twin porch.
Tiverton, R.I. (Baptist).
WHITMAN, MASS.

1808 BETHANY, CONN. (Anglican) (Christ Church). 48×36, then 48 "proportioned" to Waterbury. Architect: David Hoadley.
Boston, Mass. (First Church), IV. Architect: Asher Benjamin.
Coventry, R.I. ("Tin Top"). 60×40. Gallery. Floated down from Providence.
HADLEY, MASS., III.
JAMAICA, VT. Sinnott: type 3. Town meetings once held "below."
JEFFERSON, MAINE (Baptist).
NEWTOWN, CONN., II. 60×40. Belfry and cupola. Builder: Isaac Scudder.
Northborough, Mass., II. 56×56; projection 34×15. Builder: John Ames, Capt. Brooks.
Preston, Conn., III.
STOUGHTON, MASS. Cupola, belfry, dome.
Stratford, N.H. Moved 1820 to central location.
WESTWOOD, MASS. Builder: Benjamin Robbins.
WINDSOR, CONN. (Anglican) (St. John's). Compass windows.

1809 Abington, Mass. (South Parish). "Two turrets connected by piazza and pediment."
ASHBY, MASS., II.
Boston, Mass. (Irish or Presbyterian), III. Gothic revival.
BOSTON, MASS. (Congregational) (Park Street Church). Brick.
FREETOWN, MASS. (Assonet) (Congregational), II (North Church). Sinnott: type 3.
LYME, N.H., II. Builder: John Thompson Jr. Sinnott: type 3.
MANCHESTER, MASS., IV.
Middletown, Conn. (Baptist), I. 53×38.
Moriches, L.I. (Union Church).
NANTUCKET, MASS. (Unitarian). 3-story porch and bell tower (like Bedford).
Newburyport, Mass. (Congress Street) (Baptist)
Otis, Mass., I. Burned shortly after it was raised.
PROVIDENCE, R.I. (Beneficent Congregational). Dome and 4 columns. Much remodeled. Stone and brick.
SOUTH YARMOUTH, MASS. (Quaker).
WAREHOUSE POINT, CONN. (Anglican).
Westford, Vt. (formerly held in a barn). Replaced 1840.
West Greenwich, R.I. (Union). 38×32, 19 posts.

1810 EAST SANDWICH, MASS. (Quaker). Single porch.
FAIRFIELD, MAINE. Sinnott: type 3.

KILLINGWORTH, CONN. (Anglican).
ORANGE, CONN. (Milford Third Parish). Architect: David Hoadley.
PROVIDENCE, R.I. (Anglican). Stone. Gothic windows.
RUMFORD, R.I. (Newman Congregational).
UNITY, N.H. (Baptist).

1811 Boston, Mass., III. (Hollis Street). Brick. 2-tier porch. Single 4-tier tower.
BRIDGTON, MAINE (Methodist).
CARLISLE, MASS. (Unitarian), II. Builder: Joseph Wyman, John Sawyer of Templeton. Light straw color with mahogany doors.
CHELSEA, VT. Sinnott: type 3.
Hanover, Mass. (Anglican), II. Cost: $5,000.
Littleton, N.H.
MONROE, CONN.
MONROE, CONN. (Anglican) (St. Peter's). Compass windows.
Northampton, Mass., IV. 100×76, 30 posts. (seated 1,000). Steeple 140 ft. Architect: Asher Benjamin, Isaac Damon. Cost: $22,174. Burned 1878.
TEMPLETON, MASS., II. 65×55. Builder: Elias Carter.
WHITING, VT. Committee member went to Boston for advice.

1812 ASHFIELD, MASS., II. Builder: John Ames. Sinnott: type 3. Now town hall.
Brookhaven, L.I., III.
Burlington, Vt. (First Calvinist Congregational). Wood. Burned 1829.
Chatham, Conn.
EAST BLACKSTONE, MASS. (Quaker).
GUILFORD, CONN. (Third or North Parish), II. 48×38. Steeple "8 ft within . . . & 4 do. Without." Builder: Abraham Coan.
LYME, CONN. (Congregational) (Grassy Hill).
Lynn, Mass. (Methodist), II.
Mt. Holly, Vt. (Baptist). Large gallery and pulpit and sounding board.
Nashua Village, N.H. (formerly Dunstable) ("Old South").
NEW HAVEN, CONN. (Fair Haven and White Haven) (United Church). Brick. Architect: David Hoadley.
New Ipswich, N.H., IV. 92×69. Architect: Seth Nason. Builders: John Butman, Capt. Roffe.
OXFORD, CONN. (Quaker's Farm) (Anglican) (Christ Church). Gothic. Architect: George Boult.
Poultney, Vt.
PRESTON, CONN. (Baptist).
Westfield, Conn. (Baptist). 36×26.
Westhampton, Mass., II.
Wilmington, Mass., III. 56×49. Porch 8×31.

1813 Great Barrington, Mass., II.
Medway, Mass., III. 53×53, 29 posts. Porch 15×30. Builder: Malachi Bullard.
MEDWAY, MASS. (Second or West Parish), II. 53×53, 19 posts. Medway III imitated it.

NEW HAVEN, CONN., IV (Center Church). 100×70. Brick. Architect: Ithiel Town.
NEW HAVEN, CONN. (Anglican), II. Stone. About 100×70. Architect: Ithiel Town.
NORFOLK, CONN., II. 60×45. Architect: David Hoadley. Greek Revival portico.
OTIS, MASS., II. 50×45. 1789 Bulfinch type. Copied Winsted, Conn.
RICHMOND, VT. (Union) ("Old Round Church"). "sixteen sides." Builder: William Rhodes.
STRATFIELD, CONN. (Baptist), II. 40×35.
WESTPORT, MASS. (Quaker).

1814 Boston, Mass. (New South Society). Stone. Architect: Charles Bulfinch.
BRISTOL, R.I. (Baptist). Stone. Wooden tower.
CANTON, CONN., II.
CASCO, MAINE (Quaker).
CHAPLIN, CONN.
HUNTINGTON, CONN. (Anglican). "Shingled."
New Shoreham, R.I. (Block Island) (Baptist), II. Became town hall.
NORTH GUILFORD, CONN. (Anglican).
SUDBURY, MASS. (Wayland), V. Architect: "Andrews Palmer from Asher Benjamin design."
TROY, N.H., II. Builder: from Sullivan, N.H. Finish carpenter: Samuel Morse, Templeton, Mass. Lower floor became firehouse.

1815 ALLENSTOWN, N.H. Low and very plain. Ground floor seats on incline.
BRATTLEBORO, VT., II. Tower. Quoins. Lock stage.
BRENTWOOD, N.H., III. 50×45. Remodeled 1847. Church below, town hall above.
Goffstown, N.H., II.
LANCASTER, MASS., IV. Architect: Charles Bulfinch.
LYME, CONN. (Congregational) (Hamburg Church). Church above, town hall below.
OAKHAM, MASS., II. 60×45 including porch.
WASHINGTON, VT.

1816 ADDISON, VT. (Baptist).
BEDFORD, MASS., II. Wood. Architect: Asher Benjamin. Similar to Old West and Charles Street.
BETHEL, VT. Brick.
BURLINGTON, VT. (Congregational). Brick. Architect: Peter Banner.
Dorchester, Mass., V. 73×62, 32 posts. Tower height 129 ft. Cost: $20,188.
Exeter, R.I. (Chestnut Hill) (Baptist), II. 40×34. Gallery. Builder: Daniel Spink.
Fitzwilliam, N.H., II. Builder: Killburn and Jonathan Cutting. Burned 1816.
Lynn, Mass. (Quaker), II.
Medway, Mass. (West Parish), II.
New Sharon, Maine.
NORTH WOODBURY, CONN., I.
PLAINFIELD, CONN., II. 60×50? Stone.
PROVIDENCE, R.I. (First Unitarian). Architect: John Holden Green.
SEYMOUR, CONN. (Anglican).
SOUTH BARNSTEAD, N.H.

THOMPSON, CONN., II. Architect: Ithiel Town. Builder: Elias Carter.
Wickford, R.I. (Baptist). 50 × 40.

1817 Attleborough, Mass. (North Baptist). Transitional?
BLUE HILL, MAINE (Baptist).
Dartmouth, Mass. (New Bedford), II. 48 × 60. 7-ft. portico.
EAST HARPSWELL, MAINE (Baptist). No galleries.
KILLINGWORTH FARMS, CONN. (Killingworth), II. Architect: Ithiel Town (probable).
Lyme, Conn., IV. Brick?
NORWICH, VT.
PRESTON, CONN. (Second or Long Society), II. 52 × 40? Builder: George W. Willard. Sinnott: type 2.
Searsport, Maine (Second Congregational).
SOUTH DARTMOUTH, MASS.
Wellfleet, Mass. (Methodist Episcopal). 48 × 38.
WEST TOWNSEND, VT.
WOODBURY, CONN. Designer: Harman Stoddard.

1818 BELFAST, MAINE.
Dublin, N.H., II. Copied Fitzwilliam, N.H. Builder: J. Cutting, S. Kilburn. Dismantled 1852.
FITZWILLIAM, N.H., III. Town house 1868.
Foxborough, Mass. (Baptist). 40 × 36. No belfry. Pulpit in front between doors.
Hubbardston, Vt. (Congregational).
KILLINGLY, CONN. (Putnam Heights), IV. Architect-builder: Elias Carter.
NORTH BRANFORD, CONN. (Anglican). Builder: Abraham Coan.
North Yarmouth, Maine, II. 60 × 55. 2 porches on front (twin porch?). Gallery. Abandoned 1868. Torn down 1879.
PORTER, MAINE (Baptist) ("Old Bullockite Church"). Plain. Used for town meeting.
SOUTH PARIS, MAINE (Congregational).
SPRINGFIELD, MASS., IV. 90 × 72, 30 posts. Architect-builder: Isaac Damon.
THETFORD, VT. (Post Mills). Sinnott: "Steeple suggests Asher Benjamin design."
WARNER, N.H.
Warren, N.H. 50 × 40. Moved and remodeled 1859.

1819 AVON, CONN., II. Architect: David Hoadley. Sinnott: "Windows . . . at pulpit end now closed."
BOSTON, MASS. (Anglican) (St. Paul's). Stone. Architect: Alexander Parris, Solomon Willard.
BRISTOL, VT. (Baptist).
CRAFTSBURY COMMON, VT.
DEDHAM, MASS. (Congregational) (Allin Church).
DERBY, CONN., III. 50 × 40, 24 posts. Builder: Amos Williams, Nathaniel. Barnum. Sinnott: "Hoadley type."
EASTPORT, MAINE (Baptist).

GARDINER, MAINE (Anglican). Gothic. Unhammered granite.
GREENFIELD, MASS., II. Architect: Isaac Damon.
HAMDEN, Conn. (Anglican) (Grace Church). Architect: David Hoadley?
HANCOCK, N.H., II. Copied Dublin, N.H. Builder: Jacob Ames, Samuel Kilbourn. Church above, town hall below.
LINCOLNVILLE, MAINE. Plain. No belfry.
MILFORD, MASS., II. Architect: Elias Carter (vote: "A skillful and faithful architect").
SHARON, CONN. (Anglican). Brick.
SOUTH DARTMOUTH, MASS. (Quaker). Organ.
WARREN, CONN., II. 56 × 42. "taking of Seven feet for a steeple." Builder: James Jennings.

1820 ACWORTH, N.H. (Quaker). 2 doors, "the women's wider."
Charlestown, N.H., III. Brick. 70 × 60, 32 posts. Cost: $7,500. Organ 1829.
HAVERHILL, MASS. Brick.
KINGSTON, R.I.
Marlborough, Vt., II.
MENDON, MASS., V. Architect: Elias Carter. Cost: $7,619.
Mt. Holly, Vt. (Union Church). Portico. Large columns in style of Pantheon.
NORTH BARNSTEAD, N.H. 1 story. "Perfectly plain."
NORTH BUXTON, MAINE.
Pittsfield, Vt. Cost: $1,000.
Salisbury, N.H. (East Village, now Franklin).
Southampton, L.I., IV.
SOUTH DEERFIELD, MASS.
UNITY, N.H. (Quaker). "Two doors, wider one for women."
WINDSOR, VT. (Anglican).

1821 ACWORTH, N.H., II. Templeton type.
BRIDGEWATER, MASS. (Scotland Parish) (Trinitarian).
Eastham, Mass. (Methodist).
GLOCESTER, R.I. (Chepachet) (Baptist). Architect: Elias Carter. Builder: Clark Sayles.
Leominster, Mass., III. 75 × 62. Projecting porch, Ionic order.
NEWBURY VILLAGE, N.H. (Baptist).
Salisbury, Mass. (Baptist), I. 50 × 42.
Scituate, R.I. (Baptist) II.
Topsham, Maine, II.
WEATHERSFIELD CENTER, VT. Brick.
WOODSTOCK, CONN. Sinnott: "like...Putnam Heights church."

1822 EAST BERKSHIRE, VT.
EAST CANAAN, CONN. Sinnott: "Resembles Avon church."
EAST HAVERHILL, MASS. (Baptist).
EAST MONTPELIER, VT. (Methodist). Used for town meetings until 1847.
Goshen, Mass. (Baptist).

GRANBY, MASS., II. Builder: Elias Carter (like Mendham).
HOLLISTON, MASS., II.
Lynn, Mass. (Second Congregational became Unitarian).
MARBLE DALE, CONN. (Anglican). Brick. Gothic.
New Britain, Conn., II. (Old North Church).
NEWPORT, N.H., III. Brick.
North Providence, R.I. (Baptist).
Salem, Mass. (Methodist).
SALISBURY, CONN. (Anglican). Brick.
SOUTH BUXTON, MAINE ("Tory Hill").
Tewksbury, Mass., II.
WEST GREENWICH, R.I. (Baptist), II (Plain Meeting House). 1 story. Remodeled 1856.
Westerly, R.I. (Union Church). Steeple. Architect: Benjamin Palmer. Bass viol.

1823 BETHEL, VT. (Anglican).
BLANDFORD, MASS., II.
Calais, Vt. 42 × 40. 2 floors.
EAST WINTHROP, MAINE (Baptist). Sinnott: type 3.
MILFORD, CONN., III. Greek Revival portico. Architect: David Hoadley. Builder: Elias Carter.
NANTUCKET, MASS. (Methodist).
NEW BOSTON, N.H., III. 60 × 69, 30 posts. $5\frac{1}{2} \times 36$ porch. Stone and brick. Mason: John Leach.
NEWPORT, N.H. (Second Parish), I. Builder: John Leach.
NORTH BROOKFIELD, MASS. (Second Parish). Much like Mendon, Mass.
SOUTH BERWICK, MAINE.
SWANTON, VT.
WEBSTER, N.H.

1824 CALAIS, VT. Sinnott: transitional.
CARVER, MASS. ("Old Meeting House"). Cranberry barn in 1963.
CLARENDON, VT. Brick.
DEERFIELD, MASS., IV. Brick. Architect: Winthrop Clapp.
Dorchester, Mass. (Canton), III. 46 × 34.
HARVARD, MASS. (Congregational).
Hawley, Mass., II.
JERICHO, VT., II. Brick.
MARBLEHEAD, MASS., III. Stone.
Salem, Mass. (Independent Congregationalist).
SHARON, CONN., III. Brick. Builder: Hiram Vail. Mason: William Watson. Finish carpenter: James Jennings.
SOUTHWICK, MASS., III.
STOCKBRIDGE, MASS., III. Brick with wood steeple. Builder: Ralph Bigelow.
WEST TAUNTON, MASS. Small. Simple.
WINTHROP, MAINE (South Parish), III. 3 accidental deaths at raising.

1825 Attleborough, Mass. (Second Parish), II. Copied North Baptist meetinghouse, Providence.
Barnstable, Mass. (Hyannis) (Baptist). Replaced "ancient Baptist meeting-house."
BURKE HOLLOW, VT. ("Old Union"). Builder: Ira Armington, Seth Clark Jr.
COHASSET, MASS. (Congregational).
FRAMINGHAM, MASS. (Baptist). Architect: Solomon Willard, Boston.
HEBRON, CONN. (Anglican). "Rose colored" brick.
KINGSTON, N.H.
Nashua, N.H. ("Olive Street").
NEW PRESTON, CONN., III ("Old Congregational Church"). 54×44. Stone.
NORTH CORNWALL, CONN. 50×40. "steeple projecting 6 feet." Builder: Hiram Vail.
NORTH SANDWICH, N.H. (Baptist).
PETERBOROUGH, N.H. Brick.
POLAND, MAINE (Congregational).
PORTLAND, MAINE (Unitarian) (First Church). 102×66. Stone (granite).
SOUTH BRITAIN, CONN., II. 50×40. Porch 7 ft. Builder: Hall and Winton.
SOUTH WINDHAM, VT. Brick.
STOCKBRIDGE, MASS. (Interlaken). Brick.
WENTWORTH, N.H.
Winthrop, Maine (Methodist).

1826 AMESBURY, MASS. (Unitarian became Congregational).
AMHERST, MASS. (Johnson Chapel, Amherst College). Brick.
ANDOVER, MASS. (West Parish) (Congregational). Stone (granite).
Antrim, N.H., II. Brick. Templeton style. Standing in 1880.
BELGRADE, MAINE (Baptist) ("Old South Church").
BELLINGHAM, MASS. (Baptist), II. "Three round-topped doors."
BERLIN, MASS., II.
CHESHIRE, CONN., III. Greek Revival. Portico. Hoadley type. Builder: Hall, Winton.
CHICOPEE, MASS. (Second, formerly Fifth Parish in Springfield), II.
DIGHTON, MASS. (Congregational).
Farmington Falls, Maine (Union).
GILMANTON, N.H., II. Round-topped windows.
GILMANTON, N.H. (Iron Works Village).
Greenville, R.I. (Baptist).
KENNEBUNK, MAINE (Union).
KENT, CONN. (Anglican). Stone.
LEICESTER, VT. Design adopted from St. Albans, Vt.
MANOMET, MASS. (Second Congregational Church of Plymouth).
NEW LONDON, N.H. (Baptist).
NORTH AMHERST, MASS. Builder: Winthrop Clapp.
Plymouth, Mass. (Cole's Hill) (Universalist).
PORTLAND, MAINE ("Abyssinian Meeting House"). Vacant since 1991.
PORTSMOUTH, N.H. ("Old South"). 92×66. Granite. Architect: Alexander Parris.
Russell, Mass., II (Baptist).

Salem, Mass. (Second Baptist Church).
SCITUATE, MASS.
SHUTESBURY, MASS., II.
SOUTH HANSON, MASS.
SOUTHWICK, MASS. (Methodist Episcopal).
WATERVILLE, MAINE (Baptist).
WESTHAMPTON, MASS., III.
WOODSTOCK, VT. Brick. Now Masonic temple.

1827 ACTON CORNER, MAINE. Very plain.
ASHFIELD, MASS. (Anglican).
ATHOL, MASS., II ("Old Meeting House"). "Like Templeton, N.H."
BRISTOL, N.H.
FRANKLIN, VT. Very plain. Had "horse block" in 1963.
GREENE, MAINE (Universalist).
GREENSBORO, VT.
HARTFORD, CONN. (Second Parish), III. Brick. Builder: William Hayden.
HAVERHILL, N.H. Brick.
HOPKINGTON, N.H. (Anglican) (St. Andrew's). Stone (granite).
HUBBARDSTON, MASS. (Evangelical).
LOUDON, N.H., II.
MATTAPOISETT, MASS. (Quaker). Hipped roof changed to pitched roof.
MIDDLEBURY, VT. (Anglican).
NASHUA, N.H. Attributed to Asher Benjamin. Doric columns.
Newmarket, N.H. (Freewill Baptist).
Newmarket, N.H. (Methodist Episcopal).
OSSIPEE, N.H.
READFIELD, MAINE. Brick. Builder: Richard Mace, Jere Page, and Francis Hunt.
TRURO, MASS.
VERNON, CONN., II.
WEBSTER CORNER, MAINE. Architect: Sampson Colby.

1828 Amherst, Mass., III. 80×65. Brick.
Arlington, Mass. (Baptist), II.
Athol, Mass., IV. Templeton type.
ATTLEBOROUGH, MASS. (Second or East Parish), II. 2-story shallow portico. Tower.
BENTON FALLS, MAINE. "last bell by the Revere family."
BETHLEHEM, CONN. (Anglican). Brick.
Brookfield, Mass. (Evangelical).
CHESTER, VT. Steeple copied Peterborough, N.H.
Dedham, Mass. (South Parish or Norwood).
EAST LONGMEADOW, MASS.
EDGARTOWN, MASS.
GUILFORD, CONN., III. 80×60. Wood. Projecting porch. Builder: Ira Atwater, Wilson Booth.
HAMPTON FALLS, N.H. (Baptist).

HARTFORD, CONN. (Anglican), II. Stone. Gothic. Architect: Ithiel Town. Builder: James Chamberlain.
HARTFORD, VT. (Second Congregational Church).
HOLDEN, MAINE.
HOPKINTON, N.H. (Anglican) (St. Andrew's). Stone. Builder: John Leach.
KENNEBUNKPORT, MAINE (Second Congregational Church).
LANESBOROUGH, MASS. (Baptist).
LEBANON, N.H.
MACHIASPORT, MAINE (Congregational).
MIDDLEBOROUGH, MASS., III. Sinnott: "Good example of Greek Revival."
Middletown, Conn. (Methodist), II. 75 × 55, 30 posts.
MILLBURY, MASS.
NATICK, MASS. (Eliot Church).
NEW CASTLE, N.H. Builder: Thomas Foye. Finish carpenter: Andrew Venard.
NEW HARTFORD, CONN. Brick.
NEWMARKET, N.H., III.
NORTH ATTLEBOROUGH, MASS.
NORTH READING, MASS. Church above, town hall below.
Otis, Mass. (Anglican) (St. Paul's).
Providence, R.I. (Richmond Street), II. 75 × 65. Wood.
QUINCY, MASS. (Braintree), IV. Stone. Architect: Alexander Parris.
SOMERSWORTH, N.H.
SOUTH ACTON, MAINE (Baptist).
SOUTHINGTON, CONN. Imitated Cheshire.
STONINGTON, CONN. (Road Church).
Worcester, Mass. (Unitarian), II. Architect-builder: Elias Carter.

1829 ARLINGTON, VT. (Anglican). Stone. Gothic tower.
BILLERICA, MASS. (Congregational).
Boston, Mass. (Baptist), III. Brick.
CASTINE, MAINE (Congregational).
COVENTRY, VT.
DEERING CENTER, N.H.
DIXFIELD, MAINE. No galleries.
DOVER, N.H. Brick.
EASTFORD, CONN., II.
Eastham, Mass., IV.
EASTPORT, MAINE (Congregational).
KINGSTON, MASS.
LITCHFIELD, CONN. 70 × 50. Like Cheshire and Southington. Greek Revival portico.
LIVERMORE, MAINE (Norland Meeting House, "Devil's Roosting Place").
LYNDON, VT.
Middletown, Conn. (African Methodist Episcopal). 39 × 30.
ORLEANS, MASS.
Perry, Maine.
RIVERTON, CONN. (Union). Stone.

South Kingstown, R.I. (Wakefield) (First Baptist). Moved across street 1852; converted to dwelling house.
SUTTON, MASS.
TISBURY, MASS. (Christiantown Chapel).
WEST HAMPTON, MASS. Builder: Caleb Loud.
WESTMINSTER, VT.

1830 ANNISQUAM, MASS.
Ashford, Conn., III.
EAST GRANBY, CONN. (Congregational). Stone. Architect: Isaac Damon.
Lynn, Mass. (Third Methodist).
MERIDEN, CONN. (Congregational). Greek Revival portico.
PLYMPTON, MASS., IV.
Rutland, Mass. III. 77 × 48, 20 posts. Tower.
SIMSBURY, CONN., III. Architect: Isaac Damon [and Hayden] of Northampton.
SOUTHOLD, L.I. (Mattatuck), II.
TAUNTON, MASS. Stone. Gothic. Pinnacle at every corner.
TOWNSEND, MASS. Brick. Wooden steeple.
WESTON, CONN. (Norfield Congregational Church).

APPENDIX C

# Pinnacles, pyramids, and spires, 1651–1709

This information is gathered from New England town and parish records, indentures, contracts, invoices, and contemporary images.

1651  Dedham, Mass., I. Raised 1638. 36 × 20, 12 posts. Daubed, thatched 1651: "[install] one pyramedy at the south end and shingle the penthouse."

1652  Sudbury, Mass., II. Raised 1653. 40 × 24, 12 posts. "& pinacles both at each end & each gable wth a clear story."

1658  Roxbury, Mass., I. Raised 1632, repaired 1646, 1656. Gallery, plaster, turret "pinakle[s]" added 1658: "That some pinakle or other ornament be set upon each end of the howse."

1669  Boston, Mass. (Third Church), I. Raised 1669. 75 × 51. 3 porches. Cupola. Pinnacles seen on 1725 Burgis-Price view of Boston.

1672  Haddam, Conn., I. 28 × 24, 13 posts. Raised 1673. 8 windows. John Clark instructed to put up "tooe pramedyes at each end" of the meetinghouse.

1682  New London, Conn., II. Raised 1697. 40 × 40, 20 posts. 4 gables. Turret. Galleries. Town voted to "set up on all the four gables of the house, pyramides comely and fit for the work upon each end of the house."

1682  Simsbury, Conn., I. Raised 1683. 28 × 24, 14 posts. From an indenture with Thomas Barber: "put up Flue Boards at each end, and piramides also."

1694  Northampton, Mass., II. Raised 1661. Joseph Parson's account for repair: "sawing two stocks for Preamady."

1704  Hartford, Conn. (First Church), II. Raised 1638. Rev. William Davenport arranged "for setting up the speer & vain" on the turret of the 1638 meetinghouse.

1705  Norwich, Conn., II. Raised 1673, enlarged 1689. Town voted "to mend the pyramid and to close the leanto roofs where they joine to the bodie of the meetinghouse."

1709  Norwalk, Conn., I. Raised 1659. Samuel Keeler Jr. to build belfry, "and at ye top of ye turret a good sufficient cedar stump to fix a weathercock on, if ye town see cause; or a pinnicle."

APPENDIX D

# Enlargements of meetinghouses in New England by cutting the frame, 1723–1824

1723  Barnstable, Mass. (West Parish). 1719 meetinghouse enlarged by 2 bays.
1737  Newburyport, Mass. 1725 meetinghouse enlarged to 80×60.
1742  Rowley, Mass. (Second Parish, Georgetown). 1729 meetinghouse enlarged 13 ft. 4 in.
1745  Scituate, Mass. 1707 meetinghouse enlarged 13 ft.
1750  (estimated date) Salem, Mass. (Middle Precinct, later Peabody). Meetinghouse enlarged twice by Daniel Spofford, first crosswise, later lengthwise.
1754  Duxbury, Mass. 1706 meetinghouse enlarged 15 or 17 ft.
1756  Barnstable, Mass. (Second or East Parish). 1719 meetinghouse enlarged 15 ft. by cutting; belfry added.
1756  Sandwich, Mass. 1703 meetinghouse divided in center and lengthened 15 ft.
1759  Falmouth, Maine. 1740 meetinghouse (Old Jerusalem) enlarged by sawing "through on both sides of the pulpit and each end was moved from the pulpit twelve feet," creating 28 new pews on lower floor.
1761  Yarmouth, Mass. (Second or East Parish, Dennis). 1721 meetinghouse enlarged.
1762  North Yarmouth, Maine. 1727 meetinghouse, 50×40, cut in the middle and the western half moved 40 ft. to create a building 45×94. One source says 28 ft. 28 pews added.
1764  Hanover, Mass. (Central Meeting House). Town voted to open its 1728 meetinghouse "in two parts and put in a new piece in the middle 13 feet or 15 feet in length"; subsequently voted for a new meetinghouse, 62×43, 22 posts.
1765  Truro, Mass. 1720 meetinghouse enlarged and repaired.
1768  Plympton, Mass. (Second or South Parish or Carver). Town voted "to cut the [1732] meeting house in two in the middle of the broad alley and put in fifteen feet."
1768  West Tisbury, Mass. Town voted to cut the 1733 meetinghouse in the middle and enlarge it by 15 ft., and enlarge it an additional 2 ft. on the back.
1768  Yarmouth, Mass. 1716 meetinghouse enlarged 15 ft.
1769  Killingly, Conn. (Second, North, or Thompson Parish). 1729 meetinghouse cut into two parts and enlarged 14 ft.
1769  Sherburne, Mass. 1723 meetinghouse enlarged by 20 ft.; town voted "that the Peace be put in the middle." Another description: "this was done by sawing the house in two in

the middle, moving the western half to the distance desired, and connecting the two parts together by a new piece."

1770 Salem, Mass. (Second or East Parish). 1717 meetinghouse enlarged by inserting 14 ft. in the center.

1772 Westborough, Mass. Town voted to expand its 1749 meetinghouse and look at examples of cutting and filling in to make enlargements. Voted in 1774 to "split the meeting house & put in 14 feet."

1772 Woburn, Mass. Town voted to "open the [1748] Meeting House in said Parish, and move to the West eighteen feet & a half; and move the Pulpit to the middle of the House on the North Side."

1773 Chatham, Mass. 1730 meetinghouse enlarged "east and west" by the addition of 17 ft. and a 9 x 10 porch.

1775 Watertown, Mass. 1723 meetinghouse enlarged (before 1775) by extending the pulpit side about 18 ft., adding 16 pews and creating a structure like a lean-to on the pulpit side.

1781 Cummington, Mass. Meetinghouse moved and enlarged (after 1781) by the addition of a section in the middle.

1782 Lynnfield, Mass. Town voted to enlarge its 1715 meetinghouse by cutting it into two pieces and adding 14 ft. Bentley's diary says in 1813 that it was enlarged.

1787 Holliston, Mass. Town voted to add 14 ft. to the center of its 1725 meetinghouse, increasing it from 40 × 32 to 54 × 30.

1792 Mendon, Mass. (Second or East, Milford). Town added 14 ft. to its 1741 meetinghouse.

1795 Dorchester, Mass. 1743 meetinghouse enlarged "by first dividing it along the ridge pole, and moving off one half 14 ft., and then building an addition in the middle; after which the tower and steeple were moved, standing, seven feet, to bring it to the center of the end."

1796 Harwich, Mass. 1723 meetinghouse enlarged by opening the frame to new dimensions 72 × 45.

1801 Newburyport, Mass. 1756 Presbyterian meetinghouse was "cut open with the purpose of enlarging it. It was open exactly in front of the front gallery."

1804 Sandwich, Mass. 1703 meetinghouse enlarged 15 ft. a second time, this time in width. Another source says: "deepened by another 12½ feet, through moving the entire north wall with pulpit and pews that much father north. The front roof and ridge from the belltower remained in place, so that the back roof slope became flatter."

1824 Londonderry, N.H. (East Parish). 1769 meetinghouse enlarged by "cutting it through the middle, moving the eastern end 24 feet, and finishing between the posts."

# APPENDIX E

# Citations of exterior painting, 1678–1828

When the color vote, application, or purchase is unknown, the meetinghouse date is indicated with an asterisk (*).

Abington, Mass. 1764. "Colored" white; paint analysis: sandstone or light yellow on the corner boards, doors a rich green.

Alstead, N.H. 1794. Painted red ochre (copied by Washington, N.H.)

Amesbury, Mass. 1788. "The West Parish meeting house . . . was painted this year, and it required 33 2-3 bushels of flax seed to make the 'oyl.'"

Arlington, Mass. 1795. "paint the outside . . . the same color as Mr. Thomas Russells."

Arlington, Mass. 1805. "painted white."

Ashburnham, Mass. 1798. Voted that "the color should be pea green": reconsidered earlier vote and decided on "white."

Barnstable, Mass. (Baptist). 1788.* "a great porch all painted red."

Barnstead Parade, N.H. 1799. "The body . . . was painted yellow; the roof red."

Bedford, Mass. 1780. "covered with a coating of 'Bedford Yellow,' a sort of mineral paint found in the town"; beginning of the nineteenth century described as being "dark, dirty yellow."

Bedford, N.H. 1762. "finished mixing 40 pounds of paint for the Meeting house."

Berlin, Mass. 1794. Committee report: "65 gallons linseed oil . . . two barrals fish oil . . . 500½ white lead . . . Verdigrea 6½ lb. . . . 5 hundred Spanish brown . . ."

Bernardston, Mass. 1793. "painted of a light colour, and very agreeable."

Bernardston, Mass. 1794. "colored yellow."

Bethany, Conn. 1774. "that the meetinghouse be colored blue, and the windows white"; shortly thereafter vote changed to "white."

Bluehill, Maine. 1793. "that the body of the meeting house be painted a yellow stone color and the roof to be painted with oil, turpentine and Spanish brown."

Boston, Mass. (First Church). 1714. Edward Pell paid "for painting ye Brick meeting house."

Boston, Mass. (First Church). 1801. Brick sides light stone color in James Brown Marston's painting *State Street*.

Boxborough, Mass. 1784. "get the outside of the meeting-house painted."

Boxford, Mass. 1736. "newly painted of an olive color."

Boxford, Mass. Circa 1800. Painted "stone-color."
Bradford, Mass. (East Parish). 1822. Moved "to have the meeting-house painted twice over with good white lead and linseed oil with colouring so as to make it a handsome stone colour. The windows and frames to be white."
Braintree, Mass. (Randolph). 1796. "Voted, to build two porches to the meeting-house . . . both to be finished off and painted handsomely."
Branford, Conn. 1797. "painted, or whitewashed, both inside and out, and the roof . . . coated 'with Spanish Brown laid on with Linseed oil.'"
Branford, Conn. 1812. "painted white."
Bridgewater, Mass. (North Parish). 1788. "Window frames and sashes be painted white."
Bridgewater, Mass. (South Parish). 1773. "paint the outside . . . as much as has been painted before."
Bridgewater, Mass. (South Parish). 1802. "white, one shade on the yellow."
Brimfield, Mass. 1761. "to color the outside of the meeting-house."
Bristol, Conn. 1770. Body "spruce yellow"; "Dores and windows . . . white"; roof, Spanish Brown."
Brookfield, Conn. 1769. "oyl and culler the windows and doors, and corner-boards."
Brookfield, Mass. (Second or North Parish). 1756. "voted to color the clapboards of same."
Brooklyn, Conn. 1762. "bright orange," doors chocolate, with white.
Brooklyn, Conn. 1771. Meetinghouse to be "colored white."
Brooklyn, Conn. 1788. Voted in September $100 "to be paid in Flaxseed or any other Material proper for Painting & Repairing the Meeting-house"; voted in November to paint the exterior "of a light Stone colour."
Brunswick, Maine (Baptist). 1795.* Called "Old Yellow Meeting House."
Burrillville, R.I. (Quaker). 1791* "only a modest brown coat upon the exterior."
Camden, Maine. 1799.* "The outside was clap-boarded and painted yellow."
Canaan, N.H. 1792. "painting of the outside exactly like the lower meeting house in Salisbury."
Canaan, N.H. 1794. "that the sides and wall of the house be colored a stone couler, the roof Spanish Brown, and the doors a sky blue."
Canaan, N.H. 1812. Meetinghouse painted with "white lead and a Red Rough."
Candia, N.H. 1795. "house was clapboarded, [and] painted white."
Canton, Conn. 1763. Voted "to coller the Meeting house."
Carlisle, Mass. 1811.* "The body a light straw color with white trimmings; the roof painted a chocolate color, and the doors imitation mahogany."
Centerbrook, Conn. 1797. Voted "to coulour the Meeting House."
Charlestown, N.H. (North Parish). 1801. Meetinghouse painted "tawdry" yellow.
Charlestown, N.H. (North Parish). 1825. Tax bill: $125 paid for painting the meetinghouse.
Chatham, Mass. 1773. "To paint . . . the frunt and the two Gable Ends . . . a Stone Couler and the Porch, back side and all over the Roofe with Spanish Brown."
Chelmsford, Mass. 1793. Bentley describes meetinghouse as "painted well without."
Claremont, N.H. (Union Episcopal Church). 1801. "Gorgeous in its yellow paint."
Claremont, N.H. 1826. Voted $200 for repairing and painting the meetinghouse.
Cohasset, Mass. Circa 1812. Ink and watercolor mourning picture depicts green meetinghouse with white trim.
Colrain, Mass. 1764. Voted "to colour the meeting house . . . Blew."
Columbia, Conn. (Second Parish in Lebanon or Lebanon Crank). 1753. "Collour the Meeting House sky collour."

Concord, Mass. Before 1842. Nineteenth-century model and architectural drawing of meetinghouse colored yellow.

Cummington, Mass. 1806. "voted to paint the meeting house anew, and to paint it white."

Danvers, Mass. 1803. "yellow stone color, with the 'cornices, weather boards, window frames and sashes' white."

Deerfield, Mass. 1769. "Body Dark stone Colour, ye Window frames white; ye Doors a Chocolate."

Deerfield, Mass. 1791. £40 "raised to paint the house"; "remembered by the old folks as being yellow, when taken down in 1824."

Douglas, Mass. 1793. Voted to have meetinghouse "colored."

Dracut, Mass. (Second Parish or Lowell). 1794.* Known in nineteenth century as the "Old Yellow Meeting House"; yellow in 1963.

Dudley, Mass. 1768. Warrant "to See if the Town will agree to Cholour the body of our meeting house"; "Voted to Cholour our meeting house with an orange Cholour."

Dunbarton, N.H. 1789. "The outside of said house to be painted with a good stone color."

Durham, N.H. 1792.* Plastered belfry arch "painted a sky color interspersed with scattered clouds."

East Hampton, L.I. 1801. Subscription circulated to paint the meetinghouse "light Red or Peach Bloe."

East Hartford, Conn. 1754. Meetinghouse "colored."

East Haven, Conn. 1748. "to Cullor the meating house claboards wit sume Cullor sutable for the house of God."

East Plymouth, Conn. (St. Matthew's Episcopal Church). 1791? "an original coat of red" under the present white.

Enfield, Mass. 1787.* Painted "a dingy sulphur color."

Exeter, N.H. 1762. "that it be painted according to custom."

Framingham, Mass. 1772. Meetinghouse built 1735, not painted until 1772.

Gardner, Mass. Circa 1788. "That the color, for the meeting-house, the ground work, to be a stone color the window frames and sashes, and weather-boards and girt, be white, the doors green."

Gilead, Conn. (Second Parish or Hebron). 1749. Society voted to paint the meetinghouse "sky color."

Gilsum, N.H. 1791. Outside to be "a Bright Orring, Only the doors . . . Stone Gray the gets and Cornishes and windows . . . white."

Goshen, Conn. 1770. "voted that the committee paint the body of the [meeting]house white, also paint the roof."

Goshen, Conn. 1771. "voted that the body of the new meeting house be made a spruce yellow."

Greenfield, N.H. 1795. Painted white; roof "Spanish Brown darkt by lamp black."

Griswold, Conn. 1767.* Meetinghouse colored; hamlet later known as "Blue Pachaug."

Groton, Mass. Circa 1800. Meetinghouse described in the beginning of the nineteenth century as "straw, trimmed with white"; traces of yellow paint under more recent white found on the late-eighteenth century steeple finial from the 1755 meetinghouse.

Guilford, Conn. 1787. Permission given "to any person or persons to color the walls of the meeting house & steeple white provided they will do it on their own cost."

Hadley, Mass. 1753. "cover the body of the meeting-house with quarter-boards and color it."

Hadley, Mass. 1771. "vote in March, 1771, to color the meeting-house. . . . It was colored."

Hampton, Conn. 1768. "to color the same [meetinghouse] something like the color of Pomfret meeting house."

Hampton, Conn. 1805. Meetinghouse to be painted "on the roof and back side red, the foreside & ends Stone yellow, the window frames white, the door & bottom boards of a chocolate color."

Hancock, N.H. 1793. "The groundwork on the outside to be white, and the roof to be Spanish brown."

Hancock, N.H. 1806. Voted to paint the meetinghouse "white."

Hancock, N.H. 1807. Vote changed to "straw color."

Hanover, Mass. 1789. Voted to paint the meetinghouse "stone yellow, the roof spanish brown, and the corner boards and window frames and sashes white."

Hanover, N.H. 1794. "the whole of the outside . . . to be painted [as] in well finished meeting houses."

Hanover, N.H. 1795. Roof of steeple "slate color"; steeple underside "white with light tinge of blue."

Harvard, Mass. 1793. "The Meeting House . . . lately painted white makes a pleasing object."

Harwich, Mass. (Second or South Parish). 1792. New meetinghouse to be painted "above the jets red"; "foreside porch, the two ends with yellow oker"; back side "red as the roof"; "the jets, corner boards, weather boards, window frames, door casings, and window sashes with white lead"; "ground boards and doors . . . of a chocolate color."

Hatfield, Mass. 1793. "entered Hatfield, whose M. House benefitted by changing a red paint for a more ornamental."

Haverhill, Mass. 1790. "Congregational Church is painted white."

Hawley, Mass. 1798. "to raise fifty pounds to paint the meeting house"; "painted yellow."

Hingham, Mass. 1682. Joshua Lincoln paid for "collering the casements and other wood-work."

Hollis, N.H. Circa 1804. Meetinghouse remembered as "painted white" when first finished.

Holliston, Mass. 1787. "outside [of the meetinghouse] to be an orange color."

Hopkinton, Mass. 1773. 1725 meetinghouse painted for the first time in 1773.

Huntington, Conn. 1783. (St. Paul's Church). "voted to pay Andrew Shelton 'four shillings a Day for . . . Colloring the Church.'"

Ipswich, Mass. 1755. Thomas Lawlor paid for "priming painting & Gilden the Inside Doars & Casing of the outside of the first parrish . . . 52½ lb of White & Stone Collor . . . 1 Gallon ½ of Boyld oyl . . . 1 quart & a pint [boiled oil] . . . 1 Do. [quart and a pint] Turpentine . . . 6½ lb of Chocolate . . . 3 pints of Boyld Oyl turpentine."

Ipswich, Mass. 1763. "steeple and house painted with white lead and oil."

Ipswich, Mass. 1764. "Dummer Jewett . . . provided white lead and oil for painting the meeting house of the First Parish in July."

Jaffrey, N.H. 1774. "the outside . . . Collored like Rindge meeting-house."

Jaffrey, N.H. 1796. "painted with a light stone color," "White lead," paid for kettles and firewood.

Keene, N.H. 1786.* "painted white, or light yellow, with green doors."

Kensington, Conn. 1789. "To paint the meeting house, the body thereof and the roof"; remembered as "dull yellow."

Kensington, N.H. 1823. Meetinghouse depicted in surveyor's drawing as yellow with bright orange doors and Spanish brown roof.

Kent, Conn. 1773. "voted that we will color the new meeting house a dark green colour."

Kent, Conn. 1790. "voted to new paint the meeting house . . . with white lead and spanish white."

Killingly, Conn. (Second, North, or Thompson Parish). 1769. "that the cullering of the body of our meeting house shall be like Pomfret, and the Roff shall be cullured Read."

Killingworth, Conn. Circa. 1770. Meetinghouse painted "peach-blossom color."

Lebanon, Conn. 1758. "to new Clapboard the west end of sd House . . . & To Collour the same with the Colour of the Tower."

Leominster, Mass. 1753. "to finish the outside of the meeting-house and to color it."

Lexington, Mass. 1794. To decide "whether it should be painted 'pea-green' or some other color."

Lexington, Mass. 1795. "The former House had two galleries, without a steeple & was painted yellow. The present House is ornamented with a Steeple, & is painted green. . . . The Sashes & Corners of the House are painted white."

Litchfield, Conn. 1772. Tax levied for "colouring the house."

Litchfield, Conn. 1790. "to paint the meeting house and the roof if the Comte think it proper."

Littleton, N.H. 1815. Meetinghouse received a "coat of white paint."

Lyme, Conn. 1817? Meetinghouse to be painted "with a bright straw color or white."

Madison, Conn. 1742. "to collour our new meeting-house a lead collour."

Malden, Mass. 1728. Contract with Aaron Cleveland "to colour the outside said House as followeth with a lead colour. Viz., the Steeple and Galleries and all the Mundillions and the fatheers Weather Boards and Window frames with the cases Troughs & Trunks with the Shells over each Door all the above mentioned particulars to be of a lead colour."

Manchester, Conn. (Orford Parish). Before 1794. "Voted, . . . the red paint covered on the front side of said house."

Mansfield, Mass. 1788. "voted to build and sell four pews in meeting-house, and with the proceeds to paint the house."

Marblehead, Mass. Well after 1715. "Externally the church was painted of a clapboard color."

Marlborough, Conn. 1789. "outside doors were painted."

Marlborough, Conn. After 1794. Meetinghouse painted "on the outside."

Mason, N.H. Circa 1795. "the outside . . . painted, the color having a slight tinge of yellow, making a straw color."

Mendon, Mass. (Second Parish). 1748. Voted to "color the Meeting House doors, window frames, weather boards, corner boards eve troughs and the two bottom boards."

Middletown, Vt. 1796. "The body of the house shall be painted white, and the roof red."

Milford, Conn. After 1728. "large, two-galleried blue church" referred to in the genealogy of Martha Beard.

Milton Green, Conn. (Litchfield Third Society). 1795.* Painted yellow, called "Old Yaller."

Monroe, N.H. Circa 1800. "yellow coat of paint"; called "Old Yellow."

Montague, Mass. 1793. "to Cullor the meeting-house the same of Sunderland."

Morris, Conn. 1785. "New meeting house shall be painted white leaving colour of door to discretion of workman."

Morris, Conn. 1794. "voted to paint the meeting house white."

Natick, Mass. 1799. Remembered in 1856 as "two stories high and painted yellow."

New Braintree, Mass. After 1772. "The [meeting] house was colored a dingy yellow."

New Britain, Conn. 1755. "Whether they would culler the Meeting House, viz: the Windows and coverings and Doors, &c. Voted in ye affirmative, Mr. Joseph Clark was chosen to procuer colering stuff and culler the Meeting house, agreeable to vote above."

New Britain, Conn. 1756. Account from Joseph Clark for "three Galons of Linset Oyle & for 24 pounds White Lead & 2 p'd of Spanish White & for 2 pounds of Spanish Brown."

New Britain, Conn. 1785. "Coller the same [meetinghouse] with a Fashenable Collor."

Newburyport, Mass. (First Society). 1820. Account for "two coats of stone color paint."

New Haven, Conn. (White Haven Society). 1761. "This Society being Senceable yt ye meeting house wants Colouring . . . if there be money Subscribed Sufficient . . . that ye Same be paid to the Society Comtt to be by them Laid out for the purposes aforesd."

New Haven, Conn. (White Haven Society). Circa 1762. "completed in 1748 and painted an azure blue."

New Haven, Conn. (White Haven Society). After 1764. Called the "Blue Meeting-house."

New Ipswich, N.H. 1812.* "originally painted cream-color . . . when . . . necessary to apply a new coat, the dirty and dismal coating of yellow ochre was put upon it. . . . It has now stood thirty-eight years."

New London, Conn. 1788. "Paint the Outside and inside twice over with such colours as the Society shall direct."

New Preston, Conn. 1771. "that we couller ye Meeting House on ye oute Side with White Lead and Oyle."

Newtown, Conn. 1762. "And ye society voted to go on and finish ye steeple and culler ye house . . . according to ye proposal."

Newtown, Conn. 1781. Committee "to procure flax seed to exchange for oil to paint the meeting house"; "new painting of ye outside of ye same [meetinghouse]."

Newtown, Conn. 1781? "that the Meeting House should be colored tan with cornice, pilasters, windows and door frames dark brown."

Norfolk, Conn. 1761. "received the coat of peach blow pink paint."

Norfolk, Conn. Circa 1770. "painted . . . with what was called a peach-blow color."

Norfolk, Conn. 1793. Meetinghouse "painted white."

Northampton, Mass. 1788. Voted to paint the meetinghouse; estimate of expenses to paint the meetinghouse: "140 gall. oil . . . 700 lbs white lead . . . 200 lbs. spruce yellow . . . 6 bb. lampblack. . . ."

Northborough, Mass. After 1744. Secondhand report: "painted a dingy yellow."

North Branford, Conn. (Zion Episcopal Church). 1827. "that a subscription paper be circulated through the Parish for the purpose of raising money to paint the Church."

North Branford, Conn. (Zion Episcopal Church). 1828. "Paid for 75 lbs. white lead & 5 gal. oil," "Paid for 40 lbs. of spanish white . . . for 2 books of gold leaf."

North Brookfield, Mass. 1756. "to color the clapboards of the same [meetinghouse]."

Northfield, Mass. 1788. Farmers' surplus flax seed exchanged in Boston for paint and oil.

Northfield, Mass. 1789. Meetinghouse "colored in the summer."

Norwalk, Conn. 1771. "to colour ye sd house."

Norwich, Conn. 1752. Entries in treasurer's accounts for "pigments, such as white lead, Spanish white, 'lamblack' and 'yellow oaker.'"

Oxford, Mass. 1792. "met Nov. 8, 1792, for the purpose of painting the meeting-house."

Oxford, Mass. 1825. "traces of a coat of yellow paint."

Pelham, Mass. 1741. Contract with Thomas and John Dick "to Paint ye Windows, Doors wether boords Trouses & Corness with Askie Coler."

Pepperell, Mass. 1769.* Called "a plain yellow building with belfry and two porches."
Petersham, Mass. 1738. Thomas Dick paid "for coloring the meeting-house."
Pomfret, Conn. 1762. "voted that the new meeting-house should be colored on the outside of an orange color—the doors and bottom boards of a chocolate color—windows, jets, corner boards and weather boards, colored white."
Pomfret, Conn. 1773. "Voted to new color the meeting house."
Princeton, Mass. 1770. "to paint the meeting house, provided Mr. Moses Gill finds paint."
Providence, R.I. (First Baptist Church). 1774 "paint the roof with Tar & Spannish Brown."
Reading, Mass. (Wakefield). 1768. Voted "not to paint the clapboards, or do the roof with rosin, tar, and pitch."
Rehoboth, Mass. (Second Parish). 1773.* Called the "Yellow Meeting House."
Rindge, N.H. 1773. "voted to cover the wooden shingles of their meeting house roof with pitch and sand."
Rindge, N.H. Before 1839. Watercolor map shows yellow meetinghouse (built in 1796) with red roof.
Rowe, Mass. 1793.* Voted for "cream color with red roof and green doors."
Rowe, Mass. 1814. "Voted to paint the body a French Yellow, the roof a chocolate Colour."
Rowley, Mass. 1764. £8 set aside for "painting the Windows, Doors, Covers, Corner Boards, Wash boards & Spouts of the Meetinghouse."
Rowley, Mass. (Second Parish or Georgetown). 1744. Samuel Harriman paid £20 for "Redding the meeting-house."
Roxbury, Conn. 1794. "voted to give its new building three coats of paint: white on the building's facades and red on the roof."
Sanbornton, N.H. 1796. Voted "to . . . paint the Rough."
Sanbornton, N.H. 1797. Voted "to clapboard and paint the meeting-house this year."
Sandown, N.H. 1774. "To color the meeting house the color of Chester meeting house."
Scituate, Mass. 1774.* "body . . . a 'Dark Stone Color, roof red and Doors a Chocolate Colour,' with white trim."
Shirley, Mass. 1795. "the Meeting house . . . beautifully painted white on the sides & even over the roof. The doors were green."
Shrewsbury, Mass. 1766.* Remembered as yellow; lowest layer of paint from a window cornice dentil analyzed as ochre in 1978.
Shrewsbury, Mass. 1808. "to paint & . . . Repair the Meeting house": To 29½ Gal. of Linseed Oil . . . 32 Gal. Of fish Oil . . . 2–3 grs of white lead . . . 20 wt. of Spruce Yellow, & small paints . . . William Rice Acct. of Painting & graining doors."
Simsbury, Conn. 1782. "to Couler the Meeting House & that the Couler shall be White."
Springfield, Mass. 1678. John Gilbert paid for "Pining the Casemts . . . & for 2 quts of oile."
Stockbridge, Mass. 1784.* "house was white without."
Sullivan, N.H. 1822. "paint the meeting house like the one in Keene": "yellowish tint with white trimmings."
Surry, N.H. 1789. "the outside of said Meeting house is to be glaised and painted like Keene meetinghouse."
Temple, N.H. 1781. "To colour ye Meeting-house, in its several parts, agreeable to Wilton meeting-house colours, or as near as may be."
Templeton, Mass. 1792. Voted to paint it for the first time "of the color of Leominster."
Tewksbury, Mass. 1741. "to clapboard the sides . . . collering the window with Spanish Brown."

Tewksbury, Mass. 1791. "voted to repaint the meeting house and to inquire of the painter what 'coller is the most durable to paint the meeting-house' . . . proved to be stone color."

Topsfield, Mass. 1721. "The Town allowed Natl Capen 9s–6d for work iron and oyl & Spanish Brown to sit up the meeting house vein."

Topsfield, Mass. 1732. "The Town allowed four pounds Nine shillings to Ens Ivory Hovey for work done by Nathan Hood on ye Meeting house & for oyl, Nails & Spanish brown in 1732."

Topsham, Maine. (First Baptist). 1795.* Known as "Old Yellow Meeting-House."

Townsend, Mass. 1771. "the window, and door frames, and the doors, were painted on the outside during the summer of 1771"; paint analysis from clapboarding in 1978 revealed dirty orange or dark yellow under twelve layers of whites and creams.

Troy, N.H. 1779. "to finish Cleapboording the meeting house and colour it."

Troy, N.H. 1814.* "painted on the outside at least."

Trumbull, Conn. 1773. "coller the outside and finish the inside of said meeting-house."

Tyngsborough, Mass. 1797. "It [the meetinghouse] is painted white."

Wallingford, Conn. (New Cheshire Parish). 1735.* "it was agreed to put on a good handsome painte on ye meeting-house: in order to preserve ye same from ye wether."

Walpole, Mass. 1783. "to paint the outside of the meeting house 'Except the Roof.'"

Walpole, N.H. 1789. "painted its meetinghouse 'straw color.'"

Washington, N.H. 1794. "the walls the colour of Alsted Meetinghouse [red ochre?] & the roof Spanish brown."

Watertown, Mass. 1721. Paid George Adams 2½ days' work and "for oile and Spanish Brown."

Wells, Maine (Second Parish). 1804. "Exterior of the house and steeple was painted a dark yellow."

Westborough, Mass. (First Precinct). 1754. Precinct refused to "culler the outside of the meeting-house."

Westbrook, Conn. 1763. "to paint the clapboards sky colour, and the doors and sash white."

Westford, Mass. 1793. "Voted to Culler the meeting-house this season and make it neer the Culler of Chelmsford meeting-house. Voted the ruf of the meeting house be tard or Cullered as the Committee think best"; "The Meeting House soon presented, painted white."

West Tisbury, Mass. 1769. Painted "with Tarr and Oker to Preserve the Shingles."

West Woodstock, Conn. (New Roxbury Society). 1791. Roof to be painted "Spanish Brown" and "the sides and ends with a stone color so called."

Wilmington, Mass. 1765. "When it was finished, in 1765, . . . painted in light yellow."

Wilton, Conn. 1801. Voted to paint the exterior "yellow ochre and the roof Spanish brown"; vote rescinded and white chosen.

Wilton, N.H. 1773.* "Nineteenth-century meetinghouse model painted dirty-yellow or ochre with white trim."

Winchendon, Mass. 1802. "to paint the meeting-house, next season, a bright stone color."

Windham, Conn. 1762. "at Pomfret and Windham . . . painted a brilliant yellow"; "the orange or bright yellow of Pomfret, Windham, and Killingly."

Wolcott, Conn. 1794. "that the body of the house be painted white and the roof red."

Woodbury, Conn. 1789. Meetinghouse to be painted "up to the square . . . the same color it was before."

Woodbury, Conn. 1790. "that the color of the meeting house be near the color of Mr. Timy Tomlinsons except it be a little more greenish as it."

Woodstock, Conn. 1790. Meeting warned to vote if they would "also new color the outside."

Woodstock, Conn. 1795. Money from sale and rent of pews allocated "for the expense of Painting the Meeting House white"; roof to be painted also.

Woodstock, Conn. 1821. "to paint the meeting house white to prime with French Yellow & boiled oil; also to paint the roof."

Woodstock, Vt. 1808. "painted outside and within . . . the outside of the body of the house being painted white"; called the "White Meeting House" or the "Old White."

Wrentham, Mass. 1766.* "a large wooden building painted yellow."

Yarmouth, Mass. 1768. "lower room of the porch . . . to be sealed with planed boards, and the doors to be with handsome wainscot work, and colored in chocolate color."

APPENDIX F

# Citations of interior painting, 1656–1817

When the coloring date is unknown, the date of the meetinghouse is given and indicated with an asterisk (*).

Abington, Conn. 1802. Pulpit and architraves painted a mustard color; red paint on interior woodwork; trompe l'oeil window lights.

Amesbury, Mass. (West Salisbury, Rocky Hill) (survival). 1784.* Whitish green; pillars and pulpit window marbleized with blue.

Andover (South or Second Parish). 1793. Bentley: Inscribed over the pulpit, "Holiness becomes thy house O Lord, Forever"; "I. H. S." painted on the front of the pulpit.

Arlington, Mass. 1775. In 1813 Bentley remembered that during the British occupation of Boston the pulpit of the first meetinghouse was painted "of a chocolate colour."

Arlington, Mass. 1795. Voted to paint "the inside a stone color."

Barkhamsted, Conn. 1784.* Pulpit and gallery front blue or lead colored paint.

Barnstead Parade, N.H. 1799. "The sounding board was like the pulpit, a clay color."

Bedford, N.H. 1767. Paint pulpit "the same color as Rev. Mr. McGregor's pulpit is, in Londonderry."

Berlin, Mass. Circa 1787. Pineapple finial, probably from 1787 pulpit, repainted green and gold in 1955.

Beverly, Mass. 1770.* Stair baluster painted gray-white.

Bluehill, Maine. 1798. "Voted, that the Pulpit pillars, posts and front of the Gallery be painted."

Boston (King's Chapel). 1713. "Voted that the Pillers, Capitalls, and Cornish of the Church be painted wainscott Colur."

Boston (Christ Church). 1727. Ropes painted "supporting the brass branches or chandeliers, — 'prussian blue picked in with vermillion'"; cherubs' heads and "fusthoons" on the panels; "painting and gilding of the tables of the law."

Boston (Christ Church). 1736. Backdrop of the organ loft "bright red," gilding.

Bradford, Mass. 1793. Bentley: gold lettering over the pulpit, "O worship the Lord in the beauty of holiness."

Branford, Conn. 1746. "Coulering ye inside of ye meeting house."

Branford, Conn. 1797. Painted or whitewashed inside and out.

Bridgewater, Mass. (South Parish). 1773. Voted to paint "the canopy, pulpit, the front work of the galleries, the pillars under the galleries, the posts and braces."

Brooklyn, Conn. 1772. Voted "to leave it with the Society and Building Committees, with the Painter to ditermine what colour the insid of the Meeting-house and Pulpit shall be."

Burrillville, R.I. 1770?* Probably painted in early nineteenth century. Above the pulpit "a painting representing cherubim, but a most rude and shabby daub."

Chatham, Mass. 1773. "The Pulpit and frunt of the Gallers and the Sids all with Stone Couller."

Chelmsford, Mass. 1793. Bentley: pulpit and gallery fronts painted, gilding below pulpit panels in "chinese work."

Concord, Mass. Circa 1744. Flame finial, painted gold and red with a blue base from the sounding board of the 1711 meetinghouse.

Deerfield, Mass. 1729.* Pulpit and canopy painted "a dark olive-green."

Dorchester, Mass. Circa 1750. Finial probably from the 1743 meetinghouse, painted gray.

East Hampton, L.I. 1756. Molding with vine-and-grape motif and carved pilaster capital painted with red, black, yellow, and green colors from the 1756 pulpit.

Fairfield, Conn. 1785. Pulpit painted "light stone color."

Gilead, Conn. 1761. Pulpit, breastwork, canopy, pillars "light red slightly striped with white."

Gilsum, N.H. 1791. "Inside to Be a Stone Gray only the Canopy to Be a Prussian Blue."

Greenwich, Conn. (Second Parish). 1716.* Pulpit "bluish color."

Hadley, Mass. 1739. "color the facing of the gallery"; "M. R. H." [March] 1739" on the canopy.

Hanover, N.H. 1794. Voted, "so much of the inside as is usual to be painted in well finished meeting houses."

Harpswell, Maine. 1757.* Dark green pulpit said to be original color.

Harwich, Mass. (Second or South). 1792.* Recollection: Pulpit and desk "rich sea green"; deacons' seat "Dark Spanish Brown."

Hatfield, Mass. 1755. Casings of timbers in the meetinghouse to be "decently colored."

Hatfield, Mass. 1750.* Possibly painted after 1779 or 1793; building survived until 1982. Canopy and probably the pulpit: robin's egg blue.

Haverhill, Mass. 1734.* Nineteenth-century reminiscence: Faces of two cherubs (one with blue eyes, the other with brown) painted on either side of the pulpit window.

Henniker, N.H. 1787.* Gilt acorn finial from the sounding board.

Hingham, Mass. 1682. Joshua Lincoln (1645–1694) paid for "Collering the the casements and other wood-work."

Hingham, Mass. (Old Ship). Circa 1720 to 1730. Red sponge painting on whitewashed posts.

Holliston, Mass. 1787. The inside to be a "stone color."

Holland, Mass. 1794. "brest work pillers and Pulpit, to be coulloured a good hansome pee green."

Ipswich, Mass. (South Parish). 1747. "unpretentious pine pulpit, painted white, at the north end."

Ipswich, Mass. (First Parish). 1749. Surviving pulpit painted mahogany grain.

Ipswich, Mass. (First Parish). 1755. "Painting & Gilding the inside doors & Casing of the outside" (white, stone color, chocolate) by Thomas Lawlor.

Ipswich, Mass. (First Parish). 1756. Richard Manning paid to gild the baptismal basin and the hourglass.

Ipswich, Mass. (First Parish). 1767. "Mr. Knowlton was paid for 'painting the canopy.'"

Kensington, Conn. 1793. To "give liberty to have the meeting house painted withinside ... provided it be done without charge to the society."

Killingly, Conn. (Second, North, or Thompson Parish). 1817. Trompe l'oeil painting under pulpit of a "stairway partly veiled with crimson drapery," by Harvey Dresser (1789? –1835).

Leicester, Mass. 1784.* Pulpit and columns "painted in ... pointed block-work of shaded marble."

Lempster, N.H. Circa 1795. Surviving pulpit window casing painted light greenish-gray over light blue.

Lexington, Mass. 1763. "to coulior ye meeting house att ye back of the Pulpit the same coulior the Pulpit is coulioured."

Lexington, Mass. 1795. Bentley: "House within is of a light stone colour."

Litchfield, Conn. Circa 1762. Two pilaster capitals with rose motif, painted or dyed red; fragment of carved vine from the pulpit of the 1762 meetinghouse.

Litchfield, Conn. 19th century reminiscence; Harriet Beecher Stowe: "How did I wonder at the panels on either side of the pulpit [ca. 1762], in each of which was carved and painted a flaming red tulip...."

Loudon, N.H. 1797. "pulpit and surrounding were painted of a lead color ... tables ... dark brown"; top of interior posts in the lower part painted with figures "1797."

Malden, Mass. 1728. Contract with Aaron Cleveland: "also to lath and plaister all over head and under each Gallery and Whitewash all the plaistering."

Marblehead, Mass. After 1780. Below the canopy a "frieze ... on which a blue or black ground were 13 gilt stars."

Marlborough, Conn. 1789. "inside of the house and the outside doors were painted."

Medfield, Mass. After 1655. Surviving decorative pulpit insets have "traces of verdigris coloring."

Middletown, Vt. 1794. Canopy, turned pillars under the galleries, and breastwork "shall be painted blue."

Newbury, Mass. (Second Parish or West Newbury). 1759.* Canopy's lower "panel work painted white"; upper part of canopy "colored blue ... with gilt finial, acorn-shaped."

Newbury, Vt. 1790.* Reminiscence: "The sounding board with the ornament on its top decorated with red white and blue and gold stripes."

Newburyport, Mass. (St. Paul's). 1801. Bentley: "On the front Gallery there is a tribute of respect to Timothy Dexter.... Over the altar & above the bread & Commandments is a spread eagle holding the Bible & the Common Prayer.... Walls as high as the Arch are covered with paper & painted blue"; pews, "faint green with caps of orange colour. The arches are pure white as are the paintings of the gallery."

New Haven, Conn. 1761. "ye Pulpit to be finished & Coloured, and the breast work of ye gallery, and Pillars to be Coloured ... if there be money."

New Ipswich, N.H. 1770. Vote to paint the interior; gallery breastwork, cornice, and posts "poppy-red and grained in imitation of marble or mahogany ... curious gilded canopy."

New London, Conn. 1788. "Paint the Outside and inside twice over with such colours as the Society shall direct except the ceiling under the windows the inside of the pews below and above."

Newmarket, N.H. (East and West Societies, Newfields). 1792. Written in gilt letters on a black ground: "O Thou that hearest prayer / Unto thee shall all flesh Come. Ps. LXV.2 / 1792."

Newport, N.H. (Baptist) 1810. "elevated pulpit, sky blue in color."

Newtown, Conn. 1762. "ye society voted to go on and finish ye steeple and culler ye house and ye pulpit according to ye proposal."

Newtown, Conn. 1786. Pews to be "painted a proper color for the inside of such a building."

Northampton, Mass. 1735. "1735" written on the sounding board.

Portsmouth, N.H. 1806. "walls and ceilings tinted with indigo blue wash; the seats painted green; and the high pulpit decorated with splendid crimson silk draperies."

Providence, Mass. 1796.* Reminiscence: "it is said that back of the pulpit there were some paintings 'supposed to represent angel faces,' and over the window caps on each side, was a figure, of a cherub perhaps."

Providence, R.I. (First Baptist) 1775.* Surviving interior wood fragment painted grayish-green.

Rowe, Mass. 1814. "Voted to paint . . . the inside a Light Blue."

Rowley, Mass. (Second Parish or Georgetown). 1744. "to paint the pulpit."

Sandown, N.H. 1773.* Survival: Pulpit and gallery front, "cedar-grained"; "Two sets of pilasters on the pulpit and the columns which support the galleries are veined in dark blue on an oyster white ground."

Shirley, Mass. (Shaker) 1795. Bentley: "Within the wood work is painted of a deep blue, & the seats are of a chocolate colour."

Shrewsbury, Mass. 1766.* Canopy finial base dark green, leaves dark and light green, inside leaves white, red interior; underside rosette from canopy has red petals, green pointed leaves, gold background, white and gray circles.

Southington, Conn. Circa 1757. Surviving pulpit base painted yellowish brown.

Springfield, Mass. 1677. John Gilbert paid to paint window casements.

Sterling, Mass. Circa 1800. Two angels painted on wall behind pulpit, singing "Glory to God in the highest" and "On earth peace and goo[d] will to men."

Stockbridge, Mass. 1784.* "unpainted," except high pew, pulpit and canopy.

Sullivan, N.H. 1807.* Pulpit front, the stairs, balustrade, gallery fronts, and supporting columns "light blue."

Sutton (North), N.H. 1795.* Meetinghouse completed about 1797. Gallery pillars, front of gallery, Communion table, deacons' seat, pulpit and sounding board "brilliant green"; walls white.

Swanzey, N.H. 1796.* "Representations of seraphs or angelic beings" painted on the wall above the pulpit.

Topsfield, Mass. 1703. "The Town agreed to allow Mr Capen; one Pound & 6 shillings for varnishing the Pulpit."

Topsfield, Mass. 1729. "The Town Allowed to Nathll Capen five shillings for Cullouring the pulpit before Ordination of Mr Emerson."

Wells, Maine. (Second Parish). 1774.* "The front part of the galleries was painted . . . the pulpit . . . the deacon's seat, just under it . . . and the pew of Dimon Hubbard."

Westborough, Mass. (First Precinct). 1754. Refused to paint the breastwork of the galleries; voted to paint the pulpit.

Westfield, Mass. 1697. Repair and paint gallery: "comely and comfortable."

Weymouth, Mass. (South). 1785. Inside: girts, posts, plate, gallery front, pulpit, sounding board, and window picked out in lead color; sashes white, ceiling plaster and walls whitewashed.

Wilmington, Mass. 1766. "to paint the breast-works of the galleries, the pillars and the pulpit."

Wilmington, Mass. 1767. Second vote to paint the gallery breastwork, pillars, and pulpit; between 1767 and 1813. Interior the "dull red of old mahogany"; pulpit "nicely grained in imitation of mahogany"; "sounding-board . . . a very light red."

Winchendon, Mass. 1793. "paint the outside [of the pulpit] green."

Windham, Conn. (Second Society or Canada). 1753.* "Holiness unto the Lord" inscribed on the sounding board.

Worcester, Mass. 1733. "that the front of the gallery, the pulpit, and pillars, be colored and varnished."

Yarmouth, Mass. Enlarged 1768. Sounding board to be "colored with a fashionable color, with a deacon seat and communion table . . . colored fashionably also, and they are to be in the form and fashion as Barnstable East Precinct have their's in."

APPENDIX G

# Meetinghouse replications in New England, 1647–1828

Listed chronologically by town or parish vote to copy the dimensions, design features, or colors of their own or other meetinghouses.

Date in parentheses indicates construction date of the prototype.

Measure of miles indicates distance to prototype in another community (0 indicates that the prototype is within the community).

1647 Wethersfield, Conn. Seats to have wainscot "according to the seats [in the] Hartford Meeting House" (1638): 5 miles. Kelly, *Early Connecticut Meetinghouses*, 2:287.

1651 New London, Conn. Meetinghouse to be "about the same demention of Mr. Parke's his barne": 1 mile. Caulkins, *History of New London*, 9.

1654 Sudbury, Mass. "to appoint a man to remove the pulpit and the deacons' seat out of the old meeting house into the new" (1642); "to build seats after the same fashion as in the old meeting house" (1642): 0. Hudson, *History of Sudbury*, 190.

1654 Watertown, Mass. "Cambridge meeting house shall be our pattern in all poynts" (1651): 4 miles. Watertown Records, 14 August 1654, 2:37.

1659 Rehoboth, Mass. Enlargement to be "shingled as well as Goodman Payne's house": 1 mile. Newman, *Rehoboth in the Past*, 17.

1672 Westfield, Mass. "for form like the Hatfield meeting house" (1668): 20 miles. *History of the Connecticut Valley*, 384.

1678 Norwalk, Conn. Roof "to be built after the manner of Faierfield meeting house" (1668): 9 miles. Hall, *Ancient Historical Records*, 71.

1679 Ipswich, Mass. (Second Parish or Essex). Turret to be built "after the fashion, and in proportions of the turret in Andover" (1661): 24 miles. Crowell, *History of Essex*, 84.

1680 Hingham, Mass. Three men "to view some other meeting houses in some other Townes . . . they may better inform themselves . . . how big a house may be suteable": within 10 miles. Hingham Town Meeting Records, 2:93, courtesy of Robert B. St. George.

1681 Norwalk, Conn. To remove the "deske, and seates, and plankes of the ould meeting house [1659] to the new": 0. Hall, *Ancient Historical Records of Norwalk*, 76.

1684 Windsor, Conn. "the form of the house according to the Meeting House at Springfield" (1677): 19 miles. Kelly, *Early Connecticut Meetinghouses*, 2:305.

1686 Sudbury, Mass. "to erect a meeting-house, just like the new one in Dedham" (1673): 15 miles. Drake, *History of Middlesex County*, 2:468.

1688 Sudbury, Mass. To follow "in all respects for dimentions, strength, shape . . . and conveniences, as Dedham" (1673): 15 miles. Hudson, *History of Sudbury*, 265; Hudson, *Annals*, 47.

1689 Marlborough, Mass. Its old meetinghouse and pulpit "were improved in the meetinghouse, for carrying on the finishing of that" (1677): 0. Hudson, *History of the Town of Marlborough*, 88.

1692 Manchester, Mass. "roof . . . to be of the same form of Beverly [1682] or Wenham [1663]": 7 miles (Beverly); 8 miles (Wenham). *Early Records of the Town of Manchester*, 44–45.

1693 Billerica, Mass. Reading to be "the pattern in most respects" (1689): 13 miles. Hazen, *History of Billerica*, 168.

1694 Deerfield, Mass. Meetinghouse to be "ye bigness of Hatfield" (1668): 11 miles. Sheldon, *History of Deerfield*, 1:202.

1695 Rowley, Mass. Committee to view Wenham (1663) and Beverly (1682) and report on size: 10 miles (Wenham); 13 miles (Beverly). Jewett and Jewett, *Rowley, Massachusetts*, 106.

1696 Deerfield, Mass. Seating to follow "ye present modell of Hatfield Meeting House Seats" (1668): 11 miles. Sheldon, *History of Deerfield*, 1:203.

1696 Haverhill, Mass. "to look and view some meeting houses for dimensions"; July report: "seats, pulpit, galleries, windows, doors, floors and stairs" to be like those in Beverly (1682): 22 miles; sides to be modeled after those of meetinghouse in Reading (1689): 22 miles. Hurd, *History of Essex County*, 1947–48.

1699 Boxford, Mass. Pulpit to be "as good as Topsfield's" (1663): 3 miles; pews "to be set as in Andover" (1669): 11 miles. Perley, *History of Boxford*, 127.

1701 Newbury, Mass. Canopy of "old pulpit given by the town to the west part of Newbury for their pulpit" (1661): 9 miles. Coffin, *A Sketch of the History of Newbury*, 168.

1701 West Tisbury, Mass. "a new meeting-house after the manner and dementions of the meeting-house in Chilmark" (ca. 1690): 14 miles. Banks, *History of Martha's Vineyard*, 2:46, 78.

1702 Topsfield, Mass. "ye Town did agree yt ye seats shall be plased after ye maner as thay be placed in Rowley meeting house and ye five seates before ye Pulpit is to be sixteen foot long" (1697): 8 miles. Dow, *Town Records of Topsfield*, 1:119.

1703 Springfield, Mass. (Second or West Parish). "that the Meeting-House be seated In form according to the moddle of the east side Meeting-House, proportionate according to the room" (1677): 5 miles. *History of the Connecticut Valley*, 907.

1703 Topsfield, Mass. "that the new Meeting House should be Seated after the maner as Ipswich new meeting House is seated leavening no room for Puese except Mr Capens Pue" (1699): 7 miles. Dow, *Town Records of Topsfield*, 1:129.

1707 Narragansett, R.I. (St. Paul's Church). Meetinghouse to resemble first King's Chapel (Boston) according to "contract" (1688): 72 miles. Dorsey, *Early English Churches in America*, 166.

1711 Andover, Mass. (North Parish). "ye old pulpit in the North Precinct shall be set in our new meeting-house" (1669): 0. Bailey, *Historical Sketches of Andover*, 430.

1711 Andover, Mass. (North Precinct). "ye model of ye seats to be like Bradford" (1706): 9 miles; meetinghouse to have "a Roofe like Salem-village" (Danvers) (1701): 12 miles. Bailey, *Historical Sketches of Andover*, 430.

1713 Brookline, Mass. To have the same dimensions as meetinghouse in Roxbury (1674): 3 miles. Hurd, *History of Norfolk County*, 807.

1713 East Windsor, Conn. "roof of the new meeting house shall be as this is" (1695): 0. Stiles, *History of Ancient Windsor*, 1:232.

1713 Lexington, Mass. To build meetinghouse "on the plan of the one at Concord" (1711): 6 miles. Hudson, *History of Lexington*, 57.

1714 Middletown Upper Houses, Conn. (North or Cromwell Parish). To finish the meetinghouse "after same manner the meeting house in South Society, that is the two ends of it" (Middletown [First], 1679): 3 miles. Adams, *Middletown Upper Houses*, 31.

1715 Framingham, Mass. Roof to be "the same form and workmanship" as that in Marlborough (1688): 8 miles; "a good floor, a table, and . . . seats . . . as in Sudbury meeting house" (1688): 7 miles. Temple, *History of Framingham*, 144–45.

1717 Norwich, Conn. (West Farms or Franklin). To use Norwich pews, pulpit, galleries, and other woodwork (1673): 7 miles. Kelly, *Early Connecticut Meetinghouses*, 2:111.

1717 Wallingford, Conn. Meetinghouse "form to be like Gilford meeting house" (1712): 17 miles. Perkins, *Historical Sketches of Meriden*, 34.

1718 Northfield, Mass. Meetinghouse to "be of the dimensions of Swamfield (Sunderland)" (1717): 21 miles. Temple and Sheldon, *History of Northfield*, 147.

1719 Durham, N.H. Frame and belfry "being in figure" like those of the new meetinghouse in Hampton (1715): 19 miles. Stackpole and Thompson, *History of Durham*, 1:173.

1719 East Haven, Conn. "the pulpit and seats shall be in the form of Branford meeting house" (1699): 5 miles. Havens, *Stone Meeting House*, 21.

1720 Kensington, Conn. Galleries to be finished like those in Farmington (1709): 8 miles. Kelly, *Early Connecticut Meetinghouses*, 1:243.

1721 Amesbury, Mass. (Second, East, or Jamaco Parish). Meetinghouse to have same dimensions as Amesbury (1715): 3 miles. Merrill, *History of Amesbury*, 175.

1721 Watertown, Mass. (West Parish). To purchase, move, and rebuild Newton's meetinghouse (1697): 4 miles. *Records of the West Precinct of Watertown*, 18.

1725 Sudbury, Mass. (Wayland). Committee to "make it as near as they can like the new house in the West Precinct [Sudbury, Second Parish]" and have same number of pews but "handsomer" steps (1724): 4 miles. Drake, *History of Middlesex County*, 2:469.

1726 Guilford, Conn. To copy "Fashion and proportion of the Belfry & Spire at [Trinity Church, Newport] Rhode Island" (1725): 80 miles; 1724 bell like that of "Mr. Colman's meeting house in Boston" (1716): 129 miles. Belfry and spire: Kelly, *Early Connecticut Meetinghouses*, 1:172; Bell: Steiner, *History of the Plantation of Menunkatuck*, 275.

1729 Killingly, Conn. (Second, North, or Thompson Parish), "make Woodstock meetinghouse their pattern to go by" (1720): 7 miles. Larned, *History of Windham County*, 1:310.

1730 Chatham, Mass. Dimensions the same as those of "the south meeting house in Eastham" (1723): 12 miles. Smith, *History of Chatham*, 270.

1731 Killingly, Conn. (Second, North, or Thompson Parish). "Body of seats . . . after the form" of those in Woodstock (1720): 7 miles. Larned, *History of Windham County*, 1:316.

1731 Sturbridge, Mass. "to be finished according to articles drawn to finish the meeting house at Hassanamisco [Grafton]" (1730): 24 miles. *History of Worcester County*, 2:364.

1734 Andover, Mass. (Second or South Parish). To build new meetinghouse "after the same form and fashion as the old" (1709): 0. Bailey, *Historical Sketches of Andover*, 442.

1734 Killingly, Conn. (Second, North, or Thompson Parish). To build seats in the gallery after "ye form of Woodstock seats in their Gallery" (1720): 7 miles. Larned, *History of Windham County,* 1:317.

1735 Tewksbury, Mass. Committee "to view Andover [South Parish] old meeting-house frame" (1709): 6 miles. Pride, *Tewksbury: A Short History,* 17.

1736 Boscawen, N.H. Meetinghouse to have same width as Rumford, but "two feet. Higher . . . of logs" [Concord] (1727): 7 miles. Walker, *First Congregational Society, Concord,* viii.

1737 Columbia, Conn. (Second Parish in Lebanon or Lebanon Crank). Voted to follow "the rule by which . . . Old Society" sings: 5 miles. *One Hundred and Fiftieth Anniversary of the Organization of the Congregational Church in Columbia,* 49.

1738 Becket, Mass. Meetinghouse (built 1761) to be finished "as well as the Meeting House in Grafton" (1730): 87 miles. Archer, *Bicentennial History of Becket,* 35.

1739 Killingworth, Conn. (Second Society or Killingworth Farms). Posts "two feet shorter than those in the First Society" (1730): 5 miles. Kelly, *Early Connecticut Meetinghouses,* 1:249.

1741 Wilton, Conn. (Second Parish in Norwalk). Meetinghouse to be finished on the "former model" of First Parish in Norwalk (1723): 7 miles. Kelly, *Early Connecticut Meetinghouses,* 2:298.

1743 Killingworth, Conn. (Second Society or Killingworth Farms). The seats and pews to be "dignified by the same rules" as East Guilford (Madison) (1737): 4 miles. Kelly, *Early Connecticut Meetinghouses,*1:249.

1743 Pelham, Mass. Glass and pulpit and canopy to be the same as that in Harvard (1732): 50 miles; pulpit to be in "Dignitee like unto Hadley third precinct" (1738): 7 miles. Parmenter, *History of Pelham,* 79.

1747 Ipswich, Mass. (South Parish). Drew on one of Boston's "artificers in building a pulpit" (1747): 28 miles. Kimball, *Last Sermon Preached,* 10–11.

1749 Abington, Conn. To have "the same dimensions as that of Pomfret" (1714): 4 miles; to build seats "after the form" of Woodstock (1720): 7 miles. Dimensions: Kelly, *Early Connecticut Meetinghouses,* 1:5; form: Larned, *History of Windham County,* 1:316.

1749 Berwick, Maine (North Parish). Meetinghouse to be "the same size" as Berwick South Parish (1702): 8 miles. Mitchell and Campbell, *Berwick Register,* 50.

1749 Woodstock, Conn. (Second Parish). "Build the two fore-seats like those in the first parish . . . and have as many pews as in the first parish" (1720): 4 miles. Larned, *History of Windham County,* 1:498.

1752 Windsor Conn. (Scantic or North Parish). Meetinghouse to have "same length and breadth" as Second Parish in Windsor (East Windsor) (1714): 3 miles. Stiles, *History of Ancient Windsor,* 2:295.

1753 Manchester, Mass. Steeple to be "near the forme of Gloucester New Meeting House" (1752): 7 miles. *Early Records of Manchester,* 65.

1753 Springfield, Mass. (Fifth or Chicopee Parish). "'seat men and women together' as in the new Meeting House in Springfield" (1752 for seating): 4 miles. Quotation from Palmer, *Annals of Chicopee Street,* 36; Green, *Springfield, 1636–1886,* 259.

1756 Nottingham, N.H. "all pews shall be built in the same manner in fassion and workmanship" as Epping (1741): 6 miles. Cogswell, *History of Nottingham,* 117–18.

1757 Dover, N.H. "a plan of Berwick [Maine] lower meeting house . . . be accepted" (1750): 5 miles. Wadleigh, *Notable Events in the History of Dover,* 147.

1760 Falmouth, Maine. Spire to be "copied from the one at York" (1747): 50 miles. Goold, *Portland in the Past,* 289.

1761 Bridgewater, Mass. (Fourth or North Parish). Pews to be sold according to the layout of those of South Parish in Bridgewater (1759); meetinghouse to have "the same Demenshons of the South Meeting House, in Bridgewater": 5 miles. Hurd, *History of Plymouth County*, 565.

1764 Bethlem, Conn. Meetinghouse to be "just as high as ye Meeting House in ye old Society" in Woodbury (1747): 8 miles. Cothren, *History of Ancient Woodbury*, 1:248.

1764 Holland, Mass. Meetinghouse to be the "same [dimensions] as Wales" (1764): 5 miles. *History of the Connecticut Valley*, 1104.

1765 Southbury, Conn. (Second Parish in Woodbury). "that we will build the house according to the Demensions of Litchfield present Meeting House in bigness and Form" (1762): 19 miles. Warren, "The First Two Southbury Meeting Houses, Part 2," 25.

1766 Boston. New Brick Church. Deacons' seat "as lately been done at Mr. Cooper's and Old North churches" (about 1764): 1 mile. Robbins, *History of the Second Church in Boston*, 316.

1767 Bedford, N.H. Pulpit to be painted "same color the Rev. Mr. McGregor's ... in Londonderry" (1721): 16 miles. *History of Bedford*, 328.

1767 Deerfield, Mass. "Erect a Steeple ... in the same proportion as the Steeple of Northfield Meeting house is to the body of that house" (1762): 16 miles. Sheldon, *History of Deerfield*, 1:474.

1767 Dunstable, Mass. "Build the pulpit like that in Pepril" (1745): 6 miles. Nason, *History of Dunstable*, 104.

1767 South Britain, Conn. (Parish in Southbury). "in length & heath & breadth of Roxbury [Conn.] Meating House" (1745): 8 miles. Kelly, *Early Connecticut Meetinghouses*, 2:201.

1767 Stratham, N.H. Meetinghouse to be "finished much after the same manner as Greenland" (1756): 5 miles. Nelson, *History of Stratham*, 247.

1767 Watertown, Mass. (West Parish or Waltham). "Interior finish ... like that of Watertown" (1723): 4 miles; "arrangement of the interior" like that of Roxbury (1746): 7 miles. Sanderson, *Waltham as a Precinct of Watertown*, 53.

1768 Ashford, Conn. Pews to be "as like the pews in the meeting house at Union" (1739): 11 miles. Larned, *History of Windham County*, 2:25.

1768 Hampton, Conn. Meetinghouse to be "something like the color" of Pomfret (painted 1762): 11 miles. Bayles, *History of Windham County*, 384.

1768 Salisbury, N.H. Meetinghouse to have "the same bigness" as Second Parish in Kingston (1738): 55 miles; "the pulpit to be of the same size as the one at Hawke [Danville]" (1755): 50 miles. Dearborn, *History of Salisbury*, 132.

1768 Yarmouth, Mass. "a new sounding-board, with iron-work thereto that is needful and fashionable, and colored a fashionable color, with a deacon seat and communion table, they being fashionable and colored fashionably also, and they are to be in the same form and fashion as Barnstable East Precinct have their's in." (1756): 3 miles. Dodge, *History of the First Congregational Church, Yarmouth*, 33.

1769 Killingly, Conn. (Second, North, or Thompson Parish). "that the cullering of the body of our meeting house should be like Pomfret" (1762): 8 miles. Larned, *History of Windham County*, 2:81.

1770 Westford, Mass. To "build the pews ... and seats and alleys ... as they are in Medford" (1769): 22 miles. Hodgman, *History of Westford*, 100.

1771 Amherst, N.H. To follow plan of Old North meetinghouse in Concord (1751): 31 miles. Locke, *Colonial Amherst*, 18.

1771 Brookline, Mass. Steeple "not higher than Doctor Boyles Steeple is" on Hollis Street meetinghouse in Boston (1731): 5 miles. *Muddy River and Brookline Records*, 231.

1771 Kensington, N.H. To build "as near as may be after the pattern of the North-Hill [North Hampton] Meeting House" (1761): 10 miles. Sawyer, *History of Kensington*, 157.

1772 Francestown, N.H. "sat up ye frame as Long and Good as Lyn Borough [Lyndeborough]" (1772): 9 miles. Cochrane, *History of Francestown*, 46.

1772 Goffstown, N.H. "pulpit to be built as well as that in the church at Atkinson" (1769): 30 miles. Hadley, *History of Goffstown*, 1:374.

1772 Westborough, Mass. "Committy to Vue sum meeting houses that hav ben Cut in two & a pece put in ye meedel": unknown distance. DeForest, *Early History of Westborough*, 154.

1773 Bernardston, Mass. Pews "built the same for largeness" as those in Greenfield (1760): 7 miles. *History of the Connecticut Valley*, 692.

1773 Leominster, Mass. Meetinghouse to be "the same bigness with Lunenburg" (1749): 6 miles. Gardner, *A Discourse in Two Parts*, 5.

1773 Needham, Mass. Committee to view "One or more of the meeting Houses in the Neighboring Towns": 5 miles. Clarke, *History of Needham*, 201.

1774 Boxford, Mass. (Second Parish), "same plan" as New Rowley [Georgetown] without the steeple (1769): 5 miles. Perley, *History of Boxford*, 245.

1774 Jaffrey, N.H. Meetinghouse exterior to be "Collored like Rindge" and have a "Pulpit like that in Rindge" (1764): 5 miles. Cutter, *History of Jaffrey*, 60.

1774 Providence, R.I. (First Baptist) Committee "to view the different churches and meeting-houses there, and to make a memorandum of their several dimensions and forms of architecture" in Boston: 42 miles. Isham, *Meeting House*, xvi.

1774 Salem, Mass. Tabernacle said to be "like Whitefield's in London" (1756). Worcester, *Memorial of the Old and New Tabernacle*, 21.

1774 Sandown, N.H. Meetinghouse to be "the color of Chester" (1774): 5 miles. Little, *American Decorative Wall Painting*, 12.

1775 Boxborough, Mass. To form "a Committee for purchasing Harvard old meatting-House" (1732): 4 miles. Hager, *Boxborough*, 15; Drake, *History of Middlesex County*, 1:271–72.

1775 Providence, R.I. (First Baptist). Architect Joseph Brown used a bell tower design taken from the 30th plate of James Gibbs's *Book of Architecture*, 1728. Little, *Life and Works of James Gibbs*, 187; Benes and Zimmerman, *New England Meeting House and Church*, 28–29.

1775 Harvard, Mass. (Baptist). To purchase Leominster meetinghouse (1742): 10 miles. Wilder, *History of Leominster*, 156.

1775 Rochester, N.H. Meetinghouse to be "the same dimensions" as Dover (1758): 10 miles. McDuffee, *History of Rochester*, 100.

1777 Loudon, N.H. Meetinghouse to have "the same size of the Epsom house" (1764): 9 miles. Hurd, *History of Merrimack County*, 490.

1778 Eastford, Conn. To build meetinghouse "of equal bigness with Woodstock's West Society's" (1743): 5 miles. Larned, *History of Windham County*, 2:34.

1780 Goshen, Mass. Meetinghouse "with posts two feet shorter than Chesterfield" (1768): 4 miles. Barrus, *History of the Town of Goshen*, 19.

1781 Hubbardston, Mass. Pulpit to be "the fashion of the Pulpit in the old Rutland meeting house" (1759): 9 miles; Pulpit to be "equal" to that in First Parish in Shrewsbury (1766): 21 miles. Stowe, *History of Hubbardston*, 125.

APPENDIX G

1781 Temple, N.H. "to color ye Meeting-house, in its several parts, agreeable to Wilton meeting-house colours, or as near as may be" (1773): 7 miles. Blood, *History of Temple*, 135.

1781 Walpole, Mass. Meetinghouse to have "a plan that was drawn of Mansfield Meeting House" (1764): 9 miles. Lewis, *History of Walpole*, 128.

1783 Pittsfield, N.H. Meetinghouse to be the "same bigness of Hampton Falls" (1780): 40 miles. Hurd, *History of Merrimack County*, 593.

1784 Antrim, N.H. Meetinghouse to be "patterned after" the one in Londonderry (1769): 40 miles. Cochrane, *History of Antrim*, 179.

1784 Stoddard, N.H. Meetinghouse to be "the same bigness of the one in Packersfield [Nelson]" (1776): 8 miles. Gould, *History of Stoddard*, 28.

1785 Milford, N.H. Meetinghouse size to be same as Mont Vernon (1779): 4 miles. Ramsdell, *History of Milford*, 61.

1785 Salisbury, Mass. (Rocky Hill). Meetinghouse to be "patterned after" Kensington, N.H. (1771): 6 miles. Sawyer, *History of Kensington*, 157.

1785 Weymouth, Mass. (Second or South Parish). Pulpit, canopy, and deacons' seat "to be Executed in the same manner they are in the Revd Mr. Taft's Meeting house [Braintree First Parish, now Quincy]"; front of the gallery "to be finished like the front of the gallery of Rev Mr Tafts Meetinghouse" (1732): 7 miles; "Pulpit window to be cased like the pulpit window in Mr. Wibard's Meeting-house [Braintree Third Parish, now Randolph]" (1763): 8 miles. Contract, Records of the South Precinct, 1785, 22.

1786 Bow, N.H. Meetinghouse to be "as large as Mr. Colbies" in Pembroke (1759): 12 miles. Hurd, *History of Merrimack County*, 272.

1786 Milford, N.H. "to accept the plan of the porches of the Temple meeting-house" (1781): 11 miles. Ramsdell, *History of Milford*, 64.

1787 Amherst N.H. (Second Parish). To build porches like those in Temple (same builder) (1781): 14 miles. Secomb, *History of Amherst*, 84.

1787 Andover, Mass. (South Parish). Meetinghouse to be "modeled after that in the North Parish" (1753) and to have "ground pinnings as good as" those of the North Parish: 3 miles. Mooar, *Historical Manual*, 32.

1787 Rockingham, Vt. To be "as large as Charlestown [N.H.] Meeting House, as to the square of it" (1767): 10 miles. Hayes, *History of Rockingham*, 143.

1787 Westminster, Mass. Meetinghouse to be finished "after the style of" Leominster (1774): 11 miles. Heywood, *History of Westminster*, 274.

1787 Wolfeborough, N.H. Plan to be like the meetinghouse in Middleton with ... amendments" (1787): 11 miles. Parker, *History of Wolfeborough*, 256.

1788 Hancock, N.H. "to be in all parts both as to size and goodness equal to the frame of Packerfield [Nelson]" (1776): 11 miles. Hayward, *History of Hancock*, 103.

1789 Gardner, Mass. To be finished inside "as Westminster meeting-house is finished" (1788): 5 miles. Herrick, *History of Gardner*, 487.

1789 Pittsfield, Mass. "Col. Bulfinch of Boston" to furnish the designs (1789): 130 miles. Smith, *History of Pittsfield*, 441.

1789 Surry, N.H. "That the whole of Said House be finished in the same form and as Near Like Keen Meetinghouse as the Bigness of Said house will admit of . . ."; glazing, exterior paint, pulpit window, canopy, and painting and numbering of pews like Keene (1786): 7 miles. Kingsbury, *History of Surry*, 174–75.

1789 Wilton, Conn. To be built "upon the construction of the Norwalk meeting-house" (1783): 6 miles. Kelly, *Early Connecticut Meetinghouses*, 2:298.

1790 Woodbury, Conn. "that the color of the meeting house be near the color of mr. Timy Tomlinsons" (1790): 1 mile. Kelly, *Early Connecticut Meetinghouses*, 2:320. See also Cothren, *History of Ancient Woodbury*, 3:1575.

1791 Gilsum, N.H. "Pulpit and Canopy to Be made Like Surry's" (1771, pulpit and canopy "finished" about 1790): 4 miles. Hayward, *History of Gilsum*, 102.

1791 Oxford, Mass. (Universalist). To build "in the Tuscan order, equal to the Ward meetinghouse in quality" (Auburn, 1773): 3 miles. Daniels, *History of the Town of Oxford*, 89.

1792 Canaan, N.H. "painting of the outside is to be done in the same manner and exactly like the lower meeting house in Salisbury as to color" (1791): 28 miles; "The Pews are to be made and placed exactly according to the plan by which they are sold, and the inside work to be . . . in every respect equal to the upper meeting house in Salisbury" (1791): 25 miles. Wallace, *History of Canaan*, 146.

1792 Durham, N.H. Meetinghouse to be "like that at Amherst" (contract with the same builder, Edmund Thompson) (1771): 49 miles. Stackpole and Thompson, *History of Durham*, 1:173.

1792 New Durham, N.H. "pulpit and canopy be built according to that . . . in Gilmanton" (1774): 15 miles. Jennings, *History of New Durham*, 44.

1792 Templeton, Mass. Meetinghouse to be painted "of the color of Leominster" (1774): 20 miles. Adams, *Historical Discourse, Templeton*, 112.

1793 Dracut, Mass. (Second Parish or Lowell). "to build a house of the same bigness as the one in Pelham, [N.H.]" (1746): 7 miles. Coburn, *History of Lowell and Its People*, 68.

1793 Hampton, Conn. Lightning rod "be made like that lightning rod of Scotland Steple" (Third Parish in Windham, 1774): 5 miles. Kelly, *Early Connecticut Meetinghouses*, 1:187.

1793 Kensington, Conn. Meetinghouse to be painted "within side similar to Worthington" (1774): 3 miles. Kelly, *Early Connecticut Meetinghouses*, 1:245.

1793 Montague, Mass. "Cullor the meeting-Hous the same of Sunderland" (1793): 6 miles. *History of the Connecticut Valley*, 637.

1793 Westford, Mass. "to Culler the meeting-house . . . neer the Culler of Chelmsford"; to build a belfree . . . in the same form as Chelmsford" (1792): 5 miles. Hodgman, *History of Westford*, 151.

1794 Canaan, N.H. Pulpit and canopy to be not like those in Salisbury (1791): 28 miles; to be "exactly the Pulpit and canopee of Chelmsford" (1792): 65 miles. Wallace, *History of Canaan*, 149.

1794 Dunstable, Mass. "breastwork in the Gallery not inferior to that in the meeting house in Tyngsborough" (1755): 3 miles. Nason, *History of Dunstable*, 155.

1794 Greenfield, N.H. Frame to be similar to that of Temple (1781): 11 miles. Hopkins, *Greenfield*, 21.

1794 Richmond, Mass. Meetinghouse to be built "similar to the large meeting house in Pittsfield" (1790): 9 miles. Annin, *Richmond*, 62.

1794 Sutton, N.H. (North). "the house was to be built according to New London meetinghouse with some small alterations" (1786): 7 miles. Quotation from Worthen, *History of Sutton*, 328; Sinnott, *Meetinghouse and Church*, 67.

1794 Washington, N.H. "the walls the colour of Alsted Meetinghouse & the roof Spanish brown" (1788, painted by 1793): 19 miles. Jager and Krone, *"A Sacred Deposit,"* 55.

1794 Westford, Mass. "Pulpit, canapy, and Dean Seete be nearly in the form that Chelmsford meeting house is" (1792): 5 miles. Hodgman, *History of Westford*, 152.

1794 Windsor, Conn. To contract with Ebenezer Clark, who designed Pittsfield; To build square tower and cupola "from plans . . . from the meeting-house in Pittsfield" (1790): 57 miles. Kelly, *Early Connecticut Meetinghouses*, 2:308; *Quarter Millennial Anniversary*, 70.

1795 Arlington, Mass. "To paint the outside . . . the same color as Mr. Thomas Russell's" (unknown, probably domestic): unknown distance.

1796 Barnstable (Centerville), Mass. Meetinghouse to be painted "in the manner as the house is that stands near Jabez Howes in Yarmouth": 9 miles. Trayser, *Barnstable*, 74–75.

1796 Candia, N.H. To send John Lane, who added the steeple, "to Chester to view the meeting house" (1774): 10 miles. Moore, *History of Candia*, 62.

1796 Fitchburg, Mass. "to model meetinghouse after the one in Leominster" (1774 twin porch): 6 miles; to model the meetinghouse after the one . . . at Ashburnham" (1791 three porches): 7 miles. Torrey, *History of the Town of Fitchburg*, 117.

1796 Gill, Mass. Meetinghouse to be painted "same color as church in Sunderland" (1793): 14 miles. Stoughton, "History of Gill, Massachusetts," 1:48.

1796 Methuen, Mass. Meetinghouse to be "upon the plan of the new Meeting House lately finished in the lower Parish of Bradford" (Second Parish or Groveland) (1790): 11 miles. Bentley, *Diary*, 19 April 1796 (2:179).

1796 Middletown, Vt. Meetinghouse to be "painted equal to Graham's old house [domestic], in Rutland and the joiner work shall be equal to that of the west parish meeting house in Rutland" (1789): 30 miles. Frisbie, *History of Middletown*, 92.

1797 Hinsdale, Mass. Exterior to be similar to Chester (1793): 16 miles; interior to be similar to Pittsfield (1790): 9 miles. *Commemoration of the Centennial of the Congregational Church, Hinsdale*, 34. See also Sinnott, *Meetinghouse and Church*, 92.

1797 Ryegate, Vt. Meetinghouse modeled after Newbury (twin porch), "considered one of the best in the state" (1790): 10 miles. Miller and Wells, *History of Ryegate*, 107.

1798 Salisbury, Conn. To "be modeled after the recently erected meetinghouse at Richmond, Massachusetts" (1794): 31 miles. Kelly, *Early Connecticut Meetinghouses*, 2:176.

1798 Warren, N.H. Meetinghouse to be the same size as Rumney (1795): 13 miles. Little, *History of Warren*, 358.

1799 Hollis, N.H. Meetinghouse plan to copy Billerica, Mass. (1797): 23 miles. Worcester, *History of Hollis*, 245.

1799 Lee, Mass. Meetinghouse to be like Richmond (1794): 10 miles. Field, *History of the County of Berkshire*, 2:139.

1800 Agawam, Mass. Purchased and moved separatist meetinghouse in Suffield, Conn. (1763): 6 miles. Sinnott, *Meetinghouse and Church*, 221; "Agawam, Massachusetts," 12–13; Trumbull, *Memorial History of Hartford County*, 2:393.

1800 Newburyport, Mass. St. Paul's Church. Builders to copy the reading desk and pulpit of Trinity Church in Boston (1734): 34 miles. Benes, *Old Town and the Waterside*, 179.

1802 Milford, N.H. Belfry to be "similar to that in Francestown" (1801): 15 miles. Ramsdell, *History of Milford*, 64.

1802 Roxbury, Mass. Meetinghouse to be similar to Newburyport "with a few alterations" (1801): 37 miles. Thwing, *History of the First Church*, 171.

1803 Westfield, Mass. "the dimensions of the meeting-house when built be the same of that procured from Mr. Bulfinch of Boston" (designed 1789): 97 miles. Lockwood, *Westfield*, 2:235. Citation courtesy of Kevin Sweeney.

1804 Canterbury, Conn. Rustication and ornaments "to be the same as the new meeting house in Norwich Town"; "the steple end to be the whol width same as Norwich Town Meeting house" (1801): 13 miles. Kelly, *Early Connecticut Meetinghouses*, 1:61.

1805 Rocky Hill, Conn. Meetinghouse to be built with a projection on the plan of Middletown (1804): 10 miles. Kelly, *Early Connecticut Meetinghouses*, 2:165.

1807 Bridgewater, Conn. Building committee "to go and view New Stratford & other Meeting houses" for dimensions: 9 miles. Kelly, *Early Connecticut Meetinghouses*, 1:31.

1807 Claremont, N.H. Addition "to be modeled after Concord meeting house" (1751, semicircular addition in 1802): 47 miles. Spofford, *Old Meeting House*, 1–8.

1808 Bethany, Conn. Anglican church to be "proportioned as to Length and Bredth after . . . Waterbury" (1795): 12 miles. Kelly, *Early Connecticut Meetinghouses*, 1:21.

1809 Lyme, N.H. "Order and stile of both the inside and outside work of the church be according to the plan on which the meeting house at Dartmouth College in Hanover was built" (1795): 11 miles. Cole, *Patterns and Pieces*, 308.

1809 Methuen, Mass. (Second Parish). Pulpit to be dressed "as high as the First parish meetinghouse dressing cost." First Parish in Methuen (1796): 3 miles. "Second Parish Methuen, 1784–1846," (entry under 4 April 1809), unpaginated.

1809 South Abington, Mass. To be "modelled upon the South Meeting in Boston [Hollis]" (Bulfinch, 1788): 20 miles. Bentley, *Diary*, 3 October 1809 (3:465).

1810 Northampton, Mass. Meetinghouse to be built "After a plan drawn by Mr. Asher Benjamin" (cost of plan, $45.00) (1809); contract to build "in a manner equal to that of Mr. Emerson's meeting house in Boston" (1808): 93 miles. Plan by Benjamin: *First Parish, Northampton*, 21, 29; equal to Mr. Emerson's: 25.

1811 Whiting, Vt. Committee member to go to Boston for advice (1811): 172 miles. Sinnott, *Meetinghouse and Church*, 239.

1812 Troy, N.H. Committee "to go to Templeton [Mass.] and to examine a model house . . . just completed" (1811); to ask a committee to draw a plan of a meetinghouse they had seen at Templeton: 19 miles. Caverly, *History of Troy*, 131; Stone, *History of Troy*, 133.

1812 Wilmington, Mass. Committee to "view the neighboring meeting house lately built in order of drawing a plan of said house" (possibly Carlisle) (1811): 12 miles. Simmons, *History, Yearbook and Church Directory*, unpaginated.

1813 Medway, Mass. Meetinghouse to be built with minor changes "after the plan of the new meeting-house then building in West Medway" (1813): 2 miles. Jameson, *History of Medway*, 113.

1813 New Haven, Conn. (First Church of Christ, Congregational). Two men to look at Northampton "with a view of ascertaining . . . that work" (1811): 76 miles; to hire "Mr. Benjamin" of Boston to design new meetinghouse: 137 miles. Kelly, *Early Connecticut Meetinghouses*, 2:12–13.

1813 Otis, Mass. Meetinghouse to be of "the same construction as the one in Winsted, Conn." (1800): 25 miles. Field, *History of the County of Berkshire*, 261–62.

1816 Goshen, N.H. To be "somewhat similar to the Lempster Meeting House" (1794): 6 miles. Nelson, *History of Goshen*, 202.

1817 Dublin, N.H. Meetinghouse to be "after the plan of Ashby, or Fitzwilliam" (1816): 12 miles. Mason, *History of Dublin*, 205.

1817 E. Avon, Conn. "not inferior to the workmanship of Norfolk Meeting House" (1813): 26 miles. Kelly, *Early Connecticut Meetinghouses*, 1:9.

1819 Hancock, N.H. Meetinghouse to be "nearly the size, construction, and form of the Congregational meeting house in Dublin" (1818): 8 miles. Hayward, *History of Hancock*, 143.

1820 Derby, Conn. Ornamentation of "the exterior of sd Building Steeple Belfry & Lantern shall be modern & conformed . . . to the style adopted in finishing the same parts of a Meeting House in . . . Warren built by Jennings" (1819): 36 miles. Kelly, *Early Connecticut Meetinghouses*, 1:97.

1820 Woodstock, Conn. Meetinghouse to be "the size and form of the one lately built in Killingly" (1818): 11 miles. Kelly, *Early Connecticut Meetinghouses*, 2:331.

1822 Sullivan, N.H. "to paint the meetinghouse like the one in Keene" (1786): 6 miles. Seward, *History of Sullivan*, 1:394.

1825 South Britain, Conn. To have "slips," "Globe arch," galleries, windows, and steeple-end pulpit as at Derby (1819): 16 miles; to have cornices "in Ionic order or like those in Warren"; "steeple inclosed like that in Warren" (1819): 22 miles. Kelly, *Early Connecticut Meetinghouses*, 2:204.

1826 Attleborough, Mass. To heat the church "with a furnice or like the new meetinghouse in Taunton" (1792): 13 miles. Daggett, *Sketch of the History of Attleborough*, 266.

1828 Attleborough, Mass. (Second Parish). "take the North Baptist meeting house at the North end of Providence for a sampl with some variations" (1822): 9 miles. Daggett, *Sketch of the History of Attleborough*, 264.

1828 Guilford, Conn. Meetinghouse to be "finished nearly in the same style with the new churches in Milford and Cheshire" (1823): 24 miles; meetinghouse to be "finished nearly in the same style" as Milford and Cheshire (1826): 23 miles. *New Haven Register*, 12 December 1828, cited in Kelly, *Early Connecticut Meetinghouses*, 1:174.

1828 Southington, Conn. Meetinghouse to have "the same size and dimensions and after a plan similar to the new Congregational meeting house lately erected in Cheshire" (1826): 7 miles. Kelly, *Early Connecticut Meetinghouses*, 2:220.

# Notes

### Introduction: A New England Icon Reconsidered

1. The story of the sounding board and the hinged seats appears in Clark, *Historical Address*, 45–46. The *Boston News-Letter* of 23 April 1773 reports that the iron hooks holding the canopy at Grafton, Mass., gave way when the meetinghouse was not in use, crushing the pulpit desk. Note: Spellings in quotations cited in the text of this work are generally modernized except where the meaning is unclear or subject to interpretation.

2. Speare, *Colonial Meeting-Houses*, 67; Davis, *History of Wallingford*, 196; Perkins, *Historical Sketches of Meriden*, 52–53; Coffin, *History of Newbury*, 175–84; Kelly, *Early Connecticut Meetinghouses*, 2:33, 195; Hine, *Early Lebanon*, 71–84; Baldwin, "'Devil Begins to Roar'"; *History of the Connecticut Valley*, 353; Hurd, *History of Worcester County*, 1:382.

3. Parmenter, "Old Meeting-House at Pelham."

4. Bliss, *History of Rehoboth*, 214–28.

5. Torrey, *History of the Town of Fitchburg*, 118.

6. Winthrop, *Journal*, 19 March 1632 (64).

7. *Confession of Faith*, 38, cited in Winslow, *Meetinghouse Hill*, 52.

8. Chauncy, *Divine Institution*, 2–3. The misattribution of Chauncy's remark "There is no just grounds . . ." began with Noah Porter, who, in "New England Meetinghouse," 306, cites Richard Mather as the author and adds the parenthetical note "Ratio Disciplinae, 5." This citation, however, alludes to Cotton Mather's *Ratio Disciplinae*, 5, which has the same meaning but does not use the same wording. Alice Earle, in *Sabbath*, 1, picks up from Porter but erroneously cites Cotton Mather as the author. The phrase is correctly attributed to Chauncy in Cummings, *Dictionary of Congregational Usages*, 52 and 228. Born in Hertfordshire, Isaac Chauncy (1632–1712) attended Harvard College, but returned to England to serve as a pastor for the remainder of his life.

9. "Synagogue" appears in the town records of Amherst, Mass., in 1749. Gay, *Gazetteer of Hampshire County*, 167.

10. Sprunger, *Dutch Puritanism*, 50–51, 83–84.

11. Burrage, *Early English Dissenters*, 2:48; Rogers, *Diary*, lxii, 79, 81, 128, 174.

12. The 1593 law restricting Christian fellowship is cited in the *Oxford English Dictionary*, 2d ed., under "meeting" 3b; it disallowed being "present at any unlawful Assemblies,

Conventicles, or Meetings, under Colour or Pretence of any Exercise of Religion." The author wishes to thank Christopher King for this research.

13. Stiles, *Itineraries*, 450; "Diary of Mary Vial Holyoke," 7 August 1776 (94); Johnson, *Rhode Island Baptists*, 122.

14. Place, "From Meeting House to Church," 69. The "main alley" design was far from common in New England or indeed the American colonies.

15. Congregational and Presbyterian societies enjoyed the privilege to tax in all New England states except Rhode Island. While both denominations were based on Reformed Calvinistic beliefs (the terms *Congregational* and *Presbyterian* were sometimes used interchangeably), Congregational churches were wholly independent and followed the Cambridge platform of 1648, whereas Presbyterians organized their churches around regional councils of elders; in Connecticut Presbyterians organized under the 1708 Saybrook platform.

16. Gage, *History of Rowley*, 38–39, 101–4.

17. Earle's study, like most of her work, lacks footnotes but is among the wittiest treatments of the subject written to date; Winslow's is equally brilliant and much more erudite.

18. Sinnott, *Meetinghouse and Church*, 16.

19. Dean, Review of Donnelly, *New England Meeting Houses*, 159.

20. Sweeney, "Meetinghouses, Town Houses, and Churches," 61.

21. Garvan, *Architecture and Town Planning*, 141.

22. Coolidge, "Hingham Builds a Meetinghouse," 460–61.

23. *Vernacular* means native to a region or a district (rather than a literary, cultivated, or school-taught convention) or a tradition that draws on an unwritten body of agricultural, architectural, or mechanical practices. This study presents evidence that early New England meetinghouses were based on barn-making, bridge-making, and mill-making traditions while also conforming to a loosely defined but articulate concept of European Protestant ecclesiastic architecture.

24. *Platform of Church Discipline*, chap. 3, sec. 4.

25. North, *History of Berlin*, 153; Stiles, *Itineraries*, 244.

26. Biglow, *History of Sherburne*, 43.

27. Smith, *History of Pittsfield*, 1:447.

28. Trumbull, *History of Northampton*, 2:529.

29. *Berkshire Genealogist* 21, no. 1 (2000): 36.

## Chapter 1. The Meetinghouse and the Community

1. "Hovels" served to protect horses (Lockwood, *Westfield and Its Historic Influences*, 1:315). "To Sargt Samll Foster for the Decense of the meeting House," Chelmsford, Mass., 1701. Cited in Waters, *History of Chelmsford*, 675. A "necessary" was located near the Methodist meetinghouse. Map of Lynn Common, Mass., ca. 1827, collection of the Peabody Essex Museum, Salem, Mass.

2. Mitchell, *History of New Haven County*, 290.

3. Lead weights cited by Caulkins, *History of Norwich*, 340; Usher, *History of Medford*, 399; warnings against "cutting the seats" in Medford, Mass., Earle, *Sabbath*, 58.

4. Kilde, *When Church Became Theatre*, chap. 1.

5. For example, in 1663 Lydia Wardwell, a Quaker convert, entered naked into the meetinghouse in Newbury, Mass. Coffin, *History of Newbury*, 66.

6. Stone, *History of Beverly*, 247; Hurd, *History of Essex County*, 1:714.

7. Sewall, *History of Woburn*, 547, cites the use of meetinghouses as temporary barracks. Stiles, Literary *Diary*, 2:473, cites their use as hospitals.

8. Dunlap, *History of the Rise and Progress of the Arts of Design*, 344: historical painter William Dunlap reports hired "churches," 22 June 1822. *Very Poor and of Lo Make*, 23 March 1779 (238): Psalmodist Andrew Law holds a final singing meeting at the Keene, N.H., meetinghouse.

9. Mitchell, *History of the United Church of New Haven*, 125.

10. Brian Powell and Andrea Gilmore argue persuasively that the name "the Old Ship" was bestowed in the early twentieth century. Powell and Gilmore, "Old Ship Meeting House," 1:7–9. The Hingham artist Hosea Sprague, who illustrated this meetinghouse in the mid-nineteenth century, called it the "Old North."

11. "Tunnel" was meant in its archaic sense of a funnel. See Lewis and Newhall, *History of Lynn*, 278.

12. *Centennial History of the Town of Millbury*, 308. Some Anglican churches in America's middle and southern colonies were known by their location ("Middle Church"), by their material ("Brick Church"), or by a geographical feature ("Swamp Church"). Carl Lounsbury to the author, 20 January 2010.

13. Quotation taken from Wight, *Some Old Time Meeting Houses*, 87.

14. Washburn, *Historical Sketches*, 104; Bliss, *Side Glimpses*, 106–7, cites the Reading example.

15. Newhall, *Liñ, or, Jewels of the Third Plantation*, 70–71. Newhall edited a second issue of Alonzo Lewis's *History of Lynn Including Nahant* and wrote *Liñ*, in which excerpts from the fictitious diary were published, as a companion volume.

16. South Bridgewater: Stiles, *Itineraries*, 232; Livermore: Sinnott, *Meetinghouse and Church*, 218; Peterborough: Morison, *Address Delivered*, 25.

17. Gage, *History of Washington*, 31.

18. *First Church, Killingly* 12; Stiles, *Itineraries*, 149, 321. For other examples of this practice, see *Bicentennial, First Congregational Church, Danbury*, 13; Cooley, *Granville Jubilee*, 43.

19. *Sandwich and Bourne*, 7.

20. Hudson, *History of Sudbury*, 124–25, 285–89; Brigham, *History of the Brigham Family*, 70–71; Powell, *Puritan Village*, 126–27.

21. Coffin, *History of Newbury*, 175–84.

22. Kelly, *Early Connecticut Meetinghouses*, 1:263.

23. Kelly, *Early Connecticut Meetinghouses*, 1:263–74; Webb, "Plan of the Third Society"; Hine, *Early Lebanon*, 71–84; Thompson, *Maps of Connecticut*, 36, 38; Garvan, *Architecture and Town Planning*, 63–65.

24. Depew, *Proceedings* (Williamstown, Mass.), kindly provided by Carl A. Westerdahl.

25. Kelly, *Early Connecticut Meetinghouses*, 1:4–5.

26. Davis, *History of Chelmsford*, 48, 410–11. Suffield, Conn., used a red flag as "a sign" in 1685. Sheldon, *Documentary History*, 18.

27. Kelly, *Early Connecticut Meetinghouses*, 1:195.

28. Stiles and Dams, *History of Ancient Wethersfield*, 2:223.

29. Quotation taken from *Quarter Millennial Anniversary*, 56; Kelly, *Early Connecticut Meetinghouses*, 1:308, 2:87; Tucker, "Hope Atherton," 388.

30. Jones, *Stockbridge Past and Present*, 59; Johnson, *Historic Hampshire*, 159; Burnham, *History and Traditions of Shelburne*, 10; Packard, *History of the Churches*, 323. *History of the Connecticut Valley*, 628; Johnson, *Historic Hampshire*, 243; *History of the Town of Amherst*, opp. 39.

31. Thompson, *History of Greenfield*, 1:539.
32. Whately: Crafts, *History of Whately*, 161; Sunderland: Smith, *History of Sunderland*, 161.
33. Sewall, *History of Woburn*, 82n14.
34. Kelly, *Early Connecticut Meetinghouses*, 2:133, 197.
35. *Records of the Town of Braintree*, 36; *Records of the Town of Plymouth*, 2:204; Cutter, *History of the Town of Jaffrey*, 64; Dole, *Windham in the Past*, 116.
36. Jewett and Jewett, *Rowley*, 105 (Ipswich Town Records, 3 March 1644; Hampton Records, 1644).
37. Woodstock quotation taken from Larned, *History of Windham County*, 2:368; Earle, *Sabbath*, 12.
38. *Boston Post-Boy*, 25 October 1736.
39. Goold, *Portland in the Past*, 296.
40. Sewall, *Diary*, 10 May 1717 (2:854).
41. Clapp, *History of the Town of Dorchester*, 358.
42. Lynde and Lynde, *Diaries*, 96, 100, 151, 197.
43. Waters, *Ipswich*, 2:443; Plummer, "Dying Confession of Pomp."
44. Rhode Island, where religious toleration had been practiced since the founding of the colony in the seventeenth century, did not allow compulsory religious taxation.

## Chapter 2. The Meetinghouse and the Church

1. Presbyterians in New England were always a small minority, chiefly Scottish and Scotch-Irish immigrants, organizing their Reformed churches around the teachings of John Calvin and John Knox, who allowed greater connectivity between congregations and greater control of churches by elders; some Congregationalists, particularly those in Connecticut, who followed these practices were called Presbyterians but were in fact independent Congregationalists.
2. Samuel Sewall never mentions crying children in his diary, and Mary Goodhue's narrative (ca. 1680) suggests she rarely came to the meetinghouse during her many pregnancies. David D. Hall to the author, 16 November 2008.
3. Cited in Hambrick-Stowe, *Practice of Piety*, 105.
4. Danckaerts, *Journal of a Voyage*, 28 June 1680 (380).
5. Cited in Hambrick-Stowe, *Practice of Piety*," 105.
6. Smith, *Journals*, 11 January 1759 (278).
7. In 1817 Thaddeus Harris, a historian of Dorchester, Mass., wrote, in his *Valedictory Sermon*, "The *stand* of curiously wrought iron, which supported the Hour Glass in the pulpit, has been preserved, and is now deposited in the vestry of the meeting house erected in the year 1816."
8. Bliss, *Side Glimpses*, 253; Winthrop, *Journal*, 26 May 1639 (297).
9. Hambrick-Stowe, *Practice of Piety*, 111.
10. Stiles, *Itineraries*, 237.
11. Estes, *History of Holden*, 95.
12. DeForest, *Early History of Westborough*, 140.
13. Sewall, *Diary*, 26 February 1688 (1:161).
14. Stout, *New England Soul*, 127–31.
15. Ainsworth, *Apologie*.
16. Ainsworth and Broughton, *Certayne questions*.
17. Wilder, *History of Leominster*, 155.

18. A notice in the *Massachusetts Spy*, 3 January 1788, reveals that the new Brattle Square structure was the only meetinghouse in Boston to be heated by stoves.

19. Peterson, *Price of Redemption*, 67; *Records of the Church of Christ at Cambridge*, 28–29; Winslow, *Meetinghouse Hill*, 40–47.

20. Stiles, *Itineraries*, 246.

21. *Manifesto Church*, 4–5.

22. *Milton Town Records*, 368.

23. Ware, *Two Discourses*, 6; Ward, "'In a Feasting Posture,'" 20; Thwing, *History of the First Church in Roxbury*, 42, 116.

24. *Records of the Church of Christ at Cambridge*, 232.

25. Flaherty, *Privacy in Colonial New England*, 643.

26. *Records of the Church of Christ at Cambridge*, 121–22; "True Copy," 87.

27. Data drawn from Oberholzer, *Delinquent Saints*, 23–24; Flaherty, *Privacy in Colonial New England*, 138–51; and individual parish histories.

28. *Manifesto Church*," pts. 5, 6.

29. Stoddard, *Inexcusableness;* Holifield, "Intellectual Sources."

30. Orcutt, *History of the Towns of New Milford and Bridgewater*, 52.

31. Stiles, *Literary Diary*, 6 September 1773 (1:411).

32. Homes quotation taken from Frothingham, *History of Charlestown*, 200, and Felt, *Annals of Salem from Its First Settlement*, 625. Cotton Mather said "There is perfect Charity" in the practice of reading Scripture and "To put the Term of *dumb Reading* on it is esteemed improper and indecent." Mather, *Ratio Disciplinae*, 67.

33. Chandler, *History of the Town of Shirley*, 222.

34. Stiles, *Itineraries*, 299–300. Stiles notes that some parishes such as the second in Preston, Conn., read "in summer."

35. Ward, "'In a Feasting Posture'"; Sewall, *Diary*, 6 December 1724 (1023).

36. Hambrick-Stowe, *Practice of Piety*, 113.

37. Foote, *Three Centuries*, 54.

38. Scholes, *Oxford Companion to Music*, 501. See also John Cotton, *Singing of Psalms a gospel ordinance* (London: J. R. Alley, 1650), whose final section, "Touching the manner of singing," advocates the practice of lining out in churches where psalters are lacking or in which illiteracy is a problem.

39. Updike, *History of the Episcopal Church of Narragansett*, 435.

40. Hood, *History of Music in New England*, 141. Buechner, "Thomas Walter"; Buechner, *Yankee Singing Schools*, chaps. 1, 2.

41. Gay, *Farmington Papers*, 23–39.

42. Paige, *History of Hardwick*, 185–86; *Proceedings at the One Hundred and Fiftieth Anniversary* (Randolph, Mass.), 93; Estes, *History of Holden*, 91; Nason, *History of Dunstable*, 153; Rice, *Proceedings at the Celebration* (First Parish at Salem Village), 88.

43. Gay, *Farmington Papers*, 39; Chipman, *History of Harwinton*, 112–13.

44. Buechner, *Yankee Singing Schools*, 117–18.

45. Kingman, *History of North Bridgewater*, 95.

46. *Two Hundredth Anniversary*, Kensington, 38; *One Hundred Fiftieth Anniversary of the Town of Sterling*, 10; Tarbox, "Musical History," 114.

47. Stiles, *Itineraries*, 225. William Billings has generally been credited with the first use of a pitch pipe and the introduction of the bass viol into American church worship, though there is no indication to that effect in Boston church records. Silverman, *Cultural History*, 193–94; *Grove's Dictionary of Music and Musicians*, s.v. "Church Music."

48. Waters, *Ipswich*, 2:443.

49. Noyes, *Memorial of the Town of Hampstead*, 0:168; Thomas and Benes, "Amzi Chapin," 85.

50. Jackson, *History of Littleton*, 2:236; Hurd, *History of Rockingham and Strafford Counties*, 69.

51. Foote, *Annals of King's Chapel*, 1:211. King's Chapel later passed the organ to Anglican churches in Newburyport, Mass., and Portsmouth, N.H.

52. Shepard, *History of St. Mark's*, 93–94.

53. Reported by Ezra Stiles, who is cited in Foote, *Three Centuries*, 85.

54. Foote, *Three Centuries*, 80–85; Lothrop, *History of the Church in Brattle Street*, 147.

55. Caulkins, *History of Norwich*, 341.

56. Quotation taken from *Account of the Observance of the One Hundred and Fiftieth Anniversary*, 28; Jackson, *History of Littleton*, 2:329.

57. *Manifesto Church*, 5; Foote, *Annals of King's Chapel*, 1:207–11; Robbins, *History of the Second Church*, 184; Hill, *History of the Old South Church*, 2:39; Ellis, *History of the First Church*, 205.

58. Benes, "Psalmody."

59. Chandler, *History of the Town of Shirley*, 228.

60. Thwing, *History of the First Church in Roxbury*, 340–41; Wood, *History of the First Baptist Church*, 307; Moe, *Three Centuries of Church Music*; Bayles, *History of Windham County*, 891.

61. Flaherty, *Privacy in Colonial New England*, 149.

## Chapter 3. The Builders

1. This term was cited 22 December 1719 in the *Early Records of Manchester, Massachusetts*, 1:147.

2. Herrick, *History of Gardner*, 484.

3. Sewall, *Diary*, 20 June 1716 (2:822).

4. Hazen, *History of Billerica*, 169.

5. Upham, *Principles*, 57; Goodell, *First Meeting House in Salem*, 45.

6. Trumbull, *History of Northampton*, 2:67–72; *First Parish, Northampton*, 11–12.

7. *First Parish, Northampton*, 27.

8. Dow, *History of Hampton*, 3.

9. Marvin, *History of Winchendon*, 159.

10. Blood, *History of Temple*, 133–34.

11. Hurd, *History of Hillsborough County*, 334.

12. Lewandoski, "Historic American Timber-Framed Steeples," 22; Sobon, "English Barn in America."

13. Waters, *History of Chelmsford*, 677; Hodgman, *History of the Town of Westford*, 98; Cummings, *Framed Houses*, 63.

14. Perley, *History of Boxford*, 114, 127–28; Sewall, *History of Woburn*, 312.

15. Clark, *Meetinghouse Tragedy*, 35–46.

16. Secomb, *History of Amherst*, 239; Watkins, "Malden's Old Meetinghouses," 38.

17. Hazen, *History of Billerica*, 169.

18. Fitts, *History of Newfields*, 315.

19. Pride, *Tewksbury*, 20; Harlow, "Shrewsbury Meeting-house," 2; Hodgman, *History of the Town of Westford*, 98.

20. Sawtelle, *History of Townsend*, 142–43; Hurd, *History of Hillsborough County*, 334.
21. Willis, *History of Portland*, 358; Hall, *Report of the Celebration*, 17–18.
22. Roy, *History of East Brookfield*, 33.
23. Porter, *Historical Discourse*, 9–11.
24. Ibid., 10–11; see also Kelly, *Early Connecticut Meetinghouses*, 1:162.
25. Among the master builders known to have been responsible for multiple structures are Elias Carter (fifteen structures), David Hoadley (fourteen), Isaac Damon (thirteen), Asher Benjamin (thirteen), Charles Bulfinch (ten), John Ames (six), Lavius Fillmore (five), and Ithiel Town (three).
26. The close relation of bridge building to meetinghouse building is revealed in one unusual instance in which the same timber components that went into making a meetinghouse frame were used for a bridge. The town of Raymond, New Hampshire, erected a frame for a meetinghouse in 1774; within a year, the town changed its mind, dismantled the frame, and used the timber to build a bridge spanning the Lamprey River. The town had to wait another twelve years before a new meetinghouse was raised. Hurd, *History of Rockingham and Strafford Counties*, 449.
27. Coolidge, "Hingham Builds a Meetinghouse," 446; Powell and Gilmore, "Old Ship Meetinghouse," vol. 1. Caulkins, *History of New London*, 108, 191–92; Caulkins, *History of Norwich*, 216, 282; Kelly, *Early Connecticut Meetinghouses*, 2:108–11.
28. McIntyre, *Old First Church*, [4].
29. Kelly, *Early Connecticut Meetinghouses*, 2:114; Andres, "Lavius Fillmore," 41.
30. Howes, *History of Ashfield*, 260.
31. Andrew H. Ward, *History of the Town of Shrewsbury*, cited in Harlow, "Shrewsbury Meeting-house," 4; *Road We Have Travelled*; Howes, *History of Ashfield*, 260.
32. Coffin, *History of Newbury*, 64, 116.
33. Quotation taken from *History of the First Parish, Newbury*, 31–32; see also Currier, *History of Newbury*, 337, and Marlowe, *Churches of Old New England*, 193.
34. *History of the Connecticut Valley*, 761; Willson, *Address Delivered in Petersham*, 26; *History of Bolton*, 63–64.
35. Pelham's meetinghouse building contract with Thomas and John Dick of Bolton, Mass., required that their work be finished by 1 February 1741. (A fragment of the contract is in the James Gibson Papers, Pelham Records, 1743–1779, Special Collections and University Archives, W. E. B. Du Bois Library, University of Massachusetts Amherst.)
36. *History of the Connecticut Valley*, 715–16; *Centennial Anniversary, Heath, Mass.*, 21. Never completed, the 1762 meetinghouse was sold seven years later to a farmer who moved it and remodeled it for a dwelling house.
37. Five generations of Spoffords kept the Rowley mill in operation until 1925, when the machinery was sold to the Henry Ford Museum.
38. Spofford, *Genealogical Record*, 47, 454–58.
39. Spofford, *Family Record*, 26.
40. Bentley, *Diary*, 19 December 1813 (4:221); Sinnott, *Meetinghouse and Church*, 86. Pettingell, "West Parish of Salisbury," 36; Annett and Lehtinen, *History of Jaffrey*, 172–74. Speare, *Colonial Meeting-Houses*, 191.
41. Speare, *Colonial Meeting-Houses*, 116. The frontispiece of a copy of Langley's work that Timothy Carter used is illustrated in Wight, *Some Old Time Meeting Houses*, opp. 4.
42. Forbes, "Elias Carter."
43. *Annals of Brimfield*, 43.
44. Sinnott, *Meetinghouse and Church*, 95–96.

45. Kelly, *Early Connecticut Meetinghouses*, 2:149.
46. Adams, *Historical Discourse* (Templeton, Mass.), 50.
47. A hipped roof has no gables and comes to a peak in the center. It is also known as a "gathered," "four-sided," "four square," or "bevel" roof.
48. *Springfield Records*, 2:157–63.
49. Heywood, *History of Westminster*, 274.

## Chapter 4. Seating the Congregation

1. Spicer, "'Accommodating of Thame Selfis to Heir the Worde.'"
2. For a contemporary calculation of sizes, see Stiles, *Literary Diary*, 1:80–81; Atwater, *History of the Colony of New Haven*, 542–54; *Proceedings at the Centennial Celebration, Town of Longmeadow*, 154.
3. Sewall, *History of Woburn*, 315.
4. Craig, *Reformation, Politics, and Polemics*, 29–30.
5. Earle, *Sabbath*, 66.
6. Kimball, *A Sketch*, 12.
7. *Records of the Town of Cambridge*, 354; Paige, *History of Cambridge*, 262–63, 532, 673.
8. Atwater, *History of the Colony of New Haven*, 546.
9. Walker, *History of First Church in Hartford*, 231; Lockwood, *Westfield and Its Historic Influences*, 1:143–45; *Milton Town Records*, 204.
10. Stone, *History of Beverly*, 14–16, 24.
11. Roads, *History and Traditions of Marblehead*, 17, 25.
12. *Record of the Services Held at the Congregational Church of Windsor*, 65–66.
13. Smith, *History of Sunderland*, 53–54.
14. Dinkin, "Seating the Meeting House," 453, who cites Sewall, *History of Woburn*, 84; and Chase, *History of Haverhill*, 141.
15. Grobel, *History of the First Church of Stafford*, 30.
16. Shaw, *Belchertown in the Eighteenth Century*, 36.
17. *History of the Connecticut Valley*, 196.
18. Stone, *History of Beverly*, 251–52.
19. *Proceedings at the Celebration of the 250th Anniversary of the First Church of Christ in Milford*, 162.
20. *Record of the Services Held at the Congregational Church of Windsor*, 65.
21. "The Second Meeting-House in Lexington," 130.
22. Thompson, *History of Long Island*, 1:271.
23. Copeland, *"Our Country and Its People,"* 2:385–86; Lockwood, *Westfield and Its Historic Influences*, 1:314–16 (quotations taken from 315–16); Mooar, *Historical Manual*, 28.
24. Lockwood, *Westfield and Its Historic Influences*, 1:144.
25. Dinkin, "Seating the Meeting House," 459; Smith, *History of Sunderland*, 53; *Records of the Society or Parish of Turkey Hills*, 19.
26. Todd, *History of Redding*, 88; Timlow, *Ecclesiastical and Other Sketches*, 185–90.
27. Draper, "Wayland Local History," no. 3.
28. Usher, *History of Medford*, 391–94, 399.
29. Ware, *Two Discourses*, 45n4.
30. *Manual of the Church of Christ, Framingham*, 21–22.
31. Coffin, *History of Newbury*, 72, 119. The men were sentenced in Salem to be whipped or pay a fine of ten pounds.

32. Quotations taken from Kelly, *Early Connecticut Meetinghouses*, 2:140; Hyde, *Historical Celebration*, 119.

33. For example, Woodbury, Conn., voted in 1775 "to seat the Meeting House Promiscuously by Men and Women together." Kelly, *Early Connecticut Meetinghouses*, 2:320.

34. Steiner, *History of the Plantation* (Guilford and Madison), 275; Quotation taken from Kelly, *Early Connecticut Meetinghouses*, 1:172; Orcutt, *History of the Old Town of Stratford*, 483.

35. Hurd, *History of Norfolk County*, 646; Gay, *Gazetteer of Hampshire County*, 167.

36. Stiles, *History of Ancient Windsor*, 1:357.

37. Norton, *History of Fitzwilliam*, 156–57.

38. Probate inventory, Abel Flint, 1789, Middlesex County Courthouse, Boston, Mass.

39. *One Hundred Fiftieth Anniversary, First Church of Christ in Pomfret*, 43.

40. Jackson, *History of Early Settlement*, 143.

41. Hurd, *History of Norfolk County*, 808.

42. Thwing, *History of the First Church in Roxbury*, 139–40.

43. *Manual of the Church of Christ, Framingham*, 22.

44. *Centennial History of the Town of Millbury*, 309.

45. Kimball, *Sketch*, 8–9, states, "The aristocracy of that day chose the wall pews, and the two wall pews next to the front door on each side commanded the highest price." See also *Old Records of the Town of Duxbury*, 326; Paige, *History of Cambridge*, 292–93.

46. Copeland, *History of the Town of Murrayfield*, 86, 166.

47. Timlow, *Ecclesiastical and Other Sketches*, 183–90; Orcutt, *History of the Towns of New Milford and Bridgewater*, 184, 260–67.

48. *Records of the Town of Lee*, 104; Hyde, *Centennial Celebration*, 230. The plan for the location of pews in Lee was later supplanted by a town vote to build by subscription.

49. Thwing, *History of the First Church in Roxbury*, 270, 310 (pew prices itemized 271–316).

50. *Columbian (Mass.) Centinel*, 9 January 1805.

51. Andrews, *Centennial Discourse*, 22.

52. Chandler, *History of the Town of Shirley*, 208.

53. Butler, *History of the Town of Groton*, 151.

54. Damon, *History of Holden*, 55.

55. Stowe, *History of the Town of Hubbardston*, 128.

56. Hudson, *History of Sudbury*, 130.

## Chapter 5. Meetinghouses of the Seventeenth Century

1. *The Directory for the Public Worship of God* (1649), cited in Garvan, *Architecture and Town Planning*, 141. The best critique of Garvan's point of view is Trent, "Marblehead Pews."

2. A fourteenth-century "Great Barn" with a hipped roof and oak frame still survives at Wanborough Manor, Guildford, England.

3. *Records of the Town of Cambridge*, 85: "Voted . . . that the meeting house shall be repaired with a 4:square roof." See also Bailey, *Beginning of the First Church*, 1. Evidence from the Chesapeake area suggests that "4:square" may also signify a "true pitch" of forty-five degrees.

4. Sprunger, *Dutch Puritanism*, 103; *Commemorative Exercises of the First Church of Christ in Hartford*, 143–59; quotations taken from Kelly, *Early Connecticut Meetinghouses*, 1:191–94; Wadsworth, *Diary*, 30 August 1737 (12).

5. Donnelly, *New England Meeting Houses*, 15.

6. *Records of the Colony and Plantation of New Haven*, 25, 145, 304–5; *New Haven Town Records*, 1:49, 115, 270–74; Kelly, *Early Connecticut Meetinghouses*, 2:3–5.

7. Winthrop, *Journal*, September 1639, 2 February 1641, 17 September 1644 (309–10, 344, 553); Donnelly, *New England Meeting Houses*, 122; Turell, *Benjamin Colman*, 179.

8. Ellis, *History of the First Church*, 170.

9. Cummings, *Framed Houses*, chap. 1.

10. Stell, *An Inventory of Nonconformist Chapels and Meeting-houses*; Stell, "Puritan and Nonconformist Meetinghouses in England."

11. Powell and Gilmore, in "Old Ship Meetinghouse," 1:9–11, were the first to address the American origin of the term *meetinghouse*, proposing it as evidence the meetinghouse form was also American.

12. Donnelly, *New England Meeting Houses*, chap. 2; Garvan, *Architecture and Town Planning*, chap. 6, esp. 140–43. For background see also Laurent, *Promenade à travers les temples de France*, 64, 298.

13. Hamberg, *Temples for Protestants*, 22–23, 36–43, 126–29; Perret's quotation taken from 37.

14. Guicharnaud, "Introduction," 135, 143; Laurent, *Promenade à travers les temples de France*, 11–25. Laurent illustrates long temples at La Rochelle and Gironde, 228, 234; six-sided temples at Bergerac, 240; round temples at Quevilly, Montauban, and Lyon, 18, 263, 298; octagonal temples at Caen and La Rochelle, 18, 228; a square temple at Metz, 128; and a rectangular temple at Charenton, 16, 64.

15. Sprunger, "Puritan Church Architecture," 52–53; Sprunger, *Dutch Puritanism*, 66, 91–92.

16. Quotation taken from Spicer, *Calvinist Churches*, 114.

17. First noticed among American scholars by Donald R. Friary, the Burntisland kirk is also cited by Kevin Sweeney in "Meetinghouses, Town Houses, and Churches," 61.

18. Drummond, *Church Architecture*, 48–49; Hay, *Architecture of Scottish Post-Reformation Churches*, 32–34; Glendinning et al., *History of Scottish Architecture*, 626; Groome, *Ordnance Gazetteer of Scotland*.

19. Spicer, *Calvinist Churches*, 57–60. Archbishop William Laud (1573–1645) dismissed the Burntisland kirk as a "square theatre."

20. "Brief History of Old Bergen Church," 2–3.

21. Alexander, "Religion in Rensselaerswijck"; Prime, *History of Long Island*, 341; *Appleton's Cyclopedia*, s.v. "Schoonmaker"; Stiles, *History of the City of Brooklyn*, 355; Hamilton, *Itinerarium*, 167; Hempstead, *Diary*, 12 July 1749 (519).

22. Davies, *Worship of American Puritans*, 235.

23. "Rook Lane Chapel." Information kindly provided by Donald R. Friary.

24. Foote, *Three Centuries*, 54–55.

25. Three men involved in the construction of the Huguenot temple at Amentières escaped to England in the late sixteenth century. Spicer, *Calvinist Churches*, 114.

26. Hamberg, *Temples for Protestants*, 40, 128; Laurent, *Promenade à travers les temples de France*, 228; Guicharnaud, "Introduction," 144.

27. Peterson, *Price of Redemption*, 8; Garvan, *Architecture and Town Planning*, 46–48. The 1641 Brockett map of New Haven is illustrated in Osterweis, *Three Centuries of New Haven*.

28. Donnelly, *New England Meeting Houses*, 135n31.

29. *Bicentennial Book of Malden*, 124–25.

30. The town of Farmington, for example, repaired a "court chamber" on the third floor of its four-square meetinghouse in 1762. Kelly, *Early Connecticut Meetinghouses*, 2:289.

31. Powell, "Exhuming Old Ship"; Coolidge, "Hingham Builds a Meetinghouse." According to Coolidge, the committee was also instructed "to view some other meeting houses in some other Towns, and comparing their number of inhabitants with ours, they may better inform themselves how big a house may be suitable for this town."

32. Winiarski, "Gendered 'Relations,'" 58.

33. The 1696 contract reads, "with 2 [or] 3 gables on every side." Cited in Hurd, *History of Essex County*, 1:583.

34. *First Church in Middleborough*, 5.

35. From Ayer, *South Meeting-House*, 3: "We know who was the builder, for in the Braintree Records occurs the following entry: 'Lievt. Robert Tweld, who erected the South Church at Boston died March 9th, 1696/7, aged 77 or thereabout.'" *Records of the Town of Braintree*, 17, 693.

36. Ayer, *South Meeting-House*; Donnelly, *New England Meeting Houses*, 66, 67; Hill, *History of the Old South Church*, 1:139–46; Hull, *Diaries*, 6 February, 12 March, and 17 September 1669 (229–30); Peterson, *Price of Redemption*, 44–45. Quotations taken from Hill, 145–46.

37. William Burgis, *Boston N Engd. Planted A.D. MDCXXX*. Boston, 1728. Library of the Boston Athenaeum, Boston, Mass.

38. Ellis, *History of the First Church in Boston*, 170–73; *Records of the First Church*, 1:123–26, 145. According to the *New England Weekly Journal* for 5 June 1727, "this day is Published A Draught of the Meeting House of the Old Church in Boston, with the New Spire and Gallery and are to be sold by Mr. Price, over against the town House." No trace of this print has been found. *Records of the First Church in Boston*, 1:xxix. Quotation from Ellis, 171.

39. Simonds, *First Church and Society of Branford*, 48. Branford's "long brick house" was not built because the town was also considering a square wood-frame forty-by-forty alternative and drew lots to decide. They chose a "square house." Donnelly, in *New England Meeting Houses*, calls these meetinghouses "rectangular."

40. Banks, *History of Martha's Vineyard*, 2:146; Roads, *History and Traditions of Marblehead*, 14–24; Judd, *History of Hadley*, 42; Caulkins, *History of Norwich*, 126.

41. Green, *Springfield*, 75.

42. Donnelly, *New England Meeting Houses*, 122; Dow, *History of the Town of Hampton*, 351.

43. *Two Hundred and Fiftieth Anniversary of the First Church of Christ, Old Saybrook*, 23; *Quarter Millennial Anniversary*, 59–61.

44. *Early Records of the Town of Dedham*, 3:38–39, 48, 115, 196–97, 187–88. For a comparison see Butler, *History of the Town of Groton*, 139.

45. Caulkins, *History of New London*, 108; Newman, *Rehoboth in the Past*, 17.

46. "The Lord's Barn" is cited in *Centennial History of the Town of Millbury*, 309. One of the meanings of the term *barn* in the *Oxford English Dictionary*, 2d ed. (2010), is a "building for worship" (1689). European associations between barns and early Protestant houses of worship are cited in Craig, *Reformation, Politics, and Polemics*, 125; Guicharnaud, "Introduction," 135, 143; Spicer, *Calvinist Churches*, 97, 115, 179, 199. For New England and Long Island, see *Proceedings of the Celebration of the Two Hundred and Fiftieth Anniversary of the First Church of Christ in Milford*, 7, 46; Underhill, *Descendants of Edward Small*, 745; Jones, *Stockbridge Past and Present*, 59; Hurd, *History of Worcester County*, 2:1103; Smith and Rann,

*History of Rutland County,* 600; Swift, *History of the Town of Middlebury,* 308–9; Drake, *History and Antiquities,* 576; Child, *Gazetteer and Business Directory of Chittenden County,* 256; Lambert, *History of the Colony of New Haven,* 53; Speare, *Colonial Meeting-Houses,* 44; Stiles, *History of Ancient Windsor,* 1:324–25; Adams, *History of the Town of Southampton,* 156. In Essex, Mass., a private barn was temporarily fitted with an old pulpit and singing pews during renovations of the meetinghouse. Crowell, *History of the Town of Essex,* 244.

47. Yates, *Buildings, Faith, and Worship,* 27–36.

48. Stell, "Puritan and Nonconformist Meetinghouses in England," 51.

49. Sprunger, "Puritan Church Architecture," 36.

50. Quotation taken from *Ancient Historical Records of Norwalk,* 49; Donnelly, "Seventeenth-Century Meeting House Turrets"; Craig Chartier, "Duxbury Second Meeting House Dig 2008," Plymouth Archaeological Rediscovery Project, described in *Duxbury Clipper,* 15 October 2008; Sewell, *History of Woburn,* 78–79; Hazen, *History of Billerica,* 168–69; Deetz, *In Small Things Forgotten,* 98–99, 102.

51. Shurtleff, *Log Cabin Myth;* Bradford, *History of Plymouth Plantation,* 1:275–76.

52. Adams, *Historical Discourse* (Portsmouth, N.H.), 24–25.

53. Wadleigh, *Notable Events,* 70; Jewett and Jewett, *Rowley,* 104.

54. Walker, *Our Four Meeting Houses,* 3–4.

55. Hurd, *History of Merrimack and Belknap Counties,* chapters on "Chichester" (235–62) and "Pembroke" (560–88); Price, *Chronological Register,* 28.

56. Candee, "Wooden Buildings."

57. Burnham, *History and Traditions of Shelburne,* 9; *History of Windsor County,* 578–80.

58. William Andrews and Ensign Munson reported to the town of New Haven "they thought it good that the upper Turret be taken Down." *New Haven Town Records* (11 August 1662), 2:5. Copeland, *"Our Country and Its People,"* 3:242, describes the West Springfield meetinghouse.

59. Hurd, *History of Worcester County,* 1:381.

60. *Records of the Town of Cambridge,* 4; *Watertown Records,* 1:17.

61. *Springfield Records,* 1:157.

62. Sewall, *History of Woburn,* 32n15; *Records of the West Precinct of Watertown,* 33.

63. Smith, *History of Newton,* 52. The meetinghouse referred to is the one Watertown bought in 1721.

64. Donnelly, *New England Meeting Houses,* 50; for "pyks" see Earle, *Sabbath,* 7.

65. Harris and Lever, *Illustrated Glossary,* 48.

66. Cummings, *Framed Houses,* 144.

67. Trumbull, *History of Northampton,* 1:121.

68. See the detail of the Old Cedar in Boston (Third Church) in chapter 7.

69. Caulkins, *History of Norwich,* 216; Donnelly, *New England Meeting Houses,* 127; *Ancient Historical Records of Norwalk,* 104.

70. Donnelly, "New England Pyramids," 76–77.

71. Tapley, *St. Peter's Church in Salem,* 11–20. Donnelly, "New England Pyramids," 76–77.

72. *Springfield Records,* 2:157–63.

73. St. George, "Style and Structure"; *Bicentennial Book of Malden,* 123–25; Tilden, *History of the Town of Medfield,* 63. The guidebook at Blythburgh, however, says the pulpit dates from 1670 to 1675.

74. The author is indebted to Giovanna Vitelli for pointing out this pulpit and to Jennifer H. Hanes of the Natick Historical Society and to Robert F. Trent for providing an initial analysis.

75. Quotation from *Bicentennial Book of Malden*, 125; *Historical Manual of the Congregational Church of Topsfield*, 7; Sewall, *History of Woburn*, 84–85.

76. *Records of the Town Meeting of Lynn*, 1:9, states that Thomas Farrar Sr., Crispus Brewer, Allen Bread Sr., Clement Coldom, Robert Rand Sr., Johnathan Hudson, Richard Hude Sr., and Sergant Heaven should "set in the pulpit."

77. Atwater, *History of the Colony of New Haven*, 248–49.

78. Adams, *Historical Discourse* (Portsmouth, N.H.), 25; *Historical Manual of the Congregational Church of Topsfield*, 7.

79. Stiles, *Itineraries*, 164.

80. Eliot, *Historical Notices*, 17.

81. Reymond, *L'Architecture religieuse*, 33. Reymond cites a 1586 drawing in *Chronique du chanoine* by Johannes Wick.

82. Watkins, "Three Contracts," 27.

83. Yates, *Buildings, Faith, and Worship*, 29; Reymond, *L'Architecture religieuse*, 30 (a late example in Scotland is Ardchattan Parish Church, Argyll).

84. Brookhaven quotation taken from Thompson, *History of Long Island*, 1:271; Dorchester quotation taken from *Records of the First Church in Dorchester*, 243; Harris, *Valedictory Sermon*, 27.

85. Waters, *History of Chelmsford*, 48.

86. Ward, "'In a Feasting Posture,'" 12–14; Stiles, *Literary Diary*, 6 September 1773 (1:411).

87. *Record of the Services Held at the Congregational Church of Windsor*, 59.

88. Trent, "Marblehead Pews."

89. Kelly, *Early Connecticut Meetinghouses*, 2:304; Adams, *Historical Discourse* (Portsmouth, N.H.), 25, 35; *Records of the Town of Braintree*, 36.

90. *Ancient Historical Records of Norwalk*, 80–81.

91. Wethersfield: Kelly, *Early Connecticut Meetinghouses*, 2:287; Portsmouth: Adams, *Historical Discourse*, 25; Malden: *Bicentennial Book of Malden*, 125; Garvan, "Protestant Plain Style," 5–13.

## Chapter 6. Meetinghouses of the Eighteenth Century

1. Foote, *Annals of King's Chapel*, 1:205; Isham, *Trinity Church in Newport*, 8; Lounsbury, "Anglican Church Design," 25–28. Of the two Anglican church designs cited in the Chesapeake region by Lounsbury, King's Chapel probably resembled the later eighteenth-century Maryland type. Quotation taken from Watkins, "Three Contracts," 31–32.

2. Bushman, *Refinement of America*, 174; Nissenbaum, *Battle for Christmas*, chap. 1.

3. Lounsbury, "Anglican Church Design."

4. Rose, *Colonial Houses of Worship*, 408. Stuart Feld argues that most early Anglican churches followed "meetinghouse type" models, including the first King's Chapel and the first Trinity in Boston. Feld, "St. Michael's Church," 103–5. For more on this subject see MacSparran, *Letter Book and Abstract of Out Services*.

5. Feld, "St. Michael's Church," 97; Marblehead Church to Sir Francis Nicholson, 27 November 1714, Society for the Propagation of the Gospel in Foreign Parts, cited at http://stmichaels1714.org.

6. Tapley, *St. Peter's Church in Salem*, frontispiece and 49.

7. Bateman, "National Register Nomination Information."

8. *Trinity Church in the City of Boston*, 6–7.

9. Stell, "Puritan and Nonconformist Meetinghouses," 54–55. For a discussion of the compass-headed window in the ecclesiastical architecture of the southern American colonies, see Nelson, *Beauty of Holiness*, 146–52. Nelson notes that the New England founders of Protestant congregations in South Carolina and Georgia typically built brick meetinghouses with flat windows rather than the "arch'd" windows favored by the Anglicans.

10. Benes and Zimmerman, *New England Meeting House and Church*, entry 58.

11. A pitched roof extends from one end of the gable to the other. Besides "flat," eighteenth-century documents called them "barn-fashion roofs," "flattish roofs, "long roofs," "straight roofs," and "English roofs."

12. "Manifesto or Declaration, Set forth by the Undertakers of the New Church," in Lothrop, *History of the Church in Brattle Street*, 20–25. Lothrop cites the diary of Josiah Cotton of Marblehead, Mass., where "Manifesto Church" is used as a contemptuous term (39–40, 44–45). Ezra Stiles measured this meetinghouse in 1751. Stiles, *Itineraries*, 97.

13. Providence Baptists, for example, worshiped after 1700 in a house shaped like a "hay cap." Tillinghast and Tillinghast, *Little Journey*, 13.

14. Durham, Conn., for example, built a forty-by-forty-foot meetinghouse in 1709 with a "flat roof, and turret." Fowler, *History of Durham*, 92–93.

15. Deane, *History of Scituate*, 37.

16. Bailey, *Historical Sketches of Andover*, 427–30.

17. Tucker, "Meeting Houses of the First Parish," 306–28.

18. Waters, *History of Chelmsford*, 677.

19. Forrey, "Meeting House at Rumney Marsh," 89; Sewall, *Diary*, 10 July 1710 (2:639).

20. Hudson, *History of the Town of Lexington*, 57.

21. Eliot, *Historical Notices*, 6.

22. Hadley: Judd, *History of Hadley*, 318; Middletown: Adams, *Middletown Upper Houses*, 31; Stratfield: Orcutt, *History of the Old Town of Stratford*, 480–82; East Haven: Havens, *Historical Discourse*, 19; Wallingford: Perkins, *Historical Sketches of Meriden*, 52–53; Westfield: Lockwood, *Westfield and Its Historic Influences*, 1:311; *History of the Connecticut Valley*, 947.

23. Currier, *History of Newbury*, 337; *Centennial Discourse*, 12–20; *First Church in Middleborough*, 5.

24. Jameson, *History of Medway*, 108–9.

25. Stiles, *History of Ancient Windsor*, 1:232.

26. Temple, *History of Framingham*, 145.

27. *Milton Town Records*, 251.

28. Waters, introduction to *Diary of William Bentley*, xli; Smith, *History of Chatham*, 147, 268–69.

29. Usher, *History of Medford*, 400.

30. Gage, *History of Rowley*, 17; Waters, *History of Chelmsford*, 687; Brown, *History of the Town of Bedford*, frontispiece; *Lexington: A Handbook*, 8.

31. Cheyney, *Readings in English History*, 516. For a New England viewpoint see Gilbert, *Annals of an Old Parish*, 41: "'The steeple house' was the common name given to one of our Churches by the Puritans."

32. Bentley, *Diary*, 8 August 1797 (2:231); 18 August 1793 (2:40–41).

33. Judd, *History of Hadley*, 310.

34. Waters, *History of Chelmsford*, 677: "Voted a concurrence to the committee's proposals in all things as to finishing the meeting house which we have agreed to build in

Chelmsford except the steeple." This may be the first known use of the term *steeple* in New England by a Reformed parish.

35. "Battlements" were cited by Boston selectmen giving the New North permission to build in 1713. Thwing, *Inhabitants and Estates*, entry 46760.

36. Holman, "William Price"; Reps, "Boston by Bostonians."

37. Minor quoted in Cothren, *History of Ancient Woodbury*, 1:139; see also Kelly, *Early Connecticut Meetinghouses*, 2:319.

38. Foote, *Annals of King's Chapel*, 105.

39. Watkins, "Three Contracts," 31.

40. Lounsbury, "Anglican Church Design," 25.

41. Quotation taken from Thwing, *Inhabitants and Estates*, entry 46760; Eliot, *Historical Notices*, 8; Fuller, *Historical Discourse*, 48n.

42. Ellis, *Commemorative Discourse*, 7.

43. Sewall, *Diary*, 24 June 1717 (2:857).

44. An alternate view of Brattle's bell tower is also known. William Bentley, who was thirteen years old when the structure was pulled down in 1772, writes in his diary that the bell tower on the 1743 Separate church in Exeter, N.H., "exactly resembles the tower and steeple of the former Brattle Street Church in Boston." A painted view of the Exeter meetinghouse reveals a bell mounted on top of the tower and protected by a high steeple. It is likely the Brattle's tower had been taken down and redesigned before Bentley saw it. Bentley, *Diary*, 14 September 1801 (2:392).

45. For example, St. Swithin was designed by Christopher Wren. See Taylor, *Towers and Steeples*, opp. 22 and 26.

46. Babcock, *Christ Church*, 32.

47. J. Gwilt, *The Encyclopaedia of Architecture*, 1867, cited in Lewandoski, "Historical American Timber-Framed Steeples," 18.

48. Sinnott, *Meetinghouse and Church*, 44–46; Hill, *History of the Old South Church*, 1:431–57; Wisner, *History of the Old South Church*, 26–28; Smith, *Beacon Guide*, 60; Betlock et al., *Old South*, 8–9.

49. Mason, *Annals of Trinity Church*, 41–51; Sinnott, *Meetinghouse and Church*, 186–87.

50. Quotations taken from Kelly, *Early Connecticut Meetinghouses*, 1:172; see also Steiner, *History of the Plantation of Menunkatuck*, 275.

51. Porter, *Historical Discourse*, 12. Rev. Thomas Ruggles to Rev. Thomas Prince, 10 June 1729, cited in *Connecticut Historical Society Collections*, 3:287. "Steeple was 120 foot high and was the first in Connecticut." According to Edith Nettleton and Ruth Nettleton of Guilford, Rev. William C. H. Moe, who served as minister of the parish between 1925 and 1948, said Hubbard followed "details [that] were told him by aged people who had worshipped in the building." See Moe, "Second Meeting House."

52. *Commemoration of the 250th Anniversary of the First Church of Charlestown*, 39.

53. Hurd, *History of Norfolk County*, 751; Bell, *History of Exeter*, 179–80; Hazlett, *History of Rockingham County*, 162–63.

54. Kelly, *Early Connecticut Meetinghouses*, 1:307; *History of Milford, Connecticut*, 51; Perkins, *Historical Sketches of Meriden*, 34–36. Early bell towers were also built in Old Lyme and Hartford's First Society: Cary, *Memorial Discourse of the First Congregational Church*, 4; Wadsworth, *Diary*, 29 May 1738 (25).

55. Rose, *Colonial Houses of Worship*, 412–13.

56. Tapley, *St. Peter's Church in Salem*, 11–20.

57. A "paster" was a small patch designed to be attached to an existing view in order to update it. See Reps, "Boston by Bostonians," 38–39.

58. *Records of Trinity Church*, 1:427.

59. Goelet, *Voyage and Travels*, 14 October 1750.

60. Babcock, *Christ Church*, 181–90; Foley, "Christ Church, Boston," 77–80.

61. Watkins, "Malden's Old Meetinghouses," 39.

62. The author is indebted to Richard M. Candee for locating this drawing in the town of Kittery archives and for his research on John Godsoe. Candee, "Land Surveys."

63. *Proceedings at the Centennial Celebration, Town of Longmeadow*, 158.

64. Fuller, *Historical Discourse*, 48. See also Reps, "Boston by Bostonians," 34–49, which illustrates William Burgis's *A North East View of the Great Town of Boston*, 1723; William Burgis and William Price's *A South East View of the Great Town of Boston in New England in America*, 1725, 1736, 1743; James Turner's *View of Boston*, 1743, 1744, 1750; Paul Revere's *Perspective View*, 1770; *A View of Part of the Town of Boston in New England and British Ships Landing their Troops 1768*, 1770; and *A View of Boston with Several Ships of War*, 1774.

65. Benes and Zimmerman, *New England Meeting House and Church*, 122–23; Tatham, "Lithographs of Benjamin Champney," 4, and cover illustration. A print by Benjamin Johnson of Newburyport, Massachusetts, in 1774 (see fig. 9.7) reveals three such belfries dominating the town's skyline. Smith, *History of Newburyport*, opp. 61.

66. Merrill, *History of Amesbury*, 217; Coffin, *History of Newbury*, 240.

67. According to Harry Eversull, the first steeple of the stone meetinghouse erected in East Haven, Conn., in 1772 "was of the type known as the Squaw's cap." Eversull, *Evolution of an Old New England Church*, 73. The term was interpreted with the assistance of Kevin M. Sweeney.

68. Stiles, *Itineraries*, 29 (28 September 1762).

69. Kelly, *Early Connecticut Meetinghouses*, 2:286–90.

70. Kevin M. Sweeney to the author, 16 August 1978.

71. *Proceedings at the Centennial Celebration, Town of Longmeadow*, 158.

72. Merrill, *History of Amesbury*, 316.

73. *Town Records of Manchester*, 2:65. Manchester later changed its mind and voted to build its steeple "from the ground upwards"—that is, a standing bell tower, probably one that imitated Gloucester's first parish, built in 1738.

74. *Muddy River and Brookline Records*, 231.

75. Davis, *History of Wallingford*, 121.

76. Kelly, *Early Connecticut Meetinghouses*, 1:196.

77. Ibid., 2:112.

78. Guild, *James Manning*, 229; Isham, *Meeting House*; Detwiller, "Thomas Dawes's Church in Brattle Square." Gibbs (1682–1754) published *A Book of Architecture* in 1728.

79. Cited in Kelly, *Early Connecticut Meetinghouses*, 2:290. For an earlier version of the arguments presented in this section see Benes, "Twin-Porch versus Single-Porch Stairwells."

80. Roads, *History and Traditions of Marblehead*, 24; Judd, *History of Hadley*, 42; Chapin, *Glastenbury*, 58.

81. *New Haven Town Records*, 154 (19 September 1699).

82. Eliot, *Historical Notices*, 17.

83. Ruell, "'Round' Meetinghouses," 171–74, 178–82; Waite, *History of Claremont*, 127, 353; Walker, *Our Four Meeting Houses*, 10.

84. Caulkins, *History of New London*, 488; Metcalf, *Annals of the Town of Mendon*, 158; Mendon's text reads, "A Rooff to cripple on upon the Ruff of the former house att each end."

85. Clapp, *History of the Town of Dorchester*, 307; Harris, *Valedictory Sermon*, 28–32.

86. Bates, *History of Westborough*, 154.

87. Vail, "American Sketchbooks," no. 780.

88. Usher, *History of Medford*, 349.

89. *Mattapoisett and Old Rochester*, 76; Earle, *Sabbath*, 63.

90. Hurd, *History of Norfolk County*, 646.

91. Lewis, *History of Walpole*, 94–95.

92. Lancaster, *History of Gilmanton*, 184.

93. Hurd, *History of Middlesex County*, 3:439.

94. Bourne, *History of Wells and Kennebunk*, 438; Trayser, *Barnstable*, 57.

95. Paine, *History of Harwich*, 256–57.

96. Ibid., 157; Smith, *History of Chatham*, 333.

97. Blake, *Annals of the Town of Dorchester*, 58.

98. Thwing, *History of the First Church in Roxbury*, 250.

99. Briggs, *Church and Cemetery Records*, 1:8.

100. Marvin, *History of Worcester County*, 2:120–25; *Account of the Observance of the One Hundred and Fiftieth Anniversary*, 27.

101. Perley, *History of Boxford*, 245.

102. Four small- to moderate-sized New Hampshire towns that chose twin-porch plans were Dublin (1771), Hudson (1771), Chester (1773), and Westmoreland (1779).

103. Wallace, *History of Canaan*, 146.

104. Ramsdell, *History of Milford*, 63–64; 66.

105. Stearns, *History of Ashburnham*, 294.

106. Kelly, *Early Connecticut Meetinghouses*, 1:36, 165, 264–65; 2:294.

107. Stiles, *Itineraries*, 109–10.

108. Merrill, *History of Amesbury*, 236, 318.

109. Candage, *Historical Sketkches of Bluehill*, 44–45.

110. Watkins, "Malden's Old Meetinghouses," 39.

111. Records of the South Precinct, Weymouth, Mass., 23 May 1785. (Copy courtesy of Chester B. Kevitt, Weymouth Historical Commission.)

112. Herrick, *History of Gardner*, 484–85.

113. Stark, *History of Dunbarton*, 156–59; Blake, *History of the Town of Warwick*, 71–72.

114. For the full text of Dunlap's specifications, see Parsons, *The Dunlaps*, 45–52.

115. Quotation taken from Kelly, *Early Connecticut Meetinghouses*, 1:243; see also *Two Hundredth Anniversary, Kensington*, 37.

116. Larned, *History of Windham County*, 1:53.

117. Hamilton, *Itinerarium*, 109.

118. Quotation taken from Kelly, *Early Connecticut Meetinghouses*, 1:135; see also Benes and Zimmerman, *New England Meeting House and Church*, 37–38 (fig. 73); Havens, *Historical Discourse*, 21.

119. Benes and Zimmerman, *New England Meeting House and Church*, 40–44 (figs. 74a, 74b); Kimball, *Last Sermon*, 10. The best description of the circumstances surrounding the Knowlton pulpit are found in Nelson, "Capt. Abraham Knowlton," 46–53.

120. Waters, *Ipswich in the Massachusetts Bay Colony*, 2:261, 440, 473–74; Bentley, *Diary*, 21 June 1810 (3:526).

121. Benes and Zimmerman, *New England Meeting House and Church,* 39; Gould and Kidder, *History of New Ipswich,* 157.

122. Worcester, *Memorial of the Old and New Tabernacle,* 25; Hurd, *History of Cheshire and Sullivan Counties,* 475. A dove represents the Holy Spirit in Christian iconography.

123. Merrill, *History of Amesbury,* 232; Benes, *Old-Town and the Waterside,* entry 156.

124. Benes and Zimmerman, *New England Meeting House and Church,* 39.

125. Porter, *Historical Discourse,* 11.

126. Quotation taken from Kelly, *Early Connecticut Meetinghouses,* 1:277; see also Stowe and Stowe, *Harriet Beecher Stowe,* 29.

127. Speare, *Colonial Meeting-Houses,* 186.

128. White, *History of the Town of Litchfield,* 29. The author is indebted to the late N. Sherrill Foster of East Hampton, L.I., for pointing out the Buell pulpit and pilaster fragment.

129. Wight, *Some Old Time Meeting Houses,* 12.

130. Forbes, *Gravestones,* 108–9, 130; Sikes quotation taken from Noon, *History of Ludlow,* 29, 185.

131. Earle, *Sabbath,* 17.

132. Photocopy of 1743 meetinghouse building contract, James Gibson Papers, Pelham Records, 1743–79, Special Collections and University Archives, W. E. B. Du Bois Library, University of Massachusetts Amherst; Parmenter, *History of Pelham,* 79. See also Benes, "Essay."

133. Weis, *Colonial Clergy,* vol. 2, s.v. "Moses Taft" and "Anthony Wibard."

134. For an earlier discussion of meetinghouse colors, see Benes, "Sky Colors and Scattered Clouds." Color analysis on a dentil from a window cornice of the 1766 meetinghouse in Shrewsbury, Mass., was done in 1979 by Historic New England. Their report identified the lowest layer of paint as an "ochre," Munsell Code 10YR 5/6. Benes and Zimmerman, *New England Meeting House and Church,* entry 60.

135. *Springfield Records,* 2:157; Joshua Lincoln is cited in Marble, "Old Ship" (citation courtesy of Robert B. St. George); Benes and Zimmerman, *New England Meeting House and Church,* 5, 36, 131, 136.

136. Bates, *Westfield Jubilee,* 62.

137. Cummings, "Decorative Painters and House Paintings," 113; James Brown Marston, *State Street,* 1801, oil on canvas, Massachusetts Historical Society, Boston.

138. Often applied to meetinghouse roofs, Spanish brown was made using red lead and generally had a very reddish hue. The state architectural historian James L. Garvin reports that in 1773 the town of Rindge, N.H., voted to cover the wooden shingles of their meetinghouse with pitch and sand; other towns considered but rejected this treatment (Garvin to Jim Derby and Vernacular Architecture Forum, 15 March 2010, author's archives). In 1768 the town of Reading, Mass., voted "not to paint the clapboards, or do the roof with rosin, tar, and sand." Hamilton, *Commemorative Address Delivered in Wakefield,* 28.

139. *Records of the West Precinct of Watertown,* 30, 35.

140. Watkins, "Malden's Old Meetinghouses," 39.

141. Mitchell, *History of New Haven County,* 289.

142. Petersham: Willson, *Address Delivered in Petersham,* 26; Madison: Evarts, *History of the First Congregational Church,* 18; Pelham: Pelham meetinghouse building contract, James Gibson Papers, Pelham Records, 1743–79, Special Collections and University Archives, W. E. B. Du Bois Library, University of Massachusetts Amherst; Rowley: Henry M. Nelson, "Georgetown," in Hurd, *History of Essex County,* 2:820; Gage, *History of Rowley,* 92–93; 38–40.

143. Ballou, *History of Milford*, 70.

144. Deforest, *Early History of Westborough*, 139.

145. Jewett and Jewett, *Rowley*, 110.

146. Ipswich: Thomas Lawlor's account, 19 September 1755, archives of the First Parish, Ipswich, Mass. Leominster: Stebbins, *Centennial Discourse*, 19. Hadley: Judd, *History of Hadley*, 314. North Brookfield: Temple, *History of North Brookfield*, 251; Lebanon and East Haven: Kelly, *Early Connecticut Meetinghouses*, 1:265; 2:138.

147. Temple and Sheldon, *History of Northfield*, 316; Annett and Lehtinen, *History of Jaffrey*, 316. Berlin: "To the Inhabitants of the District of Berlin." Shrewsbury: "Report of the Committee."

148. Reynolds, *Directions of House and Ship Painting*, 8, 13; First Parish, Northampton, 14.

149. Nelson, *Beauty of Holiness*, 19–20, 123; Upton, *Holy Things and Profane*, 103.

150. Paine, *History of Harwich*, 251.

151. Bentley, *Diary*, August 1793 (2:56).

152. Cummings and Candee, "Colonial and Federal America," 27–28. The exteriors of most homes in eighteenth-century New England were unpainted; barns were painted even less often. Paint analysis on about a dozen churches (almost all brick) in the Chesapeake region reveal that the earliest finish on exterior trim was reddish brown. Documentary research reveals there were also white, stone, and ochre. Carl Lounsbury to the author, 20 January 2010; Nelson, *Beauty of Holiness*, 119–120, 123.

153. Killingworth: Miller, *Historical Discourse*, 31; Norfolk: Roys, *History of the Town of Norfolk*, 11; East Hampton: Rattray, *Discovering the Past*, 204.

154. Watercolor mourning picture, Joseph Joy (1784–1812), in the collection of the Gore Place House Museum, Waltham, Mass., cited in Benes and Zimmerman, *New England Meeting House and Church*, 24. The provenance of this watercolor has been inferred from genealogical evidence in Joy, *Thomas Joy and His Descendants*, 92.

155. Bentley, *Diary*, 14 July 1795 (2:147); Kelly, *Early Connecticut Meetinghouses*, 2:320; Stearns, *History of Ashburnham*, 296. Timothy Tomlinson (1757–1821), born in Derby, Connecticut, was a private householder in Woodbury in 1790 (Cothern, *History of Ancient Woodbury*, 3:75–76, 258).

156. See, for example, Somersworth, N.H., in Hayward, *New England Gazetteer*. "Red and yellow ochre, also iron ore, have been found in this town. The ochre has been used in painting houses, and has been found to make a durable paint."

157. Sinnott, *Meetinghouse and Church*, 223; *Map of Kensington*, by Thomas Rand, 1823, New Hampshire Historical Society, Concord. The Dracut meetinghouse is now painted white.

158. Benes and Zimmerman, *New England Meeting House and Church*, 21.

159. Hampton: Kelly, *Early Connecticut Meetinghouses*, 1:188; Scituate: Waite, *First Trinitarian Congregational Church*, 41; Canaan: Wallace, *History of Canaan*, 149.

160. *One Hundred Fiftieth Anniversary, First Church of Christ in Pomfret*, 43–44.

161. "Deep" orange: Larned, *History of Windham County*, 2:3; "newest, biggest, and yallowest": Earle, *Sabbath*, 15.

162. Windham: Mitchell, *History of the United Church of New Haven*, 125; Brooklyn: Fogg, *Memorial Sermon*, 10, where Godfrey Malbone, who opposed in 1668 the building of a new meetinghouse in Brooklyn, Conn., is quoted as complaining that the parish wanted to "boast, I suppose, a newer, a larger, and a yellower one than the other [in Pomfret], and for a pretext they say it is not big enough." See also Blake, *Chronicles of New Haven Green*, 94; Kelly, *Early Connecticut Meetinghouses*, 1:xlvii, 46; Earle, *Sabbath*, 15. While the infor-

mation for Brooklyn (Earle and Blake) is questionable, it is included here because it may be accurate.

163. Hampton: Bayles, *History of Windham County*, 384; Dudley: *Dudley Town Records*, 113; Killingly (Second, North, or Thompson Parish): Larned, *History of Windham County*, 2:81; Bayles, *History of Windham County*, 644.

164. Hurd, *History of Middlesex County*, 3:435–39; Hayward, *Address Delivered*, 19.

165. Hayward, *History of Gilsum*, 18, 188–250.

166. Beard, *Genealogy*, 9; Guilford: Gallup, *Historical Discourse*, 24.

167. Stiles quotation taken from Kelly, *Early Connecticut Meetinghouses*, 2:34; Blake, *Chronicles of New Haven Green*, 94; Benes, *New England Prospect*, entry 65.

168. Gilead: Mack, *Historical Sketch*, 10; Lebanon Crank: *One Hundred Fiftieth Anniversary of the Organization of the Congregational Church in Columbia*, 35; Westbrook: *Two Hundred and Fiftieth Anniversary of the First Church of Christ Congregational, Old Saybrook, Connecticut*, 123; Bethany: Sharpe, *Bethany Sketches and Records*, 7; Griswold: Phillips, *Griswold*, 58.

169. Nelson, *Beauty of Holiness*, 155, 200–201.

170. Blake, *Chronicles of New Haven*, 93–94; *Boston Gazette*, 16 March 1761; Mitchell, *History of New Haven County*, 290. Blake writes that blue "has greatly puzzled the historians. Mr. Barber says it was caused by mixing too much lampblack with the white.... Others have suggested that the color symbolized the orthodoxy of the worshippers."

171. Stilgoe, *Common Landscape of America*, 167–68.

172. Andrews, *Shaker Meeting House*, 4.

173. Stiles, *Itineraries*, 285 (1769); Benes, "Psalmody," 128–31; Benes, "Distinguishing Signs," 141–43. Revival-related motifs appear notably in the work of Nathaniel Fuller, Jacob Vinal Jr., and Obadiah Wheeler.

174. Stiles, *Itineraries*, 299 (1769); Eliot, "Diary," 28 March 1742–5 June 1742.

175. Foote, *Annals of King's Chapel*, 1:294; Powell and Gilmore, "Old Ship Meeting House," 58–59.

176. Examined and photographed by the author in 1980.

177. Gilsum: Hayward, *Address Delivered*, 110; Newport: Wheeler, *History of Newport*, 110; Portsmouth: Hazlett, *History of Rockingham County*, 163; Rowe: *History and Proceedings of the Pocumtuck Valley Memorial Association* 7 (1922): 103.

178. Greens: Hurd, *History of Merrimack and Belknap Counties*, 631; Paine, *History of Harwich*, 256–57; Wheeler and Wheeler, *History of Brunswick*, 436; Lovering, *History of Holland*, 189; Sheldon, *History of Deerfield*, 1:472. Stone colors: Bentley, *Diary*, 14 July 1795 (2:147); Smith, *History of Chatham*, 333; Perry, *Old Burying Ground of Fairfield*, 229; lead colors: Hurd, *History of Merrimack and Belknap Counties*, 490; Lee, *Centennial Celebration of Barkhamsted*, 54; Records of the South Precinct, Weymouth, Mass., 23 May 1785.

179. Bentley, *Diary*, 19 December 1813 (4:221).

180. Simmons, *History*.

181. Gould and Kidder, *History of New Ipswich*, 153.

182. Washburn, *Historical Sketches*, 104.

183. Records of the South Precinct, Weymouth, Mass., 23 May 1785.

184. Dodge, *History of First Congregational Church*, 33.

185. *History of Bedford*, 328.

186. Waters, *Ipswich*, 2:440.

187. Gould and Kidder, *History of New Ipswich*, 153; Secomb, *History of Amherst*, 241; Jewett and Jewett, *Rowley*, 109; First Parish, Northampton, 12.

188. *Bicentennial of the First Congregational Church, Marblehead;* Wells, *History of Newbury,* 137.

189. Mack, *Historical Sketch,* 10, 13.

## Chapter 7. Meetinghouses of the Early Nineteenth Century

1. Nylander, "Towards Comfort and Uniformity"; Bushman, *Refinement of America,* 335–48; Kelly, *Early Connecticut Meetinghouses,* 1:176.

2. William Bentley noted that the 1793 pulpit in Chelmsford, Mass., was "gilded below the panels in chinese work." Bentley, *Diary,* 19 August 1793 (2:40–41). Westford, Mass., ordered builders in 1794 to "dress the Pulpit and Dress it in Crimson Color." Hodgman, *History of the Town of Westford,* 96.

3. Middle and Hanover Streets are cited in the records. Booth, *Story of the Second Church,* 22.

4. *New England Weekly Journal,* 28 April 1729, cited in Ayer, *South Meeting-House,* 4.

5. Wisner, *History of the Old South Church,* 27.

6. Eaton, *Famous Mather Byles,* opp. 66.

7. Wood, *History of the First Baptist Church,* 265.

8. Phillips, *Salem in the Eighteenth Century,* 344; *First Centenary, the North Church,* 21–23, 183; "Diary of Mary Vial Holyoke," 14, 16, and 17 July 1772 (78). A map prepared by Ezra Stiles indicates the North meetinghouse overlooked the drawbridge in Salem where Col. Alexander Leslie's 240 men arrived to take possession of illegal ordinance on 25 February 1775. Col. Thomas Pickering of Salem drew a line and said "no farther." The English eventually left without it. Stiles, *Diary,* 7 March 1775 (1:523).

9. Detwiller, "Thomas Dawes's Church"; *Boston Post-Boy,* 19 October 1772; *Providence Gazette,* 31 July 1773.

10. Isham, *Meeting House,* xvi, xviii.

11. Ibid., 24–25; Little, *Life and Work of James Gibbs,* 186–87; Guild, *James Manning,* 229.

12. Worcester, *Memorial of the Old and New Tabernacle,* 18–27.

13. Jones, *Stockbridge Past and Present,* 184.

14. Stiles, *Literary Diary,* 2:358–59.

15. Budington, *History of the First Church,* 235.

16. Speare, *Colonial Meeting-Houses,* 212–13. The Fairfield pulpit was to be painted a "light stone color," Perry, *Old Burying Ground of Fairfield,* 229.

17. Cummings, "Meeting and Dwelling House," 11–12; Kirker, *Architecture of Charles Bulfinch,* 17–19. Codman, *Hollis Street Church, Boston Records,* "Introduction."

18. Drawn from receipts and vouchers from Hollis Street Church (Boston, Mass.) Records, 1787–1879, Andover-Harvard Theological Library, Harvard Divinity School, Cambridge, Mass. (Call no. bMS 5). "To Painting and Glittering two Record Books . . . £0.11.8." The receipt was signed by Enoch Lane, 1 September 1788.

19. Kirker and Kirker, *Bulfinch's Boston,* 281. Little, *Life and Work of James Gibbs,* 186–87.

20. Bentley, *Diary,* 3 October 1809 (3:465); 10 June 1806 (3:234). *Report of the Proceedings . . . Kingston, Mass.,* 122.

21. *Proceedings in Commemoration of the Organization in Pittsfield,* 26–31.

22. Sinnott, *Meetinghouse and Church,* 76–80. Sinnott believes this design was influenced by Asher Benjamin's *Country Builder's Assistant* (1797), but at least two were erected before its publication. Joel Dickinson: Smith, *History of Pittsfield,* 441.

23. Sinnott called these designs "transitional." *Meetinghouse and Church,* 73–74.
24. Asher Benjamin and Daniel Raynerd, *The American Builder's Companion* (Boston, 1806). In the second edition of this work (issued by Benjamin in Charlestown, Mass., in 1811) the West Church design appears as plate 57. See also Vose, "Asher Benjamin's West Church."
25. Kelly, *Early Connecticut Meetinghouses,* 2:119.
26. Sinnott, *Meetinghouse and Church,* 111, 154.
27. Hodgman, *History of the Town of Westford,* 151–52; Bentley, *Diary,* 8 August 1797 (2:231).
28. *Commemoration of the Centennial of the Congregational Church, Hinsdale,* 33–35.
29. Kelly, *Early Connecticut Meetinghouses,* 2:165.
30. *First Parish, Northampton,* 21–30; quotation on 25.
31. *Proceedings in Commemoration of the Organization in Pittsfield,* 29.

## Chapter 8. Some Theoretical Models

1. Sprunger, "Puritan Church Architecture," 36–41; Barrow quotations on 40. See also White, "From Protestant to Catholic Plain Style," 460; Hammond, *Liturgy and Architecture,* 84–85.
2. Sanford, "Entering into Covenant," 29–33; Mason, *Annals of Trinity Church,* 51.
3. Babcock, *Christ Church,* 185; Wight, *Some Old Time Meeting Houses,* opp. 4; Little, *Life and Work of James Gibbs,* 187; Shaw, *Topographical and Historical Description,* 253.
4. The process described here had clear parallels elsewhere in the American colonies, but these may not have matched the scale of New England's practices where decisions were made by town or parish meetings rather than vestry committees. For specifications for Anglican parish churches in Virginia and the Carolinas, see Upton, *Holy Things and Profane,* 29–32; Nelson, *Beauty of Holiness,* 118–19.
5. Kingsbury, *History of the Town of Surry,* 175.
6. Kelly, *Early Connecticut Meetinghouses,* 1:173, 2:164.
7. Guilford imitating Newport: ibid., 1:172; Mason, *Annals of Trinity Church,* 40.
8. *First Parish, Northampton,* 21–30.
9. Archer, *Bicentennial History of Becket,* 35.
10. Dearborn, *History of Salisbury,* 132–40.
11. Adams, *Middletown Upper Houses,* 31; Hughes, *History of East Haven,* 77.
12. Stiles, *History of Ancient Windsor,* 1:232.
13. Chatham: Smith, *History of Chatham,* 170; Killingworth: Kelly, *Early Connecticut Meetinghouses,* 1:249.
14. "Essay on the Laying Out of Towns," 475.
15. Quotation taken from *Watertown Records,* 1:37; Drake, *History of Middlesex County,* 2:448.
16. *History of the Connecticut Valley,* 384–85; *Quarter Millennial Anniversary,* 64; Peterson, *Price of Redemption,* 53.
17. Hazen, *History of Billerica,* 168; Hurd, *History of Essex County,* 1:1947; *History of the Connecticut Valley,* 613.
18. Kelly, *Early Connecticut Meetinghouses,* 1:205, 2:297–99.
19. *Ancient Historical Records of Norwalk,* 71; *Town Records of Manchester,* 1:44–45.
20. West Springfield: *History of the Connecticut Valley,* 907; Boxford: Perley, *History of Boxford,* 127; Andover: Bailey, *Historical Sketches of Andover,* 430.
21. Quotation taken from Hurd, *History of Essex County,* 1:1947–48; Noyes, *Memorial of the Town of Hampstead,* 2:8–9; Mirick, *History of Haverhill,* 84, 100–101.

22. Gage, *History of Rowley*, 17; Jewett and Jewett, *Rowley*, 106.

23. New Haven 1639; Hartford Second 1670; Wethersfield 1686; Stamford 1702; Farmington 1709; Norwich 1711. See Donnelly, *New England Meeting Houses*, 122, 128; Kelly, *Early Connecticut Meetinghouses*, 1:157, 205; Huntington, *History of Stamford*, 134–36.

24. Watertown in 1656; Woburn in 1672; Gloucester in 1697; Framingham in 1698. See *Records of the Town of Cambridge*, 85; Donnelly, *New England Meeting Houses*, 124, 130.

25. Hurd, *History of Cheshire and Sullivan Counties*, 225; Blood, *History of Temple*, 135; Little, *American Decorative Wall Painting*, 60; Kingsbury, *History of the Town of Surry*, 175.

26. Pittsfield: Smith, *History of Pittsfield*, 441; Richmond: Annin, *Richmond, Massachusetts*, 62; Hinsdale: *Commemoration of the Centennial of the Congregational Church, Hinsdale*, 33–35; Salisbury: Kelly, *Early Connecticut Meetinghouses*, 2:176; Lee: *Records of the Town of Lee*, 97; Winsted: *History of Litchfield County*, 212; Barber, *Connecticut Historical Collections*, 503; Washington: Kelly, *Early Connecticut Meetinghouses*, 2:257; South Canaan: ibid., 2:210–11; Westfield: Lockwood, *Westfield and Its Historic Influences*, 2:235; Lenox: Sinnott, *Meetinghouse and Church*, 82; Otis: Field, *History of Berkshire County*, 2:261–62.

27. John Hulett of Watertown, Conn., built the meetinghouses, Lee (1800) and Lenox (1805) and possibly worked on Richmond (1794). Annin, *Richmond, Massachusetts*, 59; Hyde, *Centennial Celebration*, 226–27; Sinnott, *Meetinghouse and Church*, 77–78, 82.

28. Sinnott, *Meetinghouse and Church*, 96–99; Adams, *Historical Discourse* (Templeton, Mass.), 50; Leonard and Seward, *History of Dublin*, 29; Mason, *History of Dublin*, 205; Hayward, *History of Hancock*, 1:143.

29. Caverly, *Historical Sketch of Troy*, 130–32; *Annals of Brimfield*, 43. John Warner Barber's imprecise sketch of the Brimfield meetinghouse in 1832 provides no indication that the belfry and spire conformed to the Templeton model; see Barber, *Historical Collections of Massachusetts*, 277.

30. Mason, *History of Dublin*, 205.

31. Benes, "Templeton 'Run' and the Pomfret 'Cluster,'" 6–9.

32. Hayward, *History of Hancock*, 143.

33. Of the eight Templeton-model steeples and porches erected in 1811–1823, only the Templeton original was contracted to the architect-builder Elias Carter. The remaining seven were apparently contracted to others at a time when Carter himself had been hired to build the meetinghouses at Mendon, Mass., and Milford Conn., where he used a different design. See Forbes, "Elias Carter," 60–61.

34. Cochrane, *Antrim*, 179.

35. Robbins, *History of the Second Church*, 316.

36. Crowell, *History of Essex*, 84.

37. Kelly, *Early Connecticut Meetinghouses*, 2:111.

38. Bailey, *Historical Sketches of Andover*, 430.

39. Bliss, *History of Rehoboth*, 174.

40. Orcutt, *History of the Towns of New Milford and Bridgewater*, 184.

41. *Records of the West Precinct of Watertown*, 26–35.

42. Agawam, Massachusetts, purchased Suffield's frame in 1800, later converting it to a meetinghouse; Boxborough, Massachusetts, acquired nearby Harvard's first meetinghouse in 1775; and Harvard's Baptists acquired Leominster's first meetinghouse in 1775. Sinnott, *Meetinghouse and Church*, 221; *History of the Connecticut Valley*, 1049; Drake, *History of Middlesex County*, 1:271–72; Hagar, *Boxborough*, 15; Wilder, *History of Leominster*, 156.

## Chapter 9. Meetinghouse Architecture as Puritan Ecclesiology

1. Cothren, *History of Ancient Woodbury*, 1:139.
2. Cited by Sweeney, "Meetinghouses, Town Houses, and Churches," 63; Brattle Street: *Manifesto Church*, 4; Westfield: Lockwood, *Westfield and Its Historic Influences*, 1:323–24.
3. Norwalk: Sweeney, "Meetinghouses, Town Houses, and Churches," 59; Leominster: Wilder, *History of Leominster*, 155; Bedford: Mansur, *New England Church*, 156.
4. Quotation taken from Coolidge, "Hingham Builds a Meetinghouse," 445.
5. Bushman, *Refinement of America*, 170.
6. Buggeln, *Temples of Grace*, 74, 130.
7. Stiles, *Literary Diary*, 26 February 1772 (1:214).
8. Sanford, "Entering into Covenant," app. A.
9. Tillinghast and Tillinghast, *Little Journey*, 13; Isham, *Meetinghouse*, 1.
10. Sweeney, "Meetinghouses, Town Houses, and Churches," 65, 79.
11. Lounsbury, "God Is in the Details," 18.
12. The phrase "pure primitive Church" appears in a deacon's record in Roxbury, Mass., in 1788; quotation taken from Thwing, *History of the First Church in Roxbury*, 341.
13. Under some circumstances, the congregation or precinct supported conservative practices, especially when they were threatened by the disestablishment of state and church.
14. Bushman, *Refinement of America*, 174.
15. Foote, *Three Centuries*, 65. Turell, *Benjamin Colman*; Lothrop, *History of the Church in Brattle Street*, 44–45.
16. Turell, *Life and Character of the Reverend Benjamin Colman*, 180.
17. *Manifesto Church*, broadside reproduction between 4 and 5.
18. *Manifesto Church*, 5, 14, 27, 37–38; Hood, *History of Music in New England*, 141, citing Timothy Burbank's diary for the first music school in New England; Foote, *Three Centuries*, 100.
19. Stiles, *Itineraries*, 284.
20. Ware, *Two Discourses*, 29.
21. Robbins, *History of the Second Church*, 180; Chaney, *Hollis Street Church*, 6.
22. Fuller, *Historical Discourse*, 5.
23. Emerson, *Historical Sketch*, 163.
24. Hill, *History of the Old South Church*, 2:19–20; Eliot, *Sermon*, 22–23; Robbins, *History of the Second Church*, 180–84; Foote, *Three Centuries*, 159; Foote, *Annals of King's Chapel*, 1:205.
25. Eaton, *Famous Mather Byles*.
26. Ward, "'In a Feasting Posture,'" 17.
27. *Massachusetts Spy*, 3 January 1788.
28. Ellis, *History of the First Church*, 172, 200, 204–5; Wisner, *History of the Old South Church*, 119n62.
29. Ware, *Two Discourses*, 49.
30. Robbins, *History of the Second Church in Boston*, 36; Mather, *Diary*, 5 January 1700 (1:329); Ware, *Two Discourses*, 53; Wisner, *History of the Old South Church*, 119n62.
31. Wisner, *History of the Old South Church*, 26–27, 119.
32. Kelly, *Early Connecticut Meetinghouses*, 1:172; Moe, *Three Centuries*, 8–10. The author is indebted to Edith Nettleton and Ruth Nettleton of Guilford, who provided a copy of William Moe's publication.

33. Mitchell, *History of New Haven County*, 291; Perkins, *Historical Sketches of Meriden*, 34–37; Davis, *History of Wallingford*, 118–21.

34. Quotations taken from Kelly, *Early Connecticut Meetinghouses*, 1:306–7; *Proceedings at the Celebration of the 250th Anniversary of the First Church of Christ in Milford*, 162.

35. Ford, *Historical Sketches*, 51; Orcutt, *History of the Old Town of Stratford*, 299–307.

36. Kelly, *Early Connecticut Meetinghouses*, 2:3–11.

37. Stiles, *Itineraries*, 321, 284.

38. Blake, *Chronicles of New Haven Green*, 85–97; Stickney cited in Kelly, *Early Connecticut Meetinghouses*, 2:35.

39. Barthelemy, "History of the Painting *South Danvers in 1828*."

40. Upham, *Principles*, 50; see also Whitmore, *Abel Bowen*. Another example of a centrally located belfry or "spire" was the 1729 Deerfield meetinghouse. This design is said to have "sagged, and spread the walls" of the building and was replaced with an attached side tower in 1768. Sheldon, *History of Deerfield*, 1:474.

41. Essex, Mass., built a fifty-two-by-forty-two-foot meetinghouse in 1719 whose bell rope was suspended "in the middle of the house below." Crowell, *History of the Town of Essex*, 128.

42. Felt, *Annals of Salem*, 2d ed., 2:623; Oberholzer, *Delinquent Saints*, 23–24.

43. Upham, *Address at the Rededication*, 44.

44. Quotation taken from Hurd, *History of Essex County*, 1002. See also Wells, *Peabody Story*, 196–99; and Hurd, *History of Essex County*, 989–1007.

45. Upham, *Address at the Rededication*, 43; Bentley, *Diary*, 1:xli. Perley, "Historical Sketch," 154; Cooke, *Century of Puritanism*, 198–202. Lynn continued to worship at the Old Tunnel meetinghouse until 1827 when the structure was moved and rebuilt with a steeple. In 1837 the first parish sold it to the Second Christian (Universalist) Society.

46. Stiles, *Itineraries*, 244, 237.

47. Abbot, *History of Andover*, 81, 88.

48. Stiles, *Literary Diary*, 12 June 1771 (1:109).

49. Sprague, *Annals of the American Pulpit*, 1:273–75.

50. Winslow, *Meetinghouse Hill*, 210.

51. Phillips, *Discourse*, 58.

52. Mooar, *Historical Manual*, 100.

53. Quotations taken from Bailey, *Historical Sketches of Andover*, 427, 428, 430, 442; see also Mooar, *Historical Manual*, 28.

54. Patten, *History of the Town of Tewksbury*, 5–12.

55. Mooar, *Historical Manual*, 32. In the same vein, "and the work to be done decent and plain," Wolcott, Conn., 1771. Orcutt, *History of the Town of Wolcott*, 43.

56. Bailey, *Historical Sketches of Andover*, 452.

57. Little and Ilsley, *First Parish*, 32–35; Hovey, *Old South Meetinghouse*, 10, 17; Currier, *History of Newbury*, 337; Currier, "Ould Newbury," 435; Atkinson, *History of the First Religious Society*, 9.

58. *Plymouth Church Records*, 1:257, 278; 2:333–36, 366, 57; Cuckson, *Brief History*, 76; "Third Meetinghouse in Plymouth" and "View of the Town Square in Plymouth about 1828" are reproduced in *Plymouth Church Records*, 2:288, 3:578.

59. Gomes, "Churches of the Not-So-Standing Order."

60. Eaton, "First Church," 222.

61. Updike, *History of the Episcopal Church*, 435; Foote, *Three Centuries*, 383–86.

62. Phillips, *Salem in the Eighteenth Century*, 344; Frederic Detwiller to the author, 25 January 1979; *First Centenary, the North Church*, 21, 183–84. See also Stiles, *Literary Diary*, 27 April 1772 (1:229).

63. Felt, *Annals of Salem*, 2d ed., 2:625; *First Centenary, the North Church*, 158; Oberholzer, *Delinquent Saints*, 23–24.

64. Taylor, *History of Great Barrington*, 176. Barrington and Pittsfield were then competing to become the county seat.

65. Spalding, *Centennial Discourse*, 16.

66. Fuller, *History of Warwick*, 312. Merrill, *History of Amesbury*, 296–97. Writing in the 1870s, Joseph Merrill was one of the few historians in New England who used the term *hopper-roof* to describe the hipped or four-square roof, applying it not only to seventeenth-century structures, but also to the one built by Hibbert. The separatist church in Amesbury soon became disenchanted with Hibbert, and the meetinghouse was converted into a barn.

67. Sinnott, *Meetinghouse and Church*, 197, 202–3.

68. Bentley, *Diary*, 3 October 1809 (3:464).

69. Stiles, *Literary Diary*, 12 June 1771 (1:108). "From all I can learn *this Chh.* & that at *Hingham* are in the best State of any—& nearly as perfect as this World will admit."

## Chapter 10. A Fleeting Image

1. Bentley, *Diary*, 23 and 24 April 1793 (2:16–19).

2. Benes and Zimmerman, *New England Meeting House and Church*, 83. The IHS cipher Bentley found was one of two done in gold leaf and paid for by the new clergyman in return for his being given a pew. See Jonathan French to Zebadiah Abbot, 8 December 1788, cited in Mooar, *Historical Manual*, 54.

3. Hyde, *Historical Celebration*, 123;

4. Earle, *Sabbath*, 17.

5. *Two Babes in the Wood: together with Divine Songs for Children*.

6. Walker, *Flaming Sword*, 3.

7. Leamon, "Jacob Bailey and the Ladies," 147.

8. Staples, "Sketch of the History of Lexington Common," 131. Canopies suspended by hands are known in Pomfret, Vt., 1791, in Thomaston, Maine, in 1796, and Strafford, Vt., in 1799: Eaton, *History of Thomaston*, 226; Smith, *Town House*, 73–74.

9. Burrillville: Keach, *Burrillville as It Was*, 34; *Historical Pascoag [R.I] Herald*, 1894, Burrillville Historical and Preservation Society, Pascoag; West Haverhill: *One Hundred and Fiftieth Anniversary of the West Congregational Church*, 12; Swansea: Read, *History of Swansea*, 169; Princeton: Blake, *History of Princeton*, 164; Sterling: *One Hundred Fiftieth Anniversary of the Town of Sterling*, 35; New Ipswich: Phelps, *Historic New Ipswich*, 21.

10. Stackpole and Thompson, *History of Durham*, 1:201.

11. Brooke-Stewart, "John Colby."

12. Norton, "Anglican Embellishments"; Babcock, *Christ Church*, 244; Burroughs, *Historical Account*, 18.

13. Henry Guionneau inventory, 1730, John Liddel, inventory, 1755, Anthony Stoddard, inventory, 1748, Suffolk County Probate Court, Boston, Mass. (microfilm copy at Boston Public Library), 28:235, 49:803–8, 41:160–75.

14. Taylor, *The Poems of Edward Taylor*, 38, 213. Meditations 23 and 78. The lines read: "That my dull Soule, might be inflamde to See / How Saints and Angells ravisht are in

Glee" and "My Gold-Finch't Angell Feathers dapled in / Hells Scarlet Dy fat, blood red grown with sin."

15. Two other gravestones that use the image of bubbling suns are known, one in Braintree, Mass., and the other in Bristol, R.I.

16. See, for example, the cherub in the center of a pieced and appliquéd quilt, Leverett and Saltonstall families of Massachusetts, eighteenth century, in Bassett, *Massachusetts Quilts*, fig. 6, p. 11.

17. Winthrop, *Journal*, 15 October 1640 (340–41).

18. Cited in Weisman, *Witchcraft, Magic, and Religion*, 230n31.

19. "Commonplace Book of Joseph Green," teacher at the Roxbury Latin School, 1696. Cited in Demos, *Remarkable Providences*, 417.

20. Mixer, *Account*, 2.

21. Hutchins, *Hutchins Improved*, title page.

22. Walker, *Flaming Sword*, 7–8.

23. Swan's *Remarkable Visionary Dreams* is an imprint at the American Antiquarian Society. The text was kindly posted on line by John Salliant, History Department, Brown University.

24. Quotations taken from Upton, *Holy Things and Profane*, 119–20, based on Gabriel Williamson Galt to Elizabeth J. Galt, 10 January 1840, transcript in Bruton Parish Church file. See also Nelson, *Beauty of Holiness*, 157.

## Epilogue

1. Powell and Gilmore, "Old Ship Meeting House," 13.
2. *Watertown Records*, 1:37–38.
3. *Records of the West Precinct of Watertown*, 18.
4. Prime, *History of Long Island*, 132.
5. Cothren, *History of Ancient Woodbury*, 941; Kelly, *Early Connecticut Meetinghouses*, 2:319.
6. Kelly, *Early Connecticut Meetinghouses*, 1:280.
7. Staples, *Annals of Providence*, 456. A photograph and description of the Chester Meeting House appears at www.chesterct.com/articles/meeting_house.htm.
8. Kelly, *Early Connecticut Meetinghouses*, 2:308.
9. Daniels, *History of the Town of Oxford*, 363.
10. Ruell, "'Round' Meetinghouses," 178.
11. Information courtesy of Donald R. Friary.
12. North, *History of Berlin*, 153.
13. Sinnott, *Meetinghouse and Church*, 232.
14. Bailey, *Historical Sketches of Andover*, 451–52; Bacon, *History of Natick*, 109.
15. *First Centenary*, 23.
16. Kirker, *Architecture of Charles Bulfinch*, 17–19; Smith, *History of Pittsfield*, 425, 446–47.
17. Parke, *Epic of Unitarianism*, 19–96.
18. Quotation taken from Speare, *Colonial Meeting-Houses*, 33. See also Secomb, *History of Amherst*, 244–48.
19. Jager and Krone, "Sacred Deposit," chaps. 11–15.
20. Sinnott, *Meetinghouse and Church*, 232; Smith, *History of the Town of Mont Vernon*, 83, 87; Ramsdell, *History of Milford*, 204, 359–61.

21. Wellman, *History of the Town of Lynnfield*, 281; MacKenzie, "First Parish Meetinghouse."

22. Sinnott, *Meetinghouse and Church*, 68.

23. Rose, *Colonial Houses of Worship*, 221; Sinnott, *Meetinghouse and Church*, 166.

24. McChesney, *History of Ludlow*, 24–25. Still visible on the Lempster, N.H., meetinghouse is a large sign over the main door reading, "Silver MT Grange, No. 196."

25. Little, "Treasurer's Book," 48.

26. James L. Garvin to Elizabeth Marshall, 9 October 1995, together with 1982 National Register of Historic Places Inventory Nomination Form, author's archives, courtesy of William Gard, 20 May 2010.

27. For an excellent photographic compilation of many surviving New England meetinghouses, see Wainwright, *Space for Faith*.

28. *History of the West Parish*.

29. Betlock et al., *Old South*, chaps. 4, 5; Phillips, *Old South Meeting House;* Holleran, *Boston's "Changeful Times*," 94–104.

30. Lincoln, *Discourse*, 39.

# Works Cited

Abbot, Abiel. *History of Andover from Its Settlement to 1829*. Andover, Mass.: Flagg and Gould, 1829.

*Account of the Observance of the One Hundred and Fiftieth Anniversary of the Incorporation of the Town of New Braintree, Mass.* Worcester, Mass.: Press of Charles Hamilton, 1902.

Adams, Charles Collard. *Middletown Upper Houses*. Canaan, N.H.: Ranney Genealogical Fund, 1983.

Adams, Edwin G. *An Historical Discourse . . . First Congregational Church in Templeton, Massachusetts*. Boston: Crosby, Nichols, 1857.

Adams, George M. *An Historical Discourse: 250th Anniversary of the North Church, Portsmouth, New Hampshire*. Portsmouth: Robinson, 1871.

Adams, James T. *History of the Town of Southampton*. Bridgehampton, L.I.: Hampton, 1918.

"Agawam, Massachusetts, over the Span of a Century, 1855–1955." Agawam Anniversary Celebrations. http://magemuseum.smugmug.com.

Ainsworth, Henry. *An apologie or defence of such true Christians as are commonly (but unjustly) called Brownists*. Amsterdam, 1604.

Ainsworth, Henry, and Hugh Broughton. *Certayne questions. . . .* Amsterdam: Giles Thorp, 1605.

Alexander, Robert. "Religion in Rensselaerswijck." In *A Beautiful and Fruitful Place*, edited by Nancy Zeller, 309–15. Albany, N.Y.: New Netherlands, 1991.

*Ancient Historical Records of Norwalk, Connecticut*. Edited by Edwin Hall. Norwalk: Mallory, 1847.

Andres, Glenn M. "Lavius Fillmore and the Federal Style Meeting House." In Benes, *New England Meeting House and Church*, 32–40.

Andrews, David. *Centennial Discourse, Pepperell, Massachusetts*. Boston: Wright, 1847.

Andrews, Edward D. *A Shaker Meeting House and Its Builder*. Hancock, Mass.: Shaker Community, 1962.

*Annals of Brimfield*. Springfield, Mass.: Bowles, 1856.

Annett, Albert, and Alice Lehtinen. *History of Jaffrey, New Hampshire*. Jaffrey: privately printed, 1937.

Annin, Katharine H. *Richmond, Massachusetts: The Story of a Berkshire Town and Its People, 1765–1965*. Richmond: Richmond Civic Association, 1964.

Archer, Cathaline. *A Bicentennial History of Becket*. Becket, Mass.: Becket Historical Society, 1964.

Atkinson, Minnie. *A History of the First Religious Society in Newburyport, Mass.* 1933. Reprint, Newburyport: First Religious Society, 2001–3.

Atwater, Edward E. *History of the Colony of New Haven.* New Haven, Conn.: privately printed, 1881.

Austin, Richard C. "The Meetinghouse of Colonial New England as an Expression of Puritan Theology." Bachelor of Divinity thesis, Union Theological Seminary, 1959.

Ayer, Mary Farwell. *The South Meeting-House, Boston, 1669–1729.* Boston: Clapp, 1905.

Babcock, Mary Kent Davey. *Christ Church, Salem Street, Boston. . . .* Boston: Thomas Todd, 1947.

Bacon, Oliver N. *History of Natick, Massachusetts, from Its First Settlement in 1651.* Boston: Damrell, 1856.

Bailey, Sarah L. *Historical Sketches of Andover, Massachusetts.* Boston: Houghton, Mifflin, 1880.

Bailey Hollis R. *Beginning of the First Church in Cambridge.* Cambridge, Mass.: privately printed, 1932.

Baldwin, Eric. "'The Devil Begins to Roar': Opposition to Methodism in New England." *Church History* 75, no. 1 (2006): 94–119.

Ballou, Adin. *History of Milford, Massachusetts.* Boston: Franklin, 1882.

Banks, Charles. *History of Martha's Vineyard.* 3 vols. Edgartown, Mass.: Dukes County Historical Society, 1966.

Banks, Charles E. *History of York, Maine.* Boston, Caulkins, 1931.

Banks, William N. "History in Towns: Temple, New Hampshire." *Magazine Antiques,* October 1975, 712–29.

Barber, John W. *Connecticut Historical Collections.* New Haven: Durrie and Peck, 1836.

———. *Historical Collections of Massachusetts.* Worcester, Mass.: Lazell, 1844.

Barrus, Hiram. *History of the Town of Goshen.* Boston: privately printed, 1881.

Barry, John S. *A Historical Sketch of the Town of Hanover, Mass.* Boston: Drake, 1853.

Barry, William. *A History of Framingham, Massachusetts: Including the Plantation.* Boston: Munroe, 1847.

Barthelemy, Nancy. "The History of the Painting *South Danvers in 1828.*" *South Danvers Observer* 4, no. 4 (Summer 2010): 1–4. www.peabodylibrary.org.

Bassett, Lynn Z., ed. *Massachusetts Quilts: Our Common Wealth.* Hanover, N.H.: University Press of New England, 2009.

Bateman, Nell M. "National Register Nomination Information: Union Episcopal Church, West Claremont, New Hampshire." Claremont, N.H., prepared March 1977. Excerpted at www.crjc.org/heritage/NO7-3.htm.

Bates, Edmund C. *History of Westborough, Massachusetts.* Westborough: Town, 1891.

Bates, William G. *Westfield Jubilee. . . .* Westfield, Mass.: Clark and Story, 1870.

Bayles, Richard M. *History of Windham County, Connecticut.* New York: Preston, 1889.

Beard, Ruth. *A Genealogy of the Descendants of Widow Martha Beard of Milford, Connecticut.* Ansonia, Conn.: Emerson, 1915.

Bell, Charles H. *History of Exeter, New Hampshire.* 1888. Reprint, Bowie, Md.: Heritage Books, 1979.

Benes, Peter. "'Distinguishing Signs of Truly Gracious and Holy Affections': Revival Motifs in Eighteenth-Century New England Gravestone Carvings." In *Mirror and Metaphor: Material and Social Constructions of Reality,* edited by Daniel W. Ingersoll Jr. and Gordon Bronitsky, 161–70. Latham, Md.: University Press of America, 1987.

———. "Essay." In Wainwright, *A Space for Faith*, 87–107.

———, ed. *New England Meeting House and Church, 1630–1650. The Dublin Seminar for New England Folklife: Annual Proceedings, 1979.* Boston: Boston University Scholarly Publications, 1980.

———. *New England Prospect: A Loan Exhibition of Maps at the Currier Gallery of Art, Manchester, New Hampshire.* Boston: Boston University Scholarly Publications, 1981.

———. *Old-Town and the Waterside.* Newburyport, Mass.: Historical Society of Old Newbury, 1986.

———. "Psalmody in Coastal Massachusetts and the Connecticut River Valley." In *The Bay and the River, 1600–1900. The Dublin Seminar for New England Folklife: Annual Proceedings, 1981,* edited by Peter Benes, 117–31. Boston: Boston University Scholarly Publications, 1982.

———. "Sky Colors and Scattered Clouds: The Decorative and Architectural Painting of New England Meeting Houses, 1738–1834." In Benes, *New England Meeting House and Church*, 51–69.

———. "The Templeton 'Run' and the Pomfret 'Cluster': Patterns of Diffusion in Rural New England Meetinghouse Architecture, 1647–1822." *Old-Time New England* 68 (Winter–Spring 1978): 1–21.

———. "Twin-Porch versus Single-Porch Stairwells: Two Examples of Cluster Diffusion in Rural Meetinghouse Architecture." *Old-Time New England* 69 (Winter–Spring 1979): 44–68.

Benes, Peter, and Philip D. Zimmerman. *New England Meeting House and Church: 1630–1850: A Loan Exhibition Held at the Currier Gallery of Art, Manchester, New Hampshire.* Boston: Boston University Scholarly Publications, 1979.

Bentley, William. *The Diary of William Bentley D.D., Pastor of the East Church, Salem, Massachusetts.* 4 vols. Salem: Essex Institute, 1905.

Betlock, Lynn, et al. *Old South: An Architectural History of the Old South Meeting House.* Boston: Old South Association in Boston, 1993.

*Bicentennial Book of Malden, Massachusetts.* Boston: Rand, 1850.

*Bicentennial, First Congregational Church, Danbury.* Danbury, Conn.: News Book, 1896.

*Bicentennial of the First Congregational Church, Marblehead, Massachusetts.* Marblehead: Church, 1884.

Biglow, William. *History of Sherburne, Massachusetts.* Milford, Mass.: Ballou, 1880.

Blake, Francis E. *History of Princeton, Massachusetts.* Princeton, Mass.: privately printed, 1915.

Blake, Henry T. *Chronicles of New Haven Green from 1638 to 1862. . . .* New Haven, Conn.: Tuttle, Morehouse and Taylor, 1898.

Blake, James. *Annals of the Town of Dorchester.* 1750. Reprint, Boston: Clapp, 1846.

Blake, Jonathan. *History of the Town of Warwick, Massachusetts.* Boston: Noyes, 1873.

Bliss, Leonard. *History of Rehoboth, Massachusetts.* Boston: Otis, 1836.

Bliss, William R. *Side Glimpses from the Colonial Meeting-house.* Boston: Houghton Mifflin, 1894.

Blood, Henry A. *History of Temple, New Hampshire.* Boston: Rand and Avery, 1860.

Booth, John N. *The Story of the Second Church in Boston.* Boston, 1960.

Bourne, Edward E. *The History of Wells and Kennebunk from the Earliest Settlement.* Portland, Maine: B. Thurston, 1875.

Bradford, William. *History of Plymouth Plantation, 1620–1647.* 2 vols. [Boston]: Massachusetts Historical Society, 1912.

"Brief History of Old Bergen Church." MS, 12 January 1976. Joan D. Lovero Collection, New Jersey Room, Jersey City Free Public Library, Jersey City, N.J.

Briggs, L. Vernon. *Church and Cemetery Records of Hanover, Massachusetts*. 2 vols. Boston: W. Spooner, 1895–1904.

Brigham, W. I. Tyler. *History of the Brigham Family*. New York: Grafton, 1907.

Brooke-Stewart, Jeff. "John Colby, Preacher of the Gospel." chepachetfreewill.org/john-colby.htm.

Brown, Abram E. *History of the Town of Bedford*. Bedford, Mass.: privately printed, 1891.

Brown, Jerald E. *The Years of the Life of Samuel Lane, 1718–1806*. Edited by Donna-Belle Garvin. Hanover, N.H.: University Press of New England, 2000.

Budington, William I. *The History of the First Church, Charlestown, in Nine Lectures*. Boston: Charles Tappan, 1845.

Buechner, Alan C. "Thomas Walter and the Society for Promoting Regular Singing in the Worship of God: Boston, 1720–1723." In *New England Music: The Public Sphere, 1600–1900. The Dublin Seminar for New England Folklife: Annual Proceedings, 1996*, edited by Peter Benes, 48–60. Boston: Boston University Scholarly Publications, 1998.

———. *Yankee Singing Schools and the Golden Age of Choral Music in New England, 1760–1800*. Boston: Boston University Scholarly Publications, 2003.

Buggeln, Gretchen T. *Temples of Grace: The Material Transformation of Connecticut's Churches, 1790–1840*. Hanover, N.H.: University Press of New England, 2003.

Burnham, Mrs. Walter E. *History and Traditions of Shelburne*. Shelburne, Mass.: Town, 1958.

Burrage, Champlin. *The Early English Dissenters in Light of Recent Research (1550–1641)*. 2 vols. 1912. Reprint, New York: Russell and Russell, 1967.

Burroughs, Henry. *A Historical Account of Christ Church, Boston*. Boston: A. Williams, 1874.

Bushman, Richard L. *The Refinement of America: Persons, Houses, Cities*. New York: Knopf: 1992.

Butler, Caleb. *History of the Town of Groton, including Pepperell and Shirley. . . .* Boston: Press of T. K. Marvin, 1848.

Candage, R. G. F. *Historical Sketches of Bluehill, Maine*. Ellsworth, Maine: Hancock, 1905.

Candee, Richard M. "Land Surveys of William and John Godsoe of Kittery, Maine: 1689–1769." In *New England Prospect. The Dublin Seminar for New England Folklife: Annual Proceedings, 1980*, edited by Peter Benes, 9–46. Boston: Boston University Scholarly Publications, 1980.

———. "Wooden Buildings in Early Maine and New Hampshire: A Technological and Cultural History, 1600–1720." Ph.D. diss., University of Pennsylvania, 1976.

Card, Marian. "A Small New England Church." *Old-Time New England* 43 (July 1952): 4–6.

Cary, William B. *Memorial Discourse of the First Congregational Church, 1693–1876, of Old Lyme, Conn., July 9, 1876*. Hartford: Case, Lockwood, and Brainard, 1876.

Caulkins, Frances Manwaring. *History of New London, Connecticut*. New London, Conn.: Utley, 1895.

———. *History of Norwich, Connecticut*. Hartford, Conn.: privately printed, 1866.

Caverly, A. M. *History of Troy, New Hampshire*. Keene, N.H.: Sentinel, 1895.

*Centennial Anniversary, Heath, Massachusetts, 1785–1885*. Boston, 1885.

*Centennial Discourse, Congregational Church of Mansfield Center, Connecticut*. 1876.

*Centennial History of the Town of Millbury, Massachusetts*. Millbury: Town, 1915.

Chandler, Seth. *History of the Town of Shirley, Massachusetts*. Shirley: privately printed, 1883.

Chaney, George L. *Hollis Street Church . . . 1732–1861: Two Discourses. . . .* Boston: Ellis, 1877.

Chapin, Alonzo. *Glastenbury for Two Hundred Years: A Centennial Discourse.* . . . Hartford, Conn.: Case, Tiffany, 1853.

Chapman, Edward. *First Church of Christ, Saybrook, Connecticut.* New Haven, Conn. 1947.

Chase, Benjamin. *History of Old Chester [N.H.] from 1719 to 1869.* Auburn, N.H.: privately printed, 1869.

Chase, George Wingate. *History of Haverhill, Massachusetts.* . . . Haverhill: privately printed, 1861.

Chauncy, Isaac. *The Divine Institution of Congregational Churches, Ministry, and Ordinances.* . . . London: Hiller, 1697.

Cheyney, Edward P. *Readings in English History from the Original Sources.* Boston: Ginn, 1908.

Child, Hamilton. *Gazetteer and Business Directory of Chittenden County, Vermont, for 1882–83.* Syracuse, N.Y.: Journal Office, 1882.

Chipman, R. Manning. *The History of Harwinton, Connecticut.* Hartford, Conn.: Williams, Wiley and Turner, 1860.

Clapp, Ebenezer. *History of the Town of Dorchester, Massachusetts.* Boston: Clapp, 1859.

Clark, Charles E. *The Meetinghouse Tragedy [Wilton, N.H.]: An Episode in the Life of a New England Town.* Hanover, N.H.: University Press of New England, 1998.

Clark, Frank G. *Historical Address Given at the 150th Anniversary of the Settlement of the Town of Lyndeborough, New Hampshire.* Concord, N.H.: Republican Press Association, 1891.

Clarke, George K. *History of Needham, Massachusetts, 1711–1911.* Cambridge, Mass.: University Press, 1912.

Coburn, Frederick W. *History of Lowell and Its People.* New York: Lewis Historical, 1920.

Cochrane, W. R. *History of Francestown, New Hampshire.* . . . Nashua, N.H.: Barker, 1895.

———. *History of the Town of Antrim, New Hampshire, from Its Earliest Settlement, to June 27, 1877.* Manchester, N.H.: Town, 1880.

Codman, Ogden, ed. *Hollis Street Church, Boston: Records of Admissions, Baptisms, and Deaths, 1732–1887.* Boston: New England Historic Genealogical Society, 1998.

Coffin, Joshua. *A Sketch of the History of Newbury, Newburyport, and West Newbury, from 1635 to 1845.* Boston: Drake, 1845.

Cogswell, Elliott C. *History of Nottingham, Deerfield, and Northwood.* Manchester, N.H.: Clarke, 1878.

Cole, Luane, ed. *Patterns and Pieces: Lyme, New Hampshire, 1761–1976.* Canaan, N.H.: Lyme Historians, 1976.

*Commemoration of the Centennial of the Congregational Church, Hinsdale, Massachusetts.* . . . Pittsfield, Mass.: Sun Printing Company, 1896.

*The Commemoration of the 250th Anniversary of the First Church of Charlestown.* Charlestown, Mass.: privately printed, 1882.

*Commemorative Exercises of the First Church of Christ in Hartford, Connecticut.* Hartford: Case, Lockwood and Brainard, 1883.

*Confession of Faith, Owned and Consented unto by the Elders and Messengers of the Churches Assembled at Boston in New England, on May 12, 1680. Being the Second Session of that Synod.* Boston, 1725.

Cooke, Parsons. *A Century of Puritanism and a Century of Its Opposites.* Boston: S. K. Whipple, 1855.

Cooley, Timothy M. *Granville Jubilee.* Springfield, Mass.: Taylor, 1845.

Coolidge, John. "Hingham Builds a Meetinghouse." *New England Quarterly* 34, no. 4 (1961): 435–61.

Copeland, Alfred M. *A History of the Town of Murrayfield*. . . . Springfield, Mass.: Bryan, 1892.

———. *"Our Country and Its People": A History of Hampden County, Massachusetts*. 3 vols. Boston: Century, 1902.

Copeland, Jennie F. *Mansfield 150th Anniversary Program for August 23–26, 1925*. Mansfield, Mass., 1925.

*Copy of the Old Records of the Town of Duxbury, Mass., from 1642 to 1770*. Plymouth, Mass.: Avery and Doten, 1893.

Corse, Murray P. "The Old Ship Meeting-House in Hingham, Mass." *Old-Time New England* 21, no. 1 (July 1930): 19–31.

Cothren, William. *History of Ancient Woodbury, Connecticut*. 3 vols. (paged continuously). Waterbury, Conn.: Bronson, 1854–79.

Crafts, James M. *History of Whately, Massachusetts*. Orange, Mass.: Crandall, 1899.

Craig, John. *Reformation, Politics, and Polemics: The Growth of Protestantism in East Anglican Market Towns, 1500–1610*. Aldershot: Ashgate, 2001.

Crawford, Mary Caroline. *The Romance of Old New England Churches*. Boston: Page, 1903.

Crowell, Robert. *History of the Town of Essex: from 1634–1868 . . . with Sketches of the Soldiers in the War of the Rebellion, by Hon. David Choate*. Essex, Mass.: Town, 1868.

Cuckson, John. *A Brief History of the First Church of Plymouth*. Boston: Ellis, 1902.

Cummings, Abbott L. "Decorative Painters and House Paintings at the Massachusetts Bay, 1630–1725." In *American Paintings to 1776: A Reappraisal*. Winterthur, Del.: University Press of Virginia for the Winterthur Museum, 1971.

———. *The Framed Houses of Massachusetts Bay, 1625–1725*. Cambridge, Mass.: Harvard University Press, 1979.

———. "Meeting and Dwelling House: Interrelationships in Early New England." In Benes, *New England Meeting House and Church*, 4–17.

Cummings, Abbott L., and Richard M. Candee. "Colonial and Federal America: Accounts of Early Painting Practices." In *Paint in America: The Colors of Historic Buildings*, edited by Roger W. Moss. New York: Wiley and Sons, 1994.

Cummings, Preston. *A Dictionary of Congregational Usages and Principles*. Boston: Whipple, 1852.

Currier, John J. *History of Newbury, Massachusetts, 1635–1902*. Boston: Damrell, 1902.

———. *History of Newburyport, Mass., 1764–1905*. Newburyport, Mass.: privately printed, 1906.

———. *"Ould Newbury": Historical and Biographical Sketches*. Boston: Damrell, 1896.

Cutter, Daniel B. *History of the Town of Jaffrey, New Hampshire, . . . 1790–1880*. Concord, N.H.: Republican Press Association, 1881.

Daggett, John. *A Sketch of the History of Attleborough from Its Settlement to the Division*. Boston: S. Usher, 1894.

Damon, Samuel C. *The History of Holden, Massachusetts, 1667–1841*. [Worcester, Mass.: Wallace and Ripley], 1841.

Daniels, George F. *History of the Town of Oxford, Massachusetts*. Oxford: Town, 1892.

Davies, Horton. *The Worship of the American Puritans, 1629–1730*. New York: Peter Lang, 1990.

Davis, Charles H. S. *History of Wallingford, Connecticut*. Meriden, Conn.: privately printed, 1870.

Dean, Edgar P. Review of *The New England Meeting Houses of the Seventeenth Century*, by Marian C. Donnelly. *New England Quarterly* 43, no. 1 (1970): 158–59.

Deane, Samuel. *History of Scituate, Massachusetts.* Boston: Loring, 1831.

Dearborn, John. *History of Salisbury, New Hampshire.* Manchester, N.H.: Moore, 1890.

Deetz, James. *In Small Things Forgotten: The Archeology of Early American Life.* Garden City, N.Y.: Doubleday / Anchor Press, 1977.

DeForest, Heman. *Early History of Westborough, Massachusetts.* Westborough: Town, 1891.

Demos, John, comp. *Remarkable Providences, 1600–1760.* New York: Braziller, 1972.

Depew, John. *The Proceedings in Commemoration of the One Hundred Fiftieth Anniversary of the First Congregational Church, Williamstown, Massachusetts.* Pittsfield, Mass.: Sun Printing Company, 1915.

Detwiller, Frederic C. "Thomas Dawes's Church in Brattle Square." *Old-Time New England* 69 (Winter–Spring 1979): 1–17.

Dexter, Henry Martyn. "Meeting-Houses: Considered Historically and Suggestively." *Congregational Quarterly* 1 (April 1859): 186–214.

"Diary of Mary Vial Holyoke." In *The Holyoke Diaries, 1709–1856.* Salem, Mass.: Essex Institute, 1913 (47–138).

Dinkin, Robert J. "Seating the Meeting House in Early Massachusetts." *New England Quarterly* 43, no. 3 (1970): 450–64.

Dodge, John W. *History of the First Congregational Church, Yarmouth, Massachusetts.* Yarmouthport, Mass.: Register, 1873.

Dole, Frederick H. *Windham in the Past.* Auburn, Maine: Merrill, 1916.

Donnelly, Marian Card. *The New England Meeting Houses of the Seventeenth Century.* Middletown, Conn.: Wesleyan University Press, 1968.

———. "New England Meetinghouses in the Seventeenth Century." *Old-Time New England* 47 (Spring 1957): 85–99.

———. "New England Pyramids, 1651–1705." *Journal of the Society of Architectural Historians* 19 (May 1960): 76–77.

———. "Seventeenth-Century Meeting House Turrets." *Old-Time New England* 65 (Summer–Fall 1974): 10–11.

Dorsey, Stephen P. *Early English Churches in America, 1607–1807.* New York: Oxford University Press, 1952.

Dow, George Francis. *Town Records of Topsfield, Massachusetts.* Vol. 1, *1659–1739.* Topsfield, Mass.: Topsfield Historical Society, 1917.

Dow, Joseph. *History of Hampton, New Hampshire.* Salem, Mass.: Salem Press, 1893.

Drake, Francis P. *The Town of Roxbury: Its Memorable Persons and Places.* Roxbury, Mass.: privately printed, 1878.

Drake, Samuel A. *History and Antiquities of Boston.* Boston: Stevens, 1856.

———. *History of Middlesex County, Massachusetts.* 2 vols. Boston: Estes and Lauriat, 1880.

Draper, James S. "Wayland Local History" [Mounted newspaper slips from the *Waltham Free Press*]. Waltham, Mass.: Waltham, 1867. Widener Library, Harvard College Library.

Drummond, Andrew L. *The Church Architecture of Protestantism: An Historical and Constructive Study.* Edinburgh: Clark, 1934.

*Dudley Town Records, 1754–1794.* Pawtucket, R.I.: Adams Sutcliffe Co., 1894.

Dunlap, William. *A History of the Rise and Progress of the Arts of Design in the United States.* 3 vols. Boston: Goodspeed, 1918.

Earle, Alice Morse. *The Sabbath in Puritan New England.* New York: Charles Scribner's Sons, 1891.

*The Early Records of the Town of Dedham, Massachusetts, 1636–1659.* Vol. 3 of the printed records of the Town of Dedham. Edited by D. Gleason Hill. Dedham: Dedham Transcript, 1892.

*Early Records of the Town of Manchester, formerly Derryfield, N.H., 1751. . . .* Manchester, N.H.: Manchester Historic Association, 1905.

Eaton, Arthur Wentworth Hamilton. *The Famous Mather Byles, the Noted Boston Tory Preacher, Poet, and Wit, 1707–1788.* Boston: Butterfield, 1914.

———. "The First Church Founded by New-England People in Kings County, Nova Scotia." *New England Historical Genealogical Society Register* 46 (July 1892): 219–26.

Eaton, Cyrus. *History of Thomaston, Rockland, and South Thomaston, Maine.* Hallowell, Maine: Masters, Smith, 1865.

Eliot, Ephraim. *Historical Notices of the New North Religious Society.* Boston: Phelps and Farnham, 1822.

Eliot, Jacob. "Diary." *Historical Magazine* 2d ser., 5 (January 1869): 33–34.

Eliot, John. *Sermon Delivered before the New North, May 2, 1804.* Boston, 1804.

Ellis, Arthur B. *History of the First Church in Boston, 1630–1880.* Boston: Hall and Whiting, 1881.

Ellis, George E. *Commemorative Discourse on the New South Church, December 25, 1864.* Boston: Dutton, 1865.

Emerson, William. *An Historical Sketch of the First Church in Boston.* Boston: Munroe and Francis, 1812.

"Essay on the Laying Out of Towns." *Collections of the Massachusetts Historical Society,* 5th ser., 1 (1871): 474–80.

Estes, David F. *History of Holden, Massachusetts, 1684–1894.* Worcester, Mass.: Town, 1894.

Evarts, Mary. *History of the First Congregational Church.* Madison, Conn., 1955.

Eversull, Harry Kelso. *The Evolution of an Old New England Church.* East Haven, Conn., 1924.

Feld, Stuart P. "St. Michael's Church, Marblehead, Massachusetts, 1714." *Old-Time New England* 52 (Spring 1962): 91–113; 53 (Fall 1962): 31–47.

Felt, Joseph B. *Annals of Salem, from Its First Settlement.* Salem, Mass.: Ives, 1827.

———. *Annals of Salem, Massachusetts.* 2d ed. 2 vols. Salem, Mass.: Ives, 1845–49.

Field, D. D., ed. *History of Berkshire County, Massachusetts.* 2 vols. New York: J. B. Beers, 1885.

Finney, Paul Corby, ed. *Seeing Beyond the Word: Visual Arts and the Calvinist Tradition* Grand Rapids, Mich.: W. B. Eerdmans, 1999.

*First Centenary, the North Church and Society, Salem, Massachusetts.* Salem, Mass.: North Church and Society, 1873.

*The First Century of the History of Springfield: The Official Records from 1636 to 1736.* 2 vols. Edited by Henry M. Burt. Springfield, Mass.: Burt, 1899.

*First Church in Middleborough, Massachusetts.* Boston: Moody, 1854.

*First Church, Killingly, Connecticut.* Danielson, Conn.: Parish House Association, 1901.

*First Parish, Northampton, Massachusetts. Meeting Houses and Ministers from 1653 to 1878.* Northampton, Mass.: Gazette Printing Company, 1878.

Fitts, James H. *History of Newfields, New Hampshire.* Concord, N.H.: Rumford Press, 1912.

Flaherty, David H. *Privacy in Colonial New England.* Charlottesville: University Press of Virginia, 1972.

Fogg, Thomas B. *A Memorial Sermon Delivered by Thomas Brinley Fogg in Old Trinity Church, Brooklyn, Connecticut, on the Hundredth Anniversary of Its Opening, April 12th, 1871.* Hartford, Conn.: Church Press, n.d.

Foley, Suzanne. "Christ Church, Boston." *Old-Time New England* 51 (Winter 1961): 67–85.

Foote, Henry Wilder. *Annals of King's Chapel from the Puritan Age of New England to the Present Day.* 2 vols. Boston: Little, Brown, 1882.

———. *Three Centuries of American Hymnody.* 1940. Reprint, Archon Books, 1968.

Forbes, Harriette M. "Elias Carter, Architect of Worcester, Massachusetts." *Old-Time New England* 2 (Fall 1920): 58–71.

———. *Gravestones of Early New England and the Men Who Made Them, 1635–1800.* 1927. Reprint, New York: Da Capo, 1967.

Ford, George H. *Historical Sketches of the Town of Milford, Connecticut.* Hartford, Conn.: Tuttle Morehouse, 1914.

Forrey, Robert. "The Meeting House at Rumney Marsh." *Essex Institute Historical Collections* 128, no. 1 (1987): 88–102.

Fowler, William Chauncey. *History of Durham, Connecticut.* Hartford, Conn.: Town, 1866.

Freeman, Frederick. *The History of Cape Cod.* 2 vols. Boston: Piper, 1869.

Friary, Donald R. "The Architecture of the Anglican Church in the Northern American Colonies: A Study of Religious, Social, and Cultural Expression." Ph.D. diss., University of Pennsylvania, 1971.

Frisbie, Barnes. *The History of Middletown, Vermont, in Three Discourses.* Rutland, Vt.: Tuttle, 1867.

Frothingham, Richard. *The History of Charlestown, Massachusetts.* Boston: Little, Brown, 1845.

Fuller, Arthur B. *Historical Discourse, New North Church.* Boston: Crosby, 1854.

Fuller, Oliver P. *The History of Warwick, Rhode Island. . . .* Providence, R.I.: Angell, Burlingame, 1875.

Gage, George N. *History of Washington, New Hampshire.* Claremont, N.H.: Claremont Manufacturing Company, 1886.

Gage, Thomas. *History of Rowley, Massachusetts; Anciently including Bradford, Boxford, and Georgetown, from the Year 1639 to the Present Time. . . .* Boston: Andrews, 1840.

Gallup, James A. *Historical Discourse, Congregational Church in Madison, Connecticut, 1707–1877.* New Haven, Conn.: Punderson and Crisand, 1878.

Gardner, Francis. *A Discourse in Two Parts Delivered in Leominster, Massachusetts, December 27, 1812.* Leominster, Mass.: Wilder, 1813.

Garvan, Anthony N. B. *Architecture and Town Planning in Colonial Connecticut.* New Haven, Conn.: Yale University Press, 1951.

———. "The Protestant Plain Style before 1630." *Journal of the Society of Architectural Historians* 9 (October 1950): 5–13.

Gay, Julius. *Farmington Papers.* Hartford, Conn.: Case, Lockwood and Brainard, 1929.

Gay, W. B. *Gazetteer of Hampshire County, Massachusetts, 1654–1887.* Syracuse, N.Y.: W. B. Gay, 1892.

Gibbs, James. *Book of Architecture Containing Designs of Buildings and Ornaments.* London, 1728.

Glendinning, Miles, et al. *A History of Scottish Architecture: From the Renaissance to the Present Day.* Edinburgh: Edinburgh University Press, 1996.

Goelet, Francis. *The Voyage and Travels of Francis Goelet, 1746–1758.* Edited by Kenneth Scott. [Flushing, N.Y.]: Queens College Press, 1970.

Gomes, Peter. "Churches of the Not-So-Standing Order." *Pilgrim Society Notes* 18 (September 1966): 1–14.

Goodell, Abner C. *The First Meeting House in Salem, Massachusetts. . . .* Salem: Essex Institute, 1900.

Goold, William. *Portland in the Past*. Portland, Maine: Thurston, 1886.

Gould, August, and Frederic Kidder. *History of New Ipswich, New Hampshire*. Boston: Gould and Lincoln, 1852.

Gould, Isaiah. *History of Stoddard, Cheshire County, 1774–1854*. Marlborough, N.H.: Metcalf, 1897.

Green, Mason A. *Springfield, 1636–1886*. Springfield, Mass.: Nichols, 1938.

Grobel, Kendrick. *History of the First Church of Stafford, Connecticut. . . .* Stafford Springs, Conn.: Women's Council of the Congregational Church, 1942.

Groome, Francis H., ed. *The Ordnance Gazetteer of Scotland*. 2d ed. London, Mackenzie, 1894–95.

Guicharnaud, Hélène. "An Introduction to the Architecture of Protestant Temples Constructed in France before the Revocation of the Edict of Nantes." In *Seeing beyond the Word: Visual Arts and the Calvinist Tradition*, edited by Paul Corby Finney, 133–55. Grand Rapids: W. B. Eerdmans, 1999.

Guilbert, Edmund. *Annals of an Old Parish: Historical Sketches of Trinity Church, Southport, Connecticut, 1725 to 1848*. New York: T. Whittaker, 1898.

Guild, Reuben A. *Life, Times, and Correspondence of James Manning*. Boston: Gould and Lincoln, 1864.

Hadley, George P. *History of Goffstown, New Hampshire, 1733–1920*. 2 vols. Concord, N.H.: Rumford, 1922.

Hager, Lucie C. *Boxborough: A New England Town and Its People*. Philadelphia: J. W. Lewis, 1891.

Hall, Edwin. *The Ancient Historical Records of Norwalk, Connecticut. . . .* Norwalk: J. Mallory and Company, 1847.

Hall, Mary. *Report of the Celebration of the Centennial of the Incorporation of the Town of Marlborough*. Hartford, Conn.: Press of the Case, Lockwood, and Brainard Company, 1904.

Hamberg, Per Gustaf. *Temples for Protestants: Studies in the Architectural Milieu of the Early Reformed Church and the Lutheran Church*. Translated by Nancy Adler, Kerstin W. Wallin, and Catriona MacLellan. Göteborg, Sweden: Acta Universitatis Gothoburgensis, 2002. Originally published as *Tempelbygge för Protestanter* (Stockholm, 1955).

Hambrick-Stowe, Charles E. *The Practice of Piety: Puritan Devotional Disciplines in Seventeenth-Century New England*. Chapel Hill: University of North Carolina Press, 1982.

Hamilton, Alexander. *Itinerarium*. Chapel Hill: University of North Carolina Press, 1948.

Hamilton, Samuel K. *Commemorative Address Delivered at the Celebration by the First Parish in Wakefield, Massachusetts. . . .* Wakefield: Parish, 1919.

Hammond, Peter. *Liturgy and Architecture*. New York: Columbia University Press, 1961.

Harlow, Hiram. "The Shrewsbury Meeting-house of 1766." Fourteen-page manuscript (1924). Collection of the author.

Harris, John, and Jill Lever. *Illustrated Glossary of Architecture, 830–1830*. New York: Potter, 1966.

Harris, Thaddeus M. *A Valedictory Sermon, First Parish in Dorchester*. Boston: Eliot, 1817.

Havens, D. William, *Historical Discourse, Centennial Celebration of the Stone Meeting House in East Haven*. New Haven, Conn.: Punderson and Crisand, 1876.

Hay, George. *The Architecture of Scottish Post-Reformation Churches, 1560–1843*. Oxford: Clarendon Press, 1957.

Hayes, Lyman Simpson. *History of the Town of Rockingham, Vermont. . . .* Bellows Falls, Vt.: privately printed, 1907.

Hayward, John. *The New England Gazetteer*. Concord, N.H.: Boyd and White, 1839.

Hayward, Silvanus. *Address Delivered at the Centennial of the Congregational Church at Gilsum, New Hampshire*. Dover, N.H.: Goodwin, 1873.

———. *History of Gilsum, New Hampshire*. Manchester, N.H.: privately printed, 1881.

Hayward, William W. *History of Hancock, New Hampshire, 1764–1889*. 2 vols. Lowell, Mass.: Vox, 1889.

Hazen, Henry A. *History of Billerica, Massachusetts*. Boston: Williams, 1883.

Hazlett, Charles. *History of Rockingham County, New Hampshire, and Representative Citizens*. Chicago: Richmond-Arnold, 1915.

Hempstead, Joshua. *The Diary of Joshua Hempstead*. New London, Conn.: New London County Historical Society, 1999.

Herrick, William D. *History of Gardner, Massachusetts*. Gardner, 1878.

Heywood, William S. *History of Westminster, Massachusetts, 1728–1893*. Lowell, Mass.: Vox Populi, 1893.

Hill, Hamilton A. *History of the Old South Church (Third Church) Boston, 1669–1884*. 2 vols. Boston: Houghton, Mifflin, 1890.

Hine, Orlo D. *Early Lebanon*. Hartford, Conn.: Case, Lockwood, and Brainard, 1880.

Hingham Town Meeting Records, Town Records Office, Hingham, Mass.

Historic American Buildings Survey (HABS) collection. Library of Congress, Washington, D.C.

*Historic New Ipswich, New Hampshire*. Edited by Abbie L. Phelps. [Milford, N.H.: Cabinet Press], 1936.

*Historical Manual of the Congregational Church of Topsfield, Massachusetts, 1663–1907*. Topsfield: privately printed, 1907.

*History of Bedford, New Hampshire, from 1737*. Concord, N.H.: Rumford Press, 1903.

*History of Bolton, 1738–1938*. Bolton, Mass., 1938.

*History of Litchfield County, Connecticut*. Philadelphia: J. W. Lewis, 1881.

*History of Milford, Connecticut, 1639–1939*. Bridgeport, Conn.: Press of Braunworth, 1939.

*History of the Connecticut Valley in Massachusetts*. 2 vols. bound as 1. [Vol. 1: *History of Hampshire County*; vol. 2: *History of Franklin County. History of Hampden County*.] Philadelphia: Everts, 1879.

*History of the First Parish, Newbury*. Newburyport, Mass., 1935.

*History of the Town of Amherst, Massachusetts, 1731–1896*. Amherst: Carpenter and Morehouse, 1896.

*The History of the West Parish*. Barnstable, Mass.: West Parish Memorial Foundation, 1953.

*History of Windsor County, Vermont*. Edited by Lewis Cass Aldrich and Frank R. Holmes. Syracuse, N.Y.: Mason and Company, 1891.

*History of Worcester County, Massachusetts*. . . . 2 vols. Boston: C. F. Jewett, 1879.

Hodgman, Edwin R. *History of the Town of Westford, in the County of Middlesex, 1659–1883*. Lowell, Mass.: Westford Town History Association, 1883.

Holifield, E. Brooks. "The Intellectual Sources of Stoddardeanism." *New England Quarterly* 45, no. 3 (1972): 373–92.

Holleran, Michael. *Boston's "Changeful Times": Origin of Preservation and Planning in America*. Baltimore: Johns Hopkins University Press, 1998.

Holman, Richard B. "William Burgis." In *Boston Prints and Printmakers, 1670–1775*, 57–81. Boston: Colonial Society, 1973.

Homes, William. *A discourse concerning the publick reading of the Holy Scriptures*. . . . Boston: B. Green, 1720.

Hood, George. *History of Music in New England*. Boston: Wilkins, Carter and Company, 1846.

Hopkins, Doris E. *Greenfield, New Hampshire: Story of a Town, 1791–1976*. Greenfield: Greenfield Historical Society, 1977.

Hovey, Horace C. *Old South Meeting House in Newburyport*. Newburyport, Mass., 1907.

Howes, Frederick G. *History of Ashfield*. Ashfield, Mass.: Town, 1910.

Howie, Robert L., Jr. *Architecture and Liturgy in St. Michael's Church*. [Marblehead, Mass.], 1976.

Hudson, Alfred S. *The Annals of Sudbury, Wayland, and Maynard, Middlesex County, Massachusetts*. [Ayer, Mass.]: privately printed, 1891.

———. *The History of Sudbury, Massachusetts*. Sudbury: Bodgett, 1889.

Hudson, Charles. *History of the Town of Lexington, Middlesex County, Massachusetts....* Boston: Wiggin and Lunt, 1868.

———. *History of the Town of Marlborough, Middlesex County*. Boston: Martin, 1862.

Hughes, Sarah E. *History of East Haven*. New Haven, Conn.: Tuttle, 1908.

Hull, John. "The Diaries of John Hull, Mint-Master and Treasurer of the Colony of Massachusetts Bay." *Transactions and Collections of the American Antiquarian Society* 3 (1857): 109–316.

Huntington, Elijah B. *History of Stamford, Connecticut*. Stamford: privately printed, 1868.

Hurd, D. Hamilton. *History of Cheshire and Sullivan Counties, New Hampshire*. Philadelphia: J. W. Lewis: 1886.

———. *History of Essex County, Massachusetts*. 2 vols. Philadelphia: J. W. Lewis, 1888.

———. *History of Hillsborough County, New Hampshire*. Philadelphia: J. W. Lewis, 1885.

———. *History of Merrimack and Belknap Counties, New Hampshire*. Philadelphia: J. W. Lewis, 1885.

———. *History of Middlesex County, Massachusetts*. 3 vols. Philadelphia: J. W. Lewis, 1890.

———. *History of Norfolk County, Massachusetts*. Philadelphia: J. W. Lewis, 1884.

———. *History of Plymouth County, Massachusetts*. Philadelphia: J. W. Lewis, 1884.

———. *History of Rockingham and Strafford Counties, New Hampshire, with Biographical Sketches*. Philadelphia: J. W. Lewis, 1882.

———. *History of Worcester County, Massachusetts*. 2 vols. Philadelphia: J. W. Lewis, 1889.

Hutchins, John N. *Hutchins Improved: Being an Almanack and Ephemeris... 1792*. New York: Gaine, 1791.

Hyde, Charles M. *The Centennial Celebration and Centennial History of the Town of Lee, Massachusetts*. Springfield, Mass.: Bryan, 1878.

———. *Historical Celebration: Town of Brimfield, Massachusetts*. Springfield, Mass.: Bryan, 1879.

Isham, Norman. *The Meeting House of the First Baptist Church in Providence: A History of the Fabric*. Providence, R.I.: Charitable Baptist Society, 1925.

———. *Trinity Church in Newport, Rhode Island: A History of the Fabric*. Boston: Updike, 1936.

Jackson, Francis. *History of Early Settlement, Newton, Mass.* Boston: Stacy, 1854.

Jackson, James R. *History of Littleton, New Hampshire*. 3 vols. Cambridge, Mass.: Town, 1905.

Jager, Ronald, and Sally Krone. "...A Sacred Deposit": The Meetinghouse in Washington, New Hampshire. Washington, N.H.: Randall, 1989.

Jameson, Ephraim O. *History of Medway, Massachusetts*. Providence, R.I.: Reid, 1886.

Jennings, Ellen C. *The History of New Durham, New Hampshire*. . . . Manchester, N.H.: Fitzpatrick Printers, 1962.

Jewett, Amos, and Emily Jewett. *Rowley, Massachusetts*. Rowley: Jewett, 1946.

Johnson, Clifton. *Historic Hampshire in the Connecticut Valley*. Springfield, Mass.: Milton Bradley, 1932.

Johnson, Katharine W. *Rhode Island Baptists: Their Zeal, Their Times*. Valley Forge, Pa.: Judson, 1975.

Jones, Electa F. *Stockbridge Past and Present*. Springfield, Mass., Bowles, 1854.

Joy, James Richard. *Thomas Joy and His Descendants*. New York: privately printed, 1900.

Judd, Sylvester. *History of Hadley, Massachusetts*. Northampton, Mass.: Metcalf, 1863.

Keach, Horace A. *Burrillville as It Was and as It Is*. Providence, R.I.: Knowles, 1856.

Kelly, J. Frederick. *Early Connecticut Meetinghouses*. 2 vols. New York: Columbia University Press, 1948.

Kilde, Jeanne H. *When Church Became Theatre: The Transformation of Evangelical Architecture and Worship in Nineteenth-Century America*. New York: Oxford, 2002.

Kimball, David T. *The Last Sermon Preached in the Ancient Meeting House of the First Parish in Ipswich, February 22, 1846*. Boston: Temperance Standard Press, 1846.

———. *A Sketch of the Ecclesiastical History of Ipswich*. Haverhill, Mass.: Gazette and Patriot Office, 1823.

Kingman, Bradford. *History of North Bridgewater, Massachusetts*. Boston, 1866.

Kingsbury, Frank B. *History of the Town of Surry, Cheshire County, New Hampshire*. . . . Surry, N.H.: Town, 1925.

Kirker, Harold. *The Architecture of Charles Bulfinch*. Cambridge, Mass.: Harvard University Press, 1969.

Kirker, Harold, and James Kirker. *Bulfinch's Boston, 1787–1817*. New York: Oxford University Press, 1964.

Lambert, Edward R. *History of the Colony of New Haven*. New Haven, Conn.: Hitchcock and Stafford, 1838.

Lancaster, Daniel. *The History of Gilmanton, New Hampshire*. . . . Gilmanton: Prescott, 1845.

Larned, Ellen D. *History of Windham County, Connecticut*. 2 vols. Worcester, Mass.: Hamilton, 1847–80.

Laurent, René. *Promenade à travers les temples de France*. Montpellier, France: Languedoc, 1996.

Leamon, James. "Jacob Bailey and the Ladies." In *In Our Own Words: New England Diaries, 1600 to the Present. The Dublin Seminar for New England Folklife: Annual Proceedings, 2006–2007*, edited by Peter Benes, 139–48. Boston: Boston University Scholarly Publications, 2009.

Lee, William Wallace. *Barkhamsted, Conn., and Its Centennial, 1879*. Meriden [Conn.]: Republican Steam Print, 1881.

Leonard, Levi W., and Josiah L. Seward. *History of Dublin*. Dublin, N.H.: Town, 1920.

Lewandoski, Jan. "The Erection of Church Steeples in 18th- and 19th-century New England." *Timber Framing*, June 1995, 6–7.

———. *Historic American Roof Trusses*. Edited by Ken Rowen. Illustrated by Jack Sobon. Becket, Mass.: Timber Framers Guild, 2006.

———. "Historic American Timber-Framed Steeples." *Timber Framing*, March 2007, 18–27; September 2007, 6–15; December 2007, 24–29.

Lewis, Alonzo. *History of Lynn Including Nahant.* Boston: Dickinson, 1844.

Lewis, Alonzo, and James R. Newhall. *History of Lynn, Essex County, Massachusetts: Including Lynnfield, Saugus, Swampscot, and Nahant.* Boston: Shorey, 1865.

Lewis, Isaac N. *History of Walpole, Massachusetts.* Walpole: Walpole Historical Society, 1905.

*Lexington: A Handbook of Its Points of Interest.* Boston: Clarke, 1891.

Lincoln, Calvin. *Discourse, First Parish in Hingham, Massachusetts.* Hingham: First Parish, 1873.

Little, Bryan. *The Life and Work of James Gibbs, 1682–1754.* London: Batsford, 1955.

Little, Eliza E., and Lucretia L. Ilsley. *The First Parish, Newbury, Massachusetts, 1635–1935.* Newburyport, Mass., 1935.

Little, Nina F. *American Decorative Wall Painting, 1700–1850.* New York: Dutton, 1972.

———. "The Treasurer's Book of the Rocky Hill Church." *Old-Time New England* 57 (Fall 1966): 46–48.

Little, William. *The History of Warren: A Mountain Hamlet Located among the White Hills of New Hampshire.* Manchester, N.H.: Moore, 1870.

Locke, Emma P. Boylston. *Colonial Amherst: The Early History, Customs, and Homes....* Milford, N.H.: [W. B. and A. B. Rotch], 1916.

Lockwood, John H. *Westfield and Its Historic Influences.* 2 vols. Springfield, Mass.: privately printed, 1922.

Lothrop, Samuel K. *History of the Church in Brattle Street.* Boston: Crosby, 1851.

Lounsbury, Carl. "Anglican Church Design in the Chesapeake." In *Constructing Image, Identity, and Place,* edited by Alison K. Hoagland and Kenneth A. Breisch, 22–38. Perspectives in Vernacular Architecture 9. Knoxville: University of Tennessee Press, 2003.

———. "God Is in the Details: The Transformation of Ecclesiastical Architecture in Early-Nineteenth-Century America." *Vernacular Architecture Journal* 13, no. 1 (2006): 1–21.

Lovell, Russell A. *Sandwich, a Cape Cod Town.* Sandwich, Mass.: Town, 1984.

Lovering, Martin. *History of Holland, Massachusetts.* Rutland, Vt.: Tuttle, 1915.

Lynde, Benjamin, and Benjamin Lynde Jr. *Diaries of Benjamin Lynde and Benjamin Lynde, Jr.* Boston: Riverside Press, 1880.

Mack, Josiah A. *Historical Sketch, Congregational Church in Gilead, Connecticut.* Hartford, Conn.: Moseley, 1878.

MacKenzie, Neil D. "The First Parish Meetinghouse, Lynnfield Center, Massachusetts." *Old-Time New England* 45, no. 4 (April 1955): 103–6.

MacSparran, James. *A Letter Book and Abstract of Out Services: Written during the Years 1743–1751.* Boston: Merrymount Press, 1899.

Mallary, Peter T. *New England Churches and Meetinghouses, 1680–1830.* New York: Vendome Press, 1985.

*The Manifesto Church: Records of the Church in Brattle Square, Boston, 1699–1872.* Boston: Benevolent Fraternity, 1902.

Mansur, Ina. *A New England Church* [Bedford, Mass.]. Freeport, Maine: Bond Wheelwright, 1974.

*Manual, First Congregational Church, Haddam, Connecticut.* Haddam, 1902.

*Manual of the Church of Christ, Framingham, Massachusetts.* Boston: Wright and Potter, 1870.

*Manual of the Congregational Church at Thompson, Connecticut, 1730–1901.* Worcester, Mass.: Hamilton, 1901.

Marble, Arthur. "The Old Ship, The Ancient Meeting House of the First Parish in Hingham." First Parish Office, Hingham, Mass., n.d., unpaginated.
Marlowe, George F. *Churches of Old New England.* New York: Macmillan, 1947.
Marvin, Abijah P. *History of Winchendon, Massachusetts.* Winchendon: privately printed, 1868.
———, comp. *History of Worcester County, Massachusetts.* 2 vols. Boston: C. F. Jewett, 1879.
Mason, Charles. *History of Dublin, New Hampshire.* Boston: John Wilson, 1855.
Mason, Ellen. "The Old Meeting-House of North Yarmouth, Maine." *Old Times in North Yarmouth, Maine* 2 (1878): 175–82.
Mason, George C. *Annals of Trinity Church, Newport, Rhode Island.* Newport: Mason, 1890.
Massachusetts Historical Commission. Town Reconnaissance Survey Reports. www.sec.state.ma.us/mhc/mhchpp/TownSurveyRpts.htm.
Mather, Cotton. *Diary of Cotton Mather.* 2 vols. New York: Ungar, 1957.
———. *Ratio Disciplinae Fratrum Nov-Anglorum.* Boston: Gerrish, 1726.
*Mattapoisett and Old Rochester, Massachusetts.* New York: Grafton, 1907.
McChesney, Herbert L. *A History of Ludlow, Massachusetts, 1774–1974.* Longmeadow, Mass.: Otto, 1978.
McDuffee, Franklin. *History of Rochester, New Hampshire.* Manchester, N.H.: Clarke, 1892.
McIntyre, Ruth A. *Old First Church: The Fourth Meetinghouse (1819).* Springfield, Mass.: First Congregational Church, 1962.
Merrill, Joseph. *History of Amesbury, Massachusetts.* Haverhill, Mass.: Stiles, 1880.
Metcalf, John G. *Annals of the Town of Mendon, Massachusetts.* Providence, R.I.: Freeman, 1880.
Miller, Edward, and Frederic P. Wells. *History of Ryegate, Vermont.* St. Johnsbury, Vt.: Caledonian, 1913.
Miller, William. *Historical Discourse of the Congregational Church in Killingworth, Connecticut.* New Haven, Conn.: Hoggson and Robinson, 1870.
*Milton Town Records, 1662–1729.* Boston: Sherrill Press, 1930.
Mirick, Benjamin L. *The History of Haverhill, Massachusetts.* Haverhill: Thayer, 1832.
Mitchell, H. E., and E. M. Campbell. *Berwick Register.* Kents Hill, Maine: H. E. Mitchell Publishing Company, 1904.
Mitchell, Mary H. *The History of New Haven County, Connecticut.* Boston: Pioneer Historical, 1930.
———. *History of the United Church of New Haven.* New Haven, Conn.: United Church of New Haven, 1942.
Mixer, Elisabeth. *An Account of Some Spiritual Experiences and Rapturous and Pious Expressions.* New London, Conn.: T. Green, 1736.
Moe, William C. H. "The Second Meeting House." Undated typescript at the First Congregational Church archives, Guilford, Conn.
———. *Three Centuries of Church Music.* Guilford, Conn.: privately printed, 1938.
Mooar, George. *Historical Manual of the South Church in Andover, Mass.* Andover: Draper, 1859.
Moore, Jacob Bailey. *History of the Town of Candia, Rockingham County, N.H., from Its First Settlement to the Present.* Manchester, N.H.: G. W. Browne, 1893.
Morison, John H. *Address Delivered to the Centennial Celebration in Peterborough, New Hampshire.* Boston: Butts, 1839.
*Muddy River and Brookline Records, 1634–1838.* Brookline: Farwell, 1875.

Nason, Elias. *History of Dunstable, Massachusetts.* Boston: Mudge, 1877.
National Register of Historic Places. Inventory, Nomination Form. Danville Meeting House, Danville, N.H. Listed 19 April 1982.
Nelson, Charles. B. *History of Stratham, New Hampshire, 1631–1900.* Somersworth, N.H.: New Hampshire Publishing Co., 1965.
Nelson, John. *Pastor's Memorial* [Leicester, Mass.]. Boston: Mudge, 1862.
Nelson, Louis P. *The Beauty of Holiness: Anglicanism and Architecture in Colonial South Carolina.* Chapel Hill: University of North Carolina Press, 2008.
Nelson, Susan S. "Capt. Abraham Knowlton, Joiner, and the Seminal Woodworkers of Ipswich, Massachusetts." In *Rural New England Furniture: People, Place, and Production. The Dublin Seminar for New England Folklife: Annual Proceedings 1998,* edited by Peter Benes, 42–59. Boston: Boston University Scholarly Publications, 2000.
Nelson, Walter R. *History of Goshen, New Hampshire: Settled, 1769, Incorporated, 1791.* Concord, N.H.: Evans Print Co., 1957.
Newhall, James Robinson. *Liñ, or, Jewels of the Third Plantation.* Lynn, Mass.: T. Herbert and J. M. Munroe, 1862.
*New Haven Town Records, 1649–1769.* 3 vols. Edited by F. B. Dexter. New Haven, Conn.: New Haven Colony Historical Society, 1917–1962.
Newman, Sylvanus C. *Rehoboth in the Past.* Pawtucket, R.I.: Sherman, 1860.
Nissenbaum, Stephen. *The Battle for Christmas.* New York: Knopf, 1996.
Noon, Alfred. *History of Ludlow, Massachusetts.* Springfield, Mass.: Bryan, 1875.
North, Catharine M. *History of Berlin, Connecticut.* New Haven, Conn.: Tuttle, 1916.
Norton, Bettina A. "Anglican Embellishments: The Contributions of John Gibbs, Junior, and William Price to the Church of England in Eighteenth-Century Boston." In Benes, *New England Meeting House and Church,* 70–85.
Norton, John F. *History of Fitzwilliam, New Hampshire.* New York: Burr, 1888.
*Notes on the History of the First Parish Church, Sandwich, Massachusetts.* Sandwich: Bicentennial Committee, 1975.
Noyes, Harriette E., comp. *A Memorial of the Town of Hampstead, New Hampshire.* . . . 2 vols. Boston: Reed, 1899.
Nylander, Jane C. "Toward Comfort and Uniformity in New England Meeting Houses, 1750–1850." In Benes, *New England Meeting House and Church,* 86–100.
Oberholzer, Emil. *Delinquent Saints: Disciplinary Action in the Early Congregational Churches of Massachusetts.* New York: Columbia University Press, 1956.
*One Hundred and Fiftieth Anniversary of the Organization of the Congregational Church in Columbia, Connecticut.* Hartford, Conn.: Case, Lockwood, 1867.
*One Hundred and Fiftieth Anniversary of the West Congregational Church, Haverhill.* Haverhill, Mass.: C. C. Morse and Son, 1886.
*One Hundred Fiftieth Anniversary of the Organization of the First Church of Christ in Pomfret, Connecticut.* Danielsonville, Conn.: Transcript Printers, 1866.
*One Hundred Fiftieth Anniversary of the Town of Sterling, Massachusetts.* Sterling, 1931.
Orcutt, Samuel. *A History of the Old Town of Stratford and the City of Bridgeport, Connecticut.* 2 vols. New Haven, Conn.: Fairfield County Historical Society, 1886.
———. *History of the Town of Wolcott (Connecticut).* . . . Waterbury, Conn.: Press of the American Printing Company, 1874.
———. *History of the Towns of New Milford and Bridgewater, Connecticut, 1703–1882.* Hartford, Conn.: Press of the Case, Lockwood, and Brainard Company 1882.

Osterweis, Rollin. *Three Centuries of New Haven, 1738–1938.* New Haven, Conn.: Yale University Press, 1953.
Packard, Theophilus. *History of the Churches and Ministers in Franklin County, Massachusetts.* Boston: Whipple, 1854.
Paige, Lucius R. *History of Cambridge, Massachusetts, 1630–1877.* Boston: Houghton, 1877.
———. *History of Hardwick, Massachusetts.* Boston: Houghton-Mifflin, 1883.
Paine, Josiah. *History of Harwich, Barnstable County, Massachusetts, 1620–1800.* Rutland, Vt.: Tuttle, 1937.
Palmer, Clara Skeele. *Annals of Chicopee Street: Records and Reminiscences of an Old New England Parish for a Period of Two Hundred Years.* Springfield, Mass.: H. R. Johnson, 1899.
Parke, David B. *The Epic of Unitarianism: Original Writings for the History of Liberal Religion.* Boston: Beacon Press, 1960.
Parker, Benjamin Franklin. *History of Wolfeborough (New Hampshire).* [Cambridge, Mass.: Caustic and Claflin], 1901.
Parmenter, C. O. *History of Pelham, Massachusetts, from 1738 to 1898, Including the Early History of Prescott.* Amherst, Mass.: Carpenter and Morehouse, 1898.
———. "Old Meeting-House at Pelham." *Springfield [Mass.] Sunday Republican,* 8 November 1903, 10.
Parsons, Charles S. *The Dunlaps and Their Furniture.* Manchester, N.H.: Currier Gallery, 1970.
Patten, Harold J., comp. *"Ask Now of the Days That Are Past": A History of the Town of Tewksbury, Massachusetts, 1734–1964.* Tewksbury, 1964.
Patten, Matthew. *The Diary of Matthew Patten of Bedford, N.H. from Seventeen Hundred Fifty-four to Seventeen Hundred Eighty-eight.* Concord, N.H.: Rumford Press, 1903.
Perkins, G. W. *Historical Sketches of Meriden.* Meriden, Conn.: Hinman, 1849.
Perley, Sidney. "Historical Sketch of the First Church in Lynn." *Essex Antiquarian* 1, no. 10 (October 1897): 151–57.
———. *History of Boxford.* Boxford, Mass.: privately printed, 1880.
Perry, Kate E. *The Old Burying Ground of Fairfield, Conn.* Hartford: American Publishing Co., 1882.
Peterson, Mark A. *The Price of Redemption: The Spiritual Economy of Puritan New England.* Stanford: Stanford University Press, 1997.
Pettingell, Charles I. "The West Parish of Salisbury, Massachusetts, and the Rocky Hill Meetinghouse." *Old-Time New England* 57 (Fall 1966): 29–46.
Phillips, Daniel L. *Griswold: A History.* New Haven, Conn.: Tuttle, 1929.
Phillips, James D. *Salem in the Eighteenth Century.* Boston: Houghton Mifflin, 1937.
Phillips, Samuel. *A Discourse Delivered at Boston.* Boston: Kneeland and Adams, 1766.
Phillips, Wendell. *The Old South Meeting House.* Address given 14 June 1876. Old South Leaflets, no. 202. Boston, n.d.
Place, Charles A. "From Meeting House to Church New England." *Old-Time New England* 13 (October 1922): 69–77; (January 1923): 110–23; (April 1923): 149–64; 14 (July 1923): 3–20.
*A Platform of Church Discipline: Gathered out of the Word of God.* Cambridge, Mass.: Samuel Green, 1649.
Plummer, Jonathan. "The Dying Confession of Pomp." Broadside. Newburyport, Mass., 1795.
*Plymouth Church Records, 1620–1859.* 2 vols. Publications of the Colonial Society of Massachusetts. Boston: Colonial Society of Massachusetts, 1920, 1923.

Porter, Noah. *An Historical Discourse Delivered at the Celebration of the One Hundredth Anniversary of the Congregational Church in Farmington, Connecticut.* Hartford, Conn.: Lockwood and Brainard, 1873.

———. "The New England Meeting House." *New Englander,* n.s., 6 (1883): 303–38.

Powell, Brian. "Exhuming Old Ship: New Evidence for Original Features." Paper presented at the New England Chapter of the Vernacular Architectural Forum, Sturbridge, Mass., 3 March 2007.

Powell, Brian, and Andrea Gilmore. "Old Ship Meeting House, First Parish, Hingham, Massachusetts: Historic Structure Report." 4 vols. Dedham, Mass., Building Conservation Associates, 2007. Copy available at the Hingham Public Library.

Powell, Sumner C. *Puritan Village: The Formation of a New England Town.* Middletown, Conn.: Wesleyan University Press, 1963.

Price, Ebenezer. *A Chronological Register of Boscawen.* Concord, N.H.: Moore, 1823.

Pride, Edward W. *Tewksbury: A Short History.* Cambridge, Mass.: Riverside Press, 1888.

Prime, Nathaniel S. *History of Long Island.* New York: R. Carter, 1845.

*Proceedings at the Celebration of the Two Hundred Fiftieth Anniversary of the First Church of Christ in Milford, Connecticut.* Milford, Conn.: Ansonia Sentinel, 1890.

*Proceedings at the Centennial Celebration, Town of Longmeadow, Massachusetts.* Longmeadow: Town, 1884.

*Proceedings at the One Hundred and Fiftieth Anniversary of the Organization of the First Congregational Church: Randolph, Mass. . . .* Boston: T. Todd, 1881.

*Proceedings in Commemoration of the Organization in Pittsfield . . . of the First Church of Christ.* Pittsfield, Mass.: Sun Printing Company, 1889.

*Quarter Millennial Anniversary: The Ancient Church in Windsor, Connecticut.* Windsor, Conn.: Church, 1880.

Quinan, Jack. "Asher Benjamin and Charles Bulfinch: An Examination of Baroque Forms in Federal Style Architecture." In Benes, *New England Meeting House and Church,* 18–29.

Ramsdell, George A. *The History of Milford, New Hampshire.* Concord, N.H.: Rumford Press, 1901.

Rattray, Jeannette E. *Discovering the Past: The Writings of Jeannett Edwards Rattray, 1893–1974, Relating to the History of the Town of East Hampton.* Edited by Thomas Twomey. New York: Newmarket Press, 2001.

Read, Benjamin. *History of Swansea, New Hampshire.* Salem, Mass.: Salem Press, 1892.

*Records of the Church in Brattle Square, Boston, 1699–1872.* Boston: Benevolent Fraternity, 1902.

*Records of the Church of Christ at Cambridge in New England, 1632–1830.* Boston: Putnam, 1906.

*Records of the Colony and Plantation of New Haven, from 1638 to 1649.* Edited by C. J. Hoadly. Hartford, Conn., 1857.

*The Records of the First Church in Boston, 1630–1868.* 3 vols. Edited by Richard D. Pierce. Boston: Colonial Society, 1961.

*Records of the First Church in Dorchester in New England, 1636 to 1734.* Boston: Ellis, 1891.

*A Record of the Services Held at the Congregational Church of Windsor, Connecticut.* Windsor: Congregational Church of Windsor, 1880.

*Records of the Society or Parish of Turkey Hills, Now the Town of East Granby, Connecticut, 1737–1791.* Edited by Albert C. Bates. Hartford, Conn., 1901.

Records of the South Precinct, Weymouth, Mass. Transcript of selected records, collection of the author.

*Records of the Town Meeting of Lynn, Massachusetts,* [1691–1783]. 7 vols. Lynn: Lynn Historical Society, 1949–1971.
*Records of the Town of Braintree.* Edited by Samuel A. Bates. Randolph, Mass.: D. H. Huxford, 1886.
*Records of the Town of Cambridge (formerly Newtowne), Massachusetts, 1630–1703.* Cambridge: Cambridge City Council, 1901.
*Records of the Town of Lee, Massachusetts.* Lee, Mass.: Gleaner, 1900.
*Records of the Town of Plymouth.* Edited by William T. Davis. 3 vols. Plymouth, Mass.: Avery and Doten, 1889–1903.
*Records of the West Precinct of Watertown, Massachusetts.* Waltham, Mass.: Aldermen, 1913.
*Records of Trinity Church, Boston, 1728–1830.* Edited by Andrew Oliver and James Bishop Peabody. 2 vols. Boston: Colonial Society of Massachusetts, 1980.
"Report of the Committee for the Meeting House Repairs." Transcript of document dated 4 March 1808 in Shrewsbury, Mass., in possession of the author.
*Report of the Proceedings and Exercises at the One Hundred and Fiftieth Anniversary of the Incorporation of the Town of Kingston, Mass.: June 27, 1877.* Boston: Stillings, 1876.
Reps, John W. "Boston by Bostonians: The Printed Plans and Views of the Colonial City." *Boston Prints and Printmakers, 1670–1775.* Boston: Colonial Society, 1973.
Reymond, Bernard. *L'Architecture religieuse des protestants.* Geneva, Switzerland: Labor et Fides, 1996.
Reynolds, Hezekiah. *Directions for House and Ship Painting.* Facsimile of 1812 edition. Worcester, Mass.: American Antiquarian Society, 1978.
Rice, Charles B. *Proceedings at the Celebration of the Two Hundredth Anniversary of the First Parish at Salem Village, Now Danvers, October 8, 1872. . . .* Boston: Congregational Publishing Society, 1874.
Rich, Shebnah. *Truro—Cape Cod; or, Land Marks and Sea Marks.* Boston: Lothrop, 1883.
*The Road We Have Travelled.* Shrewsbury, Mass.: First Church, 1963.
Roads, Samuel Jr. *History and Traditions of Marblehead, Massachusetts.* Boston: Houghton, Osgood, 1880.
Robbins, Chandler. *History of the Second Church or Old North, in Boston: To which is added a History of the New Brick Church.* Boston, 1852.
Robinson, G. Frederick, and Ruth Robinson Wheeler. *Great Little Watertown: A Tercentenary History.* Watertown, Mass.: Historical Society, 1930.
Rogers, Samuel. *The Diary of Samuel Rogers, 1638–1639.* Edited by Tom Webster and Kenneth Shipps. Woodbridge, GB: Boydell, 2004.
*Rook Lane Chapel, Frome [Somerset County]: A Short History, 1707–1993.* Frome, England: Somerset Building Preservation Trust, 1993.
Rose, Harold Wickliffe. *The Colonial Houses of Worship in America.* New York: Hastings, 1963.
Roy, Louis E. *The History of East Brookfield, Massachusetts, 1686–1970.* Brookfield: Heffernan, 1970.
Roys, Auren. *History of the Town of Norfolk, Connecticut.* New York: Ludwig, 1847.
Ruell, David. "The 'Round' Meetinghouses of New Hampshire and Vermont." *Historical New Hampshire* 36 (1981): 171–94.
Sanderson, Edmund L. *Waltham as a Precinct of Watertown and as a Town, 1630–1884.* Waltham, Mass.: Waltham Historical Society, 1936.
*Sandwich and Bourne, Colony and Town Records.* Yarmouthport, Mass.: Swift, 1912.
Sanford, Don A. "Entering into Covenant: The History of the Seventh Day Baptists in Newport [Rhode Island]." *Newport History* 66 (Summer 1994): 1–47.

Sanger, Abner. *Very Poor and of a Lo Make: The Journal of Abner Sanger.* Edited by Lois K. Stabler. Portsmouth, N.H.: Peter E. Randall, 1986.

Sawyer, Roland D. *History of Kensington, New Hampshire, 1663–1945.* Farmington, Maine: Knowlton, 1946.

Scholes, Percy A. *The Oxford Companion to Music.* London: Oxford University Press, 1970.

Scott, Jonathan. "The Early Colonial Houses of Martha's Vineyard." 2 vols. Ph.D. diss., University of Minnesota, 1985.

Secomb, Daniel F. *History of Amherst, New Hampshire, 1728–1882.* Concord, N.H.: Evans, 1885.

"The Second Meeting-House in Lexington, Erected by the Town in 1714." *Proceedings of the Lexington Historical Society, 1886–1889,* 129–30. Lexington, Mass.: Lexington Historical Society, 1890.

"Second Parish, Methuen, 1784–1846." *Essex-County Historical and Genealogical Register* 1–2 (1894–1895), unpaginated.

Sewall, Samuel. *The Diary of Samuel Sewall, 1674–1729.* 2 vols. Edited by M. Halsey Thomas. New York: Farrar, Straus and Giroux, 1973.

Sewall, Samuel. *The History of Woburn, Middlesex County, Massachusetts. From the Grant of its Territory to Charlestown, in 1640, to the Year 1860.* Boston: Wiggin and Lunt, ca. 1868.

Seward, Josiah L. *History of Sullivan, New Hampshire.* 2 vols. Keene, N.H.: Seward, 1921.

Sharpe, W. C. *Bethany Sketches and Records.* Seymour, Conn.: Record Print, 1908.

Shaw, Charles. *A Topographical and Historical Description of Boston.* Boston: Spear, 1817.

Shaw, William E. *History of Belchertown in the Eighteenth Century.* Amherst, Mass.: Newell, 1968.

Sheldon, George. *A History of Deerfield, Massachusetts.* 2 vols. Greenfield, Mass.: Press of E. A. Hall and Co., 1895.

Sheldon, Hezekiah S. *Documentary History of Suffield.* Springfield, Mass.: Clark W. Bryan, 1879–1888.

Shepard, James. *History of St. Mark's.* New Britain, Conn., 1907.

Shurcliff, Margaret H. "English Bells." *Old Time New-England* 49, no. 3 (1958): 57–71.

Shurtleff, Harold R. *The Log Cabin Myth: A Study of the Early Dwellings of the English Colonies in North America.* Cambridge, Mass.: Harvard University Press, 1939.

Silverman, Kenneth. *A Cultural History of the American Revolution.* New York: Columbia University Press, 1987.

Simmons, Arthur A. *History, Yearbook and Church Directory, First Congregational Church in Wilmington, Massachusetts.* Unpaginated. Wilmington, Mass., 1933.

Simonds, J. Rupert. *A History of the First Church and Society of Branford, Connecticut.* New Haven, Conn.: Tuttle, 1919.

Sinnott, Edmund W. *Meetinghouse and Church in Early New England.* New York: Bonanza Books, 1963.

Smith, Charles James. *History of the Town of Mont Vernon, New Hampshire.* Boston: Blanchard, 1907.

Smith, E. Vale. *History of Newburyport.* Newburyport, Mass., 1854.

Smith, G. E. Kidder. *The Beacon Guide to New England Houses of Worship.* Boston: Beacon Press, 1989.

Smith, Gwenda. *The Town House.* Strafford, Vt.: Strafford Historical Society, 1992.

Smith, H. C., and W. S. Rann. *History of Rutland County, Vermont.* Syracuse, N.Y.: Mason, 1886.

Smith, J. E. A. *History of Pittsfield, Massachusetts.* 2 vols. Boston: Lee, 1869.

Smith, John Montague. *History of Sunderland, Massachusetts.* Greenfield, Mass.: E. A. Hall, 1899.
Smith, Samuel F. *History of Newton, Massachusetts.* Boston: American, 180.
Smith, Thomas. *Journals of the Rev. Thomas Smith and the Rev. Samuel Deane, pastors of the First Church in Portland.* Portland, Maine: Bailey, 1849.
Smith, William C. *A History of Chatham, Massachusetts.* Chatham, Mass.: Historical Society, 1971.
Sobon, Jack A. "The English Barn in America: IV. Raising the Frame." *Timber Framing,* March 2007, 12–17.
South Plympton Precinct Book. Typescript copy, 1732–1896. Library, New England Historic Genealogical Society, Boston.
Spalding, A. F. *The Centennial Discourse on the One Hundredth Anniversary of the First Baptist Church, Warren, R.I.* Providence, R.I.: Knowles, Anthony and Co., 1865.
Speare, Eva A. *Colonial Meeting-Houses of New Hampshire.* Littleton, N.H.: D.C.W., 1938.
Spicer, Andrew. "'Accommodating of Thame Selfis to Heir the Worde': Preaching, Pews, and Reformed Worship in Scotland, 1560–1638." *History: Journal of the Historical Association* 88 (1991): 405–22.
———. *Calvinist Churches in Early Modern Europe.* Manchester and New York: Manchester University Press, 2007.
Spofford, Charles B. *The Old Meeting House, Claremont, N.H., 1792–1895.* [S.l.: s.n., 1895?].
Spofford, Jeremiah. *A Family Record of the Descendants of John Spofford, and Elizabeth his wife.* Haverhill, Mass.: Frothingham, 1851.
———. *A Genealogical Record . . . of [the] Descendants of John Spofford and Elizabeth Scott.* Boston: A. Mudge and Son, 1888.
Sprague, William B. *Annals of the American Pulpit.* New York: Carter, 1857.
Sprunger, Keith L. *Dutch Puritanism: A History of English and Scottish Churches of the Netherlands in the Sixteenth and Seventeenth Centuries.* Leiden: Brill, 1982.
———. "Puritan Church Architecture and Worship in a Dutch Context." *Church History* 66, no. 1 (1997): 36–63.
St. George, Robert B. "Style and Structure in the Joinery of Dedham and Medfield, Massachusetts, 1635–1685." *Winterthur Portfolio* 13 (1979): 1–46.
Stackpole, Everett S., and Lucien Thompson. *History of the Town of Durham, New Hampshire. . . .* 2 vols. [Durham, N.H.?]: Town: [1913].
Staples, C. A. "A Sketch of the History of Lexington Common." In *Proceedings of the Lexington Historical Society, 1886–1889:* 16–27. Lexington, Mass.: Lexington Historical Society, 1890.
Staples, William R. *Annals of Providence.* Providence, R.I.: Knowles, 1843.
Stark, Caleb. *History of Dunbarton, New Hampshire.* Concord, N.H.: G. Parker Lyon, 1860.
Stearns, Ezra S. *History of Ashburnham, Massachusetts.* Ashburnham, Mass.: Town, 1887.
Stebbins, Rufus P. *Centennial Discourse, Leominster, Mass.* Boston: Little Brown, 1843.
Steiner, Bernard C. *A History of the Plantation of Menunkatuck and of the original town of Guilford, Connecticut: comprising the present towns of Guilford and Madison.* Baltimore: privately printed, 1897.
Stell, Christopher. *An Inventory of Nonconformist Chapels and Meeting-houses in Central England.* London: HMSO, 1991.
———. "Puritan and Nonconformist Meetinghouses in England." In *Seeing beyond the Word: Visual Arts and the Calvinist Tradition,* edited by Paul Corby Finney. Grand Rapids: W. B. Eerdmans, 1999.

Stiles, Ezra. *Extracts from the Itineraries.* New Haven, Conn.: Yale University Press, 1916.
———. *The Literary Diary of Ezra Stiles. D.D., LL.D.* 5 vols. New York: Scribner's, 1901.
Stiles, Henry R. *History of Ancient Windsor, Connecticut.* 2 vols. New York: C. B. Norton, 1859.
———. *History of the City of Brooklyn. Including the Old Town and Village of Brooklyn, the Town of Bushwick, and the Village and City of Williamsburg.* Brooklyn, N.Y.: Published by subscription, 1867–1870.
Stiles, Henry R., and Sherman W. Adams. *The History of Ancient Wethersfield.* 2 vols. New York: Grafton Press, 1904.
Stilgoe, John R. *Common Landscape of America, 1580–1845.* New Haven, Conn.: Yale University Press, 1982.
Stoddard, Solomon. *The Inexcusableness of Neglecting the Worship of God under Pretence of Being in an Unconverted Condition.* Boston: Green 1708.
Stone, Edwin M. *History of Beverly, Massachusetts.* Boston: Munroe, 1843.
Stone, Melvin T. *Historical Sketch of the Town of Troy, New Hampshire, 1764–1897.* Keene, N.H.: Press of the Sentinel Printing Co., 1897.
Stoughton, Ralph M. "History of Gill, Massachusetts," 1:48. Typescript, New England Historic Genealogical Society Library, Boston, Mass.
Stout, Harry S. *The New England Soul: Preaching and Religious Culture in Colonial New England.* New York: Oxford University Press, 1986.
Stowe, Charles Edward, and Lyman Beecher Stowe. *Harriet Beecher Stowe: The Story of Her Life.* Boston: Houghton Mifflin, 1911.
Stowe, John M. *History of the Town of Hubbardston, Worcester County, Mass.* Hubbardston, Mass.: The Committee, 1881.
Swan, Frederick W. *Remarkable Visionary Dreams, of a Mulatto Boy, in Northfield, Mass. . . .* [Chesterfield, N.H.]: Merriam, 1822.
Sweeney, Kevin M. "Meetinghouses, Town Houses, and Churches: Changing Perceptions of Sacred and Secular Space in Southern New England, 1720–1850." *Winterthur Portfolio* 28, no. 1 (Spring 1993): 59–93.
Swift, Charles F. *History of Old Yarmouth: Comprising the Present Towns of Yarmouth and Dennis.* Yarmouth, Mass.: privately printed, 1884.
Swift, Samuel. *History of the Town of Middlebury.* Middlebury, Vt.: Copeland, 1859.
Tapley, Harriet S. *St. Peter's Church in Salem, Massachusetts, before the Revolution.* Salem, Mass.: Essex Institute, 1944.
Tarbox, Increase N. "Musical History." In *One Hundredth Anniversary of the Congregational Church in West Newton.* Boston: Beacon, 1882.
Tatham, David. "The Lithographs of Benjamin Champney." *Old-Time New England* 67 (Summer–Fall 1976): 1–6.
Taylor, Andrew. *Towers and Steeples designed by Sir Christopher Wren.* London: B. T. Batsford, 1881.
Taylor, Charles James. *History of Great Barrington (Berkshire) Massachusetts.* [Great Barrington]: Town, 1928.
Taylor, Edward. *The Poems of Edward Taylor.* New Haven, Conn.: Yale University Press, 1960.
Temple, J. H. *Early Ecclesiastical History of Whately.* Northampton, Mass., Metcalfe, 1849.
———. *History of Framingham, Massachusetts.* Framingham, Mass., Town, 1887.
———. *History of North Brookfield, Massachusetts.* North Brookfield, Mass.: Town, 1887.

Temple, J. H., and George Sheldon. *History of Northfield, Massachusetts.* Albany, N.Y.: Munsell, 1875.

Thomas, David C., and Peter Benes. "Amzi Chapin: A New England Cabinetmaker Singing and Working in the South and Trans-Appalachian West." In *Rural New England Furniture: People, Place, and Production. The Dublin Seminar for New England Folklife: Annual Proceedings, 1998,* edited by Peter Benes, 76–99. Boston: Boston University Scholarly Publications, 2000.

Thompson, Benjamin F. *History of Long Island: Containing an Account of the Discovery and Settlement.* 2 vols. New York: Gould, Banks, 1843.

Thompson, Edmund. *Maps of Connecticut before the Year 1800.* Windham, Conn.: Hawthorne House, 1940.

Thompson, Francis M. *History of Greenfield, Massachusetts.* 2 vols. Greenfield, Mass., 1904.

Thwing, Annie H. *Inhabitants and Estates of the Town of Boston, 1630–1800.* CD. Boston: New England Historic Genealogical Society with the Massachusetts Historical Society, 2001.

Thwing, Walter E. *History of the First Church in Roxbury, 1630–1904.* Boston: Butterfield, 1908.

Tilden, William S. *History of the Town of Medfield, Massachusetts, 1650–1886. . . .* Boston: Ellis, 1887.

Tillinghast, John A., and Frederick W. Tillinghast. *A Little Journey to the Home of Elder Pardon Tillinghast.* Providence, R.I.: Standard Printing Company, 1908.

Timlow, Heman R. *Ecclesiastical and Other Sketches of Southington, Connecticut.* Hartford, Conn.: Case, 1875.

"To the Inhabitants of the District of Berlin in Town Meeting Assembled." Account of a committee to finish the Berlin meetinghouse, dated 19 November 1794. Berlin Historical Commission, Berlin, Mass.

Todd, Charles B. *History of Redding, Connecticut.* New York: Gray, 1880.

Torrey, Rufus C. *History of the Town of Fitchburg, Massachusetts.* Fitchburg, Mass.: Centennial Committee, 1865.

*Town Records of Manchester, Massachusetts.* 2 vols. Salem, Mass.: Salem Press, 1891.

Trayser, Donald G. *Barnstable: Three Centuries of a Cape Cod Town.* Hyannis, Mass.: Goss, 1939.

Trent, Robert F. "The Marblehead Pews." In Benes, *New England Meeting House and Church,* 101–11.

*Trinity Church in the City of Boston, Massachusetts.* Boston: Wardens, 1933.

"A True Copy of the 'Ancient Book of Records' of the First Church of Christ, Rochester, Mass." Copied by Alice M. Bolles, 1900. Plumb Memorial Library, Rochester, Mass.

Trumbull, James R. *History of Northampton, Massachusetts, from Its Settlement in 1654. . . .* 2 vols. Northampton: Gazette Printing Company, 1898–1902.

Trumbull, J. Hammond. *Memorial History of Hartford County, Connecticut.* Boston: Osgood, 1886.

Tucker, Arthur H. "Hope Atherton and His Times." In *History and Proceedings of the Pocumtuck Valley Memorial Association* (Deerfield, Mass.) 7 (1921–1929): 371–423.

Tucker, Edgar W. "The Meeting Houses of the First Parish." In *The Meeting House on the Green: A History of the First Parish in Concord and Its Church.* Concord, Mass.: First Parish, 1985.

Turell, Ebenezer. *The Life and Character of the Reverend Benjamin Colman.* Boston: Rogers and Fowle, 1749.

*The Two Babes in the Wood: Together with Divine Songs for Children.* Broadside, 1760. (Listed in Evans, *Early American Imprints, Series I, 1639–1800,* no. 49234.)

*Two Hundred and Fiftieth Anniversary of the First Church of Christ Congregational, Old Saybrook, Connecticut.* Middletown, Conn.: Stewart, 1896.

*Two Hundredth Anniversary, Kensington Congregational Church.* Kensington, Conn., 1912.

Underhill, Lora A. W. *Descendants of Edward Small of New England and the Allied Families.* . . . Rev. ed. Boston, New York: Houghton Mifflin, 1934.

Updike, Wilkins. *History of the Episcopal Church of Narragansett, Rhode Island.* New York: Onderdonk, 1847.

Upham, Charles W. *Address at the Rededication of the Fourth Meeting House of the First Church of Salem.* Salem, Mass.: Gazette, 1867.

———. *Principles of the Reformation: A sermon preached November 16, 1826, at . . . the First Congregational Society in Salem.* . . . Salem, Mass.: Warwick Palfray, Jr., 1826.

Upton, Dell. *Holy Things and Profane: Anglican Parish Churches in Colonial Virginia.* Cambridge: MIT Press, 1986.

Usher, James M. *History of Medford, Massachusetts.* Boston: Franklin, 1886.

Vail, R. W. G. "The American Sketchbooks of Charles Alexandre Lesueur." *American Antiquarian Society Proceedings* 48 (1938): 59–155.

Vose, Nancy S. "Asher Benjamin's West Church: A Model for Change." *Old-Time New England* 67 (Summer–Fall 1976): 7–15.

Wadleigh, George. *Notable Events in the History of Dover, New Hampshire.* Dover, N.H.: Tufts College Press, 1913.

Wadsworth, Daniel. *Diary of Rev. Daniel Wadsworth, 1737–1747.* Hartford, Conn.: Case, Lockwood and Brainard, 1894.

Wainwright, Paul. *A Space for Faith: The Colonial Meetinghouses of New England.* Portsmouth, N.H.: Peter E. Randall Publisher / Jetty House, 2009.

Wainwright, Paul (photographer). "Colonial Meetinghouses of New England." colonialmeetinghouses.com, 2008.

Waite, Clarence M. *First Trinitarian Congregational Church, Scituate, Massachusetts.* Scituate, Mass., 1967.

Waite, Otis. *History of Claremont, New Hampshire.* Manchester, 1895.

Walker, George L. *History of First Church in Hartford, 1633–1883.* Hartford, Conn.: Brown and Gross, 1884.

Walker, Joseph B. *Our Four Meeting Houses: First Congregational Society, Concord, New Hampshire.* Concord N.H.: Evans, 1888.

Walker, Timothy P. *The Flaming Sword, or, A Sign from Heaven: Being a Remarkable Phenomenon, seen in the state of Vermont.* Norwich, Conn., 1799.

Wallace, William A. *History of Canaan, New Hampshire.* Concord, N.H.: Rumford Press, 1910.

Ward, Barbara M. "'In a Feasting Posture': Communion Vessels and Community Values in Seventeenth- and Eighteenth-Century New England." *Winterthur Portfolio* 23, no. 1 (Spring, 1988): 1–24.

Ware, Henry. *Two Discourses containing the history of the Old North and New Brick Churches.* Boston: Burditt, 1821.

Warren, William L. "The First Two Southbury Meeting Houses." *Connecticut Antiquarian* 33, no. 1 (1981): 22–32.

———. "The Oxford Meeting House." *Connecticut Antiquarian* 33 (1981): 4–9.

Washburn, Emory. *Historical Sketches of the Town of Leicester, Massachusetts.* Boston, Wilson, 1860.

Waters, Joseph G. Introduction to *Diary of William Bentley,* 1:xli–xlii. Gloucester, Mass.: Smith, 1962.

Waters, Thomas F. *Ipswich in the Massachusetts Bay Colony.* 2 vols. Ipswich, Mass.: Ipswich Historical Society, 1905–1917.

Waters, Wilson. *History of Chelmsford, Massachusetts.* Lowell, Mass.: Courier-Citizen, 1917.

*Watertown Records, Prepared for Publication by the Historical Society.* 8 vols. Watertown, Mass.: Historical Society, 1894–1939.

Watkins, Walter K. "Malden's Old Meetinghouses." *Register of the Malden [Massachusetts] Historical Society* 2 (1911–1912): 33–53.

———. "Three Contracts for Seventeenth Century Building Construction in Massachusetts." *Old-Time New England* 12 (July 1921): 27–32.

Webb, Nathaniel. "Plan of the Third Society in Lebanon." 1769. Connecticut Historical Society.

Weis, Frederick. *The Colonial Clergy and the Colonial Churches of New England.* 2 vols. Lancaster, Mass., 1936.

Weisman, Richard. *Witchcraft, Magic, and Religion in Seventeenth-Century Massachusetts.* Amherst; University of Massachusetts Press, 1984.

Wellman, Thomas B. *History of the Town of Lynnfield, Massachusetts, 1635–1895.* Boston: Blanchard and Watts, 1895.

Wells, Frederic P. *History of Newbury, Vermont.* St. Johnsbury, Vt.: Caledonian, 1902.

Wells, John. *Peabody Story: Events in Peabody's History, 1626 to 1972.* Salem, Mass.: Essex Institute, 1972.

Wheeler, Edmund. *History of Newport, New Hampshire.* Concord, N.H.: Republican Press Association, 1879.

Wheeler, George Augustus, and Henry Warren Wheeler. *History of Brunswick, Topsham, and Harpswell, Maine, including the ancient territory known as Pejepscot.* Boston: Mudge, 1878.

White, Alain C. *History of the Town of Litchfield, Connecticut, 1720–1920.* Litchfield, Conn., 1920.

White, James F. "From Protestant to Catholic Plain Style." In *Seeing beyond the Word: Visual Arts and the Calvinist Tradition,* edited by Paul Corby Finney. Grand Rapids: W. B. Eerdmans, 1999.

Whitmore, William H. *Abel Bowen, Engraver.* Boston: Rockwell and Churchill, 1884.

Wight, Charles A. *Some Old Time Meeting Houses of the Connecticut Valley.* Chicopee Falls, Mass.: Wight, 1911.

Wilder, David. *History of Leominster, Massachusetts.* Fitchburg, Mass.: Reveille, 1853.

Willis, William. *History of Portland, Maine.* Portland, Maine: Bailey, 1865.

Willson, Edmund. *Address Delivered in Petersham, Massachusetts.* Boston: Crosby, 1855.

Winiarski, Douglas L. "Gendered 'Relations' in Haverhill, Massachusetts, 1719–1742." In *In Our Own Words: New England Diaries, 1600 to the Present. The Dublin Seminar for New England Folklife: Annual Proceedings, 2006–2007,* edited by Peter Benes, 58–78. Boston: Boston University Scholarly Publications, 2009.

Winslow, Ola E. *Meetinghouse Hill, 1630–1783.* 1952. Reprint, New York: Norton, 1972.

Winthrop, John. *The Journal of John Winthrop, 1630–1649.* Edited by Richard S. Dunn, James Savage, and Laetitia Yeandle. Cambridge, Mass.: Harvard University Press, 1996.

Wisner, Benjamin B. *The History of the Old South Church in Boston.* Boston: Crocker, 1830.

Wood, Nathan. *The History of the First Baptist Church, Boston (1665–1899).* Philadelphia: American Baptist, 1899.

Woodbridge, Dudley. Journal, 1–10 October 1728. 5 pages. Massachusetts Historical Society, Boston, Mass.

Worcester, Samuel M. *Memorial of the Old and New Tabernacle, Salem, Massachusetts.* Boston: Crocker, 1855.

Worcester, Samuel T. *History of Hollis, New Hampshire, from Its First Settlement to the Year 1879.* Boston: Williams, 1879.

Worthen, Augusta H. *History of Sutton, New Hampshire.* Concord, N.H.: Republican Press, 1890.

Yates, Nigel. *Buildings, Faith, and Worship.* Oxford: Oxford University Press, 1991.

Zeiller, Martin. *Topographia Galliae, oder Beschreibung und Contrafaitung der Vornehmbsten und bekantisten Oerter in dem mächitgen under gassen Königreich Franckreich.* 4 vols. Frankfurt am Main: Caspar Merian, 1655–1661.

Zimmerman, Philip D. "Ecclesiastical Architecture in the Reformed Tradition in Rockingham County, New Hampshire, 1790–1850." Ph.D. diss., Boston University, 1985.

# Acknowledgments

The following individuals and institutions have greatly assisted the research and writing of this book.

## Individuals

Glenn M. Andres, William N. Banks, Georgia B. Barnhill, William L. Baughan, Ross W. Beales Jr., Emilie Žadna Beneš, Květa Emilie Beneš, Jane Montague Beneš, Harry Breger, Rutheva Brockett, Alan Clark Buechner, Raymond Cable, Richard M. Candee, Nancy C. Carlisle, Abbott L. Cummings, Arthur Deming, Frederick C. Detwiller, Robert M. Doty, Peter Drummey, Barry W. Eager, Jonathan K. Fairbanks, Daniel and Jessie Farber, Anne Farnam, Donald R. Friary, Donna-Belle B. Garvin, James L. Garvin, Anne Grady, Gerald J. Gross, David D. Hall, Charles Hambrick-Stowe, Charles Hammond, Russell G. Handsman, Henry J. Harlow, Margaret H. Hepler, Alvan Hill, William N. Hosley Jr., Robert L. Howie Jr., John Kendall, Chester B. Kevitt, Christopher King, Arthur J. Krim, Sally Krone, Gregory H. Laing, Wilhelmina Lunt, Ina Mansur, Herbert McChesney, Ethel Hedman Montague, Edith Nettleton, Ruth Nettleton, Bettina A. Norton, Jane C. Nylander, Frances E. O'Donnell, Morgan Phillips, Brian Powell, David R. Proper, Milena Beneš Rosecan, Jack Quinan, Robert Blair St. George, Gwenda Smith, Stephen M. Straight, Kevin M. Sweeney, Robert F. Trent, Edgar Wesley Tucker, Giovanna Vitelli, Paul Wainwright, William L. Warren, Ola E. Winslow, Harold F. Worthley, Philip D. Zimmerman.

At the University of Massachusetts Press: Dennis Anderson, Mary Bellino, Carol Betsch, Clark Dougan, Jack Harrison, Sally Nichols, Debby Smith, and Bruce Wilcox.

## Institutions

American and New England Studies Program, Boston University; American Antiquarian Society; Boston Athenaeum; Concord Free Public Library, Concord, Mass.; Congregational Library; Currier Gallery of Art, Manchester, N. H.; Harvard University library system: Andover-Harvard Theological Library, Fine Arts Library, Loeb Design Library, and Widener Library; Historical Society of Old Newbury; Keene Public Library; Library of the Massachusetts Historical Society; Library of the New England Historical and Genealogical Society; Mugar Memorial Library, Boston University; The National Endowment for the Humanities (1979).

# Index

Abbott, Deacon I., 254
Abington, Conn., 23
acrobat, 149
Acworth, N.H., 232
Adam, Robert and James, 210
Adams, George, 192
Adams, Rev. Joseph, 255
Adams, Samuel (brother-in-law of Jeremiah Spofford; builder), 59
Agawam, Mass., 397n42
Ainsworth, Henry, 34, 83, 258
aisle, main, 73, 133–34, 204–5, 213
Albany, N.Y., 84–85
Allis, John (builder), 61, 108–9, 227
Allis, Samuel (brother of John; turner), 61
Alna, Maine, 125, 278
Alstead, N.H., 195
altar, in Anglican churches, 117, 204
*American Builder's Companion* (A. Benjamin), 215
American Revolution, 18, 37, 54, 119, 149, 209, 217, 226
Ames, Jacob (builder), 235
Ames, John (builder and cabinetmaker), 57, 381n2
Amesbury, Mass., 17, 151–52, 154, 156, 182. *See also* Rocky Hill meetinghouse, West Salisbury (Amesbury), Mass.
Amherst, Mass., 24, 70, 151, 225
Amherst, N.H., 202, 276
Andover, Mass., First or North Parish: architectural decisions, 255; liturgical practices, 254; as model, 227, 237; painted cipher in, 265, 400n2; parish division, 130–31; pews reused in, 275; pulpit reused in, 236; roof selection, 130–31
Andover, Mass., Second or South Parish: architectural decisions, 242, 255, 263; liturgical practices, 254–55; refusal to sell pew spaces, 280; religious maxim in, 264; seating, 68; services, 32–33; triple-porch meetinghouse, 58–59, 172
Andrews, Nathan (son of William; joiner), 94, 113, 160
Andrews, William (builder), 65, 79, 89, 91, 94, 105, 113, 386n58
Andros, Edmund, 118
angels, 267–72
Anglican churches: altar in, 117, 204; architectural forms of, 121, 387n4; bell towers on, 138; influence of, 7, 261, 263; influence of on meetinghouse architecture, 120, 204–5, 208–10, 217, 230; names of, 18, 377n12; placement of pulpit in, 117; relative permanence of, 273; survival rates of, 5
Anglican ecclesiastic forms, used by Congregationalists, 34, 154
Anglican parishes: liturgical changes in, 260–61; numbers of in New England, 174
"Anglicization," 34
Antinomian controversy, 246
Antrim, N.H., 18, 235
Appleton, Rev. Nathaniel, 32
Apponaug (Warwick), R.I., 262
Apthorpe, Charles, 209–10
architects: early European, 81–84; full involvement by, 239–41; role of designers as, 127, 139, 143, 146, 204–5, 209; working without, 216, 255
architectural concepts, regionwide exchange of, 133, 253–54
architectural copybooks, 157–58, 190, 230
architectural innovations: rate of adaptation of, 221, 223; replications of, 225
architectural styles, meetinghouse: evolution of, 204–5; influence of private money on, 241; and liturgical practices, 243, 246–63; local transmission of, 240; patterns of transmittal of, 240–43; periods of, 242; subregional variations in, 240; transitions between, 246, 250, 262

architecture, English, 2, 157–58, 208, 223, 246, 263
architecture, Anglican and Reformed similarities, 120–24
Arlington, Mass., 59, 201
Arnold, John (builder), 262
"artificial workmen," 49
artisanal traditions, 117
Ashburnham, Mass., 171–72, 196
Ashby, Mass., 235
Ashfield, Mass., 57
Atwater, Edward, 113
axial plan, 4, 118, 121, 204–7, 246, 261. *See also* church plan
axis, architectural, 134–45

Bacon, Timothy (builder), 61
Bailey, Rev. Jacob, 265
Bailey, Sarah L., 255
"bakehouse," 3
balustrade, 128
banns boxes, 25
baptism: 16, 33, 36–38, 222
baptismal basins, 114, 202, 387n7
Barker, Ephraim (builder), 52
Barnard, Rev. Thomas, 130, 205
Barnard, Vt., 105
barns, 19, 77, 81, 92, 102, 383n2, 385–86n46
Barnstable, Mass.: East Precinct, 166, 202, 228; West Precinct, 278
barracks, meetinghouses as, 16
Barrow, Henry, 3, 221
bass viol, 44–45, 47, 249, 379n47
batten construction, 177, 180, 182
Bay Psalm Book, 41, 89, 245, 247–48, 258
Becket, Mass., 224
Bedford, Mass., 135, 217, 229, 240
Bedford, N.H. (Presbyterians), 202
Beecher, Rev. Lyman, 183–84
Belchertown, Mass., 66
belfry: centrally mounted, 85, 91, 94, 100–102, 108, 252, 399nn40–41; freestanding, 135, 229; on Hartford meetinghouse, 79; open, 142; painted images on, 267; terms for, 137; turret-mounted, 139
bell deck, 138–40, 152
Bellingham, Richard, 98
bell ropes, 106, 134, 252, 262
bells: meetinghouses with, 2, 79, 85, 101, 106, 156; renunciation of, 135; uses of, 50, 106
bell tower additions, 57, 213, 223
bell towers: in Boston, 138–43; dissemination of, 138, 146, 156; ecclesiological significance of, 135; erection of by private wealth, 241; European influence on, 91, 158; imitations of, 156; on long side of meetinghouse, 215, 259; numbers of with bells, 135; origins of, 135; with pinnacles, 107; replication of, 138; roof styles on, 138; sectarian differences in, 158
bell towers, self-standing, 119
bell towers, standing, 135–60, 246, 257, 390n73
Benjamin, Asher (architect), 50, 213–15, 217, 235, 240, 263–64, 280, 381n25
Bennington, Vt., 44
Bentley, Rev. William: on Abraham Knowlton, 181; on Arlington pulpit color, 201; on Brattle Street bell tower, 389n44; on Chelmsford pulpit, 395n2; on East Parish meetinghouse, 34, 182, 252; on Hatfield colors, 195; on Kingston meetinghouse, 211; on Lexington exterior color, 196; on Quaker meetinghouse roofs, 262; on religious maxims, 264–65, 400n2; on South Abington meetinghouse, 211; on Westford steeple, 137
"bents," 51–52
Bergen, N.J., 85
Berlin, Mass., 182, 193–94
Bethany, Conn., 200
Beverly, Mass.: First Parish, 66–68, 227–28, 240; Second or North Parish, 252
Bible reading, 34, 38, 46, 244
Billerica, Mass., 50, 52, 104, 227
Billings, William, 44, 47, 379n47
Bingham, James Harvey, 44
Bird, Rev. Samuel, 37
Bird meetinghouse, Nashua (formerly Dunstable), N.H., 274–75
Blake, Francis E., 267
Blake, Henry T., 199
Blake, James, 167
Blanchard, Joshua (mason), 143
block houses, 104–5
*The Bloody Massacre perpetrated in King Street Boston on March 5th 1770* (H. Pelham), 101
blue, lead-color, or sky-color exteriors, 192, 199–200
Bluehill, Maine, 176–77
Blue Meeting-house, 16, 37, 199
Blue Pachaug, 200
Boardman, Rev. Daniel, 38
Bolton, Mass., 57–58
Bonner, John, 205
*Book of Architecture* (J. Gibbs), 157
*Book of Psalmes: Englished both in prose and meter* (H. Ainsworth), 258
Boscawen, N.H., 105
Boston, Mass., First Baptist Church, 41, 47, 205
Boston, Mass., First Society: liturgical practices, 246–48; long-term conservatism of, 246–7; organ acquisition, 46; singing school, 247; termination of lining out by, 47; use of term *meetinghouse* in, 80

# INDEX

Boston, Mass., meetinghouses of the First Society: stone construction of I, 121; additional balcony tiers in II, 164; II as possible model, 79; private funding for II, 241; conservative architectural decisions for III, 242; exterior paint for III, 191; four-square vote for III, 132; names of III, 16; A. Benjamin design for IV, 215, 217; imitations of IV, 16, 25, 217. *See also* Old Brick, Boston, Mass.; Old Meeting House, Boston, Mass.

Boston, Mass., Second or North Society, 26, 35, 69, 246–47. *See also* Old North, Boston, Mass.

Boston, Mass., Third Society: abandonment of Old South, 279; adoption of halfway covenant, 36; Anglican services in meetinghouse, 118; Anthony Stoddard as member, 269; architectural decisions, 248–49; formation of, 37, 244, 246; last ruling elder in, 36; liturgical practices, 247–48; meetinghouse names, 16; use of private funding by, 241. *See also* Old Cedar, Boston, Mass.; Old South meetinghouse, Boston, Mass.

Boston, Mass.: West Society or Lynde Street: adoption of *New Version of the Psalms* by, 41; architectural decisions, 246; A. Benjamin meetinghouse design, 215; liturgical practices, 245; meetinghouse interior, 177, 179; meetinghouse as model, 217

*Boston News-Letter*, 94

Boston Synod of 1662, 36, 47

*Boston Weekly News-Letter*, 100

Bowen, Abel, 252

Boxborough, Mass., 397n42

Boxford, Mass.: First Parish, 52, 227; Second Parish, 169

Bradford, Mass., 4, 227, 264

Bradford, William, 104

Braintree, Mass.: First Parish, 25, 115, 121, 190; Second Parish, 261

Braintree (Randolph), Mass., Third Parish, 190

Bramhope Chapel, 102–4

Branford, Conn., 102, 225, 385n39

Brattle, Thomas, 46, 244

Brattleboro, Vt., 54, 61

Brattle Square meetinghouse I, Boston, Mass.: bell tower, 139, 246; called a "church," 239; description of, 128; as model, 222, 235, 237; roof, 128, 130; spire type, 149

Brattle Square meetinghouse II, Boston, Mass.: alignment of, 208; building committee, 208; compass-headed windows, 127; interior, 208; as model, 222; plans for, 208; use of stoves, 34, 246, 379n18

Brattle Square Society, Boston, Mass.: adoption of dumb reading, 47; architectural decisions, 246; Benjamin Colman as minister of, 144; child baptism, 37; Communion, 37; first singing school, 42; lack of ruling elders in, 36; legitimacy challenged, 247; liturgical practices, 244–45, 247; Manifesto, 35; members, 208, 244; proprietors, 128–29; termination of lining out by, 47; use of private funding, 241

bridge-building, 54, 59, 77, 92, 105

Bridgewater, Mass., 42

"Brief History of Old Bergen Church," 85

Brimfield, Mass., 20, 60, 70, 234, 265, 397n29

Bristol, Maine, 278

"broadsides," 51

Brockett, John (surveyor), 89

Brookhaven, L.I., 68, 114

Brookline, Mass., 72, 156

Brooklyn, Conn., 173, 198, 278, 393n162

Brown, John, 242

Brown, Joseph (architect), 128, 157, 208, 223

Brownist sects, 34, 83

Brunswick, Maine, 196

Bruton Parish Church, Williamsburg, Va., 271

Buckland, Mass., 57

Buell, Rev. Samuel, 185

Buell, William (joiner), 25, 115

Buell pulpit, 185–86

builders, master: background of in structural carpentry, 54, 381n26; English domestic traditions of, 77; experience of as millwrights and bridge mechanics, 54; families of, 57; military and naval experience of, 55–56; names of, 1791–1830, 54, 381n25; numbers of, 1791–1830, 54; occasional, 53; political experience of, 55; professional, 54, 61; raising and joining techniques of, 49; in seventeenth and eighteenth centuries, 53

building committees: preference for local models by, 216, 235, 240; reliance on old models by, 237; use of innovative guidelines by, 132, 149, 154, 177, 224–27, 242

building rates, 4–5, 209, 213

Bulfinch, Charles (architect): and Hollis Street design, 210–11, 246; influence of, 263–64; multiple structures by, 215, 381n25; and Pittsfield design, 10, 211–13, 230, 240, 261; and ties to Thomas Dawes, 6, 210; and Trinity Church, Boston, spire, 149; and Westfield, Mass., design, 230

Bullock, Elder Jeremiah, 16

Burgis, William (artist), 137, 150

Burgis-Price views, 99, 106, 127–28, 138–39, 146, 149–50

Burgis 1728 map of Boston, 101

Burntisland kirk, Fife, Scotland, 11, 80, 84–85, 384n17, 384n19

Bushwick (Brooklyn), L.I., 85, 87

Bruton Parish Church, Williamsburg, Va., 271

Burrillville, R.I., Baptist meetinghouse, 267–68

433

burying ground, 13, 16, 185, 221
Byles, Rev. Mather, 156, 205, 245–46, 263

cages, 25
Canaan, N.H., 171, 198
Calvin, John, 378n1
Calvinist architectural radicalism, 80
Cambridge, Mass.: baptism rates, 37; bell, 106; desirable locations of seating in, 72; four-square roof, 78, 383n3; meetinghouse as model, 226, 228; optional relations in, 37; seating assignments, 65, 67; use of term *meetinghouse* in, 80
Cambridge platform (1648), 9, 35, 244, 263, 376n15
canopies: as focus, 13; forms of, 182; maxims on, 264–65; ornamental hangers for, 266, 400n8; painted, 180, 201–3; over pews, 182; stories about, 1
canopy finials, 182, 188–90, 392n122
Cape Cod, Mass., 134, 166, 171
Carolinas, exterior ecclesiastic colors in, 194
Carter, Benjamin (son of Timothy; builder), 59–60
Carter, Elias (son of Timothy; woodworker, builder, and architect), 20, 59–60, 215, 237, 239, 264–65, 381n25, 397n33
Carter, Timothy (builder), 59–60, 223
Carter, Timothy, Jr. (son of Timothy; builder), 59
Carter and Carter, firm of, 60
Carter and Cutting, partnership of, 60
Carter and Hulett, partnership of, 60
ceiling, vaulted, 241
chairs, 10, 14, 70, 133
Champney, Benjamin (lithographer), 150
Chapin, Amzi, 32, 44
Charenton, France, 1623 Huguenot temple at, 8, 81, 91, 260
Charlemont, Mass., 58
Charles Street Church, Boston, 215
Charleston, S.C., 115
Charlestown, Mass.: adoption of halfway covenant, 36; bell tower, 146; Bulfinch bell tower design, 210; gallery tiers, 164; meetinghouse raising, 49; minister selection criticized in, 249; pitched roof, 131; use of term *meetinghouse* in, 80
Chatham, Mass., 167, 195, 225
Chauncy, Rev. Charles, 46, 246–47, 255
Chauncy, Rev. Isaac, 2–3, 240, 273, 375n8
Chelmsford, Mass.: bellhouse, 135; bell tower as model, 137; Communion table, 114; description of meetinghouse in, 131; halfway covenant in, 36; meetinghouse raising, 51; as model, 217; pulpit, 395n2; replication in, 237; separated belfry, 229; use of flag in, 23
Chelsea, Mass., 252

cherubim, 267–70, 401n16
Chesapeake region, 120, 383n3, 387n1, 393n152
Cheshire, John (architect), 154, 160
Chester, Conn., 274
Chester, Mass., 217, 230
Chester, N.H., 42, 44, 391n102
Chichester, N.H., 105
Child, Thomas, 191
Chilmark, Mass., 38
Christ Church, Boston, Mass.: church plan, 118; compass-headed window, 125; design, 142; as model, 222–23, 241, 249; painted cherubim in, 268; spire design, 158; steeple, 148–49
Christ Church, Cambridge, Mass., 210
Christ Church, Middletown, Conn., 46
church: and changes in making decisions, 35; definition of, 2; formation of, 29; membership of, 36–38; and selection of officers, 35; and transformations in authority, 34; use of term, 135, 239
church plan: conservative attitudes towards, 253, 275; definition of, 135, 209, 213–16; dispersal of, 118, 230, 237, 243, 261, 264; seating in, 73. *See also* axial plan
*The City and Country Builder's and Workman's Treasury of Designs* (B. Langley), 59, 223
Claremont, N.H., 44, 121, 161, 273
Clark, Ebenezer (builder), 213
clergymen, hiring of, 29
Cleveland, Aaron, 52, 149, 177, 192
"cluster" dissemination, 191, 228–29, 240
"The Coffin," Orford, N.H., 17
Cohasset, Mass., 125, 151, 195–96, 278
Colman, Rev. Benjamin, 79, 139, 144, 156, 237, 239–46, 263
colors, exterior. *See* paint, exterior
colors, interior. *See* paint, interior
*Columbian Magazine of Philadelphia*, 210
Communion, 33, 36–40, 114, 124
Communion ware, 38–39, 246, 265
Communion tables: European antecedents for, 81, 88; folding, 14, 114, 117, 174, 221; long form, 114–15; part of pulpit group, 108; seating at, 68, 113
compass-headed pulpit windows. *See* pulpit windows
conch, 2, 23–24
Concord, Mass., 131, 164, 182, 237, 265
Concord, N.H., 105, 161, 171, 177, 194
"coneys." *See* cupolas
Connecticut General Assembly, 21
Connecticut Valley: bell towers, 154; decorative motifs, 182–90; exclusion of porch stairwells in, 172–73; liturgical practices, 42, 46–47; open Communion in, 38; pulpit forms, 182–83, 185, 190; replication in, 228; roof selection in, 133; townhouses and town halls, 7

consecration of meetinghouses, 34
conservative aesthetic, influence of, 236–37
construction, meetinghouse, subcontracting of, 61
conversion, 31, 33, 36–37
Coolidge, John, 6, 8, 385n31
Cooper, Rev. Samuel, 235
Copley, John Singleton, 208
Cotton, Rev. John, 37, 246, 379n38
*The Country Builder's Assistant* (A. Benjamin), 213, 215, 395n22
covenant, 2, 29, 33, 38
Coverly, Nathaniel, 28
cultural shifts, in Boston, 118–21
cupolas: 101, 106, 130, 133–35, 157, 210–11
curtains, 179, 205, 210
Cutler, Rev. Timothy, 149
Cutting, Jonathan, Jr. (builder), 60, 231

Damon, Isaac (architect, builder): 50, 54, 61, 215, 217, 239, 381n25
dancing schools, 118, 227
Danckaerts, Jasper, 30
Danvers, Mass., 37, 251
Danville, N.H., 181, 278
Davenport, Rev. John, 79, 89
Dawes, Thomas (architect, mason), 6, 205, 208–10, 246, 263
deacons' pew, 14, 221, 253
deacons' seat, 113–14, 174, 190, 202, 217, 235, 237
de Brosse, Salomon (architect), 81, 91
Dedham, Mass., 26–27, 35, 37, 101, 107, 109, 276
Deerfield, Mass., 94, 149, 227, 399
derricks, 51–52
design conduits, 217, 225–27
design dispersal: exceptions to patterns of, 235; of stairwell forms, 171; rate of, 226; regional leaders of, 228; role of financial investment in, 235–36; role of geography, class, and social standing in, 237. *See also* "cluster" dissemination; design conduits; neighbor-to neighbor routes; replications; "runs" or running diffusion
"Design for a Church," 215
Dickinson, Joel (builder), 213
desk. *See* pulpits
"Devil's Roosting Place," 19
Dexter, Henry M., 5, 36
dial post, 25
Dick, John (builder), 57–58, 190, 225, 381n35
Dick, Thomas (builder), 57–58, 190, 225, 381nn35–36
dignifying the meetinghouse, 68–74
dignity, 64, 67–68, 72–74, 190–91, 225, 240
*Directions for House and Ship Painting* (H. Reynolds), 194
disestablishment laws, 27, 35, 240, 275–76, 398n13

Divine eye, 265
dogs, 18, 239
Dominion of New England, 118
Doolittle, Amos, 135
Dorchester, Mass.: canopy finial, 182; frame enlargement, 161–62; halfway covenant in, 36; meetinghouse cited in Winthrop's journal, 2–3, 80; pew at the Communion table, 114; stairwell porch, 167; trial in, 26
Dover, N.H., 105
Doxology, 18
Dracut, Mass., 196, 393n157
Drowne, Shem (coppersmith), 140
Drowne, Thomas (son of Shem; coppersmith), 152
drums, 2, 23–24, 50, 106
Dublin, N.H., 47, 232, 235, 391n102
"dumb reading," 38, 46–47, 379n32
Dudley, Mass., 198
Dudley, Paul, 167
Dunlap, John (furniture maker), 177
Durham, N.H., 267
Dutch Reformed American meetinghouses, 8, 81, 87, 88, 128–30, 261
Dutch Reformed European meetinghouses, 84–85, 89, 134–35
Dutton, Thomas (builder), 213, 230
Duxbury, Mass., 72, 104

"earthfast" structures, 104
earthquakes, 37, 139, 145
East Braintree (part of Weymouth), Mass., 275
East Granby, Conn., Turkey Hills Society, 69
Eastham, Mass., 225
East Hampton, L.I., 183–85, 195
East Hartford, Conn., 19
East Haven, Conn., 121, 123, 133, 179–80, 193, 225
East Plymouth, Conn., 195
East Sandwich, Mass., Quaker meetinghouse, 262
East Windsor, Conn., 43, 225
Eaton, Theophilus, 79
Edgartown, Mass., 101
Edict of Nantes, 81
Edwards, Jonathan, 38
egalitarianism, 33–34
Elderkin, John (builder), 54
Elderkin, John, II (son of John; builder), 54, 236
elders, 34–37, 64–65, 111, 113–14, 124, 180, 243–45, 247
Eliot, Rev. Jacob, 200–201
Emerson, Rev. William, 217, 224
Emmes, Nathaniel (mason), 143
English influence: in Boston, 33; on meetinghouse architecture, 177, 264
enlargements, meetinghouse, 59, 113, 133–34, 160–74, 198

"*en manière de théâtre*," 81, 92
entries to meetinghouse, separate, 34, 262
Episcopal Trinity Church, New York City, N.Y., 43
Essex, Mass., 252, 385–86n46, 399n41
Exeter, N.H., First Parish, 146, 215, 389n44
European origin, of American meetinghouses, 8–9, 80–89, 91
executions, 26
exhibitions, 16
exiting the meetinghouse, 74

Fairbanks, Jason, 26
Fairfield, Conn., 87, 210, 227, 395n16
Falmouth, Maine, 26, 53, 156
Falmouth, Mass., 26, 133
Farmington, Conn., 42, 53, 94, 173, 183, 278, 385n30
Farrar, Daniel W., 235
Federal-period architectural style, 73, 198, 204, 239, 246, 263–64, 277
Federal taste, influence of, 215, 222–23
Fillmore, Lavius (architect, builder), 55, 381n25, 215
finish carpentry, 14, 61, 120, 174, 176, 179, 190, 235
finishing academies, 119
"finishing" the meetinghouse, 53, 174–88, 190–91
First Baptist Church, Providence, R.I., 242
First Baptist meetinghouse, Providence, 2, 128, 157–58, 208–9, 222–23, 237
first-period meetinghouses: changes in, 119–20; numbers of, 77; style of, 5, 120, 130, 280; two principal forms of, 77
Fitchburg, Mass., 2
Fitzwilliam, N.H., 71, 232, 235
Five Nations, chief of, 25–26
flags, 2, 23, 106, 151, 377n26
Flint, Abel, 71
foot warmers, 14, 258
"four-decker" meetinghouse, 260
four-square meetinghouses: 77–78, 92–101, 120, 130, 258, 383n3
frame, steps in making, 49
Framingham, Mass.: 69, 72, 134, 165
Freemasonry, 265
Fremont, N.H., 169, 278
Frisbie, Rev. Levi, 26
Frizell, John, 139
Fuller, Capt. Isaac, 235
Fuller, Gen. John (builder), 20
funerals, 1, 26, 106, 276–77
furnishings, reuse of, 236

gables, 96–97, 99, 106, 385n33
galleries: 77, 81, 89, 94, 100, 130, 163–64
games, 10
Gardner, Mass., 177

Gay, Fisher (builder), 54
Gay, Rev. Ebenezer, 255, 263
General Court of Massachusetts, 21
Georgetown, Mass., 44
Georgian decorative and architectural modes: 157–58, 175–80, 182, 198, 203–4, 222, 241, 249, 263–64
Georgian design, vocabulary of, 176–77, 179–80
Georgian style, 123, 143, 203
Ghent, Belgium, 84
Gibbs, James (English architect), 1, 157, 209, 223
Gibbs, John (painter-stainer), 268
Gibbs, John, Jr. (son of John; artist), 268
Gilbert, John (iron- and glassworker), 106, 191
Gilead, Conn., 33, 203
Gilead, Conn., Hebron Second Parish, 199–200
Gilsum, N.H., 199, 201, 229
gin pole, 51–52, 236
Glastonbury, Conn., 160
Glocester, R.I., 267
Gloucester, Mass.: First Parish, 252, 390n73; Fourth Parish, 156
"God's House," 34
"God's Old Barn," 18
"God's Tabernacle," 34
Godsoe, John, 149
Goelet, Francis, 147
Gomes, Peter, 259
Goodhue, Mary, 378n2
*The Gospel Order Revived* (T. Brattle et al.), 247
governance, changes in, 34–35
graffiti, 14
Grafton, Mass., 224, 375n1
graining, 181, 201
gravestones, 185–87, 200, 269–70, 394n173, 400n15
Great Awakening, 38, 41, 200
Great Meeting-House, Boston, Mass. *See* Old Brick, Boston, Mass.
Great Meeting House, Salem, Mass., 250. *See also* Salem, Mass., First Parish
Greek Revival style, 204, 264, 277
Green, Joseph, 270–71
green exteriors, 194–96
Greenfield, Mass., 24
Greenfield, N.H., 51, 53
Gregg, William (builder), 235
Griswold, Conn., 200
Grossmünster church, Zurich, Switzerland, 114
Groton, Mass., 19, 74, 277
Groveland, Mass., Bradford East Parish, 59
Guilford, Conn.: architectural decisions, 249; bass viol, 47; bell purchase, 144; bell tower, 143–46, 156, 241, 389n51; bell tower as model, 152, 228, 237; liturgical practices, 249; mixed seating in, 70; replication in, 224, 237; roof selection, 133; stone meetinghouse, 121

Guilford (Madison), Conn., Second Parish, 199
Guionneau, Henry, 269
gunpowder storage, 16
Guyhirn, Cambridgeshire, England, 104

Hadley (Amherst), Mass., Third Parish, 190
Hadley, Mass., First Parish: 101, 133, 137, 160, 193
halfway covenant, 36–38, 46–47, 243, 246–47, 249–50, 253, 258
Halifax, Nova Scotia, 259–60
Hamilton, Alexander, 87, 177, 179
Hamilton, Mass., 167
Hammond, Jonathan, 208
Hampstead, N.H., 151
Hampton, Conn., 195, 198
Hampton, N.H., 25, 50, 101, 133
Hampton Falls, N.H., 17
Hancock, John, 241
Hancock, N.H., 232, 235
hands, ornamental, 266, 400n8
Hanover, Mass., 168
Harriman, Samuel, 192
Harris, John (engraver), 137
Harris, Thaddeus, 378n7
Harrison, Peter (architect), 210
Hartford, Conn., First Society, 23, 65, 72, 78–79, 117, 157, 227–28, 241
Hartford, Conn., South or Second Society, 227, 249
Harvard, Mass., 225, 397n42
Harwich, Mass.: First Parish, 166; Second Parish, 195, 227
Haskell, Joseph (builder), 59
Hatfield, Mass., 23, 106, 154, 195, 201, 227–28, 274
Haverhill, Mass., 66, 227, 240, 252, 269
"hay cap," 242, 388n13
Hawke (Danville), N.H., 225, 278
Hebron, Conn., and Gilsum, N.H., proprietors, 199
Hemenway, Daniel (builder), 57
Hemlock meetinghouse, Colebrook, Conn., 17
Hempstead, Joshua, 87
Henniker, N.H., 182, 215, 277–78
Hibbert, Rev. Thomas, 262, 400n66
Hinsdale, Mass., 217, 230
*Historical Pascoag Herald*, 267
Hoadley, David (architect, builder), 215
Holden, Mass., 33, 74
Holliman, John (gravestone maker, painter-stainer), 146
Hollis Street meetinghouses: I, 156; II, 210–11, 222–23, 241, 275
Hollis Street Society, Boston, Mass., 47, 245–46
Holliston, Mass., 162, 166, 199, 229
Holyoke, Mary Vial, 3

Holy Trinity Church, Blythburgh, Suffolk, England, 109
Homes, Rev. William, 38
Honeyman, Rev. James, 143
Hooker, Rev. Thomas, 30, 78
Hopkinton, N.H., 215
hospitals, meetinghouses as, 16
Houghton, John (carpenter), 109–10
hourglasses, 30, 202
hourglass holders, 30, 114, 174, 378n7
Housatonic Valley, Mass., 261
hovels, 13, 376n1
Hubbard, Charles D., 145
Hubbardston, Mass., 74
Huchinson, John (builder), 104, 117
Hudson, N.H., 391n102
Huguenot temples, 8, 81–84, 89, 384n14, 384n25
Hulett, John (builder), 60, 213, 230, 397n27
Hull, John, 270
Hunt, David, 50
Hunt, Dea. Ebenezer, 50

Indicott, John (builder), 148
innovations: high-style architectural, 230; liturgical, 46–48; musical, 40–46; vernacular, 228
interiors: first-period, 108–17; second-period, 176–91; third-period, 204–5, 239
Ipswich, Mass., 25, 29
Ipswich, Mass., First Parish: funeral sermon in, 26; lore, 19; meetinghouse III, 89, 96–97, 385n33; meetinghouse IV, 26, 127; musical instruments, 44; paint in meetinghouse IV, 193, 202; pew rights, 72; pulpit in meetinghouse IV, 180–82; rift in, 180; tithingmen, 65
Ipswich, Mass., Second Parish, 234, 237

Jaffrey, N.H., 25, 59, 182, 193–94, 198, 229, 232, 278
Jamaica, L.I., 87, 121
James II, 118, 120
Jameson, Ephraim, 134
Jaques, Henry (nephew of Stephen Sr.; builder), 57
Jaques, Henry (son of Richard; woodworker), 57
Jaques, John (grandnephew of Stephen Sr.; turner), 57
Jaques, Richard (father of Henry), 57
Jaques, Stephen (son of Henry; builder, millwright, and woodworker), 57, 97, 114, 133, 257
Jaques, Stephen (son of Stephen Sr.; turner), 57
Jennings, Joshua (joiner), 117
Johnson, Bradbury (joiner), 215
Johnson, Rev. Francis, 3, 83
Joy, Joseph, 195–96

Keach, Horace A., 267
Keene, N.H., 223–44
Kensington, Conn., 43, 45, 177, 274
Kensington, N.H., 196
Kilburn, Samuel (builder), 235
Killingly, Conn.: First Parish, 19, 60; Second, North, or Thompson Parish, 198
Killingworth, Conn.: First Society, 225; Second Society or Killingworth Farms, 195, 225
Kimball, David, 180
King Philip's War, 33, 36
King's Chapel, Boston, Mass.: bell tower on I, 138; compass-headed windows in I, 124; connections of Gibbs artists to, 268; design for I, 118, 387n1; design for II, 121, 210; donation of organ by, 380n51; effect of on meetinghouse architecture, 120; gift of organ to, 45–46; interior paint in I, 201; lining out in, 47; name of, 18; *New Version of the Psalms* in, 41, 260
Kingsley, Peleg (builder), 61
Kingston, Mass., 211
Kingston, N.H., 225
Kittery, Maine, Spruce Creek meetinghouse, 149
Knowlton, Abraham (joiner), 180–81
Knowlton, Abraham (son of Abraham; joiner), 180
Knox, John, 378n1

Lakeman, Nathan, 251
Lane, Job, 93, 111, 117
Langley, Batty (English architect), 59
Langley, Samuel (builder), 177
"lanthornes." *See* cupolas
La Rochelle, France, Huguenot temples at, 89
Lawlor, Thomas, 193, 202
lead weights, 14
lean-tos, 101–2, 113, 115, 160–61
Lebanon (Columbia), Conn., Second Society or Lebanon Crank, 200
Lebanon, Conn., First Society, 21, 173, 193, 200
lectures, 30, 277
Lee, Mass., 73, 230, 383n48, 397n27
Leicester, Mass., 60, 188, 202
Lenox, Mass., 230, 261, 397n27
Leominster, Mass., 193, 240, 397n42
Leonard, Rev. Nathaniel, 258–59
Le Petit-Quevilly, Huguenot temple at, 89
Lesueur, Charles-Alexandre, 162–63
Lexington, Mass.: 67, 132, 135–36, 164, 196, 229, 237
Liddell, John, 269
lightning, 94, 146
Lincoln, Calvin, 280
Lincoln, Joshua, 191
Lincoln, Mass., 71

Line meeting house, Fall River, Mass., and Tiverton, R.I., 17
lining out, 41–42, 45–47, 70, 245, 249, 252, 379n38
Litchfield, Conn., 167, 183–84, 274
Little Compton, R.I., 269
Littleton, N.H., 44, 46
liturgical perspectives, transference of, 253–54
liturgical practices: and architectural change, 243, 246–63; and Communion, 38–40; effect of disestablishment on, 398n13; evolution of, 243–49; and music, 40–46; and seating, 65–69
liturgy, changes in, 34
Livermore, Maine, 19
"living saints," 36, 270
"logg houses," 104–5, 123
Londonderry, N.H., 177, 202, 235
long houses, 77, 101–4
Long Island, six-and eight-sided meetinghouses in, 85–87
Longmeadow, Mass., 23, 62, 154
Lord, Joseph, 26
"The Lord's Barn," 102, 385n46
Lord's Prayer, 34, 38, 124, 244
lore, 18–20
Ludlow, Mass., 182–83, 185–87, 278
Lyman, Theodore, 208
Lynde, Benjamin, 26
Lynde, Benjamin, Jr. (son of Benjamin), 26
Lynn, Mass., First Parish, 78, 105–6. *See also* Old Tunnel, Lynn, Mass.
Lynnfield, Mass., 237, 276–77
Lyon, France, 8

Machias, Maine, 260
Mackmallun, Jonathan (turner), 146
MacSparran, Rev. James, 41, 260
Madison, Conn., 192
mahoganized finishes, 176, 180, 201–2
Malden, Mass., 92–94, 111, 113, 149, 177, 192
Manchester, Conn., Orford Parish, 195
Manchester, Mass., 227–29, 252, 390n73
Manifesto Church. *See* Brattle Square Society, Boston, Mass.
Manning, Elder James, 262
Mansfield, Conn., 133
Marblehead, Mass.: First Parish, 66, 115, 160, 202; Second Parish, 182
marbleizing, 176, 201–3
Margaret of Parma, 84
Marlborough, Conn., 53
Marlborough, Mass., 57, 134
Marston, James Brown, 192
Maryland, 121
Massachusetts Bay charter, 33, 118, 120
Mather, Rev. Cotton: 3, 38, 245, 373n8, 379n32
Mather, Rev. Increase, 30, 247
Mather, Rev. Richard, 3, 88, 124, 375n8

May, Hezekiah (builder), 154
Maynard, Mass., 20
mbira, 44
McGregor, Rev. David, 202
McIntire, Samuel (architect), 209
Medfield, Mass., 109, 113, 180, 191, 386n73
Medford, Mass., 69, 135, 150, 163, 252, 271
Medway, Mass., 133–34
*meeting*, use of term in England, 3; use of term in New England, 3
meetinghouse: as American form, 7, 80, 88; civic functions of, 16–17; dedicated for worship, 34; as defensive fort, 105; differences from Anglican and Catholic structures, 221; as European form, 7–9, 80–84, 89–92; evolution of ecclesiastic role, 239–40; evolution of form, 29; interior conditions, 2, 3; legal requirements for, 20; as municipal building, 16; numbers raised, 4; regional variety of, 222; similarity of to bridge building, 5, 381n26; subcontracting of, 61; as symbol, 1–2; as temporary structure, 1; as a term, 2, 80–81, 87, 384n11; transformation of, 264; uniformity in, 238
meetinghouse interiors, 15, 81, 92, 117, 217, 222
meetinghouse plan, 4, 77, 121, 135
meetinghouse purchases, 236, 397n42
meetinghouse sources, linguistic evidence of, 80–81
meetinghouses, nineteenth- and twentieth-century: abandonment of, 275, 278; effect of disestablishment on, 275–76; impermanence of, 273; owners of, 275–76; relocation of, 274–75, 277; reuse of, 273–80; sale of, 274–75; survival of, 5, 277–80; turning of, 277
meetinghouse to church paradigm, 7
melodeon, 46
Mendon, Mass., 60, 106, 161, 391n84, 397n33
Mendon (Milford), Mass., Second Parish, 192–93
Mendon (Millville), Mass., Third or South Parish, 127, 182
Merrimack, N.H., 278
Mico, John, 244
Middleborough, Mass., 97, 133
Middletown, Conn.: First Society, 133, 217; South Society, 133, 225
Middletown Upper Houses, Conn., North or Cromwell Society, 225
Milford, Conn., 67, 146, 152, 199, 249, 397n33
Milford, N.H., 171, 276
Millbury, Mass., 72
Millville, Maine, 278
millwrights, as meetinghouse builders, 54, 57–58
Milton, Mass., 35, 65, 134, 146
Milton, N.H., 172, 215
Milton Green, Conn., 196
minister, selection of, 29, 35

ministerial routines, 30–31
Minor, Joseph, 138, 239
Mistley, Essex, England, 210
Mitchell, James (builder), 154
Mitchell, Mary, 192
Mixer, Elisabeth, 271
money, private, 156, 174, 235, 241, 249
Monroe, N.H., 196
Montague, Mass., 24
Mont Vernon, N.H., 276
Morse, Samuel (carpenter), 235
M-shaped gables, 99, 102
Mulliken, Jonathan, 101
Munday, Richard (architect), 128, 143, 180, 223, 241
Murrayfield (Chester), Mass., 40–46, 72
musical instruments, 43–46, 249, 256. *See also* bass-viol; mbira; melodeon; organ

names of meetinghouses, colloquial, 16–18, 196, 199, 262
Nantucket, Mass., 26, 217
Natick, Mass., 275
Native Americans, 25–26, 61, 70, 110–11, 239
"necessaries," 13, 376n1
neighbor-to-neighbor routes, 156, 216–17, 237–38
New, James, gravestone-making family of, 269–70
New Bedford, Mass., 162
New Braintree, Mass., 169
New Brick, Boston, Mass.: affiliation with Second Society, 247; architectural decisions, 246; compass-headed windows, 127; description of, 139; dumb reading in, 47; lining out in, 47; liturgical practices, 245; meetinghouse alignment, 205; *New Version of the Psalms* in, 41; replication in, 235
Newbury, Mass., Church of England in, 21
Newbury, Mass., First Parish: architectural decisions, 257; contract, 97; liturgical practices, 256; precinct dispute, 21; pyramid, 152; religious protests, 376n5; roof modifications, 133; shared ownership of pews in, 69–70; steeple, 152; weathercock, 152
Newbury, Mass., West Precinct, 182
Newbury, Vt., 203
Newburyport, Mass., 18, 58–59, 182, 256–57
New England prototypes, 88
"New England Version," 41, 254, 256
Newhall, James Robinson, 18–19
New Hampshire, semicircular lean-tos in, 160–61
New Haven, Conn., meetinghouses of the First Society: design for I, 79, 89–92, 105; seating practices for I, 65, 68, 72, 113; architectural decisions for expanding II, 249–50; design for II, 96; floor plan for II, 62; lean-to for II, 160; design for III, 127, 152

New Haven, Conn., First Society: liturgical practices, 48, 249; musical practices, 250; split in, 37
New Haven, Conn., White Haven Society, 16, 37, 199, 200, 250
New Ipswich, N.H., 182, 201–2, 267
New Jersey, six- and eight-sided meetinghouses in, 84–85
New London, Conn., First Parish, 102, 161
New London (Montville), Conn., North Parish, 173
Newmarket (Newfields), N.H., 52
New Milford, Conn., 38, 73, 236
New North, Boston, Mass., 113–14, 127, 132, 139, 149–50, 246, 389n35
*A New Plan of the Great Town of Boston* (J. Bonner), 205
Newport, N.H., 201, 232
Newport, R.I.: First and Second Congregational Parishes, 146; Seventh-Day Baptists, 241–42; spired meetinghouses in, 146
New Preston, Conn., 236
New Rowley (Georgetown), Mass., 169
New South, Boston, Mass., 16, 133, 139, 150, 156, 245–46, 249
Newton, Mass., 71, 106, 236, 274
Newtown, Conn., 23
Newtowne (Cambridge), Mass., 35
New Utrecht, L.I., 85, 121
*New Version of the Psalms* (N. Tate and N. Brady), 41, 42, 47, 245
Norfolk, Conn., 195
Northampton, Mass., meetinghouses: accessories in II, 106–7; decorative canopy of III, 202; exterior painting of III, 194; frame for III raised, 50; prohibition against games near III, 10; seating plans in III, 66; design for IV, 217, 224; frame for IV raised, 50, 61
Northborough, Mass., 57
North Bridgewater, Mass., 42
North Brookfield, Mass., 193
North Church, Boston, Mass., 132
Northey, Abijah, 206
Northfield, Mass., 193
North Guilford, Conn., 23
North Haven, Conn., 19
North Pembroke, Mass., Quaker meetinghouse, 262
Norwalk, Conn., 104, 108, 115, 227, 239–40
Norwich, Conn., 46, 48, 54, 108, 157
Norwich (Franklin), Conn., West Farms, 54, 236
notetaking, 31
Nothingarians, 27
Noyes, Rev. Joseph, 200

octagonal structures, 8, 81, 84–85, 87, 89, 91
Ohio Meeting House, 17

Old Brick, Boston, Mass., 16, 25, 73, 85, 100–101, 209, 385n38. *See also* Boston, Mass., meetinghouses of the First Society
Old Brick Church (St. Luke's Church), Isle of Wight County, Va., 138
Old Bullockite meetinghouse, Porter, Maine, 16
Old Cedar, Boston, Mass.: builder, 98, 385n35; four-square plan, 130; name, 16; pinnacles, 107; raising, 98; as site of Old South, 205; size, 128; timbers, 100. *See also* Boston, Mass., Third Society
Old German Meeting House, Alna, Maine, 16
Old Jerusalem, Falmouth, Maine, 53
Old Meeting, Norwich, England, 88, 104
Old Meeting House, Boston, Mass., 79, 130. *See also* Boston, Mass., meetinghouses of the First Society
Old North, Boston, Mass., 130, 235. *See also* Boston, Mass., Second or North Society
"old of the moon," 19
Old Round, Richmond, Vt., 17
Old Ship meetinghouse, Hingham, Mass.: archaeological investigation, 9; building committee, 94, 240, 383n31; casements, 191; contract 1680, 54; interior paint, 201; name, 16, 377n10; preservation effort for, 280; pulpit windows, 125; reuse of 1635 materials in, 273
Old Sloop, Scituate, Mass., 16, 198
Old South Association, Boston, Mass., 280
Old South meetinghouse, Boston, Mass.: alignment, 205; bell-tower design, 158; compass-headed windows, 125, 127–28; description of, 143; lining out in, 47; as model, 250; name, 16; preservation effort for, 279–80; private funding of, 269; renovation, 209. *See also* Boston, Mass., Third Society
Old Tabernacle, Salem, Mass., 182, 209, 253. *See also* Salem, Mass., Third or Presbyterian Society
Old Tin Top, Providence, R.I., 17, 274
"Old Town" district, Newbury, Mass., 256
Old Tunnel, Lynn, Mass., 16, 112–13, 252–53, 275, 377n11, 387n76, 399n45
"Old Yellow" meetinghouses, 196
Orange, Conn., Milford Third Parish, 215
orange exteriors, 198–99, 229
*The Order of the Gospel* (I. Mather), 247
organ, 2, 45–46, 147, 245, 256, 380n51
Ormsbee, Caleb (architect), 210
Otis, Mass., 230
oxen, 51, 161–63, 274
Oxford, Mass., 274

Paget, John, 83
Paine, Robert T., Jr., 73
paint, 120, 191–203

paint, exterior: in Chesapeake region, 393n152; chronological distribution of, 196, 198–200; evolution of use, 191–93, 203; geographic distribution of, 195–96, 198–200; imitations of, 198; sources of evidence for, 194; symbolic use of, 200, 394n170; use of on roofs, 392n138
paint, interior, 183–88, 190–91, 193, 201–3
palisades, 105
Palladian window, 135, 208, 213, 246
Palmer, Ambrose (brother of Timothy; builder), 59–60
Palmer, Andrew (brother of Timothy; builder), 59
Palmer, Cotton (designer), 146, 157
Palmer, Timothy (bridge designer, builder), 59, 215
Palmer family, 58–60
Paradis, Lyon, France, 1566 Huguenot temple at, 81, 84, 89, 160, 172
parishes: conservative, 46, 243–49, 255–56, 258, 263; formation of, 2, 20; progressive, 46, 243–46, 249, 252, 257, 263
Parkman, Rev. Ebenezer, 23, 33
Parsons, Joseph (carpenter), 107
patterns of diffusion, 227–35
Pelham, Henry, 101
Pelham, Mass., 57–58, 192, 225, 381n35
Pell, Edward (designer, painter-stainer), 139, 191–92, 205
Pembroke, N.H., 105
penthouse. *See* turret
Pepperell, Mass., 74
Perkins, Abraham (builder), 97
Perkins, George Augustus, 146
Perret, Jacques (architect, city planner), 8, 81
Peterborough, N.H., 19
Petersham, Mass., 57, 192
pew associations, 70–71, 120
pew building, permission for, 69–70
pew doors, outside, 69
pew plans. *See* seating plans
pew space, 69, 120, 165, 169, 280
pewing, private, 40, 46, 70–71
pews: arranged *"en manière de théâtre,"* 81, 92; auctions of, 71; with canopies, 182; distribution of, 71; families sitting in, 34; highest ranked, 64–65; hinged, 1; lowest ranked, 64–65; private construction of, 69, 165–66; seventeenth-century, 115; shared ownership of, 69; third-floor, 163–64
Phelps, Abbie L., 267
Phelps, Elizabeth Porter, 32
Phillips, James D., 261
Phillips, Rev. George, 114
Phillips, Rev. Samuel, 33, 254–55, 263
pick poles, 51–52
Pierce, Col. Samuel, 26

pillories, 25
pinnacles, 89, 106–9, 118, 136, 139, 146, 154
pitch, 392n138
pitch pipe, 43, 249, 379n47
Pittsfield, Mass., meetinghouse: architectural decisions, 242; Book of Credits, 217; Bulfinch design, 211–12, 261; replications of, 212–13, 217, 230, 237, 240; reuse of, 275
"Pittsfield run," 230
Place, Charles A., 5
plans: axial, 246; basilican, 81, 142; longitudinal, 207–8; rectangular and square, 77
plate heights, 101, 131, 163–65, 173, 240
Plymouth, Mass., 25, 102, 166, 257–59
Pollio, Marcus Vitruvius, 89, 91
Pomfret, Conn., 71, 198, 229
Pomfret, Vt., 400n8
Pomp, execution of, 26
Poplin (Fremont), N.H., 169
population growth, effect of on meetinghouse construction, 160
populist imagery, 264
Porter, Maine, 127, 213
Porter, Noah, 5, 7, 375n8
Portsmouth, N.H., 25, 104, 113, 115, 117, 146, 241
postholes, 104
Potash meetinghouse, Rochester, Vt., 17
Powell, Peter (builder), 213
prayer, 30–31, 33–34, 38, 124, 244, 258
praying town, 110
precinct, 20–21, 275
Presbyterians, as a minority, 378n1
Preston, Conn., 70, 213
Price, William (cabinet maker, designer), 137, 147–48, 153–54, 223
Prime, Nathaniel S., 85
Prince, Rev. Thomas, 248
Princeton, Mass., 267
promiscuous seating, 34, 46, 70, 72, 243. *See also* seating, of men and women together
proprietors, role of, 23, 128, 152, 199, 210
"Protestant plain style," 6, 8, 117, 236
Protestant ecclesiastic architecture, 8, 84, 89, 91
Protestant worship, in Flanders and Holland, 84
prototypes, 6, 88, 128, 224, 228–30, 237
Providence, R.I., First Congregational Society, 46, 210
*Providence Gazette*, 157
"Providences," 270–71
psalmody, 32–34, 43, 47
psalmody translations, imported into England, 89
psalms: reading of, 33, 41; singing of, 32
*Psalms and Hymns* (I. Watts), 47
*Psalms of David Imitated* (I. Watts), 41, 47, 245
public notices, 25

pulpit, traveling, 111
pulpits: attached, 113; capsule, 109, 386n73; decorative treatments of, 175–90; elevated, 13; forms of, 179–83; freestanding, 109, 113; Huguenot, 110; importance in dignifying the meetinghouse, 62; inscriptions and maxims on, 264–65; as liturgical center, 221–22; for multiple occupants, 111–12; painted, 180, 183–85, 188, 191, 193, 201–3; placement of, 113, 117; placement of in Anglican churches, 111, 117; realignment of, 213; seventeenth-century, 108–14; tiers of, 113
pulpit windows, 93–94, 102, 105, 108, 125–28
pulpit window surrounds, 182
punishments, 25
"pyks." *See* pyramids
pyramids, 102, 106–8, 136–37, 152, 154

Quaker meetinghouse design, 84, 262
Quakers, 62, 135, 376n5
Quinipiack, Conn., 79, 89

raisings, 19–20, 49–53
rank, assessment of, 67
Raymond, N.H., 381n26
Read, Benjamin, 267
Reading, Mass., 18, 36, 227–28, 392n138
Redding, Conn., 69
red or peach-blossom exteriors, 192, 195, 261
Reformed religion: changes in, 34; worshiping practices in, 30
Reforming Synod (1679–80), 2, 35–36, 65
regular singing. *See* singing by rule
Rehoboth, Mass.: First Parish, 1–2, 102, 236; Second Parish, 196, 236
relations: definition of, 33; ending of, 261; geographical spread of, 47–48; made optional, 46; seventeenth-century practices of, 37; spoken retained, 246, 248, 254; written retained, 246–52, 254, 258–59
religious imagery, 264–65, 267–72
religious maxims, 264–65
religious practices: conservative, 221, 243–44, 246–47, 249–52; progressive, 243–46, 249, 252
religious protests, 16, 376n5
religious societies, liturgical differences between, 7, 262–63
*Remarkable Visionary Dreams of a Mulatto Boy, in Northfield, Mass.* (F. Swan), 271
Remonstrants' temple, Amsterdam, the Netherlands, 89
replications: age of models, 236–37; of architectural features, 223, 225; cluster distribution of, 228–29; effects of economics on, 226, 230; of exterior painting, 229; of finish carpentry, 190–91; first period, 78–80, 226–27; geographic, 237; as high-style innovations, 230; influence of conservatism on, 236; key models of, 237; local models of, 225–26, 236–38; long distance, 224–26, 230–32, 235–36; of non-architectural features, 223; numbers of, 223, 225; patterns of diffusion of, 223–26, 228; rate of dispersal of, 226, 230, 234; role of private money in, 235, 237; sources of prototypes of, 228; as vernacular transmission, 225
Restoration fashion, 222
Revere, Paul, 101, 149
Reynolds, Hezekiah, 194
Rice, Ens. David (builder), 51
Richardson, Ebenezer, 247
Richmond, Mass., 230, 397n27
Rindge, N.H., 171, 196, 229, 392n138
Robbins, Rev. Chandler, 259
Roche, John (builder, mason), 84
Rochester, Mass.: First Parish, 163–64; Second Parish, 37
Rockingham, Vt., 20, 89, 125, 278
Rocky Hill, Conn., 217
Rocky Hill meetinghouse, West Salisbury (Amesbury), Mass., 58–59, 125, 174, 181, 278
Rogers, Rev. John, 156
Rogers, Samuel, 3
Rolfe, Rev. Benjamin, 228
roof, "bevel," 131, 244, 382n47; dormer, 81, 89, 94, 130–31; gabled, 99, 102, 176, 252; gambrel, 121; gathered, 130–31, 133–34, 161, 280, 382n47; "hopper," 262, 400n66; "pyramidical," 79; "tunnel," 16, 134, 252
roof, "English," 131, 133–34, 139, 222, 246, 280. *See also* roof, pitched
roof, first-period. *See* roof, hipped
roof, "flat." *See* roof, pitched
roof, four-square. *See* roof, hipped
roof, hipped: on bell towers, 138; as current style, 77, 79, 94, 128, 130, 382n47, 383n3; on English barns, 383n2; late examples of, 255, 262; modifications to, 133; in Scotland, 84; shift away from, 128, 130, 133
roof, pitched: as common type, 134; explanation of, 128, 388n11; impact of, 134; numbers of, 134; in Plymouth, Mass., 102; preference for, 130–31, 133, 241, 246, 257, 388n14; resistance to, 134; shift towards, 119, 128–30; spread of, 133; votes for, 131–33
roof, sheet-leaded, 241
roof design, arguments over, 130–31
roof fixtures, ornamental, 106
"roof pews," 163–64
Rook Lane Chapel, Frome, Somerset County, England, 88–89
Rotterdam Scottish Church, the Netherlands, 84–85
"round" (sixteen-sided) structures, 17, 81, 274

round-top windows. *See* windows, compass-headed
Rowley, Mass., 4, 58, 228–29
Roxbury, Mass., 36, 47, 72–73, 106
Rowe, Mass., 201
Rowley, Mass.: First Parish, 135, 193, 202; Second Parish (Georgetown), 192
Roxbury, Mass., 36, 42, 47, 72, 106, 167
Rumney Marsh (Revere), Mass., 131
"runs" or running diffusion, 230
Rutter, John (builder), 5

Sabbath-day houses, 13
Sabbath exercises, 29–33
Salem, Mass., First Parish, 25, 50, 134, 164, 205, 252–53
Salem (Peabody), Mass., Middle Parish, 59, 164, 251, 253
Salem, Mass., North or Lynde Street meetinghouse, 128, 205–7, 213, 237, 275, 395n8
Salem, Mass., North or Lynde Street Society, 253, 261
Salem, Mass., Second or East Parish, 134, 182, 253
Salem, Mass., Third or Presbyterian Society, 209
Salem Village (Danvers), Mass., 130, 251
Salem, N.H., 277
Salisbury, Conn., 204, 230
Salisbury (Amesbury), Mass. West Parish, 58–59, 125, 174, 181, 278
Salisbury, N.H., 225
sand, 392n138
Sandown, N.H., 125, 181, 202, 230, 278
Sandwich, Mass., 20
Sandy Hill meetinghouse, Amesbury, Mass., 182
Satan, 19, 271
Saybrook, Conn.: First Society, 101; West Society or Westbrook, 200
Saybrook platform (1708), 35, 376n15
Scituate, Mass., Quaker meetinghouse, 262
Scituate, Mass., Second or South Parish, 130–31
Scripture reading, 38, 46
seating: Anglican emphasis on, 74; best locations of, 62, 72–73, 383n45; of clergymen, 70, 72; at Communion table, 68, 113–15, 253; in conservative parishes, 46; according to dignity, 64; evolution of, 73; for the hearing impaired and visitors, 62; influence of on Sabbath service, 40; of men and women separately, 34, 39, 62, 68, 253; of men and women together, 34, 39–40, 46, 70–72, 383n33; merit-based system of, 62; in progressive parishes, 46; rules concerning, 67; of servants, slaves, and boys, 67, 70; shifts in policies of, 39–40; of singers together, 42, 47; social leveling through, 68
seating capacity, 26–27, 62, 160, 164
seating committees, 65–69, 73
seating plans, 2, 62, 64–65, 67–68, 73, 113, 165, 206–7
seats, round, 115
Second Boston synod. *See* Reforming Synod (1679–80)
second-period meetinghouses: height of style of, 213; numbers of, 5, 209; survival rate of, 5; survivals of, 278–80; turning of, 277
sectarian controversies, 1–2
separatists, 4, 16, 28, 200, 205, 250, 274
sermons, nature and length of, 30–31
"settles," 175
Seventh-Day Baptist meetinghouse, Newport, R.I., 128, 180, 241
Sewall, Samuel: at Charlestown raising, 49; on Colman's steeple, 139; absence of crying children, 378n2; reaction to Communion and baptism, 33; on receiving Communion, 39; at Rumney Marsh raising, 131; on trial of Jeremiah Phenix, 26
Shakers, 4, 7, 200
Shelburne, Mass., 24, 105
Shepard, D. M., 252
Shepherd, Rev. Thomas, 35
Sherman, John (builder), 79, 226–28, 273–74
Shirley, Mass., 38, 47, 74, 181
Shrewsbury, Mass., 47, 53, 57, 172, 181–82, 188–90, 193, 392n134
Shutesbury, Mass., 57
signposts, 25
Sikes family, 186–87
singers, seating of, 42–43, 46–47
singing aids, objections to, 43–45
singing by rule, 41–42, 46–47
singing exhibitions, 16
singing schools, 41–42, 47, 245, 247
single-porch meetinghouses, 166–67, 171, 173–74, 262
site controversies, 2, 20–21, 23
sitting on the sills, 19
slaves, 67–68, 70
Smith, John Rubens, 101
Smith, Rev. Thomas, 30
societies, formation of, 20
sounding board. *See* canopy
South Abington, Mass., 211
South Bridgewater, Mass., 19
South Canaan, Conn., 230
*A South East View of the Great Town of Boston in New England in America* (W. Price), 137
South Hadley, Mass., 24
South Harwich, Mass., 166–67
Southington, Conn., 69, 73, 182

Southold, L.I., 274
South Weymouth, Mass., contract, 177, 190, 202
Spanish brown, 192, 194–95, 198
spike poles, 51–52
spire, "common form," 150–52; conical, 152; cupola, 150–52; tapering, 149
spires, types of, 149–56
Spofford, Abner (brother of Daniel; builder), 60
Spofford, Col. Daniel (millwright, builder), 58–59, 192, 251
Spofford, Jacob (nephew of Daniel; builder), 59
Spofford, Jeremiah (nephew of Daniel; builder), 59
Spofford, Moody (son of Daniel; builder), 59, 255
Spofford and Palmer, firm of, 60
Sprague, Hosea, 196, 377n10
Springfield, Mass., 54, 61, 101, 106, 108–9, 191, 217, 227–28
"Squaw's cap" steeple design, 152, 154, 390n67
St. Antholin's Church, London, England, 143
St. James's Church, Great Barrington, Mass., 261
St. James's Church, Piccadilly, London, England, 143
St. Martin-in-the-Fields, London, England, 157
St. Matthew's Church, Halifax, N.S., 259–60
St. Michael's Church, Marblehead, Mass., 18, 121, 125, 138–39, 273
St. Paul's Church, Narragansett, R.I., 41, 121, 125, 273
St. Peter's Church, Salem, Mass., 121, 138, 146, 161
St. Stephen's Church, London, England, 210
Stafford, Conn., 66
stairwell porches, 85, 120, 154, 160, 166–67, 172–73
stairwell porches: opposed with tower, 167–69; single: 166–68, 171; twin: 166, 169–72
stairwells, 165–74
stairwells, separate, 34, 168, 221
stairwells, sixteenth-century, 172
Stamford, Conn., 121
steeple, as term, 137, 388n34
steeple fires, 19
"steeplehouse," 135, 388n31
steeples: absence of in rural areas, 169, 198; designs of in Connecticut towns, 144–46; designs of in Massachusetts towns, 177, 192, 194, 209–10, 217; dispersal of in New England, 149–54, 156–57, 222–24; dominating nature of, 135–42; early Anglican examples of, 138, 143, 147–48; early Boston examples of, 138–42; in progressive or privately funded societies, 242, 246; as "pyramids," 108
Sterling, Mass., 43, 267
Sternhold (Thomas) and Hopkins (John), 40, 260

Stickney, John, 250
"sticks," 49
Stiles, Abel, 199
Stiles, Rev. Ezra: on Andover, 254–55; on church policies in Charleston, S.C., 38; on Communion table in Charleston, S.C., 115; on congregations reading Scripture, 38; on C. Whittlesey and B. Colman, 245; on E. Gay, 263; on families and meetinghouses, 9; on introduction of musical instruments, 43–44; letter from A. Stiles, 199; map locating North meetinghouse, Salem, 395n8; on Newport's Trinity Church spire, 154; number of Episcopal parishes, 174; number of New Haven structures burned by British, 209; preaching in secular locations, 3; on raising at North Haven, 19; recollection of New Haven seating plan, 62, 113; on religion in eastern Conn., 200; on S. Phillips, 32–33, 263; use of term *meetings*, 3
"The Still," Amesbury, Mass., 17
Stockbridge, Charles (builder), 54, 79
Stockbridge, Mass., 23, 209, 213, 261
stocks, 25
Stoddard, Anthony and Martha, 269
Stoddard, Rev. Solomon, 37
Stoddardism, 48
stone-color exteriors, 196–98
stone embankments, 105
stone meetinghouses, 121–22
Stout, Harry S., 33–34
stoves, 34, 246, 379n18
Stowe, Harriet Beecher, 183–84
Stowe, Mass., 20
Strafford, Vt., 213, 266, 400n8
Stratfield (Bridgeport), Conn., 70, 133, 152
Stratford, Conn., 46, 249
Stratham, N.H., 45, 47
Sudbury, Mass., 5, 20, 59, 69, 74
Suffield, Conn., 377n26, 397n42
Sullivan, N.H., 213
Sunderland, Mass., 24, 66, 69
sundials, 25
Surry, N.H., 223–24, 226, 230, 240
"swallows' nests," 163–64
Swalow, Ambrose (carpenter), 51
Swan Frederic W., 271
Swanzey, N.H., 267
Symmes, Rev. Thomas, 41
Symmes, Rev. William, 254
Symons, Samuel (joiner), 180

Tabernacle Church, London, England, 209
Taft, Rev. Moses, 190
Takawampbait, Rev. Daniel, 110–11
Tate (Nahum) and Brady (Nicholas), 41–42, 46–47, 245, 247, 254, 256, 258, 260

# Index

Taunton, Mass., 94, 212–13
taxation, 4, 20, 27–28, 35, 376n15, 378n44
Taylor, Edward, 269, 272
teacher, church, 34–35, 64, 111
Temple, N.H., 51, 171, 177, 229–30
Templeton, Mass., 60, 231, 235, 397n33
"Templeton run," 231–32, 234–35
Terry, Joseph (carpenter), 55
Terry and Fillmore, firm of, 54–55
Tewksbury, Mass., 53, 255
Thacher, Rev. Peter, 30
thatch, 102
third-period meetinghouses: characteristics of, 204–5, 239; distribution of, 213; evolution of, 213; numbers of, 209, 213; religious imagery in, 264–68, 271–72; survival rate of, 5
Thomaston, Maine, 266, 400n8
Tidewater region Virginia, 121
Tilton, Abraham (builder), 97
timber-frame meetinghouses, 4–5, 123
tithingmen, 18–19, 64–65
tobacco chewing, 14
Toleration Act of New Hampshire, 276
Topsfield, Mass., 105, 113, 167, 180, 227, 252
Topsham, Maine, 196
Tory Hill Meeting House, South Buxton, Maine, 17
Town, Ithiel (builder), 215, 381n25
town layout, hypothetical, 20, 89, 91, 226
town meeting, 16, 176, 277, 396n4
Townsend, Mass., 53, 57
Toxteth Park, Liverpool, England, stone chapel, 88
transition periods, 5, 246, 250
treaty negotiations, 25–26
trials, 25–27, 79
Trinity Church, Boston, Mass., 121, 124–25, 146–47, 268
Trinity Church, Brooklyn, Conn., 125
Trinity Church, New Haven, Conn., 152, 250
Trinity Church, Newport, R.I., 125, 143, 153–54, 156, 160, 222–24
triple-decker meetinghouses, 146, 164, 192, 249
triple-porch meetinghouses, 171–72
Troy, N.H., 232, 235
trumpets, 2, 23
tuning forks, 43
Turell, Ebenezer, 79
turrets: in Huguenot architecture, 81; on long houses, 101, 105–6; meetinghouses with, 79, 93–94, 96–97, 99, 130, 134, 258; on square-plan, 77; upper, 105, 386n58
Tweld, Robert (builder), 98, 385n35
Twelves, Robert (designer, builder), 143, 146, 205
twin-porch meetinghouses: 51, 89, 169–74, 194, 213, 391n102

Underhill, Charles (builder), 131
Union Episcopal Church, Claremont, N.H., 273
Upham, Charles, 252

Vaernewicjck, Marcus Van, 84
vanes, iron, 79, 106
vernacular, definition of, 376n23
vernacular designs, 174
vernacular tradition, 9–10, 213
Victorian style, 277–78
Virginia, exterior ecclesiastic colors in, 194

Wadsworth, Rev. Daniel, 79
Wadsworth map of New Haven, 199
wainscot, 110–11, 113, 117–18, 177, 180, 191, 201–2, 223
Waldoboro, Maine, 278
Walker, Timothy P., 271
Wallingford, Conn., 133, 146, 152, 156, 241, 249
Wallingford, Conn., New Cheshire Society, 192
Walpole, Mass., 165
Walter, Rev. Thomas, 41
Waltham, Mass., 19
Ware, Henry, 35
Wareham, Mass., 47
warning the meeting, 1, 23–24
Warren, R.I., 262
Warwick, Mass., 177
Warwick, R.I., 17, 262
Washington, Conn., 230
Washington, N.H., 19, 195, 276
watch-house, 101, 105
"Waterside" district, Newbury (Newburyport), Mass., 256
Watertown, Mass.: First Parish, 79, 106, 149, 273–74; West Parish (Waltham), 106, 192, 236, 274
Watts, Rev. Isaac, 41, 47, 245, 265
Wayland, Mass., 20, 59
weathercocks, 79, 138, 149, 151–52
weather vanes: Anglican, 146, 148, 154, 262; first period, 79, 94, 97, 106, 135, 137; second period, 143, 151, 157
Wells, Maine, Second Parish, 166
Wells, Philip (surveyor), 118
Wenham, Mass., 165, 227–28, 252
Westborough, Mass., 162, 193
Westfield, Mass., 65, 68–69, 133, 191, 239
Westford, Mass., 51–53, 137, 217, 395n2
Westhampton, Mass., 172
West Haverhill, Mass., 267
Westminster, Mass., 47, 61
The Westminster Confession of 1646, 77
Westmoreland, N.H., 182, 391n102

West Salisbury (Amesbury), Mass., 59, 174, 181, 278
West Springfield, Mass., 105, 213, 227
West Woodstock, Conn., 47
Wethersfield, Conn., meetinghouses: design for I, 94; seats for I, 117; use of drum in 1660, 23; bell tower design in II, 154; II as a survival, 278; pulpit in II, 182, 184; stairwell porches in II, 160, 173
Whately, Mass., 24
Wheaton, Comfort, 208
whipping posts, 25
white exteriors, 16, 194–96, 198, 200
Whittlesey, Rev. Chauncey, 245, 250
whistles, 43
Whitefield, Rev. George, 209
White Haven Society, 16, 199–200, 250
*Whole Book of Psalmes* (T. Sternhold and J. Hopkins), 40–41, 260
Wiggin, Henry (builder), 52
Wilton, N.H., 229–30
Willemstad Reformed Church, the Netherlands, 81, 84, 89
William III and Mary II, 118
Williamsburg, Mass., 24
Williamstown, Mass., 23
Wilmington, Mass., 201
Wilton, Conn., 25
Wilton, N.H., 52
Winchendon, Mass., 51, 198
Windham, Conn., 198, 229
Windham, Maine, 25
windows, casement, 102, 191–92
windows, compass-headed, 85, 119, 124–28, 210, 241, 246, 250, 388n9
windows, dormer, 81, 89, 94, 97, 128, 130–31, 133, 257

Windsor, Conn.: halfway covenant in, 36; "lanthorn" in, 108; meetinghouse, 101; pew associations, 71; pews, 115; relations in, 48; replication in, 227–28; reuse of separatist meetinghouse, 274; roof selection, 132; seating, 66–67; stocks, 25; use of trumpet, 23
Winsted, Conn., 230
Winthrop, John, 2–3, 30, 79–80, 241, 270
Woburn, Mass., 52, 66, 104, 106
wolves, 25
Woodbridge, Benjamin (builder), 57
Woodbridge, Dudley, 94, 105, 149
Woodbridge, Rev. Samuel, 19
Woodbury, Conn., 138, 196, 274
Woodruff, Judah (woodworker, builder), 53–54, 183
Woodstock, Conn., 25, 177
Woonsocket, R.I., Quaker meetinghouse, 262
Worcester, Mass., 26, 57, 150
Worden, Elder Peter, 262
word of God, 30, 40, 221
*Works in Architecture* (R. and J. Adam), 210
Wren, Christopher (English architect), 1, 143, 146, 210, 223, 389n45
Wrentham, Mass., 70, 165
Wright, Joseph (builder), 50
writing tables, 14
wrought iron, 30, 106, 266, 378n7

Yarmouth, Mass., 202, 228
yellow exteriors, 194–96, 198, 229–30
York, Maine, 156

Zeiller, Martin, 89
Zwingli, Huldrych, 114

BORN IN GENEVA, Switzerland, Peter Benes received his education at the Mill Hill School in London, Berkeley (California) High School, Harvard College, Harvard University Graduate School of Education, and Boston University's American and New England Studies Program. He is the cofounder (1976), director, and editor of The Dublin Seminar for New England Folklife, a continuing series of conferences, exhibitions, and publications exploring everyday life, work, and culture in New England's past. Benes's first book, *The Masks of Orthodoxy: Folk Gravestone Carving in Plymouth County, Massachusetts, 1689–1805* (University of Massachusetts Press, 1977), received the Chicago Folklore Prize. His other publications include four exhibition catalogues, two coedited volumes, and numerous articles on New England history, cartography, art, and culture. In 2011 he and his wife, Jane Montague Benes, received the Bay State Legacy Award for their contributions to Massachusetts history. Jane and Peter have two daughters and four grandchildren; they live in Concord, Massachusetts.

NHTI Library
Concord's Community College
Concord, NH 03301